PENGUIN BOOKS

THE PENGUIN GUIDE TO AMERICAN LAW SCHOOLS

Harold R. Doughty is currently a Management and Educational Consultant. He was formerly Executive Vice President and Chief Operating Officer at American Commonwealth University; Vice President for Admissions, Financial Aid and Enrollment Services at United States International University; Director of Admissions and Summer Sessions at New York University; and Director of Admissions and Freshmen Development at Adelphi University. His *Guide to American Graduate Schools* is also available from Penguin.

THE PENGUIN
GUIDE TO
AMERICAN
LAW
SCHOOLS

Harold R. Doughty

PENGUIN BOOKS

PENGUIN BOOKS
Published by the Penguin Group
Penguin Putnam Inc., 375 Hudson Street,
New York, New York 10014, U.S.A.
Penguin Books Ltd, 27 Wrights Lane,
London W8 5TZ, England
Penguin Books Australia Ltd, Ringwood,
Victoria, Australia
Penguin Books Canada Ltd, 10 Alcorn Avenue,
Toronto, Ontario, Canada M4V 3B2
Penguin Books (N.Z.) Ltd, 182–190 Wairau Road,
Auckland 10, New Zealand

Penguin Books Ltd, Registered Offices:
Harmondsworth, Middlesex, England

First published in Penguin Books 1999

1   3   5   7   9   10   8   6   4   2

LIBRARY OF CONGRESS CATALOGING IN PUBLICATION DATA
Doughty, Harold.
The Penguin guide to American law schools/
Harold R. Doughty.
p.   cm.
ISBN 0 14 046.994 X (pbk.)
1. Law schools—United States—Directories.   I. Title.
KF266.D68   1999
340'.071'173—dc21   98-28969

Printed in the United States of America
Set in Times Roman

CONTENTS

PREFACE

This Guide is designed to provide prospective law students with the basic information they need to select the appropriate law school. It describes all nationally accredited/approved law schools in the United States, each of which has been contacted at least once. Additional material was obtained from the Internet and other supplemental resources.

Each entry contains information concerning the law school's parent institution, the law school's admission and degree requirements, standards, enrollment and faculty figures, tuition charges, financial aid opportunities and deadlines, library and housing facilities and, whenever possible, material related to joint-degree programs and graduate law degrees. While this book has been prepared especially for the first-year law student, counselors, faculty, administrative officers, and potential graduate law students will also find it useful.

It should be noted that the *Penguin Guide to American Law Schools* is intended only as a first source of information. With such data the student is more fully aware of the opportunities available and can narrow the selections to the geographical area and then the institutions he or she is likely to find most suitable. The student is encouraged to seek the advice of undergraduate faculty, especially those in law-related fields, and consult catalogs, bulletins, and Web sites. Most important, the applicant must be brutally frank in his or her self-appraisal of abilities, objectives, and motives for undertaking legal study.

The author wishes to express his indebtedness to the law school deans, admission officers, and their assistants who provided the information presented. Further revisions of this volume are planned, and corrections and suggestions are welcome.

H. R. D.

INTRODUCTION

THE PROFESSIONAL SCHOOL

All study beyond the undergraduate college is essentially "professional" in nature. The graduate school of arts and sciences was created primarily to train college teachers and scholars, even though most of those who hold master's and doctoral degrees do not enter the field of teaching higher education. But graduate training in fields other than the humanities and sciences is designed for specific occupations.

Although there are no agreed demarcations, it can be stated fairly that some sixteen disciplines are the predominant arenas of postbaccalaureate professional study: architecture, business, dentistry, education, engineering, forestry, law, library science, medicine, nursing, optometry, pharmacy, public health, social work, theology, and veterinary medicine. Cases can be made for including under this label such fields as journalism and physical therapy, but for the purposes at hand these sixteen are most relevant.

Even this list could be winnowed further. The origins of formal education for just three professions predate those of all others by many decades. Training for these—law, medicine, theology—has developed independently of most forms of graduate study. Indeed, law schools still speak of work for the first law degree as "undergraduate" as if candidates could enter directly from high school.

Many other programs still struggle for full recognition of their professional status and often remain as mere departments of larger divisions.

And make no mistake, the designation of an academic subdivision as a department or institute or school or college is a distinction important beyond simple academic snobbery. Professional "schools" within broader institutions have more stature than departments. They have independent administrations and faculties, sometimes even their own boards of trustees. Often, they are able to detach their fund-raising activities from their parent institutions and thus have greater latitude in distribution of moneys separated from contributors. There is greater unity of purpose, and faculties of law schools are typically better paid than those of most other professional schools.

And in the current atmosphere of student specialization and vocationalism, professional schools have the upper hand in determining the direction of their institutions, while many liberal arts programs struggle with enrollment and fiscal problems. The following pages outline these schools and programs and briefly describe factors to be considered in selection, admission and degree requirements, and sources of financial aid.

SELECTING A LAW SCHOOL

Professional schools often have been accused of unduly restricting enrollment at times of expanding need. Now, having rushed to meet urgently expressed national needs, educational institutions find themselves the targets of the reverse criticism: they went too far and now must start reducing the number of students they will accept.

There are now oversupplies of teachers in some areas of the country, some say two for every job. Doctors and nurses are not in as much demand in some regions. Ph.D.s in some of the hard sciences are not able to find any employment even in related occupations. New members of the bar are encountering stiffer competition, and there looms the previously unbelievable prospect of a surplus of lawyers. Increasingly, formerly independent law schools are being absorbed into larger institutions or are joining with other institutions to form new entities, thereby shrinking enrollment opportunities still further. In a nation headed toward zero population growth, this oversupply prediction has been used as justification by federal agencies attempting to limit aid for graduate and professional education to loan programs.

The result of these trends will be to make professional study even more difficult to undertake than it is already. Admission standards, too, will undoubtedly escalate still further, putting even the least glossy law schools out of reach of all but the most capable applicants. Anticipating an oversupply of attorneys, a few law schools have already announced cutbacks in first-year enrollment. Still other schools are talking tentatively about charging tuition that actually covers instructional expenses, meaning annual tuition could reach as high as $30,000 at some private institutions, and this is not even counting living expenses. Financial aid is far from munificent and with additional federal cutbacks anticipated, professional education will become increasingly out of reach of even those of the more "advantaged" applicants.

In the very short-lived meantime, students of above average, if unspectacular, aptitude and credentials have reason to be hopeful about gaining entrance to a law school as long as they are not unrealistically fussy about location and "image."

COST, SIZE, LOCATION. The costs for the study of law vary widely, depending principally upon the type of institutional or state support. Annual tuition ranges from about $1,800 to $9,000 at publicly supported schools, from $15,000 to $25,000 at private schools, all escalating at an average rate of nearly 5 percent a year. In general, tuition has been increasing by 6 to 7 percent each year. Always check with the institution in question regarding current tuition charges.

Student bodies of professional schools are customarily in the 300 to 700 range, but some exceed 1,000 in enrollment. Women make up about 35 to 45 percent of the total law school enrollment and minority enrollments range between 7 and 10 percent.

There are law schools in forty-nine states, in the District of Columbia, and in Puerto Rico; only Alaska is without at least one law school. Even with this broad geographical base, full-time law students can expect to enroll at institutions farther away from home than their undergraduate colleges were.

ADMISSION

The law schools set rigorous entrance requirements and thus avoid the separate step of "admission to candidacy," not to mention the high attrition rate attributed to most other graduate schools. It is not possible, therefore, to suggest that any college graduate can gain admission to some law school. Nevertheless, admission is not always as difficult as is commonly supposed, if students are willing to consider a law school without regard to location or to presumed reputation. (Since law schools must meet fairly high minimum criteria to retain accreditation/approval by appropriate professional associations, it is probably safe to say that few truly "bad" schools exist.) Several factors influence the decisions of admission committees, and these should be understood by the potential applicant.

PREPARATION. A few schools are willing to consider applicants who do not hold a bachelor's degree certifying completion of a four-year undergraduate program. However, these schools are commonly involved with B.A., B.S.-J.D. programs with the schools/colleges within the parent institution. Undergraduate preparation need not have followed strictly the curricula laid down by preprofessional advisors. This is especially true of applicants to law schools, which are less likely to require specific undergraduate preparation.

The schools emphasize in their catalogues that general liberal arts studies are more important for their students than specialized majors in fields thought to be closely related to law. For example, a major in economics, history, English, sociology, or even business administration, with a heavy emphasis on writing, would prove to be very advantageous to a law applicant.

CREDENTIALS. In addition to official transcripts of undergraduate and any graduate study completed, applicants are nearly always expected to provide one to three letters of recommendation, LSAT scores, and a personal statement/résumé. In many cases, the letters of recommendation may be replaced totally or in part by the recommendations of the undergraduate preprofessional faculty committee. In the case of joint-degree applicants, the results of the appropriate entrance examinations prepared and/or administered by the professional associations or a testing agency may also be required. The addresses of these associations/agencies follows:

Graduate Management Admissions Test (GMAT)—applications available from Graduate Management Admissions Test, P.O. Box 6101, Princeton, NJ 08541-6101. Phone: (601)771-7330.

Graduate Record Examination (GRE)—applications available from Graduate Record Examinations, Educational Testing Service, P.O. Box 6000, Princeton, NJ 08541-6000. Phone: (609)771-7670 or in the California Bay Area, (510)654-1200.

Law School Admission Test (LSAT)—applications available from Law School Council, Box 2000, Newtown, PA 18940. Phone: (215)969-1001.

Miller Analogies Test (MAT)—applications available from The Psychological Corporation, 555 Academic Court, San Antonio, TX 78204. Phone: (800)622-3231 or (210)299-1061.

Test of English as a Foreign Language, Test of Spoken English, Test of Written English (TOEFL, TSE, TWE)—applications available from TOEFL, P.O. Box 6151, Princeton, NJ 08541-6151. Phone: (609)771-7100.

A few law schools may require an interview, by invitation, for the special applicants or special scholarship programs, but, generally speaking, not one law school uses the interview as part of any admissions decision process. However, most law schools do encourage campus tours, group informational interviews, and class visits.

DEADLINES. Law schools customarily accept applications for admission starting in September of the year preceding the proposed term of entrance. Most law schools set closing dates for the receipt of completed applications in January or February, although these dates for many schools are often flexible. An indication of this flexibility is the statements some law schools use, i.e., "priority deadline" or "applicants by a certain date given special consideration." Be sure to confirm with the institution its current deadline.

In the case of transfers or visiting students, many law schools accept applications well into the summer preceding the term of entrance, although some of the more prestigious schools have deadlines in May.

Almost all schools restrict entrance for first-year students to the fall term, or occasionally to the summer (for special admission programs or accelerated programs). Transfers can generally enroll in any term when space is available. The only restriction for a transfer applicant is usually an official transcript showing one full year of academic work, a statement of good standing at his/her previous school, and a limit on the amount of credit that can be applied toward the J.D.

COMMON APPLICATION SERVICES. In an effort to ease the burden on students intent on applying for ad-

mission (and to cut their own clerical cost) all law schools subscribe to the services of a centralized processing agency (LSDAS). This processor accepts academic credentials and other data from applicants, summarizing them in uniform formats and passing them on to the designated schools. The clearinghouse does not offer advisement or make admission decisions; that still remains the province of the schools themselves. After determining the schools in which the student is interested, he or she should write to the LSAC at:

Law School Admission Council (LSAC) Law Services, Box 2000, 661 Penn Street, Newtown, PA 18940-0977; Phone: (215)968-1314.

In addition, there is a new application process which is being used by about fifty to sixty law schools, both public and private. These law schools, listed in the Index on page 291, accept the Law Multi-App in lieu of their own institutionalized application forms. The computer software application form is available from: Law Multi-App, 740 South Chester Road, Suite F, Swarthmore, PA 19081; Phone: (800)515-2927.

There is a fee associated with these applications/services, usually escalating with the number of schools to which the materials are to be sent. Some of the schools require supplementary materials and/or an interview. All schools expect payment of application fees with admission application.

STANDARDS. It is probably safe to say that at least 30 percent to 40 percent of the applicants to most professional schools are accepted for admission. Allowing for duplication of applications, available statistics suggest that an even larger percentage of students eventually gain acceptance to some school, perhaps as many as two-thirds of all applicants.

Most law schools claim to seek students with undergraduate grade point averages of B. Depending on the degree of competition created by the number of applicants, this may be interpreted to mean an average as low as C plus or as high as A minus. It is generally agreed, in any event, that the grade point average is the single most reliable predictor of success in postbaccalaureate professional studies. While the scores on the LSAT are undeniably important in the deliberations of admissions committees, students should not expect strong scores to outweigh mediocre grades in undergraduate course work, even if the degree is from a prestigious institution.

FINANCIAL ASSISTANCE

Professional law study is expensive, and although various forms of aid are available, most students must plan to meet costs through loans or their own resources. Most law schools provide a limited numbers of scholarships, grants, and tuition waivers from institutional funds. In addition, some schools may have research assistantships/fellowships for first-year students as well as for advanced students. Low-cost loans are widely available through governmental agencies, some banks, private lending groups, professional associations, and private or community groups, in addition to the loan resources available from schools themselves.

Students apply for several governmentally- (state/federal) sponsored loan programs through the individual law schools to which they seek admission or through the parent institution's financial aid office. Information with reference to other loan programs can be obtained from banks and private agencies as well as from the law schools themselves. Many law schools assist the spouses of students in obtaining local or institutional employment. Although part-time employment is out of the question for first-year students, given the workload, this possibility should be explored in the second and third years of legal study.

THE STRUCTURE OF PROFESSIONAL STUDY OF LAW

Programs leading to the J.D. degrees require three years of full-time study or where permitted, four years in part-time attendance.

Law students can anticipate a beginning year of introductory work, usually conducted in lecture classes. The following two years permit more latitude in course selection, and seminars are more commonly available. Course work is generally supplemented by tutorial work, law clinics, pro bono legal experience, and training in research and various forms of legal writing.

Programs leading to J.D. degrees are demanding, and standards of performance are rigorous, but the rewards are substantial. If the potential student is realistic in selecting a school consistent with his/her interests and aptitudes, the experience will test his mind and spirit and lead to the kind of lifelong fulfillment few others are fortunate to enjoy.

Several law schools offer advanced study beyond the J.D. Graduate study in law may be administered by the graduate schools of the parent institution with which the law schools are affiliated, or administered by the law school's graduate division/program. In the case when graduate study is coordinated by the parent institution, students usually must meet admission and degree requirements established by both the graduate school and professional school's graduate divisions. In most law schools, however, graduate study is located in and governed by the dean and faculty of the professional school.

UNDERSTANDING THE ENTRIES

The information on the following pages describes the structure and content of the institutional entries that make up the main portion of this volume. For the entries to be of maximum value, it is important that the reader properly interpret the data provided. The entries contain the kinds of basic information a potential applicant is likely to seek in choosing a law school.

Careful examination of the school descriptions should aid the student in reaching realistic preliminary decisions. Since admission standards and requirements, course offerings, and financial aid opportunities are subject to frequent revision, it is not to be assumed that the entries can replace individual school bulletins.

Several points must be kept in mind. The listed institutions were asked to supply figures on enrollment and faculty and percentages of applications accepted and grants of financial aid awarded. When possible, informa-

tion for the 1997–98 academic year were used. All institutions in this guide are accredited by the appropriate professional accrediting associations.

Every effort has been made to render these data understandable without reference to elaborate indexes of codes and abbreviations. However, some symbols, in addition to abbreviations for degrees and commonly required entrance examinations, have been used. Another symbol regularly used throughout this book is the "diacritical" or "stroke" mark, as in "teaching/research." As employed here, the stroke means only "and/or."

The following pages describe in some detail the kinds of information to be found under each entry, in the same order. The items listed below are not included in every entry, either because they are not relevant or because specific data were not available.

GENERAL CHARACTERISTICS OF THE PARENT INSTITUTION

Name of parent institution. In the case of about 90 percent of all ABA-accredited/approved law schools, the law school is a part of a much larger institution, either a college or a university. This introductory institutional information has been included to establish a general atmosphere or ambiance (founding date, location, environment, enrollment, library size, etc.) in which the law school functions. The colleges and universities are arranged in alphabetical order according to the most important word in the title. The reader should use the table of contents to assist in locating a particular law school of interest.

Mailing address of the main campus. The name of the

city and state in which the main campus is located, plus zip code and Internet Web sites were included when available.

Founding date. Usually the year the institution was chartered, but sometimes the year classes were started or the year of the opening of another institution from which the present one developed.

Location in direction and miles from nearest major city. Direction from nearest major city is given in appropriate capital letters (NW, SE). The mileage given is approximate road distance. Often the city named is relatively small but sufficiently well known and is given only to establish the location of the main campus.

Type of control. If the institution is supported primarily by public funds it is called public. Occasionally, institutions receive substantial amounts of financial support from the state or city government but decision-making powers are retained by the board of trustees. In other cases, individual divisions of universities are totally or mostly supported by public funds. In these instances, control is often shared. When appropriate, these situations are noted.

Many private institutions are sponsored by religious denominations, and this affiliation is mentioned. Although few such colleges and universities restrict their enrollments to members of the sponsoring churches, students may be expected to adhere to certain basic or curricular requirements.

Semester, quarter, or trimester system. The semester system (the system used by almost all law schools) provides study during two terms of a nine-month academic year and, usually, during one or more summer sessions. The quarter system divides the calendar year into four equal terms, the trimester into three. Under all three systems, students typically attend classes for about nine months. For no apparent historical reason, Western colleges and universities most often operate on the quarter system, those in the East on the semester. The trimester is still relatively uncommon.

Library. This figure is the total number of bound volumes in the institution's collections; when available, figures for microforms and current periodicals/subscriptions are also included. When special collections or several libraries at different centers are available, the figure represents the combined number of volumes. Information concerning the number of computer workstations is also included when available.

Other graduate schools/colleges. To provide a sense of the educational environment in which the law school functions, this graduate information is included. The total university/college enrollment figure furnishes yet another aspect of the environmental milieu in which the law school will be operating.

GENERAL CHARACTERISTICS OF THE LAW SCHOOL

Name of the law school. The law schools are arranged in alphabetical order according to the main institutional affiliation. An index with cross references to help the reader locate a law school by either its major institutional name or its specific law school name is found at the end of this book. For example, Boalt Law, see University of California, Berkeley. Several other institutional indexes can be found in the back of the book to provide for further assistance in locating a specific law school.

Mailing address of the law school. The name, post office box, street, city, and state in which the school/college is located, plus the zip code, phone, Internet Web sites, and E-mail address are included when available.

Founding date. This is usually the year the law school was chartered/founded/established or the year classes were started or the year of the opening of another institution from which the present one developed. Occasionally historical data or other points of interest are included.

Location. Most law schools are affiliated with a university or college located on the main campus. For law schools not on the main campus, the location is given in miles from nearest major city. Direction from nearest major city is given in appropriate capital letters (NW, SE).

ABA/AALS information. This information is included to place the law school in a historical perspective.

Full-time, part-time study. Full- and part-time study indicates the options available at a particular law school. In general, the newer law schools, which tend to be located in urban areas, are more receptive to the part-time student.

Semester, quarter, or trimester system. Almost all law schools operate on a semester basis, even if the main campus uses another system. If there is a scheduling difference it is usually between beginning and ending dates of the quarter and semester system, and this is only a problem if a law student is participating in joint- or concurrent-degree programs. While it does add a complication to the process, it does not necessarily increase the time needed to complete both degrees.

Library. This figure is the total number of bound volumes in the law school's collections; when available, figures for microforms, current periodicals/subscriptions, and computer workstations is included.

Special facilities programs. Included under this category are special centers, institutes, summer abroad programs, faculty/student exchanges, internships/externships. This list is not intended to be exhaustive but only to note distinctive offerings and to suggest their scope. Since this information is not always available, its absence does not necessarily mean that special facilities/ programs do not exist at a given institution.

Annual tuition charges for full-time students. Many public institutions use the term "fees" rather than "tuition," often with additional "tuition" for out-of-state students. This semantic distinction is often employed to maintain the illusion of low tuition cost institutions. The cost of tuition/fees at public institutions is always greater for nonresidents than for residents, while there is no such distinction at private colleges and universities. On occasion, a third level of tuition may be charged for foreign students. When no flat-rate tuition is set for full-time students, the per hour charge is given. Throughout this book, "annual" refers to the academic, not the calendar year. It also should be remembered that tuition charges are constantly on the rise, increasing at an annual rate at most institutions. This fact has been anticipated when possible, and the charges indicated are customarily for the 1997–98 year.

Part-time tuition charges. Schedules of charges are per credit (semester or quarter) hour. As above, charges are indicated for both resident and nonresident students, when appropriate.

On- and off-campus housing availability and housing contacts. Many institutions are unable to provide data for housing available to law students per se. In this event, it may be assumed that law students are eligible for some on-campus housing. The figure given for married student housing should be interpreted as family units (apartments), while the figure for single students refers to individual spaces only. "On-campus housing" means institutionally owned or controlled housing and does not include private accommodations. (Only one or two colleges indicate that nearby, privately owned, off-campus housing was not available.) Law students who choose to live in institutional housing must remember that they are usually expected to observe the restrictions in force for all residents and there may be housing application deadlines.

Annual on- and off-campus housing expenses. This figure is for the academic year and relates only to the cost of university-owned or -operated housing, not to private accommodations. The cost described is generally for the mid range, and cost variations depend upon the nature of accommodations. Unless otherwise specified, figures are for rent or room charges only, not board.

Housing deadlines and contacts. This notes the deadlines, if applicable, and the office to contact for both on- and off-campus housing information. If only one office is mentioned, it generally provides information for both institutional and private accommodations. If no housing information is supplied, it should be understood that the admissions office is the appropriate office to contact for either on- or off-campus housing information.

Enrollment. Figures are for J.D. students only. (The LL.M. Index provides graduate enrollment figures.) The figures are usually broken down into full- and part-time enrollments and the percentages of men and women for the combined total. On occasion, the latter figures refer either to the full- or part-time figure. Beginning with "Statistics," the enrollment information refers to total and not just first-year enrollment data.

Faculty. This is the total number of faculty teaching law courses on a full- and/or part-time basis. This is often the least reliable statistic of all, for obvious reasons. In general, full-time represents permanent faculty, part-time represents part-time or adjunct appointments.

Types of degrees conferred. Abbreviations are used for all law and joint-degree programs. At the graduate level the same abbreviations often have different meanings. Please consult the Key to Degree Abbreviations and the LL.M. Index for specific definitions.

Recruitment practices. This section is included to add one more dimension to the question of whether a particular law school is a local, regional, or nationally recognized school and to indicate the extent of the school's recruitment efforts. There are six national forums held each year across the U.S. (Atlanta, Boston, Chicago, Houston, Los Angeles, New York City), and most nationally recognized law schools attend them all. Regional and local schools will be selective with reference to which national forums they will attend as well as how many local on-campus conferences they will attend. Almost all law schools have extensive on-campus activities. As soon as the applicant requests information from a law school, he/she will be placed on the school's mailing list and begin to receive invitations to a multitude of on- and off-campus conferences, tours, group meetings, etc. Therefore, early contact with the law schools of choice will be to the applicant's advantage.

ADMISSION REQUIREMENTS

Credentials required in support of application. This paragraph lists all documents, entrance examinations, and other requirements needed for an admission decision. In general, the application, recommendations, and financial aid requests should be sent directly to the law school. Test scores are sent to the LSDAS and then forwarded on to the law school. All law schools expect applicants to hold a bachelor's degree from an accredited institution. Only two or three schools admit students with fewer than four years of undergraduate study and these schools generally have combined degree programs with a parent institution's undergraduate schools/ colleges. Official transcripts of previous undergraduate and graduate study (when applicable) are always required in support of applications for admission. Applicants must submit one official transcript from each college/university attended directly to the LSDAS.

The LSAT is required for all accredited/approved law schools and in most cases it is to the student's advantage to take this entrance exam early (preferably in June or October). Each law school treats multiple test results differently; some average the scores, and others take the highest. Always contact the law schools you are considering before retaking the LSAT to ensure that the results will be used to your advantage.

Many schools request one or more letters of recommendation. Ordinarily, the applicant must use a recommendation form found in the application materials and is asked to have the recommendations sent directly to the school. In some cases, the names of the persons willing to send recommendations is requested in the application, and the school takes the responsibility of obtaining the letters. In a few cases, recommendations are encouraged but not required.

Additional requirements for admission. Personal statements, essays, and résumés are also given consideration. In general, if these supplementary materials are requested, they are used by the school to add another dimension to applicants' profiles. The school is interested in such things as curricular and extracurricular activities, ethnic/racial background, individual character and personality, work experience, community activities, state residency, difficulties overcome or anything else that would distinguish or separate the candidate from the rest of the applicant pool.

International applicants. International students are more likely to apply to and enroll in graduate programs than they are to enter a J.D. program. Nevertheless, information with reference to TOEFL/TSE/TWE and services which will translate and evaluate foreign credentials has been included. Many institutions have their own international application and an international students office. The international applicant should consult with this office early in the process for the most comprehensive and current information pertaining to the process and the application deadlines and application fees. In most cases, the international applicant must demonstrate English proficiency and the ability to pay all school expenses (room, board, tuition, etc.) in U.S. currency before his/her application can be considered complete, reviewed for admission and, if accepted, have the necessary entry documents (visas) issued.

Joint/concurrent-degree programs. In almost every case, a joint-degree applicant must apply to and be accepted by both schools or both degree programs. In some cases the LSAT can be substituted for the master's entrance exam while other joint-degree programs require both the LSAT and the GRE/GMAT/MAT. At some institutions the decision to combine degrees can be put off until the end of the first semester. Several other schools have the accepted joint-degree students start the master's program in the summer prior to enrollment in the law school in an attempt to accelerate both degree programs.

Transfer applicants and visiting students. Law schools accept transfer applicants from other ABA-accredited or AALS-approved institutions. Transfer students are accepted on a space available basis only and even then only under certain extenuating circumstances. Acceptance is based primarily upon whether the school would have accepted the applicant as a first-year student. In almost all cases, an official transcript from the candidate's current law school showing a full year of academic work and class ranking is required. Generally speaking, no more than one third of the total course work for the J.D. degree is allowed for work completed at other law schools. Several law schools are willing to consider transfer applicants but will grant advanced standing only after a semester or year in residence has been completed.

Office and dates of application. This refers to the office of the school from whom application forms can be obtained. The completed forms and supporting documents are customarily returned to the same office. Closing dates for filing applications should be carefully observed. All supporting credentials should also be received by these deadlines, but there is in most cases greater flexibility with receipt of test scores and the LSDAS. In some cases, no firm deadlines are set but priority/preferred dates are suggested. The applicant is advised to apply well in advance of these dates. In addition, the applications for both admission and financial aid should be submitted by the date indicated in the financial aid section. Information on closing dates for all terms was not always available, so it should not be assumed that a spring or summer term does not exist for transfer applicants simply because a closing date is not mentioned for that term.

Application fee. This information was not always available. Its absence does not necessarily mean that no application fee is required.

Phone and fax numbers and E-mail addresses. The numbers listed in both the Admission Requirements and the Financial Aid sections are general contact numbers for both the law school and, in many cases, the university, and are supplied for a preliminary applicant's convenience only.

Master's and doctoral degree programs. As is the case with all entries in this guide, the application requirements listed are not definitive but only provide a starting point. The final word in all admissions matters rests solely with the law school's director of graduate studies, the appropriate graduate admissions office, and in some cases, an official of the admissions office of the graduate school of the university. Usually, the supporting credentials requested are official copies of all undergraduate and J.D. transcripts, a copy of the LSAT (in most cases), several recommendations, a résumé/curriculum vitae, and a personal statement. In the case of a research LL.M., a thesis/project proposal is usually required. There is a wide variety of LL.M. programs listed in the LL.M. degree index. This is not a exhaustive list, and the candidate will need to contact the individual law/graduate school to obtain the latest degree/program information. Most doctoral candidates are selected from promising LL.M. students already enrolled in the law school awarding the doctoral degree and applications are not generally accepted from other law school candidates.

ADMISSION STANDARDS

Law school quality can be assessed in a variety of ways. The ABA fiercely resists any rating of law schools and indeed their Section on Legal Education firmly expresses that there should be "no rating of law schools beyond the simple statement of accreditation . . . Qualities that make one kind of school good for one student may not be as important to another." The quality of credentials of the groups of applicants to different institutions varies widely, and the degree of difficulty of admission must be interpreted accordingly. In other words, the most highly regarded institutions naturally attract applications from superior students in greater numbers than do less favored schools. Therefore, the standards at a top law school cannot be assumed to be dealing with the same level of applicants as those at less prestigious institutions.

Caution must be taken in equating difficulty of admission with quality of program. While there is clearly some relationship between the strength of the student body and the effectiveness of the program, this is less true on the professional school level than on the undergraduate level. Limited facilities may restrict enrollment and therefore produce an image of quality due to the low number of applicants accepted. On the other hand, some schools may be able to accept larger proportions of applicants without a reduction in the quality of the student body. Contrary to the assumption of many applicants, the grade point average and LSAT median scores stated are not absolute "floors" or cutoff scorers. Scores for the candidates in the top 75th percent of the entering class are reported in order to correct this misinterpretation and misinformation. As with the descriptions of admissions policies, information about attrition rates, ranking, and ratings is offered merely as a guide to help the applicant begin to focus his/her search for the right school.

Prospective law students should consider a variety of factors in choosing where to apply. This section presents many factors to assist the reader in determining the appropriate institutional fit. Among these factors are the number of applications accepted, the median LSAT and GPA, the scores of the student in the top 75th percent of all accepted students, the attrition rates, and the two ranking/rating sources. However, these are only a few pieces of the puzzle. What school is best for me is a complex question. A Selection Checklist at the end of this introduction section helps the reader pull together the remaining factors needed to start the selection process.

FINANCIAL AID

The basic philosophy behind financial aid/student assistance as it is practiced at most law schools is quite simple. The assumption is that four not-so-equal partners will support the law student's educational endeavor: the first one is the student, then the parents and the law school, and by far the largest partner is the lender, which may or may not include the federal government. The reader can discover just what a school's potential financial assistance will be by simply looking at the size of the average scholarship/grant listed in this section and then doing a little basic arithmetic. It should become quite clear that the foundation undergirding most financial aid policy is that the student is expected to finance his/her legal education with only a minimum reliance on institutional scholarships/grants, tuition waivers, etc. Only the most highly endowed schools are able to extend sizable amounts of merit-based funding to members of the incoming class and even then it is almost always part of an aid package with as much as a 50 to 70 percent loan.

Types of aid administered by the school/college. Scholarships, fellowships, grants-in-aid, assistantships, and tuition waivers are the most common forms of aid available (very few schools have all the above mentioned forms of gift aid). As listed here, the merit-based grants are offered by institutional funds, gifts, contributions, or aid programs administered by the law school or the university. Most have to be renewed each year. Federal work-study programs are only offered to second- and third-year students. Since scholarships/fellowships generally include renewals for returning students as well, it should not be assumed that all those listed are solely for entering students.

Nevertheless, some conclusions can be drawn about actual aid available. Scholarships rarely have service requirements, and the term "fellowship" is often used in lieu of "scholarship." Thus, an entry reading "Scholarships, fellowships, grants, tuition waivers, teaching/research assistantships" means that no service is required in exchange for the first four forms of aid, while those who hold assistantships are expected to assume some additional responsibilities. Duties may involve direct assistance in research to a particular faculty member or general responsibilities within a faculty area, such as grading papers or assisting in demonstrations. Fellowships and assistantships typically carry a tuition remission privilege plus an annual stipend. Since fellowships are generally regarded as the more prestigious of the two types of award, the stipend is often larger than for assistantships, and the tasks assigned may be more challenging in nature. This is subject to broad variations between faculty specialties and schools. Many schools award assistantships and fellowships and generally assist students to obtain internships and externships.

To whom to apply and the closing date. It is often necessary to apply to different persons or offices for the several kinds of aid available. If no deadline date is set, it is wise to apply as soon as possible after January 1 but certainly no later than February 1. Early applications receive maximum consideration. Scholarships and fellowships are often awarded through a central committee of the law school; assistantships may also be granted by the graduate department offering study in the proposed joint-degree field. As a result, it may be necessary to contact as many as two or three persons or offices to obtain information about various forms of aid at the law school and in the university/college. In general, an applicant applies to the law school via the admission/financial aid application for scholarships, fellowships, grants, tuition waivers and to the university/college for federally sponsored programs/ loans. In some instances (depending upon history and tradition), the law school may administer all aspects of the financial aid process. In all cases, the second, if not the first, step in the process is to

submit the FAFSA. This federal document is used by all schools/colleges/universities to determine an accepted student's need to attend a particular law school. In this entry the phrase "use" or "submit FAFSA" means that the applicant should submit the FAFSA in time for the processing center to return the necessary information to the school/university (processing generally take six weeks) prior to the financial aid deadline. Many schools have merit- and need-based scholarship programs and an accepted student is automatically considered for this form of aid. For some schools a special scholarship/fellowship application is required. In all cases, the final authority is the law school's admission/ financial aid office and they must be contacted to receive the most current information.

Percentage of students receiving aid other than loans. The percentage given here relates to the number of students awarded scholarships, fellowships, assistantships, and other grants (but not loans) from both internal and external sources. The latter includes grants provided by private and governmental agencies. In this entry are the percentages of grant/scholarship recipients for full-time first-year students and if part-time data was available it is also included. A percentage of financial assistance for the total student population is also listed.

When the information was available, a figure for total indebtedness for three years of law school was shown. A general rule of thumb for finding your debt picture after three years of law school would be take the total financial aid budget used by the law school for one year and multiply it by between two and two and one half; this will be your debt picture upon graduation. A loan repayment/forgiveness program for public interest employment is available at a few of the larger law schools, but each program is unique; therefore, the financial aid office must be contacted for current information.

Aid available to part-time students. It is by no means a universal practice to make aid, even loans, available to part-time students. This line states whether or not such aid, including loans, is offered.

Aid available for graduate study. Fellowships, teaching/research assistantships, and grants are the most common forms of aids, though funds are limited. Institutional, private loans, and, in some special cases, federal loans may be available to U.S. citizens. In addition, international applicants must produce documentation that they have sufficient funds to support one full year of law study.

DEGREE REQUIREMENTS

For J.D. degrees. As used throughout this book, "residence" refers to credit hours completed while in full- or part-time attendance at the law school granting the degree. This section begins with the minimum total number of credit (semester or quarter) hours that must be completed, followed by the minimum number of hours to be completed in residence at the institution granting the degree. Therefore, the difference in credit hour requirements between the minimum number for the degree and the number to be completed "in residence" is the number of hours that may be accepted in transfer from other ABA/AALS approved schools. The J.D. full-time program is normally completed in three years, or six semesters; the part-time program may be accomplished in as few as four years or eight semesters. In many schools, this time frame can be accelerated by attendance during summer sessions. For joint-degree programs the time needed to accomplish both degrees is usually reduced by between one half and one full year, and the number of credits required for both degrees is also reduced. On the other hand, concurrent-degree programs may reduce the time required to complete both degrees, but the number of credits for each degree is generally not reduced.

For master's degrees. This section begins with the total number of credit (semester or quarter) hours that must be completed, followed by the minimum number of hours to be completed in residence at the institution granting the degree. In those cases where residence credit hours must be completed while in attendance as a full-time student, the entry reads "at least 24 in full-time residence." If the residence and full-time attendance requirements differ, this is normally stated as "at least 24 in residence and 18 in full-time attendance." If a student may elect whether or not to complete a thesis in partial fulfillment of degree requirements, both options are stated in terms of minimum total and residence credit hours. For example, "24 credit hours plus thesis, at least 18 in residence, or 30 hours without thesis, at least 24 in residence." These options are stated in different ways, generally in accordance with the terminology of the law school/graduate school being reported.

Listed next are additional degree requirements: qualifying, candidacy, or final exams; thesis or final projects. If any of these requirements are only for a particular LL.M., this fact is noted: "thesis for LL.M. (Research); final oral exam (Taxation)," etc. Most graduate programs stress that the requirements specified are minimums only and that additional credit hours, exams, or the like may be stipulated, depending upon the candidate's previous background, his performance in, or the special nature of, a particular program. In practice, such variations are more likely to occur at the doctoral rather than the master's level.

Many graduate programs point out that admission to graduate study does not imply automatic admission to candidacy. Advancement to formal candidacy for the degree depends upon successful completion of a variety of requirements, such as the filing of an acceptable thesis plan, appointment of a faculty thesis committee, or candidacy exams. This is true for both the master's and doctoral degrees.

For doctoral degrees. As with the LL.M. (Research), the number of hours is given as total credits beyond the J.D. or beyond the master's. However, many institutions do not specify a set number of credits for the doctorate, choosing instead to state the residence requirements in terms of semesters or years. (This is occasionally true of the master's as well.) In this case, it can be assumed that the years or semesters of residence required may be completed in full-time attendance only, unless otherwise specified. As mentioned above, "residence" refers to hours completed while in full- or part-time attendance at the institution granting the degree. In those cases where residence credit must be completed while in full-time attendance, the entry specifies "in full-time residence." Further, the number of hours, semesters, or years to be completed in residence is the total required for the doctorate which is in addition to the credits required for master's (LL.M., M.C.L., etc.). The nature and scope of the doctoral dissertation/thesis vary for each type of degree. The dissertation/thesis is normally expected to show technical mastery of a major or interdisciplinary field, to offer an original contribution to the existing body of legal knowledge, and to be of publishable quality.

KEY TO ABBREVIATIONS

EXAMINATIONS AND OTHER ABBREVIATIONS

AACSB	American Assembly of Collegiate Schools of Business—the American Association of Management Education
AALL	American Association of Law Libraries
AALS	Association of American Law Schools
ABA	American Bar Association
ALAS	Auxiliary Loans to Assist Students
CLEO	Council on Legal Education Opportunity
CRS	Candidate Referral Service
CSS	College Scholarship Service
EDP	Early Decision Program
ETS	Educational Testing Service
FAF	Financial Aid Form
FAFSA	Free Application for Federal Student Aid
FFS	Family Financial Statement
FWSP	Federal Work-Study Program
GMAT	Graduate Management Admissions Test
GRE	Graduate Record Examination
GPA	Grade Point Average
GSL	Guaranteed Student Loans
LSAT	Law School Admissions Test
LSDAS	Law School Data Assembly Service
MELAB	Michigan English Language Assessment Battery
MLK	Martin Luther King
N.A.L.P.	National Association for Law Placement
PAEG	Prueba de Admisiones para Estudios Graduados
PHEAA	Pennsylvania Higher Education Assistance Agency
SAAC	Student Aid Application for California
TOEFL	Test of English as a Foreign Language
TSE	Test of Spoken English
TWE	Test of Written English
UGPA	Undergraduate Grade Point Average
WS	Work Study
WES	World Education Service

DEGREES

A.M.	Master of Arts
A.M.I.R.	Master of Arts in International Relations
D.C.L.	Doctor of Civil Law
D.C.L.	Doctor of Comparative Law
D.V.M.	Doctor of Veterinary Medicine
J.D.	Doctor of Jurisprudence
J.S.D.	Doctor of the Science of Law
J.S.M.	Master of the Science of Law
LL.B.	Bachelor of Laws
LL.M.	Master of Laws
M.A.	Master of Arts
M. Acct.	Master of Accountancy
M.A.L.D.	Master of Arts in Law and Diplomacy
M.A.I.R.	Master of Arts in International Relations

M.A.L.I.R.	Master of Arts in Labor and Industrial Relations
M.A.P.A.	Master of Arts in Public Administration
M.A.S.	Master of Accounting Science
M.B.A.	Master of Business Administration
M.B.T.	Master of Business Taxation
M.C.J.	Master of Criminal Justice
M.C.L.	Master of Comparative Law
M.C.P.	Master of City Planning
M.C.P.	Master of Community Planning
M.C.R.P.	Master of City and Regional Planning
M.D.	Doctor of Medicine
M.D.	Master of Divinity
M.Ed.	Master of Education
M.E.M.	Master of Environmental Management
M.E.S.	Master of Environmental Studies
M.F.A.	Master of Fine Arts
M.F.	Master of Forestry
M.F.S.	Master of Forest Studies
M.H.A.	Master of Health Administration
M.H.S.A.	Master of Health Services Administration
M.I.A.	Master of International Affairs
M.I.L.R.	Master of Industrial and Labor Relations
M.I.M.	Master of International Management
M.I.P.	Master of Intellectual Properties
M.J.	Master of Jurisprudence
M.L.S.	Master of Legal Studies
M.L.S.	Master of Library Science
M. L. & T.	Master of Law and Taxation
M.M.	Master of Management
M.N.M.	Master of Nonprofit Management
M.N.O.	Master of Nonprofit Organization
M.O.B.	Master of Organizational Behavior
M.P.A.	Master of Professional Accountancy
M.P.A.	Master of Public Administration
M.P.H.	Master of Public Health
M.P.P.	Master of Public Policy
M.P.P.A.	Master of Public Policy Administration, Master of Public Policy and Administration
M.P.P.M.	Master of Public and Private Management
M.R.P.	Master of Regional Planning
M.S.	Master of Science
M.S.A.	Master of Sports Administration
M.S.E.L.	Master of Science in Environmental Law
M.S.L.	Master of Studies in Law
M.S.P.H.	Master of Science in Public Health
M.S.S.A.	Master of Science in Social Administration
M.S.W.	Master of Social Work
M.Tax.	Master of Taxation
M.T.S.	Master of Theological Studies
M.U.P.	Master of Urban Planning
M.U.R.P.	Master of Urban and Regional Planning
Pharm.D.	Doctor of Pharmacy
Ph.D.	Doctor of Philosophy
S.J.D.	Doctor of Jurisprudence

KEY ORGANIZATIONS AND WEB SITES

American Bar Association (ABA)
Section of Legal Education and Admissions to the Bar
North Lake Shore Drive
Chicago, Illinois 60611
Phone: (312)988-5000
http://www.abanet.org

Founded in 1878. Nationally recognized accrediting agency for Professional Schools of Law.

Association of American Law Schools (AALS)
1201 Connecticut Avenue, NW, Suite 800
Washington, DC 20036-2605
Phone: (202)296-8851
http://www.aals.org

An association of law schools dedicated to the improvement of the legal profession through legal education.

Health Resource Center
One Dupont Circle, NW, Suite 800
Washington, DC 20036-1193
Phone: (202)939-9320

The American Council on Education operates this national clearinghouse so individuals with disabilities can obtain information related to their concerns.

Law School Admission Council (LSAC)
Box 2000
Newton, PA 18940-0998
Phone: (215)968-1001
http://www.lsac.org

A nonprofit corporation composed of 194 American and Canadian law schools which provide the following services (1) Law School Admissions Test (LSAT), (2) Law School Data Assembly Services (LSDAS), (3) Candidate Referral Services (CRS).

Law Multi-App
740 South Chester Road, Suite F
Swarthmore, PA 19081
Phone: (800)515-2927
http://www.multi-app.com/multi-app

A private corporation which supplies a software package containing a generic law school application accepted by about sixty private/public law schools in lieu of their own individual applications.

National Association for Law Placement
1666 Connecticut Avenue, Suite 325
Washington, DC 20009-1039
Phone: (202)667-1666
http://www.nalp.org

A professional organization of law schools and legal employers established to provide information, coordination, and standards for fair recruitment for all participants in the employment process.

Test of English as a Foreign Language (TOEFL)
P.O. Box 6154
Princeton, NJ 06854-6154
Phone: (609)771-7100
http://www.toefl.org

U.S. Department of Education
Federal Student Aid Information Center
P.O. Box 84
Washington, DC 20044
Phone: (800)4-Fed-Aid
http://www.ed.gov/offices/OPE/Students

A resource for general financial aid information. Financial aid publications (including the FAFSA) may be requested from this resource as well.

World Education Service (Midwest Office)
P.O. Box 11623
Chicago, IL 60661-0623
Phone: (312)222-0882, fax: (312)222-1217

World Education Service (New York City Office)
P.O. Box 745 Old Chelsea Station
New York, NY 10113-0745
Phone: (212)966-6311, fax: (212)966-6395

An organization widely recommended and utilized for translation and evaluation of foreign credentials.

SELECTED PRIVATE LENDING ORGANIZATIONS

The Access Group
1411 Foulk Road
P.O. Box 7430
Wilmington, DE 19803-0430
Phone: (800)282-1550, fax: (302)477-4080

Law Loans
P.O. Box 64337
St. Paul, MN 55164-0337
Phone: (800)984-0190

LawEXCEL
50 Braintree Hill Park, Suite 300
Braintree, MA 02184
Phone: (800)EDU-LOAN

Citi Assist
P.O. Box 22945
Rochester, NY 14692
Phone: (800)745-5473

Law School

Name of Law School	1st Choice:	2nd Choice:	3rd Choice	4th Choice
Geographic Location				
Public/Private				
Size of Parent Institution				
Year Law School Founded				
Size of Law School				
Full-Time Study Only				
Part-Time Study				
Library Size				
Special Facilities				
Special Programs				
Costs				
On-Campus Housing Available				
Total Enrollment				
Number of Full-Time Faculty				
Degrees Offered				
Application Deadline				
Number of Full-Time Applications				
Number of Part-Time Applications				
Number of Full-Time Acceptances				
Number of Part-Time Acceptances				
Number of Full-Time Enrollees				
Number of Part-Time Enrollees				
Median LSAT Scores				
Median GPA				
LSAT Score at 75th Percentile				
GPA at 75th Percentile				
% of 1st Year Class Receiving Scholarships/Grants				
% of Total Enrollment Receiving Financial Aid				
Average Size of Scholarship/Grants				
Number of On-Campus Interviews				
% of Graduates Employed in State				
% of First-Time Bar Exam Takers to Pass Bar Exam				
Average State Passage Rate				

Selection Checklist

ᵗʰ Choice	6ᵗʰ Choice	7ᵗʰ Choice	8ᵗʰ Choice	9ᵗʰ Choice	10ᵗʰ Choice

THE PENGUIN
GUIDE TO
AMERICAN
LAW
SCHOOLS

UNIVERSITY OF AKRON

Akron, Ohio 44325-0001

Internet site: http://www.uakron.edu

Founded 1870. Located 45 miles S of Cleveland. Municipal control. Semester system. Library: 1,078,00 volumes; 1,626,100 microforms; 6,800 periodicals/subscriptions; 120 computer workstations.

University's other graduate colleges/schools: Buchtel College of Arts and Sciences, College of Business, College of Education, College of Engineering, College of Fine and Applied Arts, College of Nursing, College of Polymer Science and Polymer Engineering. Total university enrollment: 25,000.

School of Law

Akron, Ohio 44325-2901

Phone: (800) 4AKRON-U

Internet site: http://www.uakron.edu/law/index.html

E-mail: lawadmissions@uakron.edu

Founded 1921. Merged with University of Akron 1959. Located in the C. Blake McDowell Law Center at corner of Wolf Ledges and University Avenue on main campus. ABA approved 1961. AALS member. Semester system. Full- and part-time study—both day and evening available. Law library: 243,968 volumes; 3,174 periodicals/subscriptions; has LEXIS, NEXIS, WESTLAW, Ohio-LINK; is a Federal Government Depository. The law students' microcomputer network has 12 workstations with complete Internet access.

Annual tuition: resident full-time $6,785, part-time $5,297; nonresident full-time $11,633, part-time $9,085. Limited on-campus housing for single students, none for married students. Annual on-campus housing cost: $5,016 (including board). For on-campus housing information contact Office of Residential Life and Housing. Phone: (216)972-7800. Affordable housing opportunities within walking distance of campus available. Off-campus housing costs: approximately $10,300. For off-campus housing information contact Off-Campus Housing Referral. Phone: (216)972-6636. Additional costs: books approximately $500.

Enrollment: first-year class 150 day, 65 evening; total day and evening 630 (men 60%, women 40%). In first-year class statistics: 15% from out of state; 19 states and 2 foreign countries represented; the average age full-time 24, part-time 28; 40% women; 7.8% minority; more than 60 different majors; 100 different undergraduate institutions; average first-year section sizes full-time 50 students, part-time 63 students.

Faculty: full-time 16, part-time 32; 40% female; 15% minority; student/faculty ratio 30 to 1. Number of upper divisional courses offered after first year 40.

Degree conferred: J.D., J.D.-M.B.A., J.D.-M.P.A., J.D.-M.Tax.

ADMISSION REQUIREMENTS FOR FIRST-YEAR APPLICANTS. LSDAS law school report, LSAT, two recommendations, bachelor's degree from accredited institution, personal statement required with application. Applicants must have received bachelor's degree prior to enrollment. In addition, international applicants must submit TOEFL and TSE before application can be considered. Interview not required. Apply to Admission Director as early as possible after September 1, before March 1 (priority deadline). Applicants admitted fall semester only (mid August). Rolling admissions process notification begins in late November/early December. Application fee $35. Phone: (216)972-7331, 7334. Fax (215)258-2343. Acceptance of offer and first deposit due in April.

ADMISSION REQUIREMENTS FOR TRANSFER APPLICANTS. Accepts transfer applicants from other ABA-accredited schools. Admission limited to space available. At least one year of enrollment, letter from current dean indicating applicant is in good standing, LSAT, LSDAS report (photocopy of original acceptable), personal statement, current law school transcript required in support of application. Submit course descriptions/syllabi for all courses taken at current law school. Apply to Admission Director by May 1 (decision made by mid July). Application fee: $35. Will consider visiting/transient students.

ADMISSION STANDARDS. Number of full-time applicants 1,194, part-time 224; Number accepted 575 full-time, 96 part-time; enrolled 155 full-time, 66 part-time. Median LSAT score 153 (75% of full-time/part-time class have a score at or above 150; median GPA 3.1 (A = 4) (75% of full-time class have a GPA at or above 2.78, 75% of part-time class have a score at or above 2.71). Attrition rate: 5.8%. Gorman ranking: 2.89. *U.S. News & World Report* ranking in the fourth tier of all law schools.

FINANCIAL AID. Scholarships, need and merit-based loans. Assistantships available for upper divisional joint-degree candidates. Apply after January 1 but prior to May 1 (priority deadline) to the university's Office of Student Financial Aid. Phone: (800) 621-3847 or (216) 972-733 1. Use FAFSA (FAFSA code #003123). Information from the College Scholarship Service regarding the applicant's financial need must be received before a financial aid offer can be extended. Approximately 30% of students receive full or partial scholarships. Financial assistance available for part-time students. Average grant full-time $3,000, part-time $1,500. Average debt after graduation $35,000.

DEGREE REQUIREMENTS. For J.D.: 88 credits (44 required) with a 2.0 (A = 4) GPA, plus an upper divisional writing requirement; 3-year day program, 4-year evening program; accelerated J.D. program available. On-campus summer sessions available. Upper divisional students may attend an ABA accredited law school's "Summer Abroad Program" as long as it does not effect the J.D. degree residency requirements. For J.D.-M.B.A.: total 103 credits (J.D. 78 credits, M.B.A. 25 credits). For J.D.-M.P.A.: total 109 credits (J.D. 77 credits, M.P.A. 32 credits). For J.D.-M.Tax.: total 98 (J.D. 78 credits, M.Tax. 20 credits).

CAREER AND PLACEMENT. Approximated 75% of graduates are employed in state. More than 60% of graduates are practicing law; 6% in business; 12% in government; 2% in academia. Approximately 90% of the University of Akron's first-time bar exam takers pass the Ohio Bar Exam; Ohio's passage rate for all first-time takers from ABA-approved schools is 90%. Graduates are eligible to take bar exams in all 50 states.

UNIVERSITY OF ALABAMA
P.O. Box 870188
Tuscaloosa, Alabama 35487-0118
Internet site: http://www.ua.edu

Founded 1831. Located 50 miles SW of Birmingham. Public control. Semester system. Library: 1,860,000 volumes; 2,560,000 microforms; 16,000 periodicals/subscriptions.

University's other graduate colleges/schools: College of Arts and Sciences, College of Communication, College of Education, College of Engineering, College of Human Environmental Sciences, Manderson Graduate School of Business, School of Library & Information Studies, School of Social Work.

Total university enrollment: 13,000.

School of Law
P.O. Box 8703825
Tuscaloosa, Alabama 35487-0382
Phone: (205)348-5440
Internet site: http://www.law.ua.edu
E-mail: bmcginle@law.ua.edu

Established 1872. Located at Tuscaloosa. ABA approved since 1926. AALS member. Semester system. Full-time, day study only. Law library: 227,900 volumes; 95,000 microforms; 3,000 current periodicals; has LEXIS, NEXIS, WESTLAW, DIALOG, OCLC; is a Federal Government Depository. Special programs: summer study abroad at University of Freiburg, Switzerland; externships.

Annual tuition: resident $3,578, nonresident $8,382. On-campus housing available for both single and married students. Annual on-campus housing cost: single students $1,990 (room only), married students $3,375. Housing deadline June 1. Contact Office of Housing and Residential Life, University of Alabama. Phone: (205)348-8086. Law students tend to live off-campus. Off-campus housing cost: approximately $8,200. Additional cost: books approximately $500.

Enrollment: first-year class 191; total full-time 548 (men 57%, women 43%); no part-time students. First-year statistics: 15% out of state, 10 states and foreign countries represented; 40% women; 12% minority; average age 23; 52 undergraduate institutions represented; range of first-year section sizes 16–96 students; number of upper division courses offered after first year 83.

Faculty: full-time 28, part-time 31; 22% female; 7% minority; student/faculty ratio 19 to 1.

Degrees conferred: J.D., J.D.-M.B.A., LL.M. (Tax), M.C.L. (only for persons who have completed a basic legal education and received a university degree in law in another country).

RECRUITMENT PRACTICES AND POLICIES. Attends national law school forums. School has diversity program and actively recruits women/minority applicants.

ADMISSION REQUIREMENTS FOR FIRST-YEAR APPLICANTS. LSDAS law school report, LSAT (not later than December test date, if more than one LSAT, highest is used), bachelor's degree from an accredited institution, transcripts (must show all schools attended and at least three years of study) required in support of application. Applicants must have received bachelor's degree prior to entrance. Interview not required but may be requested by school. In addition, international applicants must submit TOEFL (not older than two years). Apply to Admission Coordinator after September 1, before March 1. First-year students admitted fall only. Rolling admissions process, notification starts in November and is finished by late April. Acceptance of offer and first deposit deadline May 1. School does maintain a waiting list. Application fee $25. Phone: (205)348-5440. E-mail: admissions@law.ua.edu. Admission deadline for M.C.L. February 1.

ADMISSION REQUIREMENTS FOR TRANSFER APPLICANTS. Accepts transfers from other ABA-accredited schools. Admission limited to space available. At least one year of enrollment, in good standing, prefer applicants in the top quarter of first-year class, and submit LSAT, LSDAS, personal statement regarding reason for transfer request. Apply to Admission Coordinator by June 1. Application fee $25.

ADMISSION STANDARDS. Number of full-time applicants 814; number accepted 304; number enrolled 191; median LSAT 156 (75% of class have a score at or above 153); median GPA 3.4 (A = 4) (75% of class have a GPA at or above 3.16). Attrition rate 3.5%. Gorman ranking 3.24; *U.S. News & World Report* ranking is in the second tier of all law schools.

FINANCIAL AID. Scholarships, merit scholarships; loans and federal WS offered through university's Financial Aid Office. For scholarships (selection criteria place heavy reliance on LSAT and undergraduate GPA), apply to Assistant Dean of school after January 1 before May 1. Phone: (205)348-4508. Use Schools FAF. For all other programs apply to Director of Student Financial Services, University of Alabama, P.O. Box 870162. Phone: (205)348-6756. Use FAFSA (FAFSA code #001051). Approximately 25% of students receive scholarships. Average scholarship grant $2,000. Average debt after graduation $29,015.

DEGREE REQUIREMENTS. For J.D.: 90 credits (36 required) with a 2.0 (A = 4) GPA, plus completion of upper divisional writing course; 3-year program. Accelerated J.D. with 1 summer of course work. For J.D.-M.B.A.: total 108 credits (J.D. approximately 80 credits, M.B.A. approximately 38). For LL.M. (Tax): 24 credits. For M.C.L. (International): 30 credits; at least two semesters in residence; GPA of 2.5 (A = 4) required.

CAREER AND PLACEMENT INFORMATION. Approximately 78% of graduates are employed in state. More than 80% of graduates are practicing law; 8% are in business; 10% in government; 2% in academia. Approximately 90% of the University of Alabama's first-time state bar exam takers pass the Alabama State Bar Exam; Alabama's state passage rate for all first-time takers from ABA-approved schools is 90%.

THE AMERICAN UNIVERSITY
Washington, D.C. 20016-8111
Internet site: http://www.american.edu

Founded 1893. Located 3 miles W of downtown. Private control. Semester system. Library: 580,000 volumes; 715,000 microforms; 3,000 periodicals/subscriptions; 53 computer workstations.

University's other graduate colleges/schools: College of Arts and Sciences, College of Education, Kogod College of Business Administration, School of Communication, School of International Service, School of Public Affairs.

Total university enrollment: 9,928.

Washington College of Law
4801 Massachusetts Avenue, NW
Washington, D.C. 20016-8186
Phone: (202)274-4101
Internet site: http://www.wcl.american.edu
E-mail: wcladmit@wcl.american.edu

Established 1896. Located on main campus. ABA approved since 1940. AALS member. Semester system. Full-time, part-time, day, evening study. Law library: 404,890 volumes; 6,181 current periodicals; has LEXIS, NEXIS, WESTLAW, DIALOG, OCLC; is a Federal Government Depository. Special programs: Program for Advanced Studies in the Federal Regulatory Process (summer); independent study, externships. LL.M. specializations include International Trade and Banking, International Organizations, International Environmental Law, International Protection of Human Rights.

Annual tuition: full-time $21,894; part-time per credit $799. Off-campus housing only. Off-campus housing costs (includes room, board, transportation): approximately $12,734. Additional cost: books approximately $540.

Enrollment: first-year class 374, day 286, evening 88; total 870 (men 49%, women 51%). First-year statistics: 35 states and foreign countries represented; 51% women; 23% minority; average age 24; 160 undergraduate institutions represented.

Faculty: full-time 55, part-time 163; 32% female; 8% minority; student/faculty ratio 24 to 1; number of upper division courses offered after first year 160; part-time 67.

Degrees conferred: J.D., J.D.-M.B.A. (Kogod College of Business Administration), J.D.-M.A. (School of International Affairs), J.D.-M.S. (School of Public Affairs in Law Justice and Society), LL.M. (International Legal Studies, a 1-year program for both U.S. and international attorneys).

RECRUITMENT PRACTICES AND POLICIES. Attends local and national law school forums. Conducts on-campus information sessions. College does have diversity program and actively recruits women/minority applicants.

ADMISSION REQUIREMENTS FOR FIRST-YEAR APPLICANTS. LSDAS law school report, LSAT (not later than February test date), bachelor's degree from an accredited institution, two recommendations required in support of application. Applicants must have received bachelor's degree prior to entrance. In addition, international applicants must submit TOEFL (minimum acceptable score 600), certified transcript and evaluation of all foreign documents from a member association of the National Association of Credential Evaluation Services (NACES). Joint-degree applicants must apply to and be accepted by both schools; GRE required for J.D.-M.S. Apply to Office of Admission after October 1, before March 1. First-year students admitted fall only. Rolling admission process; notification starts as early as mid-December. Acceptance of offer and first deposit due date April 15. School does maintain a waiting list. Application fee $55. Phone: (202)274-4101. Fax: (202)274-4107. E-mail: wcladmit@wcl.american.edu.

ADMISSION REQUIREMENTS FOR TRANSFER APPLICANTS. Accepts transfers from other ABA-accredited schools. Admission limited to space available. At least one year of enrollment, in good standing, LSAT, dean's statement indicating applicant's eligibility to return, transcripts of all schools/colleges attended required in support of application. Apply to Office of Admission by May 1. All transfer decisions made by mid-July. Application fee $55.

ADMISSION STANDARDS. Number of full-time applicants 4,054, part-time 512; number accepted full-time 1,643, part-time 225; number enrolled full-time 286, part-time 88; median LSAT full-time 158 (75% of full-time class have a score at or above 155), part-time 152 (75% of part-time class have a score at or above 149); median GPA 3.32 (A = 4) (75% of full-time class have a GPA at or above 3.07, 75% of part-time class have a GPA at or above 2.66). Attrition rate: 1.9%. Gorman ranking 3.84; *U.S. News & World Report* ranking is in the second tier of all law schools.

FINANCIAL AID. Washington College of Law Grants, scholarships, minority scholarships, federal loans, private loans. Apply to Financial Aid Office of school after January 1, before March 1. Phone: (202)274-4040. Use FAFSA (due by March 1) (FAFSA code #001434), Access disk due by February 1 for grants and scholarships. Approximately 84% of first-year students receive aid. Approximately 73% receive loans. Average scholarship/grant $6,587. Financial aid available for part-time study. Average debt after graduation $66,000.

DEGREE REQUIREMENTS. For J.D.: 86 credits (34 required) with a 2.0 (A = 4) GPA, plus completion of upper divisional writing course; 3-year full-time, 4-year part-time program. For J.D.-M.B.A.: total 108 credits (J.D. 80 credits, M.B.A. approximately 32-41 credits). For J.D.-M.A.: total 101 credits (J.D. 80 credits, M.A. 21 credits; approximately 3½ years). For J.D.-M.S.: total 113 credits (J.D. 80 credits, M.S. 33 credits). For LL.M.: 24–31 credits.

CAREER AND PLACEMENT INFORMATION. About 125–130 employers conducted on-campus interviews. Approximately 79% of graduates are employed in Maryland, New York, Virginia; more than 62% are practicing law; 8% are in business; 12% in government; 2% in academia. Approximately 67% (MD), 68% (VA), 70% (NY) of the Washington College of Law's first-time state bar exam takers pass the bar exam; the passage rate for all first-time takers from ABA-approved schools is 75% (MD), 76% (VA), 78% (NY). Graduates are eligible to take the bar exam in all 50 states.

ARIZONA STATE UNIVERSITY
Tempe, Arizona 85287-1003
Internet site: http://www.asu.edu/

Founded 1885. Located 10 miles E of Phoenix. Public control. Semester system. Library: 2,712,000 volumes; 4,150,000 microforms; 32,241 periodicals/subscriptions; 190 workstations.

University's other graduate colleges/schools: College of Architecture and Environmental Design, College of Business, College of Education, College of Engineering and Applied Sciences, College of Fine Arts, College of Liberal Arts and Sciences, College of Nursing, College of Public Programs, School of Social Work.

Total university enrollment: 42,185.

School of Law
Armstrong Hall
P.O. Box 877906
Tempe, Arizona 85287-7906
Phone: (602)965-6181. Fax: (602)965-2427
Internet site: http://www.asu.edu/law

Established 1967. Located on the main campus. ABA approved since 1969. AALS member since 1969. Semester system. Full-time, day study only. Law library: 340,000 volumes and microforms; 6,400 current periodicals/subscriptions; has LEXIS, WESTLAW. Special programs: Indian Legal program, Center for the Study of Law, Science and Technology, externships in prosecution and defender clinics.

Annual tuition: resident $4,059, nonresident $10,711. On-campus housing available for single students only. Annual on-campus housing costs: single students $3,460 (room only). Law students tend to live in nearby off-campus housing. Average off-campus housing costs: $10,765. Contact the Office of Residential Life for both on- and off-campus housing information. Phone: (602)965-3515. Additional costs: books approximately $600.

Enrollment: first-year class 150; total full-time 500 (men 60%, women 40%); no part-time students. First-year statistics: 24% out of state, 79 states and foreign countries represented; 47% women; 25% minority; average age 28; 100 undergraduate institutions represented; range of first-year section sizes 30–125 students; number of upper division courses offered after first year 92.

Faculty: full-time 33, part-time 26; 27% female; 16% minority; student/faculty ratio 16 to 1.

Degrees conferred: J.D., J.D.-M.B.A., J.D.-M.H.S.A., J.D.-Ph.D. (Justice)

RECRUITMENT PRACTICES AND POLICIES. Attends national law school forums. School does have diversity program and actively recruits women/minority applicants.

ADMISSION REQUIREMENTS FOR FIRST-YEAR APPLICANTS. Application available online, must have Adobe Acrobat Reader. Application materials available in September. Submit LSDAS law school report (completed by December), LSAT (not later than December test date and include writing sample), bachelor's degree from an accredited institution, domicile affidavit, personal statement (no longer than three pages), transcripts (must show all schools attended and at least three years of study) required in support of application. Recommendations not required but considered important. Applicants must have received bachelor's degree prior to enrollment. In addition, international applicants must submit a preliminary application, TOEFL (not older than two years), TSE, TWE. Apply to Admission Committee after October 1, before March 1. First-year students admitted fall only. Most students will be notified of acceptance in April. Application fee $35. Phone: (602)965-1474.

ADMISSION REQUIREMENTS FOR TRANSFER APPLICANTS. Accepts transfers from other ABA-accredited schools. Admission limited to space available. Admits both fall and spring. Applicants should have at least one year of enrollment, be in good standing, and rank in the top 10 percent of first-year class. LSAT, LSDAS, personal statement regarding reason for transfer, current law school transcript required in support of application. Apply to Admission Committee by October 1 (spring), July 1 (fall). Application fee $35. Will consider visiting/transient applicants.

ADMISSION STANDARDS. Number of full-time applicants 1,795; number accepted 378; number enrolled 150; median LSAT 161 (75% of class have a score at or above 156); median GPA 3.4 (A = 4) (75% of class have a GPA at or above 3.19). Attrition rate 4.6%. Gorman ranking 3.3; *U.S. News & World Report* ranking is in the top 45 of all law schools.

FINANCIAL AID. For financial aid information contact the College of Law's Assistant Dean. Phone: (602)965-6380. Financial aid includes grants, merit scholarships, institutional loans, private loans, federal loans. All students are automatically considered for merit scholarships by college's Admissions Committee during the decision process. For all other aid apply to university's Student Financial Assistance Office after January 1, before May 1. Phone: (602)965-3355. Use FAFSA (FAFSA code #001081). Approximately 82% of first-year class received aid. Approximately 45% receive some form of grant. Average scholarship/grant $3,000. Average debt after graduation $23,000.

DEGREE REQUIREMENTS. For J.D.: 87 credits (34 required) with a 2.0 (A = 4) GPA; 3-year program. For J.D.-M.B.A.: total 117 credits (J.D. 80 credits, M.B.A. 37 credits); approximately 4–5 years to complete. For J.D.-M.H.S.A.: total 117 (J.D. 80 credits, M.H.S.A. 37 credits); approximately 4 years to complete. For J.D.-Ph.D.: joint-degree programs individually designed in consultation with candidate.

CAREER AND PLACEMENT INFORMATION. Approximately 83% of graduates are employed in state. More than 74% of graduates are practicing law; 9% are in business; 17% in government; none in academia. Approximately 85% of Arizona State University's first-time state bar exam takers pass the Arizona state bar exam; Arizona's passage rate for all first-time takers from ABA-approved schools is 84%.

UNIVERSITY OF ARIZONA

Tucson, Arizona 95721
Internet site: http://www.Arizona.edu

Founded 1885. Located 100 miles SW of Phoenix, near the international border. Public control. Semester system. Library: 3,907,000 volumes; 4,624,000 microforms; 26,000 periodicals/ subscriptions.

University's other graduate colleges/schools: College of Agriculture, College of Architecture, College of Business and Public Administration, College of Education, College of Engineering and Mines, College of Fine Arts, College of Humanities, College of Nursing, College of Pharmacy, College of Science, College of Social and Behavioral Sciences, School of Health Related Professions; College of Medicine.

Total university enrollment: 34,777.

College of Law

Tucson, Arizona 95721
Phone: (502)621-3477
Internet site: http://www.law.Arizona.edu
E-mail: admission@law.arizona.edu

Established 1915. Located at corner of Mountain and Speedway. ABA-approved since 1930. AALS member since 1931. Semester system. Full-time, day study only. Law library: 362,000 volumes and microforms; 4,121 current periodicals/subscriptions; 28 computer workstations; has LEXIS, NEXIS, WESTLAW, DIALOG, OCLC. Special programs: LL.M. (open to both U.S. and international attorneys), several congressional internships, a state legislative internship, internships programs with Navajo, Pascua Yaqui, White Mountain Apache, and Tohono O'Odham tribal governments.

Annual tuition: resident $4,060, nonresident $10,712. On-campus housing available for both single students. Annual on-campus housing costs: single students $8,094 (including board). Contact Residence Life Office for both on-and off-campus housing information. Phone: (520)621-6500. Law students tend to live off-campus. Off-campus housing costs: approximately $11,740. Additional costs: books approximately $600.

Enrollment: first-year class 151; total full-time 472 (men 51%, women 49%); no part-time students. First-year statistics: 21% out of state, 45 states and foreign countries represented; 45% women; 27% minority; average age 26; 160 undergraduate institutions represented; range of first-year section sizes 25–75 students; number of upper division courses offered after first year 97.

Faculty: full-time 30, part-time 59; 30% female; 9% minority; student/faculty ratio 16 to 1.

Degrees conferred: J.D., J.D.-M.B.A., J.D.-M.P.A., J.D.-M.A. (Economics, American Indian Studies), LL.M. (International Trade Law), J.D.-Ph.D. (Economics, Philosophy, Psychology).

RECRUITMENT PRACTICES AND POLICIES. Attends national law school forums. School does have diversity program and actively recruits women/minority applicants.

ADMISSION REQUIREMENTS FOR FIRST-YEAR APPLICANTS. LSDAS law school report, LSAT (not later than December test date, if more than one LSAT, scores are averaged), bachelor's degree from an accredited institution, domicile affidavit, résumé, personal statement, two recommendations, prelaw advisor recommendation, transcripts (must show all schools attended and at least three years of study) required in support of application. Applicants must have received bachelor's degree prior to enrollment. Interview not required. In addition, international applicants must submit TOEFL (not older than one year) and transcript with an explanation of grading system and detailed written analysis of transcript by an objective agency. Apply to Assistant Dean after December 1, before March 1. First-year students admitted fall only (mid August start). Rolling admission process. Acceptance of offer and first deposit due date May 1. School does maintain a waiting list. Application fee $45. Phone: (520)621-3477; E-mail: admissions@law.arizona.edu.

ADMISSION REQUIREMENTS FOR TRANSFER APPLICANTS. Accepts transfers from other ABA-accredited schools. Admission limited to space available. At least one year of enrollment, in good standing. Prefer applicants in top quarter (residents), top 10 percent (nonresidents) of first-year class, LSAT, LSDAS, personal statement regarding reason for transfer, domicile affidavit, current law school transcript including grades and class rank through final semester of study required in support of application. Apply to Assistant Dean by December 1 (spring), July 15 (fall). Admission decisions made by December 15 (spring), August 1 (fall). Application fee $45. Will consider visiting/transient applicants.

ADMISSION REQUIREMENTS FOR LL.M. Transcripts including evidence of graduation with J.D. (or equivalent); two recommendations; evidence of interest and ability in international law; evidence of a commitment to teach at a law school level; involvement in government service or international law; fluency in Spanish or Portuguese; current résumé; personal statement; LSAT scores if taken, domicile affidavit required in support of application. In addition, international candidates for whom English is not their first language, a TOEFL is required (usual minimum TOEFL score is 600). Apply by February 28 to Director, Graduate Studies in Law. Earlier applications are encouraged. Application fee $45. Phone: (520)621-1801. Fax: (520)621-9836. E-mail: gavit@ Law.arizona.edu.

ADMISSION STANDARDS. Number of full-time applicants 1,773; number accepted 478; number enrolled 151; median LSAT 162 (75% of class have a score at or above 156); median GPA 3.4 (A = 4) (75% of class have a GPA at or above 3.12). Attrition rate 1.7%. Gorman ranking 3.33; *U.S. News & World Report* ranking is in the top 38 of all law schools.

FINANCIAL AID. Scholarships, merit scholarships, institutional loans, federal loans, and federal WS offered through university's Office of Student Financial Aid. For scholarships (selection criteria place heavy reliance on LSAT and undergraduate GPA), apply to Financial Aid Office of college after January 1, before March 1. Phone: (520)621-3477. Use school's FAF. For all other programs apply to Director of the Office of Student Financial Aid. Phone: (520)621-1858. Use FAFSA (FAFSA code #001083). Approximately 55% of first-year class received aid. Average scholarship/grant $2,000. Average debt after graduation $23,000.

DEGREE REQUIREMENTS. For J.D.: 85 credits (39 required) with a 2.0 (A = 4) GPA, plus completion of upper divisional writing course; 3-year program. For J.D.-M.B.A.: total 125 credits (J.D. minimum of 80 credits, M.B.A. minimum of 45 credits), 4-year program. For J.D.-M.P.A.: total 119 credits (J.D. minimum of 80 credits, M.P.A. minimum of 39 credits), 4-year program. For J.D.-M.A.: total 105 credits (J.D. minimum of 80 credits, M.A. minimum of 25 credits, thesis may be required). For J.D.-M.S.: total 105 credits (J.D. minimum of 80 credits, M.S. minimum of 25 credits, thesis may be required). For LL.M.: a minimum of 24 credits beyond J.D.; several legal research papers may be required.

CAREER AND PLACEMENT INFORMATION. Approximately 68% of graduates are employed in state. More than 65% of graduates are practicing law; 12.5% are in business; 21% in government; 1.5% in academia. Approximately 90% of the University of Arizona's first-time state bar exam takers pass the Arizona Bar Exam; Arizona's passage rate for all first-time takers from ABA-approved schools is 84%.

UNIVERSITY OF ARKANSAS
Fayetteville, Arkansas 72701-1201
Internet site: http://www.uark.edu

Founded 1871. Located 200 miles NW of Little Rock. Public control. Semester system. Library: 1,452,000 volumes; 860,675 microforms; 16,298 periodicals/subscriptions; 150 computer workstations.

University's other graduate colleges/schools: College of Business Administration, College of Education, College of Engineering, Dale Bumpers College of Agricultural, Food and Life Sciences, J. William Fulbright College of Arts and Sciences.

Total university enrollment: 14,692.

School of Law
Robert A. Leflar Law Center
Fayetteville, Arkansas 72701-1201
Phone: (501)575-3102
Internet site: http://Law-gopher.uark.edu

Established 1924. Located on main campus. Environment: small town. ABA-approved since 1926. AALS member since 1927. Semester system. Full-time, day study only. Law library: 238,000 volumes and microforms; 2,200 current periodicals/subscriptions; has LEXIS, WESTLAW, Legistate; is a Federal and State Government Depository. Special programs: LL.M. in Agricultural Law.

Annual tuition: resident $3,613, nonresident $8,101. LL.M. tuition charges: residents $3,264, nonresidents $4,032. On-campus housing available for both single and married students. Annual on-campus housing cost: single students $2,700 (room only), $4,400 (includes board), married students approximately $3,000. Contact Residence Life and Dining Services. Phone: (501)575-3951. Off-campus housing costs: approximately $10,464. Additional costs: approximately $1,231 for J.D.; approximately $1,000 for LL.M.

Enrollment: first-year class 156; total full-time 394 (men 63%, women 37%); no part-time students. First-year statistics: 20% out of state, 33 states and foreign countries represented; 40% women; 10% minority; average age 26; 126 undergraduate institutions represented; range of first-year section sizes 25–75 students; number of upper division courses offered after first year 101.

Faculty: full-time 32, part-time 11; 22% female; 11% minority; student/faculty ratio 12 to 1.

Degrees conferred: J.D., J.D.-M.B.A., LL.M. (Agricultural Law).

RECRUITMENT PRACTICES AND POLICIES. Attends national law school forums. School does have diversity program and actively recruits women/minority applicants.

ADMISSION REQUIREMENTS FOR FIRST-YEAR APPLICANTS.

LSDAS law school report, LSAT (not later than February test date), bachelor's degree from an accredited institution, transcripts (must show all schools attended and at least three years of study) required in support of application. Applicants must have received bachelor's degree prior to enrollment. Interview and additional information may be may be requested by school for some state residents. In addition, international applicants must submit TOEFL. Apply to Dean of Admission after October 1, before April 1. Admission materials available in September. Early applications encouraged; preferably by January 1. Applicants after April 1 considered on a space available basis only. Out-of-state applicants considered on basis of LSAT and undergraduate GPA only. First-year students admitted fall only. Rolling admission process, notification starts in January and is finished by late April. Acceptance of offer and first deposit due date May 1. Application fee none. Phone: (501)575-5601.

ADMISSION REQUIREMENTS FOR TRANSFER APPLICANTS.

Accepts transfers from other ABA-accredited schools. Admission limited to space available. At least one year of enrollment, in good standing, prefer applicants in the top quarter of first-year class, LSAT, LSDAS, personal statement regarding reason for transfer, current law school transcript required in support of student's application. Apply to Admission Coordinator by June 1. Will consider visiting/transient applicants.

ADMISSION REQUIREMENTS FOR LL.M.

Cover letter including statement of purpose, evidence of law degree, three letters of recommendation, University of Arkansas Application for admission plus graduate program's application. In addition, international applicants should submit TOEFL, TSE if English is not first language, TOEFL scores should arrive by April 15 (TOEFL score required 600, scores below 600 may be accepted on a conditional basis; TSE score required between 55 and 60), official transcript with English translation and certificate of authenticity, total of 4 letters of recommendation, evidence of adequate funding for entire LL.M. program required in support of application. Apply to Director, Graduate Agricultural Law Program, University of Arkansas School of Law. Phone: (501)575-3706. Fax: (501)575-2053. Telex: 314000. E-mail: LBEARD@ MERCURY.UARK.EDU.

ADMISSION STANDARDS.

Number of full-time applicants 733; number accepted 356; number enrolled 156; median LSAT 153 (75% of class have a score at or above 147); median GPA 3.19 (A = 4) (75% of class have a GPA at or above 2.88). Attrition rate 8.6%. Gorman ranking 2.86; *U.S. News & World Report* ranking is in the third tier of all law schools.

FINANCIAL AID.

Scholarships, minority scholarships, institutional loans, federal loans and federal WS offered through university's Financial Aid Office. For scholarships (selection criteria place heavy reliance on LSAT and undergraduate GPA), apply to Director of Financial Aid of school after January 1, before April 1. Phone: (501)575-3806. Use FAFSA. Approximately 24% of first-year class received scholarships, 63% receive loans. Average scholarship/grant $2,250. For LL.M. applicants: graduate assistantships, waiver of nonresident tuition charge. Apply to Director, Graduate Program in Agricultural Law with application for admission.

DEGREE REQUIREMENTS.

For J.D.: 90 credits (44 required) with a 2.0 (A = 4) GPA; 3-year program. Accelerated J.D. with 1 summer of course work. Transfer must complete at least 2 semesters in residence. For J.D.-M.B.A.: total 110 credits (J.D. 86 credits, M.B.A. 24 credits). For LL.M. (Agriculture Law): 24 credits, at least 3 credits taken in College of Agriculture; GPA of 2.75 (A = 4); completion within 4 years.

CAREER AND PLACEMENT INFORMATION.

Approximately 42% of graduates are employed in state. More than 72% of graduates are practicing law; 12% are in business; 14% in government; 1% in academia. Approximately 84% of the University of Arkansas' first-time state bar exam takers pass the Arkansas Bar Exam; Arkansas' passage rate for all first-time takers from ABA-approved schools is 84%.

UNIVERSITY OF ARKANSAS

Little Rock, Arkansas 72204-1099
Internet site: http://www.ualr.edu

Located in the city of Little Rock. Public control. Semester system. Library: 394,780 volumes; 691,612 microforms; 2,626 periodicals/subscriptions; 100 computer workstations.

University's other graduate colleges/schools: College of Arts, Humanities and Social Sciences, College of Business Administration, College of Education, College of Professional Studies, College of Sciences and Engineering Technology.

Total university enrollment: 11,000.

School of Law

1201 McAlmont Street
Little Rock, Arkansas 72202-5142
Phone: (501)324-9434
Internet site: http://www.ualr.edu

Established 1965. Moved in 1992 to a location 6 miles from main campus. ABA approved since 1969. AALS member. Semester system. Full-time, part-time study. Law library: 249,000 volumes and microforms; 3,183 current periodicals/subscriptions; 64 computer workstations; has LEXIS, WESTLAW, DIALOG; is both a Federal and State Government Depository.

Annual tuition: full-time resident $4,206, nonresident $9,274; part-time resident $136 per credit, nonresident $308 per credit. On-campus housing available for single students. Annual on-campus housing cost: single students $8,900 (includes room and board). Law students tend to live off-campus. For both on- and off-campus information contact Graduate Student Housing. Phone: (501)569-3392. Off-campus housing cost: approximately $9,517. Additional costs: books approximately $700.

Enrollment: first-year class full-time 86, part-time 43; total full-time 263, part-time 154 (men 52%, women 48%). First-year statistics: 20% out of state; 18 states and foreign countries represented; 48% women; 12% minority; average age 27; 98 undergraduate institutions represented; average first-year section sizes full-time 75 students, part-time 50 students; number of upper division courses offered after first year full-time 44, part-time 34.

Faculty: full-time 25, part-time 22; 30% female; 10% minority; student/faculty ratio 15 to 1.

Degrees conferred: J.D., J.D.-M.B.A.

RECRUITMENT PRACTICES AND POLICIES. Attends national law school forums. On-campus informational sessions. School does have diversity program and actively recruits women/minority applicants.

ADMISSION REQUIREMENTS FOR FIRST-YEAR APPLICANTS. LSDAS law school report, LSAT, bachelor's degree from an accredited institution, personal statement, interview, two recommendations, transcripts (must show all schools attended and at least three years of study) required in support of application. Applicants must have received bachelor's degree prior to enrollment. Interview not required but may be requested by school. In addition, international applicants must submit TOEFL.

Apply to Director of Admission and Registrar after October 1, before April 1. First-year students admitted fall only. Rolling admission process. Application fee $40. Phone: (501)324-9439. Fax: (601)324-9433. E-mail: admissions@ualr.edu.

ADMISSION REQUIREMENTS FOR TRANSFER APPLICANTS. Accepts transfers from other ABA-accredited schools. Admission limited to space available. At least one year of enrollment, in good standing, LSAT, LSDAS, personal statement regarding reason for transfer, current law school transcript required in support of application. Apply to Director of Admission and Registrar by June 1. Application fee $40. Will consider visiting/transient applicants.

ADMISSION STANDARDS. Number of full-time applicants 317, part-time 150; number of full-time accepted 181, part-time 65; number of full-time enrolled 86, part-time 49; median LSAT 156 (75% of class have a score at or above 153); median GPA 3.1 (A = 4) (75% of class have a GPA at or above 2.91). Attrition rate 6.8%. Gorman ranking 2.47; *U.S. News & World Report* ranking is in the fourth tier of all law schools.

FINANCIAL AID. Scholarships, merit scholarships, institutional loans, federal loans and federal WS offered through university's Financial Aid Office. For scholarships, apply to Assistant Dean of school after January 1, before April 1. Phone: (501)324-9434. For all other programs apply to university's Director of Financial Aid. Phone: (501)569-3392. Use FAFSA. Approximately 22% receive scholarships. Average scholarship/grant full-time $1,500, part-time $1,135. Financial aid available for part-time students. Additional financial aid available for second- and third-year students.

DEGREE REQUIREMENTS. For J.D.: 87 credits (50 required) with a 2.0 (A = 4) GPA, plus completion of upper divisional writing course; full-time 3-year program, part-time 4-year program. Accelerated J.D. with 1 summer of course work. For J.D.-M.B.A.: total 102–123 (J.D. 78 credits, M.B.A. 24–45 credits, depending previous business background) credits.

CAREER AND PLACEMENT INFORMATION. Approximately 77% of graduates are employed in state. More than 56% of graduates are practicing law; 28% are in business; 11% in government; 3% in academia. Approximately 85% of the University of Arkansas at Little

Rock's first-time state bar exam takers pass the Arkansas Bar Exam; Arkansas's passage rate for all first-time takers from ABA-approved schools is 84%.

UNIVERSITY OF BALTIMORE

Baltimore, Maryland 21201-5779
Internet site: http://www.ubalt.edu

Founded 1925. Located in the heart of Baltimore's cultural district. Public control, part of the University of Maryland system. Semester system. Library: 410,000 volumes; 53,100 microforms; 1,400 periodicals/subscriptions.

University's other graduate colleges/schools: College of Liberal Arts, School of Business.

Total university enrollment: 5,000.

School of Law

1420 North Charles Street
Baltimore, Maryland 21201-5779
Phone: (410)837-4458
Internet site: http://www.ubalt.edu/www/law

Established 1925. Joined University of Maryland system in 1988. Located in midtown area in the John and Frances Angelos Law Center. ABA approved since 1972. AALS member. Semester system. Full-time, part-time, day, evening study. Law library: total of 285,000 volumes including microforms; 3,272 current periodicals; 55 computer workstations; has LEXIS, WESTLAW, DIALOG, CARL. Special programs: Center for International and Comparative Law; summer abroad at the University of Aberdeen, Scotland; special program in summer for conditionally admitted students.

Annual tuition: full-time resident $8,352, nonresident $14,480; part-time resident $6,878, nonresident $11,318. No on-campus housing available. Law students live off-campus. Contact School of Law for off-campus information. Off-campus housing cost: approximately $10,480. Additional costs: books approximately $600.

Enrollment: first-year class 310 (day 224, evening 86); total 650 (men 52%, women 48%). First-year statistics: 20% out of state, 22 states and foreign countries represented; 45% women; 20% minority; average age full-time 27, part-time 29; 60 undergraduate institutions represented; average first-year section size 75 students; number of upper division courses offered after first year 69 day, 82 evening.

Faculty: full-time 39, part-time 57; 35% female; 12% minority; student/faculty ratio 19 to 1.

Degrees conferred: J.D., J.D.-M.B.A., J.D.-M.P.A., J.D.-M.S. (Criminal Justice), LL.M. (Tax), J.D.-Ph.D. (Policy Science).

RECRUITMENT PRACTICES AND POLICIES. Attends some national law school forums. On-campus informational sessions. School does have diversity program and actively recruits women/minority applicants.

ADMISSION REQUIREMENTS FOR FIRST-YEAR APPLICANTS. LSDAS law school report, LSAT (not later than February test date), bachelor's degree from an accredited institution, personal statement, two recommendations, transcripts (must show all schools attended and at least three years of study) required in support of application. Applicants must have received bachelor's degree prior to enrollment. In addition, international applicants must submit TOEFL (not older than two years), supplemental international application; call International Student Advisor for SIA. Phone: (410)837-4756. Apply to Director of Admission after September 30, before April 1. Applicants for graduate/J.D. programs must apply to and be accepted by each school. First-year students admitted fall only. Rolling admission process, notification starts in January and is finished by late April. School does maintain a waiting list. Application fee $35. Phone: (410)837-4459. Fax: (410)837-4450. E-mail: lwadmiss@ubmail.ubalt.edu. For LL.M. information, call (410)837-4470.

ADMISSION REQUIREMENTS FOR TRANSFER APPLICANTS. Accepts transfers from other ABA-accredited schools. Admission limited to space available. At least one year of enrollment, in good standing, personal statement regarding reason for transfer, current law school transcript required in support of application. Apply to Director of Admission by June 1. Admission decisions made by mid July. Application fee $35. Will consider visiting students.

ADMISSION STANDARDS. Number of applicants day 1,484, evening 378, total 1,862; number of accepted day 821, evening 171, total 992; number enrolled day 224, evening 86, total 310; median LSAT 153 (75% of class have a score at or above 149); median GPA 3.13 (A = 4) (75% of class have a GPA at or above 2.8). Attrition rate 2.6%. Gorman ranking 2.58; *U.S. News & World Report* ranking is in the fourth tier of all law schools.

FINANCIAL AID. Private loans, federal loans, and Federal WS offered through university's Financial Aid Office. Submit university's Financial Aid Form at the same time as the application for admission preferably before April 1, but send it directly to the Director of Financial Aid. Phone: (410)837-4763. Use FAFSA; a copy of the FAFSA must be sent to the School of Law's Financial Aid Office as well (FAFSA code #002105). In addition have your financial aid transcript sent directly to the university's Financial Aid Office. Approximately 10% of full-time and 13% of part-time first-time students receive scholarships. Approximately 65% of current students received aid. Average scholarship/grant full-time $1,500, part-time $1,200.

DEGREE REQUIREMENTS. For J.D.: 90 credits (39 required) with a 2.0 (A = 4) GPA, plus completion of upper divisional writing course; 3-year day program, 4-year evening program. Accelerated J.D. with 1 summer of course work. For J.D.-M.B.A.: total 117 credits (J.D. 81 credits, M.B.A. 36 credits). For J.D.-M.P.A.:total 115 credits (J.D. 81 credits, M.P.A. 34 credits). For J.D.-M.S.: total 108 credits (J.D. 81 credits, M.S. 27 credits, plus either a comprehensive exam or defense of master's thesis). For J.D.-Ph.D.: 9 graduate credits accepted toward the J.D., 12–15 law credits accepted toward the Ph.D. For LL.M. (Tax): 30 credits.

CAREER AND PLACEMENT INFORMATION. About 30 employers conducted on-campus interviews. Approximately 80% of graduates are employed in state. More than 60% of graduates are practicing law; 18% are in business; 19% in government; 1% in academia. Approximately 82% of the University of Baltimore's first-time state bar exam takers pass the Maryland Bar Exam; Maryland's passage rate for all first-time takers from ABA-approved schools is 75%.

BAYLOR UNIVERSITY

Waco, Texas 76798
Internet site: http://www.baylor.edu

Founded 1985. Located 90 miles S of Dallas/Fort Worth. Private control. Semester system. Library: 1,531,000 volumes; 1,047,100 microforms; 10,500 periodicals/subscriptions; 67 computer workstations.

University's other graduate colleges/schools: Academy of Health Science, College of Arts and Sciences, George W. Truett Seminary, Hankamer School of Business, College of Education, College of Engineering and Computer Science, School of Music, School of Nursing.

Total university enrollment: 12,200.

BAYLOR UNIVERSITY LAW SCHOOL
P.O. Box 97288
Waco, Texas 76798-7288
Phone: (817)755-1911
Internet site: http://www.baylor.edu/baylor/
    Departments/acad/law
E-mail: law_support@baylor.edu

Established 1587, the oldest law school in Texas. ABA approved since 1931. AALS member. Quarter system. Full-time, day study only. Law library: 160,940 volumes and microforms; 2,113 current periodicals/subscriptions; 30 computer workstations; has LEXIS, NEXIS, WESTLAW, DIALOG. Special programs: study abroad in Guadalajara, Mexico for second- and third-year students.

Annual tuition: $11,839. No on-campus housing available. Law students live off-campus. Contact Law School for off-campus information. Off-campus housing cost: approximately $12,300. Additional costs: books approximately $700.

Enrollment: first-year class 65–70 (spring), 30–35 (summer), 60–70 (fall); total full-time 410 (men 63%, women 37%); no part-time students. First-year statistics: 20% out of state, 27 states and foreign countries represented; 37% women; 14% minority; average age 25; 130 undergraduate institutions represented; average first-year section size 45 students; number of upper division courses offered after first year 63.

Faculty: full-time 16, part-time 8; 23% female; 4% minority; student/faculty ratio 21 to 1.

Degrees conferred: J.D., J.D.-M.B.A., J.D.-M.P.P.A. (Political Science), J.D.-M.Tax.

RECRUITMENT PRACTICES AND POLICIES. Attends national law school forums. Two on-campus informational sessions. School does have diversity program and actively recruits women/minority applicants.

ADMISSION REQUIREMENTS FOR FIRST-YEAR APPLICANTS. LSDAS law school report, LSAT (not later than December test date, if more than one LSAT, highest is used), bachelor's degree from an accredited institution, personal statement, three recommendations in support of application. Applicants must have received bachelor's degree prior to enrollment. GMAT required for M.B.A., M.Tax., GRE required for M.P.P.A. In addition, international applicants must submit TOEFL. Apply to Admission Director before March 1 (fall), November 1 (spring), February 1 (summer). Notification date is 4–6 weeks after application deadline. Application fee $40. Phone: (800) BAYLOR-U (option 3) or (817)755-1911. E-mail: law_support@baylor. edu.

ADMISSION REQUIREMENTS FOR TRANSFER APPLICANTS. Accepts transfers from other ABA-accredited schools. Admission limited to space available. At least one year of enrollment, in good standing (prefer applicants with a GPA of 3.0 [A = 4]), LSAT, LSDAS, personal statement regarding reason for transfer, current law school transcript required in support of application. Apply to Admission Director at least two months prior to expected date of enrollment. Application fee $40. Will consider visiting/transient applicants.

ADMISSION STANDARDS. Number of full-time applicants 792; number accepted 310, number enrolled 75; median LSAT 160 (75% of class have a score at or above 157); median GPA 3.48 (A = 4) (75% of class have a GPA at or above 3.28). Attrition rate 6.5%. Gorman ranking 3.31; *U.S. News & World Report* ranking is in the second tier of all law schools.

FINANCIAL AID. Scholarships, merit scholarships, Texas Tuition Grants, institutional loans, federal loans, and Federal WS offered through university's Financial Aid Office. For scholarships (selection criteria place heavy reliance on LSAT and undergraduate GPA) apply to Law School Financial Aid before May 1 (fall), January 1 (spring), April 1 (summer). Phone: (800) BAYLOR-U. For all other programs apply to university's Director of Student Financial Aid, P.O. Box 97028. Use FAFSA (FAFSA code #003545). Approximately 87% of first-year class received aid. Approximately 10% receive scholarships. Average scholarship/grant $2,745. Average debt after graduation $35,335.

DEGREE REQUIREMENTS. For J.D.: 120 quarter credits (76 required) with a 2.0 (A = 4) GPA, plus completion of upper divisional writing course; 3-year program. Accelerated J.D. available. For J.D.-M.B.A.: total 140 quarter credits equivalent (J.D. 108 quarter credits, M.B.A. 32 semester credits). For J.D.-M.P.A.: total 140 quarter credits equivalent (J.D. 108 quarter credits, M.P.A. 32 semester credits). For J.D.-M.Tax: 133 quarter credits equivalent (J.D. 108 quarter credits, M.Tax 25 semester credits).

CAREER AND PLACEMENT INFORMATION. Approximately 92% of graduates are employed in state. More than 86% of graduates are practicing law; 5% are in business; 8% in government; 1% in academia. Approximately 94% of Baylor University's first-time state bar exam takers pass the Texas Bar Exam; Texas passage rate for all first-time takers from ABA-approved schools is 82%.

BOSTON COLLEGE

Chestnut Hill, Massachusetts 02167-9991
Internet site: http://www.bc.edu

Founded 1863. Located 8 miles W of Boston. Private control (Roman Catholic affiliation). Semester system. Library: 1,590,000 volumes; 2,540,000 microforms; 17,489 periodicals/subscriptions.

College's other graduate schools: Graduate School of Arts and Sciences, Graduate School of Education, Graduate School of Social Work, School of Nursing, Wallace E. Carroll Graduate School of Business.

Total college enrollment: 14,695.

Boston College Law School

885 Centre Street
Newton, Massachusetts 02159-1163
Phone: (617)522-8550
Internet site: http://www.bc.edu
E-mail: bclawadm@bc.edu

Established 1929. Located W of Boston. ABA approved since 1932. AALS member. Semester system. Full-time, day study only. Law library: 362,111 volumes and microforms; 5,700 current periodicals/subscriptions; 95 computer workstations; has LEXIS, NEXIS, WEST-LAW, DIALOG. Special programs: summer study abroad program at the University of London.

Annual tuition: $22,360. Law students live off-campus. Contact the college's Office of Off-Campus Housing for off-campus information. Phone: (617)552-3075. Off-campus housing cost: approximately $12,225. Additional costs: books approximately $700.

Enrollment: first-year class 269; total full-time 830 (men 52%, women 48%); no part-time students. First-year statistics: 37 states and foreign countries represented; 46% women; 18% minority; average age 24; 209 undergraduate institutions represented; range of first-year section sizes 35–100 students; number of upper division courses offered after first year 122.

Faculty: full-time 59, part-time 46; 27% female; 11% minority; student/faculty ratio 17 to 1.

Degrees conferred: J.D., J.D.-M.B.A., J.D.-M.S.W.

RECRUITMENT PRACTICES AND POLICIES. Attends national law school forums. On-campus informational sessions. School does have diversity program and actively recruits women/minority applicants.

ADMISSION REQUIREMENTS FOR FIRST-YEAR APPLICANTS. LSDAS law school report, LSAT (not later than December test date), bachelor's degree from an accredited institution, personal statement, two recommendations, transcripts (must show all schools attended and at least three years of study) required in support of application. Applicants must have received bachelor's degree prior to enrollment. International applicants must submit TOEFL if they graduated from a foreign university where the primary mode of instruction was not English. In addition, they must submit transcripts of all post-secondary education which must be reviewed by a U.S. transcript evaluation service certifying that they are equivalent to a U.S. baccalaureate degree. Applications available in September. Apply to Admission Director after November 1, before March 1. Early notification program—if complete application is received by November 26, decisions will be mailed out by December 16. Applicants for joint-degree programs must apply to and be accepted to both schools. First-year students admitted fall only. Rolling admission process. Application fee $65. Phone: (617)552-4350. Fax: (617)552-2615. E-mail: bclawadm@bc.edu.

ADMISSION REQUIREMENTS FOR TRANSFER APPLICANTS. Accepts transfers from other ABA-accredited schools. Admission limited to space available. At least one year of enrollment, in good standing, LSAT, LSDAS, dean's recommendation, personal statement regarding reason for transfer, current law school transcript required in support of application. Apply to Admission Coordinator by July 1. Admission decisions made by August 1. Application fee $50. Will consider visiting/transient applicants.

ADMISSION STANDARDS. Number of full-time applicants 4,644; number accepted 1,225; number enrolled 269; median LSAT 162 (75% of class have a score at or above 159); median GPA 3.42 (A = 4) (75% of class have a GPA at or above 3.17). Attrition rate 3.7%. Gorman ranking 4.29; *U.S. News & World Report* ranking is in the top 22 of all law schools.

FINANCIAL AID. Scholarships, minority scholarships, public interest loan program, private and federal loans, Federal WS. Apply January 1, before March 15. For all programs apply after January 1, before March 15 to College's Director of Financial Aid. Phone: (800)284-0294; (617)353-3163. Use FAFSA (FAFSA code #002128), CSS/analysis profile, needs Access diskette. Approximately 80% of first-year class received aid. Approximately 35% receive scholarships. Average scholarship/grant $7,000. Federal loan forgiveness program available. Average debt after graduation $60,500.

DEGREE REQUIREMENTS. For J.D.: 85 credits (38 required) with a 2.0 (A = 4) GPA, plus completion of upper divisional writing course; 3-year program. Accelerated J.D. with 1 summer of course work. For J.D.-M.B.A.: total 116 (J.D. 73 credits, M.B.A. 43 credits) credits. For J.D.-M.S.W.: total 116 (J.D. 73 credits, M.S.W. 43 credit) credits. Both joint-degree programs can be accomplished in 4 years instead of the usual 5 years needed if degrees taken separately.

CAREER AND PLACEMENT INFORMATION. About 147 employers conducted on-campus interviews. Approximately 50% of graduates are employed in state. More than 75% of graduates are practicing law; 9.5% are in business; 14% in government; 1% in academia. Approximately 92% of Boston College's first-time state bar exam takers pass the Massachusetts Bar Exam; Massachusetts passage rate for all first-time takers from ABA-approved schools is 85%. Graduates are eligible to take the bar exam in all 50 states.

BOSTON UNIVERSITY
Boston, Massachusetts 02215
Internet site: http://www.bu.edu

Founded 1839. Located in the city of Boston. Private control. Semester system. Library: 1,949,000 volumes; 3,444,000 microforms; 28,800 periodicals/subscriptions.

University's other graduate colleges/schools: College of Communication, College of Engineering, Graduate School of Arts and Sciences, Henry M. Goldman School of Graduate Dentistry, Metropolitan College, Sargent College of Allied Health Professions, School for the Arts, School of Education, School of Management, School of Medicine, School of Social Work, School of Theology.

Total university enrollment: 30,400.

School of Law
765 Commonwealth Avenue
Boston, Massachusetts 02215
Phone: (617)353-3112
Internet site: http://web.bu.edu/LAW
E-mail: bulawadm@bu.edu

Established 1872. Located in downtown Boston. ABA approved since 1925. AALS member. Semester system. Full-time, day study only. Law library: 500,000 volumes/microforms; 6,300 current periodicals/subscriptions; 101 computer workstations; has LEXIS, NEXIS, WEST-LAW, DIALOG. Special programs: summer study abroad at Oxford University in England, Université Jean Moulin in Lyon, France, University of Leiden, Netherlands, University of Tel Aviv, Israel.

Annual tuition: $22,268. On-campus housing available for both single and married students. Annual on-campus housing cost: single students $7,040 (room and board), married students $4,040. Contact the Office of Housing for both on- and off-campus housing information. Phone: (617)353-3511. Law students generally live off-campus. Off-campus housing and personal expenses: approximately $12,532. Additional costs: books approximately $700.

Enrollment: first-year class 340; total full-time 1,066 (men 52%, women 48%); no part-time students. First-year statistics: 76% out of state, 66 states and foreign countries represented; 48% women; 18% minority; average age 23; 298 undergraduate institutions represented; range of first-year section sizes 35–100 students; number of upper division courses offered after first year 112.

Faculty: full-time 59, part-time 86; 35% female; 9% minority; student/faculty ratio 17 to 1.

Degrees conferred: J.D., J.D.-M.B.A. (Management, Health Care Management), J.D.-M.A. (International Relations, Mass Preservation), J.D.-M.S. (Mass Communication), J.D.-M.P.H. (Public Health), LL.M. (American Banking Law, International Banking, Taxation, American Law).

RECRUITMENT PRACTICES AND POLICIES. Attends national law school forums. Has on-campus informational sessions. School does have diversity program and actively recruits women/minority applicants.

ADMISSION REQUIREMENTS FOR FIRST-YEAR APPLICANTS. LSDAS law school report, LSAT (not later than February test date, bachelor's degree from an accredited institution, résumé, personal statement, two recommendations, transcripts (must show all schools attended and at least three years of study) required in support of application. Applicants must have received bachelor's degree prior to enrollment. Interview not required but visits to the school are encouraged. In addition, international applicants must submit TOEFL (not older than two years), unless the applicant has received a bachelor's degree from a U.S. college or university, and financial support document. (For dual-degree programs, applicant must apply to and be accepted by both schools and observe the appropriate deadlines for each school. GMAT and GRE may be required.) Apply to Admission Office after September 30, before March 1. First-year students admitted fall only. Rolling admission process, notification starts in November and is finished by late April. Acceptance of offer and first deposit due date April 1. Application fee $50. Phone: (617)353-3100. Fax: (617)353-2547. E-mail: bulawadm@bu.edu.

ADMISSION REQUIREMENTS FOR TRANSFER APPLICANTS. Accepts transfers from other ABA-accredited schools. Admission limited to space available. At least one year of enrollment, in good standing, LSAT, LSDAS, personal statement regarding reason for transfer, and current law school transcript (showing all courses taken) required in support of application. Apply to Admission Office by June 1. Application fee $50. Will consider visiting/transient applicants.

ADMISSIONS REQUIREMENTS FOR LL.M. APPLICANTS. For LL.M. (Taxation): applicants must have a degree from a law school approved by the Section of Legal Education of the ABA and be in good standing with a state bar association. Official transcripts and two letters of recommendation required in support of graduate application. In addition, international applicants whose native language is not English must submit TOEFL and TWE. Apply to the Graduate Tax Program by July 31 (fall), December 1 (spring). Application fee $50. Phone: (617)353-3105. E-mail: gradtax@bu.edu. For LL.M. (American, International Banking): applicants must have a degree from a law school approved by the Section of Legal Education of the ABA and be in good standing with a state bar association. Official transcripts and two letters of recommendation required in support of graduate application. In addition, international applicants whose native language is not English must submit TOEFL and TWE. Apply to the Graduate Banking Program by July 31 (fall), December 1 (spring). Application fee $50. Phone: (617)353-3023. E-mail: gradbanking@bu.edu. For LL.M. (American Law): Applicants must be graduates of a foreign law program equivalent to an American J.D., submit an International Student Data Form, personal statement, official transcripts with explanation, and TOEFL and TWE for those applicants whose native language is not English. Two letters of recommendation required in support of international application. Admits fall and spring. Apply to Office of Foreign Programs, Room 1240, School of Law. Phone: (617)353-5323. Fax: (617)353-3077. E-mail: aucoinfp@bu.edu.

ADMISSION STANDARDS. Number of full-time applicants 4,585; number accepted 1,576; number enrolled 340; median LSAT 160 (75% of class have a score at or above 159); median GPA 3.33 (A = 4) (75% of class have a GPA at or above 3.17). Attrition rate 3.7%. Gorman rating 4.48; *U.S. News & World Report* ranking places Boston University among the top 35 of law schools.

FINANCIAL AID. Scholarships, minority scholarships, MLK Fellowships, loans, federal loans, and Federal WS offered through university's Financial Aid Office. Assistantships may be available for upper divisional joint-degree candidates. For scholarships, apply to Financial Aid Office of school after January 1, before April 1. For all other programs apply to university's Director of Financial Aid. Phone: (617)353-2697. Use FAFSA (FAFSA code #002130), submit CSS profile. Approximately 35% of first-year class receive scholarships. Average scholarship/grant $7,000. Approximately 80% of all students receive some form of aid.

DEGREE REQUIREMENTS. For J.D.: 84 credits (33 required) with a 2.0 (A = 4) GPA, plus completion of upper divisional writing course; 3-year program. Accelerated J.D. with 1 summer of course work. In general, for all dual-degree programs up to 12 credits may be used for J.D. and between 9 and 15 credits may be used for master's. For J.D.-M.A. (Mass Preservation Studies, International Relations): 3½-year programs instead of 4½-year programs. For J.D.-M.B.A. (Management, Health Care Management): 4-year programs instead of 5-year programs. For J.D.-M.P.H. (Public Health): 3½-year program instead of 4½-year program. For J.D.-M.S. (Mass Communication): 3½-year program instead of 4½-year program. For LL.M. (Tax): 24 credits. For LL.M.: 24 credits; at least 2 semesters in residence carrying 10 credits each.

CAREER AND PLACEMENT INFORMATION. Approximately 50% of graduates are employed in state. More than 75% of graduates are practicing law; 10% are in business; 14% in government; 1% in academia. Approximately 92% of Boston University's first-time state bar exam takers pass the Massachusetts Bar Exam; Massachusetts's passage rate for all first-time takers from ABA-approved schools is 85%. Graduates are eligible to take the bar exam in all 50 states.

BRIGHAM YOUNG UNIVERSITY
Provo, Utah 84602-1001
Internet site: http://www.byu.edu

Founded 1875. Located 50 miles S of Salt Lake City. Private control (Church of Jesus Christ of Latter-day Saints—Mormon Church). Trimester system. Library: 2,372,000 volumes; 2,133,000 microforms; 17,000 periodicals/subscriptions; 680 computer workstations.

University's other graduate colleges/schools: College of Biological and Agricultural Sciences, College of Education, College of Engineering and Technology, College of Family, Home and Social Sciences, College of Fine Arts and Communication, College of Humanities, College of Nursing, College of Physical Education, College of Physical and Mathematical Sciences, Marriott School of Management.

Total university enrollment: 31,540.

J. Reuben Clark Law School
340 JRCB
P.O. Box 28000
Provo, Utah 84602-8000
Phone: (801)378-4276
Internet site: http://www.law.byu.edu
E-mail: wilcockl@lawgate.byu.edu

Established 1971. Located on main campus. ABA approved since 1974. AALS member. Semester system. Full-time, day study only. Law library: 395,700 volumes/microforms; 5,980 current periodicals/subscriptions; 63 computer workstations; has LEXIS, NEXIS, WESTLAW, RLIN, Notis. Special programs: Pre-Law Summer Institute for American Indians.

Annual tuition: Church members $4,970, nonmembers $7,450; per semester credits: church members $275, nonmembers $412. On-campus housing available for both single and married students. Annual on-campus housing cost: single students $3,930 (room and board), married students $2,800. Contact Director of Housing Service. Phone: (801)378-2611. Contact Off-Campus Housing Manager for off-campus information. Phone: (801)378-5066. Off-campus housing and personal expenses: approximately $10,940. Additional costs: books approximately $600.

Enrollment: first-year class 161; total full-time 469 (men 66%, women 34%). First-year statistics: 50% out of state, 42 states and foreign countries represented; 34% women; 13% minority; average age 25; 71 undergraduate institutions represented; range of first-year section sizes 25–125 students; number of upper division courses offered after first year 47.

Faculty: full-time 29, part-time 30; 20% female; 5% minority; student/faculty ratio 18 to 1.

Degrees conferred: J.D., J.D.-M.B.A., J.D.-M.P.A., J.D.-M.Acc., J.D.-M.Ed., J.D.-M.O.B. LL.M. (American and Comparative Legal Studies; only for persons who have completed a basic legal education and received a university degree in law in another country).

RECRUITMENT PRACTICES AND POLICIES. Attends national law school forums. On-campus informational sessions. School does have diversity program and actively recruits women/minority applicants.

ADMISSION REQUIREMENTS FOR FIRST-YEAR APPLICANTS. LSDAS law school report, LSAT (scores from the last three years acceptable, if more than one LSAT, average is used), LSAT writing sample, bachelor's degree from an accredited institution, personal statement, two recommendations, transcripts (must show all schools attended and at least three years of study) required in support of application. Applicants must have received bachelor's degree prior to enrollment. In addition, international applicants must submit TOEFL (not older than two years), TSE (strongly recommended for students whose native language is not English), Financial Certification Form (this form is sent to Office of Graduate Studies). Apply to Admission Director after October 1, before February 15. First-year students admitted fall only. Rolling admission process, notification starts in November and is finished by late April. Acceptance of offer and first deposit due date April 1. School does maintain a waiting list. Application fee $30. Phone: (801)378-4277. E-mail: wilcorkl@lawgate.byu.edu.

ADMISSION REQUIREMENTS FOR TRANSFER APPLICANTS. Accepts transfers from other ABA-accredited schools. Admission limited to space available. At least one year of enrollment, in good standing (prefer applicants in the top third of first-year class), LSAT, LSDAS, personal statement regarding reason for transfer, current law school transcript, undergraduate transcript showing degrees conferred required in support of application. Apply to Admission Director by March 1. Admission decisions made by July 1. Application fee $30. Will not consider visiting/transient applicants.

ADMISSION REQUIREMENTS FOR LL.M. APPLICANTS. Cover letter including a statement of purpose, evidence of law degree, official transcripts with English translations and certificate of authenticity, evidence of adequate financial support for entire program, three letters of recommendation required in support of LL.M. application. In addition, if English is not first language, TOEFL, TWE scores should be submitted. Scores should arrive no later than April 15. Apply to Admissions Office by March 15. Application fee $30.

ADMISSION STANDARDS. Number of full-time applicants 710; number accepted 222; number enrolled 161; median LSAT 160 (75% of class have a score at or above 156); median GPA 3.52 (A = 4) (75% of class have a GPA at or above 3.28). Attrition rate 0.4%. Gorman rating 3.63; *U.S. News & World Report* ranking is in the top 33 of all law schools.

FINANCIAL AID. Scholarships, merit scholarships, minority scholarships, institutional loans, federal loans, and Federal WS offered through university's Financial Aid Office. For scholarships apply to law school after January 1, before June 1. For all other programs apply to university's Director of Financial Aid. Phone: (801)378-4104. Use FAFSA (FAFSA code #003670) and BYU Touch-Tone FA Application. Approximately 51% of first-year students receive scholarships. Average first-year scholarship/grant $1,500. Approximately 79% of all students received some financial assistance. Average debt after graduation $23,000.

DEGREE REQUIREMENTS. For J.D.: 90 credits (36 required) with a 2.0 (A = 4) GPA, plus completion of upper divisional writing course; 3-year program. Accelerated J.D. with 1 summer of course work. For J.D.-master's programs: a maximum of 6 credits may be used toward J.D.; at least 5 semesters in residence at law school; usual completion time is 4 years instead of 5 years. For LL.M.: at least 24 credits and 2 semesters in residence.

CAREER AND PLACEMENT INFORMATION. Eighty-six to ninety employers conducted interviews on campus. Approximately 44% of graduates are employed in state. More than 68% of graduates are practicing law; 17% are in business; 10% in government; 3% in academia. Approximately 90% of Brigham Young University's first-time state bar exam takers pass the Utah state bar exam; Utah's passage rate for all first-time takers from ABA-approved schools is 90%.

BROOKLYN LAW SCHOOL

250 Joralemon Street
Brooklyn, New York 11201-3798
Phone: (718)625-2200
Internet site: http://www.brooklaw.edu
E-mail: admitq.brooklaw@pcm.brooklaw.edu

Established 1901. Located between historic Brooklyn Heights and the Brooklyn Civic Center. ABA approved since 1937. AALS member. Semester system. Students attend full-time day; part-time day; part-time evening; part-time day/evening. Law library: 435,000 volumes/microforms; 4,875 current periodicals/subscriptions; 45 computer workstations; has LEXIS, NEXIS, WESTLAW, DIALOG. Special programs: Center for the Study of International Business Law.

Annual tuition: full-time $20,740, nonresident $15,580. Law school housing available for both single and married students in Brooklyn Heights. Annual housing and personal expenses: $16,506. For housing information contact Law School Admissions Office. Additional costs: books approximately $700.

Enrollment: first-year class full-time 281, part-time 187; total full-time 967, part-time 487 (men 53%, women 47%). First-year statistics: 15 out of state, 37 states and foreign countries represented; 47% women; 19% minority; average age full-time 24, part-time 26; 265 undergraduate institutions represented; range of first-year section sizes 31–97 students; number of upper division courses offered after first year full-time 68, part-time 61.

Faculty: full-time 62, part-time 86; 37% female; 6% minority; student/faculty ratio 21 to 1.

Degrees conferred: J.D., J.D.-M.B.A. (Baruch College), J.D.-M.P.A. (Baruch College), J.D.-M.A. (Brooklyn College), J.D.-M.U.P. (Hunter College), J.D.-M.S. (Library and Information Science, City and Regional Planning, Pratt Institute), Program for Foreign Trained Lawyers (only for persons who have completed a basic legal education and received a university degree in law in another country).

RECRUITMENT PRACTICES AND POLICIES. Attends national law school forums. On-campus informational sessions. School does have diversity program and actively recruits women/minority applicants.

ADMISSION REQUIREMENTS FOR FIRST-YEAR APPLICANTS. LSDAS law school report, LSAT (not later than December test date, if more than one LSAT, highest is used), bachelor's degree from an accredited institution, résumé, personal statement, transcripts (must show all schools attended and at least three years of study) required in support of application. Letters of reference not required but strongly recommended. Applicants must have received bachelor's degree prior to enrollment. Interview not required but may be requested by applicants or school. In addition, international applicants whose degree is from an institution located in a foreign country must submit translation and evaluations from a recognized evaluation service, and the degree must be certified to be equivalent in quality and duration to a U.S. baccalaureate degree. Apply to Admission Office for Category I by February 1, LSAT by December; Category II apply between February 2 and April 1, LSAT no later than February; Category III apply between April 2 and August 1, LSAT no later than June. First-year students admitted fall only. Rolling admission process, notification starts in March and is finished by late August. Acceptance of offer and first deposit due date for Category I April 1. School does not maintain a waiting list. Application fee $60. Phone: (718)780-7906. Fax: (718)780-0395. E-mail: admitq.brooklaw@pcm.brooklaw.edu.

ADMISSION REQUIREMENTS FOR TRANSFER APPLICANTS. Accepts transfers from other ABA-accredited schools. Admission limited to space available. At least one year of enrollment, dean's letter indicating applicant is in good standing, LSAT, LSDAS, personal statement regarding reason for transfer, current law school transcript (by July 1) required in support of application. Apply to Dean of Admission by May 15. Admission decisions made by mid August. Application fee $60. Will consider visiting/transient applicants.

ADMISSION REQUIREMENTS FOR FOREIGN-TRAINED LAWYERS PROGRAM. Provision of a letter from the New York State Board of Law Examiners indicating that applicant would qualify for the New York Bar Examination if applicant completes 24 credits at an accredited U.S. law school, a translation and evaluation from a recognized evaluation service that the foreign degree is certified as equivalent in quality and duration to a U.S. baccalaureate degree, TOEFL, TWE, TSE required in support of application. Apply by May 1 to Office of Admission. Application fee $60.

ADMISSION STANDARDS. Number of applicants full-time 2,229, part-time 476; number accepted full-time 1,125, part-time 411; number enrolled full-time 281, part-time 187; median LSAT full-time 157, part-time 154 (75% of full-time class have a score at or above 152, part-time 149); median GPA full-time 3.3, part-time 3.11 (A = 4) (75% of full-time class have a GPA at or above 2.99, part-time 2.76). Attrition rate 3.0%. Gorman rating 3.62; *U.S. News & World Report* ranking is in the second tier of all law schools.

FINANCIAL AID. Scholarships, institutional loans, federal loans, and Federal WS. For scholarships (selection criteria place heavy reliance on LSAT and undergraduate GPA) apply to Admissions Office after January 1, before April 1 (priority deadline). Phone: (718)780-7915. Use FAFSA (FAFSA code #E00057) and institutional FA application, submit copy of 1040, FA transcript. Approximately 44% full-time, 19% part-time of first-year class receive scholarships. Average scholarship grant full-time $5,251, part-time $4,138.

DEGREE REQUIREMENTS. For J.D.: 86 credits (34 required) with a 2.0 (A = 4) GPA, plus completion of upper divisional writing course; 3-year program, 4-year program (part-time). Accelerated J.D. with 1 summer of course work. For J.D.-master's programs: the J.D. program will accept 9 credits towards degree and for the master's programs it ranges from 9 to 15 depending on degree requirements. For Foreign Trained Lawyers Program: 24 credits.

CAREER AND PLACEMENT INFORMATION. Approximately 99 employers conducted job interviews on campus. Approximately 92% of graduates are employed in state. More than 66% of graduates are practicing law; 17% are in business; 15% in government; 1% in academia. Approximately 86% of Brooklyn Law School's first-time state bar exam takers pass the New York state bar exam; New York's passage rate for all first-time takers from ABA-approved schools is 78%.

UNIVERSITY AT BUFFALO, STATE UNIVERSITY OF NEW YORK

Buffalo, New York 14260-1608
Internet site: http://www.buffalo.edu

Founded 1846. Located approximately 3 miles N of Buffalo. Public control. Semester system. Library: 2,937,000 volumes; 4,565,000 microforms; 21,818 periodicals/subscriptions; 261 computer workstations.

University's other graduate colleges/schools: Faculty of Arts and Letters, Faculty of Natural Sciences and Mathematics, Faculty of Social Sciences, Graduate Programs in Biomedical Sciences at Roswell Park, Graduate School of Education, School of Architecture and Planning, School of Dental Science, School of Engineering and Applied Sciences, School of Health Related Professions, School of Information and Library Studies, School of Management, School of Medicine, School of Nursing, School of Pharmacy, School of Social Work.

Total university enrollment: 24,400.

School of Law

319 O'Brian Hall
Amherst Campus
Buffalo, New York 14260
Phone: (716)645-2053
Internet site: http://www.buffalo.edu/law
E-mail: mcook@msmail.buffalo.edu

Established 1887. Located on Amherst campus. ABA approved since 1936. AALS member. Semester system.

Full-time, day study only. Law library: 488,500 volumes/microforms; 5,291 current periodicals/subscriptions; 34 computer workstations; has LEXIS, WESTLAW, RLIN, LRS, QUICKLAW (Canadian Database); is a Federal Government Depository. Special facility: Baldy Center for Law and Social Policy, Buffalo Criminal Law Center, Buffalo Human Rights Center. Special programs: Government Law Program (Public Service); public service summer internships, externships in public interest.

Annual tuition: resident $8,075, nonresident $12,725. On-campus housing available for both single and married students. Annual on-campus housing cost: single students $3,125 (room only), $4,155 (room and board); married students $6,500. Housing deadline May 1. Contact University Residence Hall for on-campus information. Phone: (716)645-2171. Law students tend to live off-campus. For off-campus housing information contact the Office of Off-Campus Housing (a student-run organization). Phone: (716)829-2224. Off-campus housing and personal expenses: approximately $9,855. Additional costs: books approximately $800.

Enrollment: first-year class 208; total full-time 515 (men 53%, women 47%); no part-time students. First-year statistics: 20% out of state; 47% women; 21% minority; average age 26; average first-year section size 100 students; number of upper division courses offered after first year 151.

Faculty: full-time 51, part-time 62; 39% female; 14% minority; student/faculty ratio 14 to 1.

Degrees conferred: J.D., J.D.-M.B.A., J.D.-M.S.W., J.D.-Ph.D. (Anthropology, Environmental Studies, Philosophy, Sociology).

RECRUITMENT PRACTICES AND POLICIES. Attends local and selected national law school forums. Has on-campus informational sessions. School does have diversity program and actively recruits women/minority applicants.

ADMISSION REQUIREMENTS FOR FIRST-YEAR APPLICANTS. LSDAS law school report, LSAT (not later than December test date, if more than one LSAT, average is used), bachelor's degree from an accredited institution, personal statement, two recommendations, transcripts (must show all schools attended and at least three years of study) required in support of application. Applicants must have received bachelor's degree prior to enrollment. Interview not required. In addition, international applicants whose native language is not English must submit TOEFL (not older than two years, minimum score required 630), TWE (minimum score required 5.0);

submit evidence of financial support. Joint-degree applicants must apply to and be accepted by both schools. Apply to Office of Admission after September 1, before February 1. First-year students admitted fall only. Rolling admission process, notification starts in February and is finished not later than June 15. Acceptance of offer and first deposit due date April 1. School does maintain a waiting list. Application fee $50. Phone: (716)645-2061. E-mail: mscook@msmail.buffalo.edu.

ADMISSION REQUIREMENTS FOR TRANSFER APPLICANTS. Accepts transfers from other ABA-accredited schools. Admission limited to space available. At least one year of enrollment, dean's letter indicating applicant is in good standing (prefer applicants in the top quarter of first-year class), LSAT, LSDAS, personal statement regarding reason for transfer, two recommendations, undergraduate transcript, current law school transcript required in support of application. Apply to Admission Office by June 1. Admission decisions made between mid July and mid August. Application fee $50. Will consider visiting students.

ADMISSION STANDARDS. Number of full-time applicants 1,023; number accepted 527; number enrolled 208; median LSAT 155 (75% of class have a score at or above 148); median GPA 3.33 (A = 4) (75% of class have a GPA at or above 2.99). Attrition rate 3.3%. Gorman rating 4.32; *U.S. News & World Report* ranking is in the second tier of all law schools.

FINANCIAL AID. Need-based scholarships, merit scholarships, diversity scholarships, assistantships, fellowships, private loans, state programs, federal loans, and Federal WS offered through university's Financial Aid Office. All accepted students are considered for scholarships (selection criteria place heavy reliance on LSAT and undergraduate GPA); contact the law school's Financial Aid Office for further information. Phone: (716)645-2907. For all other programs apply as soon as possible after January 1, before March 1, to university's Office of Financial Aid. Phone: (716)829-3724. E-mail: dewaal@msmail.buffalo.edu. Submit TAP application and CSS Form; the FAFSA for all federal programs (Title IV School code #002837). Also submit Financial Aid Transcript, federal income tax forms. Approximately 53% of first-year class received scholarships/grants. Approximately 85% of current students receive some form of financial assistance. Average scholarship/grant $500.

DEGREE REQUIREMENTS. For J.D.: 87 credits (35 required) with a 2.0 (A = 4) GPA, plus completion of upper divisional writing course; 3-year program. Accelerated J.D. with 1 or 2 summers of course work. For J.D.-M.B.A.: 123 total credits (J.D. 72–74 credits, M.B.A. 48 credits). For J.D.-M.S.W.: a 4-year program rather than the usual 5 years needed if both degrees taken separately. For J.D.-Ph.D.: Individually designed programs, generally 6-year programs rather than the usual 7-year programs needed if both degrees taken separately.

CAREER AND PLACEMENT INFORMATION. About 50–60 employers conducted on-campus interviews. Approximately 74% of graduates are employed in state. More than 74% of graduates are practicing law; 14% are in business; 11% in government; 1% in academia. Approximately 72% (NY), 86% (CT), 80% (PA) of University of Buffalo's first-time state bar exam takers pass the bar exam; the passage rate for all first-time takers from ABA-approved schools is 78% (NY), 78% (CT), 73% (PA). Graduates are eligible to take the bar exam in all 50 states.

UNIVERSITY OF CALIFORNIA, BERKELEY

Berkeley, California 94720-7200
Internet site: http://www.berkeley.edu

Founded 1868. Located 12 miles E of San Francisco. Public control. Semester system. Library: 7,000,000 volumes; 3,000,000 microforms; 100,000 periodicals/subscriptions.

University's other graduate colleges/schools: College of Chemistry, College of Engineering, College of Environmental Design, College of Letters and Sciences, College of Natural Resources, Graduate School of Journalism, Graduate School of Public Policy, Haas School of Business, School of Education, School of Information Management and Systems, School of Optometry, School of Public Health, School of Social Work.

Total university enrollment: 30,300.

School of Law (Boalt Hall)

220 Boalt Hall
Berkeley, California 94720-7200
Phone: (510)642-2274
Internet site: http://www.law.berkeley.edu
E-mail: admissions@boalt.berkeley.edu

Established 1912. Located on main campus. ABA approved since 1923. AALS member. Semester system. Full-time, day study. Law library: 750,000 volumes/microforms; 7,500 current periodicals/subscriptions; 79

computer workstations; has LEXIS, NEXIS, WEST-LAW, INNOPAC, MELVYL; is a Federal Government Depository. Special programs: combined degree programs with Fletcher School of Law and Diplomacy, Tufts University, John F. Kennedy School of Government, Harvard University.

Annual tuition: resident $10,800, nonresident $19,784. On-campus housing available. Annual on-campus housing and personal expenses: $12,344. Law students tend to live off-campus. Contact Office of Graduate Housing Services for off-campus information. Phone: (510)642-7781. Off-campus housing and personal expenses: approximately $12,344. Additional costs: books approximately $600.

Enrollment: first-year class 623; total full-time 838 (men 50%, women 50%); no part-time students. First-year statistics: 25% out of state, 50 states and foreign countries represented; 50% women; 36% minority; average age 25; 87 undergraduate institutions represented; range of first-year section sizes 30–100 students; number of upper division courses offered after first year: 118.

Faculty: full-time 67, part-time 68; 28% female; 12% minority; student/faculty ratio 17 to 1.

Degrees conferred: J.D., J.D.-M.B.A., J.D.-M.P.P., J.D.-M.A. (Asian Studies, Economics), J.D.-M.C.R.P., J.D.-M.S., J.D.-M.S.W., J.D.-M.J., J.D.-Ph.D. (Economics, History, Jurisprudence and Social Policy), LL.M., J.S.D.

RECRUITMENT PRACTICES AND POLICIES. Attends national law school forums. On-campus informational sessions and special visitation program. School does have diversity program and actively recruits women/minority applicants.

ADMISSION REQUIREMENTS FOR FIRST-YEAR APPLICANTS. LSDAS law school report, LSAT (not later than December test date, if more than one LSAT, average is used), bachelor's degree from an accredited institution, résumé, personal statement, interview, two recommendations, transcripts (must show all schools attended and at least three years of study) required in support of application. Applicants must have received bachelor's degree prior to enrollment. In addition, international applicants must submit TOEFL (not older than two years). Apply to Admission Office after September 30, before February 1. First-year students admitted fall only. Rolling admission process, notification starts in January and most are sent out by May. School does not maintain a waiting list. Application fee $40. Phone: (510)642-2273. E-mail: admissions@boalt.berkeley.edu.

ADMISSION REQUIREMENTS FOR TRANSFER APPLICANTS. Accepts transfers from other ABA-accredited schools. Admission limited to space available. At least one year of enrollment, in good standing (prefer applicants in the top 5% of first-year class), LSAT, LSDAS, personal statement regarding reason for transfer, current law school transcript required in support of application. Apply to Admission Office by June 1. Admission decision made by mid July. Application fee $40.

ADMISSION STANDARDS. Number of full-time applicants 4,624; number accepted 855; number enrolled 263; median LSAT 163 (75% of class have a score at or above 161); median GPA 3.63 (A = 4) (75% of class have a GPA at or above 3.55). Attrition rate 2.8%. Gorman rating 4.89; *U.S. News & World Report* ranking is in the top 9 of all law schools.

FINANCIAL AID. Grants-in-aid, all other aid is need based. Federal loans and Federal WS also offered. Apply to Financial Aid Office of school after January 1, before March 1. Phone: (510)642-1563. Use FAFSA (FAFSA code #001312). Current federal income tax return required. Approximately 60% of first-year class received grants-in-aid. Approximately 85% of all students received financial assistance. Average scholarship/grant $6,000. Average debt after graduation $24,000.

DEGREE REQUIREMENTS. For J.D.: 85 credits (30 required) with a 2.0 (A = 4) GPA, plus completion of upper divisional writing course; 3-year program. For J.D.-master's program: most joint-degree master's programs can be completed in 4 years instead of the usual 5 years. For J.D.-Ph.D.: individualized programs, time frame is usually 6–7 years. For LL.M.: individually designed degree programs in consultation with a faculty member; 20 academic units usually taken during 1 year in residence; research and writing project. For J.S.D.: individually designed programs in preparation for a career in academia or legal scholarship; must complete LL.M.; minimum of 20 credits; dissertation suitable for publication; oral defense.

CAREER AND PLACEMENT INFORMATION. About 316 employers conducted interviews on campus. Approximately 70% of graduates are employed in state. More than 88% of graduates are practicing law; 4% are in business; 7% in government; 1% in academia. Approximately 90% of the University of California, Berkeley's first-time state bar exam takers pass the California Bar Exam; California's passage rate for all first-time takers from ABA-approved schools is 83%. Graduates are eligible to take the bar exam in all 50 states.

UNIVERSITY OF CALIFORNIA, DAVIS

Davis, California 95616-5201
Internet site: http://www.ucdavis.edu

Founded 1868. Located 12 miles W of Sacramento. Public control. Quarter system. Library: 2,700,000 volumes; 3,450,000 microforms; 47,100 periodicals/subscriptions.

University's other graduate colleges/schools: College of Engineering, Graduate School of Management, School of Medicine, School of Veterinary Medicine.

Total university enrollment: 23,100.

School of Law (King Hall)

King Hall
Davis, California 95616-5201
Phone: (916)752-0243
Internet site: http://kinghall.ucdavis.edu
E-mail: admissions@kinghall.ucdavis.edu

Established 1965. Located on main campus. ABA approved since 1968. AALS member. Semester system. Full-time, day study only. Law library: 392,000 volumes/microforms; 5,470 current periodicals/subscriptions; 59 computer workstations; has LEXIS, NEXIS, WEST-LAW, MELVYL; is both a Federal and State Government Depository. Special programs: integrated civil rights curriculum, public interest law program.

Annual tuition: resident $10,843, nonresident $19,827. On-campus housing available for both single and married students. Annual on-campus housing: single students $6,180 (room and board), married students $5,473. Housing deadline April 1 (students are encouraged to apply early). Contact Student Housing Office. Phone: (916)752-2033. Law students tend to live off-campus. Contact Student Housing Office for off-campus information. Phone: (916)752-2033. Off-campus housing and personal expenses: approximately $10,263. Additional costs: books approximately $700.

Enrollment: first-year class 152; total full-time 489 (men 54%, women 46%); no part-time students. First-year statistics: 9% out of state, 15 states and foreign countries represented; 46% women; 33% minority; average age 25; 118 undergraduate institutions represented; range of first-year section sizes 25–80 students; number of upper division courses offered after first year 79.

Faculty: full-time 30, part-time 12; 20% female; 8% minority; student/faculty ratio 15 to 1.

Degrees conferred: J.D., J.D.-M.B.A., J.D.-M.A. (Anthropology, Economics, International Agricultural Development, Philosophy, Rhetoric, Sociology).

RECRUITMENT PRACTICES AND POLICIES. On-campus informational sessions are held in October, November, December, January. School does have diversity program and actively recruits women/minority applicants.

ADMISSION REQUIREMENTS FOR FIRST-YEAR APPLICANTS. LSDAS law school report, LSAT (not later than December test date, if more than one LSAT, the average is used), bachelor's degree from an accredited institution, personal statement, two recommendations, transcripts (must show all schools attended and at least three years of study but prefer fall grades) required in support of application. Applicants must have received bachelor's degree prior to enrollment. Interview not required but may be requested by School. In addition, international applicants must submit TOEFL (not older than two years and a score of 600 or higher). Apply to Admission Office after October 1, before February 1 (firm date). First-year students admitted fall only. Rolling admission process. Use either the Law Multi-App or law school application. Application fee $40. Phone: (619)752-6477. E-mail: admissions@cawadmin.ucdavis.edu.

ADMISSION REQUIREMENTS FOR TRANSFER APPLICANTS. Accepts transfers from other ABA-accredited schools. Admission limited to space available. At least one year of enrollment, dean's letter indicating applicant is in good standing, prefer applicants in the top quarter of first-year class, LSAT, LSDAS, personal statement regarding reason for transfer, current law school transcript required in support of application. Apply to Admission Office between June 1 and June 30. Admission decisions made by late July, early August. Application fee $40. Will consider visiting/transient applicants.

ADMISSION STANDARDS. Number of full-time applicants 2,621; number accepted 833; number enrolled 152; median LSAT 162 (75% of class have a score at or above 158); median GPA 3.4 (A = 4) (75% of class have a GPA at or above 3.15). Attrition rate 3.0%. Gorman rating 4.43; *U.S. News & World Report* ranking is in the top 40 of all law schools.

FINANCIAL AID. Scholarships, federal loans, and Federal WS offered through university's Financial Aid Office. Apply to School of Law for scholarships after January 1, before March 2. Phone: (916)752-6573. Use FAFSA (FAFSA code #001313). Approximately 60% of first-year class received scholarships/grants-in-aid. Approximately 87% of current students receive some form of financial assistance. Average scholarship/grant $3,776. Average debt after graduation $28,000.

DEGREE REQUIREMENTS. For J.D.: 88 credits (33 required) with a 2.0 (A = 4) GPA, plus completion of upper divisional writing course; 3-year program. For J.D.-master's joint-degree program: 3½ to 4 years to complete instead of the usual 4½ to 5 years to complete if degrees taken separately.

CAREER AND PLACEMENT INFORMATION. About 42 employers conducted on-campus interviews. Approximately 90% of graduates are employed in state. More than 68% of graduates are practicing law; 3% are in business; 21% in government; 2% in academia. Approximately 93% of the University of California, Davis' first-time state bar exam takers pass the California Bar Exam; California's passage rate for all first-time takers from ABA-approved schools is 83%. Graduates are eligible to take the bar exam in all 50 states.

UNIVERSITY OF CALIFORNIA
HASTINGS COLLEGE OF LAW
200 McAllister Street
San Francisco, California 94102
Phone: (415)565-4623
Internet site: http://www.uchastings.edu
E-mail: admiss@uchastings.edu

Established 1878 as the University of California's first law school. Located at San Francisco's Civic Center. ABA approved since 1937. AALS member. Semester system. Full-time, day study only. Law library: 575,600 volumes/microforms; 8,370 current periodicals/subscriptions; 98 computer workstations; has LEXIS, NEXIS, WESTLAW, DIALOG, INFOTRAC, LEGITECH, FIRST SEARCH, EPIC; is a State and Federal Government Depository. Special programs: concentrations in civil litigation, international law, public interest law, taxation; exchange programs with Leiden University, Netherlands, University of British Columbia, Vermont Law School. Special facilities: Land Conservation Institute, Public Law Research Institute, Public Interest Clearinghouse.

Annual tuition: resident $11,167, nonresident $19,559. On-campus housing available for both single and married students (250 apartments from efficiencies to two bedrooms). Average for both on- and off-campus housing and personal expenses: $15,704. Contact Housing Office for both on- and off-campus housing information. Phone: (415)557-0985. Additional costs: books approximately $700.

Enrollment: first-year class 492; total full-time 1,291 (men 52%, women 48%); no part-time students. First-year statistics: 9% out of state, 47 states and foreign countries represented; 47% women; 37% minority (approximately 20% of class is from LEOP program); average age 27; 200 undergraduate institutions represented; range of first-year section sizes 16–85 students; number of upper division courses offered after first year 130.

Faculty: full-time 50, part-time 45; 30% female; 16% minority; student/faculty ratio 25 to 1.

Degrees conferred: J.D., J.D.-M.B.A., J.D.-M.P.P.M., J.D.-M.Ed.

RECRUITMENT PRACTICES AND POLICIES. Attends national law school forums. On-campus informational sessions. School does have diversity program and actively recruits women/minority applicants.

ADMISSION REQUIREMENTS FOR FIRST-YEAR APPLICANTS. LSDAS law school report, LSAT (not later than December test date), bachelor's degree from an accredited institution, personal statement, two recommendations, transcripts (must show all schools attended and at least three years of study), Statement of Legal Residency required in support of application. Applicants must have received bachelor's degree prior to enrollment. Interview not required but may be requested by school. In addition, international applicants must submit TOEFL (not older than two years), TSE, TWE, supplemental application. Apply to Admission Office after September 30, before February 15. First-year students admitted fall only. Rolling admission process, notification starts in December and is finished by mid April. Application fee $40. Phone: (415)565-4623. E-mail: admiss@uchastings.edu.

ADMISSION REQUIREMENTS FOR TRANSFER APPLICANTS. Accepts transfers from other ABA/AALS-accredited/approved schools. Admission limited to space available. At least one year of enrollment, in good standing (prefer applicants with 3.0 GPA [A = 4]), LSAT, LSDAS, personal statement regarding reason for transfer, current law school transcript required in support of application. Apply to Admission Office by May 1. Admission decision made by July 1. Application fee $40. Will consider visiting/transient applicants.

ADMISSION STANDARDS. Number of full-time applicants 4,350; number accepted 1,773; number enrolled

492; median LSAT 162 (75% of class have a score at or above 149); median GPA 3.38 (A = 4) (75% of class have a GPA at or above 2.94). Attrition rate 2.6%. Gorman rating 4.62; *U.S. News & World Report* ranking is in the second tier of all law schools.

FINANCIAL AID. Scholarships, grants-in-aid, private loans, federal loans, Federal WS. Apply to Financial Aid Office after January 1, before February 15. Phone: (800)433-3243. Use FAFSA (FAFSA code #GO3947). Approximately 81% of first-year class received scholarships/grants-in-aid. Approximately 82% of current students receive some form of financial assistance. Average scholarship/grant $3,350. Loan forgiveness program available. Average debt after graduation $40,500.

DEGREE REQUIREMENTS. For J.D.: 86 credits (36 required) with a 2.0 (A = 4) GPA, plus completion of upper divisional writing course; 3-year program. For J.D.-master's: individualized programs; no more than 10 credits may be credited toward J.D.; combined degree programs may reduce the amount of time required to complete both degrees by as much as 1 year.

CAREER AND PLACEMENT INFORMATION. About 175 employers conducted on-campus interviews. Approximately 65% of graduates are employed in state. More than 73% of graduates are practicing law; 12% are in business; 12% in government; 3% in academia. Approximately 79% of the Hastings College of Law's first-time state bar exam takers pass the California Bar Exam; California's passage rate for all first-time takers from ABA-approved schools is 83%.

UNIVERSITY OF CALIFORNIA, LOS ANGELES

Los Angeles, California 90024-1301
Internet site: http://www.ucla.edu

Founded 1919. Located in the Westwood section of Los Angeles. Public control. Quarter system. Library: 6,200,000 volumes; 6,300,000 microforms; 94,000 periodicals/subscriptions.

University's other graduate colleges/schools: College of Letters and Sciences, Graduate School of Education and Information Science, John E. Anderson School of Management, School of Engineering and Applied Science, School of Nursing, School of Public Health, School of Public Policy and Social Research, School of the Arts and Architecture, School of Theater, Film and TV, School of Dentistry, School of Medicine.

Total university enrollment: 32,625.

School of Law
71 Dodd Hall
Box 951445
Los Angeles, California 90095-1445
Phone: (310)825-4041
Internet site: http://www.law.ucla.edu
E-mail: admissions@law.ucla.edu

Established 1947. Located on main campus. ABA approved since 1950. AALS member. Semester system. Full-time, day study only. Law library: 524,300 volumes/microforms; 6,880 current periodicals/subscriptions; 100 computer workstations; has LEXIS, NEXIS, WEST-LAW, DIALOG, CIS; is a Federal Government Depository. Special programs: Environmental Law, Public Interest Law and Policy; concurrent-degree programs with the Fletcher School of Law and Diplomacy, Tufts University, Nitze School of Advanced International Studies, Johns Hopkins University, School of Foreign Service, Georgetown University, Woodrow Wilson School of International Studies, Princeton University.

Annual tuition: resident $10,917, nonresident $19,901; LL.M. $19,941. On-campus housing available for both single and married students. Annual on-campus housing cost: single students $9,703 (room and board), married students $3,500–$5,000. Contact Office of Residential Life. Phone: (310)825-4941. Law students tend to live off-campus. Contact UCLA Community Housing Office for off-campus information. Phone: (310)825-4491. Or Housing Assignment Office. Phone: (310)825-4271. Off-campus housing and personal expenses: approximately $13,838. Additional costs: books approximately $800.

Enrollment: first-year class 307; total full-time 919 (men 50.5%, women 49.5%); no part-time students. First-year statistics: 20% out of state, 27 states and foreign countries represented; 49% women; 44% minority; average age 24; 90 undergraduate institutions represented; range of first-year section sizes 27–67 students; number of upper division courses offered after first year 103. LL.M.: approximately 10 students per year.

Faculty: full-time 51, part-time 8; 30% female; 4% minority; student/faculty ratio 15.5 to 1.

Degrees conferred: J.D., J.D.-M.B.A., J.D.-M.A. (Urban Planning, American Indian Studies), LL.M. (for persons who have completed a basic legal education and received a university degree in law in another country, are not currently living in the U.S., and plan to return to their home country upon graduation).

RECRUITMENT PRACTICES AND POLICIES.

Attends local and national law school forums. Has on-campus informational sessions. School does have diversity program and actively recruits women/minority applicants.

ADMISSION REQUIREMENTS FOR FIRST-YEAR APPLICANTS.

LSDAS law school report, LSAT (not later than December test date, if there are multiple test scores, the average is used), bachelor's degree from an accredited institution, transcripts (must show all schools attended and at least three years of study) required in support of application. Two or three recommendations are encouraged, a personal statement is optional. Applicants must have received bachelor's degree prior to enrollment. In addition, international applicants must submit TOEFL (not older than two years), TSE, TWE, certified translations and evaluations of all foreign credentials. Will accept the Law Multi-App in lieu of UCLA application. Apply to Admission Office after September 30, before January 15. First-year students admitted fall only. Rolling admission process, notification starts in February and is finished by May. Application fee $40. Phone: (310)825-4041. E-mail: admissions@law.ucla.edu.

ADMISSION REQUIREMENTS FOR TRANSFER APPLICANTS.

Accepts transfers from other ABA-accredited schools. Admission limited to approximately 20 spaces. At least one year of enrollment, dean's letter indicating applicant is in good standing (prefer applicants in the top quarter of first-year class), LSAT, LSDAS, personal statement regarding reason for transfer, two letters of recommendation, undergraduate transcript, current law school transcript required in support of application. Apply to Admission Office after May 1, before July 1. Admission decisions made by the end of July. Application fee $40. Will consider visiting/transient applicants.

ADMISSION REQUIREMENTS FOR LL.M. APPLICANTS (international lawyers).

Certified English translations and evaluations of all foreign credentials, three letters of recommendation, TOEFL (institutional code #4837, minimum score required 590), statement of objectives and research topic, financial resources statement required in support of LL.M. application. Apply by March 1 to Director Graduate LL.M. Program, 405 Hilgard Avenue, Los Angeles, CA 90095-1476.

ADMISSION STANDARDS.

Number of full-time applicants 4,417; number accepted 1,009; number enrolled 307; median LSAT 162 (75% of class have a score at or above 159); median GPA 3.57 (A = 4) (75% of class have a GPA at or above 3.42). Attrition rate 2.6%. Gorman rating 4.75; *U.S. News & World Report* ranking is in the top 20 of all law schools.

FINANCIAL AID.

Scholarships, merit scholarships, minority scholarships, grants-in-aid; assistantships, institutional loans; federal loans and Federal WS offered through university's Financial Aid Office. For scholarships, assistantships apply to Financial Aid Office of school after January 1, before March 1. Phone: (310)825-2260. For all other programs apply to university's Director of Financial Aid, A1295 Murphy Hall. Phone: (310)206-0400. Use FAFSA (FAFSA code #001315), submit CSS analysis, submit Financial Aid Transcript, federal income tax forms. Approximately 51% of first-year class received scholarships/grants-in-aid. Approximately 80% of current students receive some form of financial assistance. Average scholarship/grant $4,250. Federal loan forgiveness program available. Average debt after graduation $45,000. For LL.M. information contact the university's Financial Aid Office after acceptance. However, it is expected that all LL.M. candidates are financially self-supporting.

DEGREE REQUIREMENTS.

For J.D.: 87 credits (33 required) with a 2.0 (A = 4) GPA, plus completion of upper divisional writing course and professional responsibility course; 3-year program. Accelerated J.D. with 1 summer of course work. For J.D.-master's: individualized programs, but no more than 10 credits can be credited toward J.D.; combined programs may reduce the 2 degrees by up to 1 year. For LL.M.: 2 semesters in full-time residence; a 20-credit program plus a research project and scholarly work written in English.

CAREER AND PLACEMENT INFORMATION.

About 250 employers conducted on-campus interviews. Approximately 83% of graduates are employed in state. More than 85% of graduates are practicing law; 3% are in business; 9% in government; 1% in academia. Approximately 89% of the University of California, Los Angeles' first-time state bar exam takers pass the California Bar Exam; California's passage rate for all first-time takers from ABA-approved schools is 83%. Graduates are eligible to take the bar exam in all 50 states.

CALIFORNIA WESTERN SCHOOL OF LAW

225 Cedar Street
San Diego, California 92101-3046
Phone: (800)255-4252, (619)239-0391
Internet site: http://www.cwsl.edu
E-mail: admissions@cwsl.edu

Established 1958. Located in downtown San Diego. ABA approved since 1962. AALS member since 1967. Trimester system. Full-time, day study only. Law library: 233,000 volumes/microforms; 3,000 current periodicals/subscriptions; 46 computer workstations; has LEXIS, NEXIS, WESTLAW, DIALOG.

Annual tuition: $19,820. Law students have to live off-campus. Contact Housing Coordinator in Admissions Office for off-campus information. Phone: (800)255-4252. Off-campus housing and personal expenses: approximately $13,120. Additional costs: books approximately $650.

Enrollment: first-year class 247; total full-time 710 (men 53%, women 47%); no part-time students. First-year statistics: 45% out of state, 43 states and foreign countries represented; 47% women; 26% minority; average age 27; 291 undergraduate institutions represented; average first-year section size 85 students; number of upper division courses offered after first year 122.

Faculty: full-time 46, part-time 34; 44% female; 5% minority; student/faculty ratio 20 to 1.

Degrees conferred: J.D., J.D.-M.S.W. (San Diego State University).

RECRUITMENT PRACTICES AND POLICIES. Attends national law school forums. On-campus informational sessions. School does have diversity program and actively recruits women/minority applicants.

ADMISSION REQUIREMENTS FOR FIRST-YEAR APPLICANTS. LSDAS law school report, LSAT (fall applicants not later than December test date, spring applicants not later than June, if more than one LSAT is available, last score is used), bachelor's degree from an accredited institution, personal statement, two recommendations, transcripts (must show all schools attended and at least three years of study) required in support of application. Applicants must have received bachelor's degree prior to enrollment. Campus visits are encouraged. In addition, international applicants whose native language is not English must submit TOEFL (not older than two years), transcripts with certified evaluation and statement indicating degree is equivalent to a U.S. degree. Ap-

ply to Admission Office before April 1 (fall), November 1 (spring). First-year students admitted fall and spring. Rolling admission process. Acceptance of offer and first deposit due date May 1 (fall), November 15 (spring). Application fee $45. Phone: (800)255-4252, (619)239-0391. E-mail: admissions@cwsl.edu.

ADMISSION REQUIREMENTS FOR TRANSFER APPLICANTS. Accepts transfers from other ABA-accredited schools. Admission limited to space available. At least one year of enrollment, dean's letter indicating applicant is in good standing, prefer applicants in the top quarter of first-year class, LSAT, LSDAS, personal statement regarding reason for transfer, two letters of recommendations, current law school transcript required in support of application. Apply to Admission Office by July 15 (fall), November 15 (spring), April 15 (summer). Admission decisions made within one month of file being completed. Application fee $45. Will consider visiting/transient applicants.

ADMISSION STANDARDS. Number of full-time applicants 1,934; number accepted 1,258; number enrolled 297; median LSAT 153 (75% of class have a score at or above 148); median GPA 3.11 (A = 4) (75% of class have a GPA at or above 2.84). Attrition rate 11%. Gorman rating 3.05; *U.S. News & World Report* ranking is in the fourth tier of all law schools.

FINANCIAL AID. Scholarships, Academic Scholars Program, state grants, institutional loans; federal loans, Federal WS. Apply to Admissions Office. Use FAFSA (FAFSA code #G13103), submit CSS analysis. Approximately 34% of first-year class received scholarships/grants-in-aid. Approximately 85% of current students receive some form of financial assistance. Average scholarship/grant $9,100. Average debt after graduation $78,000.

DEGREE REQUIREMENTS. For J.D.: 89 credits (43 required) with a 2.0 (A = 4) GPA, plus completion of upper divisional writing course; 3-year program. For J.D.-M.S.W.: up to 12 credits may be credited toward J.D.; 4- to 5-year program.

CAREER AND PLACEMENT INFORMATION. About 7 employers conducted on-campus interviews. Approximately 65% of graduates are employed in state. More than 59% of graduates are practicing law; 16% are in business; 20% in government; 1% in academia. Approximately 82% of the California Western School of Law's first-time state bar exam takers pass the California Bar Exam; California's passage rate for all first-time takers from ABA-approved schools is 83%.

CAMPBELL UNIVERSITY

Buies Creek, North Carolina 27506
Phone: (910)893-1200
Internet site: http://Webster.campbell.edu

Founded 1887. Located 30 miles SE of Raleigh and 30 miles N of Fayetteville. Rural setting. Buies Creek has a population of 2,000. Independent control (Southern Baptist affiliation). Semester system. Library: 338,000 volumes; 711,000 microforms; 3,161 periodicals/subscriptions; 46 computer workstations.

University's other graduate schools: Lundy-Fetterman School of Business, Pharmacy School.

Total university enrollment: 2,700.

Norman Adrian Wiggins School of Law

P.O. Box 158
Buies Creek, North Carolina 27506
Phone: (910)893-1750
Internet site: http://Webster.campbell.edu/culawsch.htm

Established 1976. Located on main campus. ABA approved since 1979. Semester system. Full-time, day study only. Law library: 156,000 volumes/microforms; 2,346 current periodicals/subscriptions; 10 computer workstations.

Annual tuition: $15,733. On-campus housing available for both single and married students. Annual on-campus living expenses: $9,500. Contact Residential Life Office. Phone: (910)893-1200. Single law students required to live on campus. Contact Director of Married Housing for both married and off-campus information. Phone: (910)893-1616. Off-campus housing and personal expenses: approximately $12,330. Additional costs: books approximately $500.

Enrollment: first-year class 119; total full-time 331 (men 60%, women 40%); no part-time students. First-year statistics: 25% out of state, 40% women; 11% minority; average age 25; range of first-year section sizes 25–50 students; number of upper division courses offered after first year 61.

Faculty: full-time 20, part-time 15; 15% female; 7% minority; student/faculty ratio 19 to 1.

Degrees conferred: J.D., J.D.-M.B.A.

RECRUITMENT PRACTICES AND POLICIES. Attends national law school forums. On-campus informa-

tional sessions. School does have diversity program and actively recruits women/minority applicants.

ADMISSION REQUIREMENTS FOR FIRST-YEAR APPLICANTS. LSDAS law school report, LSAT (not later than December test date, if more than one LSAT, the average is used), bachelor's degree from an accredited institution, résumé, personal statement, personal interview, two recommendations, transcripts (must show all schools attended and at least three years of study) required in support of the comprehensive application. Applicants must have received bachelor's degree prior to enrollment. Personal interview requested of all finalist candidates. In addition, international applicants must submit TOEFL. Apply to Dean of Admission after August 1, preferably by March 1. First-year students admitted fall only. Rolling admission process. Application fee $40. Phone: (910)893-1754.

ADMISSION REQUIREMENTS FOR TRANSFER APPLICANTS. Accepts transfers from other ABA-accredited schools. Admission limited to space available. At least one year of enrollment, letter from dean indicating candidate is in good standing, LSAT, LSDAS, personal statement regarding reason for transfer, current law school transcript required in support of application. Apply to Dean of Admission by June 1. Admission decisions made by July 15. Application fee $40. Will consider visiting/transient applicants.

ADMISSION STANDARDS. Number of full-time applicants 800; number accepted 206; number enrolled 119; median LSAT 153 (75% of class have a score at or above 150); median GPA 3.0 (A = 4) (75% of class have a GPA at or above 2.62). Attrition rate 3.4%. Gorman rating 2.16; *U.S. News & World Report* ranking is in the third tier of all law schools.

FINANCIAL AID. Scholarships, assistantships, loans; federal loans and Federal WS offered through university's Financial Aid Office. For scholarships apply to Dean of School after January 1, before May 1. Phone: (910)893-1750. For all other programs apply to Director of Financial Assistance. Phone: (910)893-1200. Use FAFSA (FAFSA code #002913). Approximately 15% of first-year class received scholarships. Approximately 95% of current students receive some form of financial assistance. Average scholarship/grant $2,500.

DEGREE REQUIREMENTS. For J.D.: 90 credits (70 required) with a 70 (Scale 0–100) GPA, plus completion of upper divisional writing course; 3-year program. For J.D.-M.B.A.: total 114 credits (J.D. 90 credits, M.B.A. 24 credits).

CAREER AND PLACEMENT INFORMATION. Approximately 91% of graduates are employed in state. More than 95% of graduates are practicing law; 1% are in business; 4% in government; none in academia. Approximately 97% of Campbell University's first-time state bar exam takers pass the North Carolina Bar Exam; North Carolina's passage rate for all first-time takers from ABA-approved schools is 85%. Graduates are eligible to take the bar exam in all 50 states.

CAPITAL UNIVERSITY
Columbus, Ohio 43209-2394
Internet site: http://www.capital.edu

Founded 1830. Private control, Lutheran affiliation. Semester system. Library: 400,000 volumes; 102,000 microforms; 2,866 periodicals/subscriptions; 74 computer workstations.

University's other graduate schools: Graduate School of Administration, School of Nursing.

Total university enrollment: 4,000.

School of Law
303 East Broad
Columbus, Ohio 43215-3201
Phone: (614)236-6310; Fax: (614)236-6972
Internet site: http://www.capital.edu/law/law.hlm
E-mail: law-admissions@capital.edu

Established 1903. Located downtown in the Discovery District, adjacent to German Village. ABA approved since 1950. AALS member. Semester system. Full-time, part-time study available. Law library: 237,000 volumes/microforms; 2,000 current periodicals/subscriptions; has LEXIS, NEXIS, WESTLAW, INFOTRAC. Special facilities: Center for Dispute Resolutions, The Ethic Institute, Institute for Citizen Education, Institute for International Legal Education. Special programs: externships.

Annual tuition: full-time $14,933, part-time $9,823; LL.M., M.T. per credit $620. Contact Law School Admissions Office for off-campus information. Off-campus housing and personal expenses: approximately $10,585. Additional costs: books approximately $600.

Enrollment: first-year class 277; total full-time 472, part-time 342 (men 55%, women 45%). First-year statistics: 45% out of state, 40 states and foreign countries represented; 45% women; 9% minority; average age 25; 150 undergraduate institutions represented; average first-year section sizes full-time 88 students, part-time 95 students; number of upper division courses offered after first year full-time 36, part-time 73.

Faculty: full-time 31, part-time 53; 10% female; 5% minority; student/faculty ratio 20 to 1.

Degrees conferred: J.D., J.D.-M.B.A., J.D.-M.S.A. (Sports Administration with Ohio University), J.D.-M.N.S., J.D.-LL.M. (Tax), LL.M. (Business and Taxation), M.T. (for accountants only).

RECRUITMENT PRACTICES AND POLICIES. Attends national law school forums. On-campus informational sessions. School does have diversity program and actively recruits women/minority applicants.

ADMISSION REQUIREMENTS FOR FIRST-YEAR APPLICANTS. LSDAS law school report, LSAT (not later than December test date, if more than one LSAT, average is used), bachelor's degree from an accredited institution, personal statement, two recommendations, transcripts (must show all schools attended and at least three years of study) required in support of application. Applicants must have received bachelor's degree prior to enrollment. Interview not required but may be requested by school. Joint-degree applicants must apply to and be accepted by both schools. Apply to the Office of Admission after September 30, before May 1. First-year students admitted fall only. Rolling admission process. Application fee $35. Phone: (614)236-6310. Fax: (614)236-6972. E-mail: law-admissions@capital.edu.

ADMISSION REQUIREMENTS FOR TRANSFER APPLICANTS. Accepts transfers from other ABA-accredited schools. Admission limited to space available. At least one year of enrollment, dean's letter indicating candidate is in good standing, LSAT, a copy of LSDAS report, personal statement regarding reason for transfer, current law school transcript required in support of application. Apply to the Office of Admission by June 1. Admission decisions made by early August. Application fee $35. Will consider visiting students.

ADMISSION REQUIREMENTS FOR LL.M., M.T. APPLICANTS. For LL.M.: applicant must have an LL.B. or J.D. from an approved ABA law school; submit official transcript showing rank in class (prefer upper half of class), transcripts from all post-secondary institutions attended (at least one course in basic income tax law), résumé, personal statement or any published written works required in support of LL.M. application. Letters of recommendations not required but will be carefully considered. Personal interviews are strongly encouraged, contact Graduate Tax Program directly at (614)236-6444. E-mail: gradtax@capital.edu In addition, international applicants whose native language is not English must submit TOEFL; in lieu of TOEFL a GRE or LSAT score may be substituted. Admits fall and spring. Apply to Office of Graduate Studies at least 6 weeks prior to desired term of entrance. Application Fee $25. Phone: (614)236-6444.

For M.T.: an undergraduate degree in accounting required: submit official transcripts from all post-secondary institutions attended, résumé, personal statement required in support of application. Letters of recommendations not required but will be carefully considered. Personal interviews are strongly encouraged, contact Graduate Tax Program directly at (614)236-6444. E-mail: gradtax@capital.edu. In addition, international applicants whose native language is not English must submit TOEFL; in lieu of TOEFL a GRE or LSAT score may be substituted. Admits fall and spring. Apply to Office of Graduate Studies at least 6 weeks prior to desired term of entrance. Application Fee $25. Phone: (614)236-6444.

ADMISSION STANDARDS. Number of full-time applicants 754, part-time 201; number accepted full-time 528, part-time 125; number enrolled full-time 175, part-time 100; median LSAT 152 (75% of class have a score at or above 147); median GPA 3.1 (A = 4) (75% of class have a GPA at or above 2.76). Attrition rate 8.7%. Gorman rating 2.78; *U.S. News & World Report* ranking is in the fourth tier of all law schools.

FINANCIAL AID. Scholarships, assistantships, minority scholarships, institutional and privately funded loans; federal loans and Federal WS offered through university's Financial Aid Office. For scholarships, assistantships (selection criteria place heavy reliance on LSAT and undergraduate GPA), apply to Director of Admissions and Financial Aid Office of school after January 1, before April 1. Phone: (614)236-6350. Use school's FA application. For all other programs apply to university's Director of Financial Aid. Phone: (800)289-6289. Use FAFSA. Approximately 35% full-time, 26% part-time in the first-year class received scholarships/grants-in-aid. Approximately 80% of current students receive some form of financial assistance. Average scholarship/grant full-time $3,000, part-time $2,500. Average debt after graduation $43,000.

DEGREE REQUIREMENTS. For J.D.: 86 credits (42 required) with a 2.0 (A = 4) GPA, plus completion of upper divisional writing course; 3-year program, 4-year program (part-time). For J.D.-M.B.A.: total combined degree program is reduced by up to 18 credits. For J.D.-M.S.A.: individualized program, total time for both degrees may be reduced by as much as 1 year. For J.D.-M.N.S.: individually designed programs which significantly reduce number of credits for each degree. For J.D.-LL.M. (Tax): combined program is reduced by 12 credits. For LL.M., M.T.: 24-credit program; 2.75 (A = 4) GPA required; up to 4 hours of graduate business law courses may be included in degree program; successful completion of Taxation Research II, Tax Policy seminar, and dissertation.

CAREER AND PLACEMENT INFORMATION. Approximately 81% of graduates are employed in state. More than 60% of graduates are practicing law; 21% are in business; 16% in government; 3% in academia. Approximately 94% of Capital University's first-time state bar exam takers pass the Ohio Bar Exam; Ohio's passage rate for all first-time takers from ABA-approved schools is 90%. Graduates have taken the bar exam in more than 30 states and are eligible in all 50 states.

CASE WESTERN RESERVE UNIVERSITY
Cleveland, Ohio 44106
Internet site: http://www.cwru.edu

Formed as a result of a merger between Case Institute of Technology and Western Reserve University in 1967. Located 3 miles E of Cleveland. Private control. Semester system. Library: 1,900,000 volumes; 2,181,000 microforms; 14,100 periodicals/subscriptions; 45 computer workstations.

University's other graduate schools: Frances Payne Bolton School of Nursing, Mandel School of Applied Sciences, School of Dentistry, School of Graduate Studies, School of Medicine, Weatherhead School of Management.

Total university enrollment: 9,750.

School of Law
11075 East Boulevard
Cleveland, Ohio 44106-7148
Phone: (216)368-3600
Internet site: http://lawwww.cwru.edu
E-mail: lawadmissions@PO.cwru.edu

Established 1892. Located on main campus, 20 minutes from downtown. ABA approved since 1923. AALS charter member. Semester system. Full-time, limited number of part-time con-sidered. Law library: 347,700 volumes/microforms; 4,600 current periodicals/subscriptions; 62 computer workstations; has LEXIS, NEXIS, WESTLAW; library has access to over 700 databases. Special facilities: Frederich K. Cox International Law Center. Special programs: Canada-U.S. Law Institute (sponsored with the University of Western Ontario), Russian Legal Studies Program (affiliated with St. Petersburg University).

Annual tuition: $19,540, per credit $813. On-campus housing available for single students only. Annual on-campus housing cost: single students $3,700 (room only), $5,800 (room and board). Housing deadline May 1. Contact Graduate Housing Office. Phone: (216)368-3780. Law students tend to live off-campus in Cleveland Heights. Contact university's Off-Campus Housing Bureau for off-campus information. Phone: (216)368-4390. Off-campus housing and personal expenses: approximately $10,430. Additional costs: books approximately $600.

Enrollment: first-year class 225; total full-time 632 (men 57%, women 43%). First-year statistics: 52% out of state, 44 states and foreign countries represented; 43% women; 14% minority; average age 25; 134 undergraduate institutions represented; range of first-year section sizes 28–100 students; number of upper division courses offered after first year 97.

Faculty: full-time 32, part-time 38; 23% female; 4% minority; student/faculty ratio 15 to 1.

Degrees conferred: J.D., J.D.-M.B.A. (Management), J.D.-M.A. (Legal History, Bioethics), J.D.-M.S.S.A., LL.M. (Tax), LL.M. (only for persons who have completed a basic legal education and received a university degree in law in another country).

RECRUITMENT PRACTICES AND POLICIES. Attends national law school forums. On-campus informational sessions. School does have diversity program and actively recruits women/minority applicants.

ADMISSION REQUIREMENTS FOR FIRST-YEAR APPLICANTS. LSDAS law school report, LSAT (not later than February test date [test results are valid for three years], if more than one LSAT, average is used), bachelor's degree from an accredited institution, personal statement, three recommendations, transcripts (must show all schools attended and at least three years of study) required in support of application. Applicants must

have received bachelor's degree prior to enrollment. In addition, international applicants must submit TOEFL (not older than two years), certified translation and evaluation of all non-English transcripts. Apply to Admission Office after September 30, before April 1. First-year students admitted fall only. Rolling admission process, notification starts in January and is finished by May 1. School does maintain a waiting list. Application fee $40. Phone: (800)756-0036. E-mail: lawadmissions@PO.cwru.edu. Admission Deadline for LL.M. is March 1.

ADMISSION REQUIREMENTS FOR TRANSFER APPLICANTS. Accepts transfers from other ABA-accredited schools. Admission limited to space available. At least one year of enrollment, in good standing, official class rank, LSAT, LSDAS, personal statement regarding reason for transfer, current law school transcript required in support of application. Apply to Admission Office by July 1. Admission decisions made by August 1. Application fee $40. Will consider visiting students.

ADMISSION STANDARDS. Number of full-time applicants 1,458; number accepted 864; number enrolled 225; median LSAT 158 (75% of class have a score at or above 154); median GPA 3.36 (A = 4) (75% of class have a GPA at or above 3.02). Attrition rate 3.4%. Gorman rating 3.74; *U.S. News & World Report* ranking is in the top 50 of all law schools.

FINANCIAL AID. Scholarships, diversity grants, private loans; federal loans and Federal WS offered through university's Financial Aid Office. For scholarships (selection criteria place heavy reliance on LSAT and undergraduate GPA) apply to School of Law's Financial Aid Office after January 1, before May 1 (priority date February 1). E-mail: lawmoney@PO.cwru.edu. Use school's FA application. Use FAFSA for all federal programs (FAFSA Title IV code #E00082); submit latest federal income tax form, Financial Aid Transcript. Approximately 37% of first-year class received scholarships/grants-in-aid. Approximately 79% of current students receive some form of financial assistance. Average scholarship/grant $9,700.

DEGREE REQUIREMENTS. For J.D.: 88 credits (33 required) with a 2.0 (A = 4) GPA, plus completion of upper divisional writing course; 3-year program. For J.D.-master's: a maximum of 9 credits may be used toward J.D.; 4-year program. For LL.M. (Tax): 24 credits. For

LL.M. (International): 30 credits; at least 2 semesters in residence; mentorship with a Cleveland law firm or corporation.

CAREER AND PLACEMENT INFORMATION. Approximately 67% of graduates are employed in state. More than 75% of graduates are practicing law; 14% are in business; 11% in government; none in academia. Approximately 94% of Case Western Reserve University's first-time state bar exam takers pass the Ohio Bar Exam; Ohio's passage rate for all first-time takers from ABA-approved schools is 90%. Graduates are eligible to take the bar exam in all 50 states.

THE CATHOLIC UNIVERSITY OF AMERICA
Washington, D.C. 20064
Internet site: http://www.cua.edu

Founded 1887. Located in suburban Washington on a 154-acre campus. Private control (Catholic affiliation). Semester system. Library: 1,365,000 volumes; 1,230,000 microforms; 9,450 periodicals/subscriptions; 100 computer workstations.

University's other graduate schools: National Catholic School of Social Services, School of Architecture and Planning, School of Arts and Sciences, School of Engineering, School of Library and Information Science, School of Nursing, School of Philosophy, School of Religious Studies, The Benjamin T. Rome School of Music.

Total university enrollment: 6,100.

Columbus School of Law
Cardinal Station
Washington, D.C. 20064
Phone: (202)319-5140
Internet site: http://www.law.cua.edu
E-mail: sokatch@law.cua.edu

Established 1897. Located on main campus. ABA approved since 1925. AALS member since 1921. Semester system. Full-time, part-time study. Law library: 264,400 volumes/microforms; 5,200 current periodicals/subscriptions; 33 computer workstations; has LEXIS, NEXIS, WESTLAW, DIALOG. Special facilities: Institute for Communications Law Studies, Comparative and International Law Institute, Law and Public Policy Program. Special programs: summer study abroad at Jagiellonia University, Cracow, Poland; Preface Program; externships.

Annual tuition: full-time $22,412, part-time $17,065. Limited on-campus housing available. Annual on-campus housing cost: $6,200–$8,000 including board. Contact Director of Housing for on-campus housing information. Phone: (202)319-5615. Law students tend to live off-campus. Contact Admissions Office for off-campus information. Phone: (202)319-5151. Off-campus housing and personal expenses: approximately $12,790. Additional costs: books approximately $700.

Enrollment: first-year class 300; total full-time 693, part-time 287 (men 54%, women 46%). First-year statistics: 96% out of state, 50 states and foreign countries represented; 46% women; 16% minority; average age 23; 276 undergraduate institutions represented; range of first-year section sizes 30–70 students; number of upper division courses offered after first year full-time 83, part-time 73.

Faculty: full-time 44, part-time 84; 12% female; 5% minority; student/faculty ratio 19 to 1.

Degrees conferred: J.D., J.D.-M.A. (Economics, History, Politics, Philosophy), J.D.-M.S.W., J.D.-M.L.S., J.D.-M.Div.

RECRUITMENT PRACTICES AND POLICIES. Attends national law school forums. On-campus informational sessions. School does have diversity program and actively recruits women/minority applicants.

ADMISSION REQUIREMENTS FOR FIRST-YEAR APPLICANTS. LSDAS law school report, LSAT (not later than December test date, if more than one LSAT, the average is used), bachelor's degree from an accredited institution, personal statement, interview, two recommendations, transcripts (must show all schools attended and at least three years of study) required in support of application. Applicants must have received bachelor's degree prior to enrollment. Interview not required but may be requested by school. In addition, international applicants whose native language is not English applicants must submit TOEFL (not older than two years). Apply to Office of Admission after September 30, before March 1. First-year students admitted fall only. Rolling admission process, notification starts in December and is finished when class is filled. Application fee $55. Phone: (202)319-5151. E-mail: sokatch@law.cua.edu.

ADMISSION REQUIREMENTS FOR TRANSFER APPLICANTS. Accepts transfers from other ABA-accredited schools. Admission limited to space available. At least one year of enrollment, dean's letter indicating

candidate is in good standing (prefer applicants in the top quarter of first-year class), LSAT, LSDAS, personal statement regarding reason for transfer, official undergraduate transcript, current law school transcript required in support of application. Apply to Office of Admission by July 15. Admission decisions made by August 15. Application fee $55. Will consider visiting/transient applicants.

ADMISSION STANDARDS. Number of full-time applicants 1,848, part-time 425; number of accepted full-time 911, part-time 205; number of enrolled full-time 221, part-time 79; median LSAT 156 (75% of class have a score at or above full-time 151, part-time 148); median GPA 3.17 (A = 4) (75% of class have a GPA at or above full-time 2.8, part-time 2.6). Attrition rate 3.5%. Gorman rating 3.89; *U.S. News & World Report* ranking is in the second tier of all law schools.

FINANCIAL AID. Scholarships, minority scholarships, grants-in-aid, institutional loans; federal loans and Federal WS offered through university's Financial Aid Office. Assistantships may be available for upper divisional joint-degree candidates. For scholarships (selection criteria place heavy reliance on LSAT and undergraduate GPA) apply to Assistant Director of Admissions of school after January 1, before March 1. Phone: (202)319-5151. For all other programs apply to university's Office of Financial Aid. Phone: (202)319-5057. Use FAFSA (FAFSA code #001437), Access Disk. Approximately 33% of full-time, 3% of part-time students in first-year class received scholarships/grants-in-aid. Approximately 80% of current students receive some form of financial assistance. Average scholarship/grant $3,500 for full-time, $1,500 for part-time. Average debt after graduation $66,800.

DEGREE REQUIREMENTS. For J.D.: 84 credits (33 required) with a 70 (scale 0–100) GPA, plus completion of upper divisional writing course; 3-year program, 4-year program (part-time). Accelerated J.D. with 1 summer of course work. For dual-degree programs: candidates must satisfy all degree requirements for each degree.

CAREER AND PLACEMENT INFORMATION. About 53 employers conducted on-campus interviews. Approximately 50% of graduates are employed in metropolitan D.C. More than 70% of graduates are practicing law; 18% are in business; 11% in government; 1% in academia. Approximately 70% of the Catholic University of America's first-time bar exam takers pass the Maryland or Virginia bar exam; the passage rate for all first-time takers from ABA-approved schools is 75%.

UNIVERSITY OF CHICAGO
Chicago, Illinois 60637-1513
Internet site: http://www.uchicago.edu

Founded 1890. Private control. Quarter system. Library: 5,850,000 volumes; 2,178,000 microforms; 45,500 periodicals/subscriptions; 158 computer workstations.

University's other graduate divisions/schools: Divinity School, Division of Social Sciences, Division of the Humanities, Division of the Biological Sciences, Division of Physical Sciences, Graduate School of Business, Pritzker School of Medicine, School of Social Services Administration, Irving B. Harris Graduate School of Public Policy Studies.

Total university enrollment: 12,200.

Law School
111 East 60th Street
Chicago, Illinois 60637
Phone: (773)702-9484
Internet site: http://www.law.uchicago.edu

Established 1902. Located in the Hyde Park area of Chicago. ABA approved since 1923. AALS charter member. Quarter system. Full-time, day study only. Law library: 600,000 volumes/microforms; 7,000 current periodicals/subscriptions; 43 computer workstations; has LEXIS, NEXIS, WESTLAW, DIALOG. Special programs: Legal History Program, Law and Government Program, Law-Economics Program. Special facilities: Center for Studies in Criminal Justice, Center for Constitutionalism in Eastern Europe.

Annual tuition: $24,138. On-campus housing available for both single and married students. Annual on-campus housing cost: single students $6,500 (room and board), married students $6,000–$7,000. Housing deadline July 1. Contact Office of Neighborhood Student Apartments for on- and off-campus housing information. Phone: (312)753-2218. Law students tend to live off-campus. Off-campus housing expenses: approximately $355–$817 per month. Additional costs: books approximately $600–$700.

Enrollment: first-year class 180; total full-time 542 (men 59%, women 41%); no part-time students. First-year statistics: 85% out of state, 46 states and foreign countries represented; 41% women; 22% minority; average age 24; 170 undergraduate institutions represented;

average first-year section size 88 students; number of upper division courses offered after first year 69.

Faculty: full-time 39, part-time 25; 20% female; 8% minority; student/faculty ratio 19 to 1.

Degrees conferred: J.D., J.D.-M.B.A., J.D.-M.A. (Public Policy), LL.M./M.Comp.L. (for those with an American or foreign first degree in law from an approved school of law), J.S.D./D.Comp.L.

RECRUITMENT PRACTICES AND POLICIES. Attends national law school forums. On-campus informational sessions. School does have diversity program and actively recruits women/minority applicants.

ADMISSION REQUIREMENTS FOR FIRST-YEAR APPLICANTS. LSDAS law school report, LSAT (not later than December test date, if more than one LSAT, consider the first score unless a later score is substantially higher), bachelor's degree from an accredited institution, personal statement, two recommendations, transcripts (must show all schools attended and at least three years of study) required in support of application. Applicants must have received bachelor's degree prior to enrollment. Interview not required but may be requested by school. In addition, international applicants must submit TOEFL (not older than two years), TSE, TWE. Apply to Admission Office after September 30, priority date February 15 (applications received after February 15 not considered until late April). First-year students admitted fall only. Rolling admission process, notification starts in late November and is finished by early May. School does maintain a waiting list. Application fee $60. Phone: (773)702-9484.

ADMISSION REQUIREMENTS FOR TRANSFER APPLICANTS. Accepts transfers from other ABA-accredited schools. Admission limited to space available. At least one year of enrollment, in good standing (prefer applicants in the top quarter of first-year class), LSAT, LSDAS, personal statement regarding reason for transfer, current law school transcript required in support of application. Apply to Admission Office by July 15. Admission decisions made by mid August. Application fee $60. Will consider visiting students.

ADMISSION STANDARDS. Number of full-time applicants 2,476; number accepted 642; number enrolled 180; median LSAT 170 (75% of class have a score at or above 166); median GPA 3.75 (A = 4) (75% of class have a GPA at or above 3.54). Attrition rate 1.5%. Gorman rating 4.90; *U.S. News & World Report* ranking is in the top 4 of all law schools.

FINANCIAL AID. Scholarships, merit scholarships, grants, institutional loans; federal loans offered through university's Financial Aid Office. Assistantships may be available for upper divisional joint-degree candidates. For scholarships (selection criteria place heavy reliance on LSAT and undergraduate GPA) apply to Admissions Office of school after January 1, before March 15. For all other programs apply to university's Director of Financial Aid. Use FAFSA (FAFSA code #001774), Access Disk. Approximately 46% of first-year class received scholarships/grants-in-aid. Approximately 80% of current students receive some form of financial assistance. Average scholarship/grant $8,000.

DEGREE REQUIREMENTS. For J.D.: 105 quarter credits (40 required) with a 68% (scale 0–100%) GPA, plus completion of upper divisional writing course and professional responsibility class; 3-year program (9 quarters). Advanced degree programs in many areas accelerated through 1 summer quarter of course work. For J.D.-master's: individual designed 4-year programs. For LL.M./M.Comp.L: 27 quarter credits, three quarters in residence. For J.S.D./D.Comp.L.: at least 27 quarter credits in full-time residency; at least a 78% (scale 0–100%) GPA; dissertation.

CAREER AND PLACEMENT INFORMATION. About 330 employers conducted on-campus interviews. Approximately 39% of graduates are employed in state. More than 92% of graduates are practicing law; 4% are in business; 2% in government; 2% in academia. Approximately 97% of the University of Chicago's first-time state bar exam takers pass the Illinois Bar Exam; Illinois' passage rate for all first-time takers from ABA-approved schools is 87%. Graduates are eligible to take the bar exam in all 50 states.

UNIVERSITY OF CINCINNATI

Cincinnati, Ohio 45221
Internet site: http://www.cu.edu

Founded 1819. Private control. Quarter system. Library: 1,980,000 volumes; 2,919,000 microforms; 21,500 periodicals/subscriptions; 436 computer workstations.

University's Division of Research and Advanced Studies includes: College-Conservatory of Music, College of Business Administration, College of Design, Architecture, Art and Planning, College of Education, College of Engineering, College of Nursing and Health, College of Pharmacy, McMicken College of Arts and Sciences, School of Social Work, College of Medicine.

Total university enrollment: 35,500.

School of Law
P.O. Box 210040
Cincinnati, Ohio 45221-0040
Phone: (513)556-6805
Internet site: http://www.la.wcu.edu
E-mail: Admissions@Law.CU.Edu

Established 1833. First law school west of the Appalachian Mountains, fourth oldest law school in the U.S. Located in the historic Clifton Area of Cincinnati, 10 miles N of downtown. ABA approved since 1923. AALS charter member. Semester system. Full-time, day study only. Law library: 361,500 volumes/microforms; 2,440 current periodicals/subscriptions; 44 computer workstations; has LEXIS, NEXIS, WESTLAW, DIALOG, OCLC, UCLIO, OHIOLINK, DATATIMES, DIANA; is a Federal Government Depository. Special facilities: Urban Morgan Institute for Human Rights, Center for Corporate Law.

Annual tuition: resident $7,245, nonresident $14,076. On-campus housing available for both single and married students. Annual on-campus apartments cost: single students $5,181 (room only), married students $5,181. Housing deadline July 1. Contact Housing Office for both on- and off-campus information. Phone: (513)556-6461. Law students tend to live off-campus. Off-campus housing and personal expenses: approximately $10,256. Additional costs: books approximately $700.

Enrollment: first-year class 124; total full-time 375 (men 44%, women 56%); no part-time students. First-year statistics: 33% out of state, 19 states and foreign countries represented; 56% women; 10% minority; average age 27; 68 undergraduate institutions represented; average first-year section size 22 students; number of upper division courses offered after first year 107.

Faculty: full-time 26, part-time 60; 27% female; 4% minority; student/faculty ratio 16 to 1.

Degrees conferred: J.D., J.D.-M.B.A., J.D.-M.C.P., J.D.-M.A. (Women's Studies).

RECRUITMENT PRACTICES AND POLICIES. Attends national law school forums. On-campus informational sessions. School does have diversity program and actively recruits women/minority applicants.

ADMISSION REQUIREMENTS FOR FIRST-YEAR APPLICANTS. LSDAS law school report, LSAT (not later than December test date (test scores are valid for up to 4 years), if more than one LSAT, the average is used), bachelor's degree from an accredited institution, résumé, personal statement (optional), two recommendations, transcripts (must show all schools attended and at least three years of study) required in support of application.

Applicants must have received bachelor's degree prior to enrollment. In addition, international applicants must submit TOEFL (not older than two years). Apply to Admission Committee after September 30, before April 1. First-year students admitted fall only. Rolling admission process, notification starts in December and is finished by late May. Acceptance of offer and first deposit due date March 15. School does maintain a waiting list after May 1. Application fee $35. Phone: (513)556-6805. E-mail: Admissions@Law.CU.Edu.

ADMISSION REQUIREMENTS FOR TRANSFER APPLICANTS. Accepts transfers from other ABA-accredited schools. Admission limited to space available. At least one year of enrollment, dean's letter indicating candidate is in good standing, prefer applicants in the top quarter of first-year class, LSAT, LSDAS, personal statement regarding reason for transfer, two recommendations, current law school transcript (including rank in class) required in support of application. Apply to Admission Committee by August 1. Admission decisions made by mid August. Application fee $35. Will consider visiting students.

ADMISSION STANDARDS. Number of full-time applicants 995; number accepted 424; number enrolled 124; median LSAT 160 (75% of class have a score at or above 154); median GPA 3.47 (A = 4) (75% of class have a GPA at or above 3.24). Attrition rate .5%. Gorman rating 3.28; *U.S. News & World Report* ranking is in the top 50 of all law schools.

FINANCIAL AID. Scholarships, merit scholarships, grants, institutional loans; federal loans offered through university's Financial Aid Office. For scholarships (selection criteria place heavy reliance on LSAT and undergraduate GPA) apply to Admissions Committee of school after January 1, before March 1. For all other programs apply to university's Director of Financial Aid. Phone: (513)556-6982. Use FAFSA (FAFSA code #003125). Approximately 64% of first-year class received scholarships/grants. Approximately 60% of current students receive some form of financial assistance. Average scholarship grant $3,000.

DEGREE REQUIREMENTS. For J.D.: 88 credits (34 required) with a 2.0 (A = 4) GPA, plus completion of upper divisional writing course and professional responsibility course; 3-year program. For J.D.-M.B.A.: 4-year program. For J.D.-M.C.P.: 4-year program. For J.D.-M.A.: 3½-year program.

CAREER AND PLACEMENT INFORMATION. About 55 employers conducted on-campus interviews. Approximately 72% of graduates are employed in state. More than 66% of graduates are practicing law; 21% are in business; 11% in government; 2% in academia. Approximately 95% of the University of Cincinnati's first-time state bar exam takers pass the Ohio Bar Exam; Ohio's passage rate for all first-time takers from ABA-approved schools is 90%. Graduates are eligible to take the bar exam in all 50 states.

CLEVELAND STATE UNIVERSITY
Cleveland, Ohio 44115
Internet site: http://www.csuohio.edu

Founded 1964. Located in downtown Cleveland. Public control. Quarter system. Library: 879,000 volumes; 633,600 microforms; 6,500 periodicals/subscriptions; 143 computer workstations.

University's College of Graduate Studies includes: College of Arts and Sciences, College of Education, Fenn College of Engineering, James J. Nance College of Business Administration, Maxine Goodman Levin College of Urban Affairs.

Total university enrollment: 15,670.

Cleveland-Marshall College of Law
1801 Euclid Avenue
Cleveland, Ohio 44115
Phone: (216)687-2304
Internet site: http://www.csuohio.edu/law/
E-mail: mmcnally@trans.csuohio.edu

Established 1897 as Cleveland Law School, joined with John Marshall Law School in 1946. Joined Cleveland State University in 1969. Located at East 18th Street and Euclid Avenue. ABA approved since 1957. AALS member. Semester system. Full-time, part-time study. Law library: 410,000 volumes/microforms; 2,140 current periodicals/subscriptions; 20 computer workstations; has LEXIS, NEXIS, WESTLAW, DIALOG.

Annual tuition: resident $7,145, nonresident $14,250; part-time resident $5,495, nonresident $10,960. On-campus housing available for single students only. Annual on-campus housing cost: single students $2,624 (room only). Housing deadline July 1. Contact Department of Residence Life. Phone: (216)687-5196. Law students tend to live off-campus. Contact Department of Student Life for off-campus information. Phone: (216)687-5196. Off-campus housing and personal expenses: approximately $9,700. Additional costs: books approximately $500.

Enrollment: first-year class 260; total full-time 572, part-time 307 (men 54%, women 46%). First-year statistics: 19% out of state, 25 states and foreign countries represented; 46% women; 12% minority; average age 27; 150 undergraduate institutions represented; average first-year section sizes full-time 70 students, part-time 40 students; number of upper division courses offered after first year full-time 46, part-time 55.

Faculty: full-time 38, part-time 31; 32% female; 9% minority; student/faculty ratio 19 to 1.

Degrees conferred: J.D., J.D.-M.B.A., J.D.-M.P.A., LL.M. (for graduates of approved American and foreign law schools).

RECRUITMENT PRACTICES AND POLICIES. Attends several national law school forums. On-campus informational sessions. School does have diversity program and actively recruits women/minority applicants.

ADMISSION REQUIREMENTS FOR FIRST-YEAR APPLICANTS. LSDAS law school report, LSAT (not later than December test date), bachelor's degree from an accredited institution, personal statement, interview, two recommendations, transcripts (must show all schools attended and at least three years of study) required in support of application. Applicants must have received bachelor's degree prior to enrollment. In addition, international applicants must submit TOEFL (not older than two years). Apply to Office of Law School Admission after September 1, before March 1. First-year students admitted fall only. Rolling admission process, notification starts in January and is finished by late May. Application fee $35. Phone: (216)687-2304. E-mail: mmcnally@trans.csuohio.edu.

ADMISSION REQUIREMENTS FOR TRANSFER APPLICANTS. Accepts transfers from other ABA-accredited schools. Admission limited to space available. At least one year of enrollment, in good standing (prefer applicants in the top quarter of first-year class), LSAT, LSDAS, personal statement regarding reason for transfer, current law school transcript required in support of application. Apply to Office of Law School Admission by June 1 (fall), December 1 (spring). Admission decisions made as soon as application is complete. Application fee $35. Will consider visiting special students.

ADMISSION REQUIREMENTS FOR LL.M. APPLICANTS. Official transcript with translations and evaluations if needed, personal statement, two recommendations, interview may be requested in support of application. TOEFL required of all applicants whose native language is not English. Apply to Assistant Dean by March 1 (fall), October 1 (spring). Application fee $35.

ADMISSION STANDARDS. Number of full-time applicants 1,136, part-time 265; number accepted full-time 655, part-time 131; number enrolled full-time 180, part-time 80; median LSAT 151 (75% of class have a score at or above full-time 145, part-time 147); median GPA 3.18 (A = 4) (75% of class have a GPA at or above full-time 2.93, part-time 2.81). Attrition rate 6%. Gorman rating 2.8; *U.S. News & World Report* ranking is in the fourth tier of all law schools.

FINANCIAL AID. Scholarships, grants, private loan, federal loans, Federal WS. For all programs apply to Financial Aid Office of college after January 1, before March 1. Phone: (216)687-2317. Use FAFSA (FAFSA code #003032). Approximately 50% of full-time, 22% of part-time students in first-year class received financial assistance. Approximately 70% of current students receive some form of financial assistance. Average scholarship/grant $1,000. Average debt after graduation $42,000.

DEGREE REQUIREMENTS. For J.D.: 87 credits (32 required) with a 2.0 (A = 4) GPA, plus completion of upper divisional writing course; 3-year full-time program, 4-year part-time program. Accelerated J.D. with summer course work. For J.D.-M.B.A.: 4-year program. For J.D.-M.P.A.: 4-year program. For LL.M.: 20 credits for graduates of American law schools; 24 credits for graduates of foreign law schools; 3.0 GPA (A = 4); thesis.

CAREER AND PLACEMENT INFORMATION. About 10 employers conducted on-campus interviews. Approximately 88% of graduates are employed in state. More than 75% of graduates are practicing law; 12% are in business; 11% in government; 2% in academia. Approximately 91% of Cleveland State University's first-time state bar exam takers pass the Ohio Bar Exam; Ohio's passage rate for all first-time takers from ABA-approved schools is 90%.

UNIVERSITY OF COLORADO AT BOULDER
Boulder, Colorado 80309
Internet site: http://www.colorado.edu

Founded 1876. Located 28 miles NW of Denver. Public control. Semester system. Library: 2,500,000 volumes; 5,319,000 microforms; 28,400 periodicals/subscriptions; 500 computer workstations.

University's other graduate colleges/schools: College of Arts and Sciences, College of Engineering and Applied Sciences, College of Music, School of Education, School of Journalism and Mass Communication; Graduate School of Business Administration.

Total university enrollment: 24,440.

School of Law
Campus Box 403
Boulder, Colorado 80309-0401
Phone: (303)492-8047
Internet site: http://www.colorado.edu/law

Established 1892. Located on main campus. ABA approved since 1923. AALS member. Semester system. Full-time, day study only. Law library: 346,300 volumes/microforms; 3,316 current periodicals/subscriptions; 20 computer workstations; has LEXIS, NEXIS, WESTLAW. Special facilities: Natural Resources Law Center.

Annual tuition: resident $4,953, nonresident $16,171. On-campus housing available for both single and married students. Annual on-campus housing cost: single students $6,273 (room and board), married students $5,100. Contact Assistant Director of Housing for on-campus housing information. Phone: (303)492-6384. Law students tend to live off-campus. Contact Off-Campus Housing Office for off-campus information. Phone: (303)492-7053. Off-campus housing and personal expenses: approximately $10,633. Additional costs: books approximately $600.

Enrollment: first-year class 167; total full-time 497 (men 57%, women 43%); no part-time students. First-year statistics: 45% out of state, 30 states and foreign countries represented; 43% women; 19% minority; average age 25; 96 undergraduate institutions represented; range of first-year section sizes 24–80 students; number of upper division courses offered after first year 89.

Faculty: full-time 43, part-time 28; 17% female; 14% minority; student/faculty ratio 16 to 1.

Degrees conferred: J.D., J.D.-M.B.A., J.D.-M.P.A.

RECRUITMENT PRACTICES AND POLICIES. Attends national law school forums. On-campus informational sessions. School does have diversity program and actively recruits women/minority applicants.

ADMISSION REQUIREMENTS FOR FIRST-YEAR APPLICANTS. LSDAS law school report, LSAT (not later than December test date, if more than one LSAT, highest is used), bachelor's degree from an accredited institution, personal statement, two recommendations, transcripts (must show all schools attended and at least three years of study) required in support of application. Applicants must have received bachelor's degree prior to enrollment. Interview not required but may be requested by school. In addition, international applicants must submit all documentation in English, financial affidavit. Apply to Admission Office after September 30, before February 15. First-year students admitted fall only. Rolling admission process, notification starts in November and is finished in May. School does maintain a waiting list. Application fee $45. Phone: (303)492-7203.

ADMISSION REQUIREMENTS FOR TRANSFER APPLICANTS. Accepts transfers from other ABA-accredited schools. Admission limited to space available. At least one year of enrollment, dean's letter indicating candidate is in good standing (prefer applicants in the top 22% of first-year class), LSAT, LSDAS, personal statement regarding reason for transfer, current law school transcript required in support of application. Apply to Admission Office by July 1. Admission decisions made by mid August. Application fee $45. Will consider visiting students.

ADMISSION STANDARDS. Number of full-time applicants 2,299; number accepted 680; number enrolled 167; median LSAT 162 (75% of class have a score at or above 160); median GPA 3.52 (A = 4) (75% of class have a GPA at or above 3.33). Attrition rate 1.2%. Gorman rating 3.50; *U.S. News & World Report* ranking is in the top 42 of all law schools.

FINANCIAL AID. Scholarships, merit scholarships, minority scholarships, grants-in-aid, institutional loans; federal loans and Federal WS offered through university's Financial Aid Office. For scholarships (selection criteria place heavy reliance on LSAT and undergraduate GPA) apply to Dean's Office after January 1, before March 1. Phone: (304)492-7203. For all other programs apply to university's Director of Financial Aid. Phone: (303)492-5091. Use FAFSA (FAFSA code #001370). Approximately 50% of first-year class received scholarships/grants-in-aid. Approximately 80% of current students receive some form of financial assistance. Average scholarship/grant $1,750. Federal loan forgiveness program available. Average debt after graduation $46,000.

DEGREE REQUIREMENTS. For J.D.: 89 credits (45 required) with a 72–75% (Scale 0–100%, A = 93–100%) GPA, plus completion of upper divisional writing course; 3-year program. Accelerated J.D. with 1 summer of course work. For J.D.-M.B.A.: individualized programs; J.D. accepts up to 12 business credits, M.B.A. accepts up to 15 credits. For J.D.-M.P.A.: individualized programs; J.D. accepts up to 12 public administration credits, M.P.A. accepts up to 12 credits.

CAREER AND PLACEMENT INFORMATION. About 27 employers conducted on-campus interviews. Approximately 70% of graduates are employed in state. More than 65% of graduates are practicing law; 17% are in business; 13% in government; 5% in academia. Approximately 92% of the University of Colorado at Boulder's first-time state bar exam takers pass the Colorado Bar Exam. Graduates are eligible to take the bar exam in all 50 states.

COLUMBIA UNIVERSITY
New York, New York 10027
Internet site: http://www.columbia.edu

Founded 1754. Located in Morningside Heights area of Manhattan. Private control. Semester system. Library: 6,260,000 volumes; 4,460,000 microforms; 63,400 periodicals/subscriptions.

University's other graduate colleges/schools: College of Physicians and Surgeons, Graduate School of Architecture, Planning and Preservation, Graduate School of Arts and Sciences, Graduate School of Business, Graduate School of Journalism, School of Dental and Oral Surgery, School of Engineering and Applied Science, School of International and Public Policy, School of Nursing, School of Public Health, School of Social Work, The School of the Arts, Teachers College.

Total university enrollment: 19,900.

School of Law
435 West 116th Street
New York, New York 10027-7297
Phone: (212)854-2670,7678.
Internet site: http://www.columbia.edu/cu/law

Established 1858. ABA approved since 1923. AALS member. Semester system. Full-time, day study only. Law library: 949,100 volumes/microforms; 6,822 current periodicals/subscriptions; 20 computer workstations; has LEXIS, NEXIS, WESTLAW, DIALOG; is a Federal Government Depository.

Annual tuition: $25,666. On-campus housing available for both single and married students. Annual on-campus housing cost: single students $4,200 (room only), married students $6,700. Contact Graduate Housing Office Phone: (212)854-9300. Law students tend to live off-campus. Contact the Office of Institutional Real Estate for off-campus information. Off-campus housing and personal expenses: approximately $13,800. Additional costs: books approximately $700.

Enrollment: first-year class 346; total full-time 1,073 (men 56%, women 44%); no part-time students. First-year statistics: 75% out of state, 48 states and foreign countries represented; 44% women; 34% minority; average age 24; 209 undergraduate institutions represented; range of first-year section sizes 30–116 students; number of upper division courses offered after first year 76.

Faculty: full-time 75, part-time 76; 23% female; 10% minority; student/faculty ratio 15 to 1.

Degrees conferred: J.D., J.D.-M.A., J.D.-M.B.A., J.D.-M.I.A. (International and Public Affairs and M.I.A. with Princeton University's Woodrow Wilson School of Public and International Affairs), J.D.-M.S. (Architecture Planning and Preservation, Journalism), J.D.-M.F.A. (Theatre Arts), J.D.-M.S.W., LL.M., J.S.D.

RECRUITMENT PRACTICES AND POLICIES. Attends national law school forums. On-campus informational sessions. School does have diversity program and actively recruits women/minority applicants.

ADMISSION REQUIREMENTS FOR FIRST-YEAR APPLICANTS. LSDAS law school report, LSAT (not later than December test date, if more than one LSAT, average is used), bachelor's degree from an accredited institution, personal statement, two recommendations, transcripts (must show all schools attended and at least three years of study) required in support of application. Applicants must have received bachelor's degree prior to enrollment. In addition, international applicants must submit TOEFL (not older than two years), TSE, TWE. Apply to Admission Office after September 1, before February 1. First-year students admitted fall only. Early decision candidates apply by December 1. Notification starts mid December and is completed by March. All other admission decisions made by early April. School does maintain a waiting list ("reserve" group). Application fee $65. Phone: (212)854-2670.

ADMISSION REQUIREMENTS FOR TRANSFER APPLICANTS. Accepts transfers from other ABA-accredited schools. Admission limited to space available (approximately thirty accepted each year). At least one year of enrollment, in good standing (prefer applicants in the top quarter of first-year class), LSAT, LSDAS, personal statement regarding reason for transfer, current law school transcript required in support of application. Apply to Admission Office at least six weeks prior to either autumn or spring term. Admission decisions made about one month prior to beginning of term. Application fee $65. Will consider visiting students.

ADMISSION REQUIREMENT FOR LL.M., J.S.D. APPLICANTS. Earned basic U.S. or foreign equivalent law degree, prefer at least two years of significant professional experience. International applicants: TOEFL is required for those for whom English is not their native language (620 or better required); written statement outlining how applicant expects to meet the cost of three years of law school. Apply to Executive Secretary Office of Graduate Legal Studies (Columbia Mail Code 4035) by December 15. Admits fall only. Application fee $75.

ADMISSION STANDARDS. Number of full-time applicants 5,510; number accepted 1,087; number enrolled 347; median LSAT 167 (75% of class have a score at or above 164); median GPA 3.6 (A = 4) (75% of class have a GPA at or above 3.35). Attrition rate .03%. Gorman rating 4.87; *U.S. News & World Report* ranking is in the top 5 of all law schools.

FINANCIAL AID. Scholarships, merit scholarships, minority scholarships, grants-in-aid, private and institutional loans, federal loans, Federal WS. For scholarships (selection criteria place heavy reliance on LSAT and undergraduate GPA) apply to Dean's Office of school after January 1, before March 1. Early decision candidates apply by mid November. Phone: (212)854-7730. Fax: (212)854-7946. Use school's FA questionnaire and loan application. For all other programs apply to Director of Financial Aid. Use FAFSA (FAFSA code #E00488), submit Access Disk, Financial Aid Transcript and federal income tax report. Approximately 22% of first-year class received scholarships/grants-in-aid. Approximately 70% of current J.D. students receive some form of financial assistance. Average scholarship/grant $9,125. Public Interest Loan Forgiveness Program available. Average debt after graduation $58,600. For LL.M., J.S.D. candidates: loans, 2-year associateships available; office space generally provided for J.S.D. candidates.

DEGREE REQUIREMENTS. For J.D.: 83 credits (35 required) with a 2.0 (A = 4) GPA, plus completion of upper divisional writing course; 3-year program. For J.D.-master's: individualized programs, most can be completed within a 4- or 5-year time frame. For LL.M.: 1 full year in residency; essay (master's essay or writing project); up to 6 credits may be taken in other Columbia University graduate schools. For J.S.D.: at least 1 full year in residency, doctoral seminar, publishable dissertation, oral exam (dissertation defense); 5-year time limit following completion of residency.

CAREER AND PLACEMENT INFORMATION. About 110 employers conducted on-campus interviews. Approximately 65% of graduates are employed in state. More than 90% of graduates are practicing law; 6% are in business; 2% in government; 3% in academia. Approximately 93% of Columbia University's first-time state bar exam takers pass the New York Bar Exam; New York's passage rate for all first-time takers from ABA-approved schools is 78%. Graduates are eligible to take the bar exam in all 50 states.

UNIVERSITY OF CONNECTICUT
Storrs, Connecticut 06269
Internet site: http://www.uconn.edu

Founded 1881. Located 30 miles E of Hartford. Public control. Semester system. Library: 2,444,000 volumes; 2,465,000 microforms; 18,615 periodicals/subscriptions; 131 computer workstations.

University's other graduate colleges/schools: College of Agriculture and Natural Resources, College of Liberal Arts and Sciences, School of Allied Health Professions, School of Business Administration, School of Education, School of Engineering, School of Family Studies, School of Fine Arts, School of Nursing, School of Pharmacy, School of Social Work.

Total university enrollment: 23,500.

School of Law
55 Elizabeth Street
Hartford, Connecticut 06105-2296
Phone: (860)570-5100
Internet site: http://www.law.uconn.edu
E-mail: admit@brandeis.law.uconn.edu

Established 1921. Located 2 miles from center of Hartford. ABA approved since 1933. AALS member. Semester system. Full-time (day), part-time (evening) study. Law library: 433,000 volumes/microforms; 6,165 current periodicals/subscriptions; has LEXIS, NEXIS, WESTLAW, DIALOG. Special programs: student-faculty exchange programs with University of Leiden (Netherlands), University of Exeter (United Kingdom), University of Puerto Rico, The University of International Business and Economics (People's Republic of China), Trinity College (Dublin, Ireland), Aix-en-Provence (France).

Annual tuition: full-time resident $10,928, nonresident $22,718; part-time resident $7,658, nonresident $15,878. No on-campus housing available for married students. Annual on-campus housing cost: single students $2,990 (room only), $5,598 (room and board). Housing deadline April 1. Contact Housing Office. Phone: (860)486-3430. Law students tend to live off-campus. Contact law school for off-campus information. Off-campus housing and personal expenses: approximately $12,800. Additional costs: books approximately $700.

Enrollment: first-year class 180; total full-time 431, part-time 181 (men 54%, women 46%). First-year statistics: 34% out of state, 18 states and foreign countries represented; 46% women; 16% minority; average age 25; 182 undergraduate institutions represented; range of first-year section sizes 25–70 students; number of upper division courses offered after first year full-time 70, part-time 38.

Faculty: full-time 43, part-time 42; 20% female; 10% minority; student/faculty ratio 14 to 1.

Degrees conferred: J.D., J.D.-M.B.A., J.D.-M.P.A., J.D.-M.P.H., J.D.-M.A. (Public Policy with Trinity College), J.D.-M.S.W., J.D.-M.L.S. (with Southern Connecticut State University), LL.M. (only for persons who have completed a basic legal education and received a university degree in law in another country).

RECRUITMENT PRACTICES AND POLICIES. Attends national law school forums. On-campus informational sessions. School does have diversity program and actively recruits women/minority applicants.

ADMISSION REQUIREMENTS FOR FIRST-YEAR APPLICANTS. LSDAS law school report, LSAT (not later than February test date, if more than one LSAT, highest is used), bachelor's degree from an accredited institution, résumé, essay, two recommendations, residence affidavit, transcripts (must show all schools attended and at least three years of study) required in support of application. Applicants must have received bachelor's degree prior to enrollment. Interview not required but may be requested by school. In addition, international applicants must submit TOEFL (not older than two years). Apply to Admission Office after September 30, before April 1. First-year students admitted fall only. Rolling admission process, notification starts in December and is finished by late May. School does maintain a waiting list. Application fee for day or evening $30, for both day and evening $45. Phone: (860)570-5127. E-mail: admit@ brandeis.law.uconn.edu.

ADMISSION REQUIREMENTS FOR TRANSFER APPLICANTS. Accepts transfers from other ABA-accredited schools. Admission limited to space available. At least one year of enrollment, in good standing, LSAT, LSDAS, personal statement regarding reason for transfer, current law school transcript required in support of application. Apply to Admission Office by July 1. Admission decisions made by mid August. Application fee $30. Will consider visiting students.

ADMISSION STANDARDS. Number of day applicants 939, evening 412; number accepted day 359, evening 167; number enrolled day 125, evening 65; median LSAT day 159, evening 157 (75% of class have a score at or above day 156, evening 512); median GPA day 3.29, evening 3.23 (A = 4), (75% of class have a GPA at or above day 3.03, evening 3.08). Attrition rate 1.1%. Gorman rating 3.38; *U.S. News & World Report* ranking is in the top 35 of all law schools.

FINANCIAL AID. Scholarships, merit scholarships, tuition remission grants, private loan programs, federal loans. For scholarships (selection criteria place heavy reliance on LSAT and undergraduate GPA) apply to Financial Aid Office of school after January 1, before March 1. Use FAFSA (FAFSA code #E00387). Approximately 33% of first-year class received scholarships/grants-in-aid. Approximately 67% of all current students receive some form of financial assistance. Average scholarship/grant $9,000. Federal loan forgiveness program available. Average debt after graduation $35,500. Limited financial aid available for part-time students.

DEGREE REQUIREMENTS. For J.D.: 86 credits (36 required) with a 2.0 (A = 4) GPA, plus completion of upper divisional writing course; 3-year program, 4-year program (part-time). Accelerated J.D. with 1 summer of course work. For J.D.-master's: Individually designed programs; generally not more than 6 credits may be applied to J.D.; usual reduction in time is between 6 months and 1 year depending on program. For LL.M. (for graduates of foreign legal programs): 24–30 credits; at least 2 semesters in residence.

CAREER AND PLACEMENT INFORMATION. About 40 employers conducted on-campus interviews. Approximately 80% of graduates are employed in state. More than 56% of graduates are practicing law; 28% are in business; 4% in government; 2% in academia. Approximately 95% of the University of Connecticut's first-time state bar exam takers pass the Connecticut Bar Exam; Connecticut's passage rate for all first-time takers from ABA-approved schools is 78%. Graduates are eligible to take the bar exam in other states.

CORNELL UNIVERSITY
Ithaca, New York 14853-0001
Internet site: http://www.cornell.edu

Founded 1865. Located in a small upstate New York City. Private control, some divisions are statutory colleges of State University of New York. Semester system. Library: 5,825,000 volumes; 6,770,000 microforms; 61,700 periodicals/subscriptions; 500 computer workstations.

University's other graduate schools: Graduate Field in the Law School, Graduate Fields of Agriculture and Life Sciences, Graduate Fields of Architecture Art and Planning, Graduate Fields of Arts and Sciences, Graduate Fields of Engineering, Graduate Fields of Human Ecology, Graduate Fields of Industrial and Labor Relations, Graduate School of Medical Sciences, Professional Field of the Johnson Graduate School of Management, Professional School of Veterinary Medicine.

Total university enrollment: 18,900.

Law School
Myron Taylor Hall
Ithaca, New York 14853-4901
Phone: (607)255-3527
Internet site: http://www.law.cornell.edu/admit/admit.htm
E-mail: lawadmit@law.mail.cornell.edu

Established 1888. Located on main campus. ABA approved since 1923. AALS member. Semester system. Full-time, day study only. Law library: 571,000 volumes and equivalent forms; 6,000 current periodicals/subscriptions; 43 computer workstations; has LEXIS, NEXIS, WESTLAW, DIALOG; is a Federal Government Depository. Special programs: Berger International Legal Studies Program; summer institute abroad at University of Paris (Panthéon-Sorbonne).

Annual tuition: resident $23,100. On-campus housing available for both single and married students. Annual on-campus housing cost: $7,150 room and board. Contact Campus Life Office for on-campus housing information. Phone: (607)255-5368. Limited off-campus housing. Estimated additional personal expense: $3,940, books approximately $700.

Enrollment: first-year class 181; total full-time 553 (men 60%, women 40%); no part-time students. First-year statistics: 75% out of state, 58 states and foreign countries represented; 40% women; 27% minority; average age 25; 250 undergraduate institutions represented; range of first-year section sizes 27–80 students; number of upper division courses offered after first year 123.

Faculty: full-time 38, part-time 22; 21% female; 5% minority; student/faculty ratio 12 to 1.

Degrees conferred: J.D., J.D.-M.B.A., J.D.-M.P.A., J.D.-M.I.L.R., J.D.-M.A., J.D.-M.R.P., J.D.-Maîtrise en Droit, J.D.-Ph.D., LL.M., J.S.D. (for both U.S. lawyers and foreign persons who have completed a basic legal education and received a university degree in law in another country, primarily for international students wishing to increase their understanding of American legal principles).

RECRUITMENT PRACTICES AND POLICIES. Attends national law school forums. On-campus informational sessions. School does have diversity program and actively recruits women/minority applicants.

ADMISSION REQUIREMENTS FOR FIRST-YEAR APPLICANTS. LSDAS law school report, LSAT (not later than December test date, if more than one LSAT, average is used), bachelor's degree from an accredited institution, personal statement, interview, two recommendations, transcripts (must show all schools attended and at least three years of study) required in support of application. Applicants must have received bachelor's degree prior to enrollment. In addition, international applicants must submit TOEFL (not older than two years). Apply to Admission Office after September 1, before February 1. First-year students admitted fall only. Joint-degree applicants must apply to and be accepted by both schools. For J.D.-Maîtrise en Droit, applicants must be fluent in both English and French; French applicants must also have the baccalauréat degree and at least two years of advanced study at a French institution. School does maintain a waiting list. Application fee $65. Phone: (607)255-5141. E-mail: admissions@lii.law.cornell.edu.

ADMISSION REQUIREMENTS FOR TRANSFER APPLICANTS. Accepts transfers from other ABA-accredited schools. Admission limited to space available. At least one year of enrollment, dean's letter indicating good academic standing (prefer applicants in the top 10% of first-year class), LSAT, LSDAS, personal statement regarding reason for transfer, two recommendations, current law school transcript, undergraduate transcript required in support of application. Apply to Admission Office by July 1. Admission decisions made by early August. Approximately 10–15 transfer applicants enrolled each year. Application fee $65. Will consider visiting students.

ADMISSION STANDARDS. Number of full-time applicants 3,400; number accepted 834; number enrolled 181; median LSAT 165 (75% of class have a score at or above 163); median GPA 3.55 (A = 4) (75% of class have a GPA at or above 3.34). Attrition rate .7%. Gorman rating 1.79; *U.S. News & World Report* ranking in top 12 of all law schools. Internet Legal Resource Guide ranks J.D.-M.B.A. among the top 40.

FINANCIAL AID. Scholarships, minority scholarships, grants-in-aid, private and institutional loans; federal loans and Federal WS offered through university's Financial Aid Office. Assistantships may be available for upper divisional joint-degree candidates. For scholarships (selection criteria place heavy reliance on LSAT and undergraduate GPA) apply to Financial Aid Office of school after January 1, before March 15. Use FAFSA (FAFSA code #002711). Submit most recent federal income tax return, Financial Aid Transcript, need Access Disk. Approximately 45% of first-year class received scholarships/grants-in-aid. Approximately 75% of current students receive some form of financial assistance. Average scholarship/grant $7,600. Public Interest Loan Reduction Program available.

DEGREE REQUIREMENTS. For J.D.: 84 credits (32 required) with a 2.0 (A = 4) GPA, plus completion of upper divisional writing course; 3-year program. Accelerated J.D. with 1 summer of course work. For J.D.-master's: both degrees can be completed in 4 years instead of the usual 5 years. J.D.-Ph.D.: both degrees can be completed in 7 years instead of the usual 8. J.D.-LL.M.: both degrees can be completed in 3 years plus 1 session at the Cornell Law School-University of Paris (Panthéon-Sorbonne) summer Institute of International and Comparative Law; thesis/nonthesis option. For J.D.-Maîtrise en Droit (French Law Degree): 4-year program, first 2 years at Cornell Law School, final 2 years at University of Paris. For LL.M.: at least 1 year of full-time study; research and publishable paper. For J.S.D.: at least 1 year of study beyond the LL.M., dissertation of publishable quality.

CAREER AND PLACEMENT INFORMATION. About 158 employers conducted on-campus interviews. Approximately 33% of graduates are employed in state. More than 84% of graduates are practicing law; 8% are in business; 7% in government; 1% in academia. Approximately 96% of Cornell University's first-time state bar exam takers pass the New York state bar exam; New York State's passage rate for all first-time takers from ABA-approved schools is 78%. Graduates are eligible to take the bar exam in all 50 states.

CREIGHTON UNIVERSITY
Omaha, Nebraska 68178-0001
Internet site: http://www.creighton.edu

Founded 1878. Located in downtown Omaha. Private control (Roman Catholic—Jesuit affiliation). Semester system. Library: 444,000 volumes; 123,100 microforms.

University's other graduate colleges/schools: College of Arts and Sciences, Eugene C. Eppley College of Business Administration, School of Dentistry, School of Medicine, School of Pharmacy and Allied Health Programs.

Total university enrollment: 6,200.

School of Law
2500 California Plaza
Omaha, Nebraska 68178-0140
Phone: (402)280-2872
Internet site: http://www.creighton.edu/CULAW
E-mail: admit@culaw.creighton.edu

Established 1904. Located on main campus. ABA approved since 1924. AALS member since 1907. Semester system. Full-time, limited part-time study. Law library: 232,000 volumes/microforms; 4,230 current periodicals/subscriptions; 41 computer workstations; has LEXIS, NEXIS, WESTLAW, DIALOG.

Annual tuition: $15,446; part-time $10,052. On-campus housing available for both single and married students. Annual on-campus housing cost: single students $2,514 (room only), $4,548 (room and board, married students $4,072. Contact Director of Housing. Phone: (402)280-3016. Off-campus housing and personal expenses: approximately $11,120. Additional costs: books approximately $600.

Enrollment: first-year class 162; total full-time 455 (men 58%, women 42%); no part-time students. First-year statistics: 63% out of state, 39 states and foreign countries represented; 42% women; 9% minority; average age 27; 182 undergraduate institutions represented; range of first-year section sizes 26–75 students; number of upper division courses offered after first year 66.

Faculty: full-time 25, part-time 36; 36% female; 2% minority; student/faculty ratio 16 to 1.

Degrees conferred: J.D., J.D.-M.B.A.

RECRUITMENT PRACTICES AND POLICIES. Attends national law school forums. On-campus informational sessions. School does have diversity program and actively recruits women/minority applicants.

ADMISSION REQUIREMENTS FOR FIRST-YEAR APPLICANTS. LSDAS law school report, LSAT (not later than February test date, December test date for scholarship applicants), bachelor's degree from an accredited institution, personal statement, two recommendations, transcripts (must show all schools attended and at least three years of study) required in support of application. Applicants must have received bachelor's degree prior to enrollment. In addition, international applicants must submit TOEFL (not older than two years). Apply to Admission Committee after September 30, before May 1 (March 1 for scholarships applications). First-year students admitted fall only. Rolling admission process, notification starts in December and is finished by late April. Acceptance of offer and first deposit due date April 15. School does maintain a waiting list. Application fee $40. Phone: (800)282-5835, (402)280-2872. E-mail: admit@culaw.creighton.edu.

ADMISSION REQUIREMENTS FOR TRANSFER APPLICANTS. Accepts transfers from other ABA-accredited schools. Admission limited to space available. At least one year of enrollment, dean's letter indicating candidate is in good standing, prefer applicants in the top quarter of first-year class, LSAT, LSDAS, personal statement regarding reason for transfer, current law school transcript required in support of application. Apply to Admission Committee by July 1. Admission decisions made by early August. Application fee $40. Will consider visiting/transient students.

ADMISSION STANDARDS. Number of full-time applicants 725; number accepted 455; number enrolled 162; median LSAT 150 (75% of class have a score at or above 147); median GPA 3.25 (A = 4) (75% of class have a GPA at or above 2.95). Attrition rate 4.8%. Gorman rating 3.09; *U.S. News & World Report* ranking is in the third tier of all law schools.

FINANCIAL AID. Scholarships, merit scholarships, private loans; federal loans and Federal WS offered through university's Financial Aid Office. For scholarships (selection criteria place heavy reliance on LSAT and undergraduate GPA) apply to Admissions Committee of school after acceptance. For all other programs apply to university's Office of Financial Aid. Phone: (402)280-2761.

Use FAFSA (FAFSA code #002542), submit Financial Aid Transcript, income tax form. Approximately 36% of first-year class received scholarships. Approximately 75% of current students receive some form of financial assistance. Average scholarship/grant $6,500.

DEGREE REQUIREMENTS. For J.D.: 94 credits (39 required) with a 2.0 (A = 4) GPA, plus completion of upper divisional writing course; 3-year program. For J.D.-M.B.A.: not more than 9 credits may be applied to the J.D., not more than 6 credits may be applied to the M.B.A.

CAREER AND PLACEMENT INFORMATION. About 12 employers conducted on-campus interviews. Approximately 53% of graduates are employed in state. More than 60% of graduates are practicing law; 23% are in business; 16% in government; 1% in academia. Approximately 93% of Creighton University's first-time state bar exam takers pass the Nebraska Bar Exam; Nebraska's passage rate for all first-time takers from ABA-approved schools is 94%.

UNIVERSITY OF DAYTON

300 College Park
Dayton, Ohio 45469-1620
Internet site: http://www.udayton.edu

Founded 1850. Located in a residential area near center of city. Private control (Roman Catholic affiliation). Semester system. Library: 1,304,000 volumes; 719,400 microforms; 3,106 periodicals/subscriptions; 84 computer workstations.

University's other graduate colleges/schools: College of Arts and Sciences, College of Business Administration, School of Education, School of Engineering.

Total university enrollment: 9,900.

School of Law
300 College Park
Dayton, Ohio 45469-1630
Phone: (937)229-3211
Internet site: http://www.udayton.edu/~law
E-mail: lawinfo@odo.law.udayton.edu/~law

Established 1974. Located on main campus. ABA approved since 1975. AALS member. Semester system. Full-time, day study only. Law library: 252,000 volumes/microforms; 4,214 current periodicals/subscriptions; 42 computer workstations; has NEXIS, WESTLAW. Special programs: externships.

Annual tuition: $18,280. No on-campus housing available. Contact Residential Services for off-campus infor-

mation. Phone: (937)229-3317. Off-campus housing and personal expenses: approximately $8,800. Additional costs: books approximately $700.

Enrollment: first-year class 191; total full-time 493 (men 57%, women 43%); no part-time students. First-year statistics: 61% out of state, 25 states and foreign countries represented; 43% women; 19% minority; average age 25; 122 undergraduate institutions represented; average first-year section size 90 students; number of upper division courses offered after first year 49.

Faculty: full-time 26, part-time 29; 31% female; 6% minority; student/faculty ratio 20.5 to 1.

Degrees conferred: J.D., J.D.-M.B.A.

RECRUITMENT PRACTICES AND POLICIES. On-campus informational sessions. School does have diversity program and actively recruits women/minority applicants.

ADMISSION REQUIREMENTS FOR FIRST-YEAR APPLICANTS. LSDAS law school report, LSAT (not later than December test date), bachelor's degree from an accredited institution, personal statement, two recommendations, transcripts (must show all schools attended and at least three years of study) required in support of application. Applicants must have received bachelor's degree prior to enrollment. In addition, international applicants must submit TOEFL (not older than two years). Apply to Admission Committee after September 1, before March 1 (for scholarship applicants), May 1 (priority deadline). First-year students admitted fall only. Rolling admission process, notification is within 6–8 weeks after completed application is filed and is finished by late May. Application fee $40. Phone: (937)229-3555. E-mail: lawinfo@odo.law.udayton.edu/~law.

ADMISSION REQUIREMENTS FOR TRANSFER APPLICANTS. Accepts transfers from other ABA-accredited schools. Admission limited to space available. At least one year of enrollment, dean's letter indicating candidate is in good standing (prefer applicants in the top quarter of first-year class), LSAT, LSDAS, personal statement regarding reason for transfer, current law school transcript required in support of application. Apply to Admission Committee by June 1. Admission decisions made by August. Application fee $40. Will consider transient students.

ADMISSION STANDARDS. Number of full-time applicants 1,559; number accepted 790; number enrolled 191; median LSAT 153 (75% of class have a score at or above 149); median GPA 3.31 (A = 4) (75% of class have a GPA at or above 2.95). Attrition rate 4.5%. Gorman rating 2.62; *U.S. News & World Report* ranking is in the fourth tier of all law schools.

FINANCIAL AID. Scholarships, merit scholarships, minority scholarships, grants-in-aid, institutional loans; federal loans and Federal WS offered through university's Financial Aid Office. For scholarships (selection criteria place heavy reliance on LSAT and undergraduate GPA) apply to Admissions Committee of school after January 1, before March 1. Phone: (937)229-3555. For all other programs apply to university's Director of Financial Aid. Phone: (937)229-4311. Use FAFSA (FAFSA code #003127). Approximately 39% of first-year class received scholarships/grants-in-aid. Approximately 85% of current students receive some form of financial assistance. Average scholarship/ grant $9,500. Federal loan forgiveness program available. Average debt after graduation $55,000.

DEGREE REQUIREMENTS. For J.D.: 87 credits (36 required) with a 2.0 (A = 4) GPA, plus completion of upper divisional writing course; 3-year program. For J.D.-M.B.A.: not more than 6 credits may be used toward J.D., not more than 9 credits may be used toward M.B.A.

CAREER AND PLACEMENT INFORMATION. About 14 employers conducted on-campus interviews. Approximately 45% of graduates are employed in state. More than 60% of graduates are practicing law; 28% are in business; 12% in government; none in academia. Approximately 94% of the University of Dayton's first-time state bar exam takers pass the Ohio Bar Exam; Ohio's passage rate for all first-time takers from ABA-approved schools is 93%.

UNIVERSITY OF DENVER
Denver, Colorado 80208
Internet site: http://www.du.edu

Founded 1864. Located in a residential area of Denver. Private control. Quarter system. Library: 1,860,000 volumes; 912,100 microforms; 5,330 periodicals/subscriptions; 72 computer workstations.

University's other graduate colleges/schools: College of Education, Daniels College of Business, Graduate School of International Studies, Graduate School of Professional Psychology, Graduate School of Social Work. Graduate Studies includes: Faculty of Arts and Humanities/Social Sciences, Faculty of Natural Science, Mathematics and Engineering.

Total university enrollment: 8,710.

College of Law
7039 E. 18th Avenue
Denver, Colorado 80220
Phone: (303)871-6135
Internet site: http://www.law.du.edu
E-mail: admissions@ad.law.du.edu

Established 1892. Located 15 minutes from downtown Denver. ABA approved since 1975. AALS member. Semester system. Full-time, part-time study. Law library: 303,540 volumes/microforms; 4,367 current periodicals/subscriptions; 90 computer workstations; has LEXIS, NEXIS, WESTLAW, DIALOG, INFOTRAC. Special programs: National Center for Preventive Law, Rocky Mountains Mineral Law Institute.

Annual tuition: Full-time $17,970, part-time $13,478, LL.M., per credit $384. On-campus housing available for both single and married students. Annual on-campus apartment costs: $5,538 (room and board). Contact Graduate Housing Office for both on-and off-campus information. Phone: (301)871-2246. Many law students live off-campus. Off-campus housing and personal expenses: approximately $11,663. Additional costs: books approximately $700.

Enrollment: first-year class full-time 277, part-time 82; total full-time 836, part-time 274 (men 55%, women 45%). First-year statistics: 48% out of state, 55 states and foreign countries represented; 45% women; 13% minority; average age 25; average first-year section size 80 students; number of upper division courses offered after first year full-time 75, part-time 59.

Faculty: full-time 40, part-time 38; 37% female; 8% minority; student/faculty ratio 23 to 1.

Degrees conferred: J.D., J.D.-M.B.A., J.D.-M.I.M. (International Management), J.D.-M.A. (History, Mineral Economics, Psychology, Sociology), J.D.-M.S.W., LL.M. (Tax), M.T.

RECRUITMENT PRACTICES AND POLICIES. Attends national law school forums. On-campus informational sessions. School does have diversity program and actively recruits women/minority applicants.

ADMISSION REQUIREMENTS FOR FIRST-YEAR APPLICANTS. LSDAS law school report, LSAT (not later than December test date, if more than one LSAT, highest is used), bachelor's degree from an accredited institution, résumé, personal statement, interview, two recommendations (optional), transcripts (must show all schools attended and at least three years of study) required in support of application. Applicants must have received bachelor's degree prior to enrollment. In addition, international applicants must submit TOEFL (not older than two years). Apply to Admission Department after September 30, before March 1. First-year students admitted fall only. Rolling admission process, notification starts in November and is finished by late April. Acceptance of offer and first deposit due date April 1. Application fee $45. Phone: (303)871-6135. E-mail: admissions@adm.law.du.edu.

ADMISSION REQUIREMENTS FOR TRANSFER APPLICANTS. Accepts transfers from other ABA-accredited schools. Admission limited to space available. At least one year of enrollment, dean's letter indicating candidate is in good standing (prefer applicants in the top quarter of first-year class), LSAT, LSDAS, personal statement regarding reason for transfer, current law school transcript required in support of application. Apply to Admission Department by May 15. Admission decisions made by July 15. Application fee $45. Will consider visiting students.

ADMISSION REQUIREMENTS FOR LL.M. (Tax), M.T. For LL.M., a J.D. or its equivalent from an ABA-accredited law school. For M.T., a baccalaureate degree from an accredited American school/college, the content of the degree must satisfy the requirements of the "Common Body of Knowledge" as defined by the AACSB. Official transcripts, two letters of recommendation, résumé, personal statement required in support of Graduate Tax Program application. Normally admits to fall, summer quarter only. Apply to the Director, Graduate Tax Program. Rolling admissions process. Application must be completed at least one month prior to beginning of quarter of preferred entrance. Application fee $25. Phone: (303)871-6239.

ADMISSION STANDARDS. Number of full-time applicants 1,905, part-time 183; number accepted full-time 1,068, part-time 115; number enrolled full-time 277, part-time 72; median LSAT 158 (75% of class have a score at or above 153 full-time, 152 part-time); median GPA 3.08 (A = 4) (75% of class have a GPA at or above 2.82 full-time, part-time 2.77). Attrition rate 3.8%. Gorman rating 3.85; *U.S. News & World Report* ranking is in the third tier of all law schools.

FINANCIAL AID. Scholarships, merit scholarships, minority scholarships, grants-in-aid, institutional and private loans; federal loans and Federal WS offered through university's Financial Aid Office. For scholarships (selection criteria place heavy reliance on LSAT and undergraduate GPA) apply to Admissions Office of school after January 1, before February 15. For all other programs apply to university's Director of Financial Aid by March 1. Phone: (303)871-2681. Use FAFSA for all federal programs (FAFSA code #001371), submit current federal income tax, Financial Aid Transcript. Approximately 29% (full-time), 25% (part-time) of first-year class received scholarships/grants-in-aid. Approximately 75% of current students receive some form of financial assistance. Average scholarship/grant $6,000. Average debt after graduation $45,000. Financial aid available for LL.M., M.T. applicants. Contact Director of Graduate Tax Program for current information.

DEGREE REQUIREMENTS. For J.D.: 90 credits (44 required) with a 2.0 (A = 4) GPA, plus completion of upper divisional writing course; 3-year program. Accelerated J.D. with summer course work. For J.D.-M.B.A., -M.I.M.: J.D. is reduced by 10 credits, the M.B.A., M.I.M. are reduced by 12 quarter credits. For J.D.-M.A.: J.D. is reduced by 10 credits, M.A. is reduced by 10 quarter credits. For J.D.-M.S.W.: J.D. is reduced by 10 credits, M.S.W. is reduced by 9 quarter credits. For LL.M. (Tax), M.T.: successful completion of 45 quarter-hour program; GPA of 77 (scale 0–100); all requirements completed within 5 years.

CAREER AND PLACEMENT INFORMATION. About 50–60 employers conducted on-campus interviews. Approximately 85% of graduates are employed in state. More than 72% of graduates are practicing law; 5% are in business; 24% in government; 1% in academia. Approximately 87% of the University of Denver's first-time state bar exam takers pass the Colorado Bar Exam. Colorado's passage rate for all first-time takers from ABA-approved schools is 87%. Graduates are eligible to take the bar exam in all 50 states.

DEPAUL UNIVERSITY
Chicago, Illinois 60604-2287
Internet site: http://www.depaul.edu

Founded 1898. Located in Chicago. Private control (Roman Catholic affiliation). Quarter system. Library: 678,200 volumes; 302,000 microforms; 9,900 periodicals/subscriptions; 275 computer workstations.

University's other graduate colleges/schools: Charles H. Kellstadt Graduate School of Business, College of Liberal Arts and Sciences, School of New Learning, School of Computer Science, Telecommunication and Information Systems, School of Education, School of Music, Theatre School.

Total university enrollment: 17,100.

School of Law
25 East Jackson Boulevard
Chicago, Illinois 60604-2297
Phone: (312)362-3867
Internet site: http://www.law.depaul.edu
E-mail: lawinfo@wppost.depaul.edu

Established 1898. Located near center of downtown Chicago. ABA approved since 1925. AALS member. Semester system. Full-time, Part-time study. Law library: 326,600 volumes/microforms; 4,938 current periodicals/subscriptions; 52 computer workstations; has LEXIS, NEXIS, WESTLAW, DIALOG, ILLINET. Special facilities: International Human Rights Law Institute, Center for Church/State Studies, Health Law Institute. Special program: externships; summer study abroad at University College (Dublin, Ireland).

Annual tuition: Full-time $18,810, Part-time $12,710. No on-campus housing available. Contact Admissions Office for off-campus information. Off-campus housing and personal expenses: approximately $12,558. Additional costs: books approximately $700.

Enrollment: first-year class 251, part-time 87; total full-time 750, part-time 331 (men 54%, women 46%). First-year statistics: 50% out of state, 29 states and foreign countries represented; 46% women; 14% minority; average age 25; 139 undergraduate institutions represented; range of first-year section sizes 20–85 students; number of upper division courses offered after first year full-time 83, part-time 83.

Faculty: full-time 51, part-time 86; 35% female; 9% minority; student/faculty ratio 22 to 1.

Degrees conferred: J.D., J.D.-M.B.A., LL.M. (Tax), LL.M. (Health Law).

RECRUITMENT PRACTICES AND POLICIES. Attends national law school forums. On-campus informational sessions. School does have diversity program and actively recruits women/minority applicants.

ADMISSION REQUIREMENTS FOR FIRST-YEAR APPLICANTS. LSDAS law school report, LSAT (not later than December test date and within the last three years), bachelor's degree from an accredited institution, personal statement, one recommendation, transcripts (must show all schools attended and at least three years of study) required in support of application. Applicants must have received bachelor's degree prior to enrollment. In addition, international applicants must submit TOEFL (not older than two years). Apply to Director of Admission after September 30, before April 1. First-year students admitted fall only. Rolling admission process, notification starts in March and is finished by late May.

Application fee $40. Phone: (312)362-6831. E-mail: lawinfo@wppost.depaul.edu.

ADMISSION REQUIREMENTS FOR TRANSFER APPLICANTS. Accepts transfers from other ABA-accredited schools. Admission limited to space available. At least one year of enrollment, dean's letter indicating candidate is in good standing (prefer applicants in the top quarter of first-year class), LSAT, LSDAS, personal statement regarding reason for transfer, current law school transcript required in support of application. Apply to Director of Admission by June 1. Admission decisions made by July 15. Application fee $40. Will consider visiting/auditing students.

ADMISSIONS REQUIREMENTS FOR LL.M. APPLICANTS. Undergraduate and J.D. transcripts, two letters of recommendation, statement of purpose required in support of application. In addition, international applicants must submit TOEFL and official transcripts with certified translation and evaluation. Admits to fall, spring, summer. Apply to Director of Admissions at least two months prior to semester of entrance. Application fee $40. Phone: (312)362-8733.

ADMISSION STANDARDS. Number of full-time applicants 2,031, part-time 418; number accepted full-time 1,180; number enrolled full-time 251, part-time 87; median LSAT 158 (75% of class have a score at or above 153 full-time, 152 part-time); median GPA 3.08 (A = 4) (75% of class have a GPA at or above 3.03 full-time, 2.75 part-time). Attrition rate 3.3%. Gorman rating 3.85; *U.S. News & World Report* ranking in the third tier of all law schools.

FINANCIAL AID. Scholarships, private loans, federal loans are administered through university's Financial Aid Office. Financial aid available for part-time students. Apply after January 1, before March 1 to university's Financial Aid Office. Phone: (312)362-8526. Use FAFSA (FAFSA code #001671). Submit federal income tax form, Financial Aid Transcript. Approximately 67% full-time, 8% part-time of first-year class received scholarships/grants-in-aid. Approximately 75% of current students receive some form of financial assistance. Average scholarship/grant $1,736.

DEGREE REQUIREMENTS. For J.D.: 86 credits (37 required) with a 2.0 (A = 4) GPA, plus completion of upper divisional writing course; 3-year program, 4-year program (part-time). Accelerated J.D. with 1 summer of course work. For J.D.-M.B.A.: not more than 6 credits accepted toward J.D., not more than 9 credits accepted toward M.B.A. For LL.M. (Tax): 24 credits; GPA of 2.5 (A = 4) required. For LL.M. (Health Law): 24 credits; GPA of 2.5 (A = 4); master's essay.

CAREER AND PLACEMENT INFORMATION. About 20 employers conducted on-campus interviews. Approximately 94% of graduates are employed in state. More than 52% of graduates are practicing law; 26% are in business; 20% in government; 2% in academia. Approximately 88% of DePaul University's first-time state bar exam takers pass the Illinois Bar Exam; Illinois' passage rate for all first-time takers from ABA-approved schools is 83%.

DETROIT COLLEGE OF LAW AT MICHIGAN STATE UNIVERSITY

N210 North Business Complex
East Lansing, Michigan 48824
Phone: (517)432-0222
Internet site: http://www.dcl.edu
E-mail: dcl@pilot.msu.edu

Established 1891. Located at Michigan State University. Private control. ABA approved since 1941. AALS member. Semester system. Full-time, part-time study. Law library: 91,640 volumes; 836,500 microforms; 2,825 current periodicals/subscriptions; 29 Value Point IBM, 6 Macintosh Quadra 610 computer workstations; has LEXIS, NEXIS, WESTLAW, INFOTRAC, MERIT. Special facilities: Center for Canadian-U.S. Law. Special program: externships; summer study abroad at University of Ottawa Canada, Babes/Balyai University, Romania.

Annual tuition: full-time $14,732, part-time $11,050. On-campus housing available for both single and married students at Michigan State University. Annual on-campus housing cost: single students $3,000 (room only), $5,000 (room and board); married students $3,400. Contact university's Housing Office for both on- and off-campus housing information. Phone: (800)678-4679; (517)355-7460. Web site http://www.hfs/msu.edu/hfs/uh. Off-campus housing and personal expenses: approximately $13,655. Additional costs: books approximately $700.

Enrollment: first-year class 148, part-time 37; total full-time 433, part-time 231 (men 62%, women 38%). First-year statistics: 18% out of state, 18 states and foreign countries represented; 38% women; 14% minority; average age 28; 150 undergraduate institutions repre-

sented; average first-year section sizes full-time 78 students, part-time 29 students; number of upper division courses offered after first year full-time 51, part-time 74.

Faculty: full-time 27, part-time 34; 13% female; 19% minority; student/faculty ratio 19.5 to 1.

Degrees conferred: J.D., J.D.-M.B.A.

RECRUITMENT PRACTICES AND POLICIES. Attends several national law school forums. On-campus informational sessions. School does have diversity program and actively recruits women/minority applicants.

ADMISSION REQUIREMENTS FOR FIRST-YEAR APPLICANTS. LSDAS law school report, LSAT (not later than December test date, if more than one LSAT, highest is used), bachelor's degree from an accredited institution, résumé, personal statement, interview, two recommendations, transcripts (must show all schools attended and at least three years of study) required in support of application. Applicants must have received bachelor's degree prior to enrollment. Interview not required but may be requested by school. In addition, international applicants for whom English is not their native language must submit TOEFL (not older than two years). Apply to Director of Admission after September 30, before April 15. First-year students admitted fall only. Rolling admission process, notification starts in November and is finished by late May. Application fee $50. Phone: (517)432-0222. E-mail: dcl@pilot.msu.edu.

ADMISSION REQUIREMENTS FOR TRANSFER APPLICANTS. Accepts transfers from other ABA-accredited schools. Admission limited to space available. At least one year of enrollment, dean's letter indicating applicant is in good standing, LSAT, LSDAS, personal statement regarding reason for transfer, current law school transcript, undergraduate transcript required in support of application. Apply to Director of Admission by June 15. Admission decisions made by mid July. Application fee $40. Enrolls between 15–20 transfer applicants each year. Will consider visiting students.

ADMISSION STANDARDS. Number of full-time applicants 740, part-time 141; number accepted full-time 848, part-time 80; number enrolled full-time 148, part-time 27; median LSAT 151 (75% of class have a score at or above 149 full-time, 147 part-time); median GPA 2.95 (A = 4) (75% of class have a GPA at or above 2.74 full-time, 2.51 part-time). Attrition rate 5.5%. Gorman rating

3.22; *U.S. News & World Report* ranking is in the fourth tier of all law schools.

FINANCIAL AID. Scholarships, minority scholarships, grants-in-aid, alternative loans, federal loans and Federal WS. For scholarships (selection criteria place heavy reliance on LSAT and undergraduate GPA) apply to Office of Financial Aid after January 1, before February 15. Phone: (517)432-5909. Fax: (517)353-5403. Use school's FAF. Use FAFSA (Title IV School code #G02254). Also submit federal income tax form, Financial Aid Transcripts. Approximately 11% full-time, 9% part-time of first-year class received scholarships/grants-in-aid. Approximately 85% of current students receive some form of financial assistance. Average scholarship/grant full-time $10,160, part-time $8,850.

DEGREE REQUIREMENTS. For J.D.: 85 credits (60 required) with a 2.0 (A = 4) GPA, plus completion of upper divisional writing course; 3-year program, 4-year program (part-time). Accelerated J.D. with 1 summer of course work. For J.D.-M.B.A.: up to 6 M.B.A. credits can be used for the J.D., up to 9 J.D. credits can be used for the M.B.A.

CAREER AND PLACEMENT INFORMATION. About 40 employers conducted on-campus interviews. Approximately 93% of graduates are employed in state. More than 63% of graduates are practicing law; 19% are in business; 17% in government; 1% in academia. Approximately 76% of the Detroit College of Law's first-time state bar exam takers pass the Michigan Bar Exam; Michigan's passage rate for all first-time takers from ABA-approved schools is 85%.

UNIVERSITY OF DETROIT MERCY
Detroit, Michigan 48219-0900
Internet site: http://www.udmercy.edu

Founded 1877. New University formed in 1990. Private control (Roman Catholic—Jesuit affiliation). Semester system. Library: 645,000 volumes; 777,000 microforms; 5,500 periodicals/subscriptions.

University's other graduate colleges/schools: College of Business Administration, College of Education and Human Services, College of Engineering and Sciences, College of Health Professions, College of Liberal Arts, School of Dentistry.

Total university enrollment: 8,000.

School of Law
651 East Jefferson Avenue
Detroit, Michigan 48226
Phone: (313)596-0200
Internet site: http://www.udmercy.edu
E-mail: udmlawao@udmercy.edu

Established 1612. Located opposite the Renaissance Center in downtown (Metro) Detroit. ABA approved since 1933. AALS member. Semester system. Full-time, part-time study. Law library: 286,000 volumes/microforms; 3,295 current periodicals/subscriptions; 39 computer workstations; has LEXIS, WESTLAW, DIALOG, INFOPAC. Special programs: London Law Programme approved by ABA, Canadian Lawyers Program, Intellectual Property Law Institute, American Indian Program, externships.

Annual tuition: full-time $15,450, part-time $11,046. Limited on-campus housing available. Annual on-campus housing cost: single students $9,790 (room and board). Contact Director of Housing for both on- and off-campus housing information. Phone: (313)933-1230. Law students tend to live off-campus. Off-campus housing and personal expenses: approximately $11,853. Additional costs: books approximately $700.

Enrollment: first-year class 108 full-time, 50 part-time; total full-time 375, part-time 238 (men 49%, women 51%). First-year statistics: 25% out of state, 51% women; 11% minority; average age 28; average first-year section sizes full-time 70 students, part-time 57 students; number of upper division courses offered after first year full-time 66, part-time 50.

Faculty: full-time 30, part-time 28; 22% female; 5% minority; student/faculty ratio 22 to 1.

Degrees conferred: J.D., J.D.-M.B.A.

RECRUITMENT PRACTICES AND POLICIES. Attends several national law school forums. Has on-campus informational sessions. School does have diversity program and actively recruits women/minority applicants.

ADMISSION REQUIREMENTS FOR FIRST-YEAR APPLICANTS. LSDAS law school report, LSAT (not later than December test date, if more than one LSAT, highest is used), bachelor's degree from an accredited institution, personal statement, two recommendations, transcripts (must show all schools attended and at least three years of study) required in support of application. Applicants must have received bachelor's degree prior to enrollment. Interview not required but may be granted upon request. In addition, international applicants must submit

TOEFL (not older than two years). Apply to Office of Admission after September 30, before April 15. First-year students admitted fall only. Rolling admission process. Application fee $50. Phone: (315)596-0264. E-mail: udmlawao@udmercy.edu.

ADMISSION REQUIREMENTS FOR TRANSFER APPLICANTS. Accepts transfers from other ABA-accredited schools. Admission limited to space available. At least one year of enrollment, dean's letter indicating applicant is in good standing (prefer applicants in the upper third of first-year class), LSAT, LSDAS, personal statement regarding reason for transfer, current law school transcript with rank in class required in support of application. Apply to Admission Office by June 30. Admission decisions made by August 1. Application fee $50. Will consider visiting students.

ADMISSION STANDARDS. Number of full-time applicants 481, part-time 310; number accepted 302 full-time, 104 part-time; number enrolled 108 full-time, 50 part-time; median LSAT 150 (75% of class have a score at or above 146 full-time, 147 part-time); median GPA 3.15 (A = 4) (75% of class have a GPA at or above 2.79 full-time, 2.66 part-time). Attrition rate 6.4%. Gorman rating 3.46; *U.S. News & World Report* ranking is in the fourth tier of all law schools.

FINANCIAL AID. Scholarships, minority scholarships, grants-in-aid, institutional loans, state and federal loans and Federal WS. For scholarships (selection criteria place heavy reliance on LSAT and undergraduate GPA) apply to Financial Aid Coordinator after January 1, before April 1. Phone: (313)596-0213. E-mail: udmlawfa@udmercy.edu. Use school's FA Scholarship Application. Submit FAFSA for all federal programs (Title IV School code #E00392). Also submit federal income tax forms. Approximately 90% (full-time), 60% (part-time) of first-year class received scholarships/grants-in-aid. Approximately 81% of current students receive some form of financial assistance. Average scholarship/grant full-time $7,500, part-time $5,390. Average debt after graduation $50,000.

DEGREE REQUIREMENTS. For J.D.: 86 credits (47 required) with a 2.0 (A = 4) GPA, plus completion of upper divisional writing course; 3-year program, 4-year program (part-time). Accelerated J.D. with 1 summer of course work. For J.D.-M.B.A.: total 108–111 credits (J.D. 72 credits, M.B.A. 36–39 credits).

CAREER AND PLACEMENT INFORMATION. Approximately 80% of graduates are employed in state. More than 50% of graduates are practicing law; 28% are in business; 20% in government; 2% in academia. Approximately 57% of the University of Detroit Mercy's first-time state bar exam takers pass the Michigan Bar Exam; Michigan's passage rate for all first-time takers from ABA-approved schools is 85%. Graduates are eligible to take the bar exam in all 50 states.

UNIVERSITY OF THE DISTRICT OF COLUMBIA
Washington, D.C. 20008-1175
Internet site: http://www.udc.edu

Founded in 1976 by the merger of District of Columbia Teachers College, Federal City College, and Washington Technical Institute. Located in NW Washington. Public control. Semester system. Library: 500,000 volumes; 200,000 microforms; 500 periodicals/subscriptions.

University's other graduate colleges/schools: School of Arts and Sciences, College of Professional Studies.

Total graduate enrollment: 552.

District of Columbia
School of Law
4250 Connecticut Avenue, NW
Washington, D.C. 20008
Phone: (202)274-7400
Internet site: http://www.udc.edu

Established 1986. Merged with University of the District of Columbia in 1996. Located on main campus. ABA approved since 1991. AALS member. Semester system. Full-time, day study only. Law library: 169,150 volumes/microforms; 2,450 current periodicals/subscriptions; 8 computer workstations; has LEXIS, WESTLAW, DIALOG, CALI. Special programs: externships, internships.

Annual tuition: resident $7,000, nonresident $14,000. No on-campus housing available. Law students live off-campus. Contact law school's Orientation Committee for off-campus information. Off-campus housing and personal expenses: approximately $18,900. Additional costs: books approximately $800.

Enrollment: first-year class 76; total full-time 226 (men 49%, women 51%); no part-time students. Statistics: 40% out of District, 29 states and foreign countries represented; 51% women; 63% minority; average age 30; 100 undergraduate institutions represented; average first-year section size 52 students; number of upper division courses offered after first year 37.

Faculty: full-time 16, part-time 9; 35% female; 39% minority; student/faculty ratio 15.7 to 1.

Degrees conferred: J.D.

RECRUITMENT PRACTICES AND POLICIES. Attends local and selected national law school forums. Has on-campus informational sessions. School does have diversity program and actively recruits women/minority applicants.

ADMISSION REQUIREMENTS FOR FIRST-YEAR APPLICANTS. LSDAS law school report, LSAT (not later than December test date, if more than one LSAT, highest is used), bachelor's degree from an accredited institution, personal statement, two recommendations, transcripts (must show all schools attended and at least three years of study) required in support of application. Applicants must have received bachelor's degree prior to enrollment. Interview not required but may be requested by school. In addition, international applicants whose native language is not English must submit TOEFL (not older than two years). Apply to Office of Admission after September 30, before April 1. First-year students admitted fall only. Rolling admission process finished when class is filled. Application fee $35. Phone: (202)274-7341.

ADMISSION REQUIREMENTS FOR TRANSFER APPLICANTS. Accepts transfers from other ABA-accredited schools. At least one year of enrollment, dean's letter indicating applicant is in good standing, prefer applicants in the top half of first-year class, LSAT, LSDAS, personal statement regarding reason for transfer, undergraduate transcript, two letters of recommendation, current law school transcript required in support of application. Apply to Admission Office by July 15. Admission decisions made by mid August. Application fee $35. Will consider visiting students.

ADMISSION STANDARDS. Number of full-time applicants 503; number accepted 143; number enrolled 76; median LSAT 144 (75% of class have a score at or above 141); median GPA 2.63 (A = 4) (75% of class have a GPA at or above 2.36). Attrition rate 20%. Gorman rating 2.10; *U.S. News & World Report* ranking is in the fourth tier of all law schools.

FINANCIAL AID. Need-based scholarships, merit scholarships, fellowships, private and institutional loans, federal loans and Federal WS available. For scholarships/fellowships (selection criteria place heavy reliance on LSAT and undergraduate GPA) apply as soon as possible after January 1, but before May 1 deadline. Phone: (202)274-7337. For all federal programs submit FAFSA (Title IV School code #B08083). Also submit Financial Aid Transcript, federal income tax forms. Approximately 63% of first-year class received scholarships/fellowships.

Approximately 88% of current students receive some form of financial assistance. Average scholarship/grant $5,000.

DEGREE REQUIREMENTS. For J.D.: 85 credits (61 required) with a 2.0 (A = 4) GPA, plus completion of upper divisional writing course; 3-year program. No accelerated J.D. program, limited number of summer courses available.

CAREER AND PLACEMENT INFORMATION. About 13–15 employers conducted on-campus interviews. Approximately 25% of graduates are employed in state. More than 59% of graduates are practicing law; 18% are in business; 22% in government; 1% in academia. Approximately 16% of the University of the District of Columbia's first-time state bar exam takers pass the District Bar Exam; the passage rate for all first-time takers from ABA-approved schools is 75%. Graduates are eligible to take the bar exam in all 50 states.

DRAKE UNIVERSITY
Des Moines, Iowa 50311-5416
Internet site: http://www.drake.edu

Founded 1881. Located 5 miles W of downtown Des Moines. Private control. Semester system. Library: 700,000 volumes; 1,600,000 microforms; 5,550 periodicals/subscriptions; 240 computer workstations.

University's other graduate colleges/schools: College of Arts and Sciences, College of Business and Public Administration, College of Pharmacy and Health Sciences, Division of Nursing, School of Education, School of Fine Arts, School of Journalism and Mass Communication.

Total university enrollment: 6,000.

School of Law
2507 University Avenue
Des Moines, Iowa 50311
Phone: (515)271-2724; (800)44-DRAKE
Internet site: http://www.drake.edu
E-mail: lawadmit@acad.drake.edu

Established 1865. Joined Drake University in 1887. Located on main campus. ABA approved since 1923. AALS charter member. Semester system. Full-time, limited part-time study. Law library: 257,400 volumes and microforms; 3,040 current periodicals/subscriptions; 104 computer workstations; has LEXIS, NEXIS, WESTLAW, DIALOG. Special facilities: Constitutional Law Center, Agricultural Law Center. Special programs: 3-3 program for completion of undergraduate degree and J.D.

Annual tuition: Full-time $16,330, per credit $550. On-campus housing available for both single and married students. Annual on-campus housing cost: single students $3,600 (room only), $4,950 (room and board) married students $3,960. Contact Drake Real Estate Office for both on- and off-campus housing information. Phone: (515)271-2196. Law students tend to live off-campus. Off-campus housing and personal expenses: approximately $10,679. Additional costs: books approximately $800.

Enrollment: first-year class 157; total full-time 444, part-time 10 (men 59%, women 41%). First-year statistics: 52% out of state, 38 states and 7 foreign countries represented; 41% women; 11% minority; average age 25; 184 undergraduate institutions represented; range of first-year section sizes 15–65 students; number of upper division courses offered after first year 106.

Faculty: full-time 22, part-time 37; 24% female; 5% minority; student/faculty ratio 21 to 1.

Degrees conferred: J.D., J.D.-M.B.A., J.D.-M.P.A., J.D.-M.A. (Mass Communication, Political Science), J.D.-M.S. (Agricultural Economics), J.D.-M.S.W. (University of Iowa).

RECRUITMENT PRACTICES AND POLICIES. Attends national law school forums. On-campus informational sessions. School does have diversity program and actively recruits women/minority applicants.

ADMISSION REQUIREMENTS FOR FIRST-YEAR APPLICANTS. LSDAS law school report, LSAT (not later than December test date, if more than one LSAT, highest is used), bachelor's degree from an accredited institution, personal statement, two recommendations, transcripts (must show all schools attended and at least three years of study) required in support of application. Applicants must have received bachelor's degree prior to enrollment. In addition, international applicants must submit TOEFL (not older than two years). Apply to Admission Committee after September 30, before February 15 (scholarship applicants), March 1 for priority consideration. First-year students admitted fall only. Rolling admission process, notification starts in January. Application fee $35. Phone: (800)44-DRAKE, Ext. 2782, (515)271-2782. E-mail: lawadmit@acad.drake.edu.

ADMISSION REQUIREMENTS FOR TRANSFER APPLICANTS. Accepts transfers from other ABA-accredited schools. Admission limited to space available. At least one year of enrollment, dean's letter indicating applicant is in good standing, LSAT, LSDAS, personal statement regarding reason for transfer, two recommendations, current law school transcript, undergraduate transcript required in support of application. Apply to Admission Committee by June 1. Admission decisions made by mid July. Application fee $35. Will consider visiting students.

ADMISSION STANDARDS. Number of full-time applicants 917; number accepted 479; number enrolled 157; median LSAT 153 (75% of class have a score at or above 150); median GPA 3.22 (A = 4) (75% of class have a GPA at or above 2.82). Attrition rate 3.7%. Gorman rating 3.35; *U.S. News & World Report* ranking is in the third tier of all law schools.

FINANCIAL AID. Scholarships, merit scholarships, minority scholarships, grants-in-aid, public interest fellowships, institutional loans; federal loans and Federal WS offered through university's Office of Financial Planning. Assistantships may be available for upper divisional joint-degree candidates. For scholarships (selection criteria place heavy reliance on LSAT and undergraduate GPA) apply after January 1, before February 15 to the Assistant Director of Admissions and Financial Aid. Phone: (800)44-DRAKE. For all other programs apply to university's Office of Financial Planning. Phone: (800)44-DRAKE, Ext. 2905. Use FAFSA (Title IV School code #001860). Also submit Financial Aid Transcript, federal income tax forms. Approximately 67% of first-year class received scholarships/grants-in-aid. Approximately 85% of current students receive some form of financial assistance, 45% receive scholarship assistance. Average scholarship/grant $4,060. Average debt after graduation $47,000.

DEGREE REQUIREMENTS. For J.D.: 90 credits (46 required) with a 2.0 (A = 4) GPA, plus completion of upper divisional writing course; 3-year program. Accelerated J.D. with 1 summer of course work. For J.D.-M.B.A.: total 108 credits (J.D. 81 credits, M.B.A. 27 credits). For J.D.-M.P.A.: total 108 credits (J.D. 81 credits, M.P.A. 27 credits). For J.D.-M.A., -M.S.: individually designed programs, can be completed in 3½ years rather than the usual 4 years needed if degrees taken separately.

CAREER AND PLACEMENT INFORMATION. Approximately 63% of graduates are employed in state. More than 63% of graduates are practicing law; 17% are in business; 19% in government; 1% in academia. Approximately 87% (IA), 100% (IL) of Drake University's first-time state bar exam takers pass the state bar exam;

the passage rate for all first-time takers from ABA-approved schools is 78% (IA), 87% (IL). Graduates are eligible to take the bar exam in all 50 states.

DUKE UNIVERSITY

Durham, North Carolina 27708-0586
Internet site: http://www.duke.edu

Founded 1838. Located in a rural area 25 miles NW of Raleigh. Private control. Semester system. Library: 4,300,000 volumes; 3,000,000 microforms; 31,800 periodicals/subscriptions; 300 computer workstations.

University's other graduate colleges/schools: Institute of Statistics and Decision Sciences, School of Engineering, Terry Sanford Institute of Public Policy, Divinity School, Fuqua School of Business, Nicholas School of the Environment, School of Medicine, School of Nursing.

Total university enrollment: 12,200.

School of Law

P.O. Box 90393
Durham, North Carolina 27708-0393
Phone: (919)613-7200
Internet site: http://www.law.duke.edu
E-mail: admissions@law.duke.edu

Established 1930. Located on main campus at Science Drive and Tower Road. ABA approved since 1931. AALS member. Semester system. Full-time, day study only. Law library: 477,000 volumes/microforms; 7,300 current periodicals/subscriptions; 100 computer workstations; has LEXIS, NEXIS, WESTLAW, DIALOG, First Search, Uncovers. Special facilities: Private Adjudication Center, Center on Law, Ethics and National Security. Special programs: Pro Bona and Public Interest Program.

Annual tuition: $24,537. On-campus housing available for both single and married students. Annual on-campus housing cost: apartments $3,500. Contact Housing Administrative Office for both on- and off-campus housing information. Phone: (919)684-4304. Law students tend to live off-campus. Off-campus housing and personal expenses: approximately $11,610. Additional costs: books approximately $700.

Enrollment: first-year class 199; total full-time 600 (men 60%, women 40%); no part-time students. First-year statistics: 88% out of state, 46 states and 15 foreign countries represented; 40% women; 20% minority; average age 23; 180 undergraduate institutions represented; range of first-year section sizes 25–80 students; number of upper division courses offered after first year 101.

Faculty: full-time 34, part-time 20; 31% female; 9% minority; student/faculty ratio 15 to 1.

Degrees conferred: J.D., J.D.-M.B.A., J.D.-M.E.M., J.D.-M.P.P., J.D.-M.A./M.S. (English, History, Humanities, Philosophy, Romance Studies, Mechanical Engineering, Cultural Anthropology, Economics, Political Science, Psychology, Forestry/Environmental Studies, Public Policy Studies), J.D.-LL.M., LL.M. (International and Comparative Law); LL.M. (U.S. law for international attorneys), S.J.D. (for international scholars who have earned a master's level degree from an accredited American law school).

RECRUITMENT PRACTICES AND POLICIES. Attends national law school forums. Has on-campus informational sessions. School does have diversity program and actively recruits women/minority applicants.

ADMISSION REQUIREMENTS FOR FIRST-YEAR APPLICANTS. LSDAS law school report, LSAT (not later than December test date, if more than one LSAT, average is used), bachelor's degree from an accredited institution, résumé, personal statement, interview, two references, transcripts (must show all schools attended and at least three years of study), Admissions Data Form, Dean's Certification Form, scholarship application form required in support of application. Applicants must have received bachelor's degree prior to enrollment. In addition, international applicants whose first language is not English must submit TOEFL (not older than two years), proof of sufficient financial support and letter from bank. For nonbinding Early Action, application must be completed by November 1, decision by December 15. For regular admission apply to Assistant Dean for Admission after September 1, before February 1 (suggested deadline). For joint-degree programs apply to both schools, take appropriate standardized test, i.e., GMAT, GRE. For accelerated summer entry joint-degree programs submit just one application. First-year students admitted fall only. Regular admission decision notification starts in late February and is finished by April 1. School does maintain a waiting list. Application fee $65. Phone: (919)613-7200. E-mail: admissions@law.duke.edu. International applicants contact Associate Dean for International Studies. Phone: (919)613-7033. E-mail: INTERNATIONAL@LAW.DUKE.EDU.

ADMISSION REQUIREMENTS FOR TRANSFER APPLICANTS. Accepts transfers from other ABA-accredited schools. Admission limited to space available. At least one year of enrollment, dean's letter indicating

applicant is in good standing, letters of recommendation form two law professors, LSAT, LSDAS, personal essay regarding reason for transfer, current law school transcript, all undergraduate and graduate transcripts required in support of application. Apply to Assistant Dean by July 1. Admission decisions made by late July. Application fee $65. Will consider visiting students.

ADMISSION REQUIREMENTS FOR LL.M. APPLICANTS. A degree in law from an approved institution in the applicant's native country, official transcripts with translation and certification of degree equivalency to American J.D., two letters of recommendation, TOEFL for those applicants whose native language is not English required in support of LL.M. application. Admits fall only. Apply by February 15 to Associate Dean for International Studies. Phone: (919)613-7033. E-mail: INTERNATIONAL@LAW.DUKE.EDU. Notification of acceptance begins in late February.

ADMISSION REQUIREMENTS FOR S.J.D. APPLICANTS. For international students who already have an LL.M. from an accredited American law school: official transcripts form all post-baccalaureate academic work, two faculty references, a sample of written work, preliminary thesis proposal. Admits fall only. Apply by February 15 to Associate Dean of International Studies. Phone: (919)613-7033. Fax: (919)613-7231. E-mail: INTERNATIONAL@LAW.DUKE.EDU.

ADMISSION STANDARDS. Number of full-time applicants 2,744; number accepted 867; number enrolled 199; median LSAT 168 (75% of class have a score at or above 164); median GPA 3.63 (A = 4) (75% of class have a GPA at or above 3.42). Attrition rate 1%. Gorman rating 4.85; *U.S. News & World Report* ranking is in the top 10 of all law schools.

FINANCIAL AID. Scholarships, merit scholarships, grants-in-aid, institutional loans, federal loans. For scholarships (selection criteria place heavy reliance on LSAT and undergraduate GPA) apply to Financial Aid Office after January 1, before February 15. Use school's scholarship application (personal financial report). For all other programs apply after January 1, before March 1. Phone: (919)613-7025. Use FAFSA for all federal programs (Title IV School code #E00167), send SAR to Financial Aid Office, submit Financial Aid Transcript, federal income tax form. Approximately 75% of first-year class received scholarships/grants-in-aid. Approximately 67% of current students receive some form of financial assistance. Average scholarship/grant $7,000.

DEGREE REQUIREMENTS. For J.D.: 84 credits (30 required) with a 2.0 (A = 4) GPA, plus completion of upper divisional writing course; 3-year program, 4-year program (part-time). Accelerated J.D. with 2 summers of course work. For J.D.-M.B.A., M.E.M., M.P.P.: normally joint-degree programs are completed in four years. For J.D.-master's: 3-year program, plus summer session prior to beginning law school degree program. For J.D.-LL.M.: 3-year program, plus 2 summers, 1 summer in either Hong Kong, or Geneva, Switzerland. For LL.M. (International and Comparative Law): 21 credits, plus 2 credits of written work. For LL.M. (international attorneys): 21 credits, including 2 credits of written work; at least 2 semesters in residence; GPA of 2.5 (A = 4.5) required. For S.J.D.: usually 1 or 2 semesters of course work; thesis; oral exam; normally completed in 2 to 3 years.

CAREER AND PLACEMENT INFORMATION. About 339 employers conducted on-campus interviews. Approximately 15% of graduates are employed in state. More than 94% of graduates are practicing law; 3% are in business; 3% in government; none in academia. Approximately 94% (NC), 98% (NY) of Duke University's first-time state bar exam takers pass the bar exam; the passage rate for all first-time takers from ABA-approved schools are 85% (NC), 83% (NY). Graduates are eligible to take the bar exam in all 50 states.

DUQUESNE UNIVERSITY
Pittsburgh, Pennsylvania 15282-0001
Internet site: http://www.duq.edu

Founded 1878. Located in downtown Pittsburgh. Private control (Roman Catholic affiliation). Semester system. Library: 628,500 volumes; 439,700 microforms; 5,742 periodicals/subscriptions; 35 computer workstations.

University's other graduate colleges/schools: Bayer School of Natural and Environmental Sciences, Graduate School of Business Administration, Graduate School of Liberal Arts and Sciences, John G. Rangos, Sr., School of Health Sciences, School of Education, School of Music, School of Nursing, School of Planning.

Total university enrollment: 9,300.

School of Law
900 Locust Street
Pittsburgh, Pennsylvania 15282
Phone: (412)396-6280
Internet site: http://www.duq.edu/law
E-mail: ricci@duq2.cc.duq.edu

Established 1911. Located on main campus. ABA approved since 1960. AALS member. Semester system. Full-time, part-time study. Law library: 211,000 volumes and equivalent microforms; 4,308 current periodicals/subscriptions; 40 computer workstations; has LEXIS, WESTLAW. Special programs: B.A.-J.D., B.S.-J.D., foreign attorneys program.

Annual tuition: full-time (day) $14,414, part-time (evening) $11,020. Limited on-campus housing available for singles only. A new Learning and Living Center is planned to open during the 1997–98 academic year. Annual on-campus housing cost: single students $3,030 (room only), $5,580 (room and board). Housing deadline May 1. Contact Office of Graduate Housing for both on- and off-campus housing information. Phone: (412)396-5028. Law students tend to live off-campus. Off-campus housing and personal expenses: approximately $9,384. Additional costs: books approximately $600.

Enrollment: first-year class full-time 113, part-time 85; total full-time 300, part-time 334 (men 58%, women 42%). First-year statistics: 30% out of state, 28 states and foreign countries represented; 42% women; 9% minority; average age 27; 181 undergraduate institutions represented; range of first-year section sizes 20–100 students; number of upper division courses offered after first year full-time 56, part-time 52.

Faculty: full-time 24, part-time 44; 14% female; 7% minority; student/faculty ratio 21 to 1.

Degrees conferred: J.D., J.D.-M.B.A., J.D.-M.S. (Environmental Science and Management), J.D.-M.Div.

RECRUITMENT PRACTICES AND POLICIES. Attends several national law school forums. On-campus informational sessions. School does have diversity program and actively recruits women/minority applicants.

ADMISSION REQUIREMENTS FOR FIRST-YEAR APPLICANTS. LSDAS law school report, LSAT (not later than December test date, if more than one LSAT, highest is used), bachelor's degree from an accredited institution, résumé (evening only), personal statement, two recommendations, transcripts (must show all schools attended and at least three years of study) required in support of application. Applicants must have received bachelor's degree prior to enrollment. Interview not required, visits are encouraged, call for appointment. Phone: (412)396-6300. In addition, international applicants whose native language is not English must submit TOEFL (not older than two years, preferred score 600). Apply to Admission Office after September 1, before April 1 (day), May 1 (evening). Applicants to the joint-degree program must apply to and be accepted by both

schools. First-year students admitted fall only. Rolling admission process, notification starts in November (day), February (evening) and both are finished by late April. Application fee $50. Phone: (412)396-6296. E-mail: ricci@duq2.cc.duq.edu.

ADMISSION REQUIREMENTS FOR TRANSFER APPLICANTS. Accepts transfers from other ABA-accredited schools. Admission limited to space available. At least one year of enrollment, dean's letter indicating applicant is in good standing, LSAT, LSDAS, personal statement regarding reason for transfer, two letters of recommendation, current law school transcript required in support of application. Apply to Admission Office by June 1. Admission decisions made by mid July. Application fee $50. Will consider visiting students.

ADMISSION REQUIREMENTS FOR FOREIGN ATTORNEY PROGRAM (For international attorneys to become eligible to sit for Pennsylvania Bar Examination). Certified transcript or diploma, documentation of admission to practice law in another country, TOEFL, letter of understanding required in support of program's application. Apply to the law school's Admissions Office by April 1 (day), May 1 (evening). Application fee $50.

ADMISSION STANDARDS. Number of full-time applicants 656, part-time 202; number accepted full-time 398, part-time 120; number enrolled full-time 113, part-time 85; median LSAT 156 (75% of class have a score at or above 150 full-time, 148 part-time); median GPA 3.25 (A = 4) (75% of class have a GPA at or above 2.92 full-time, 2.59 part-time). Attrition rate 5.1%. Gorman rating 3.32; *U.S. News & World Report* ranking is in the third tier of all law schools.

FINANCIAL AID. Scholarships, merit scholarships, minority scholarships, grants-in-aid, institutional loans; federal loans and Federal WS offered through university's Financial Aid Office. For scholarships (selection criteria place heavy reliance on LSAT and undergraduate GPA, all applicants given consideration) submit admissions application to school's Admissions Office after January 1 but as early as possible for priority consideration. For all other programs apply to university's Office of Financial Aid. Phone: (412)396-6607. Use FAFSA (Title IV School code #003258) and submit before May 31. Also submit federal income tax form, Financial Aid Transcripts, and copy of law school's letter of acceptance. Approximately 32% (day), 16% (evening) of first-year class received scholarships/grants-in-aid. Approximately 80% of current students receive some form of financial assistance. Average scholarship/grant $3,500 (day), $3,000 (evening).

DEGREE REQUIREMENTS. For J.D.: 87 credits (34 required) with a 2.0 (A = 4) GPA, plus completion of upper divisional writing course; 3-year program, 4-year program (part-time). Accelerated J.D. with 1 summer of course work. For J.D.-M.B.A.: can be completed in 4 years rather than usual 5 years (day). For J.D.-M.Div.: can be completed in 5 years (day). For J.D.-M.S. (Environmental Science and Management): can be completed in 4 years rather than usual 5 years. For Foreign Attorney Program: 39 credits, at least 2 years in residence.

CAREER AND PLACEMENT INFORMATION. About 27 employers conducted on-campus interviews. Approximately 74% of graduates are employed in state. More than 63% of graduates are practicing law; 33% are in business; 3% in government; 1% in academia. Approximately 73% of Dusquesne University's first-time state bar exam takers pass the Pennsylvania Bar Exam; Pennsylvania's passage rate for all first-time takers from ABA-approved schools is 73%.

EMORY UNIVERSITY
Atlanta, Georgia 30322
Internet site: http://www.emory.edu

Founded 1836. Located in a suburban area 6 miles NE of downtown Atlanta. Private control (Methodist affiliation). Semester system. Library: 2,200,000 volumes; 3,076,000 microforms; 24,588 periodicals/subscriptions.

University's other graduate colleges/schools: Candler School of Theology, Graduate School of Arts and Sciences, Nell Hodgson Woodruff School of Nursing, Roberto C. Goizueta Business School, School of Medicine, The Rollins School of Public Health.

Total university enrollment: 11,300.

School of Law
Gambrell Hall
1301 Clifton Road
Atlanta, Georgia 30322-2770
Phone: (404)727-6801
Internet site: http://www.law.emory.edu
E-mail: lawinfo@law.emory.edu

Established 1923. Located on main campus. ABA approved since 1923. AALS member. Semester system. Full-time, day study only. Law library: 300,000 volumes/microforms; 5,253 current periodicals/subscriptions; 80 computer workstations; has LEXIS, NEXIS, WESTLAW, DIALOG, OCLC, RUN, RLIN; is a Federal Government Depository. Special program: Certificates in Soviet, Post Soviet and East European Studies.

Annual tuition: $22,700 (Fixed Tuition Plan). On-campus housing available for both single and married students. Annual on-campus housing cost: single students $3,702 (room only), married students $6,442. Contact Residential Services for both on- and off-campus housing information. Phone: (404)727-8830. Law students tend to live off-campus. Off-campus housing and personal expenses: approximately $10,000. Additional costs: books approximately $600.

Enrollment: first-year class 208; total full-time 700 (men 52%, women 48%); no part-time students. First-year statistics: 79% out of state, 36 states and foreign countries represented; 48% women; 23% minority; average age 22; 100 undergraduate institutions represented; range of first-year section sizes 30–60 students; number of upper division courses offered after first year 89.

Faculty: full-time 40, part-time 38; 31% female; 9% minority; student/faculty ratio 22 to 1.

Degrees conferred: J.D., J.D.-M.B.A., J.D.-M.P.H., J.D.-M.T.S., J.D.-M.Div., LL.M.

RECRUITMENT PRACTICES AND POLICIES. Attends national law school forums. On-campus informational sessions. School does have diversity program and actively recruits women/minority applicants.

ADMISSION REQUIREMENTS FOR FIRST-YEAR APPLICANTS. LSDAS law school report, LSAT (not later than February test date, if more than one LSAT, highest is used), bachelor's degree from an accredited institution, personal statement, two recommendations, transcripts (must show all schools attended and at least three years of study) required in support of application. Applicants must have received bachelor's degree prior to enrollment. Interview not required, but applicants are encouraged to visit school. In addition, international applicants whose native language is not English must submit TOEFL (not older than two years). Joint-degree applicants must apply to and be accepted by both schools. Apply to Director of Admission after September 30, before March 1. First-year students admitted fall only. Modified rolling admission process, notification starts in January and is finished by May. Acceptance of offer and first deposit due immediately after acceptance notification. Application fee $50. Phone: (404)727-6801. E-mail: lawinfo@law.emory.edu.

ADMISSION REQUIREMENTS FOR TRANSFER APPLICANTS. Accepts transfers from other ABA-accredited schools. Admission limited to space available. At least one year of enrollment, dean's letter indicating applicant is in good standing (prefer applicants in the upper half of first-year class), LSAT, LSDAS, personal statement regarding reason for transfer, current law school transcript, undergraduate transcript required in support of application. Apply to Director of Admission by June 30 (fall), December 1 (spring). Admission decisions made by mid July (fall), mid December (spring). Application fee $50. Will consider guest students, apply by July 5 (fall), December 15 (spring).

ADMISSIONS REQUIREMENTS FOR LL.M. J.D. or equivalent degree from a law school that is approved by ABA and/or is a member of AALS; or equivalent degree from a foreign university that meets quality standards to those of an ABA/AALS-approved American law school, official transcripts and/or certified translation and evaluated of international transcripts/diploma, two recommendations, statement of purpose required in support of LL.M. application. Apply to Admission Office by March 1. Admits to fall semester only. Application fee $50.

ADMISSION STANDARDS. Number of full-time applicants 2,688; number accepted 1,059; number enrolled 208; median LSAT 160 (75% of class have a score at or above 158); median GPA 3.42 (A = 4) (75% of class have a GPA at or above 3.20). Attrition rate 2.3%. Gorman rating 3.90; *U.S. News & World Report* ranking is in the top 30 of all law schools.

FINANCIAL AID. Scholarships, merit scholarships, minority scholarships, grants-in-aid, institutional loans; federal loans and Federal WS offered through university's Financial Aid Office. Assistantships may be available for upper divisional joint-degree candidates. For scholarships (selection criteria place heavy reliance on LSAT and undergraduate GPA) apply to Assistant Dean for Admissions before February 15. For all other programs apply to university's Director of Admissions and Financial Aid. Phone: (404)727-1141. Use FAFSA for all federal programs (Title IV School code #001564). Also submit Financial Aid Transcript, CSS analysis, 1996 federal income tax form, and Access Disk. Approximately 54% of first-year class received scholarships/grants-in-aid. Approximately 75% of current students receive some form of financial assistance. Average scholarship/grant $11,300. Average debt after graduation $58,900.

DEGREE REQUIREMENTS. For J.D.: 88 credits (39 required) with a 72 (scale of 0–100) GPA, plus completion of upper divisional writing course; 3-year program. Accelerated J.D. with 1 summer of course work. For J.D.-M.B.A.: total 125 credits (J.D. 77 credits, M.B.A. 48 credits). J.D.-M.T.S.: total 116 credits (J.D. 77 credits, M.T.S. 39 credits; 3.0 GPA, research paper or thesis). For J.D.-M.Div.: total 148 credits (J.D. 77 credits, M.Div. 71 credits). For LL.M.: 24 credits, at least 2 semesters in residence.

CAREER AND PLACEMENT INFORMATION. About 84 employers conducted on-campus interviews. Approximately 60% of graduates are employed in state. More than 76% of graduates are practicing law; 10% are in business; 13% in government; 1% in academia. Approximately 81% of Emory University's first-time state bar exam takers pass the Georgia Bar Exam; Georgia's passage rate for all first-time takers from ABA-approved schools is 84%. Graduates are eligible to take the bar exam in all 50 states.

FLORIDA STATE UNIVERSITY
Tallahassee, Florida 32306
Internet site: http://www.fsu.edu

Founded 1957. Located in an urban area of Tallahassee. Public control. Semester system. Library: 2,116,510 volumes; 4,402,600 microforms; 18,296 periodicals/subscriptions.

University's other graduate colleges/schools: College of Arts and Sciences, College of Business, College of Communications, College of Education, College of Engineering, College of Human Science, College of Social Science, School of Criminology and Criminal Justice, School of Library and Information Studies, School of Motion Pictures, TV and Recording Arts, School of Music, School of Nursing, School of Social Work, School of Theatre, School of Visual Arts and Dance.

Total university enrollment: 30,268.

College of Law
425 West Jefferson Street
Tallahassee, Florida 32306-1034
Phone: (904)344-3400
Internet site: http://www.law.fsu.edu
E-mail: admission@law.fsu.edu

Established 1966. Located on main campus. ABA approved since 1968. AALS member. Semester system. Full-time, day study only. Law library: 390,000, volumes/microforms; 5,650 continuing subscriptions; 61 computer workstations; has LEXIS, NEXIS, WESTLAW, Legal-Trac, OCLC, RLIN. Special programs: Environmental Law, International Law Mediation, Florida Dispute Resolution Center; summer study abroad at Oxford University (England), University of West Indies (Barbados), Charles University (Prague); externships.

Annual tuition: resident $4,386, nonresident $13,930; per credit resident $124.40, nonresident $387.96. On-campus housing available for both single and married students. Annual on-campus housing cost: single students $3,180 (room only), married students $5,136. Contact university's Office of Resident Student Development for on-campus housing information. Phone: (904)644-2860. Law students tend to live off-campus. Contact Student Government Association Off-Campus Housing Office for off-campus information. Phone: (850)644-0089. Off-campus housing and personal expenses: approximately $14,034. Additional costs: books approximately $800.

Enrollment: first-year class 201; total full-time 634 (men 55%, women 45%); no part-time students. First-year statistics: 21% out of state, 45% women; 26% minority; average age 25; 68 undergraduate institutions represented; range of first-year section sizes 30–70 students; number of upper division courses offered after first year 90.

Faculty: full-time 41, part-time 7; 26% female; 14% minority; student/faculty ratio 22 to 1.

Degrees conferred: J.D., J.D.-M.B.A., J.D.-M.P.A., J.D.-Economics, International Affairs, J.D.-Urban and Regional Planning.

RECRUITMENT PRACTICES AND POLICIES. Attends national law school forums. Has on-campus informational sessions and campus visits encouraged. School does have diversity program and actively recruits women/minority applicants.

ADMISSION REQUIREMENTS FOR FIRST-YEAR APPLICANTS. LSDAS law school report, LSAT (not later than December test date, if more than one LSAT, average is used), bachelor's degree from an accredited institution, personal statement, two recommendations, transcripts (must show all schools attended and at least three years of study) required in support of application. Applicants must have received bachelor's degree prior to enrollment. Interview not required, but campus visits are encouraged. Contact Admissions Office to make arrangements. In addition, international applicants whose native language is not English must submit TOEFL (not older than two years, minimum score 550). Joint-degree program applicants must apply to and be accepted by both schools. Apply to Office of Admission after September 30, before February 15. First-year students admitted fall only. Rolling admission process, notification starts in November and is finished by late April. Application fee $20. Phone: (904)644-3787. E-mail: admissions@law.fsu.edu.

ADMISSION REQUIREMENTS FOR TRANSFER APPLICANTS. Accepts transfers from other ABA-accredited schools. Admission limited to space available. At least one year of enrollment, dean's letter indicating the applicant is in good standing (prefer applicants in the top quarter of first-year class), LSAT, LSDAS, personal statement regarding reason for transfer, current law school transcript showing completion of first year required in support of application. Apply to Admission Office by June 1 (fall), December 1 (spring) and have application completed at least one month prior to semester for which entrance is being sought. Application fee $20. Will consider visiting students.

ADMISSION STANDARDS. Number of full-time applicants 2,107; number accepted 654; number enrolled 201; median LSAT 157 (75% of class have a score at or above 153); median GPA 3.4 (A = 4) (75% of class have a GPA at or above 3.06). Attrition rate 2.1%. Gorman rating 3.42; *U.S. News & World Report* ranking is in the second tier of all law schools.

FINANCIAL AID. Scholarships, minority scholarships, grants-in-aid, institutional and private loans; federal loans and Federal WS offered through university's Financial Aid Office. Assistantships may be available for upper divisional joint-degree candidates. For scholarships (selection criteria place heavy reliance on LSAT and undergraduate GPA) apply to Committee on Scholarships and Awards after January 1, before March 1. Phone: (904)644-5716. For all other programs apply to university's Office of Financial Aid. Phone: (904)644-5871. Use FAFSA for all federal programs (Title IV School code #001489). Also submit Financial Aid Transcript, federal income tax forms. Approximately 10% of first-year class received scholarships/grants-in-aid. Approximately 75% of current students receive some form of financial assistance. Average scholarship/grant $1,200. Average debt after graduation $50,500.

DEGREE REQUIREMENTS. For J.D.: 88 credits (35 required) with a 67 (scale 0–100) GPA, plus completion of upper divisional writing course; 20 hours of pro bono work; 3-year program. Accelerated J.D. with 1 summer of course work. For J.D.-master's: individually designed degree programs, the time needed for both degrees is reduced by between 6 months and 1 year depending on master's program.

CAREER AND PLACEMENT INFORMATION. About 44 employers conducted on-campus interviews. Approximately 84% of graduates are employed in state. More than 68% of graduates are practicing law; 3% are in business; 29% in government; none in academia. Approximately 82% of Florida State University's first-time state bar exam takers pass the Florida Bar Exam; Florida's passage rate for all first-time takers from ABA-approved schools is 84%. Graduates are eligible to take the bar exam in all 50 states.

UNIVERSITY OF FLORIDA
Gainesville, Florida 32611-8140
Internet site: http://www.ufl.edu

Founded 1853. Located 75 miles SW of Jacksonville. Public control. Semester system. Library: 3,000,000 volumes; 4,200,000 microforms.

University's other graduate colleges/schools: College of Agriculture, College of Architecture, College of Business Administration, College of Engineering, College of Fine Arts, College of Health and Human Performance, College of Health Related Professions, College of Journalism and Communication, College of Liberal Arts and Sciences, College of Nursing, School of Forest Resources and Conservation, College of Dentistry, College of Medicine, College of Pharmacy.

Total university enrollment: 38,700.

College of Law
P.O. Box 117622
325 Holland Hall
Gainesville, Florida 32611-7622
Phone: (352)392-0421
Internet site: http://www.law.ufl.edu
E-mail: patrick@law.ufl.edu

Established 1909. Located on main campus. ABA approved since 1925. AALS member since 1920. Semester system. Full-time, day study only. Law library: 568,600 volumes/microforms; 7,950 current periodicals/subscriptions; 100 computer workstations; has LEXIS, NEXIS, WESTLAW, DIALOG, PLATO. Special programs: summer study abroad at Université de Montpellier.

Annual tuition: resident $4,036, nonresident $12,942. Tuition for LL.M. (Comparative Law), $13,000 per year. On-campus housing available for both single and married students. Annual on-campus housing cost: single students $2,472 (room only), married students $2,884. Contact Director of Housing for both on- and off-campus housing information. Phone: (352)392-2161. Law students tend to live off-campus. Off-campus housing and personal ex-

penses: approximately $9,110. Additional costs: books approximately $700.

Enrollment: first-year class 219 (fall), 205 (spring); total full-time 1,182 (men 59%, women 41%); no part-time students. First-year statistics: 10% out of state, 100 states and foreign countries represented; 41% women; 23% minority; average age 25; 100 undergraduate institutions represented; range of first-year section sizes 24–100 students; number of upper division courses offered after first year 70.

Faculty: full-time 76, part-time 5; 31% female; 10% minority; student/faculty ratio 20 to 1.

Degrees conferred: J.D., J.D.-M.B.A., J.D.-Accounting, J.D.-M.A., LL.M. (Tax), LL.M. (Comparative Law, for persons who have completed a basic legal education and received a university degree in law in another country).

RECRUITMENT PRACTICES AND POLICIES. Attends national law school forums. Has on-campus informational sessions conducted by Phi Alpha Delta Law Guide Service. School does have diversity program and actively recruits women/minority applicants.

ADMISSION REQUIREMENTS FOR FIRST-YEAR APPLICANTS. LSDAS law school report, LSAT (not later than December [fall], February [spring] test date [scores are valid for up to five years], if more than one LSAT, average is used), bachelor's degree from an accredited institution, personal statement, three letters of recommendation, transcripts (must show all schools attended and at least three years of study) required in support of application. Applicants must have received bachelor's degree prior to enrollment. In addition, international applicants whose native language is not English must submit TOEFL (not older than two years), submit certified translations and evaluations of all foreign credentials. Both joint- and concurrent-degree applicants must apply to and be accepted by both schools. Apply to Office of Admission after September 30, before February 1 (fall), May 15 (spring). First-year students admitted fall and spring. Rolling admission process, notification starts in November and is finished by late April (fall), by July (spring). Application fee $20. Phone: (352)392-2087. Fax: (352)392-8727. E-mail: patrick@law.ufl.edu.

ADMISSION REQUIREMENTS FOR TRANSFER APPLICANTS. Accepts transfers from other ABA-accredited schools. Admission limited to space available. At least one year of enrollment, dean's letter indicating

applicant is in good standing (prefer applicants in the upper third of first-year class), LSAT, LSDAS, personal statement regarding reason for transfer, two letters of recommendation, undergraduate transcript, current law school transcript required in support of application. Apply to Admission Office by July 1 (fall), October 1 (spring), March 1 (summer). Admission decisions made within one month from the receipt of completed application. Application fee $20. Will consider visiting students.

ADMISSIONS REQUIREMENTS FOR LL.M. (Tax). All applicants must have a J.D. or equivalent from an AALS-accredited law school. Official transcripts (both undergraduate and law school including rank in class, must be in top quarter of class), résumé, LSDAS law school report required in support of graduate application. Graduates of ABA-accredited schools or from institutions with ABA provisional accreditation may be considered. Admits fall term only (full-time), fall and spring (part-time). Apply after October 1, before June 1 (fall) to Graduate Tax Program Admissions, P.O. Box 117627. Application fee $20. Phone: (352)392-1081. Fax: (352)392-7647.

ADMISSIONS REQUIREMENTS FOR LL.M. (Comparative Law). Applicants must have a law degree with high academic standing from a recognized foreign university and a thorough knowledge of English. Official documents with certified translations and evaluations, TOEFL for those whose primary language is not English (600 minimum score, 50 on oral ability), proof of sufficient financial support for two years of study in the form of a letter of credit required in support of application. Prefers applicants with some work experience after receipt of first professional degree. Admits fall only. Apply March 15 to Director, LL.M. in Comparative Law Program, P.O. Box 117643. Phone: (352)392-0082. Fax: (352)392-3005.

ADMISSION STANDARDS. Number of full-time applicants 2,280; number accepted 512 (fall), 280 (spring); number enrolled 219 (fall), 205 (spring); median LSAT 162 (fall), 158 (spring) (75% of class have a score at or above 155 (fall), 152 (spring); median GPA 3.45 (fall), 3.35 (spring) (A = 4) (75% of class have a GPA at or above 3.26 [fall], 3.15 [spring]). Attrition rate 1.3%. Gorman rating 3.78; *U.S. News & World Report* ranking is in the second tier of all law schools.

FINANCIAL AID. Scholarships, merit scholarships, minority scholarships, grants-in-aid, private and institutional loans, federal loans available. Assistantships may be available for upper divisional joint-degree candidates. For scholarships (selection criteria place heavy reliance on LSAT and undergraduate GPA) apply to Director of Financial Aid after January 1, before April 1 (fall), July 1 (spring). Phone: (352)392-0421. Submit FAFSA for all federal programs (Title IV School code #001535). Also submit Financial Aid Transcript, federal income tax forms. Approximately 18% of first-year class received scholarships/grants-in-aid. Approximately 77% of current students receive some form of financial assistance. Average scholarship/grant $2,398. Average debt after graduation $32,500. For LL.M. (Tax); scholarships, minority fellowships (use Minority Fellowships Application); awards, assistantships, tuition waivers, loans available. Apply by February 15. All accepted students are automatically considered for all available financial assistance. For loans apply to Student Financial Affairs by June 1. Phone: (352)392-1275.

DEGREE REQUIREMENTS. For J.D.: 88 credits (34 required) with a 2.0 (A = 4) GPA, plus completion of senior writing project; 3-year program. Accelerated J.D. with summer course work. For J.D.-master's: individually designed programs which generally reduce time required for completion of both degrees by between 6 months and 1 year. For LL.M. (Tax): 26 credits with at least 2 semesters in residence plus a summer term; 3.0 (A = 4) GPA required. For LL.M. (Comparative Law): 30 credits with at least 2 semesters in residence; 3.0 (A = 4) GPA required; research project.

CAREER AND PLACEMENT INFORMATION. About 120–125 employers conducted on-campus interviews. Approximately 83% of graduates are employed in state. More than 70% of graduates are practicing law; 8% are in business; 22% in government. Approximately 92% of the University of Florida's first-time state bar exam takers pass the Florida Bar Exam; Florida's passage rate for all first-time takers from ABA-approved schools is 84%. Graduates are eligible to take the bar exam in all 50 states.

FORDHAM UNIVERSITY
New York, New York 10458
Internet site: http://www.fordham.edu

Founded 1841. Located in the Rose Hill section of the Bronx and at Lincoln Center. Private control (Roman Catholic—Jesuit affiliation). Semester system. Library: 1,233,000 volumes; 1,421,000 microforms; 5,505 periodicals/subscriptions; 30 computer workstations.

University's other graduate colleges/schools: Graduate College of Arts and Sciences, Graduate School of Business Administration, Graduate School of Education, Graduate School of Religion and Religious Education, School of Social Services.

Total university enrollment: 13,100.

School of Law
140 West 62nd Street
New York, New York 10023
Phone: (212)636-6875
Internet site: http://www.fordham.edu/law

Established 1905. Located on the island of Manhattan at Lincoln Center. ABA approved since 1936. AALS member since 1936. Semester system. Full-time, part-time study. Law library: 450,000 volumes/microforms; 3,861 current periodicals/subscriptions; 94 computer workstations; has LEXIS, NEXIS, WESTLAW, DIALOG. Special programs: Fordham Public Service Program, Fordham Center on European Community Law and International Antitrust.

Annual tuition: full-time $22,699 part-time $17,029. On-campus housing available for both single and married students. On-campus housing cost: $5,685–$6,900. Contact Admissions Office for both on- and off-campus housing information. Off-campus housing and personal expenses: approximately $16,995. Additional costs: books approximately $600–$700.

Enrollment: first-year class 343, part-time 135; total full-time 1,061, part-time 361 (men 56%, women 44%). First-year statistics: 33% out of state, 39 states and foreign countries represented; 43% women; 26% minority; average age 27; 270 undergraduate institutions represented; range of first-year section sizes for full-time 37–75 students, part-time 39–78 students; number of upper division courses offered after first year for full-time 121, part-time 99.

Faculty: full-time 60, part-time 178; 29% female; 10% minority; student/faculty ratio 20.5 to 1.

Degrees conferred: J.D., J.D.-M.B.A., J.D.-M.S.W., LL.M.

RECRUITMENT PRACTICES AND POLICIES. Attends national law school forums. On-campus informational sessions. School does have diversity program and actively recruits women/minority applicants.

ADMISSION REQUIREMENTS FOR FIRST-YEAR APPLICANTS. LSDAS law school report, LSAT (not later than February test date), bachelor's degree from an accredited institution, résumé, personal statement, two recommendations, transcripts (must show all schools attended and at least three years of study) required in support of application. Applicants must have received bachelor's degree prior to enrollment. Interview not required but may be requested by school. In addition, international applicants must submit TOEFL (not older than two years). Applicants for the joint-degree programs must apply to and be accepted by both schools. Apply to Office of Admission after September 30, before March 1. First-year students admitted fall only. Rolling admission process, notification starts in January and is finished by late May. Application fee $60. Phone: (212)636-6810.

ADMISSION REQUIREMENTS FOR TRANSFER APPLICANTS. Accepts transfers from other ABA-accredited schools. Admission limited to space available. At least one year of enrollment, dean's letter indicating applicant is in good standing (prefer applicants in the top quarter of first-year class), LSAT, LSDAS, personal statement regarding reason for transfer, current law school transcript required in support of application. Apply to Office of Admission by June 15. Admission decisions made by late July. Application fee $60. Will consider visiting students.

ADMISSION STANDARDS. Number of full-time applicants 3,916, part-time 677; number accepted full-time 1,257, part-time 227; number enrolled full-time 343, part-time 286; median LSAT 163 (75% of class have a score at or above 161 full-time, 154 part-time); median GPA 3.36 (A = 4) (75% of class have a GPA at or above 3.01 full-time, 2.86 part-time). Attrition rate 1.1%. Gorman rating 4.47; *U.S. News & World Report* ranking is in the top 30 of all law schools.

FINANCIAL AID. Scholarships, private loans; federal loans offered through university's Financial Aid Office. Most financial aid is need based. For scholarships (selection criteria place heavy reliance on LSAT and undergraduate GPA) apply to Admissions Office after January 1, before February 15. Phone: (212)636-6815. Use FAFSA for all federal programs (Title IV School code #002722). Also submit Financial Aid Transcript, CSS analysis, 1996 federal income tax form. Approximately 65% (full-time), 26% (part-time) of first-year class received scholarships/grants-in-aid. Approximately 71% of current students receive some form of financial assistance. Average scholarship/grant $6,800 (full-time), $3,500 (part-time).

DEGREE REQUIREMENTS. For J.D.: 83 credits (39 required) with a 2.0 (A = 4) GPA, plus completion of upper divisional writing course; 3-year program, 4-year program (part-time). For J.D.-master's: individually designed programs, usually takes 4 years to complete rather than 5 years. For LL.M.: 24 credits.

CAREER AND PLACEMENT INFORMATION. About 250 employers conducted on-campus interviews. Approximately 91% of graduates are employed in state. More than 70% of graduates are practicing law; 17% are in business; 12% in government; 1% in academia. Approximately 90% of Fordham University's first-time state bar exam takers pass the New York state bar exam; New York State's passage rate for all first-time takers from ABA-approved schools is 78%. Graduates are eligible to take the bar exam in all 50 states.

FRANKLIN PIERCE LAW CENTER
2 White Street
Concord, New Hampshire
Phone: (603)228-9217
Internet site: http://www.FPLC.edu
E-mail: admissions@FPLC.edu

Established 1973. Concord is the capital of New Hampshire and is 25 minutes from Manchester and one hour from Boston. ABA approved since 1974. AALS member. Semester system. Full-time, day study only. Law library: 200,000 volumes/microforms; 2,400 current periodicals/subscriptions; 28 computer workstations; has LEXIS, NEXIS, WESTLAW, DIALOG, OCLC. Special facilities: Germeshausen Center for the Law of Innovation and Entrepreneurship, Institute for Health, Law and Ethics, The Patent, Trademark, and Copyright Research Foundation. Special program: externships.

Annual tuition: $15,857, M.I.P. $19,800. There is no on-campus housing available. Law students live off-campus, 60% within walking distance of campus. Contact the Admissions Office for off-campus information. Off-campus housing and personal expenses: approximately $11,600. Additional costs: books approximately $500.

Enrollment: first-year class 151; total full-time 412 (men 65%, women 35%), no part-time students. First-year statistics: 73% out of state, 33 states and foreign countries represented; 38% women; 16% minority; average age 27; 102 undergraduate institutions represented; range of first-year section sizes 27–151 students; number of upper division courses offered after first year 90.

Faculty: full-time 18, part-time 33; 23% female; 4% minority; student/faculty ratio 18 to 1.

Degrees conferred: J D., J D.-M.I.P., M.I.P.

RECRUITMENT PRACTICES AND POLICIES. Attends national law school forums. On-campus informational sessions. School does have diversity program and actively recruits women/minority applicants.

ADMISSION REQUIREMENTS FOR FIRST-YEAR APPLICANTS. LSDAS law school report, LSAT, bachelor's degree from an accredited institution, personal statement, two recommendations, transcripts (must show all schools attended and at least three years of study) required in support of application. Applicants must have received bachelor's degree prior to enrollment. Interview not required but may be requested by school. In addition, international applicants whose native language is not English must submit TOEFL (not older than two years). Apply to Office of Admission after September 30, before May 1. First-year students admitted fall only. Rolling admissions process, notification starts in November and is finished by late April. Acceptance of offer and first deposit due date May 1. School does maintain a waiting list. Application fee $45. Phone: (603)228-1541. E-mail: admissions@FPLC.edu.

ADMISSION REQUIREMENTS FOR TRANSFER APPLICANTS. Accepts transfers from other ABA-accredited schools. Admission limited to space available. At least one year of enrollment, in good standing, LSAT, LSDAS, personal statement regarding reason for transfer, current law school transcript, undergraduate transcript required in support of application. Apply to Office of Admission; no official deadline. Admission decisions made by August 1. Application fee $45. Will consider visiting students.

ADMISSION REQUIREMENTS FOR M.I.P. (Degree is open to both nonlawyers and practicing attorneys, both U. S. and international applicants.) Official transcripts, two letters of recommendation required in support of M.I.P. application. Apply to Office of Graduate Program at least 2 months prior to expected date of entrance. Application fee $50.

ADMISSION STANDARDS. Number of full-time applicants 1,121; number accepted 533; number enrolled 151; median LSAT 155 (75% of class have a score at or above 148); median GPA 2.92 (A = 4) (75% of class have a GPA at or above 2.69). Attrition rate 6%. Gorman rating 2.60; *U.S. News & World Report* ranking is in the third tier of all law schools.

FINANCIAL AID. Merit scholarships, minority scholarships, grants-in-aid, private and institutional loans, federal loans, Federal WS. For scholarships (selection criteria place heavy reliance on LSAT and undergraduate GPA) apply to Director of Financial Aid after January 1, before February 1. Phone: (603)228-1541. Use Center's FA application. Use FAFSA for all federal programs (Title IV School code #G20979). Also submit Financial Aid Transcript, federal income tax form. Approximately 61% of first-year class received scholarships/grants-in-aid. Approximately 72% of current students receive some form of financial assistance. Average scholarship/grant $2,375. Average debt after graduation $56,300.

DEGREE REQUIREMENTS. For J.D.: 84 credits (39 required) with a 2.0 (A = 4) GPA, plus completion of upper divisional writing course; 3-year program: for M.I.P. 30 credits; research project (for non-U.S. students either an externship or substantial faculty-supervised paper).

CAREER AND PLACEMENT INFORMATION. About 12 employers conducted on-campus interviews. Approximately 32% of graduates are employed in state. More than 71% of graduates are practicing law; 19% are in business; 7% in government; 3% in academia. Approximately 73% of the Franklin Pierce Law Center's first-time state bar exam takers pass the New Hampshire Bar Exam; New Hampshire's passage rate for all first-time takers from ABA-approved schools is 73%.

GEORGE MASON UNIVERSITY
Fairfax, Virginia 22030-4444
Internet site: http://www.gmu.edu

Established as a branch of the University of Virginia in 1957, became independent in 1972. Public control. Semester system. Library: 1,635,000 volumes; 1,683,000 microforms; 9,233 periodicals/subscriptions.

University's other graduate colleges/schools: College of Arts and Sciences, College of Nursing and Health Sciences, Graduate College of Education, Institute for Computational Sciences and Informatics, Institute for Conflict Analysis and Resolution, Institute of Graduate and Professional Business Studies, Institute of Public Policy, Institute of the Arts, International Institute, School of Information Technology and Engineering.

Total university enrollment: 24,170.

School of Law
3401 N. Fairfax Drive
Arlington, Virginia 22201-4498
Phone: (703)993-8000
Internet site: http://www.gmu.edu/departments/law

Established 1979. Located in Arlington, Virginia just a Metro ride away from Washington, D.C. ABA approved since 1980. AALS member. Semester system. Full-time, part-time study. Law library: 324,000 volumes/microforms; 4,665 current periodicals/subscriptions; 21 computer workstations; has LEXIS, NEXIS, WESTLAW. Special areas of concentration; Corporate and Securities Law, Intellectual Property Law, Litigation Law, Regulatory Law. Special program: externships.

Annual tuition: resident, full-time $7,448, part-time $17,990; per credit, resident $260, nonresident $641. No on-campus housing available. Law students live off-campus. Contact Admissions Office for off-campus information. Off-campus housing and personal expenses: approximately $14,953. Additional costs: books approximately $700.

Enrollment: first-year class 216; total full-time 372, part-time 319 (men 62%, women 38%). First-year statistics: 14% out of state, 27 states and foreign countries represented; 38% women; 10% minority; average age 28; 208 undergraduate institutions represented; range of first-year section sizes (full-time) 24–151 students, (part-time) 25–69 students; number of upper division courses offered after first year 58 (full-time), 74 (part-time).

Faculty: full-time 33, part-time 28; 15% female; 7% minority; student/faculty ratio 18.7 to 1.

Degrees conferred: J.D.

RECRUITMENT PRACTICES AND POLICIES. Attends several national law school forums. On-campus informational sessions. School does have diversity program and actively recruits women/minority applicants.

ADMISSION REQUIREMENTS FOR FIRST-YEAR APPLICANTS. LSDAS law school report, LSAT (not later than February test date, if more than one LSAT, highest is used), bachelor's degree from an accredited institution, personal statement, two recommendations, transcripts (must show all schools attended and at least three years of study) required in support of application. Applicants must have received bachelor's degree prior to enrollment. Interview may be scheduled after acceptance. In addition, international applicants must submit TOEFL (not older than two years), and Certificate of Verification that degree is equivalent to a U.S. undergraduate degree. Apply to Assistant Dean for Admission after September

1, before March 1. First-year students admitted fall only. Rolling admission process, notification starts in January and is finished by June. Application fee $35. Phone: (703)993-8010. Fax: (703)993-8088.

ADMISSION REQUIREMENTS FOR TRANSFER APPLICANTS. Accepts transfers from other ABA-accredited schools. Admission limited to space available. At least one year of enrollment, dean's letter indicating applicant is in good standing (prefer applicants in the top quarter of first-year class), LSAT, LSDAS, personal statement regarding reason for transfer, two letters of recommendation, current law school transcript required in support of application. Apply to Admission Office by July 1. Admission decisions made by early August. Application fee $35. Will consider visiting students.

ADMISSION STANDARDS. Number of full-time applicants 1,540, part-time 483; number accepted full-time 608, part-time 163; number enrolled full-time 148, part-time 68; median LSAT 159 (75% of class have a score at or above 157 (full-time), 158 (part-time); median GPA 3.05 (A = 4) (75% of class have a GPA at or above 2.87 [full-time] 2.71 [part-time]). Attrition rate 2%. Gorman rating 2.73; *U.S. News & World Report* ranking in the second tier of all law schools.

FINANCIAL AID. Merit scholarships, private loans, federal loans. For scholarships (selection criteria place heavy reliance on LSAT and undergraduate GPA) apply to Associate Director of Financial Aid after January 1, before March 1. Phone: (703)993-2353. Use FAFSA for all federal programs (Title IV School code #003749). Also submit Financial Aid Transcript, federal income tax form. Approximately 4% (full-time), 3.8% (part-time) of first-year class received scholarships. Approximately 47% of current students receive some form of financial assistance. Average scholarship/grant $5,000 (full-time), $2,500 (part-time).

DEGREE REQUIREMENTS. For J.D.: 90 credits (41 required) with a 2.0 (A = 4) GPA, plus completion of upper divisional writing course; 3-year full-time program, 4-year part-time program.

CAREER AND PLACEMENT INFORMATION. About 26 employers conducted on-campus interviews. Approximately 52% of graduates are employed in state. More than 52% of graduates are practicing law; 18% are in business; 30% in government; none in academia. Approximately 80% of George Mason University's first-time state bar exam takers pass the Virginia Bar Exam; Virginia's passage rate for all first-time takers from ABA-approved schools is 76%.

GEORGE WASHINGTON UNIVERSITY
Washington, D.C. 20052
Internet site: http://www.gwu.edu

Founded 1821. Located in downtown Washington. Private control. Semester system. Library: 1,760,000 volumes; 2,016,600 microforms; 14,000 periodicals/subscriptions; 160 computer work- stations.

University's other graduate colleges/schools: Columbia College of Arts and Sciences, Elliot School of International Affairs, Graduate School of Education and Human Development, School of Business and Public Policy, School of Engineering and Applied Sciences, School of Medical and Health Sciences.

Total university enrollment: 19,670.

School of Law
2003 G Street, N.W.
Washington, D.C. 20052
Phone: (202)994-7230
Internet site: http://www.law.gwu
E-mail: jd@admit.nlc.gwu.edu

Established 1865. Located on main campus. ABA approved since 1923. AALS member. Semester system. Full-time, part-time study. Law library: 477,000 volumes/microforms; 5,732 current periodicals/subscriptions; 123 computer workstations; has LEXIS, NEXIS, WESTLAW, DIALOG, OCLC, ALADIN. Special programs: externships.

Annual tuition: full-time $22,959, part-time $16,200. Law students live off-campus. Contact Admissions Office for off-campus information. Phone: (202)944-7230. Off-campus housing and personal expenses: approximately $13,672. Additional costs: books approximately $700.

Enrollment: first-year class 453; total full-time 1,274, part-time 212 (men 55%, women 45%). First-year statistics: 94% out of state, 42 states and 6 foreign countries represented; 45% women; 30% minority; average age 24; 211 undergraduate institutions represented; average first-year section sizes (full-time) 90 students, (part-time) 50 students; number of upper division courses offered after first year 108 (full-time), 89 (part-time).

Faculty: full-time 67, part-time 176; 33% female; 9% minority; student/faculty ratio 18 to 1.

Degrees conferred: J.D., J.D.-M.B.A., J.D.-M.P.A., J.D.-M.A., J.D.-M.H.S.A., J.D.-M.P.H., LL.M. (General,

Environmental Law, Intellectual Property Law, Government Procurement Law), LL.M. (International and Comparative Law for persons who have completed a basic legal education and received a university degree in law in another country), LL.M.-M.P.A., S.J.D.

RECRUITMENT PRACTICES AND POLICIES. Attends national law school forums. On-campus informational sessions. School does have diversity program and actively recruits women/minority applicants.

ADMISSION REQUIREMENTS FOR FIRST-YEAR APPLICANTS. LSDAS law school report, LSAT (not later than December test date, if more than one LSAT, average is used), bachelor's degree from an accredited institution, personal statement, two recommendations, transcripts (must show all schools attended and at least three years of study) required in support of application. Applicants must have received bachelor's degree prior to enrollment. Personal information sessions may be requested but will have no bearing on admission decision. In addition, international applicants must submit TOEFL (not older than two years). Joint-degree applicants must apply to and be accepted by both schools. Apply to Office of Admission after September 30, before March 1. First-year students admitted fall only. Rolling admission process, notification starts in mid January and is finished by late April. School does maintain a waiting list. Application fee $55. Phone: (202)994-7230. E-mail: jd@admit.nlc.gwu.edu.

ADMISSION REQUIREMENTS FOR TRANSFER APPLICANTS. Accepts transfers from other ABA-accredited schools. Admission limited to space available. At least one year of enrollment, dean's letter indicating applicant is in good standing, LSAT, LSDAS, personal statement regarding reason for transfer, current law school transcript required in support of application. Apply to Admission Office by July 1 (fall), December 1 (spring). Admission decisions made within six weeks. Application fee $55. Will consider visiting students.

ADMISSIONS REQUIREMENTS FOR LL.M. DEGREE APPLICANTS. Official transcripts, résumé showing relevant work experience, personal statement indicating a clear demonstration of interest in a subject area required in support of application. Apply to the Graduate Programs Office June 1 (fall), November 1 (spring). Phone: (202)944-4500. E-mail: grad@main. nlc.gwu.edu. For LL.M. (International and Comparative Law): an earned law degree from a duly accredited law

faculty of a foreign university, two recommendations, TOEFL (score of 600) required for applicants whose native language is not English, official transcript signed and with seal of the registrar of the university attended required in support of graduate applicants. Admits fall only. Apply by May 1 to International Legal Studies Program. Phone: (202)944-7242. E-mail: ils@main. nlc.gwu.edu.

ADMISSION STANDARDS. Number of applicants 6,500; number accepted 1,922; number enrolled full-time 395, part-time 54; median LSAT 161 (75% of class have a score at or above 159 full-time, 155 part-time); median GPA 3.42 (A = 4) (75% of class have a GPA at or above 3.24 full-time, 2.90 part-time). Attrition rate 1.8%. Gorman rating 4.39; *U.S. News & World Report* ranking is in the top 30 of all law schools.

FINANCIAL AID. Scholarships, minority scholarships, private and institutional loans; federal loans and Federal WS offered through university's Financial Aid Office. Assistantships may be available for upper divisional joint-degree candidates. For scholarships (selection criteria place heavy reliance on LSAT and undergraduate GPA) apply to Committee on Student Financial Aid Office of the law school after January 1, before February 15. Phone: (202)944-6592. For all other programs apply to university's Office of Financial Aid. Phone: (202)944-6210. Use FAFSA for all federal programs (Title IV code #E00196). Also submit CSS profile, federal income tax form. Approximately 42% (full-time), 13% (part-time) of first-year class received scholarships/grants-in-aid. Approximately 79% of current students receive some form of financial assistance. Average scholarship/grant $8,000 (full-time), $2,000 (part-time). Average debt after graduation $67,000. Scholarships and fellowships are available for master's and doctoral programs. Apply by March 1 to law school's Financial Aid Office; submit letter with biographical data, information concerning practice, teaching or any other information that will be of assistance to the selection committee for the Loan Reimbursement Assistance Program for students who enter public interest employment.

DEGREE REQUIREMENTS. For J.D.: 84 credits (32 required) with a 2.0 (A = 4) GPA, plus completion of upper divisional writing course; 3-year full-time program, 4-year part-time program. Accelerated J.D. with 1 summer of course work. For J.D.-master's: a maximum of 6 credits can be applied to J.D. For LL.M.: 24 credits; a GPA of 2.67 (A = 4) required; thesis; 1 calendar year full-time, 2 calendar years part-time. For LL.M. (foreign law school graduates): 1 full year in residence; a GPA of 2.33 (A = 4) required; thesis/nonthesis option.

CAREER AND PLACEMENT INFORMATION. About 342 employers conducted on-campus interviews. Approximately 49% of graduates are employed in the District of Columbia. More than 72% of graduates are practicing law; 8% are in business; 19% in government; 1% in academia. Approximately 89% (MD), 92% (NY) of George Washington University's first-time state bar exam takers pass the bar exam; the passage rate for all first-time takers from ABA-approved schools is 75% (MD),78% (NY). Graduates are eligible to take the bar exam in all 50 states.

GEORGETOWN UNIVERSITY
Washington, D.C. 20057
Internet site: http://www.georgetown.edu

Founded 1789. Private control (Roman Catholic—Jesuit affiliation). Semester system. Library: 2,070,000 volumes; 2,747,000 microforms; 26,470 periodicals/subscriptions.

University's other graduate colleges/schools: Center for German and European Studies, Edmund A. Walsh School of Foreign Service, School of Business, School of Nursing, School of Medicine.

Total university enrollment: 12,618.

Law Center
600 New Jersey Avenue, N.W.
Washington, D.C. 20057
Phone: (202)662-9000
Internet site: http://www.law.georgetown.edu/lc
E-mail: admis@law.georgetown.edu

Established 1870. Located in an urban area of Washington. ABA approved since 1924. AALS member. Semester system. Full-time, part-time study. Law library: 861,200 volumes/microforms; 12,100 current periodicals/subscriptions; 125 computer workstations; has LEXIS, NEXIS, WESTLAW, DIALOG, OCLC. Special facility: Center for Applied Legal Studies. Special programs: Public Interest Law Scholars Program; externships; summer abroad programs in Florence, Italy, Heidelberg, Germany.

Annual tuition: full-time $23,375. On-campus housing available for both single and married students. Annual on-campus housing cost: $14,575. Housing deadline May 1. Contact Office of Student Affairs for both on- and off-campus housing information. Phone: (202)687-4560. E-mail: housing@law.georgetown.edu. First-year law students can live off-campus. Off-campus housing and personal expenses: approximately $14,575. Additional costs: books approximately $700.

Enrollment: first-year class 568 full-time, 131 part-time; total full-time 1,626, 486 part-time (men 54%, women 46%). First-year statistics: 95% out of state, 47 states and 6 foreign countries represented; 46% women; 24% minority; average age 24; 222 undergraduate institutions represented; range of first-year section sizes 32–125 students; number of upper division courses offered after first year 152 full-time, 108 part-time.

Faculty: full-time 88, part-time 178; 23% female; 8% minority; student/faculty ratio 18 to 1.

Degrees conferred: J.D., J.D.-M.B.A., J.D.-M.P.H. (Johns Hopkins University), J.D.-M.S.F.S., J.D.-M.A. (Philosophy), J.D.-Government, LL.M. (General, Advocacy, International and Comparative Law, Labor and Employment Law, Securities and Financial Regulations, Taxation), LL.M. (foreign attorneys who have completed a basic legal education and received a university degree in law in another country), S.J.D.

RECRUITMENT PRACTICES AND POLICIES. Attends national law school forums. On-campus informational sessions. School does have diversity program and actively recruits women/minority applicants.

ADMISSION REQUIREMENTS FOR FIRST-YEAR APPLICANTS. LSDAS law school report, LSAT (not later than December test date, if more than one LSAT, average is used), bachelor's degree from an accredited institution, personal statement, two recommendations, transcripts (must show all schools attended and at least three years of study) required in support of application. Applicants must have received bachelor's degree prior to enrollment. Interviews not required. Visits are encouraged but are not weighted by admissions committee. In addition, international applicants whose native language is not English must submit TOEFL (not older than two years). For joint degree, applicants must apply to and be accepted by both schools and should take appropriate test, i.e., GMAT, GRE. Apply to Assistant Dean for Admission after September 1, before February 1 full-time, March 1 part-time. First-year students admitted fall only. Rolling admission process, notification starts in December and is finished by mid April. Acceptance of offer and first deposit due date May 1. Application fee $60. Phone: (202)662-9010. E-mail: admis@law.georgetown.edu.

ADMISSION REQUIREMENTS FOR TRANSFER APPLICANTS. Accepts transfers from other ABA-accredited schools. Admission limited to space available.

At least one year of enrollment, dean's letter indicating applicant is in good standing, Law Center's Questionnaire, LSAT, LSDAS, personal statement regarding reason for transfer, two appraisals from current law school faculty member, current law school transcript required in support of application. Apply to Admission Office after June 1, before July 15. Admission decisions made by mid August. Application fee $60. Will consider visiting students.

ADMISSION STANDARDS. Number of full-time applicants 6,870 full-time, 660 part-time; number accepted 1,924 full-time, 230 part-time; number enrolled 568 full-time, 131 part-time; median LSAT 166 (75% of class have a score at or above 161 full-time, 160 part-time); median GPA 3.5 (A = 4) (75% of class have a GPA at or above 3.24 full-time, 3.10 part-time). Attrition rate 0.3%. Gorman rating 4.69; *U.S. News & World Report* ranking is in the top 15 law schools.

FINANCIAL AID. All financial aid is need based: a combination of federal, private, and school loans, scholarships, and Federal WS. Apply to Law Center's Financial Aid Office after January 1, before March 1. Phone: (202)662-9210. Use FAFSA for all federal programs (Title IV School code #G21075). Also submit Financial Aid Transcript, federal income tax forms, Access Disk. Approximately 30% full-time, 0.6% part-time of first-year class received scholarships/grants-in-aid. Approximately 73% of current students receive some form of financial assistance. Average scholarship/grant $8,200 full-time, $5,800 part-time. Loan Repayment Assistance Program available. Financial Aid available for part-time students and scholarships and graduate fellowships for LL.M. students.

DEGREE REQUIREMENTS. For J.D.: 83 credits (31 required) with a 2.0 (A = 4) GPA, plus completion of upper divisional writing course; 3-year full-time program, 4-year part-time program. For J.D.-M.B.A.: 122 total credits (J.D. 74 credits, M.B.A. 48 credits). For J.D.-M.P.H.: 4-year programs rather than the usual 5 years needed if both degrees taken separately. For J.D.-M.A.: 98 total credits (J.D. 74 credits, M.A. 24 credits). For J.D.-M.S.F.S.: 113 total credits (J.D. 74 credits, M.S.F.S. 39 credits). For LL.M.: 24 credits minimum all in full-time residency; minimum weighted GPA of 6.00 (scale 0–12); major paper (in the candidate's field of study) of publishable quality. For S.J.D.: exceptional students may be admitted to this degree; degree fulfillment is determined by faculty members involved with student's research proposal; dissertation of publishable quality; oral defense.

CAREER AND PLACEMENT INFORMATION. About 200 employers conducted on-campus interviews. Approximately 48% of graduates are employed in Maryland and D.C. More than 80% of graduates are practicing law; 8% are in business; 11% in government; 1% in academia. Approximately 91% (MD), 82% (NY) of Georgetown University's first-time state bar exam takers pass the bar exam; the passage rate for all first-time takers from ABA-approved schools is 78% (MD), 78% (NY). Graduates are eligible to take the bar exam in all 50 states.

GEORGIA STATE UNIVERSITY
Atlanta, Georgia 30303-3093
Internet site: http://www.gsu.edu

Founded 1913. Public control. Quarter system. Library: 1,245,600 volumes; 260,000 microforms; 11,270 periodicals/subscriptions.

University's other graduate colleges/schools: College of Arts and Sciences, College of Business Administration, College of Education, College of Health Sciences, College of Public and Urban Affairs.

Total university enrollment: 24,300.

College of Law
P.O. Box 4099
Atlanta, Georgia 30302-4037
Phone: (404)651-2096
Internet site: http://www.gsulaw.gsu.edu
E-mail: admission@gsulaw.gsu.edu

Established 1982. Located in downtown Atlanta. ABA approved since 1984. AALS member. Semester system. Full-time, part-time study. Law library: 255,400 volumes/microforms; 3,550 current periodicals/subscriptions; 16 computer workstations; has LEXIS, NEXIS, WESTLAW, DIALOG, OLLI. Special programs: externships.

Annual tuition: full-time resident $3,345, nonresident $10,429; part-time resident $2,537, nonresident $7,597. No on-campus housing available. Law students live in off-campus housing, Olympic Village is nearby. Contact Admission Office for off-campus information. Off-campus housing and personal expenses: approximately $12,705. Additional costs: books approximately $700.

Enrollment: first-year class full-time 153, part-time 65; total full-time 441, part-time 223 (men 52%, women 48%). First-year statistics: 10% out of state, 48% women; 25% minority; average age 29; range of first-year section sizes 16–133 students; number of upper division courses offered after first year full-time 70, part-time 62.

Faculty: full-time 41, part-time 30; 33% female; 15% minority; student/faculty ratio 17 to 1.

Degrees conferred: J.D., J.D.-M.B.A., J.D.-M.P.A.

RECRUITMENT PRACTICES AND POLICIES. Attends local and selected national law school forums. Has on-campus informational sessions. School does have diversity program and actively recruits women/minority applicants.

ADMISSION REQUIREMENTS FOR FIRST-YEAR APPLICANTS. LSDAS law school report, LSAT (not later than February test date, if more than one LSAT, highest is used), bachelor's degree from an accredited institution, personal statement, two recommendations, transcripts (must show all schools attended and at least three years of study) required in support of application. Applicants must have received bachelor's degree prior to enrollment. Interview not required; visit to campus are encouraged. In addition, international applicants whose native language is not English must submit TOEFL (not older than two years), certified translations and evaluation of all foreign credentials. Apply to Office of Admission after October 1, before March 15, February 1 (international applicants). First-year students admitted fall only. Rolling admission process, notification starts in January and continues until class is filled, generally mid May. Application fee $30. Phone: (404)651-2048. E-mail: admissions@gsulaw.gsu.edu.

ADMISSION REQUIREMENTS FOR TRANSFER APPLICANTS. Accepts transfers from other ABA-accredited schools. Admission limited to space available. At least one year of enrollment, dean's letter indicating applicant is in good standing (prefer applicants in the upper half of first-year class), LSAT, LSDAS, personal statement regarding reason for transfer, two letters of recommendation from current law school professors, current law school transcript required in support of application. Admits fall and spring. Apply to Admission Office by July 1 (fall), December 1 (spring). Admission decisions made within one month of the receipt of a completed application. Application fee $30. Will consider visiting students.

ADMISSION STANDARDS. Number of full-time applicants 2,020, part-time 338; number accepted 466 full-time, 84 part-time; number enrolled 153 full-time, 65 part-time; median LSAT 157 (75% of class have a score at or above 154 full-time, 153 part-time); median GPA 3.20 (A = 4) (75% of class have a GPA at or above 2.92

full-time, 2.90 part-time). Attrition rate 6.8%. Gorman rating 2.12; *U.S. News & World Report* ranking is in the third tier of all law schools.

FINANCIAL AID. Need based scholarships, merit scholarships, fee waivers, Regents Opportunity Scholarships, private loans; federal loans and Federal WS offered through university's Financial Aid Office. Assistantships may be available for upper divisional joint-degree candidates. All accepted students are automatically considered for scholarships, fee waivers (selection criteria place heavy reliance on LSAT and undergraduate GPA). For all other programs apply as soon as possible after January to university's Office of Student Financial Aid. Use university's financial aid application. Phone: (404)651-2227. Submit FAFSA for all federal programs (Title IV School code #001574). Also submit Financial Aid Transcript, federal income tax forms. Approximately 5% (full-time), 2% (part-time) of first-year class received scholarships/grants-in-aid. Approximately 45% of current students receive some form of financial assistance. Average scholarship/grant $1,634 (full-time), $1,313 (part-time).

DEGREE REQUIREMENTS. For J.D.: 90 credits (44 required) with a 70 (scale 0–100) GPA, plus completion of upper divisional writing course; 3-year program, 4-year part-time program. Accelerated J.D. with summer course work. For J.D.-M.B.A., M.P.A.: 4-year programs rather than the usual 5-year programs needed if both degrees taken separately. The College of Law will accept up to 14 credits toward degree, other graduate degree programs will accept up to 20 quarter hours.

CAREER AND PLACEMENT INFORMATION. About 40–45 employers conducted on-campus interviews. Approximately 92% of graduates are employed in state. More than 63% of graduates are practicing law; 22% are in business; 14% in government; 1% in academia. Approximately 94% of Georgia State University's first-time state bar exam takers pass the Georgia Bar Exam; Georgia's passage rate for all first-time takers from ABA-approved schools is 81%. Graduates are eligible to take the bar exam in all 50 states.

UNIVERSITY OF GEORGIA
Athens, Georgia 30602
Internet site: http://www.uga.edu

Founded 1785. Located in NE Georgia. Public control. Quarter system. Library: 3,300,000 volumes; 5,400,000 microforms; 48,100 periodicals/subscriptions; 252 computer workstations.

University's other graduate colleges/schools: College of Agriculture and Environmental Sciences, College of Arts and Sciences, College of Education, College of Environmental Design, College of Family and Consumer Sciences, School of Forest Resources, School of Journalism and Mass Communication, School of Social Work, Terry College of Business; College of Pharmacy; College of Veterinary Medicine.

Total university enrollment: 30,100.

School of Law

Athens, Georgia 30602-6012
Phone: (706)542-7140.
Internet site: http://www.lawsch.uga.edu
E-mail: jd_admissions@jd.lawsch.uga.edu

Established 1859. Located on main campus. ABA approved since 1930. AALS member. Semester system. Full-time, day study only. Law library: 458,200 volumes/microforms; 6,664 current periodicals/subscriptions; 68 computer workstations; has LEXIS, NEXIS, WESTLAW, INFOTRAC, INNOPAC; specialized European Documentation Center and Select Depository for the European Union. Special facility: Dean Rusk Center for International and Comparative Law. Special programs: summer study abroad in Belgium and England; summer clerkships; externships.

Annual tuition: resident $3,757, nonresident $12,357. On-campus housing available for both single and married students. Annual on-campus housing cost: $6,679 (room only, three quarters). Contact Department of University Housing for both on- and off-campus housing information. Phone: (706)542-1421. For family housing information contact the Office of Family Housing. Phone: (706)542-1473. Law students tend to live off-campus. Off-campus housing and personal expenses: approximately $9,328. Additional costs: books approximately $700.

Enrollment: first-year class 236; total full-time 635 (men 57%, women 43%); no part-time students. First-year statistics: 25% out of state, 26 states and foreign countries represented; 43% women; 13% minority; average age 24; 99 undergraduate institutions represented; range of first-year section sizes 10–120 students; number of upper division courses offered after first year 132.

Faculty: full-time 42, part-time 27; 29% female; 6% minority; student/faculty ratio 18.8 to 1.

Degrees conferred: J.D., J.D.-M.B.A., J.D.-M.H.P., LL.M. (About 20 candidates are enrolled each year.)

RECRUITMENT PRACTICES AND POLICIES. Attends local and national law school forums. Has on-campus informational sessions. School does have diversity program and actively recruits women/minority applicants.

ADMISSION REQUIREMENTS FOR FIRST-YEAR APPLICANTS. LSDAS law school report, LSAT (not later than December test date, if more than one LSAT, average is used), bachelor's degree from an accredited institution, personal statement, two recommendations, transcripts (must show all schools attended and at least three years of study) required in support of application. Applicants must have received bachelor's degree prior to enrollment. In addition, international applicants whose native language is not English must submit TOEFL (not older than two years), submit certified translations and evaluations of all foreign credentials. Applicants for either a joint-degree program or a concurrent-degree program must apply to and be accepted by each school. Apply to Director of Law Admission after September 30, before March 1. Apply by January 31 for scholarship consideration. First-year students admitted fall only. Rolling admission process, notification starts in November and is finished by late April. Application fee $30. Phone: (706)542-7060. E-mail: jd_admissions@jd.lawsch.uga.edu.

ADMISSION REQUIREMENTS FOR TRANSFER APPLICANTS. Accepts transfers from other ABA-accredited schools. Admission limited to space available. At least one year of enrollment, dean's letter indicating the applicant is in good standing (prefer applicants in the top quarter of first-year class), LSAT, LSDAS (certified copies acceptable), personal statement regarding reason for transfer, two letters of recommendation, official final undergraduate transcripts, current law school transcript required in support of application. Apply to Admission Office by July 1 (fall), application must be completed by July 15; November 15 (spring), application must be completed by December 1. Admission decisions within two weeks after application is completed. Application fee $30. Will consider visiting students.

ADMISSIONS REQUIREMENTS FOR LL.M. APPLICANTS. All applicants must hold either a J.D. from an ABA-accredited law school or from an AALS member law school or hold a degree equivalent to an American J.D. from a recognized international law school and have an academic record and study program acceptable to the law school faculty. Official transcripts (in English and the language of the institution), LSAT score report for U.S. law applicants, professional statement, a list of proposed courses and thesis research topic, financial assistance request, three letters of recommendation required in support of LL.M. application. In addition, TOEFL required for all applicants whose native language is not English, and certification of finances. Admits fall only. Apply before March 31 to the Director of International and Graduate Legal Studies. Application fee $30. Phone: (706)542-5211. Fax: (706)542-5556.

ADMISSION STANDARDS. Number of full-time applicants 2,314; number accepted 591; number enrolled 236; median LSAT 162 (75% of class have a score at or above 158); median GPA 3.43 (A = 4) (75% of class have a GPA at or above 3.23). Attrition rate 2.5%. Gorman rating 3.87; *U.S. News & World Report* ranking is in the top 30 of all law schools.

FINANCIAL AID. Scholarships, merit scholarships, minority scholarships, grants-in-aid, institutional loans; federal loans and Federal WS offered through university's Financial Aid Office. Assistantships may be available for upper divisional joint-degree candidates. For scholarships (selection criteria place heavy reliance on LSAT and undergraduate GPA) apply to Admissions Office by January 31. Phone: (706)542-7060. For all other programs apply to university's Office of Financial Aid. Phone: (706)542-6147. Submit FAFSA for all federal programs (Title IV School code #001598). Also submit Financial Aid Transcript, federal income tax forms. Approximately 25% of first-year class received scholarships/grants-in-aid. Approximately 71% of current students receive some form of financial assistance. Average scholarship/grant $2,500.

For LL.M. students: assistantships, waiver of out-of-state tuition, loans available for qualified candidates. Contact the Director of International and Graduate Legal Studies for specific financial need requirements.

DEGREE REQUIREMENTS. For J.D.: 88 credits (33 required) with a 2.0 (A = 4) GPA, plus completion of upper divisional writing course, one course in legal professions; 3-year program. Accelerated J.D. with summer course work. For J.D.-M.B.A., M.H.P.: 4-year programs rather than the usual 5 years needed if degrees taken separately. For LL.M.: individually designed programs; 27 credits, at least 2 semesters in full-time residence; thesis; degree approval; a 2.5 (A = 4) overall GPA, 3.0 GPA for thesis.

CAREER AND PLACEMENT INFORMATION. About 50–60 employers conducted on-campus interviews. Approximately 78% of graduates are employed in state. More than 79% of graduates are practicing law; 6% are in business; 13% in government; 2% in academia. Approximately 93% of the University of Georgia's first-time state bar exam takers pass the Georgia Bar Exam; Georgia's passage rate for all first-time takers from ABA-approved schools is 81%. Graduates are eligible to take the bar exam in all 50 states.

GOLDEN GATE UNIVERSITY
San Francisco, California 94105-2968
Internet site: http://www.ggu.edu

Founded 1853. Located in downtown San Francisco in the legal and financial district. Private control. Trimester system. Library: 260,000 volumes; 709 microforms; 1,500 periodicals/subscriptions; 25 computer workstations.

University's other graduate colleges/schools: College of Arts and Sciences, School of Business, School of Taxation, School of Technology and Industry, School of Urban and Public Policy.

Total university enrollment: 6,360.

School of Law
536 Mission Street
San Francisco, California 94105-2968
Phone: (415)442-6600
Internet site: http://www.ggu.edu/law
E-mail: lawadmit@ggu.edu

Established 1901. Located on main campus. ABA approved since 1956. AALS member. Trimester system. Full-time, part-time study. Law library: 226,000 volumes/microforms; 3,200 current periodicals/subscriptions; 54 computer workstations; has LEXIS, WESTLAW, CALI. Special programs: summer study abroad at Chulalongkorn University (Thailand), University of Malta, (Malta); externships.

Annual tuition: full-time $19,074, part-time $13,224. No on-campus housing available. Law students live off-campus. Contact University Student Services Office for off-campus information. Off-campus housing and personal expenses: approximately $11,030. Additional costs: books approximately $700.

Enrollment: first-year class, full-time 187, part-time 72; total full-time 453, part-time 260 (men 47%, women 53%). First-year statistics: 27% out of state, 39 states and foreign countries represented; 53% women; 21% minority; average age 26; 221 undergraduate institutions represented; range of first-year section sizes 26–58 students; number of upper division courses offered after first year 95 (full-time), 34 (part-time).

Faculty: full-time 36, part-time 115; 39% female; 16% minority; student/faculty ratio 15.8 to 1.

Degrees conferred: J.D., J.D.-M.B.A. (Financial Accounting, Health Services, Human Resources, International Management), J.D.-M.P.A. (International Public Services, Health Services), J.D.-TAX, J.D.-M.A. (International Relations), LL.M. (Tax), LL.M. (International Legal Studies, for persons who have completed a basic legal education and received a university degree in law in another country).

RECRUITMENT PRACTICES AND POLICIES. Attends several national law school forums. On-campus informational sessions. School does have diversity program and actively recruits women/minority applicants.

ADMISSION REQUIREMENTS FOR FIRST-YEAR APPLICANTS. LSDAS law school report, LSAT (not later than February [fall], June [mid-year]) test date, if more than one LSAT, highest is used), bachelor's degree from an accredited institution, personal statement, one recommendation, transcripts (must show all schools attended and at least three years of study) required in support of application. Applicants must have received bachelor's degree prior to enrollment. Interview not required; campus and class visitations are encouraged. In addition, international applicants whose native language is not English must submit TOEFL (not older than two years), translations and evaluation of all transcripts from non U.S. schools. Applicants interested in joint-degree programs apply after completing the first trimester of law school. Apply to Office of Admission before April 15 (fall), November 15 (mid year). First-year students admitted both fall and midyear. Rolling admission process. Application fee $40. Phone: (415)442-6630. E-mail: lawadmit@ggu.edu.

ADMISSION REQUIREMENTS FOR TRANSFER APPLICANTS. Accepts transfers from other ABA-accredited schools. Admission limited to space available. At least one year of enrollment, dean's letter indicating applicant is in good standing, a letter of recommendation from a law professor, LSAT, LSDAS, personal statement regarding reason for transfer, current law school transcript required in support of application. Apply to Admission Office by June 1 (fall), December 1 (mid-year). Admission decisions made by late July (fall), early January (mid-year). Application fee $40. Will consider visiting students.

ADMISSION REQUIREMENTS FOR LL.M. APPLICANTS. Official transcripts, proficiency in English (International Legal Studies), personal statement, one letter of recommendation required in support of graduate application. Interview is not required but may be requested. In addition, application with a degree in law from a foreign law school or university must demonstrate that academic credentials are comparable to graduates of an American law school. Apply before July 1 (fall), November 1 (mid-year) to LL.M. in Taxation Program or LL.M. in International Legal Studies. Phone: (415)442-6605 (Tax), (800)-4-TAX-LLM; (415)442-6633 (International Legal Studies). Late applicants will be considered for both programs on a space-available basis.

ADMISSION STANDARDS. Number of full-time applicants full-time 2,065, part-time 274; number accepted 1,153 full-time, 148 (part-time); number enrolled 187 (full-time), 72 (part-time); median LSAT 154 (75% of class have a score at or above 149 [full-time], 150 [part-time]); median GPA 3.02 (A = 4) (75% of class have a GPA at or above 2.76 [full-time], 2.72 [part-time]). Attrition rate 13%. Gorman rating 3.43; *U.S. News & World Report* ranking is in the fourth tier of all law schools.

FINANCIAL AID. Scholarships, merit scholarships, minority scholarships, grants-in-aid, institutional loans; federal loans and Federal WS (for upper divisional students). For scholarships (selection criteria place heavy reliance on LSAT and undergraduate GPA) apply to Financial Aid Office after January 1, before March 1 (fall), October 1 (mid-year). Phone: (415)442-6635. Use FAFSA for all federal programs (Title IV School code #001205). Also submit Financial Aid Transcript, federal income tax forms. Approximately 25% (full-time), 22% (part-time) of first-year class received scholarships/grants-in-aid. Approximately 85% of current students receive some form of financial assistance. Average scholarship/grant $6,000 (full-time), $6,000 (part-time). Public Interest Loan Assistance Program available. Average debt after graduation $67,000. Financial assistance available for LL.M. students.

DEGREE REQUIREMENTS. For J.D.: 88 credits (54 required) with a 2.0 (A = 4) GPA, plus completion of upper divisional writing course; 3-year full-time program, 4-year part-time program. For J.D.-master's: each joint degree is individually designed and generally reduces the time needed to complete both degree by between 6 months and 1 year. For LL.M. (Tax): 27 credits, a GPA of 2.5 (A = 4) required; can be completed in 3 trimesters. For LL.M. (International Legal Studies): 24 credits; at least 2 trimesters in residence; a GPA of 2.5 (A = 4) required; seminar with a substantial paper; thesis option.

CAREER AND PLACEMENT INFORMATION. Approximately 80% of graduates are employed in state. More than 61% of graduates are practicing law; 23% are in business; 13% in government; 3% in academia. Approximately 77% of Golden Gate University's first-time state bar exam takers pass the California Bar Exam; California's passage rate for all first-time takers from ABA-approved schools is 83%.

GONZAGA UNIVERSITY
Spokane, Washington 99258
Internet site: http://www.gonzaga.edu

Founded 1887. Private control (Roman Catholic—Jesuit affiliation). Semester system. Library: 550,000 volumes; 290,000 microforms; 4,200 periodicals/subscriptions; 120 computer workstations.

University's other graduate colleges/schools: College of Arts and Sciences, School of Business, School of Education, School of Engineering, School of Professional Studies.

Total university enrollment: 3,950.

School of Law
P.O. Box 3528
Spokane, Washington 99220
Phone: (800)793-1710, (509)328-5532
Internet site: http://www.law.gonzaga.edu
E-mail: admission@lawschool.gonzaga.edu

Established 1912. Located in an urban area 1½ miles from downtown. ABA approved since 1951. AALS member. Semester system. Full-time study only. Law library: 214,000 volumes/microforms; 2,880 current periodicals/subscriptions; 74 computer workstations; has LEXIS, NEXIS, WESTLAW, DIALOG, CARL. Special programs: externships.

Annual tuition: $17,030. Limited on-campus housing available for both single and married students. Annual on-campus housing cost: single students $6,600 (room and board). Contact Housing and Residential Life Office for both on- and off-campus housing information. Phone: (509)328-4220, Ext. 2212. Law students tend to live off-campus. Off-campus housing and personal expenses: approximately $12,050. Additional costs: books approximately $950.

Enrollment: first-year class 169; total full-time 517 (men 63%, women 37%); 20 part-time students. First-year statistics: 63% out of state, 38 states and foreign countries represented; 37% women; 14% minority; average age 27; 208 undergraduate institutions represented;

range of first-year section sizes 50–80 students; number of upper division courses offered after first year 75.

Faculty: full-time 36, part-time 15; 26% female; 3% minority; student/faculty ratio 20 to 1.

Degrees conferred: J.D., J.D.-M.B.A., J.D.-M.Acc.

RECRUITMENT PRACTICES AND POLICIES. Attends national law school forums. On-campus informational sessions. School does have diversity program and actively recruits women/minority applicants.

ADMISSION REQUIREMENTS FOR FIRST-YEAR APPLICANTS. LSDAS law school report, LSAT (not later than February test date, if more than one LSAT, average is used), bachelor's degree from an accredited institution, personal statement, two recommendations, transcripts (must show all schools attended and at least three years of study) required in support of application. Applicants must have received bachelor's degree prior to enrollment. Interview not required; campus and class visits are strongly encouraged. In addition, international applicants must submit TOEFL (not older than two years), statement of financial support. (International applicants should contact International Student Program for more information. Phone: [509]328-4220, Ext. 3162). Apply to Office of Admission after September 30, before March 15. Joint-degree applicants must apply to School of Business as well and take the GMAT. First-year students admitted fall only. Rolling admission process, notification starts in January and is finished by late May. Application fee $40. Phone: (509)328-4220. E-mail: admissions@lawschool.edu.

ADMISSION REQUIREMENTS FOR TRANSFER APPLICANTS. Accepts transfers from other ABA-accredited schools. Admission limited to space available. At least one year of enrollment, dean's letter indicating applicant is in good standing, LSAT, LSDAS, personal statement regarding reason for transfer, two letters of recommendation, current law school transcript required in support of application. Apply to Admission Coordinator by June 1. Admission decisions made by mid July. Application fee $40. Will consider visiting students.

ADMISSION STANDARDS. Number of full-time applicants 1,198; number accepted 805; number enrolled 169; median LSAT 155 (75% of class have a score at or above 148); median GPA 3.09 (A = 4) (75% of class have a GPA at or above 2.7). Attrition rate 8.7%. Gorman rating 3.48; *U.S. News & World Report* ranking is in the fourth tier of all law schools.

FINANCIAL AID. Scholarships, merit scholarships, diversity scholarships, grants-in-aid, private loans; federal loans and Federal WS offered through university's Financial Aid Office. For scholarships (selection criteria place heavy reliance on LSAT and undergraduate GPA) apply to Admissions Coordinator Office after January 1, before May 1 (February 15 for scholarship applicants). Phone: (509)328-4220. For all other programs apply to university's Director of Financial Aid. Phone: (509)328-4220, Ext. 3782. Use FAFSA for all federal programs (Title IV School code #003778). Also submit Financial Aid Transcript, federal income tax forms. Approximately 18% of first-year class received scholarships/grants-in-aid. Approximately 90% of current students receive some form of financial assistance. Average scholarship/grant $5,000. Average debt after graduation $65,000.

DEGREE REQUIREMENTS. For J.D.: 90 credits (20 required) with a 2.2 (A = 4) GPA, plus completion of upper divisional writing course; 3-year program. For J.D.-M.B.A.: total 114 credits. For J.D.-M.Acc.: total 111 credits. This represents a reduction of 9 credits from the number required if both degrees were taken separately.

CAREER AND PLACEMENT INFORMATION. About 20 employers conducted on-campus interviews. Approximately 48% of graduates are employed in state. More than 68% of graduates are practicing law; 15% are in business; 17% in government; none in academia. Approximately 83% of Gonzaga University's first-time state bar exam takers pass the Washington State Bar Exam; Washington's passage rate for all first-time takers from ABA-approved schools is 83%.

HAMLINE UNIVERSITY
St. Paul, Minnesota 55104-1284
Internet site: http://www.hamline.edu

Founded 1854. Located in a residential area of St. Paul. Private control (United Methodist affiliation). Semester system. Library: 312,300 volumes; 167,000 microforms; 3,753 periodicals/subscriptions; 70 computer workstations.

University's other graduate schools: Education, Liberal Arts, Public Administration.

Total university enrollment: 4,144.

School of Law
1536 Hewitt Avenue
St. Paul, Minnesota 55104
Phone: (800)388-3688, (612)641-2461
Internet site: http://www.hamline.edu
E-mail: lawadm@seq.hamline.edu

Established 1972. Located near the state capital. ABA approved since 1975. AALS member. Semester system. Full-time, day study only. Law library: 229,000 volumes/microforms; 2,680 current periodicals/subscriptions; 23 computer workstations; has LEXIS, NEXIS, WESTLAW, DIALOG. Special programs: summer study abroad at Hebrew University of Jerusalem, Israel; summer program in Oslo, Norway; externships.

Annual tuition: $15,545. On-campus housing available for single students only. Annual on-campus housing cost: single students $4,840–$5,360 (room and board). Housing deadline June 1. Contact Office of Residential Life for both on- and off-campus housing information. Phone: (612)641-2061. Law students tend to live off-campus. Off-campus housing and personal expenses: approximately $10,120. Additional costs: books approximately $700.

Enrollment: first-year class 192; total full-time 514 (men 50%, women 50%); no part-time students. First-year statistics: 50% out of state, 47 states and foreign countries represented; 50% women; 11% minority; average age 27; 188 undergraduate institutions represented; range of first-year section sizes 40–75 students; number of upper division courses offered after first year 104.

Faculty: full-time 29, part-time 44; 41% female; 8% minority; student/faculty ratio 18 to 1.

Degrees conferred: J.D., J.D.-M.B.A. (University of St. Thomas), J.D.-M.A.P.A., LL.M. (only for persons who have completed a basic legal education and received a university degree in law in another country).

RECRUITMENT PRACTICES AND POLICIES. Attends national law school forums. On-campus informational sessions. School does have diversity program and actively recruits women/minority applicants.

ADMISSION REQUIREMENTS FOR FIRST-YEAR APPLICANTS. LSDAS law school report, LSAT (not later than December test date, if more than one LSAT, highest is used), bachelor's degree from an accredited institution, personal statement, two recommendations, transcripts (must show all schools attended and at least three years of study) required in support of application. Applicants must have received bachelor's degree prior to enrollment. Interview not required but visits to school encouraged. In addition, international applicants whose native language is not English must submit TOEFL (minimum score required 600). Applicants with foreign degrees must submit certified English translations. Dual-degree applications must apply to and be accepted by both schools. J.D.-M.B.A. candidates submit GMAT scores. Apply to Office of Admission after September 1, before May 15. First-year students admitted fall only. Rolling admission process, notification starts in November and is finished by June. Application fee $30. Phone: (800)338-3688, (612)641-2461. E-mail: lawadm@seq.hamline.edu.

ADMISSION REQUIREMENTS FOR TRANSFER APPLICANTS. Accepts transfers from other ABA-accredited schools. Admission limited to space available. At least one year of enrollment, in good standing, LSAT, LSDAS, personal statement regarding reason for transfer, current law school transcript required in support of application. Apply to Office of Admission by June 1. Admission decisions made by mid July. Application fee $30. Will consider visiting students.

ADMISSION REQUIREMENTS FOR LL.M. APPLICANTS. Applicants must have a law degree with high academic standing from a recognized foreign university. Proficiency in English, two letters of recommendation, a personal statement, an official or certified-true academic record with evaluation and explanation of transcript, proof of financial support required in support of LL.M. application. Apply at least two months prior to beginning of semester. Application fee $30.

ADMISSION STANDARDS. Number of full-time applicants 1,189; number accepted 647; number enrolled 192; median LSAT 154 (75% of class have a score at or above 148); median GPA 3.12 (A = 4) (75% of class have a GPA at or above 2.86). Attrition rate 4.9%. Gorman rating 2.76; *U.S. News & World Report* ranking is in the fourth tier of all law schools.

FINANCIAL AID. Merit scholarships, minority scholarships, grants-in-aid, United Methodist Student Loans, state loan program; federal loans and Federal WS offered through university's Financial Aid Office. Assistantships may be available for upper divisional joint-degree candidates. For scholarships (selection criteria place heavy reliance on LSAT and undergraduate GPA) apply to Admissions Office after January 1, before May 15. For all other programs apply to university's Director of Financial Aid. Phone: (612)641-2280. Use FAFSA for all federal programs (Title IV School code #002354). Also submit

Financial Aid Transcript, federal income tax forms. Approximately 23% of first-year class received scholarships/grants-in-aid. Approximately 90% of current students receive some form of financial assistance. Average scholarship/grant $5,500. Average debt after graduation $60,000.

DEGREE REQUIREMENTS. For J.D.: 88 credits (33 required) with a 2.0 (A = 4) GPA, plus completion of upper divisional writing course; 3-year program. Accelerated J.D. with 1 summer of course work. For J.D.-M.B.A., M.A.P.A: individually designed programs, the time needed to complete both degrees is reduced by up to 1 academic year. For LL.M. (foreign lawyers program): 30 credits; at least 2 semesters in residence; a GPA of 2.5 (A = 4) required.

CAREER AND PLACEMENT INFORMATION. About 25 employers conducted on-campus interviews. Approximately 78% of graduates are employed in state. More than 69% of graduates are practicing law; 24% are in business; 6% in government; 1% in academia. Approximately 83% (MN), 100% (WI) of Hamline University's first-time state bar exam takers pass the bar exam; the passage rate for all first-time takers from ABA-approved schools is 90% (MN), 83% (WI). Graduates are eligible to take the bar exam in all 50 states.

HARVARD UNIVERSITY
Cambridge, Massachusetts 02138
Internet site: http://www.harvard.edu

Founded 1636. Located in Cambridge. Private control. Semester system. Library: 13,143,000 volumes; 6,755,000 microforms; 6,775 periodicals/subscriptions.

University's other graduate schools: Divinity School, Graduate School of Arts and Sciences, Graduate School of Business Administration, Graduate School of Design, Graduate School of Education, J. F. K. School of Government, Medical School, School of Dentistry, School of Public Health.

Total university enrollment: 18,310.

Law School
1563 Massachusetts Avenue
Boston, Massachusetts 02138
Phone: (617)495-3109
Internet site: http://www.law.harvard

Established 1817. The oldest law school in the U.S. Located with most of the other units of the university in Cambridge. ABA approved since 1923. AALS member.

Semester system. Full-time, day study only. Law library: 1,888,500 volumes/microforms; 14,500 current periodicals/subscriptions; 77 computer workstations; has LEXIS, NEXIS, WESTLAW, DIALOG, OCLC, RLIN, Vu/Text, among others; is a Federal Government Depository. Special programs: Criminal Justice Institute, the East Asian Legal Studies Program, the Islamic Legal Studies Program, the Human Rights Program, the Program on International Financial Systems, the European Law Research Center, the Program in Law and Economics, the Program on the Legal Profession, the Program on Negotiation.

Annual tuition: $23,466. On-campus housing available for both single and married students. Annual on-campus housing (dormitories) cost: $12,695. Housing deadline May 1. Dormitory space allocated by lottery. Law students tend to live off-campus. Contact Harvard Real Estate, Inc. for off-campus information. Phone: (617)495-5060. Off-campus housing and personal expenses: approximately $12,695. Additional costs: books approximately $800.

Enrollment: first-year class 555; total full-time 1,646 (men 59%, women 41%); no part-time students. First-year statistics: 94% out of state, 49 states and 20 foreign countries represented; 41% women; 28% minority; average age 24; 275 undergraduate institutions represented; range of first-year section sizes 45–135 students; number of upper division courses offered after first year 216.

Faculty: full-time 140, part-time 44; 27% female; 22% minority; student/faculty ratio 21 to 1.

Degrees conferred: J.D., J.D.-M.B.A. (only joint degree, all others are concurrent-degree programs), J.D.-Ed.M., J.D.-M.P.A., J.D.-M.P.P., J.D.-M.A.L.D. (Fletcher School of Law and Diplomacy), J.D.-Ph.D., J.D.-M.Div., LL.M., S.J.D.

RECRUITMENT PRACTICES AND POLICIES. Attends national law school forums. School does have diversity program and actively recruits women/minority applicants.

ADMISSION REQUIREMENTS FOR FIRST-YEAR APPLICANTS. LSDAS law school report, LSAT (not later than December test date, if more than one LSAT, average is used), bachelor's degree from an accredited institution, personal statement, interview, two recommendations, transcripts (must show all schools attended and at least three years of study) required in support of application. Applicants must have received bachelor's degree prior to enrollment. In addition, international applicants whose native language is not English must submit TOEFL (not older than two years), TSE, TWE. Apply to Office of Admission after September 30, before February

1. First-year students admitted fall only. Rolling admission process, notification starts in November and is finished by late April. Acceptance of offer and first deposit due date after receipt of financial aid decision. School does maintain a waiting list. Application fee $60. Phone: (617)495-3109. Faxes will not be accepted. For information relative to concurrent-degree programs contact the Dean of Students Office.

ADMISSION REQUIREMENTS FOR TRANSFER APPLICANTS. Will consider transfers/visiting students from other ABA-accredited schools on a very limited basis. Usually it is a case of personal hardship. Apply by mid February.

ADMISSION REQUIREMENTS FOR LL.M., S.J.D. Official transcripts from U.S. law schools showing the awarding of the J.D. or its equivalent, personal statement. For international applicants, submit transcripts, evaluation, and certification that law degree is comparable to that of a U.S. law school. Contact Division of Graduate Studies, LILC 208 for LL.M. application, descriptive materials and current deadlines. For admissions and fellowship consideration apply by December 1 (U.S. and Canadian residents) January 1 (for all other applicants). For S.J.D.: LL.M. required, usually completed at Harvard although other candidates are considered; study plan. Contact Division of Graduate Studies, LILC 208 for S.J.D. application, descriptive materials and current deadlines.

ADMISSION STANDARDS. Number of full-time applicants 6,500; number accepted 841; number enrolled 555; median LSAT 169 (75% of class have a score at or above 166); median GPA 3.8 (A = 4) (75% of class have a GPA at or above 3.70). Attrition rate 0.5%. Gorman rating 4.93; *U.S. News & World Report* ranking is in the top 2 or 3 of all law schools.

FINANCIAL AID. All aid is need based according to federal and institutional guidelines. Grants-in-aid, institutional and private loans, federal loans. Assistantships may be available for upper divisional joint- and concurrent-degree candidates. For scholarships (selection criteria place heavy reliance on LSAT and undergraduate GPA) apply to Financial Aid Office, Pound Hall as soon after January 1, as possible; use school's FAF. Use FAFSA for all federal programs (Title IV School code #002155). Also submit Financial Aid Transcript, federal income tax forms. Approximately 31% of first-year class received scholarships/grants-in-aid. Approximately 70% of current students receive some form of financial assistance.

Average scholarship/grant $8,655. Low Income Protection Program for individuals who choose to begin their careers in the public interest is available. Average debt after graduation $62,800.

DEGREE REQUIREMENTS. For J.D.: 82 credits (30 required) with a 2.0 (A+ = 8) GPA, plus completion of upper divisional writing course and 2-credit course in professional responsibility; 3-year program. For J.D.-M.B.A.: a 4-year program rather than the usual 5 years needed if both degrees taken separately. For J.D.-concurrent-degree programs: pursuing 2 degrees concurrently may not reduce the amount of time required to complete both degrees separately. For LL.M.: 1-year program; 18–20 credits, at least 2 U.S. law courses; Legal Writing Workshop; LL.M. paper (thesis); a minimum GPA 3.0 (B–) (A+ = 8). For LL.M. (non-U.S. law school graduates): 1-year program, at least 2 semesters in residence; 20–22 credits, Legal Writing Workshop; LL.M. paper (strongly encouraged) or several writing exercises; a GPA of 2.5 (A+ = 8) required. For S.J.D.: complete a minimum of 8 credits beyond the LL.M.; oral exam in 3 or 4 fields, including 1 or 2 interdisciplinary fields; 2 presentations at S.J.D. colloquia; dissertation; oral defense.

CAREER AND PLACEMENT INFORMATION. Approximately 13% of graduates are employed in state. More than 89% of graduates are practicing law; 8% are in business; 2% in government; 1% in academia. Approximately 96% (NY), 94% (MA), 95% (CA) of Harvard University's first-time state bar exam takers pass the bar exam; the passage rate for all first-time takers from ABA-approved schools is 78% (NY), 85% (MA), 82% (CA). Graduates are eligible to take the bar exam in all 50 states.

UNIVERSITY OF HAWAII AT MANOA
Honolulu, Hawaii
Internet site: http://www.hawaii.edu

Founded 1907. Located in Manoa Valley, a residential area of Honolulu. Public control. Semester system. Library: 2,860,000 volumes; 5,565,000 microforms; 22,840 periodicals/subscriptions; 105 computer workstations.

University's other graduate colleges/schools: College of Arts and Sciences, College of Business Administration, College of Education, College of Engineering, College of Health Sciences and Social Welfare, College of Tropical Agriculture and Human Resources, School of Architecture, School of Hawaiian, Asian and Pacific Studies, School of Library and Information Studies, School of Ocean and Earth Science and Technology, School of Travel Industry Management, John A. Burns School of Medicine.

Total university enrollment: 18,270.

William S. Richardson School of Law
2515 Dole Street
Honolulu, Hawaii 96822
Phone: (808)956-7966, (808)956-3000 (application request line)
Internet site: http://www.hawaii.edu
E-mail: lawadm@hawaii.edu

Established 1973. Located on main campus. ABA approved since 1974. AALS member since 1989. Semester system. Full-time, day study only. Law library: 240,000 volumes/microforms; 2,665 current periodicals/subscriptions; 11 computer workstations; has LEXIS, NEXIS, WESTLAW, INNOPAC. Special programs: Environmental/Ocean Law Program, Pacific-Asian Legal Studies; exchange program with Hiroshima, Japan Law Faculty; externships.

Annual tuition: resident $7,115, nonresident $13,547. On-campus housing available for both single and married students. Annual on-campus housing cost: single students $2,580 (room only), $4,090 (room and board), married students $5,120. Housing deadline May 1. Contact Housing Office for both on- and off-campus housing information. Phone: (808)956-8177. Law students tend to live off-campus. Off-campus housing and personal expenses: approximately $9,700. Additional costs: books approximately $850.

Enrollment: first-year class 68; total full-time 240 (men 47%, women 53%); no part-time students. First-year statistics: 14% out of state, 23 states and foreign countries represented; 53% women; 73% minority; average age 26; 98 undergraduate institutions represented; range of first-year section sizes 18–74 students; number of upper division courses offered after first year 51.

Faculty: full-time 20, part-time 28; 30% female; 23% minority; student/faculty ratio 13 to 1.

Degrees conferred: J.D., J.D.-M.B.A., J.D.-M.A. (Asian Studies), J.D.-M.U.R.P.

RECRUITMENT PRACTICES AND POLICIES. Has on-campus informational sessions. School does have diversity program and actively recruits women/minority applicants from Asian Pacific region.

ADMISSION REQUIREMENTS FOR FIRST-YEAR APPLICANTS. LSDAS law school report, LSAT (not later than December test date, if more than one LSAT, highest is used), bachelor's degree from an accredited institution, personal statement, two recommendations, transcripts (must show all schools attended and at least three years of study) required in support of application. Applicants must have received bachelor's degree prior to enrollment. Preference given to state residents and residents of Asian-Pacific region. In addition, international applicants must submit TOEFL (not older than two years). Dual-degree applications must apply to and be accepted by both schools. Apply to Office of Admission after September 30, before February 16. First-year students admitted fall only. Rolling admission process, notification starts in March and is finished by late June. Application fee $30. Phone: (808)956-8636. E-mail: lawadm@hawaii.edu.

ADMISSION REQUIREMENTS FOR TRANSFER APPLICANTS. Accepts transfers from other ABA-accredited schools. Admission limited to space available. At least one year of enrollment, dean's letter indicating applicant is in good standing, prefer state or regional residents, LSAT, LSDAS, personal statement regarding reason for transfer, current law school transcript required in support of application. Apply to Admission Office by May 1 (fall), September 1 (spring). Admission decisions made by mid June (fall), mid October (spring). Application fee $30. Will consider visiting students.

ADMISSION STANDARDS. Number of full-time applicants 668; number accepted 178; number enrolled 68; median LSAT 157 (75% of class have a score at or above 154); median GPA 3.43 (A = 4) (75% of class have a GPA at or above 3.11). Attrition rate 3%. Gorman rating 2.66; *U.S. News & World Report* ranking is in the second tier of all law schools.

FINANCIAL AID. Limited to East-West Grants, state and federal loans, Federal WS. For all programs apply to university's Financial Aid Services Office after January 1, before March 1. Phone: (808)956-7966. Use FAFSA for all federal programs (Title IV School code #001610). Also submit Financial Aid Transcript, federal income tax forms. Approximately 48% of first-year class received scholarships/grants-in-aid. Approximately 85% of current students receive some form of financial assistance. Average scholarship/grant $5,280. Average debt after graduation $42,000.

DEGREE REQUIREMENTS. For J.D.: 89 credits (42 required) with a 2.0 (A = 4) GPA, plus completion of upper divisional writing course; 60 hours of pro bono work;

3-year program. For dual-degree programs: integrated programs, generally completed in 3½ to 4 years rather than the usual 4 to 5 years needed if degrees taken separately.

CAREER AND PLACEMENT INFORMATION. About 30 employers conducted on-campus interviews. Approximately 86% of graduates are employed in state. More than 76% of graduates are practicing law; 14% are in business; 7% in government; 3% in academia. Approximately 86% of the University of Hawaii at Manoa's first-time state bar exam takers pass the Hawaiian Bar Exam; Hawaii's passage rate for all first-time takers from ABA-approved schools is 86%. Graduates are eligible to take the bar exam in all 50 states.

HOFSTRA UNIVERSITY
Hempstead, New York 11550
Internet site: http://www.hofstra.edu

Founded 1935. Located 25 miles E of New York City on Hempstead Turnpike. Private control. Semester system. Library: 1,422,500 volumes; 1,920,000 microforms; 7,017 periodicals/subscriptions; 40 computer workstations.

University's other graduate colleges/schools: College of Liberal Arts and Sciences, Frank G. Zarb School of Business, New College, School of Education.

Total university enrollment: 11,800.

School of Law
121 Hofstra University
Hempstead, New York 11550-1090
Phone: (516)463-3585
Internet site: http://www.hofstra.edu/Law
E-mail: lawall@hofstra.edu

Established 1970. Located on main campus. ABA approved since 1971. AALS member. Semester system. Full-time, day study only. Law library: 440,000 volumes/microforms; 6,100 current periodicals/subscriptions; 33 computer workstations; has LEXIS, NEXIS, WESTLAW, DIALOG. Special programs: summer study abroad at the University of Nice, France; externships.

Annual tuition: $21,182. On-campus housing available for singles only. Annual on-campus housing cost: single students $1,800–$3,175 (room only), $6,180 (room and board). Contact Housing Office for both on- and off-campus housing information. Phone: (516)463-6930. Law students tend to live off-campus. Off-campus housing and personal expenses: approximately $17,082. Additional costs: books approximately $750.

Enrollment: first-year class 254; total full-time 808 (men 56%, women 44%); no part-time students. First-year statistics: 15% out of state, 21 states and foreign countries represented; 44% women; 17% minority; average age 24; 96 undergraduate institutions represented; range of first-year section sizes 30–120 students; number of upper division courses offered after first year 100.

Faculty: full-time 39, part-time 34; 22% female; 10% minority; student/faculty ratio 23 to 1.

Degrees conferred: J.D., J.D.-M.B.A.

RECRUITMENT PRACTICES AND POLICIES. Attends several national law school forums. Has on-campus informational sessions. School does have diversity program and actively recruits women/minority applicants.

ADMISSION REQUIREMENTS FOR FIRST-YEAR APPLICANTS. LSDAS law school report, LSAT (not later than February test date, if more than one LSAT, average is used), bachelor's degree from an accredited institution, personal statement, two recommendations, transcripts (must show all schools attended and at least three years of study) required in support of application. Applicants must have received bachelor's degree prior to enrollment. In addition, international applicants must submit TOEFL (not older than two years). Joint-degree applicants must apply to and be accepted by both schools. Apply to Office of Admission after September 30, before April 15. First-year students admitted fall only. Modified rolling admission process. Application fee $60. Phone: (516)463-5916. E-mail: lawall@hofstra.edu.

ADMISSION REQUIREMENTS FOR TRANSFER APPLICANTS. Accepts transfers from other ABA-accredited schools. Admission limited to space available. At least one year of enrollment, dean's letter indicating applicant is in good standing (prefer applicants in the top quarter of first-year class), LSAT, LSDAS, personal statement regarding reason for transfer, current law school transcript required in support of application. Apply to Admission Office by June 15. Admission decisions made by mid July. Application fee $60. Will consider visiting students.

ADMISSION STANDARDS. Number of full-time applicants 1,912; number accepted 816; number enrolled 254; median LSAT 157 (75% of class have a score at or above 150); median GPA 3.30 (A = 4) (75% of class have a GPA at or above 2.97). Attrition rate 2.7%. Gorman rating 4.20; *U.S. News & World Report* ranking is in the second tier of all law schools.

FINANCIAL AID. Scholarships, state grants-in-aid, private and institutional loans, federal loans, Federal WS available. Assistantships may be available for upper divisional joint-degree candidates. For scholarships (selection criteria place heavy reliance on LSAT and undergraduate GPA) apply to Admissions Office after January 1, and as soon as possible after admissions application has been filed. Phone: (516)463-5929. Use school's FA application. Use FAFSA for all federal programs (Title IV School code #002732). Also submit Financial Aid Transcript, federal income tax forms, Access Disk. Approximately 50% of first-year class received scholarships/grants-in-aid. Approximately 70% of current students receive some form of financial assistance. Average scholarship/grant $3,716. Average debt after graduation approximately $55,000.

DEGREE REQUIREMENTS. For J.D.: 87 credits (39 required) with a 2.0 (A = 4) GPA, plus completion of upper divisional writing course; 3-year program. Accelerated J.D. with 1 summer of course work. For J.D.-M.B.A.: 4-year program, a total 105–108 credits; law school will accept up to 9 credits of approved courses, business school will accept up to 9 credits of approved courses; thesis/nonthesis options.

CAREER AND PLACEMENT INFORMATION. About 50 employers conducted on-campus interviews. Approximately 76% of graduates are employed in state. More than 73% of graduates are practicing law; 15% are in business; 11% in government; 1% in academia. Approximately 79% of Hofstra University's first-time state bar exam takers pass the New York state bar exam; New York's passage rate for all first-time takers from ABA-approved schools is 78%. Graduates are eligible to take the bar exam in all 50 states.

UNIVERSITY OF HOUSTON
Houston, Texas 77204
Internet site: http://www.uh.edu

Founded 1934. Located 3 miles S of downtown Houston. Public control. Semester system. Library: 1,835,000 volumes; 3,700,000 microforms; 12,350 periodicals/subscriptions; 300 computer workstations.

University's other graduate colleges/schools: College of Architecture, College of Business Administration, College of Education, College of Humanities, Fine Arts and Communication, College of Natural Sciences and Mathematics, College of Optometry, College of Pharmacy, College of Technology, Conrad Hilton College of Hotel and Restaurant Management, Cullen College of Engineering, Graduate School of Social Work.

Total university enrollment: 31,200.

Law Center

4800 Calhoun, Entrance 19
Houston, Texas 77204-6391
Phone: (713)743-2100
Internet site: http://www.law.uh.edu
E-mail: Info@Lawlib.UH.EDU

Established 1974. Located in metropolitan Houston. ABA approved since 1950. AALS member. Semester system. Full-time, part-time study. Law library: 400,000 volumes/microforms; 2,800 current periodicals/subscriptions; 100 computer workstations; has LEXIS, NEXIS, WESTLAW, DIALOG; is a Federal Government Depository. Special facilities: Health Law and Policy Institute, Institute for Higher Education Law and Governance, International Law Institute, Trial Advocacy Institute. Special programs: Mexican Legal Studies Program; externships.

Annual tuition: full-time resident $5,505, nonresident $9,705; part-time resident $4,049, nonresident $7,049. On-campus housing available for both single and married students. Annual on-campus housing cost: single students $2,500 (room only), $4,435 (room and board), married students $5,400 (room only), $6,900 (room and board). Housing deadline June 1. Contact Office of Residential Life and Housing for both on- and off-campus housing information. For on-campus information, Phone: (800)247-7184. Law students tend to live off-campus. For off-campus information, Phone: (713)743-6000. Off-campus housing and personal expenses: approximately $9,670. Additional costs: books approximately $750.

Enrollment: first-year class full-time 257, part-time 52; total full-time 806, part-time 257 (men 61%, women 39%). First-year statistics: 17% out of state, 20 states and 8 foreign countries represented; 39% women; 21% minority; average age 25; 129 undergraduate institutions represented; average first-year section sizes full-time 80, part-time 55 students; number of upper division courses offered after first year 168.

Faculty: full-time 48, part-time 120; 18% female; 5% minority; student/faculty ratio 20 to 1.

Degrees conferred: J.D., J.D.-M.B.A., J.D.-M.P.H. (University of Texas, School of Public Health), J.D.-M.A. (History, Rice University), LL.M. (Energy, Environmental and Natural Resources Law, Health Law, International Economic Law, Intellectual Property Law, Tax), LL.M. (Comparative Law for persons who have completed a ba-

sic legal education and received a university degree in law in another country).

RECRUITMENT PRACTICES AND POLICIES. Attends national law school forums. On-campus informational sessions. School does have diversity program and actively recruits women/minority applicants.

ADMISSION REQUIREMENTS FOR FIRST-YEAR APPLICANTS. LSDAS law school report, LSAT (not later than December test date, if more than one LSAT, average is used), bachelor's degree from an accredited institution, résumé, personal statement, two recommendations, transcripts (must show all schools attended and at least three years of study) required in support of application. Applicants must have received bachelor's degree prior to enrollment. In addition, international applicants (all students on either F-1 or J-1 visas are considered foreign students) whose native language is not English must submit TOEFL (minimum acceptable score 600); submit letters of backing, statement of understanding, official copies of transcripts/mark sheet, official translations. Apply to Office of Admission after November 1, before February 1; January 1 for applicants with foreign degrees. First-year students admitted fall (full-time) and summer (part-time). Rolling admission process, notification starts in March and is finished by May 1. Application fee $50, $75 international applicants. Phone: (713)743-1070. E-mail: SCRichardson@UH.EDU.

ADMISSION REQUIREMENTS FOR TRANSFER APPLICANTS. Accepts transfers from other ABA-accredited schools. Admission limited to space available. At least one year of enrollment, dean's letter indicating applicant is in good standing (prefer applicants in the top 10 percent of first-year class), LSAT, LSDAS, personal statement regarding reason for transfer, undergraduate transcript, current law school transcript required in support of application. Apply to Office of Admission by July 15 (fall), November 15 (spring), April 15 (summer). Admission decisions made within 30 days of the receipt of complete application. Application fee $50. Will consider visiting students; application deadlines are the same as for transfer applicants.

ADMISSION REQUIREMENTS FOR LL.M. APPLICANTS. J.D. degree or its equivalent, law school transcript including rank in class, two letters of reference, résumé, statement of purpose required in support of LL.M. application. In addition, international applicants whose native language is not English must submit

TOEFL, letter of financial backing. Admits fall and spring (U.S.), fall only (international applicants). Apply to Graduate Studies Office by March 1 (fall), October 15 (spring). Application fee $50. Phone: (713)743-2081. Web site: http://www.law.uh.edu/lawcenter/programs.

ADMISSION STANDARDS. Number of full-time applicants 2,290, part-time 310; number accepted full-time 767, part-time 86; number enrolled full-time 257, part-time 52; median LSAT 159 (75% of class have a score at or above full-time 156, part-time 154); median GPA 3.25 (A = 4) (75% of class have a GPA at or above full-time 3.04, part-time 2.98). Attrition rate 5.2%. Gorman rating 3.85; *U.S. News & World Report* ranking is in the first tier of all law schools.

FINANCIAL AID. Dean's scholarships, minority scholarships, grants-in-aid, institutional loans; federal loans and Federal WS offered through university's Financial Aid Office. Assistantships may be available for upper divisional joint- or concurrent-degree candidates. For scholarships (selection criteria place heavy reliance on LSAT and undergraduate GPA) apply to Dean's Office after January 1, before March 1. Phone: (713)743-2269. E-mail: financialaid@www.law.uh.edu. For all other programs apply to University's Financial Aid Office apply by April 1. Phone: (713)743-1010. Use FAFSA for all federal programs (Title IV School code #003652). Also submit Financial Aid Transcript, federal income tax forms. Approximately 25% of first-year class received scholarships/grants-in-aid. Approximately 80% of current students receive some form of financial assistance. Average scholarship/grant $1,250 (full-time), $1,000 (part-time). Average debt after graduation $35,000. Financial aid available for part-time students.

DEGREE REQUIREMENTS. For J.D.: 90 credits (35 required) with a 2.0 (A = 4) GPA, plus completion of upper divisional writing course; 3-year program, 4-year program. For J.D.-masters: usually both degree requirements reduced by between 6 months and 1 year; programs can be completed in 3½ rather than 4½ years. For LL.M. (U.S. candidates): 24 credits, at least 2 in residence; a GPA of 2.5 (A = 4) required; 50-page paper of publishable quality. For LL.M. (international candidates): 24 credits, at least 2 semesters in residence; a GPA of 2.0 (A = 4) required; a seminar course; American law course; legal research course required.

CAREER AND PLACEMENT INFORMATION. About 100–150 employers conducted on-campus interviews annually. Approximately 91% of graduates are employed in state. More than 76% of graduates are practicing law; 14% are in business; 9% in government; 1% in academia. Approximately 86% of the University of Houston's first-time state bar exam takers pass the Texas Bar Exam; Texas' passage rate for all first-time takers from ABA-approved schools is 82%. Graduates are eligible to take the bar exam in all 50 states.

HOWARD UNIVERSITY
Washington, D.C. 20059-0002
Internet site: http://www.howard.edu

Founded 1867. Located in an urban area of northwest Washington. Private control. Semester system. Library: 1,720,000 volumes; 1,453,000 microforms; 2,800 periodicals/subscriptions.

University's other graduate colleges/schools: College of Dentistry, College of Fine Arts, College of Medicine, College of Nursing, College of Pharmacy, Graduate School of Arts and Sciences, School of Architecture, School of Business, School of Divinity, School of Education, School of Engineering, School of Social Work.

Total university enrollment: 10,248,

School of Law
2900 Van Ness Street, N.W.
Washington, D.C. 20008
Phone: (202)806-8003
Internet site: http://www.law.howard.edu
E-mail: kgray@law.howard.edu

Established 1869. Located in NW Washington about 1½ miles from main campus. ABA approved since 1931. AALS member. Semester system. Full-time, day study only. Law library: 250,000 volumes/microforms; 1,730 current periodicals/subscriptions; 60 computer workstations; has LEXIS, NEXIS, WESTLAW, DIALOG, OCLC, CALI, LEGALTRAC. Special programs: summer study abroad at the University of Western Cape, South Africa; externships.

Annual tuition: $12,425. Limited on-campus housing available. Annual on-campus housing cost: $10,957. Contact the university's Office of Residence Life, for both on- and off-campus housing information. Phone: (202)806-5749. Law students tend to live off-campus. Off-campus housing and personal expenses: approximately $13,198. Additional costs: books approximately $800.

Enrollment: first-year class 128; total full-time 444 (men 48%, women 52%); no part-time students. First-year statistics: 80% out of the District of Columbia, 38 states and foreign countries represented; 52% women;

95% minority; average age 24; 81 undergraduate institutions represented; range of first-year section sizes 30–50 students; number of upper division courses offered after first year 64.

Faculty: full-time 23, part-time 23; 26% female; 82% minority; student/faculty ratio 15 to 1.

Degrees conferred: J.D., J.D.-M.B.A., LL.M. (General), LL.M. (Comparative and International Law for persons who have completed a basic legal education and received a university degree in law in another country).

RECRUITMENT PRACTICES AND POLICIES. Attends national law school forums. On-campus informational sessions. School does have diversity program and actively recruits women/minority applicants.

ADMISSION REQUIREMENTS FOR FIRST-YEAR APPLICANTS. LSDAS law school report, LSAT (not later than February test date, if more than one LSAT, highest is used), bachelor's degree from an accredited institution, personal statement, two recommendations, dean's survey, transcripts (must show all schools attended and at least three years of study) required in support of application. Applicants must have received bachelor's degree prior to enrollment. Interview not required but may be requested by school. In addition, international applicants whose native language is not English must submit TOEFL (not older than two years). Apply to Office of Admission after October 1, before April 30. Applicants for the J.D.-M.B.A. program must apply to and be accepted by both schools and take the GMAT. First-year students admitted fall only. Rolling admission process, notification starts in November and is finished by late May. Application fee $80. Phone: (202)806-8228. Fax: (202)806-8428. E-mail: kgray@law.howard.edu.

ADMISSION REQUIREMENTS FOR TRANSFER APPLICANTS. Accepts transfers from other ABA-accredited schools. Admission limited to space available. At least one year of enrollment, dean's letter indicating applicant is in good standing (prefer applicants in the upper one-third of first-year class), LSAT, LSDAS, personal statement regarding reason for transfer, one letter of recommendation from a law school faculty member, current law school transcript required in support of application. Apply to Office of Admission by June 1 (fall), November 1 (spring). Admission decision made within six weeks of the receipt of a completed application. Application fee $80. Will consider visiting students.

ADMISSION REQUIREMENTS FOR LL.M. APPLICANTS. Official transcripts, two recommendations, auto-biographical sketch (not more than two pages) in English, short (five typewritten pages) essay in English, TOEFL (for those applicants whose native language is not English), passport-size photo required in support of LL.M. application. Apply to the Office of Admissions by April 1 (fall), November 1 (spring). Application fee $60. Phone: (202)806-8044 or (202)806-8008.

ADMISSION STANDARDS. Number of full-time applicants 1,350; number accepted 392; number enrolled 128; median LSAT 152 (75% of class have a score at or above 148); median GPA 3.0 (A = 4) (75% of class have a GPA at or above 2.70). Attrition rate 4.4%. Gorman rating 2.87; *U.S. News & World Report* ranking is in the third tier of all law schools.

FINANCIAL AID. Scholarships, merit scholarships, grants-in-aid, private loans; federal loans and Federal WS offered through university's Financial Aid Office. International J.D. candidates are eligible for institutional financial aid funds. For scholarships (selection criteria place heavy reliance on LSAT and undergraduate GPA) apply to Financial Aid Office after January 1, before April 1. Phone: (202)806-8564. For all other programs apply to university's Financial Aid Office. Use FAFSA for all federal programs (Title IV School code #001448). Also submit Financial Aid Transcript, federal income tax forms. Approximately 48% of first-year class received scholarships/grants-in-aid. Approximately 80% of current students receive some form of financial assistance. Average scholarship/grant $9,000. There is no institutional assistance for LL.M. applicants.

DEGREE REQUIREMENTS. For J.D.: 88 credits with a GPA of at least a 70 (scale of 0–100), plus completion of upper divisional writing course; 3-year program. For J.D.-M.B.A.: a 4-year program rather than the usual 5-year program. For LL.M. (General): 24 credits; at least 2 semesters in full-time residency; fulfillment of the LL.M. writing requirement (thesis or 2 seminars). For LL.M. (Comparative and International Law): a minimum of 15 credits; at least 2 semesters in full-time residence; fulfillment of LL.M. (Comparative and International Law) writing requirement.

CAREER AND PLACEMENT INFORMATION. About 100 employers conducted on-campus interviews. Approximately 29% of graduates are employed in Maryland and New York. More than 67% of graduates are practicing law; 13% are in business; 18% in government; 2% in academia. Approximately 29% (MD), 82% (NY) of first-time state bar exam takers pass the bar exam; the passage rate for all first-time takers from ABA-approved schools is 82% (MD), 78% (NY).

UNIVERSITY OF IDAHO
Moscow, Idaho 83844
Internet site: http://www.uidaho.edu

Founded 1889. Located 90 miles SE of Spokane, Washington, 8 miles from Pullman, Washington. Public control. Semester system. Library: 975,000 volumes; 1,686,800 microforms; 13,700 periodicals/subscriptions; 168 computer workstations.

University's College of Graduate Studies includes: College of Agriculture, College of Art and Architecture, College of Business and Economics, College of Education, College of Engineering, College of Forestry, Wildlife and Range Sciences, College of Letters and Science, College of Mines and Earth Resources.

Total university enrollment: 11,700.

College of Law
6th and Rayburn
Moscow, Idaho 83844-2321
Phone: (208)885-6442, catalog requests only (208)885-2252
Internet site: http://www.uidaho.edu/law
E-mail: lawcoll@uidaho.edu

Established 1909. Located on main campus. ABA approved since 1925. AALS member since 1915. Semester system. Full-time, day study only. Law library: 161,000 volumes/microforms; 2,565 current periodicals/subscriptions; 27 computer workstations; has LEXIS, NEXIS, WESTLAW, DIALOG. Special programs: summer study abroad at Staffordshire University Law School, England; externships.

Annual tuition: resident $3,882, nonresident $9,682. Limited on-campus housing available for both single and married students. Annual on-campus housing cost: single students $3,344–$3,824 (room and board), married students $320–$515 per month. Contact Housing Services for both on- and off-campus housing information. Phone: (208)885-6574. Law students tend to live off-campus. Off-campus housing and personal expenses: approximately $10,106. Additional costs: books approximately $700.

Enrollment: first-year class 84; total full-time 268 (men 58%, women 42%); no part-time students. First-year statistics: 25% out of state, 13 states and foreign countries represented; 42% women; 10% minority; average age 25; 7 undergraduate institutions represented; average first-year section size 50 students; number of upper division courses offered after first year 50.

Faculty: full-time 23, part-time 3; 24% female; student/faculty ratio 14 to 1.

Degree conferred: J.D.

RECRUITMENT PRACTICES AND POLICIES. Attends several national law school forums. On-campus informational sessions. School does have diversity program and actively recruits women/minority applicants.

ADMISSION REQUIREMENTS FOR FIRST-YEAR APPLICANTS. LSDAS law school report, LSAT (not later than December test date, if more than one LSAT, highest is used), bachelor's degree from an accredited institution, personal statement, two recommendations, transcripts (must show all schools attended and at least three years of study) required in support of application. Applicants must have received bachelor's degree prior to enrollment. Interview not required but may be requested by school. In addition, international applicants must submit TOEFL (not older than two years). Apply to Office of Admission after September 15, before February 15 (for first wave of acceptances). First-year students admitted fall only. Rolling admission process, notification starts in November and is finished by late April. Application fee $30. Phone: (208)885-6422. E-mail: lawcoll@uidaho.edu.

ADMISSION REQUIREMENTS FOR TRANSFER APPLICANTS. Accepts transfers from other ABA-accredited schools. Admission limited to space available. At least one year of enrollment, in good standing (prefer applicants in the top half of first-year class), LSAT, LSDAS, personal statement regarding reason for transfer, current law school transcript required in support of application. Apply to Admission Office by June 30. Admission decisions made by mid August. Application fee $30. Will consider visiting students.

ADMISSION STANDARDS. Number of full-time applicants 482; number accepted 240; number enrolled 84; median LSAT 155 (75% of class have a score at or above 149); median GPA 3.22 (A = 4) (75% of class have a GPA at or above 3.02). Attrition rate 5.1%. Gorman rating 2.71; *U.S. News & World Report* ranking is in the third tier of all law schools.

FINANCIAL AID. Scholarships, grants-in-aid, institutional loans; federal loans and Federal WS offered through university's Financial Aid Office. All applicants are considered for scholarships as long as they meet the priority deadline for admission. For scholarships the selection committee places heavy reliance on LSAT and undergraduate GPA. For all other programs apply to the university's Office of Student Financial Aid Services and use the institution's financial aid application. Phone: (208)885-6312. Use FAFSA for all federal programs (Title IV School code #001626). Also submit Financial Aid Transcript, federal income tax forms. Approximately 51% of first-year class received scholarships/grants-in-aid. Approximately 70% of current students receive some form of financial assistance. Average scholarship/grant $500.

DEGREE REQUIREMENTS. For J.D.: 88 credits (31 required) with a 2.0 (A = 4) GPA, plus completion of upper divisional writing course; 3-year program.

CAREER AND PLACEMENT INFORMATION. Approximately 68% of graduates are employed in state. More than 74% of graduates are practicing law; 7% are in business; 19% in government; none are in academia. Approximately 72% of the University of Idaho's first-time state bar exam takers pass the Idaho Bar Exam; Idaho's passage rate for all first-time takers from ABA-approved schools is 75%. Graduates are eligible to take the bar exam in all 50 states.

ILLINOIS INSTITUTE OF TECHNOLOGY

Chicago, Illinois 60616
Internet site: http://www.ist.edu

Formed in 1940 by merger of Armour Institute (1890) and Lewis Institute (1896). Located three miles S of Chicago's loop. Private control. Semester system. Library: 500,000 volumes; 177,000 microforms; 750 periodicals/subscriptions.

Institute's other graduate colleges/schools: Armour College of Engineering and Sciences, College of Architecture, Institute of Design, Institute of Psychology, Stuart School of Business.

Total enrollment: 6,287.

Chicago-Kent School of Law

656 West Adams Street
Chicago, Illinois 60661-3691
Phone: (312)906-5000
Internet site: http://www.kentlaw.edu
E-mail: admitq@kentlaw.edu

Established 1887. In the late 1800s the Chicago College of Law and Kent College of Law merged to form Chicago-Kent College of Law. In 1969 Chicago-Kent College of Law became an integral part of IIT, in 1992 Chicago-Kent moved to its new quarters in downtown Chicago on Adams Street. ABA approved since 1951. AALS member. Semester system. Full-time, part-time study. Law library: 520,000 volumes/microforms; 7,560 current periodicals/subscriptions; 126 computer workstations; has LEXIS, NEXIS, WESTLAW, DIALOG, EPIC; is a Federal Government Depository. Special programs: Environmental and Energy Law, Intellectual Property Law, Labor and Employment Law; externships.

Annual tuition: full-time $19,930, part-time $14,440; LL.M. per credit $535. On-campus housing available for both single and married students at main campus. Annual on-campus housing cost: single students $5,500 (room and board), average housing costs for married students $6,500. Contact Housing Director for both on- and off-campus housing information. Phone: (312)567-5075. Law students tend to live off-campus. Off-campus housing and personal expenses: approximately $15,670. Additional costs: books approximately $700.

Enrollment: first-year class 302 full-time, 111 part-time; total full-time 853, part-time 334 (men 54%, women 46%). First-year statistics: 40% out of state, 54 states and foreign countries represented; 46% women; 16% minority; average age 26; range of first-year section sizes 30–100 students; number of upper division courses offered after first year 97 full-time, 70 part-time.

Faculty: full-time 71, part-time 74; 26% female; 6% minority; student/faculty ratio 21.8 to 1.

Degrees conferred: J.D., J.D.-M.B.A., J.D.-M.P.A., J.D.-LL.M., J.D.-M.S. (Financial Markets and Trading, Environmental Management), LL.M. (Tax and Financial Services), LL.M. (International and Comparative Law for persons who have completed a basic legal education and received a university degree in law in another country).

RECRUITMENT PRACTICES AND POLICIES. Attends national law school forums. On-campus informational sessions. School does have diversity program and actively recruits women/minority applicants.

ADMISSION REQUIREMENTS FOR FIRST-YEAR APPLICANTS. LSDAS law school report, LSAT (prefer December but will accept February test date, if more than one LSAT, average is used), bachelor's degree from an accredited institution, personal statement, two recommendations, transcripts (must show all schools attended and at least three years of study) required in support of application. Applicants must have received bachelor's degree prior to enrollment. Interview not required but may be requested by school. In addition, international applicants must submit TOEFL (not older than two years), TWE, translation and "detailed" evaluation of all academic records, affidavit of financial support. Apply to Office of Admission after October 1, before April 1. Applicants to dual-degree programs must apply to and be accepted by both schools, in addition submit current GMAT/GRE. First-year students admitted fall only. Rolling admission process, notification starts in December and is finished by late April. Application fee $40. Phone: (312)906-5020. E-mail: admitq@kentlaw.edu.

ADMISSION REQUIREMENTS FOR TRANSFER APPLICANTS. Accepts transfers from other ABA-accredited schools. Admission limited to space available. At least one year of enrollment, in good standing (prefer applicants in the top quarter of first-year class), LSAT, LSDAS, personal statement regarding reason for transfer, two letters of recommendation from current law school faculty, current law school transcript required in support of application. Apply to Admission Office by June 30. Admission decisions made by mid summer. Application fee $40. Will consider visiting students.

ADMISSION REQUIREMENTS FOR LL.M. APPLICANTS. Official law school transcripts, two letters of recommendation required in support of LL.M. application. In addition to the above requirements, international attorneys must submit translations and certification of international law degree and affidavit of financial support. Admits fall and spring. Apply to the Office of Graduate Admission at least two months prior to semester of entrance. Application $40. Phone: (312)906-5360.

ADMISSION STANDARDS. Number of full-time applicants 1,692, part-time 396; number accepted 1,202 full-time, 257 part-time; number enrolled 302 full-time, 111 part-time; median LSAT 156 (75% of class have a score at or above 150 full-time, 147 part-time); median GPA 3.20 (A = 4) (75% of class have a GPA at or above 2.88 full-time, 2.68 part-time). Attrition rate 6%. Gorman rating 3.83; *U.S. News & World Report* ranking is in the second tier of all law schools.

FINANCIAL AID. Scholarships, merit scholarships, minority scholarships, grants-in-aid, institutional/private loans, federal loans, Federal WS. Assistantships may be available for upper level students. For scholarships (selection criteria place heavy reliance on LSAT and undergraduate GPA) apply to Office of Admissions and Financial Aid after January 1, before April 15. Phone: (312)906-5180. Use school's FA application. Use FAFSA

for all federal programs (Title IV School code #001691). Also submit Financial Aid Transcript, federal income tax forms. Approximately 37% (full-time), 31% (part-time) of first-year class received scholarships/grants-in-aid. Approximately 80% of current students receive some form of financial assistance. Average scholarship/grant $6,000 (full-time), $3,225 (part-time). Loan repayment program available for public interest careers. Average debt after graduation $73,000.

DEGREE REQUIREMENTS. For J.D.: 84 credits (39 required) with a 2.0 (A = 4) GPA, plus completion of upper divisional writing course; 3-year full-time program, 4-year part-time program. Accelerated J.D. with 1 summer of course work. For J.D.-M.B.A.: up to 10-course reduction: 4-year program full time, 5½-year program part time. For J.D.-M.P.A.: up to 7 course reduction; 4-year program full-time, 5½-year program part-time. For J.D.-M.S. (Financial Marketing): up to 7-course reduction; 4-year program full-time, 5½-year program part-time. For J.D.-M.S. (Environmental Management): up to 9-course reduction; 4-year program full-time, 5½-year program part-time. For J.D.-LL.M.: up to 10 credits may be used toward J.D.; 1 additional semester for LL.M. (full-time study). For LL.M. (Tax): 24 credits; a GPA of 2.5 (A = 4) required. For LL.M. (Financial Services): 24 credits; a GPA of 3.0 (A = 4) required; publishable paper. For LL.M. (International and Comparative Law): individually designed degree depending upon previous law degree and legal experience; 1 full year in residence.

CAREER AND PLACEMENT INFORMATION. About 50 employers conducted on-campus interviews. Approximately 86% of graduates are employed in state. More than 61% of graduates are practicing law; 22% are in business; 14% in government; 1% in academia. Approximately 81% of Chicago-Kent School of Law's first-time state bar exam takers pass the Illinois Bar Exam; Illinois' passage rate for all first-time takers from ABA-approved schools is 87%. Graduates are eligible to take the bar exam in all 50 states.

UNIVERSITY OF ILLINOIS AT URBANA-CHAMPAIGN
Champaign, Illinois 61820-5711
Internet site: http://www.uiuc.edu

Founded 1867. Public control. Semester system. Library: 6,000,000 holdings.

University's other graduate colleges/schools: College of Agricultural, Consumer and Environmental Sciences,

College of Applied Life Studies, College of Commerce and Business Administration, College of Communications, College of Education, College of Engineering, College of Fine and Applied Arts, Graduate School of Library and Information Science, Institute of Labor and Industrial Relations, School of Social Work, College of Veterinary Medicine.

Total university enrollment: 36,400.

School of Law
504 East Pennsylvania Avenue
Champaign, Illinois 61820
Phone: (217)333-0931
Internet site: http://www.law.uiuc.edu
E-mail: dfalls@law.uiuc.edu

Established 1897. Located on main campus. ABA approved since 1923. AALS member. Semester system. Full-time, day study only. Law library: 660,200 volumes/microforms; 8,000 current periodicals/subscriptions; 93 computer workstations; has LEXIS, NEXIS, WESTLAW; is a Depository for European Economic Community.

Annual tuition: resident $7,646, nonresident $17,718. On-campus housing available for both single and married students. Annual on-campus housing cost: single students $2,894 (room only), $5,300 (room and board), married students $4,548. Contact Housing Information Office for both on- and off-campus housing information. Phone: (217)333-1420. Law students tend to live off-campus. Off-campus housing and personal expenses: approximately $9,632. Additional costs: books approximately $700.

Enrollment: first-year class 182; total full-time 616 (men 61%, women 39%); no part-time students. Statistics: 40% out of state, 29 states and foreign countries represented; 39% women; 28% minority; average age 26; 177 undergraduate institutions represented; range of first-year section sizes 60–65 students; number of upper division courses offered after first year 93.

Faculty: full-time 43, part-time 28; 23% female; 11% minority; student/faculty ratio 16.6 to 1.

Degrees conferred: J.D., J.D.-M.B.A., J.D.-D.V.M., J.D.-M.D., J.D.-M.A. (Labor and International Relations, Urban Planning), J.D.-M.Ed., J.D.-Ed.D., LL.M., J.S.D., S.J.D.

RECRUITMENT PRACTICES AND POLICIES. Attends local and national law school forums. Has on-campus informational sessions. School does have diversity program and actively recruits women/minority applicants.

ADMISSION REQUIREMENTS FOR FIRST-YEAR APPLICANTS. LSDAS law school report, LSAT (not later than December test date, if more than one LSAT, average is used), bachelor's degree from an accredited institution, personal statement, two recommendations, transcripts (must show all schools attended and at least three years of study) required in support of application. Applicants must have received bachelor's degree prior to enrollment. Interview not required; campus visits are encouraged. In addition, international applicants whose native language is not English must submit TOEFL (not older than two years, minimum score required 600), certified translation and evaluation of all foreign credentials. Joint-degree applicants must apply to and be accepted by both schools. Apply to Office of Admission after September 30, before March 15 (January 15 for preferred consideration). First-year students admitted fall only. Rolling admission process, notification starts in November and is finished by late April. Application fee $30, $50 for international application. Phone: (217)244-6415. E-mail: dfalls@law.uiuc.edu.

ADMISSION REQUIREMENTS FOR TRANSFER APPLICANTS. Accepts transfers from other ABA-accredited schools. Admission limited to space available. At least one year of enrollment, dean's letter indicating applicant is in good standing (prefer applicants in the top quarter of first-year class), LSAT, LSDAS, personal statement regarding reason for transfer, two letters of recommendation, undergraduate transcripts, current law school transcript required in support of application. Apply to Admission Office by July 1. Admission decisions made by early August. Application fee $30. Will consider visiting students as long as they are certified to be in good standing at current law school.

ADMISSIONS REQUIREMENT FOR LL.M. APPLICANTS. All applicants must have graduated from an AALS-approved or ABA-accredited law school with a high rank in class, prefer the top 10 percent. If from another country, the applicant must have graduated from a law school or law faculty with standards substantially equivalent to those of U.S. applicants. Official copies of all transcripts, résumé, proposed study plan, personal statement three letters of recommendation required in support of graduate application. In addition, TOEFL for those whose native language is not English; all transcripts and recommendations must be in English, evidence of financial support sufficient for one full year of academic study. Admits fall only. Request information from the Office of Graduate and International Legal Studies, College of Law. Phone: (217)333-6066. E-mail: ireynolds@

law.uiuc.edu. Submit completed application to Office of Admissions and Records, University of Illinois, 10 Henry Administration Building, 506 South Wright Street, Urbana, Illinois 61801. Apply by February 15 for scholarship/fellowship consideration. Application fee $30, $50 for international applicants. Accepts approximately thirty LL.M. students each year.

ADMISSION STANDARDS. Number of full-time applicants 1,792; number accepted 593; number enrolled 182; median LSAT 160 (75% of class have a score at or above 158); median GPA 3.41 (A = 4) (75% of class have a GPA at or above 3.07). Attrition rate 1%. Gorman rating 4.33; *U.S. News & World Report* ranking is in the top 20 of all law schools.

FINANCIAL AID. Merit scholarships, long-term loans, private loans; federal loans and Federal WS offered through university's Office of Student Financial Aid. Assistantships may be available for upper divisional joint-degree candidates. All accepted students are automatically considered for scholarships (selection criteria place heavy reliance on LSAT and undergraduate GPA) apply to admissions Office as soon as possible after January 1, before mid March. For all other programs apply to the university's Office of Student Financial Aid. Phone: (217)333-0100. Use FAFSA for all federal programs (Title IV School code #001775). Also submit Financial Aid Transcript, federal income tax forms. Approximately 44% of first-year class received scholarships. Approximately 80% of current students receive some form of financial assistance. Average scholarship/grant $5,200. Average debt after graduation $32,100. Teaching fellowships available to LL.M. students from common-law countries.

DEGREE REQUIREMENTS. For J.D.: 90 credits (39 required) with a 2.0 overall GPA, 3.0 in required courses (A = 4), plus completion of upper divisional writing course; 3-year program. Accelerated J.D. with summer course work. For J.D.-master's: individually designed programs; generally 3½- to 4-year programs rather than 4- to 5-year programs needed if both degrees taken separately. For LL.M.: individually designed programs; "Introduction to the U.S. Legal System" for all students from non-common-law countries; at least 2 semesters in residence.

CAREER AND PLACEMENT INFORMATION. About 45–50 employers conducted on-campus interviews. Approximately 74% of graduates are employed in state. More than 63% of graduates are practicing law; 18% are in business; 17% in government; 2% in academia. Approximately 96% of the University of Illinois at Urbana-Champaign's first-time state bar exam takers pass the Illinois Bar Exam; Illinois' passage rate for all first-time takers from ABA-approved schools is 87%. Graduates are eligible to take the bar exam in all 50 states.

INDIANA UNIVERSITY BLOOMINGTON

Bloomington, Indiana 47405
Internet site: http://www.indiana.edu

Founded 1820. Public control. Semester system. Library: 5,550,000 volumes; 3,445,000 microforms; 40,500 periodicals/subscriptions.

University's other graduate colleges/schools: College of Arts and Sciences, School of Fine Arts, School of Journalism, College of Business, School of Health, Physical Education and Recreation, School of Library and Information Studies, School of Music, School of Optometry, School of Public and Environmental Affairs.

Total university enrollment: 35,000.

School of Law

Law Building, Room 230
Third Street and Indiana Avenue
Bloomington, Indiana 47405-1001
Phone: (818)855-8885, fax: (812)885-0555
Internet site: http://www.law.indiana.edu
E-mail: lawadmis@indiana.edu

Established 1842. Located on main campus. ABA approved since 1923. AALS member. Semester system. Full-time, day study only. Law library: 580,000 volumes, 750,000 microforms; 6,995 current periodicals/subscriptions; 78 computer workstations; has LEXIS, WESTLAW. Special facility: Center for the Study of Law and Society. Special programs: summer study abroad in London, England; externships.

Annual tuition: resident $6,162, nonresident $15,290. On-campus housing available for both single and married students. Annual on-campus housing cost: single students $3,095 (room only), meal plans range from $1,728–$2,344, married students $409–$817 per month. Contact University Halls of Residence for both on- and off-campus housing information. Phone: (812)855-5603. The law school's Admissions Office also maintains an off-campus housing listing. Law students tend to live off-campus. Off-campus housing and personal expenses: approximately $12,127. Additional costs: books approximately $700.

Enrollment: first-year class 227; total full-time 651 (men 56%, women 44%); no part-time students. Statistics: 40% out of state, 36 states and 9 foreign countries represented; 44% women; 21% minority; average age 25; 198 undergraduate institutions represented; range of first-year section sizes 26–100 students; number of upper division courses offered after first year 94.

Faculty: full-time 43, part-time 19; 30% female; 4% minority; student/faculty ratio 16.6 to 1.

Degrees conferred: J.D., J.D.-M.B.A., J.D.-M.P.A., J.D.-M.S.E.S., J.D.-M.L.S., LL.M., M.C.L. (only for persons who have completed a basic legal education and have received a university degree in law in another country), J.S.D.

RECRUITMENT PRACTICES AND POLICIES. Attends local and national law school forums. Has on-campus informational sessions. School does have diversity program and actively recruits women/minority applicants.

ADMISSION REQUIREMENTS FOR FIRST-YEAR APPLICANTS. LSDAS law school report, LSAT (not later than December test date, if more than one LSAT, average is used), bachelor's degree from an accredited institution, personal statement, two recommendations, transcripts (must show all schools attended and at least three years of study), Application Data Sheet required in support of application. Applicants must have received bachelor's degree prior to enrollment. In addition, international applicants whose native language is not English must submit TOEFL (not older than two years), certified translations and evaluations of all foreign credentials. Apply to Office of Admission after September 30, before March 1 (for priority consideration). First-year students admitted fall only. Rolling admission process, notification starts in December and is finished by May. Application fee $35. Phone: (812)855-4765. E-mail: lawadmis@indiana.edu.

ADMISSION REQUIREMENTS FOR TRANSFER APPLICANTS. Accepts between 5 and 10 transfers from other ABA-accredited schools. Admission limited to space available. At least one year of enrollment, dean's letter indicating applicant is in good standing (prefer applicants in the top quarter of first-year class), LSAT, LSDAS, personal statement regarding reason for transfer, undergraduate transcript, current law school transcript required in support of application. Apply to Admission Office by July 1. Admission decisions made by mid August. Application fee $35. Will consider visiting students.

ADMISSION REQUIREMENTS FOR M.C.L. APPLICANTS. Must have a law degree from a foreign university. Official transcripts with certified translation and evaluation, résumé, personal statement, 2 letters of recommendation, evidence of high reading and writing skills in English required in support of graduate application. Admits fall only. Apply to the Admissions Office of the law school not later than April 1.

ADMISSION REQUIREMENTS FOR S.J.D. APPLICATIONS. LL.M. degree required. Official transcript, list of professors involved with LL.M., personal statement, any written or published work, proposal of research to be undertaken, evidence of high reading and writing skills in English. Admits fall only. Apply to the Admissions Office of the law school not later than April 1.

ADMISSION STANDARDS. Number of full-time applicants 1,524; number accepted 680; number enrolled 227; median LSAT 158 (75% of class have a score at or above 155); median GPA 3.36 (A = 4) (75% of class have a GPA at or above 3.13). Attrition rate 3.1%. Gorman rating 4.41; *U.S. News & World Report* ranking is in the top 40 of all law schools.

FINANCIAL AID. Scholarships, fellowships, grants-in-aid, private and institutional loans; federal loans and Federal WS offered through university's Financial Aid Office. Assistantships may be available for upper divisional joint-degree candidates. For scholarships/fellowships (selection criteria place heavy reliance on LSAT and undergraduate GPA) apply to Admissions Office after January 1, before March 1 (priority deadline); use law school's application for fellowships, scholarships. For all other programs apply to the university's Office of Financial Aid. Phone: (812)855-0321. Submit FAFSA for all federal programs (Title IV School code #001809). Also submit Financial Aid Transcript, federal income tax forms. Approximately 35% of first-year class received scholarships/grants-in-aid. Approximately 75% of current students receive some form of financial assistance. Average scholarship/grant $2,500. Average debt after graduation $40,000.

DEGREE REQUIREMENTS. For J.D.: 86 credits (36 required) with a 2.3 (A = 4) GPA, plus completion of upper divisional writing course and substantial research paper; 3-year program. A 27-month accelerated J.D. available. For J.D.-M.B.A.: total 118 credits (J.D. 76 credits, M.B.A. 42 credits). For J.D.-M.P.A.: total 114 credits (J.D. 78 credits, M.P.A. 36). For J.D.-M.S.E.S.: total 114 credits (J.D. 78 credits, M.S.E.S. 36 credits).

For J.D.-M.L.S.: total 120 credits (J.D. 80 credits, M.L.S. 30). For LL.M.: 30 credits, at least 2 semesters in full-time residence; thesis of publishable quality. For M.C.L. (International): 24 credits; at least 2 semesters in residence; 1 seminar. For S.J.D.: at least 1 year of full-time residence; dissertation of publishable quality; oral defense.

CAREER AND PLACEMENT INFORMATION. More than 200 employers conduct on-campus interviews each year. Approximately 46% of graduates are employed in state. More than 74% of graduates are practicing law; 13% are in business; 11% in government; 2% in academia. Approximately 82% of Indiana University Bloomington's first-time state bar exam takers pass the Indiana Bar Exam; Indiana's passage rate for all first-time takers from ABA-approved schools is 86%. Graduates are eligible to take the bar exam in all 50 states.

INDIANA UNIVERSITY–PURDUE UNIVERSITY INDIANAPOLIS

Indianapolis, Indiana 46202-2896
Internet site: http://www.iupui.edu

Located in an urban area of Indianapolis. Public control. Semester system. Library: 700,000 volumes; 970,000 microforms; 7,000 periodicals/subscriptions.

University's other graduate schools: Herron School of Art, School of Business, School of Dentistry, School of Education, School of Engineering and Technology, School of Medicine, School of Nursing, School of Public and Environmental Affairs, School of Science, School of Social Work.

Total university enrollment: 26,900.

School of Law–Indianapolis

765 West New York Street
Indianapolis, Indiana 46202-5194
Phone: (317)274-8523
Internet site: http://www.iulaw.indy.indiana.edu
E-mail: kmiller@wpo.iupui.edu

Established 1895. Located near downtown. ABA approved since 1936. AALS member. Semester system. Full-time, part-time study. Law library: 410,000 volumes/microforms; 6,880 current periodicals/subscriptions; 58 computer workstations; has LEXIS, NEXIS, WESTLAW, DIALOG, OCLC; is a U.S. Government Depository for United Nations. Special facility: Center for Law and Health. Special programs: summer study abroad in

People's Republic of China and at the Université of Lille, France; internships.

Annual tuition: full-time; resident $5,612, nonresident $13,380; part-time resident $4,059, nonresident $9,608. University-owned housing available for both single and married students but in short supply. Annual on-campus housing cost: single students $3,500 (room only), married students $4,400. Contact Housing Office for both on- and off-campus housing information. Phone: (612)274-7200. Law students tend to live off-campus. Off-campus housing and personal expenses: approximately $11,576. Additional costs: books approximately $700.

Enrollment: first-year class 179, part-time 87; total full-time 547, part-time 289 (men 55%, women 45%). First-year statistics: 16% out of state, 37 states and 3 foreign countries represented; 45% women; 11% minority; average age 27 (full-time), 32 (part-time); 163 undergraduate institutions represented; average first-year section sizes full-time 90 students, part-time 70 students; number of upper division courses offered after first year 67 full-time, 48 part-time.

Faculty: full-time 44, part-time 17; 30% female; 4% minority; student/faculty ratio 18.5 to 1.

Degrees conferred: J.D., J.D.-M.B.A., J.D.-M.P.A., J.D.-M.H.A.

RECRUITMENT PRACTICES AND POLICIES. Attends all national law school forums. On-campus informational sessions. School does have diversity program and actively recruits women/minority applicants.

ADMISSION REQUIREMENTS FOR FIRST-YEAR APPLICANTS. LSDAS law school report, LSAT (not later than December test date, if more than one LSAT, average is used), bachelor's degree from an accredited institution, personal statement, transcripts (must show all schools attended and at least three years of study) required in support of application. Recommendations are not required but are strongly encouraged. Applicants must have received bachelor's degree prior to enrollment. international applicants must submit TOEFL (not older than two years) and use the International Application form obtained from the International Affairs Office, 620 Union Drive, Indianapolis, IN 46020-2897. Joint-degree applicants must apply to and be accepted to both schools. Apply to Assistant Dean for Admission after September 30, before March 1. First-year students admitted fall only. Rolling admission process, notification starts in January and is finished by mid May. Application fee $35. Phone: (317)274-2459. E-mail: kmiller@wpo.iupui.edu.

ADMISSION REQUIREMENTS FOR TRANSFER APPLICANTS. Accepts transfers from other ABA-accredited schools. Admission limited to space available. At least one year of enrollment, dean's letter indicating applicant is in good standing (prefer applicants in the top quarter of first-year class), LSAT, LSDAS, personal statement regarding reason for transfer, current law school transcript, undergraduate transcript required in support of application. Apply to Admission Office by June 1. Admission decisions made by mid July. Application fee $35. Will consider visiting students.

ADMISSION STANDARDS. Number of full-time applicants 757, part-time 285; number accepted full-time 393, part-time 107; number enrolled full-time 179, part-time 87; median LSAT 156 (75% of class have a score at or above 152); median GPA 3.2 (A = 4) (75% of class have a GPA at or above 2.92 full-time, 2.90 part-time). Attrition rate 4.9%. Gorman rating 3.15; *U.S. News & World Report* ranking is in the second tier of all law schools.

FINANCIAL AID. Need-based scholarships, merit scholarships, diversity scholarships, grants-in-aid, private loans; federal loans and Federal WS offered through university's Financial Aid Office. For scholarships (selection criteria place heavy reliance on LSAT and undergraduate GPA) apply to Admissions Office after January 1, before March 1. For all other programs apply to university's Financial Aid Office. Phone: (317)274-4162. Use FAFSA for all federal programs (Title IV School code #001813). Also submit Financial Aid Transcript, federal income tax forms. Approximately 13% (full-time), 11% (part-time) of first-year class received scholarships/grants-in-aid. Approximately 44% of current students receive some form of financial assistance. Average scholarship/grant $1,500 full-time, $1,000 part-time. Average debt after graduation $44,000.

DEGREE REQUIREMENTS. For J.D.: 90 credits (53 required) with a 2.0 (A = 4) GPA, plus completion of upper divisional writing course; 3-year full-time program, 4-year part-time program. Accelerated J.D. with 1 summer of course work. For J.D.-M.B.A.: total 119 credits (J.D. 80 credits, M.B.A. 39 credits). For J.D.-M.P.A.: total 118 credits (J.D. 84 credits, M.P.A. 34 credits). For J.D.-M.H.A.: total 130 credits (J.D. 82 credits, M.H.A. 48 credits).

CAREER AND PLACEMENT INFORMATION. About 44 employers conducted on-campus interviews. Approximately 87% of graduates are employed in state. More than 60% of graduates are practicing law; 22% are in business; 18% in government; none are in academia. Approximately 86% of Indiana University–Purdue University Indianapolis' first-time state bar exam takers pass the Indiana Bar Exam; Indiana's passage rate for all first-time takers from ABA-approved schools is 86%. Graduates are eligible to take the bar exam in all 50 states.

INTER AMERICAN UNIVERSITY OF PUERTO RICO
Hato Rey, Puerto Rico 00191

College-level study since 1921. Private control. Semester system. Library: 100,000 volumes; 446,400 microforms; 2,000 periodicals/subscriptions; 18 computer workstations.

University's other graduate divisions: Division of Behavioral Science and Allied Professions, Division of Economics and Business Administration, Division of Education, Division of Humanities, Division of Science and Technology, School of Optometry, and a branch campus in San Germán.

Total university enrollment: 2,000.

School of Law
P.O. Box 70351
San Juan, Puerto Rico 00936-8351
Phone: (787)751-1912

Established 1961. ABA approved since 1969. AALS member. Semester system. Full-time, part-time study. Law library: 170,800 volumes/microforms; 3,900 current periodicals/subscriptions; 31 computer workstations; has LEXIS, NEXIS, DIALOG, DOBIS/LUVEN, MICROJURIS (Puerto Rican Law database).

Annual tuition: full-time $10,495, part-time $7,895. No on-campus housing available. Law students live off-campus. Contact Admission Office for off-campus information. Off-campus housing and personal expenses: approximately $8,900. Additional costs: books approximately $600.

Enrollment: first-year class 114 full-time, 103 part-time; total full-time 336, 322 part-time (men 47%, women 53%). First-year statistics: none from out of Puerto Rico; 53% women; 100% minority; average age 24; average first-year section sizes 50–55 students; number of upper division courses offered after first year 36–40.

Faculty: full-time 30, part-time 16; 33% female; 98% minority; student/faculty ratio 20 to 1.

Degree conferred: J.D.

RECRUITMENT PRACTICES AND POLICIES. On-campus informational sessions.

ADMISSION REQUIREMENTS FOR FIRST-YEAR APPLICANTS. Official transcripts, LSAT, PAEG (Prueba de Admisión para Estudios Graduados, score of 575 required), bachelor's degree from an accredited institution, personal statement, two recommendations, transcripts (must show all schools attended and at least three years of study), proficiency in Spanish required in support of application. Applicants must have received bachelor's degree prior to enrollment. Interview not required but may be requested by school. Apply to Office of Admission after September 30, before March 31. First-year students admitted fall only. Rolling admission process. Application fee $63. Phone: (787)751-1912, ext. 2013, 2012.

ADMISSION REQUIREMENTS FOR TRANSFER APPLICANTS. Accepts transfers from other ABA-accredited schools. Admission limited to space available. At least one year of enrollment, minimum of 2.5 (A = 4) GPA, LSAT, personal statement regarding reason for transfer, undergraduate transcripts, current law school transcript required in support of application. Admits fall, spring, summer sessions. Apply to Admission Office at least six weeks prior to session of entrance. Application fee $63. Will consider visiting students.

ADMISSION STANDARDS. Number of full-time applicants 447, 407 part-time; number accepted 207 full-time, 137 part-time; number enrolled 114 full-time, 103 part-time; median LSAT 138 (75% of class have a score at or above 133 for both full- and part-time); median GPA 2.85 (A = 4) (75% of class have a GPA at or above 2.59 full-time, 2.60 part-time). Attrition rate 7%. *U.S. News & World Report* ranking in the fourth tier of all law schools.

FINANCIAL AID. Honor scholarships, student incentive grant program, private loans, federal loans, Federal WS. For scholarships (selection criteria place heavy reliance on LSAT and undergraduate GPA) apply to Admissions Office after January 1, before March 31. Use FAFSA for all federal programs (Title IV School code #017202). Also submit Financial Aid Transcript, federal income tax forms. Approximately 24% (full-time), 28% (part-time) of first-year class received scholarships/grants. Approximately 71% of current students receive some form of financial assistance. Average scholarship/grant $2,250 (full-time), $420 (part-time).

DEGREE REQUIREMENTS. For J.D.: 92 credits with a GPA of at least a 2.5 (A = 4), plus completion of upper divisional writing course; 3-year full-time program, 4-year part-time program. Accelerated J.D. with 1 summer of course work.

CAREER AND PLACEMENT INFORMATION. Approximately 97% of graduates are employed in Puerto Rico. More than 73% of graduates are practicing law; 8% are in business; 19% in government; none are in academia. Approximately 60% of the Inter American University of Puerto Rico's first-time state bar exam takers pass the bar exam; the passage rate for all first-time takers from ABA-approved schools is 69%. Graduates are eligible to take the bar exam in all 50 states.

UNIVERSITY OF IOWA

Iowa City, Iowa 52242
Internet site: http://www.uiona.edu

Founded 1847. Located 125 miles E of Des Moines. Public control. Semester system. Library: 3,651,000 volumes; 5,613,200 microforms; 37,200 periodicals/subscriptions.

University's other graduate colleges: College of Business Administration, College of Education, College of Engineering, College of Liberal Arts, College of Nursing; College of Dentistry, College of Medicine.

Total university enrollment: 27,500.

College of Law

276 Boyd Law Building
Melrose and Byington Street
Iowa City, Iowa 52242-1396
Phone: (319)335-9034
Internet site: http://wwwuiowa.edu/~lawcoll
E-mail: law-admissions@uiowa.edu

Established 1865. Oldest law school west of Mississippi. Located on main campus. ABA approved since 1923. AALS member. Semester system. Full-time study only. Law library: 836,000 volumes/microforms; 7,843 current periodicals/subscriptions; 57 computer workstations; has LEXIS, NEXIS, WESTLAW, ILP. Special programs: externships.

Annual tuition: resident $5,974, nonresident $15,324. On-campus housing available for both single and married students. Annual on-campus housing cost: single students $2,468 (room only), $4,209 (room and board), married students $3,264. For on-campus housing information contact Housing Office. Phone: (319)335-3009. Contact Family Housing Office for married student housing. Phone: (319)335-3199. Contact Housing Clearinghouse for off-campus housing information. Phone: (319)335-3055. Off-campus housing and personal expenses: approximately $9,366. Additional costs: books approximately $700.

Enrollment: first-year class 51; total full-time 10 (men 56%, women 44%); no part-time students. First-year statistics: 32% out of state, 45 states and foreign countries represented; 44% women; 22% minority; average age 26; 209 undergraduate institutions represented; range of first-year section sizes 25–75 students; number of upper division courses offered after first year 127.

Faculty: full-time 51, part-time 10; 25% female; 8% minority; student/faculty ratio 13 to 1.

Degrees conferred: J.D., J.D.-joint degree with all graduate schools/colleges through the Graduate College. LL.M. (International and Comparative Law) is for both U.S. attorneys and persons who have completed a basic legal education and received a university degree in law in another country.

RECRUITMENT PRACTICES AND POLICIES. Attends national law school forums. On-campus informational sessions. School does have diversity program and actively recruits women/minority applicants.

ADMISSION REQUIREMENTS FOR FIRST-YEAR APPLICANTS. LSDAS law school report, LSAT (not later than December test date, if more than one LSAT, average is used), bachelor's degree from an accredited institution, personal statement, transcripts (must show all schools attended and at least three years of study) required in support of application. Letters of recommendation are not required but strongly encouraged. Applicants must have received bachelor's degree prior to enrollment. In addition, international applicants must submit TOEFL (not older than two years), affidavit of financial support. Preference given to Iowa residents (70% of class). For information regarding J.D.-graduate degree programs contact the Assistant Dean of Students. Phone: (319)335-9034. Apply to Office of Admission after September 30, before March 1. First-year students admitted fall only, except for summer Accelerated Candidates who begin in May. Rolling admission process, notification starts in November and is finished by late April. Application fee $20. Phone: (319)335-9142. E-mail: law-admissions@ uiowa.edu.

ADMISSION REQUIREMENTS FOR TRANSFER APPLICANTS. Accepts transfers from other ABA-accredited schools. Admission limited to space available. At least one year of enrollment, dean's letter indicating applicant is in good standing (prefer applicants in the top quarter of first-year class), LSAT, LSDAS, personal statement regarding reason for transfer, current law school transcript required in support of application. Apply to Admission Office by June 1. Admission decisions made by late July. Application fee $20. Will consider visiting students.

ADMISSION REQUIREMENTS FOR LL.M. APPLICANTS. Office transcript from ABA- or AALS-approved school, personal statement, recommendations required in support of LL.M. application. TOEFL required for international applicants from non-English-language universities (score of 575 required). Apply to Graduate Program in International and Comparative Law, Office of Admission. Phone: (319)355-9071. Fax: (319)355-9019.

ADMISSION STANDARDS. Number of full-time applicants 1,261; number accepted 542; number enrolled 219; median LSAT 158 (75% of class have a score at or above 155); median GPA 3.38 (A = 4) (75% of class have a GPA at or above 3.20). Attrition rate 2.2%. Gorman rating 4.50; *U.S. News & World Report* ranking is in the top 25 of all law schools.

FINANCIAL AID. Need-based scholarships, merit scholarships, Law Opportunity Fellowships (diversity program), grants-in-aid, institutional loans; federal loans and Federal WS offered through university's Financial Aid Office. Assistantships may be available for upper divisional joint-degree candidates. For scholarships (selection criteria place heavy reliance on LSAT and undergraduate GPA) apply to Associate Director of Admissions and Financial Aid after January 1, and as early as possible. Phone: (319)335-9142. For all other programs apply to university's Office of Financial Aid. Phone: (319)355-1450. Use FAFSA for all federal programs (Title IV School code #001892). Also submit Financial Aid Transcript, federal income tax forms. Approximately 42% of first-year class received scholarships/grants-in-aid. Approximately 85% of current students receive some form of financial assistance. Average scholarship/grant $5,166. Average debt after graduation $32,600.

DEGREE REQUIREMENTS. For J.D.: 90 credits (35 required) with a 65 (scale 0–100) GPA, plus completion of upper divisional writing course; 3-year program. Accelerated J.D. begins with first summer of course work. For J.D.-graduate degree program: up to 12 credits may be used toward J.D. and up to 12 credits may be used for the graduate degree (12–24 credits less than total of both degrees completed separately). For J.D.-LL.M.: 114 total credits. For LL.M. (International and Comparative Law): individualized programs usually require 24 credits, a combination of elective coursework, independent study, approved study abroad, approved work-study externship; comprehensive oral exam; research paper of publishable quality.

CAREER AND PLACEMENT INFORMATION. Approximately 43% of graduates are employed in state. More than 77% of graduates are practicing law; 8% are in business; 14% in government; 1% in academia. Approximately 79% of the University of Iowa's first-time state bar exam takers pass the Iowa Bar Exam; Iowa's passage rate for all first-time takers from ABA-approved schools is 78%. Graduates are eligible to take the bar exam in all 50 states.

THE JOHN MARSHALL LAW SCHOOL

315 South Plymouth Court
Chicago, Illinois 60604-3968
Phone: (800)537-4280, (312)427-2737
Internet site: http://www.jmls.edu
E-mail: 6alonzo@jmls.edu

Established 1899. Located in the heart of Chicago's legal and financial district. ABA approved since 1951. AALS member. Semester system. Full-time, part-time study. Law library: 347,000 volumes/microforms; 4,938 current subscriptions/periodicals; 20 computer workstations; has LEXIS, NEXIS, WESTLAW, CALI. Special facilities: Center for Advocacy and Dispute Resolution, Center for Information Technology and Privacy Law, Center for Intellectual Property Law, Center for International and Comparative Studies, Center for Real Estate Law, Center for Tax Law and Employees Benefits, Fair Housing Legal Support Center. Special programs: summer study abroad in Ireland, Czech Republic, Lithuania, China; externships.

Annual tuition: full-time $17,020, part-time $12,500. No on-campus housing available. All law students live off-campus. Contact the Admissions Office for off-campus information. Off-campus housing and personal expenses: approximately $13,410. Additional costs: books approximately $700.

Enrollment: first-year class 179, part-time 54; total full-time 753, part-time 357 (men 61%, women 39%). First-year statistics: 35% out of state, 31 states and foreign countries represented; 39% women; 16% minority; average age 24; 113 undergraduate institutions repre-

sented; average first-year section size 65 students; number of upper division courses offered after first year 63 full-time, 115 part-time.

Faculty: full-time 54, part-time 100; 28% female; 8% minority; student/faculty ratio 16.5 to 1.

Degrees conferred: J.D., J.D.-M.B.A. (Rosary College), J.D.-M.P.A. (Roosevelt University), J.D.-M.A. (Political Science, Roosevelt University). LL.M. (Comparative Legal Studies) for both U.S.-trained and persons who have completed a basic legal education and received a university degree in law in another country.

RECRUITMENT PRACTICES AND POLICIES. Attends national law school forums. On-campus informational sessions. School does have diversity program and actively recruits women/minority applicants.

ADMISSION REQUIREMENTS FOR FIRST-YEAR APPLICANTS. LSDAS law school report, LSAT (not later than February [fall], June [spring], if more than one LSAT, highest is used), bachelor's degree from an accredited institution, personal statement, two recommendations, transcripts (must show all schools attended and at least three years of study) required in support of application. Applicants must have received bachelor's degree prior to enrollment. Interview not required; campus visits encouraged. In addition, international applicants whose native language is not English must submit TOEFL (score of 600 required), TWE (score of 4.5 required), official transcripts translated and certified, credential evaluations, supplemental application. Joint-degree applicants must apply to and be accepted by both schools/universities. First-year students admitted both fall and spring. Apply to Office of Admission after October 1, before March 1 (fall), October 30 (spring). Rolling admission process, notification starts in November and is finished by late April. Acceptance of offer and first deposit due April 15 (fall). Application fee $50. Phone: (800)537-4280. E-mail: 6alonzo@jmls.edu.

ADMISSION REQUIREMENTS FOR TRANSFER APPLICANTS. Accepts transfers from other ABA-accredited schools. Admission limited to space available. At least one year of enrollment, dean's letter indicating applicant is in good standing (applicants should have at least a 2.5 GPA), LSAT, LSDAS, personal statement regarding reason for transfer, current law school transcript required in support of application. Apply to Admission Office by July 1 (fall), December 1 (spring). Admission decision made within six weeks of receipt of complete application. Application fee $50. Will consider visiting students.

ADMISSION REQUIREMENTS FOR LL.M. APPLI-CANTS. Official law school transcripts, two letters of recommendation required in support of LL.M. application. In addition to the above listed requirements, international attorneys must submit translations and certification of international law degree; affidavit of financial support. Admits fall and spring. Apply to Office of Graduate Admissions at least two months prior to semester of entrance. Application fee $50. Phone: (800)537-4280.

ADMISSION STANDARDS. Number of full-time applicants 179, part-time 54; number accepted 755 full-time, 260 part-time; number enrolled 179 full-time, 54 part-time; median LSAT 158 (75% of class have a score at or above 145 full-time, 145 part-time); median GPA 3.42 (A = 4) (75% of class have a GPA at or above 2.62 full-time, 2.51 part-time). Attrition rate 6%. Gorman rating 3.08; *U.S. News & World Report* ranking is in the fourth tier of all law schools.

FINANCIAL AID. Scholarships, merit scholarships, grants-in-aid, institutional loans, private loans, federal loans, Federal WS. Financial aid packets sent to all accepted students on or about March 1, return application as soon as possible. For scholarships, the selection criteria place heavy reliance on LSAT and undergraduate GPA. Use FAFSA for all federal programs (Title IV School code #G01698). Also submit Financial Aid Transcript, federal income tax forms. Approximately 16% (full-time), 14% (part-time) of first-year class received scholarships/grants-in-aid. Approximately 60% of current students receive some form of financial assistance. Average scholarship/grant $10,700 full-time, $6,200 part-time. Average debt after graduation $52,100.

DEGREE REQUIREMENTS. For J.D.: 90 credits (41 required) with a 2.0 (A = 4) GPA, plus completion of upper divisional writing course; 3-year program, 4-year program (part-time). For J.D.-graduate degree: 4-year program rather than the 5 years usually required for both degrees if taken separately. For LL.M. (Comparative Legal Studies): a minimum of 21 credits; a GPA of 2.75 (A = 4) required; externship/independent study project.

CAREER AND PLACEMENT INFORMATION. Approximately 87% of graduates are employed in state. More than 58% of graduates are practicing law; 22% are in business; 20% in government; none in academia. Approximately 87% of John Marshall Law School's first-time state bar exam takers pass the Illinois Bar Exam; Illinois' passage rate for all first-time takers from ABA-approved schools is 87%. Graduates are eligible to take the bar exam in all 50 states.

UNIVERSITY OF KANSAS
Lawrence, Kansas 66045
Internet site: http://www.ukans.edu

Founded 1886. Located 40 miles W of Kansas City. 25 miles E of Topeka (state capital). Public control. Semester system. Library: 3,379,000 volumes; 2,900,000 microforms; 32,500 periodicals/subscriptions; 250 computer workstations.

University's other graduate colleges/schools: College of Liberal Arts and Sciences, School of Architecture and Urban Design, School of Business, School of Education, School of Engineering, School of Fine Arts, School of Journalism and Mass Communication, School of Pharmacy, School of Medicine, School of Social Welfare, Graduate Studies at Medical Center—includes School of Allied Health, School of Nursing.

Total university enrollment: 27,600.

School of Law
205 Green Hall
Lawrence, Kansas 66045-2380
Phone: (913)864-4550
Internet site: http://www.law.ukans.edu
E-mail: lindeman@law.wpo.ukans.edu

Established as a Department of Law 1978, became School of Law 1981. Located on main campus. ABA approved since 1923. AALS charter member. Semester system. Full-time, day study only. Law library: 325,000 volumes/microforms; 4,330 current periodicals/subscriptions; 51 computer workstations; has LEXIS, NEXIS, WESTLAW, DIALOG. Special programs: summer study abroad in London, England as part of the London Law Consortium.

Annual tuition: resident $4,576, nonresident $11,241. On-campus housing available for both single and married students. Annual on-campus housing cost: single students $3,640 (room and board), married students $2,600. Housing deadline February 15. Contact Department of Student Housing for on-campus housing information. Phone: (913)864-4560. Law students tend to live off-campus. Contact Director Stouffer Place, Jayhawker Towers for off-campus information. Phone: (913)864-8305. Off-campus housing and personal expenses: approximately $10,391. Additional costs: books approximately $700.

Enrollment: first-year class 184; total full-time 496 (men 59%, women 41%); no part-time students. First-year statistics: 17% out of state, 36 states and foreign countries represented; 41% women; 14% minority; average age 24; 147 undergraduate institutions represented; range of first-year section sizes 20–100 students; number of upper division courses offered after first year 85.

Faculty: full-time 29, part-time 9; 30% female; 1% minority; student/faculty ratio 17.6 to 1.

Degrees conferred: J.D., J.D.-M.B.A., J.D.-M.P.A., J.D.-M.A. (Economics, Philosophy), J.D.-M.S. (Urban Planning, Health Services Administration), J.D.-M.S.W.

RECRUITMENT PRACTICES AND POLICIES. Has many on-campus informational sessions. School does have diversity program and actively recruits women/minority applicants.

ADMISSION REQUIREMENTS FOR FIRST-YEAR APPLICANTS. LSDAS law school report, LSAT (prefers December test date, if more than one LSAT, average is used), bachelor's degree from an accredited institution, personal statement, one recommendation (prefers two or three), transcripts (must show all schools attended and at least three years of study) required in support of application. Applicants must have received bachelor's degree prior to enrollment. In addition, international applicants must submit TOEFL (not older than two years). Apply to Office of Admission after September 30, before March 15 (for priority consideration apply by February 1). First-year students admitted fall only. Accelerated J.D. program begins in May. Rolling admission process, notification starts in November and is finished by late April. School does maintain a waiting list. Application fee $40. Phone: (913)864-4378. E-mail: lindeman@law.wpo.ukans.edu.

ADMISSION REQUIREMENTS FOR TRANSFER APPLICANTS. Accepts a limited number of transfers from other ABA-accredited schools. Admission limited to space available. At least one year of enrollment, dean's letter indicating applicant is in good standing, LSAT, LSDAS, personal statement regarding reason for transfer, one letter of recommendation, current law school transcript required in support of application. Apply to Admission Office at least two months prior to semester of entrance. Admission decisions made within six weeks of receipt of complete application file. Application fee $40. Will consider visiting students.

ADMISSION STANDARDS. Number of full-time applicants 819; number accepted 379; number enrolled 184; median LSAT 158 (75% of class have a score at or above 154); median GPA 3.39 (A = 4) (75% of class have a GPA at or above 3.16). Attrition rate 1.6%. Gorman rating 3.71; *U.S. News & World Report* ranking is in the second tier of all law schools.

FINANCIAL AID. Scholarships, merit scholarships, minority scholarships, grants-in-aid, institutional loans; federal loans and Federal WS offered through university's Financial Aid Office. Assistantships may be available for upper divisional joint-degree candidates. For scholarships (selection criteria place heavy reliance on LSAT and undergraduate GPA) apply to Financial Aid Office after January 1, before March 1. Phone: (913)864-4378. For all other programs apply to university's Student Financial Aid Office, Strong Hall. Phone: (913)864-4700. Use FAFSA for all federal programs (Title IV School code #001948). Also submit Financial Aid Transcript, federal income tax forms. Approximately 36% of first-year class received scholarships/grants-in-aid. Approximately 70% of current students receive some form of financial assistance. Average scholarship/grant $2,000. Average debt after graduation $25,000.

DEGREE REQUIREMENTS. For J.D.: 90 credits (43–45 required) credits with a 2.0 (A = 4) GPA, plus completion of upper divisional writing course; 3-year program. Accelerated J.D. with 2 summers of course work. For J.D.-master's: individually designed degree programs; all are 4-year programs rather than the usual five years needed if each degree taken separately.

CAREER AND PLACEMENT INFORMATION. About 140 employers conducted on-campus interviews. Approximately 48% of graduates are employed in state. More than 74% of graduates are practicing law; 11% are in business; 15% in government; none in academia. Approximately 88% of the University of Kansas' first-time state bar exam takers pass the Kansas Bar Exam; Kansas' passage rate for all first-time takers from ABA-approved schools is 82%. Graduates are eligible to take the bar exam in all 50 states.

UNIVERSITY OF KENTUCKY
Lexington, Kentucky 40506-0032
Internet site: http://www.uky.edu

Founded 1865. Located in the bluegrass horse farm region of central Kentucky. Public control. Semester system. Library: 2,556,800 volumes; 5,240,000 microforms, 26,000 periodicals/subscriptions; 1,000 computer workstations.

University's other graduate colleges/schools: College of Communication and Information Studies, College of Human Environmental Sciences, College of Nursing, College of Social Work—Graduate programs from the Colleges of Agriculture, Allied Health, Arts and Sciences, Business and Economics, Education, Engineering, Fine

Arts—College of Dentistry, College of Medicine, College of Pharmacy.

Total university enrollment: 24,400.

School of Law
209 Law Building
Lexington, Kentucky 40506-0048
Phone: (606)257-1678
Internet site: http://www.uky.edu/Law
E-mail: dbakert@pop.uky.edu

Established 1908. Located on main campus. ABA approved since 1925. AALS member since 1912. Semester system. Full-time, day study only. Law library: 350,000 volumes/microforms; 3,623 current periodicals/subscriptions; 45 computer workstations; has LEXIS, NEXIS, WESTLAW, DIALOG; is a U.S. Government Depository. Special programs: Mineral Law; externships.

Annual tuition: resident $4,956, nonresident $12,796. On-campus housing available for both single and married students. Annual on-campus housing cost: single students $4,956 (room only), married students $4,728. Contact Office of Apartment Housing for on-campus housing information. Phone: (606)257-3721. Law students tend to live off-campus. Contact Real Property Division for off-campus information. Phone: (606)257-8649. Off-campus housing and personal expenses: approximately $9,898. Additional costs: books approximately $700.

Enrollment: first-year class 133; total full-time 421 (men 63%, women 37%); no part-time students. First-year statistics: 15–22% out of state, 27 states and foreign countries represented; 37% women; 6% minority; average age 25; 127 undergraduate institutions represented; range of first-year section sizes 10–70 students; number of upper division courses offered after first year 57.

Faculty: full-time 27, part-time 30; 27% female; 7% minority; student/faculty ratio 19 to 1.

Degrees conferred: J.D., J.D.-M.B.A., J.D.-M.P.A.

RECRUITMENT PRACTICES AND POLICIES. Attends several national law school forums. Has on-campus informational sessions. School does have diversity program and actively recruits women/minority applicants.

ADMISSION REQUIREMENTS FOR FIRST-YEAR APPLICANTS. LSDAS law school report, LSAT (not later than February test date, if more than one LSAT, takes the most recent test), bachelor's degree from an accredited institution, personal statement, transcripts (must show all schools attended and at least three years of study) required in support of application. Recommendations not required but strongly encouraged. Applicants must have received bachelor's degree prior to enrollment.

Apply to Office of Admission after September 30, before March 1. First-year students admitted fall only. Applicants for joint-degree program must apply to and be accepted by both schools. Rolling admission process, notification starts in November and is finished by mid April. School does maintain a waiting list. Application fee $25. Phone: (606)257-1678. E-mail: dbakert@pop.uky.edu.

ADMISSION REQUIREMENTS FOR TRANSFER APPLICANTS. Accepts transfers from other ABA-accredited schools. Admission limited to space available. At least one year of enrollment, in good standing (present a 2.7 GPA [A = 4] or higher), LSAT, LSDAS, personal statement regarding reason for transfer, current law school transcript showing rank in class required in support of application. Apply to Admission Office by June 1 (fall), December 1 (spring), May 15 (summer). Admission decisions made on or about July 15 (fall). Application fee $25. Will consider visiting students.

ADMISSION STANDARDS. Number of full-time applicants 891; number accepted 341; number enrolled 133; median LSAT 159 (75% of class have a score at or above 156); median GPA 3.39 (A = 4) (75% of class have a GPA at or above 3.11). Attrition rate 3.2%. Gorman rating 3.26; *U.S. News & World Report* ranking is in the second tier of all law schools.

FINANCIAL AID. Scholarships, merit scholarships, minority scholarships, grants-in-aid, institutional loans; federal loans and Federal WS offered through university's Financial Aid Office. For scholarships (selection criteria place heavy reliance on LSAT and undergraduate GPA) no application is required, all accepted students are considered. For all other programs apply to university's Student Financial Aid Office, 128 Funkhouser Building, after January 1, before March 1. Phone: (606)257-3172. Use FAFSA for all federal programs (Title IV School code #001989). Also submit Financial Aid Transcript, federal income tax forms. Approximately 27% of first-year class received scholarships/grants-in-aid. Approximately 75% of current students receive some form of financial assistance. Average scholarship/grant $2,000. Average debt after graduation $36,000.

DEGREE REQUIREMENTS. For J.D.: 90 credits (34 required) with a 2.0 (A = 4) GPA, plus completion of upper divisional writing course; 3-year program. Accelerated J.D. with 1 summer of course work. For J.D.-master's: 4-year programs rather than the usual 5 years needed if both degrees taken separately.

CAREER AND PLACEMENT INFORMATION. About 56 employers conducted on-campus interviews. Approximately 86% of graduates are employed in state. More than 90% of graduates are practicing law; 6% are in business; 3% in government; 1% in academia. Approximately 92% of the University of Kentucky's first-time state bar exam takers pass the Kentucky Bar Exam; Kentucky's passage rate for all first-time takers from ABA-approved schools is 88%. Graduates are eligible to take the bar exam in all 50 states.

LEWIS AND CLARK COLLEGE

Portland, Oregon 91219-7879
Internet site: http://www.lclark.edu

Founded 1867. Located in a suburban area 6 miles from downtown Portland. Private control. Semester system. Library: 270,000 volumes; 220,000 microforms; 1,900 periodicals/subscriptions; 54 computer workstations.

The college has a Graduate School of Professional Studies in addition to its undergraduate programs.

Total college enrollment: 3,255.

Northwestern School of Law

10015 S.W. Terwilliger Boulevard
Portland, Oregon 97219-7799
Phone: (503)768-6600
Internet site: http://www.lclark.edu/LAW
E-mail: lawadmss@lclark.edu

Established 1884, became affiliated with Lewis and Clark College in 1965 and initiated a day division. ABA approved since 1970. AALS member. Semester system. Full-time (day), part-time (evening) study. Law library: 430,000 volumes/microforms; 4,312 current periodicals/subscriptions; 53 computer workstations; has LEXIS, NEXIS, WESTLAW, DIALOG, OCLC, INFOTRAC, PORTALS, CALI, WLN, INNOVATIVE, QL System; the only Patent and Trademark Depository in U.S. Special programs: Environmental and Natural Resources Law, Business and Commercial Law; externships.

Annual tuition: full-time $17,395 part-time $13,045. No on-campus housing available. Law students tend to live off-campus. Contact Admission Office for off-campus information. Off-campus housing and personal expenses: approximately $11,200. Additional costs: books approximately $700.

Enrollment: first-year class 135 full-time, 36 part-time; total full-time 481, part-time 156 (men 54%, women 46%). First-year statistics: 70% out of state, 34 states and foreign countries represented; 46% women; 14% minority; average age 26; 243 undergraduate institutions repre-

sented; range of first-year section sizes 27–60 students; number of upper division courses offered after first year 59 full-time, 48 part-time.

Faculty: full-time 35, part-time 56; 29% female; 5% minority; student/faculty ratio 18 to 1.

Degrees conferred: J.D., J.D.-M.P.A., LL.M. (Environmental and Natural Resources Law).

RECRUITMENT PRACTICES AND POLICIES. Attends several national law school forums. Has extensive on-campus informational activities and sessions. School does have diversity program and actively recruits women/minority applicants.

ADMISSION REQUIREMENTS FOR FIRST-YEAR APPLICANTS. LSDAS law school report, LSAT (not later than December test date, if more than one LSAT, highest is used), bachelor's degree from an accredited institution, personal statement, two recommendations, transcripts (must show all schools attended and at least three years of study) required in support of application. Applicants must have received bachelor's degree prior to enrollment. Interview not required. Campus and classroom visits encouraged. In addition, international applicants must submit TOEFL (not older than two years). Apply to Office of Admission after September 30, before March 15 (priority deadline). First-year students admitted fall only. Rolling admission process, notification starts in January and is finished by late April. Acceptance of offer and first deposit due within three weeks of notice of acceptance. Application fee $50. Phone: (800)303-4860, (503)768-6614. Fax: (503)768-6671. E-mail: lawadmss@lclark.edu.

ADMISSION REQUIREMENTS FOR TRANSFER APPLICANTS. Accepts transfers from other ABA-accredited schools. Admission limited to space available. At least one year of enrollment, dean's letter indicating applicant is in good standing (prefer applicants in the top quarter of first-year class), LSAT, LSDAS, personal statement regarding reason for transfer, undergraduate transcript, current law school transcript required in support of application. Apply to Office of Admission by July 15. Admission decisions made by early August. Application fee $50. Will consider visiting students.

ADMISSION REQUIREMENTS FOR LL.M. APPLICANTS. Applicants must be graduates of an ABA-accredited law school or non-U.S. law school approved under guidelines adopted by the ABA. Submit official transcripts, two letters of recommendation, writing sample or published work, personal statement indicating demonstrated interest in or academic training in environmental or natural resources law and policy. In addition, international applicants whose native language is not English must submit TOEFL and transcripts with English translations along with statement of financial support. Admits to both day and evening division. Apply to Admissions Office at least six weeks prior to semester of entrance. Application fee $50.

ADMISSION STANDARDS. Number of full-time applicants 1,637, part-time 143; number accepted 761 full-time, 81 part-time; number enrolled 135 full-time, 36 part-time; median LSAT 161 (75% of class have a score at or above 158 full-time, 156 part-time); median GPA 3.27 (A = 4) (75% of class have a GPA at or above 3.01 full-time, 2.78 part-time). Attrition rate 3.6%. Gorman rating 3.17, *U.S. News & World Report* ranking is in the second tier of all law schools.

FINANCIAL AID. Scholarships, minority scholarships, Native American scholarships, grants-in-aid, private and institutional loans; federal loans and Federal WS offered through college's Financial Aid Office. For scholarships (selection criteria place heavy reliance on LSAT and undergraduate GPA) there is no separate scholarship form. For all programs apply after January 1, before February 1 to Assistant Director of Student Financial Services. Phone: (503)768-7097. Use FAFSA for all federal programs (Title IV School code #003197). Also submit Financial Aid Transcript, federal income tax forms. Approximately 37% of first-year class received scholarships/grants-in-aid. Approximately 40% of current students receive some form of financial assistance. Average scholarship/grant full-time $6,000, part-time $5,000.

DEGREE REQUIREMENTS. For J.D.: 86 credits (34–39 required) with a 2.0 (A = 4) GPA, plus completion of 2 upper divisional writing courses; 3-year full-time program, 4-year part-time program. Accelerated J.D. with 1 summer of course work. For LL.M. (Environmental and Natural Resources Law): 26 credits including a 6-credit research paper.

CAREER AND PLACEMENT INFORMATION. About 15 employers conducted on-campus interviews. Approximately 60% of graduates are employed in state. More than 60% of graduates are practicing law; 17% are in business; 21% in government; 2% in academia. Approxi-

mately 86% of Lewis and Clark College's Northwestern School of Law's first-time state bar exam takers pass the Oregon Bar Exam; Oregon's passage rate for all first-time takers from ABA-approved schools is 85%. Graduates are eligible to take the bar exam in all 50 states.

LOUISIANA STATE UNIVERSITY & AGRICULTURAL AND MECHANICAL COLLEGE

Baton Rouge, Louisiana 70803-3103
Internet site: http://www.lsu/guests/LSU

Founded 1860. Located in an urban area of Baton Rouge. Public control. Semester system. Library: 2,778,500 volumes; 4,892,000 microforms; 14,500 periodicals/subscriptions.

University's other graduate colleges/schools: College of Agriculture, College of Arts and Sciences, College of Business Administration, College of Design, College of Education, College of Engineering, Manship School of Mass Communication, School of Library and Information Science, School of Music, School of Social Work, School of Veterinary Medicine.

Total university enrollment: 25,300.

Paul M. Hebert Law Center

210 Law Center
Baton Rouge, Louisiana 70803
Phone: (504)388-8491
Internet site: http://www.lsu/guests/LSU/LAW

Established 1906 as LSU Law School, renamed in 1979. Located on main campus. ABA approved since 1926. AALS member. Semester system. Full-time, day study only. Law library: 395,000 volumes; 840,000 microforms; 2,809 current periodicals/subscriptions; 13 computer workstations; has LEXIS, NEXIS, WESTLAW, DIALOG; is both a State and Federal Government Depository. Special facility: Center of Civil Law Studies, Louisiana Judicial College. Special programs: summer study abroad in France at University of Aix-Marseille III Law School; externships.

Annual tuition: resident $3,936, nonresident $8,923. On-campus housing available for single students only. On-campus housing cost (per semester): single students $695-$1,125 (room only). Contact Department of Residential Life for both on- and off-campus housing information. Phone: (504)388-6642. Law students tend to live off-campus. Off-campus housing and personal expenses: approximately $10,950. Additional costs: books approximately $700.

Enrollment: first-year class 262; total full-time 661 (men 55%, women 45%); no part-time students. First-year statistics: 10% out of state, 45% women; 9% minority; average age 25; range of first-year section sizes 75–80 students; number of upper division courses offered after first year 62.

Faculty: full-time 33, part-time 16; 7% female; 7% minority; student/faculty ratio 20 to 1.

Degrees conferred: J.D., J.D.-M.P.A., LL.M., M.C.L. (only for persons who have completed a basic legal education and received a university degree in law in another country).

RECRUITMENT PRACTICES AND POLICIES. Attends national law school forums. On-campus informational sessions. School does have diversity program and actively recruits women/minority applicants.

ADMISSION REQUIREMENTS FOR FIRST-YEAR APPLICANTS. LSDAS law school report, LSAT (not later than December test date, if more than one LSAT, highest is used), bachelor's degree from an accredited institution, personal statement, photograph, transcripts (must show all schools attended and at least three years of study) required in support of application. Recommendations are not required but are encouraged. In addition, international applicants whose native language is not English must submit TOEFL (preferred score 600). Applicants must have received bachelor's degree prior to enrollment. Preference given to state residents, the nonresident enrollment may not exceed 10% by statute. Joint-degree applicants must apply to and be accepted by both schools. In addition both the LSAT and GRE are required. Apply to Office of Admission after November 1, before February 1. First-year students admitted fall only. Rolling admission process, notification starts in December and is finished by late April. Application fee $25. Phone: (507)388-8646.

ADMISSION REQUIREMENTS FOR TRANSFER APPLICANTS. Accepts transfers from other ABA-accredited schools. Admission limited to space available. At least one year of enrollment, dean's letter indicating applicant is in good standing (prefer applicants in the top quarter of first-year class), LSAT, LSDAS, personal statement regarding reason for transfer, current law school transcript required in support of application. Apply to Admission Office by June 30 (fall), November 1 (spring). Admission decisions made within six weeks of receipt of completed application file. Application fee $25. Will consider visiting students.

ADMISSION REQUIREMENTS FOR LL.M./M.C.L. APPLICANTS. Official transcripts with rank in class from ABA-approved law school required in support of graduate application. In addition, TOEFL is required for international applicants whose native language is not English (a score of 600 generally required). For M.C.L. applicants must have had previous training in civil law. Apply to Graduate Studies Committee by February 1. Application fee $25.

ADMISSION STANDARDS. Number of full-time applicants 947; number accepted 541; number enrolled 262; median LSAT 153 (75% of class have a score at or above 148); median GPA 3.28 (A = 4) (75% of class have a GPA at or above 3.11). Attrition rate 15%. Gorman rating 3.39; *U.S. News & World Report* ranking is in the third tier of all law schools.

FINANCIAL AID. Scholarships, grants-in-aid, institutional and private loans; federal loans and Federal WS offered through university's Financial Aid Office. Assistantships may be available for upper divisional joint-degree candidates. For scholarships (selection criteria place heavy reliance on LSAT and undergraduate GPA) apply to Admissions Office after January 1, before April 15 and complete scholarship application on back of admission application. For all other programs apply to university's Office of Student Aid and Scholarships. Phone: (504)388-3103. Fax: (504)388-6300. Use FAFSA for all federal programs (Title IV School code #002010). Also submit Financial Aid Transcript, ACT analysis, federal income tax forms. Approximately 20% of first-year class received scholarships/grants-in-aid. Approximately 35% of current students receive some form of financial assistance. Average scholarship/grant $3,500.

DEGREE REQUIREMENTS. For J.D.: 97 credits (39 required) with a 68 (scale 0–100) GPA, plus completion of upper divisional writing course; 7 semesters in residence. For J.D.-M.P.A.: approximately 4 years of full-time study. For LL.M./M.C.L.: 24 credits, at least 2 semesters in residence; a GPA of 72 (scale 0–100) in course work, 76 (scale 0–100) in thesis/research papers; thesis of publishable quality; recommendation for degree from faculty Evaluation Committee and Graduate Studies Committee.

CAREER AND PLACEMENT INFORMATION. About 38 employers conducted on-campus interviews. Approximately 91% of graduates are employed in state. More than 83% of graduates are practicing law; 7% are in business; 10% in government; none are in academia. Approximately 79% of Louisiana State University's Paul M. Hebert Law Center's first-time state bar exam takers pass the Louisiana Bar Exam; Louisiana's passage rate for all first-time takers from ABA-approved schools is 67%. Graduates are eligible to take the bar exam in all 50 states.

UNIVERSITY OF LOUISVILLE
Louisville, Kentucky 40292-0001
Internet site: http://www.louisville.edu

Founded 1798. Located 5 miles S of downtown Louisville. Public control. Semester system. Library: 1,315,000 volumes/microforms; 12,812 periodicals/subscriptions.

University's other graduate colleges/schools: College of Arts and Sciences, College of Business and Public Administration, College of Health and Social Services, School of Education, School of Music, School of Nursing, Speed Scientific School, School of Dentistry, School of Medicine.

Total university enrollment: 21,200.

School of Law
2301 South 3rd Street
Louisville, Kentucky 40292
Phone: (502)852-6879
Internet site: http://www.louisville.edu/law
E-mail: jltorb01@ulkyvm.louisville.edu

Established 1846. Located on main campus. ABA approved since 1931. AALS member. Semester system. Full-time day; part-time evening study. Law library: 260,000 volumes/microforms; 4,800 current periodicals/subscriptions; 29 computer workstations; has LEXIS, WESTLAW, OCLC. Special facility: Center for Environmental Policy. Special programs: Samuel L. Greenebaum Public Service Program; 5 externships.

Annual tuition: resident full-time $4,850, part-time $4,060, nonresident full-time $12,690, part-time $10,590. On-campus housing available for both single and married students. Annual on-campus housing cost: single students $2,400 (room only), $3,580 (room and board), married students $3,900 (room only) $6,500 (room and board). Contact Graduate Housing Office for on-campus housing information. Phone: (502)852-6636. Law students tend to live off-campus. Contact Admissions Office for off-campus housing information. Off-campus housing and personal expenses: approximately $9,090. Additional costs: books approximately $700.

Enrollment: first-year class full-time 123, part-time 43; total full-time 419, part-time 91 (men 53%, women 47%). First-year statistics: 18% out of state, 25 states and foreign countries represented; 47% women; 6% minority; average age 25; 100 undergraduate institutions represented; range of first-year section sizes 40–60 students; number of upper division courses offered after first year full-time 63, part-time 26.

Faculty: full-time 28, part-time 20; 24% female; 11% minority; student/faculty ratio 18 to 1.

Degrees conferred: J.D., J.D.-M.B.A., J.D.-M.Div. (Louisville Presbyterian Theological Seminary).

RECRUITMENT PRACTICES AND POLICIES. Attends several national law school forums. Has on-campus informational sessions. School does have diversity program and actively recruits women/minority applicants.

ADMISSION REQUIREMENTS FOR FIRST-YEAR APPLICANTS. LSDAS law school report, LSAT (not later than December test date, if more than one LSAT, highest is used), bachelor's degree from an accredited institution, personal statement, transcripts (must show all schools attended and at least three years of study) required in support of application. Recommendation not required but encouraged. Applicants must have received bachelor's degree prior to enrollment. Interview not required; campus visits encouraged. In addition, international applicants whose native language is not English must submit TOEFL (not older than two years). Apply to Office of Admission after September 30, before February 15. Joint-degree applicants must apply to and be accepted by both schools. First-year students admitted fall only. Rolling admission process, notification starts in November and is finished by mid May. Application fee $30. Phone: (502)852-6364. E-mail: jltorb01@ulkyvm. louisville.edu.

ADMISSION REQUIREMENTS FOR TRANSFER APPLICANTS. Accepts transfers from other ABA-accredited schools. Admission limited to space available. At least one year of enrollment, dean's letter indicating applicant is in good standing (prefer applicants in the top quarter of first-year class), LSAT, LSDAS, personal statement regarding reason for transfer, current law school transcript required in support of application. Apply to Admission Office by May 15. Admission decisions made by mid July. Application fee $30. Will consider visiting students.

ADMISSION STANDARDS. Number of full-time applicants 798, part-time 124; number accepted full-time

320, part-time 65; number enrolled full-time 123, part-time 43; median LSAT 156 (75% of class have a score at or above 152 full-time, 152 part-time); median GPA 3.10 (A = 4) (75% of class have a GPA at or above 3.01 full-time, 2.80 part-time). Attrition rate 4.9%. Gorman rating 3.29; *U.S. News & World Report* ranking is in the third tier of all law schools.

FINANCIAL AID. Scholarships, merit scholarships, grants-in-aid, private and institutional loans; federal loans and Federal WS offered through university's Financial Aid Office. Assistantships may be available for upper divisional joint-degree candidates. For scholarships (selection criteria place heavy reliance on LSAT and undergraduate GPA), no financial aid application required; all accepted applicants are considered for all scholarship programs. Apply after January 1, before March 1 to the university's Office of Financial Aid for all other programs. Use FAFSA for all federal programs (Title IV School code #001999). Also submit Financial Aid Transcript, federal income tax forms. Approximately 14% (full-time), 7% (part-time) of first-year class received scholarships/grants-in-aid. Approximately 80% of current students receive some form of financial assistance. Average scholarship/grant for both full- and part-time students $4,850. Federal Loan Forgiveness Program available. Average debt after graduation $24,000.

DEGREE REQUIREMENTS. For J.D.: 90 credits (44 required) with a 2.0 (A = 4) GPA, plus completion of upper divisional writing course; 3-year program, 4-year program. For J.D.-master's: Joint-degree programs reduce the time required for completion of both degrees from 5 years to 4 years.

CAREER AND PLACEMENT INFORMATION. About 16 employers conducted on-campus interviews. Approximately 81% of graduates are employed in state. More than 74% of graduates are practicing law; 14% are in business; 11% in government; 1% in academia. Approximately 88% of the University of Louisville's first-time state bar exam takers pass the Kentucky Bar Exam; Kentucky's passage rate for all first-time takers from ABA-approved schools is 88%. Graduates are eligible to take the bar exam in all 50 states.

LOYOLA MARYMOUNT UNIVERSITY
Los Angeles, California 90045-8350
Internet site: http://www.lmu.edu

Founded 1911. Private control (Roman Catholic—Jesuit affiliation). Semester system. Library: 252,800 volumes;

94,400 microforms; 3,159 periodicals/subscriptions; 30 computer workstations.

University's other graduate colleges/schools: College of Business Administration, College of Communication and Fine Arts, College of Liberal Arts, College of Science and Engineering, School of Education.

Total university enrollment: 6,687.

Loyola Law School
919 South Albany Street
Los Angeles, California 90015
Phone: (213)736-1000
Internet site: http://www.law.lmu.edu
E-mail: lawadmis@lmulaw.lmu.edu

Established 1920. Located 1½ miles W of downtown Los Angeles. ABA approved since 1935. AALS member. Semester system. Full-time, part-time study. Law library: 414,350 volumes/microforms; 6,300 current periodicals/subscriptions; 56 computer workstations; has LEXIS, NEXIS, WESTLAW, DIALOG, C.CALI. Special facilities: Center for Conflict Resolution, Western Law Center for Disability Rights. Special Programs: summer study abroad in Costa Rica; externships.

Annual tuition: full-time $20,734, nonresident $13,922. No on-campus housing available. Law students live off-campus. Contact Admission Office for off-campus information. Off-campus housing and personal expenses: approximately $14,470. Additional costs: books approximately $700.

Enrollment: first-year class 354 full-time, 124 part-time; total full-time 963, part-time 388 (men 56%, women 44%). First-year statistics: 20% out of state, 40 states and foreign countries represented; 44% women; 39% minority; average age 24; 100 undergraduate institutions represented; range of first-year section sizes 80–100 students; number of upper division courses offered after first year 73 full-time, 80 part-time.

Faculty: full-time 65, part-time 58; 33% female; 19% minority; student/faculty ratio 22 to 1.

Degrees conferred: J.D., J.D.-M.B.A., J.D.-I. M.B.A.

RECRUITMENT PRACTICES AND POLICIES. Attends several national law school forums. Has on-campus informational sessions. School does have diversity program and actively recruits women/minority applicants.

ADMISSION REQUIREMENTS FOR FIRST-YEAR APPLICANTS. LSDAS law school report, LSAT (not later than December test date, results are valid for three years), bachelor's degree from an accredited institution, personal statement, at least one recommendation, transcripts (must show all schools attended and at least three years of study) required in support of application. Applicants must have received bachelor's degree prior to enrollment. Interview not required but may be requested by school. In addition, international applicants whose native language is not English must submit TOEFL (not older than two years; required score 600), all transcripts must have certified evaluations. Apply to Office of Admission after September 30, before February 1 (day), April 15 (evening), January 1 (scholarship applicants). Joint-degree applicants must apply to and be accepted by both schools. First-year students admitted fall only. Rolling admission process, notification starts in December and is finished by late April. School does maintain a waiting list. Application fee $50. Phone: (213)736-1180. E-mail: lawadmis@lmulaw.lmu.edu.

ADMISSION REQUIREMENTS FOR TRANSFER APPLICANTS. Accepts transfers from other ABA-accredited schools. Admission limited to space available. At least one year of enrollment, dean's letter indicating applicant is in good standing (prefer applicants in the top quarter of first-year class), LSAT, LSDAS, personal statement regarding reason for transfer, official undergraduate transcript, current law school transcript including rank in class required in support of application. Apply to Admission Office by July 15. Admission decisions made by mid August. Application fee $50. Will consider visiting students.

ADMISSION STANDARDS. Number of full-time applicants 2,588, part-time 433; number accepted full-time 999, part-time 168; number enrolled full-time 354, part-time 124; median LSAT 158 (75% of class have a score at or above 154 full- and part-time); median GPA 3.25 (A = 4) (75% of class have a GPA at or above full-time 3.05, part-time 2.93). Attrition rate 3.6%. Gorman rating 4.34; *U.S. News & World Report* ranking is in the second tier of all law schools.

FINANCIAL AID. Scholarships, merit scholarships, minority scholarships, grants-in-aid, private and institutional loans; federal loans and Federal WS offered through university's Financial Aid Office. Assistantships may be available for upper divisional joint-degree candidates. For scholarships (selection criteria place heavy reliance on LSAT and undergraduate GPA) apply to Admissions Office by January 1 (preferred date); all accepted applicants considered for scholarships. For all other programs apply by March 1. Use FAFSA for all federal programs (Title IV School code #001234). Also submit Financial Aid Transcript, federal income tax forms. Approximately 14% (full-time), 12% (part-time) of first-year class received scholarships/grants-in-aid. Approximately 89% of current students receive some form of financial assistance. Average scholarship/grant $15,000 (full-time), $10,000 (part-time). Average debt after graduation $60,000.

DEGREE REQUIREMENTS. For J.D.: 87 credits (49 required) with a 74.5 (scale 0–100) GPA, plus completion of upper divisional writing course; 40 hours of uncompensated (pro bono) public service; 3-year full-time program, 4-year part-time program. Accelerated J.D. with 1 summer of course work. For J.D.-master's: 4-year program rather than the usual 5 years needed if degrees taken separately.

CAREER AND PLACEMENT INFORMATION. About 56 employers conducted on-campus interviews. Approximately 78% of graduates are employed in state. More than 73% of graduates are practicing law; 16% are in business; 9% in government; 2% in academia. Approximately 83% of Loyola Marymount University's first-time state bar exam takers pass the California Bar Exam; California's passage rate for all first-time takers from ABA-approved schools is 83%. Graduates are eligible to take the bar exam in all 50 states.

LOYOLA UNIVERSITY CHICAGO

Chicago, Illinois 60611-2196
Internet site: http://www.luc.edu

Founded 1870. Private control (Roman Catholic—Jesuit affiliation). Semester system. Library: 1,349,000 volumes; 1,208,400 microforms; 11,454 periodicals/subscriptions; 245 computer workstations.

University's other graduate schools: Institute of Human Resources and Industrial Relations, Institute of Pastoral Studies, Marcella Niehoff School of Nursing, School of Business, School of Education, School of Social Work, Stritch School of Medicine.

Total university enrollment: 14,000.

School of Law
One East Pearson Street
Chicago, Illinois 60611
Phone: (312)915-7120
Internet site: http://www.luc.edu/schools/law
E-mail: law-admissions@luc.edu

Established 1908. Located on the Water Tower Campus about 1 mile N of downtown. ABA approved since 1925. AALS member since 1924. Semester system. Full-time, part-time study. Law library: 300,000 volumes/microforms; 3,499 current periodicals/subscriptions; 81 computer workstations; has LEXIS, NEXIS, WESTLAW. Special facilities: Institute for Consumer Antitrust Studies, Civitas Child Law Center, Institute for Health Law, Corporate Law Center, Center for Public Service. Special programs: summer study abroad in Rome at university's campus, Nottingham-Trent University (England), McGill University Center for Medicine, Ethics and Law (Montreal, Canada); externships.

Annual tuition: full-time $20,856, part-time $15,668, M.J. (evening) per credits $670, LL.M. (evening) per credit $807. Limited on-campus housing for available single students. Annual on-campus housing cost: single students $5,664 (room only). Contact Housing Office for both on- and off-campus housing information. Phone: (312)508-3300. Law students tend to live off-campus. Off-campus housing and personal expenses: approximately $13,250. Additional costs: books approximately $700.

Enrollment: first-year class 163 full-time, 83 part-time; total full-time 556, part-time 200 (men 49%, women 51%). First-year statistics: 40% out of state, 25 states and foreign countries represented; 51% women; 23% minority; average age 25; 105 undergraduate institutions represented; range of first-year section sizes 55–60 students; number of upper division courses offered after first year 93 full-time, 60 part-time.

Faculty: full-time 34, part-time 120; 36% female; 6% minority; student/faculty ratio 22 to 1.

Degrees conferred: J.D., J.D.-M.B.A., J.D.-H.S.I.R., J.D.-M.A. (Political Science), J.D.-M.S.W., LL.M. (Health Law, [full-and part-time]), M.J. (evenings), S.J.D. (Health Law and Policy), D.Law (Health Law and Policy).

RECRUITMENT PRACTICES AND POLICIES. Attends national law school forums. Informal on-campus informational sessions held on Fridays. School does have diversity program and actively recruits women/minority applicants.

ADMISSION REQUIREMENTS FOR FIRST-YEAR APPLICANTS. LSDAS law school report, LSAT (not later than December test date, if more than one LSAT, average is used), bachelor's degree from an accredited institution, personal statement, two recommendations, transcripts (must show all schools attended and at least three years of study) required in support of application. Applicants must have received bachelor's degree prior to enrollment. Interview not required but may be requested by school. In addition, international applicants whose native language is not English must submit TOEFL (not older than two years). Apply to Office of Admission after September 1, before April 1. First-year students admitted fall only. Rolling admission process, notification starts in December and is finished by mid May. School does maintain a waiting list. Application fee $45. Phone: (800)545-5744, (312)915-7170. Fax: (312)915-6215. E-mail: lawadmissions@luc.edu.

ADMISSION REQUIREMENTS FOR TRANSFER APPLICANTS. Accepts transfers from other ABA-accredited schools. Admission limited to space available. At least one year of enrollment, dean's letter indicating applicant is in good standing (prefer applicants in the top quarter of first-year class), LSAT, LSDAS, personal statement regarding reason for transfer, undergraduate transcript, current law school transcript required in support of application. Apply to Office of Admission by June 1. Admission decisions made by mid July. Application fee $45. Will consider visiting students.

ADMISSION REQUIREMENTS FOR GRADUATE LAW PROGRAMS. For M.J. (Child Law, Health Law): a bachelor's degree, experience with children and their families or be a health care professional; official transcripts, two letters of recommendation required in support of application. LSAT not required. In addition, international applicants should have graduated from a similarly accredited program in countries outside the U.S., if English is not the native language, submit TOEFL (not older than two years, 600 required), a 200-word statement (in English) indicating interest and intentions regarding either Health Law or Child Law. Apply after December 1, before March 1 to Graduate Legal Studies. Phone: (312)915-7155. M.J. candidates are notified by early April.

For LL.M. (Child Law, Health Law): A J.D. from an ABA-accredited law school, official transcripts, three letters of recommendations required in support of application. In addition, international lawyers should have graduated from a similarly accredited law program, if English is not the native language, submit TOEFL (not older than two years, 650 required), diploma or other document (with English translation) indicating completion of a first degree in law, a 200-word statement (in English) indicating interest and intentions regarding either Health Law or Child Law, an indication that applicant is eligible to sit for law licensing exam in home country. Apply by May 1 to Director of Graduate Legal Studies. Phone: (312)915-7155.

For D.Law: M.J. required, demonstrated superior research and writing skills, statement of goals and objectives required in support of application. (One applicant accepted each year.)

For S.J.D.: LL.M., M.H.A., M.P.A. degree for consideration, official transcripts, three letters of recommendation required in support of application. In addition, international lawyers should have graduated from a similarly accredited program, if English is not the native language, submit TOEFL (not older than two years, 650 required), diploma or other documents (with English translation) indicating completion of a first degree in law, a 200-word statement (in English) indicating interest and intentions regarding either Health Law or Child Law, supply information indicating that applicant is eligible to sit for law licensing exam in home country. Apply to the Director of Graduate Legal Studies. Phone: (312)915-7155.

ADMISSION STANDARDS. Number of full-time applicants 2,009, part-time 320; number accepted 755 full-time, 204 part-time; number enrolled 163 full-time, 83 part-time; median LSAT 159 (75% of class have a score at or above 154 full-time, 151 part-time); median GPA 3.27 (A = 4) (75% of class have a GPA at or above 2.95 full-time, 2.84 part-time). Attrition rate 1.4%. Gorman rating 3.49; *U.S. News & World Report* ranking is in the second tier of all law schools.

FINANCIAL AID. Scholarships, merit scholarships, grants-in-aid, private institutional loans, federal loans, Federal WS. Assistantships may be available for upper divisional joint-degree candidates. For scholarships (selection criteria place heavy reliance on LSAT and undergraduate GPA) apply to Assistant Director of Admissions and Financial Aid after January 1, before March 1 (priority deadline). Phone: (312)915-6412. Use FAFSA for all federal programs (Title IV School code #001710). Also submit Financial Aid Transcript, federal income tax forms. Approximately 39% (full-time), 23% (part-time) of first-year class received scholarships/grants-in-aid. Approximately 78% of current students receive some form of financial assistance. Average scholarship/grant $2,136 (full-time), $1,737 (part-time). Average debt after graduation $47,500. Tuition remission, fellowships available for LL.M. students, apply by June 1. For M.J. fellowships available, apply by June 1.

DEGREE REQUIREMENTS. For J.D.: 86 credits (46 required) with a 2.0 (A = 4) GPA, plus completion of upper divisional writing course and a course in philosophical and historical perspective of law; 3-year program, 4-year program. Accelerated J.D. with summer course work of up to a maximum of 9 credits. For J.D.-master's: individually designed programs, usually a 4-year program (full-time) rather than the usual 5 years needed if both degrees taken separately. For M.J. (Child Law, begins in June): 27 credits; 3-credit thesis; 2-year program. For M.J. (Health Law, begins in June): 23 credits of required course work (includes thesis), 7 credits of electives; optional externship. For LL.M. (Child Law): 21 credits; thesis; a GPA of 2.5 (A = 4). For LL.M. (Health Law): 24 credits; a GPA of 2.5 (A = 4); thesis of publishable quality. For D.Law, S.J.D.: 2-year full-time programs, thesis in first year, dissertation in second year; presentation of dissertation to law school community, health law community, and, where appropriate, the medical community.

CAREER AND PLACEMENT INFORMATION. About 40 employers conducted on-campus interviews. Approximately 93% of graduates are employed in state. More than 62% of graduates are practicing law; 22% are in business; 16% in government; none in academia. Approximately 94% of Loyola University Chicago's first-time state bar exam takers pass the Illinois Bar Exam; Illinois' passage rate for all first-time takers from ABA-approved schools is 87%. Graduates are eligible to take the bar exam in all 50 states.

LOYOLA UNIVERSITY NEW ORLEANS
New Orleans, Louisiana 70118-9195
Internet site: http://www.loyno.edu

Founded 1849. Located in uptown New Orleans, 5 miles N of the French Quarter. Private control (Roman Catholic—Jesuit affiliation). Semester system. Library: 439,000 volumes; 930,000 microforms; 1,650 periodicals/subscriptions; 35 computer workstations.

University's other graduate colleges/schools: College of Arts and Sciences, College of Music, Institute for Ministry, Joseph A. Butt, S. J. College of Business Administration.

Total university enrollment: 2,000.

School of Law
7214 St. Charles Avenue
New Orleans, Louisiana 70118
Phone: (504)861-5550
Internet site: http://www.loyno.edu

Established 1914. Located on main campus. ABA approved since 1931. AALS member since 1934. Semester system. Full-time, part-time study. Law library: 255,200 volumes/microforms; 2,594 current periodicals/subscriptions; 14 computer workstations; has LEXIS, NEXIS, WESTLAW, DIALOG. Special facility: Public Law Center. Special programs: summer study abroad at Cuernavaca, Mexico; Kyoto, Japan; Cape Town, South Africa; externships.

Annual tuition: full-time $17,975, part-time $12,179. On-campus housing available for single students only. Annual on-campus housing and personal costs: single students $11,080; room per year $2,980, board per semester $1,075–$1,200. Contact Office of Residential Life for both on- and off-campus housing information. Phone: (504)865-3735. Law students tend to live off-campus. Off-campus housing and personal expenses: approximately $11,200. Additional costs: books approximately $600.

Enrollment: first-year class 159 full-time, 47 part-time; total full-time 513, part-time 174 (men 51%, women 49%). First-year statistics: 53% out of state, 30 states and foreign countries represented; 49% women; 21% minority; average age 25; 98 undergraduate institutions represented; range of first-year section sizes 70–80 students; number of upper division courses offered after first year 62 full-time, 35 part-time.

Faculty: full-time 36, part-time 41; 20% female; 16% minority; student/faculty ratio 18 to 1.

Degrees conferred: J.D., J.D.-M.B.A., J.D.-M.P.A. (University of New Orleans), J.D.-M.A. (Communications, Religious Studies), J.D.-M.U.R.P. (University of New Orleans).

RECRUITMENT PRACTICES AND POLICIES. Attends national law school forums. Has on-campus informational sessions. School does have diversity program and actively recruits women/minority applicants.

ADMISSION REQUIREMENTS FOR FIRST-YEAR APPLICANTS. LSDAS law school report, LSAT (not later than February test date, if more than one LSAT, highest is used), bachelor's degree from an accredited institution, personal statement, three recommendations, transcripts (must show all schools attended and at least three years of study) required in support of application. Applicants must have received bachelor's degree prior to enrollment. Interview not required but may be requested by applicant. In addition, international applicants whose native language is not English must submit TOEFL (not older than two years). Joint-degree program applicants must apply to and be accepted by both schools. Apply to Office of Admission after September 30, before April 1 (priority deadline). First-year students admitted fall only. Rolling admission process, notification starts within six

weeks of receipt of completed application. Application fee $20. Phone: (504)861-5575.

ADMISSION REQUIREMENTS FOR TRANSFER APPLICANTS. Accepts transfers from other ABA-accredited schools. Admission limited to space available. At least one year of enrollment, dean's letter indication applicant is in good standing (prefer applicants in the top quarter of first-year class), LSAT, LSDAS, personal statement regarding reason for transfer, undergraduate transcript, current law school transcript required in support of application. Apply to Office of Admission by July 1. Admission decisions made by early August. Application fee $20. Will consider visiting students.

ADMISSION STANDARDS. Number of full-time applicants 1,205, part-time 136; number accepted 726 full-time, 74 part-time; number enrolled 159 full-time 47 part-time; median LSAT 153 (75% of class have a score at or above 148 both full-and part-time); median GPA 3.10 (A = 4) (75% of class have a GPA at or above 2.73 full-time, 2.71 part-time). Attrition rate 7.1%. Gorman rating 2.50; *U.S. News & World Report* ranking is in the third tier of all law schools.

FINANCIAL AID. Scholarships, merit scholarships, diversity scholarships, grants-in-aid, private and institutional loans; federal loans and Federal WS offered through Financial Aid Office. Assistantships may be available for upper divisional joint-degree candidates. For scholarships (selection criteria place heavy reliance on LSAT and undergraduate GPA) before April 1 (priority deadline); all accepted applicants are considered for scholarships. For all other programs apply after January 1, before April 1 to the university's Office of Scholarships and Financial Aid. Phone: (504)865-3231. Use FAFSA for all federal programs (Title IV School code #002016). Also submit Financial Aid Transcript, federal income tax forms. Approximately 16% (full-time) of first-year class received scholarships/grants-in-aid. Approximately 83% of current students receive some form of financial assistance. Average scholarship/grant full-time $5,500, part-time $3,000. Public Service Loan Forgiveness program established in 1991. Average debt after graduation $37,000.

DEGREE REQUIREMENTS. For J.D.: 90 credits (70 required) with a 2.0 (A = 4) GPA, plus completion of upper divisional writing course and 1 course in philosophical, historical perspective of law; 3-year program, 4-year program (part-time). Accelerated J.D. with 1 summer of course work. For J.D.-masters: individually designed programs; 3½- to 4-year program rather than the usual 5-year program needed if degrees taken separately.

CAREER AND PLACEMENT INFORMATION. About 69 employers conducted on-campus interviews. Approximately 75% of graduates are employed in state. More than 84% of graduates are practicing law; 5% are in business; 10% in government; 1% in academia. Approximately 66% of Loyola University New Orleans' first-time state bar exam takers pass the Louisiana Bar Exam; Louisiana's passage rate for all first-time takers from ABA-approved schools is 67%. Graduates are eligible to take the bar exam in all 50 states.

UNIVERSITY OF MAINE
Orono, Maine 04469-5703
Internet site: http://www.um.maine.edu

Founded 1865. Located 8 miles N of Bangor. Public control. Semester system. Library: 815,000 volumes; 1,250,000 microforms; 5,300 periodicals/subscriptions.

University's other graduate colleges/schools: College of Arts and Sciences, College of Business Administration, College of Education, College of Engineering and Technology, College of Natural Resources and Forestry and Agriculture, College of Science, College of Social and Behavioral Sciences, Institute for Quaternary Studies.

Total university enrollment: 11,500.

School of Law
246 Deering Avenue
Portland, Maine 04102
Phone: (207)780-4355
Internet site: http://www.law.usm.maine.edu
E-mail: gauditz@usm.maine.edu

Established 1962. Located in Portland. Law school is an administrative unit of the University of Southern Maine. ABA approved since 1962. AALS member. Semester system. Full-time, day study only. Law library: 280,000 volumes/microforms; 3,578 current periodicals/subscriptions; 31 computer workstations; has LEXIS, NEXIS, WESTLAW; is a Federal Government Depository and maintains an extensive collection of Canadian and British Commonwealth reports and statutes. Special facility: Marine Law Institute; Special program: externships.

Annual tuition: full-time resident $8,378, nonresident $15,994; part-time resident $6,010, nonresident $11,450. On-campus housing available for single students only. Annual on-campus housing cost: single students $2,358

(room only), $4,554 (room and board). Contact Housing Office for on-campus housing information. Phone: (207)780-5158. Law students tend to live off-campus. Contact Admission Office for off-campus information. Off-campus housing and personal expenses: approximately $7,883. Additional costs: books approximately $700.

Enrollment: first-year class 95; total full-time 284 (men 58%,women 42%); limited number of part-time students are accepted. First-year statistics: 39% out of state, 30 states and foreign countries represented; 42% women; 7% minority; average age 29; 111 undergraduate institutions represented; range of first-year section sizes 10–95 students; number of upper division courses offered after first year 49.

Faculty: full-time 16, part-time 7; 32% female; no minorities; student/faculty ratio 19 to 1.

Degree conferred: J.D.

RECRUITMENT PRACTICES AND POLICIES. Attends selected national law school forums. On-campus informational sessions available, contact Assistant Dean for information. Phone: (202)780-4345. School does have diversity program and actively recruits women/minority applicants.

ADMISSION REQUIREMENTS FOR FIRST-YEAR APPLICANTS. LSDAS law school report, LSAT (not later than December test date, if more than one LSAT, average is used), bachelor's degree from an accredited institution, personal statement, one recommendation, transcripts (must show all schools attended and at least three years of study) required in support of application. Applicants must have received bachelor's degree prior to enrollment. Interview not required but may be requested by school under certain circumstances. In addition, international applicants must submit TOEFL (not older than two years). Apply to Office of Admission after September 30, before February 15. First-year students admitted fall only. Rolling admission process, notification starts in February and is finished by April 15. Acceptance of offer and first deposit due date April 1. Application fee $25. Phone: (207)786-4341. E-mail: gauditz@usm.main.edu.

ADMISSION REQUIREMENTS FOR TRANSFER APPLICANTS. Accepts transfers from other ABA-accredited schools. Admission limited to space available. At least one year of enrollment, dean's letter indicating applicant is in good standing (prefer applicants in the top quarter of first-year class), LSAT, LSDAS, personal statement regarding reason for transfer, one recommendation, current law school transcript required in support of application. Apply to Admission Office by June 1. Admission decisions made by early August. Application fee $25. Will consider visiting students.

ADMISSION STANDARDS. Number of full-time applicants 672; number accepted 336; number enrolled 95; median LSAT 155 (75% of class have a score at or above 150); median GPA 3.24 (A = 4) (75% of class have a GPA at or above 3.09). Attrition rate 3.2%. Gorman rating 2.54; *U.S. News & World Report* ranking is in the fourth tier of all law schools.

FINANCIAL AID. Scholarships, minority scholarships, grants-in-aid, institutional loans; federal loans and Federal WS offered through university's Financial Aid Office. For scholarships (selection criteria place heavy reliance on LSAT and undergraduate GPA) apply to the university's Office of Financial Aid after January 1, before February 1. Phone: (207)581-1324. Use FAFSA for all federal programs (Title IV School code #009762). Also submit Financial Aid Transcript, federal income tax forms. Approximately 35% of first-year class received scholarships/grants-in-aid. Approximately 75% of current students receive some form of financial assistance. Average scholarship/grant $1,500. Average debt after graduation $38,000. Financial aid available for part-time students.

DEGREE REQUIREMENTS. For J.D.: 89 credits (41 required) with a 2.0 (A = 4) GPA, plus completion of upper divisional writing course; 3-year program. Accelerated J.D. with summer course work.

CAREER AND PLACEMENT INFORMATION. About 40–45 employers conducted on-campus interviews. Approximately 73% of graduates are employed in state. More than 61% of graduates are practicing law; 25% are in business; 14% in government; none are in academia. Approximately 85% of the University of Maine's first-time state bar exam takers pass the Maine Bar Exam; Maine's passage rate for all first-time takers from ABA-approved schools is 82%. Graduates are eligible to take the bar exam in all 50 states.

MARQUETTE UNIVERSITY
Milwaukee, Wisconsin 53201-1881
Internet site: http://www.mu.edu

Founded 1881. Located in an urban area adjacent to downtown, 2 miles W of Lake Michigan. Private control (Roman Catholic—Jesuit affiliation). Semester system. Library: 700,000 volumes; 268,600 microforms; 9,400 periodicals/subscriptions; 69 computer workstations.

University's other graduate colleges/schools: College of Arts and Sciences, College of Business Administration, College of Communication, College of Engineering, College of Nursing, School of Education, School of Dentistry.

Total university enrollment: 10,450.

School of Law
Sensenbrenner Hall
P.O. Box 1881
Milwaukee, Wisconsin 53201-1881
Phone: (414)288-6767
Internet site: http://www.mu.edu/dep.law
E-mail: law.admissions@marquette.edu

Established 1892. Located on main campus. ABA approved since 1925. AALS member. Semester system. Full-time, part-time day/evening (first part-time evening class admitted in 1997). Law library: 250,000 volumes/microforms; 3,100 current periodicals/subscriptions; 19 computer workstations; has LEXIS, NEXIS, WESTLAW, DIALOG, OCLC, MARQCAT, LEGALTRAC, CALI, WISCAT. Special facilities: Legal Research Center, National Sports Law Institute. Special programs: summer study abroad at University of Queensland, Australia; internships.

Annual tuition: Full-time $17,830, part-time $14,800. On-campus apartments available for both single and married students. Annual on-campus housing cost: single students $7,140 (room and board), married students $6,000–10,000. Contact Residence Life Office for on-campus housing information. Phone: (414)228-7208. Off-campus housing and personal expenses: approximately $11,990. Additional costs: books approximately $800.

Enrollment: first-year class 150 full-time, 7 part-time; total full-time 465, part-time 7 (men 58%, women 42%). First-year statistics: 34% out of state, 35 states and 3 foreign countries represented; 42% women, 13% minority; average age 25; 162 undergraduate institutions represented; range of first-year section sizes 40–75 students; number of upper division courses offered after first year 702.

Faculty: full-time 26, part-time 47; 25% female; 10% minority; student/faculty ratio 18 to 1.

Degrees conferred: J.D., J.D.-M.B.A., J.D.-M.A. (Political Science, International Affairs).

RECRUITMENT PRACTICES AND POLICIES. Attends national law school forums. Has on-campus informational sessions, contact Assistant Dean for schedule. School does have diversity program and actively recruits women/minority applicants.

ADMISSION REQUIREMENTS FOR FIRST-YEAR APPLICANTS. LSDAS law school report, LSAT (not later than February test date, if more than one LSAT, average is used), bachelor's degree from an accredited institution, personal statement, two recommendations, transcripts (must show all schools attended and at least three years of study) required in support of application. Applicants must have received bachelor's degree prior to enrollment. Interview not required but may be requested by school. In addition, international applicants whose native language is not English must submit TOEFL (not older than two years), notarized/certified English translation of all transcripts. For further information with reference to immigration status, contact the university's Office of International Programs. Phone: (414)288-7289. Applicants for joint-degree programs must apply before February 15, and apply to and be accepted by both schools. Apply to Office of Admission after October 1, before April 1. First-year students admitted fall only. Rolling admission process, notification starts in November and is finished by late May. Application fee $25. Phone: (414)288-6767. E-mail: law.admissions@marquette.edu.

ADMISSION REQUIREMENTS FOR TRANSFER APPLICANTS. Accepts transfers from other ABA-accredited schools. Admission limited to space available. At least one year of enrollment, dean's letter indicating applicant is in good standing (prefer applicants in the top quarter of first-year class), LSAT, LSDAS, personal statement regarding reason for transfer, current law school transcript required in support of application. Apply to Admission Office by July 1. Admission decisions made by early August. Application fee $25. Will consider visiting students.

ADMISSION STANDARDS. Number of full-time applicants 972, part-time 59; number accepted 459 full-time, 9 part-time; number enrolled 150 full-time, 7 part-time; median LSAT 156 (75% of class have a score at or above 153 for both full- and part-time); median GPA 3.07 (A = 4) (75% of class have a GPA at or above 2.87 full-time, 2.82 part-time). Attrition rate 2.3%. Gorman rating 4.31; *U.S. News & World Report* ranking is in the third tier of all law schools.

FINANCIAL AID. Scholarships, merit scholarships, minority scholarships, grants-in-aid, private and institutional loans; federal loans and Federal WS offered through university's Financial Aid Office. Assistantships

may be available for upper divisional joint-degree candidates. All accepted applicants are automatically considered for scholarships (selection criteria place heavy reliance on LSAT and undergraduate GPA). For all other programs apply after January 1, before March 1 to university's Student Financial Aid Office. Phone: (414)288-7390. Use FAFSA for all federal programs (Title IV School code #003863). Also submit Financial Aid Transcript, federal income tax forms. Approximately 12% of first-year class received scholarships/grants-in-aid. Approximately 85% of current students receive some form of financial assistance. Average scholarship/grant $4,261 full-time, $959 part-time. Average debt after graduation $48,000. Financial aid will be available for part-time students.

DEGREE REQUIREMENTS. For J.D.: 90 credits (33 required) with a 2.0 (A = 4) GPA, plus completion of upper divisional writing course; 3-year program, 4-year program (part-time). Accelerated J.D. with summer course work. For J.D.-master's: individually designed programs, J.D. requirements are reduced by 9 credits; a 4-year program rather than the usual 5 years needed if both degrees taken separately.

CAREER AND PLACEMENT INFORMATION. About 25–30 employers conducted on-campus interviews. Approximately 80% of graduates are employed in state. More than 72% of graduates are practicing law; 14% are in business; 14% in government. All Wisconsin law school graduates are admitted to Wisconsin bar under diploma privilege. Approximately 93% (IL), 100% (MI) of Marquette University's first-time state bar exam takers pass the bar exam; the passage rate for all first-time takers from ABA-approved schools is 87% (IL), 70% (MI). Graduates are eligible to take the bar exam in all 50 states.

UNIVERSITY OF MARYLAND AT BALTIMORE

Baltimore, Maryland 21201-1627
Internet site: http://www.umab.edu

Founded 1807. Public control. Semester system. Library: 322,500 volumes; 2,600 periodicals/subscriptions; 236 computer workstations.

University's other graduate colleges/schools: The Graduate School, Baltimore College of Dentistry, Baltimore School of Medicine, School of Pharmacy, School of Social Work.

Total university enrollment: 5,800.

School of Law
500 West Baltimore Street
Baltimore, Maryland 21201-1786
Phone: (410)706-3492
Internet site: http://www.law.umab.edu
E-mail: admissions@law.umab.edu

Established 1816. Located in downtown Baltimore in the business and legal district. ABA approved since 1930. AALS member. Semester system. Full-time (day), part-time (evening) study. Law library: 364,000 volumes/microforms; 4,048 current periodicals/subscriptions; 58 computer workstations; has LEXIS, WESTLAW, DIALOG, CARL, UMCOVER, OCLC; is a Federal Government Depository. Special programs: summer study abroad in Aberdeen, Scotland.

Annual tuition: Full-time resident $9,219, nonresident $16,603; part-time resident $6,919, nonresident $12,455. On-campus housing available for single students only. Annual on-campus housing cost: single students $2,172 (room only). Contact Office of Residential Life for both on- and off-campus housing information. Phone: (410)706-7766. Law students tend to live off-campus. Off-campus housing and personal expenses: approximately $12,630. Additional costs: books approximately $700.

Enrollment: first-year class 200 full-time, 67 part-time; total full-time 598, part-time 258 (men 49%,women 51%). First-year statistics: 25% out of state, 38 states and foreign countries represented; 51% women; 29% minority; average age 24 (full-time), 28 (part-time); 143 undergraduate institutions represented; range of first-year section sizes 23–63 (full-time) students, 34–76 (part-time) students; number of upper division courses offered after first year 113 (full-time), 37 (part-time).

Faculty: full-time 54, part-time 28; 34% female; 10% minority; student/faculty ratio 16 to 1.

Degrees conferred: J.D., Combined J.D.- B.A., B.S. (University of Maryland System only), J.D.-M.A. (Business Administration, Criminal Justice, Liberal Education, Marine/Environmental Science, Policy Sciences, Public Management, Social Work).

RECRUITMENT PRACTICES AND POLICIES. Attends national law school forums. Has on-campus informational "Open Houses"; contact Admissions Office for dates. Phone: (410)706-3492. School does have diversity program and actively recruits women/minority applicants.

ADMISSION REQUIREMENTS FOR FIRST-YEAR APPLICANTS. LSDAS law school report, LSAT (not later than February test date, if more than one LSAT, average is used), bachelor's degree from an accredited institution, personal statement, two or three recommendations, transcripts (must show all schools attended and at least three years of study) required in support of application. Applicants must have received bachelor's degree prior to enrollment. Interview not required but may be requested by school. In addition, international applicants whose native language is not English must submit TOEFL (not older than two years), international transcripts must be fully explained and have a certified evaluation. Apply to Office of Admission after September 15, before May 1 (priority date February 15). First-year students admitted fall only. Rolling admission process, notification starts in January and is finished by late April. Acceptance of offer and first deposit due date July 1. School does maintain a waiting list. Application fee $42. Phone: (410)706-3492. E-mail: admissions@law.umab.edu.

ADMISSION REQUIREMENTS FOR TRANSFER APPLICANTS. Accepts transfers from other ABA-accredited schools. Admission limited to space available. At least one year of enrollment, dean's letter indicating the applicant is in good standing (prefer applicants in the top quarter of first-year class), LSAT, LSDAS, personal statement regarding reason for transfer, current law school transcript required in support of application. Admits both fall and spring. Apply at least 2 months prior to preferred semester of entrance. Admission decision made within six weeks of the receipt of completed application. Application fee $42. Will consider visiting students.

ADMISSION STANDARDS. Number of full-time applicants 2,156, part-time 378; number accepted 840 full-time, 124 part-time; number enrolled 200 full-time, 67 part-time; median LSAT 159 (75% of class have a score at or above 152 [full-time], 153 [part-time]); median GPA 3.35 (A = 4) (75% of class have a GPA at or above 3.02 [full-time], 2.99 [part-time]). Attrition rate 4.4%. Gorman rating 3.77; *U.S. News & World Report* ranking is in the second tier of all law schools.

FINANCIAL AID. State scholarships, merit scholarships, minority scholarships, grants-in-aid, state, private and institutional loans; federal loans and Federal WS offered through university's Student Financial Aid Office. Assistantships may be available for upper divisional joint-degree candidates. For all programs apply after January 1, before March 15 to University Students Financial Aid Office. Phone: (410)455-7347. Use FAFSA for all federal programs (Title IV school code #002104). Also submit Financial Aid Transcript, federal income tax forms and university's student information form. Approximately 50% (full-time), 12% (part-time) of first-year class received scholarships/grants-in-aid. Approximately 70% of current students receive some form of financial assistance. Average scholarship/grant $2,657 (full-time), $2,324 (part-time). Assistance available for public interest employment. Average debt after graduation $34,487.

DEGREE REQUIREMENTS. For J.D.: 85 (35–38 required) credits with a 2.0 (A = 4) GPA, plus completion of upper divisional writing course; 3-year full-time program, 4-year part-time program. Accelerated J.D. with summer course work. For J.D.-master's: 3½- to 4-year programs rather than 4½- to 5-year programs if taken consecutively.

CAREER AND PLACEMENT INFORMATION. About 25–30 employers conducted on-campus interviews. Approximately 43% of graduates are employed in state. More than 57% of graduates are practicing law; 19% are in business; 22% in government; 2% in academia. Approximately 83% of the University of Maryland at Baltimore's first-time state bar exam takers pass the Maryland Bar Exam; Maryland's passage rate for all first-time takers from ABA-approved schools is 75%. Graduates are eligible to take the bar exam in all 50 states.

UNIVERSITY OF MEMPHIS
Memphis, Tennessee 38152
Internet site: http://www.memphis.edu

Founded 1912. Name changed from Memphis State University in 1994. Located in a suburban area of Memphis. Public control. Semester system. Library: 975,000 volumes; 2,634,000 microforms; 9,155 periodicals/subscriptions.

University's Graduate School includes: College of Arts and Sciences, College of Communication and Fine Arts, College of Education, Division of Audiology and Speech Pathology, Fogelman College of Business and Economics, Herff College of Engineering.

Total university enrollment: 19,977.

Cecil C. Humphreys

School of Law
3715 Central Avenue
Memphis, Tennessee 38152-6513
Phone: (901)678-2421
Internet site: http://www.people.memphis.edu
E-mail: uofmlaw@profnet.law.memphis.edu

Established 1962. Located on main campus. ABA approved since 1965. AALS member. Semester system.

Full-time, part-time study. Law library: 262,500 volumes/microforms; 3,044 current periodicals/subscriptions; 56 computer workstations; has LEXIS, NEXIS, WESTLAW, DIALOG; is a Federal Government Depository. Special programs: externships.

Annual tuition: full-time resident $4,182, nonresident $10,360; part-time resident $3,320, nonresident $8,144. On-campus housing available for both single and married students. Annual on-campus housing cost: single students $1,725 (room only), married students $2,950. Contact Office of Resident Life for both on- and off-campus housing information. Phone: (901)678-2295. Law students tend to live off-campus. Off-campus housing and personal expenses: approximately $11,090. Additional costs: books approximately $700.

Enrollment: first-year class 151 full-time, 9 part-time; total full- and part-time 423 (men 50%, women 50%); limited number of part-time students. First-year statistics: 2% out of state; 50% women; 13% minority; average age 27; 50 undergraduate institutions represented; average first-year section size 92 students; number of upper division courses offered after first year 62.

Faculty: full-time 22, part-time 27; 38% female; 4% minority; student/faculty ratio 18 to 1.

Degrees conferred: J.D., J.D.-M.B.A.

RECRUITMENT PRACTICES AND POLICIES. Attends national law school forums. Has on-campus informational sessions. School does have diversity program and actively recruits women/minority applicants.

ADMISSION REQUIREMENTS FOR FIRST-YEAR APPLICANTS. LSDAS law school report, LSAT (December test date strongly recommended, if more than one LSAT, average is used), bachelor's degree from an accredited institution, personal statement, two recommendations, dean's certification form; domicile certificate, transcripts (must show all schools attended and at least three years of study) required in support of application. Applicants must have received bachelor's degree prior to enrollment. Preference given to state residents. Apply to Office of Admission after September 1, before February 1. First-year students admitted fall only. Rolling admission process, notification starts in January and is finished by late April. 85% of admission decision is based on weighted LSAT and GPA. Application fee $10. Phone: (901)678-2073. E-mail: uolmlaw@profnet.law.memphis.edu.

ADMISSION REQUIREMENTS FOR TRANSFER APPLICANTS. Accepts transfers from other ABA-accredited schools. Admission limited to space available.

At least one year of enrollment, dean's letter indication applicant is in good standing (prefer applicants in the upper third of first-year class), LSAT, LSDAS, personal statement regarding reason for transfer, current law school transcript required in support of application. Apply to Admission Office by June 1. Admission decisions made by August. Application fee $10. Will consider visiting students.

ADMISSION STANDARDS. Number of full-time applicants 944, part-time 56; number accepted 403 full-time, 17 part-time; number enrolled 143 full-time, 9 part-time; median LSAT 153 (75% of class have a score at or above 148 for both full- and part-time); median GPA 3.19 (A = 4) (75% of class have a GPA at or above 2.91 full-time, 3.04 part-time). Attrition rate 7.1%. Gorman rating 2.63; *U.S. News & World Report* ranking is in the fourth tier of all law schools.

FINANCIAL AID. Scholarships, merit scholarships, minority scholarships, grants-in-aid, state and institutional loans; federal loans and Federal WS offered through university's Financial Aid Office. For scholarships (selection criteria place heavy reliance on LSAT and undergraduate GPA) apply to Admissions Office after January 1, before February 15; use school's scholarship form; interview may be required. For all other programs apply to university's Office of Student Aid. Phone: (901)678-4825. Use FAFSA for all federal programs (Title IV School code #003509). Also submit Financial Aid Transcript, federal income tax forms. Approximately 11% of first-year class received scholarships/grants-in-aid. Approximately 50% of current students receive some form of financial assistance. Average scholarship/grant full-time $3,880, part-time $3,524. Financial aid available for part-time students.

DEGREE REQUIREMENTS. For J.D.: 90 credits (56 required) with a 2.0 (A = 4) GPA, plus completion of upper divisional writing course; 3-year program, 4½-year program (part-time). For J.D.-M.B.A.: 4-year program rather than the 5 years usually needed if both degrees taken separately.

CAREER AND PLACEMENT INFORMATION. About 25-30 employers conducted on-campus interviews. Approximately 82% of graduates are employed in state. More than 77% of graduates are practicing law; 11% are in business; 12% in government. Approximately 81% of the University of Memphis' first-time state bar exam takers pass the Tennessee Bar Exam; Tennessee's passage

rate for all first-time takers from ABA-approved schools is 79%. Graduates are eligible to take the bar exam in all 50 states.

MERCER UNIVERSITY
Macon, Georgia 31207-0003
Internet site: http://www.mercer.edu

Founded 1833. Located in an urban area, 80 miles S of Atlanta. Private control (Baptist affiliation). Semester system. Library: 404,800 volumes; 241,000 microforms; 3,346 periodicals/subscriptions; 35 computer workstations.

University's other graduate colleges/schools: School of Education, School of Engineering, School of Medicine, Stetson School of Business and Economics.

Total university enrollment: 5,000.

Walter F. George
School of Law
1021 Georgia Avenue
Macon, Georgia 31207
Phone: (800)637-2378 (outside Georgia), (800)342-0841 (inside Georgia)
Internet site: http://www.mercer.edu/~law

Established 1873. Located on main campus. ABA approved since 1925. AALS member since 1923. Semester system. Full-time, day study only. Law library: 273,000 volumes/microforms; 2,900 current periodicals/subscriptions; 34 computer workstations; has LEXIS, NEXIS, WESTLAW, DIALOG, CALI. Special programs: on-campus summer study at the National Criminal Defense College; externships.

Annual tuition: $17,990. On-campus housing available for both single and married students. Annual on-campus housing cost: single students $1,941 (room only), $4,122 (room and board), married students $4,000–$6,000. Contact university Housing Office. Phone: (912)752-2687. Law students tend to live off-campus. Housing packets are sent to all enrolling students during the summer. Off-campus housing and personal expenses: approximately $11,000. Additional costs: books approximately $700.

Enrollment: first-year class 140; total full-time 400 (men 64%, women 36%); no part-time students. First-year statistics: 45% out of state, 28 states and foreign countries represented; 36% women; 13% minority; average age 25; 157 undergraduate institutions represented; range of first-year section sizes 25–75 students; number of upper division courses offered after first year 85.

Faculty: full-time 28, part-time 24; 27% female; 6% minority; student/faculty ratio 15 to 1.

Degrees conferred: J.D., J.D.-M.B.A.

RECRUITMENT PRACTICES AND POLICIES. Attends national law school forums. Has on-campus informational sessions. School does have diversity program and actively recruits women/minority applicants.

ADMISSION REQUIREMENTS FOR FIRST-YEAR APPLICANTS. LSDAS law school report, LSAT (not later than December test date, if more than one LSAT, highest is used), bachelor's degree from an accredited institution, personal statement, two recommendations, transcripts (must show all schools attended and at least three years of study) required in support of application. Applicants must have received bachelor's degree prior to enrollment. Interview not required. School visits encouraged. In addition, international applicants whose native language is not English must submit TOEFL (not older than two years). Joint-degree applicants must apply to and be accepted by both schools. Apply to Office of Admission after September 1, before March 15. First-year students admitted fall only. Rolling admission process, notification starts in January and is finished by late May. School does maintain a waiting list. Application fee $45. Phone: (912)752-2605.

ADMISSION REQUIREMENTS FOR TRANSFER APPLICANTS. Accepts transfers from other ABA-accredited schools. Admission limited to space available. At least one year of enrollment, dean's letter indicating the applicant is in good standing (prefer applicants in the top quarter of first-year class), LSAT, LSDAS, two letters of recommendation, personal statement regarding reason for transfer, undergraduate transcript, current law school transcript required in support of application. Admits fall only. Apply to Admission Office by June 30, applications must be completed by July 31. Admission decisions made by mid August. Application fee $45. Will consider visiting students.

ADMISSION STANDARDS. Number of full-time applicants 1,117; number accepted 481; number enrolled 143; median LSAT 154 (75% of class have a score at or above 151); median GPA 3.1 (A = 4) (75% of class have a GPA at or above 2.67). Attrition rate 4.4%. Gorman rating 2.94; *U.S. News & World Report* ranking is in the third tier of all law schools.

FINANCIAL AID. Scholarships, diversity scholarships, grants-in-aid, private and institutional loans; federal loans and Federal WS offered through university's Financial Aid Office. Assistantships may be available for upper divisional joint-degree candidates. For scholarships (selection criteria place heavy reliance on LSAT and undergraduate GPA) apply to Admissions Office after January 1, before April 1. For all other programs apply as early as possible to University's Financial Aid Office. Phone: (912)752-2429. Use FAFSA for all federal programs (Title IV School code #E00561). Also submit Financial Aid Transcript, federal income tax forms. Approximately 23% of first-year class received scholarships/grants-in-aid. Approximately 80% of current students receive some form of financial assistance. Average scholarship/grant $8,222. Average debt after graduation $53,300.

DEGREE REQUIREMENTS. For J.D.: 90 credits (52 required) with a 76 (scale 0–100) GPA, plus completion of upper divisional writing course; 3-year program. For J.D.-M.B.A.: 4-year program rather than the usual 5 years needed if both degrees taken separately.

CAREER AND PLACEMENT INFORMATION. About 15–20 employers conducted on-campus interviews. Approximately 71% of graduates are employed in state. More than 74% of graduates are practicing law; 4% are in business; 20% in government; 2% in academia. Approximately 94% of Mercer University's first-time state bar exam takers pass the Georgia Bar Exam; Georgia's passage rate for all first-time takers from ABA-approved schools is 84%. Graduates are eligible to take the bar exam in all 50 states.

UNIVERSITY OF MIAMI
Coral Gables, Florida 33124
Internet site: http://www.miami.edu

Founded 1925. Located 12 miles SW of Miami. Private control. Semester system. Library: 2,030,000 volumes; 3,130,000 microforms; 19,550 periodicals/subscriptions.

University's other graduate colleges/schools: College of Arts and Sciences, College of Engineering, Graduate School of International Studies, Rosentiel School of Marine and Atmospheric Science, School of Architecture, School of Business Administration, School of Communication, School of Education, School of Music, School of Nursing, School of Medicine.

Total university enrollment: 13,541.

School of Law

P.O. Box 248087
1311 Miller Drive
Coral Gables, Florida 33124-8087
Phone: (305)284-2394
Internet site: http://www.law.miami.edu
E-mail: admission@law.miami.edu

Established 1926. Located on main campus. ABA approved since 1941. AALS member. Semester system. Full-time (day), part-time (evening) study. Law library: 442,900 volumes/microforms; 7,265 current periodicals/subscriptions; 169 computer workstations; has LEXIS, NEXIS, WESTLAW, DIALOG, CCH. Special programs: summer study abroad at University College, London, England.

Annual tuition: full-time $21,458, part-time $15,450. On-campus housing available for both single and married students. Annual on-campus three-bedroom apartment cost: $5,154 (room only), $8,000 (room and board). Contact Department of Residence Halls. Phone: (305)284-4505. Law students tend to live off-campus. Contact Office of Student Recruitment for off-campus information. Off-campus housing and personal expenses: approximately $14,665. Additional costs: books approximately $700.

Enrollment: first-year class 378 full-time, 126 part-time; total full-time 1,251, part-time 304 (men 57%, women 43%). First-year statistics: 43% out of state, 70 states and foreign countries represented; 43% women; 33% minority; average age 26; 215 undergraduate institutions represented; range of first-year section sizes full-time 45–120 students, part-time 31–120 students; number of upper division courses offered after first year 84 full-time, 24 part-time.

Faculty: full-time 59, part-time 99; 27% female; 10% minority; student/faculty ratio 24 to 1.

Degrees conferred: J.D., J.D.-M.B.A., J.D.-M.P.H., J.D.-M.A. (Marine Affairs). LL.M. (Taxation, Estate Planning, Real Property Development), LL.M. (Inter-American Law, International Law, Ocean and Coastal Law), LL.M. (Comparative Law for persons who have completed a basic legal education and received a university degree in law in another country).

RECRUITMENT PRACTICES AND POLICIES. Attends national law school forums. Has on-campus informational sessions. School does have diversity program and actively recruits women/minority applicants.

ADMISSION REQUIREMENTS FOR FIRST-YEAR APPLICANTS. LSDAS law school report, LSAT (not later than December test date, if more than one LSAT, average is used), bachelor's degree from an accredited institution, personal statement, two recommendations, transcripts (must show all schools attended and at least three years of study) required in support of application. Applicants must have received bachelor's degree prior to enrollment. Interview not required. Campus tours are encouraged. In addition, international applicants whose native language is not English must submit TOEFL (not older than two years), all foreign transcripts must have a certified credential evaluation. Joint-degree applicants must apply to and be accepted by both schools; GMAT for Business; GRE for M.P.H. Apply to Office of Admission after September 1, before July 31 (March 7 is priority deadline). First-year students admitted fall only. Rolling admission process. Application fee $45. Phone: (305)284-6746. E-mail: admission@law.miami.edu.

ADMISSION REQUIREMENTS FOR TRANSFER APPLICANTS. Accepts transfers from other ABA-accredited schools. Admission limited to space available. At least one year of enrollment, dean's letter indicating the applicant is in good standing (prefer applicants in the top 20% of first-year class), LSAT, LSDAS, personal statement regarding reason for transfer, undergraduate transcript, current law school transcript required in support of application. Apply to Admission Office by June 15. Admission decisions made by early August. Application fee $45. Will consider visiting students.

ADMISSION REQUIREMENTS FOR LL.M. For LL.M. (Taxation, Estate Planning, Real Property Development). J.D. from accredited U.S. law school required. Official transcripts, personal statement, résumé required in support of graduate application. Admits fall only. Apply to Director of LL.M. Programs. Application fee $45. Phone: (305)284-4574 (Real Property Development), (305)284-5567 (Taxation, Estate Planning). For LL.M. (Inter-American, International Law, Ocean and Coastal Law). J.D. from an accredited U.S. law school or a law degree from a recognized foreign law school required. Official transcript, personal statement, résumé required in support of graduate application. In addition, TOEFL required for all international applicants whose native language is not English. All foreign transcripts should have a certified credential translation and evaluation. Admits fall only. Apply to Director of LL.M. Program. Application fee $45. Phone: (305)284-5497. For LL.M. (Comparative Law), for foreign lawyers with a degree from a recognized foreign law school, TOEFL required for all applicants whose native language is not English. All foreign transcripts should have a certified translation and credential evaluation. Apply by May 1 for priority consideration. Admits fall only. Application fee $50. Phone: (305)844-5402. E-mail: int-llm@law.miami.edu.

ADMISSION STANDARDS. Number of full-time applicants 2,043, part-time 333; number accepted 1,269 full-time, 200 part-time; number enrolled 378 full-time, 126 part-time; median LSAT 154 (75% of class have a score at or above 150 full-time, 145 part-time); median GPA 3.20 (A = 4) (75% of class have a GPA at or above 2.92 full-time, 2.68 part-time). Attrition rate 5.2%. Gorman rating 3.35; *U.S. News & World Report* ranking is in the second tier of all law schools.

FINANCIAL AID. Scholarships, merit scholarships, minority scholarships, grants-in-aid, institutional loans, state loans, federal loans, and Federal WS. Assistantships, scholarships, Federal WS may be available for upper divisional joint-degree candidates. All accepted applicants are automatically considered for scholarships (selection criteria place heavy reliance on LSAT and undergraduate GPA), apply to Admissions Office after January 1, before March 1 (priority deadline). Phone: (305)284-3115. Use FAFSA for all federal programs (Title IV School code #E00532). Also submit Financial Aid Transcript, federal income tax forms, use Access Disk. Approximately 28% (full-time), 2% (part-time) of first-year class received scholarships/grants-in-aid. Approximately 85% of current students receive some form of financial assistance. Average scholarship/grant $11,262 (full-time), $3,719 (part-time). Average debt after graduation $58,300. For LL.M. candidates, a limited number of fellowships, assistantships, and scholarships are available. Contact the appropriate graduate programs director for financial aid information.

DEGREE REQUIREMENTS. For J.D.: 83 credits (73 required) with a 2.0 (A = 4) GPA, plus completion of upper divisional writing course; 3-year program, 4-year program (part-time). Accelerated J.D. with summer course work. For J.D.-M.B.A., J.D.-M.A. (Marine Affairs): total 110 credits; 4-year programs rather than the usual 5 years needed if degrees taken separately. For J.D.-M.P.H.: total 115 credits; 4-year program rather than the usual 5 years needed if degrees taken separately. For LL.M. (Taxation, Estate Planning, Real Property Development): 33 credits; at least 2 semesters in full-time residence; a GPA of 2.5 (A = 4) required. For LL.M. (Inter-American, International Law, Ocean and Coastal Law): 24 credits; at least 2 semesters in full-time residence; thesis nonthesis option; a GPA of 2.5 (A = 4) required. For LL.M. (Comparative

Law): 24 credits; at least 2 semesters in residence; a GPA of 2.5 (A = 4) required.

CAREER AND PLACEMENT INFORMATION. About 25–30 employers conducted on-campus interviews. Approximately 77% of graduates are employed in state. More than 64% of graduates are practicing law; 19% are in business; 16% in government; 1% in academia. Approximately 89% of the University of Miami's first-time state bar exam takers pass the Florida Bar Exam; Florida's passage rate for all first-time takers from ABA-approved schools is 84%. Graduates are eligible to take the bar exam in all 50 states.

UNIVERSITY OF MICHIGAN
Ann Arbor, Michigan 48109
Internet site: http://www.umich.edu

Founded 1817. Located 40 miles W of Detroit. Public control. Semester system. Library: 6,133,000 volumes; 3,472,100 microforms; 67,530 periodicals/subscriptions.

University's other graduate colleges/schools: College of Architecture and Urban Planning, College of Pharmacy; Horace H. Rackham School of Graduate Studies includes the College of Engineering, College of Literature, Science and the Arts, School of Art and Design, School of Education, School of Information, School of Nursing, School of Public Policy; Medical School; School of Business Administration; School of Dentistry; School of Music; School of Natural Resources and Environment; School of Public Health; School of Social Work.

Total university enrollment: 36,600.

School of Law
Hutchins Hall
625 South State Street
Ann Arbor, Michigan 48109-1215
Phone: (313)764-1358
Internet site: http://www.law.umich.edu

Established 1869 and is one oldest law schools in the U.S. Located on main campus. ABA approved since 1923. AALS member. Semester system. Full-time, day study only. Law library: 800,100 volumes, 841,923 microforms; 10,800 current periodicals/subscriptions; 75 computer workstations; has LEXIS, NEXIS, WESTLAW, LEXCALIBUR; is a Federal Government Depository. Special programs: summer "Start Program" externships; internships.

Annual tuition: resident $17,332, nonresident $22,332. On-campus housing available for both single and married students. Annual on-campus housing cost: single students $3,825 (room only), $3,789 (room and board), married students $6,480. Contact Housing Office (Phone: [313]763-1316) or Lawyers Club (Phone: [313]764-1116) for both on- and off-campus housing information. Law students tend to live off-campus. For family housing contact Office of University Housing. Phone: (313)763-3164. Off-campus housing and personal expenses: approximately $12,250. Additional costs: books approximately $750.

Enrollment: first-year class 319; total full-time 1,068 (men 58%, women 42%); no part-time students. First-year statistics: 70% out of state, 88 states and foreign countries represented; 42% women; 21% minority; average age 24; 274 undergraduate institutions represented; range of first-year section sizes 43–85 students; number of upper division courses offered after first year 142.

Faculty: full-time 86, part-time 21; 32% female; 10% minority; student/faculty ratio 16.4 to 1.

Degrees conferred: J.D., J.D.-M.B.A., J.D.-M.H.S.A., J.D.-M.A. (Modern Middle Eastern and North African Studies, Russian and East European Studies, Law and Philosophy, History), J.D.-M.S. (Natural Resources), J.D.-M.P.P. (Public Policy), J.D.-Ph.D. (Economics), LL.M., M.C.L. (only for persons who have completed a basic legal education and received a university degree in law in another country), LL.M.-S.J.D.

RECRUITMENT PRACTICES AND POLICIES. Attends national law school forums. Has on-campus informational sessions. School does have diversity program and actively recruits women/minority applicants.

ADMISSION REQUIREMENTS FOR FIRST-YEAR APPLICANTS. LSDAS law school report, LSAT (not later than October test date, if more than one LSAT, average is most influential), bachelor's degree from an accredited institution, personal statement, one recommendation (more are encouraged), transcripts (must show all schools attended and at least three years of study) required in support of application. Two additional 250-word essays are also encouraged. Applicants must have received bachelor's degree prior to enrollment. Interview not required but law school staff will meet with any applicant. In addition, international applicants whose native language is not English must submit TOEFL (not older than two years), all undergraduate transcripts from schools outside of the U.S. and Canada must be sent directly to the law school Admissions Office. Joint-degree applicants must apply to and be accepted by both schools. Apply to Office of Admission after September 1, before February 15. First-year students admitted fall only.

Rolling admission process. School does maintain a waiting list. Application fee $70. Phone: (313)764-0537.

ADMISSION REQUIREMENTS FOR TRANSFER APPLICANTS. Accepts transfers from other ABA-accredited schools (approximately 25 each year). Admission limited to space available. At least one year of enrollment, dean's letter indicating the applicant is in good standing (prefer applicants near the top of first-year class), LSAT, LSDAS, personal statement regarding reason for transfer, undergraduate transcript, current law school transcript required in support of application. Apply to Admission Office between May 1 and August 1. Admission decisions made between July and August. Application fee $70. Will consider visiting students.

ADMISSION REQUIREMENTS FOR LL.M., M.C.L., LL.M.-S.J.D. Applicants must have an accredited B.A., B.S. degree, or its equivalent and LL.B. or J.D. from accredited law school; achieved High Honors (Order of the Coif or equivalent academic distinction); letters of recommendation from law school faculty, official transcripts should include an explanation of grading and rank in class, résumé, personal statement, a statement of purpose including academic interest and ability to benefit from graduate study are required in support of international and graduate application. In addition, international applicants from non-English-speaking countries are required to take TOEFL (usual minimum 600) or MELAB before December 1 (one calendar year before year for which admission is sought). Admits fall only. Apply by January 1 to Office of International and Graduate Programs. Phone: (313)764-0535. Fax: (313)936-1973. E-mail: law.grad. Admissions@umich.edu. Notification of decisions is generally made in March. The LL.M., M.C.L. class is between 30–35 students, the LL.M.-S.J.D. class is no more than 15 students.

ADMISSION STANDARDS. Number of full-time applicants 3,636; number accepted 1,123; number enrolled 319; median LSAT 167 (75% of class have a score at or above 164); median GPA 3.56 (A = 4) (75% of class have a GPA at or above 3.34). Attrition rate 0.4%. Gorman rating 4.92; *U.S. News & World Report* ranking is in the top 7 of all law schools.

FINANCIAL AID. Scholarships, merit scholarships, minority scholarships, grants-in-aid, private and institutional loans, state loans, federal loans, and Federal WS. Assistantships may be available for upper divisional joint-degree candidates. All accepted applicants are automatically considered for scholarships (the selection criteria place heavy reliance on LSAT and undergraduate

GPA). For all other programs apply to school's Financial Aid Office after January 1, before February 15. Phone: (313)764-5289. Use FAFSA for all federal programs (Title IV School code #E00506). Also submit Financial Aid Transcript, federal income tax forms, Access Disk. Approximately 38% of first-year class received scholarships/grants-in-aid. Approximately 85% of current students receive some form of financial assistance. Average scholarship/grant $8,688. Average debt after graduation $36,000. For graduate study: fellowships, merit-based scholarships; need-based aid may be available. Contact the International and Graduate Program Office for financial aid information.

DEGREE REQUIREMENTS. For J.D.: 83 credits (31 required) with a 2.0 (A = 4) GPA, plus completion of upper divisional writing course; 3-year program. For J.D.-master's: individually designed programs, generally completed in 3½ to 4 years rather than the usual 4½ to 5 years needed if each degree taken separately. For LL.M.: 24 credits at least 2 semesters in full-time residence; a 3.0 (A = 4) GPA required. For M.C.L. (International): 20 credits; at least 2 semesters in full-time residence; one course in U.S. constitutional law; research paper; GPA of 2.3 (A = 4) required. For LL.M.-S.J.D.: completion of an LL.M., 24 credits taken in 2 semesters; research paper, thesis project; a GPA of 3.0 (A = 4). For S.J.D.: admission to candidacy; thesis; oral exam; completion of program within 5 years.

CAREER AND PLACEMENT INFORMATION. Over 250 employers conducted on-campus interviews. Approximately 27% of graduates are employed in state. More than 88% of graduates are practicing law; 6% are in business; 5% in Government; 1% in academia. Approximately 89% (MI), 98% (IL), 76% (NY) of the University of Michigan's first-time state bar exam takers pass the bar exam; the passage rate for all first-time takers from ABA-approved schools is 70% (MI), 87% (IL), 78% (NY). Graduates are eligible to take the bar exam in all 50 states.

UNIVERSITY OF MINNESOTA

Minneapolis, Minnesota 55455-0213
Internet site: http://www.umn.edu

Founded 1851. Public control. Quarter system. Library: 5,250,000 volumes; 5,000,000 microforms; 46,000 periodicals/subscriptions.

University's other graduate colleges/schools: College of Agriculture, Food and Environmental Sciences, College of Architecture and Landscape Architecture, College of Biological Sciences, College of Education and Human Development, College of Human Ecology, College of Liberal Arts, College of Natural Resources, Hubert H. Humphrey Institute of Public Policy, Institute of Human Genetics, Institute of Technology, School of Nursing, Carlson School of Management, College of Pharmacy, College of Veterinary Medicine, Medical School, School of Dentistry, School of Public Health.

Total university enrollment: 37,000.

Law School
229 19 Avenue South
Minneapolis, Minnesota 55455
Phone: (612)625-1000
Internet site: http://sss.umn.edu./law

Established 1888. Located on main campus. ABA approved since 1923. AALS member. Semester system. Full-time, day study only. Law library: 813,800 volumes/microforms; 9,550 current periodicals/subscriptions; 32 computer workstations; has LEXIS, NEXIS, WESTLAW, LUMINA, CALI. Special programs: summer study abroad at Université Jean Moulin (Lyon, France), University of Uppsala (Sweden).

Annual tuition: resident $9,230, nonresident $15,274. On-campus housing available for both single and married students. Annual on-campus housing cost: single students $4,400 (room and board), married students $4,900. Contact Housing Office for both on- and off campus housing information. Phone: (612)624-1499. Law students tend to live off-campus. Off-campus housing and personal expenses: approximately $8,849. Additional costs: books approximately $700.

Enrollment: first-year class 250; total full-time 810 (men 54%, women 46%); no part-time students. First-year statistics: 47% out of state, 45 states and foreign countries represented; 46% women; 17% minority; average age 25; 215 undergraduate institutions represented; range of first-year section sizes 14–100 students; number of upper division courses offered after first year 142.

Faculty: full-time 42, part-time 80; 37% female; 13% minority; student/faculty ratio 16.7 to 1.

Degrees conferred: J.D., J.D.-M.B.A., J.D.-M.P.A. J.D.-M.A. (joint-degree programs available with most graduate departments/schools), LL.M. (only for persons who have completed a basic legal education and received a university degree in law in another country). LL.M. for graduates of American law schools under consideration.

RECRUITMENT PRACTICES AND POLICIES. Attends national law school forums. Has on-campus informational sessions. School does have diversity program and actively recruits women/minority applicants.

ADMISSION REQUIREMENTS FOR FIRST-YEAR APPLICANTS. LSDAS law school report, LSAT (not later than December test date, if more than one LSAT, average is used), bachelor's degree from an accredited institution, personal statement, two recommendations, transcripts (must show all schools attended and at least three years of study) required in support of application. Applicants must have received bachelor's degree prior to enrollment. Interview not required but may be requested by school. In addition, international applicants whose native language is not English must submit TOEFL (not older than two years). Joint-degree applicants must apply to and be accepted by each school. Apply to Office of Admission after November 1, before March 1. First-year students admitted fall only. Rolling admission process, notification starts one month after applicant has taken LSAT and is finished by late May. School does maintain a waiting list (deferred applicants). Application fee $40. Phone: (612)625-1000. E-mail: law@gold.tc.umn.edu.

ADMISSION REQUIREMENTS FOR TRANSFER APPLICANTS. Accepts transfers from other ABA-accredited schools. Admission limited to space available. At least one year of enrollment, dean's letter indicating the applicant is in good standing (prefer applicants in the top quarter of first-year class), LSAT, LSDAS, personal statement regarding reason for transfer, one recommendation from a current faculty member, current law school transcript required in support of application. Apply to Office of Admission by June 1. Admission decisions made by late July. Application fee $40. Will consider visiting students.

ADMISSION REQUIREMENTS FOR LL.M. Official transcripts of all university level work, résumé, two letters of recommendation, personal statement, proof of English language proficiency required in support of graduate applications. Admits fall only. Apply to Assistant Dean of International and Graduate programs. Phone: (612)625-3025. E-mail: mcqua004@gold.tc.umn.edu.

ADMISSION STANDARDS. Number of full-time applicants 1,798; number accepted 670; number enrolled 253; median LSAT 162 (75% of class have a score at or above 158); median GPA 3.61 (A = 4) (75% of class have a GPA at or above 3.27). Attrition rate 2%. Gorman rating 4.64; *U.S. News & World Report* ranking is in the top 20 of all law schools.

FINANCIAL AID. Need-based scholarships, merit-based scholarships, scholarships for American Indians, minority fellowships, grants-in-aid, private and institutional loans; federal loans and Federal WS offered through university's Student Financial Aid Office. Assistantships may be available for upper divisional joint-degree candidates. For scholarships (selection criteria place heavy reliance on LSAT and undergraduate GPA) apply to Admissions Office after January 1, before March 1. Phone: (612)625-5005. For all other programs apply after January 1, before May 1 to university's Student Financial Aid Office. Use FAFSA for all federal programs (Title IV School code #003969). Also submit Financial Aid Transcript, federal income tax forms. Approximately 36% of first-year class received scholarships/grants-in-aid. Approximately 85% of current students receive some form of financial assistance. Average scholarship/grant $6,000.

DEGREE REQUIREMENTS. For J.D.: 88 credits (32 required) with an 8.0 (Scale 4–16) GPA, plus completion of upper divisional writing course; 3-year program. Accelerated J.D. with 1 summer of course work. For J.D. master's: 4-year program rather than the usual 5 years needed if each degree taken separately. For LL.M. (graduates of foreign law schools): 24 credits; at least 2 semesters in residence; Introduction to American Law; at least 1 seminar with a research paper; thesis option.

CAREER AND PLACEMENT INFORMATION. About 125–130 employers conducted on-campus interviews. Approximately 78% of graduates are employed in state. More than 78% of graduates are practicing law; 16% are in business; 3% in government; 3% in academia. Approximately 97% of the University of Minnesota's first-time state bar exam takers pass the Minnesota Bar Exam; Minnesota's passage rate for all first-time takers from ABA-approved schools is 90%. Graduates are eligible to take the bar exam in all 50 states.

MISSISSIPPI COLLEGE
Clinton, Mississippi 39058
Internet site: http://www.mc.edu

Founded 1826. Located 5 miles W of Jackson. Private control. Semester system. Library: 240,000 volumes/microforms; 900 periodicals/subscriptions; 20 computer workstations.

College's Graduate School includes: College of Arts and Sciences, School of Business Administration, School of Education.

Total enrollment: 3,000.

School of Law
151 East Griffith Street
Jackson, Mississippi 39201
Phone: (601)925-7105
Internet site: http://www.mc.edu

Established 1975. Located in downtown Jackson. ABA approved since 1980. AALS member. Semester system. Full-time, day study only. Law library: 240,900 volumes/microforms; 3,333 current periodicals/subscriptions; 14 computer workstations; has LEXIS, NEXIS, WEST-LAW, DIALOG; is a government depository.

Annual tuition: $12,610. On-campus housing available for single students at main campus. Annual on-campus housing cost: single students $3,000 (room and board). Contact the college's Dean of Students Office for on-campus information. Phone: (601)925-3248. Law students tend to live off-campus. Contact Admissions Office for off-campus information. Off-campus housing and personal expenses: approximately $13,850. Additional costs: books approximately $850.

Enrollment: first-year class 160; total full-time 418 (men 64%, women 36%); no part-time students. First-year statistics: 55% out of state, 28 states and foreign countries represented; 36% women; 12% minority; average age 25; 28 undergraduate institutions represented; range of first-year section sizes 40–80 students; number of upper division courses offered after first year 62.

Faculty: full-time 18, part-time 19; 39% female; 9% minority; student/faculty ratio 22 to 1.

Degree conferred: J.D.

RECRUITMENT PRACTICES AND POLICIES. Attends several local and national law school forums. Has on-campus informational sessions. School does have diversity program and actively recruits women/minority applicants.

ADMISSION REQUIREMENTS FOR FIRST-YEAR APPLICANTS. LSDAS law school report, LSAT (not later than December test date, if more than one LSAT, highest is used), bachelor's degree from an accredited institution, personal statement, two recommendations, transcripts (must show all schools attended and at least three years of study) required in support of application. Applicants must have received bachelor's degree prior to enrollment. Apply to Office of Admission after September 30, before May 1. First-year students admitted fall only. Rolling admission process, notification starts in January and is finished by late May. Application fee $25. Phone: (800)738-1236, (601)925-7150.

ADMISSION REQUIREMENTS FOR TRANSFER APPLICANTS. Accepts transfers from other ABA-accredited schools. Admission limited to space available. At least one year of enrollment, dean's letter indicating the applicant is in good standing (prefer applicants in the top half of first-year class), LSAT, LSDAS, personal statement regarding reason for transfer, current law school transcript required in support of application. Apply to Admission office by June 30. Admission decisions made by early August. Application fee $25. Will consider visiting students.

ADMISSION STANDARDS. Number of full-time applicants 732; number accepted 468; number enrolled 160; median LSAT 152 (75% of class have a score at or above 145); median GPA 3.10 (A = 4) (75% of class have a GPA at or above 2.72). Attrition rate 3.4%. Gorman rating 2.14; *U.S. News & World Report* ranking is in the fourth tier of all law schools.

FINANCIAL AID. Scholarships, merit scholarships, minority scholarships, grants-in-aid, institutional loans; federal loans and Federal WS offered through college's Financial Aid Office. For scholarships (selection criteria place heavy reliance on LSAT and undergraduate GPA) apply to after January 1, before May 1 to college's Financial Aid Office. Phone: (601)944-1950. Use college's FA application. Use FAFSA for all federal programs (Title IV School code #E00479). Also submit Financial Aid Transcript, federal income tax forms. Approximately 22% of first-year class received scholarships/grants-in-aid. Approximately 81% of current students receive some form of financial assistance. Average scholarship/grant $8,181. Average debt after graduation $53,000.

DEGREE REQUIREMENTS. For J.D.: 88 credits (53 required) with a 2.0 (A = 4) GPA, plus completion of upper divisional writing course; 3-year program. Accelerated J.D. with 1 summer of course work.

CAREER AND PLACEMENT INFORMATION. About 40–45 employers conducted on-campus interviews. Approximately 51% of graduates are employed in state. More than 87% of graduates are practicing law; 6% are in business; 7% in government. Approximately 90% of Mississippi College's first-time state bar exam takers pass the Mississippi Bar Exam; Mississippi's passage rate for all first-time takers from ABA-approved schools is 87%. Graduates are eligible to take the bar exam in all 50 states.

UNIVERSITY OF MISSISSIPPI
University, Mississippi 38677
Internet site: http://www.olemiss.edu

Founded 1848. Located 180 miles N of Jackson, 75 miles SE of Memphis. Public control. Semester system. Library: 940,700 volumes; 2,788,500 microforms; 9,467 periodicals/subscriptions; 156 computer workstations.

University's other graduate colleges/schools: College of Liberal Arts, School of Accounting, School of Business Administration, School of Education, School of Engineering, School of Pharmacy.

Total university enrollment: 10,100.

School of Law
University, Mississippi 38677
Phone: (601)232-7361
Internet site: http://www.olemiss.edu
E-mail: lawmiss@sunset.backbone.olemiss.edu

Established 1854 as a department. Fourth oldest state-supported law school in U.S. Located on main campus. ABA approved since 1930. AALS member. Semester system. Full-time, day study only. Law library: 279,000 volumes/microforms; 3,355 current periodicals/ subscriptions; 36 computer workstations; has LEXIS, NEXIS, WESTLAW, DIALOG; is a Federal Government Depository.

Annual tuition: resident $3,181, nonresident $7,103. On-campus housing available for both single and married students. Annual on-campus housing cost: single students $2,105 (room only), married students $2,700. Contact university's Housing Office. Phone: (601)232-7328. Off-campus housing and personal expenses: approximately $9,600. Additional costs: books approximately $700.

Enrollment: first-year class 224; total full-time 515 (men 62%, women 38%); no part-time students. First-year statistics: 9% out of state, 21 states and foreign countries represented; 38% women; 15% minority; average age 24; 111 undergraduate institutions represented; average first-year section size 57 students; number of upper division courses offered after first year 57.

Faculty: full-time 25, part-time 9; 19% female; 15% minority; student/faculty ratio 26.5 to 1.

Degrees conferred: J.D., J.D.-M.B.A.

RECRUITMENT PRACTICES AND POLICIES. Attends several local and national law school forums. Has on-campus informational sessions. School does have diversity program and actively recruits women/minority applicants.

ADMISSION REQUIREMENTS FOR FIRST-YEAR APPLICANTS. LSDAS law school report, LSAT (not later than December test date, if more than one LSAT, average is used), bachelor's degree from an accredited institution, personal statement, two recommendations, transcripts (must show all schools attended and at least three years of study) required in support of application. Applicants must have received bachelor's degree prior to enrollment. Joint-degree applicants must apply to and be accepted by both schools. Apply to Office of Admission after September 30, before March 1. First-year students admitted fall only. Rolling admission process, notification starts in January and is finished by late May. School does maintain a waiting list. Application fee $20. Phone: (601)232-6910, 6911. E-mail: lawmiss@sunset.backbone.olemiss.edu.

ADMISSION REQUIREMENTS FOR TRANSFER APPLICANTS. Accepts transfers from other ABA-accredited schools. Admission limited to space available. At least one year of enrollment, dean's letter indicating the applicant is in good standing (prefer applicants in the top quarter of first-year class), LSAT, LSDAS, personal statement regarding reason for transfer, two letters of recommendation from current faculty, undergraduate transcript, current law school transcript required in support of application. Apply to Admission Office by June 15. Admission decisions made by mid July. Application fee $20. Will consider visiting students.

ADMISSION STANDARDS. Number of full-time applicants 1,098; number accepted 482; number enrolled 224; median LSAT 151 (75% of class have a score at or above 147); median GPA 3.20 (A = 4) (75% of class have a GPA at or above 3.02). Attrition rate 7.5%. Gorman rating 3.25; *U.S. News & World Report* ranking is in the third tier of all law schools.

FINANCIAL AID. Scholarships, merit scholarships, minority scholarships, grants-in-aid, private and institutional loans; federal loans and Federal WS offered through university's Financial Aid Office. Assistantships may be available for upper divisional joint-degree candidates. For scholarships (selection criteria place heavy reliance on LSAT and undergraduate GPA) apply to Admissions Office after January 1, before March 1. For all other programs apply to university's Office of Financial Aid. Phone: (601)232-7175. Use FAFSA for all federal programs (Title IV School code #002440). Also submit Financial Aid Transcript, federal income tax forms. Approximately 12% of first-year class received scholarships/grants-in-aid. Approximately 75% of current students receive some form of financial assistance. Average scholarship/grant $2,346.

DEGREE REQUIREMENTS. For J.D.: 90 credits (54–57 required) with a 2.0 (A = 4) GPA, plus completion of upper divisional writing course; 3-year program. Accelerated J.D. with 1 summer of course work. For J.D.-M.B.A.: 4-year program rather than the usual 5-year program needed if both degrees taken separately.

CAREER AND PLACEMENT INFORMATION. About 75–100 employers conducted on-campus interviews. Approximately 73% of graduates are employed in state. More than 81% of graduates are practicing law; 10% are in business; 8% in government; 1% in academia. Approximately 86% of the University of Mississippi's first-time state bar exam takers pass the Mississippi Bar Exam; Mississippi's passage rate for all first-time takers from ABA-approved schools is 87%. Graduates are eligible to take the bar exam in all 50 states.

UNIVERSITY OF MISSOURI—COLUMBIA

Columbia, Missouri 65211
Internet site: http://www.missouri.edu

Founded 1839. Located 120 miles W of St. Louis. Public control. Semester system. Library: 2,500,000 volumes; 4,800,000 microforms.

University's other graduate colleges/schools: College of Agriculture, College of Arts and Sciences, College of Business and Public Administration, College of Education, College of Engineering, College of Human Environmental Science, School of Health Related Professions, School of Journalism, School of Library and Information Science, School of Natural Resources, School of Nursing, College of Veterinary Medicine, School of Medicine.

Total university enrollment: 22,300.

School of Law

203 Hulston Hall
Columbia, Missouri 65211
Phone: (573)882-6487
Internet site: http://www.law.missouri.edu
E-mail: gregory@law.missouri.edu

Established 1872. Located on main campus. ABA approved since 1923. AALS charter member. Semester system. Full-time, day study only. Law library: 303,756 volumes/microforms; 4,869 current periodicals/subscriptions; 29 computer workstations; has LEXIS, NEXIS, WESTLAW, INFOTRAC, MERLIN/OCLC.

Annual tuition: resident $8,555, nonresident $16,588. On-campus housing available for both single and married students. Annual on-campus housing cost: single students $3,915 (room and board), married students $3,516. Contact Residential Life Office for both on- and off-campus housing information. Phone: (573)882-7275. Some law students do live off-campus. Off-campus housing and personal expenses: approximately $11,675. Additional costs: books approximately $700.

Enrollment: first-year class 200; total full-time 483 (men 62%, women 38%); no part-time students. First-year statistics: 15% out of state, 34 states and foreign countries represented; 38% women; 8% minority; average age 25; 121 undergraduate institutions represented; average first-year section size 75 students; number of upper division courses offered after first year 81.

Faculty: full-time 33, part-time 7; 23% female; 6% minority; student/faculty ratio 17 to 1.

Degrees conferred: J.D., J.D.-M.B.A., J.D.-M.P.A.

RECRUITMENT PRACTICES AND POLICIES. Attends national law school forums. Has on-campus informational sessions. School does have diversity program and actively recruits women/minority applicants.

ADMISSION REQUIREMENTS FOR FIRST-YEAR APPLICANTS. LSDAS law school report, LSAT (prefers December test date, if more than one LSAT, average is used), bachelor's degree from an accredited institution, transcripts (must show all schools attended and at least three years of study) required in support of application. Personal statement and recommendations are encouraged but not required. Applicants must have received bachelor's degree prior to enrollment. In addition, international applicants whose native language is not English must submit TOEFL (not older than two years) and have transcripts evaluated and translations certified. Apply to Office of Admission after September 30, before March 1 (priority deadline). First-year students admitted fall only. Rolling admission process, notification starts in December and is finished by late April. School does maintain a waiting list. Application fee $40. Phone: (573)882-6042. Fax: (573)882-9625. E-mail: gregory@law.missouri.edu.

ADMISSION REQUIREMENTS FOR TRANSFER APPLICANTS. Accepts transfers from other ABA-accredited schools. Admission limited to space available. At least one year of enrollment, dean's letter indicating

the applicant is in good standing (prefer applicants in the upper third of first-year class), LSAT, LSDAS, personal statement regarding reason for transfer, current law school transcript required in support of application. Apply to Admissions Office by June 15. Admission decisions made by late July. Application fee $40. Will consider visiting students.

ADMISSION STANDARDS. Number of full-time applicants 750; number accepted 490; number enrolled 200; median LSAT 156 (75% of class have a score at or above 151); median GPA 3.36 (A = 4) (75% of class have a GPA at or above 3.05). Attrition rate 7.4%. Gorman rating 3.79; *U.S. News & World Report* ranking is in the second tier of all law schools.

FINANCIAL AID. Need-based scholarships, minority scholarships, grants-in-aid, institutional loans; federal loans and Federal WS are administered through university's Office of Student Financial Aid. Assistantships may be available for upper divisional joint-degree candidates. All accepted applicants are automatically considered for scholarships (selection criteria place heavy reliance on LSAT and undergraduate GPA). For all programs apply after January 1, before March 1 to the university's Office of Student Financial Aid. Phone: (573)882-1383. Use FAFSA for all federal programs (Title IV School code #002516). Also submit Financial Aid Transcript, federal income tax forms. Approximately 64% of first-year class received scholarships/grants-in-aid. Approximately 80% of current students receive some form of financial assistance. Average scholarship/grant $1,000. Average debt after graduation $33,000.

DEGREE REQUIREMENTS. For J.D.: 89 credits (53 required) with a 70 (scale 0–100) GPA, plus completion of upper divisional writing course; 3-year program. Accelerated J.D. with 2 summers of course work. For J.D.-master's: 4-year program rather than the usual 5 years needed if both degrees taken separately.

CAREER AND PLACEMENT INFORMATION. About 60–70 employers conducted on-campus interviews. Approximately 89% of graduates are employed in state. More than 79% of graduates are practicing law; 5% are in business; 14% in government; 2% in academia. Approximately 90% of the University of Missouri—Columbia's first-time state bar exam takers pass the Missouri bar exam; Missouri's passage rate for all first time takers from ABA-approved schools is 92%. Graduates are eligible to take the bar exam in all 50 states.

UNIVERSITY OF MISSOURI— KANSAS CITY

Kansas City, Missouri 64110-2499
Internet site: http://www.umkc.edu

Founded 1929. Public control. Semester system. Library: 962,000 volumes; 1,813,413 microforms; 8,793 periodicals/subscriptions.

University's other graduate colleges/schools: College of Arts and Sciences, Conservatory of Music, School of Biological Sciences, School of Business and Public Administration, School of Dentistry, School of Education, School of Graduate Studies, School of Medicine, School of Nursing, School of Pharmacy.

Total university enrollment: 10,200.

School of Law

5100 Rockhill Road
Kansas City, Missouri 64110
Phone: (816)325-1657
Internet site: http://www.law.umkc.edu
E-mail: kloster@smtpgate.umkc.edu

Established 1895. Affiliated with University of Missouri in 1963. Located on main campus. ABA approved since 1936. AALS member. Semester system. Full-time, limited part-time study. Law library: 263,900 volumes/microforms; 3,857 current periodicals/subscriptions; 45 computer workstations; has LEXIS, NEXIS, WESTLAW, DIALOG.

Annual tuition: resident $8,555, nonresident $16,588. On-campus housing available for single students only. Annual on-campus housing cost: single students $4,000 (room and board). Contact Residence Housing Office for both on- and off-campus housing information. Phone: (816)235-2800. Law students tend to live off-campus. Off-campus housing and personal expenses: approximately $11,675. Additional costs: books approximately $700.

Enrollment: first-year class 163 full-time, 16 part-time; total full-time 475, part-time 45 (men 52%, women 48%). First-year statistics: 25% out of state, 22 states and foreign countries represented; 48% women; 16% minority; average age 27; 81 undergraduate institutions represented; average first-year section size 60 students; number of upper division courses offered after first year 84.

Faculty: full-time 29, part-time 33; 27% female; 5% minority; student/faculty ratio 19 to 1.

Degrees conferred: J.D., J.D.-M.B.A., J.D.-LL.M. (Taxation), LL.M. (General, Taxation).

RECRUITMENT PRACTICES AND POLICIES. Attends national law school forums. Has on-campus informational sessions. School does have diversity program and actively recruits women/minority applicants.

ADMISSION REQUIREMENTS FOR FIRST-YEAR APPLICANTS. LSDAS law school report, LSAT (not later than December test date, if more than one LSAT, average is used), bachelor's degree from an accredited institution, personal statement, two recommendations, transcripts (must show all schools attended and at least three years of study) required in support of application. Applicants must have received bachelor's degree prior to enrollment. Interview not required. Campus visits encouraged. In addition, international applicants whose native language is not English must submit TOEFL (not older than two years). Joint-degree applicants must apply to and be accepted by both schools. Apply to Office of Admission after September 30, before March 1. First-year students admitted fall only. Rolling admission process, notification starts in January and is finished by late April. Acceptance of offer and first deposit due date is April 1. Application fee $25. Phone: (816)235-1657. E-mail: kloster@smtpgate.umkc.edu.

ADMISSION REQUIREMENTS FOR TRANSFER APPLICANTS. Accepts transfers from other ABA-accredited schools. Admission limited to space available. At least one year of enrollment, dean's letter indicating the applicant is in good standing (prefer applicants in the upper third of first-year class), LSAT, LSDAS, personal statement regarding reason for transfer, undergraduate transcript, current law school transcript required in support of application. Apply to Admission Office by June 1 (fall), December 1 (spring). Admission decision made within one month after application is completed. Application fee $25. Will consider visiting students.

ADMISSION REQUIREMENTS FOR LL.M. APPLICANTS. Applicants must be graduates of an accredited American law school. Official transcripts, résumé, personal statement, letters of recommendation required in support of graduate application. Apply at least two months prior to the preferred semester of entrance. Application fee $25.

ADMISSION STANDARDS. Number of full-time applicants 726, part-time 40; number accepted 465 full-time, 26 part-time; number enrolled 163 full-time, 16 part-time; median LSAT 153 (75% of class have a score at or above 150 full-time, 146 part-time); median GPA 3.12 (A = 4) (75% of class have a GPA at or above 2.86 full-time, 2.76 part-time). Attrition rate 4.2%. Gorman rating 3.37; *U.S. News & World Report* ranking is in the third tier of all law schools.

FINANCIAL AID. Scholarships, merit scholarships, minority scholarships, grants-in-aid, private and institutional loans; federal loans and Federal WS offered through university's Financial Aid Office. Assistantships may be available for upper divisional joint-degree candidates. For scholarships (selection criteria place heavy reliance on LSAT and undergraduate GPA) submit scholarship insert from admission application for consideration. Financial aid packets are automatically sent to all accepted students and to those who are high on the wait list. Return applications to Student Financial Aid Office as soon as possible. Submit FAFSA for all federal programs (Title IV School code #002518). Also submit Financial Aid Transcript, federal income tax forms. Approximately 17% (full-time) of first-year class received scholarships/grants-in-aid. Approximately 76% of current students receive some form of financial assistance. Average scholarship/grant $3,862.

DEGREE REQUIREMENTS. For J.D.: 91 credits (52 required) with a 2.0 (A = 4) GPA, plus completion of upper divisional writing course; 3-year full-time program, 4-year part-time program. Accelerated J.D. with summer course work. For J.D.-master's: 4-year program rather than the usual 5-year program needed if both degrees taken separately. For J.D.-LL.M.: program can be completed in either 6 or 7 semesters plus 1 or 2 summer sessions. For LL.M.: 24 credits, at least 2 semesters in residence.

CAREER AND PLACEMENT INFORMATION. About 35–40 employers conducted on-campus interviews. Approximately 76% of graduates are employed in state. More than 76% of graduates are practicing law; 12% are in business; 12% in government. Approximately 95% of the University of Missouri—Kansas City's first-time state bar exam takers pass the Missouri Bar Exam; Missouri's passage rate for all first-time takers from ABA-approved schools is 92%. Graduates are eligible to take the bar exam in all 50 states.

UNIVERSITY OF MONTANA

Missoula, Montana 59812-0002
Internet site: http://www.umt.edu

Founded 1893. Public control. Semester system. Library: 564,000 volumes; 555,000 microforms; 4,347 periodicals/subscriptions.

University's Graduate School includes: College of Arts and Sciences, Division of Biological Sciences, School of Business Administration, School of Education, School of

Fine Arts, School of Forestry, School of Journalism, School of Pharmacy and Allied Health Sciences.

Total university enrollment: 11,700.

School of Law

Missoula, Montana 59812
Phone: (406)243-4311
Internet site: http://www.umt.edu/law/homepage.htm
E-mail: lawadmis@selway.umt.edu

Established 1911. Located on main campus. ABA approved since 1923. AALS member since 1914. Semester system. Full-time, day study only. Law library: 122,600 volumes/microforms; 1,673 current periodicals/subscriptions; 35 computer workstations; has LEXIS, WESTLAW.

Annual tuition: resident $6,046, nonresident $11,048. On-campus housing available for both single and married students. Annual on-campus housing cost: single students $1,926 (room only), $4,112 (room and board), married students $2,000. Housing deadline July 1. Contact Housing Officer for both on- and off-campus housing information. Phone: (406)243-2611. Law students tend to live off-campus. Off-campus housing and personal expenses: approximately $7,540. Additional costs: books approximately $700.

Enrollment: first-year class 75–80; total full-time 235 (men 56%, women 44%); no part-time students. First-year statistics: 33% out of state, 19 states and foreign countries represented; 44% women; 6.5% minority; average age 29; 41 undergraduate institutions represented; average first-year section size 25 students; number of upper division courses offered after first year 56.

Faculty: full-time 17, part-time 16; 33% female; 5% minority; student/faculty ratio 16 to 1.

Degrees conferred: J.D., J.D.-M.P.A., J.D.-M.S. (Environmental Studies).

RECRUITMENT PRACTICES AND POLICIES. Attends several local and national law school forums. Has on-campus informational sessions. School does have diversity program and actively recruits women/minority applicants.

ADMISSION REQUIREMENTS FOR FIRST-YEAR APPLICANTS. LSDAS law school report, LSAT (not later than February test date, if more than one LSAT, average is used), bachelor's degree from an accredited institution, two personal statements, three recommendations, transcripts (must show all schools attended and at least three years of study), law school application matching form required in support of application. Applicants must have received bachelor's degree prior to enrollment. Interview not required, campus visit encouraged. In addition, international applicants whose native language is not English must submit TOEFL (not older than two years), certificate of financial support. Joint-degree applicants must apply to and be accepted by both schools, GRE required for M.P.A. Apply to Office of Admission after September 30, before March 1. First-year students admitted fall only. Rolling admission process, notification starts in February and is finished by early June. School does maintain a waiting list. Application fee $60. Phone: (406)243-2698. E-mail: lawadmis@selway.umt.edu.

ADMISSION REQUIREMENTS FOR TRANSFER APPLICANTS. Accepts transfers from other ABA-accredited schools. Admission limited to space available. At least one year of enrollment, dean's letter indicating the applicant is in good standing (prefer applicants in the upper third of first-year class), LSAT, LSDAS, personal statement regarding reason for transfer, one academic reference, law school application matching form, current law school transcript required in support of application. Apply to Admission Office by June 1. Admission decisions made from April through mid July. Application fee $60. Will consider visiting students.

ADMISSION STANDARDS. Number of full-time applicants 478; number accepted 208; number enrolled 81; median LSAT 157 (75% of class have a score at or above 151); median GPA 3.20 (A = 4) (75% of class have a GPA at or above 2.98). Attrition rate 1.7%. Gorman rating 2.84; *U.S. News & World Report* ranking is in the second tier of all law schools.

FINANCIAL AID. Need-based scholarships, fee waivers, minority scholarships, private and institutional loans; federal loans and Federal WS offered through university's Financial Aid Office. Assistantships may be available for upper divisional joint-degree candidates. For scholarships (selection criteria place heavy reliance on LSAT and undergraduate GPA and are based on demonstrated need), apply by February 1. For all other programs apply after January 1, before March 1 to university's Financial Aid Office. Phone: (406)243-5373. Use FAFSA for all federal programs (Title IV School code #002536). Also submit Financial Aid Transcript, federal income tax forms. Approximately 38% of first-year class received scholarships/grants-in-aid. Approximately 85% of current students receive some form of financial assistance. Average scholarship/grant $1,482. Average debt after graduation $37,500.

DEGREE REQUIREMENTS. For J.D.: 90 credits (65 required) with a 2.0 (A = 4) GPA, plus completion of upper divisional writing course; 3-year program. For J.D.-master's: 4-year program rather than the usual 5-year program needed if both degrees taken separately.

CAREER AND PLACEMENT INFORMATION. About 20–25 employers conducted on-campus interviews. Approximately 87% of graduates are employed in state. More than 79% of graduates are practicing law; 13% are in business; 6% in government; 2% in academia. Approximately 94% of the University of Montana's first-time state bar exam takers pass the Montana Bar Exam; Montana's passage rate for all first time takers from ABA-approved schools is 90%. Graduates are eligible to take the bar exam in all 50 states.

UNIVERSITY OF NEBRASKA
Lincoln, Nebraska 68588
Internet site: http://www.unl.edu

Founded 1869. Public control. Semester system. Library: 2,330,000 volumes; 3,970,000 microforms; 20,623 periodicals/subscriptions.

University's Graduate College includes: Center of Biological Chemistry, College of Agricultural Sciences and Natural Resources, College of Architecture, College of Arts and Sciences, College of Business Administration, College of Engineering and Technology, College of Fine and Performing Arts, College of Journalism and Mass Communications, School of Biological Sciences, Teachers College.

Total university enrollment: 24,320.

College of Law
P.O. Box 830902
Lincoln, Nebraska 68583-0902
Phone: (404)472-2161
Internet site: http://www.unl.edu/lawcoll

Established 1891. Located on main campus. ABA approved since 1923. AALS member. Semester system. Full-time, day study only. Law library: 322,500 volumes/microforms; 2,794 current periodicals/subscriptions; 58 computer workstations; has LEXIS, NEXIS, WESTLAW, DIALOG.

Annual tuition: resident $4,498, nonresident $9,997; per credit, resident $97.50, nonresident $250.25. On-campus housing available for both single and married students. Annual on-campus housing cost: single students

$3,990 (room and board), married students $3,450. Contact Housing Office for both on- and off-campus housing information. Phone: (402)472-3561. Law students tend to live off-campus. Off-campus housing and personal expenses: approximately $9,005. Additional costs: books approximately $700.

Enrollment: first-year class 140; total full-time 684 (men 57%, women 43%); no part-time students. First-year statistics: 25% out of state, 23 states and foreign countries represented; 43% women; 12% minority; average age 26; 60 undergraduate institutions represented; range of first-year section sizes 25–70 students; number of upper division courses offered after first year 75.

Faculty: full-time 23, part-time 13; 23% female; 8% minority; student/faculty ratio 14.6 to 1.

Degrees conferred: J.D., J.D.-M.B.A., J.D.-M.P.Acc., J.D.-Ph.D. (Psychology), M.L.S. (for students who do not have J.D.).

RECRUITMENT PRACTICES AND POLICIES. Attends national law school forums. Has on-campus informational sessions. School does have diversity program and actively recruits women/minority applicants.

ADMISSION REQUIREMENTS FOR FIRST-YEAR APPLICANTS. LSDAS law school report, LSAT (not later than December test date, if more than one LSAT, average is used), bachelor's degree from an accredited institution, personal statement, transcripts (must show all schools attended and at least three years of study) required in support of application. Recommendations are not required but are strongly encouraged. Applicants must have received bachelor's degree prior to enrollment. In addition, international applicants whose native language is not English must submit TOEFL (not older than two years). Apply to Office of Admission after September 30, before March 1 (priority deadline). First-year students admitted fall only. Rolling admission process, notification starts in November and is finished by late April. Application fee $25. Phone: (402)472-2161. Fax: (402)472-5185. E-mail: lawadm@unlinfo.unl.edu.

ADMISSION REQUIREMENTS FOR TRANSFER APPLICANTS. Accepts transfers from other ABA-accredited schools. Admission limited to space available. At least one year of enrollment, dean's letter indicating the applicant is in good standing (prefer applicants in the top quarter of first-year class), LSAT, LSDAS, personal statement regarding reason for transfer, current law school transcript showing rank in class required in support of application. Apply to Admission Office by June

15. Admission decisions made by mid July. Application fee $25. Will consider visiting students.

ADMISSION STANDARDS. Number of full-time applicants 685; number accepted 388; number enrolled 141; median LSAT 154 (75% of class have a score at or above 151); median GPA 3.45 (A = 4) (75% of class have a GPA at or above 3.16). Attrition rate 6.5%. Gorman rating 3.23; *U.S. News & World Report* ranking is in the second tier of all law schools.

FINANCIAL AID. Scholarships, nonresident scholarships, minority scholarships, need-based grants-in-aid, private and institutional loans; federal loans and Federal WS available. Assistantships may be available for upper divisional joint-degree candidates. For scholarships (selection criteria place heavy reliance on LSAT and undergraduate GPA) apply to Admissions Office after January 1, before May 1. Use Law College Grant Application. For all other programs apply to university's Financial Aid Office before March 1. Phone: (404)472-2030. Use FAFSA for all federal programs (Title IV School code #002565). Also submit Financial Aid Transcript, FSAP (Iowa City), federal income tax forms. Approximately 55% of first-year class received scholarships/grants-in-aid. Approximately 75% of current students receive some form of financial assistance. Average scholarship/grant $2,598. Clerkships in the Public Interest Program available. Average debt after graduation $20,000.

DEGREE REQUIREMENTS. For J.D.: 96 credits (45 required) with a 4.0 (A = 8) GPA, plus completion of upper divisional writing course; 3-year program. Accelerated J.D. with 2 summers of course work. For J.D.-master's: 4-year program rather than the usual 5-year program needed if both degrees taken separately. For J.D.-Ph.D.: can be completed in 6 years rather than the usual 7 years needed if both degrees taken separately. For M.L.S.: 30 credits; at least 2 semesters in residence; a GPA of 2.5 (A = 4) required.

CAREER AND PLACEMENT INFORMATION. About 15–25 employers conducted on-campus interviews. Approximately 51% of graduates are employed in state. More than 61% of graduates are practicing law; 18% are in business; 20% in government; 1% in academia. Approximately 99% of the University of Nebraska's first-time state bar exam takers pass the Nebraska Bar Exam; Nebraska's passage rate for all first-time takers from ABA-approved schools is 94%. Graduates are eligible to take the bar exam in all 50 states.

NEW ENGLAND SCHOOL OF LAW
154 Stuart Street
Boston, Massachusetts 02116
Phone: (617)451-0010
Internet site: http://www.nesl.edu
E-mail: admit@admin.nesl.edu

Established 1908 as Portia Law School, name changed 1969. ABA approved since 1969. AALS member. Semester system. Full-time (day), part-time (evening), part-time (flexible to accommodate child-care responsibilities). Law library: 272,000 volumes/microforms, 2,997 current periodicals/subscriptions, 72 computer workstations; has LEXIS, NEXIS, WESTLAW, DIALOG, OCLC, CALI.

Annual tuition: full-time $14,350, part-time $10,880. No on-campus housing available. Law students live off-campus. Contact Admissions Office for off-campus information. Off-campus housing and personal expenses: approximately $13,450. Additional costs: books approximately $450.

Enrollment: first-year class 171, part-time 82; total full-time 561, part-time 412 (men 53%, women 47%). First-year statistics: 47% out of state, 42 states and foreign countries represented; 47% women; 15% minority; average age 27; 312 undergraduate institutions represented; range of first-year section sizes 15–115 students; number of upper division courses offered after first year 75 full-time, 71 part-time.

Faculty: full-time 39, part-time 29; 34% female; 5% minority; student/faculty ratio 20 to 1.

Degree conferred: J.D.

RECRUITMENT PRACTICES AND POLICIES. Attends national law school forums. Has on-campus informational sessions. School does have diversity program and actively recruits women/minority applicants.

ADMISSION REQUIREMENTS FOR FIRST-YEAR APPLICANTS. LSDAS law school report, LSAT (not later than February test date, if more than one LSAT, repeated scores are used if higher), bachelor's degree from an accredited institution, personal statement, two recommendations, transcripts (must show all schools attended and at least three years of study) required in support of application. Applicants must have received bachelor's degree prior to enrollment. Interview not required but may be requested by school. In addition, international applicants whose native language is not English must submit TOEFL (not older than two years), degree must be certified as equivalent to an American baccalaureate; certified transcripts must be sent directly to school. Apply to Office of Admission after September 15, before March 15 (priority deadline). Applications received between March 15 and June 1 are reviewed on a space-available basis. First-year students admitted fall only. Rolling admission process, notification starts in November and is finished by late April. Application fee $50. Phone: (617)472-7210. Fax: (617)472-7200. E-mail: admit@admin.nesl.edu.

ADMISSION REQUIREMENTS FOR TRANSFER APPLICANTS. Accepts transfers from other ABA-accredited schools. Admission limited to space available. At least one year of enrollment, dean's letter indicating the applicant is in good standing (prefer applicants in the top quarter of first-year class), LSAT, LSDAS, personal statement regarding reason for transfer, one recommendation from a current faculty member, current law school transcript required in support of application. Apply to Admissions Office by July 1. Admission decisions made by mid August. Application fee $50. Will consider visiting students.

ADMISSION STANDARDS. Number of full-time applicants 2,038, part-time 370; number accepted 1,318 full-time, 252 part-time; number enrolled 171 full-time, 82 part-time; median LSAT 150 (75% of class have a score at or above 146 for both full- and part-time); median GPA 2.92 (A = 4) (75% of class have a GPA at or above 2.59 full-time, 2.55 part-time). Attrition rate 5.5%. Gorman rating 3.07; *U.S. News & World Report* ranking is in the fourth tier of all law schools.

FINANCIAL AID. Scholarships, merit scholarships, grants-in-aid, private and institutional loans; federal loans, Federal WS available. For scholarships (selection criteria place heavy reliance on LSAT and undergraduate GPA) apply at same time as you submit admissions application. For all other programs apply after January 1, before April 1 to Financial Aid Office. Use FAFSA for all federal programs and submit to processor by February 15 (Title IV School code #G08916). Also submit Financial Aid Transcript, federal income tax forms. Approximately 48% (full-time), 13% (part-time) of first-year class received scholarships/grants-in-aid. Approximately 74% of current students receive some form of financial assistance. Average scholarship/grant $1,861 (full-time), $2,064 (part-time). Average debt after graduation $45,600.

DEGREE REQUIREMENTS. For J.D.: 84 credits (42 required) with a 2.0 (A = 4) GPA, plus completion of upper divisional writing course; 3-year full-time program, 4-year part-time program.

CAREER AND PLACEMENT INFORMATION. About 90–100 employers conducted on-campus interviews. Approximately 76% of graduates are employed in state. More than 52% of graduates are practicing law; 22% are in business; 24% in government; 2% in academia. Approximately 81% of the New England School of Law's first-time state bar exam takers pass the Massachusetts Bar Exam; Massachusetts' passage rate for all first-time takers from ABA-approved schools is 85%. Graduates are eligible to take the bar exam in all 50 states.

UNIVERSITY OF NEW MEXICO
Albuquerque, New Mexico 87131-2039
Internet site: http://www.unm.edu

Founded 1889. Located 60 miles from Santa Fe, the state capital. Public control. Semester system. Library: 1,600,000 volumes; 5,000,000 microforms.

University's other graduate colleges/schools: College of Arts and Sciences, College of Education, College of Engineering, College of Fine Arts, College of Nursing, College of Pharmacy, Robert O. Anderson Graduate School of Management, School of Architecture and Planning, School of Public Administration, School of Medicine.

Total university enrollment: 23,750.

School of Law
1117 Stanford, N.E.
Albuquerque, New Mexico 87131-1431
Phone: (505)277-2146
Internet site: http://www.unm.edu/~unmlaw

Established 1947. Located on main campus. ABA approved since 1948. AALS member. Semester system. Full-time, day study only. Law library: 351,000 volumes/ microforms; 3,145 current periodicals/subscriptions; 36 computer workstations; has LEXIS, NEXIS, WESTLAW, DIALOG, Q/L; law library is New Mexico's primary legal research center. Special facilities: American Indian Law Center, Institute of Public Law, the Natural Resources Center, International Transboundary Center, Center for Environmental Law, Center for Wildlife Law. Special programs: summer study abroad in Guanajuato, Mexico; externships.

Annual tuition: resident $3,612, nonresident $12,116. On-campus housing available for both single and married students. Annual on-campus housing cost: single students $4,500 (room and board), married students $5,000. Contact Housing Office for both on- and off-campus housing information. Phone: (505)277-4707. Law students tend to live off-campus. Off-campus housing and personal expenses: approximately $10,304. Additional costs: books approximately $700.

Enrollment: first-year class 112; total full-time 339 (men 52%, women 48%); no part-time students. First-year statistics: 9% out of state; 48% women, 39% minority; average age 28; 66 undergraduate institutions represented; range of first-year section sizes 16–56 students; number of upper division courses offered after first year 92.

Faculty: full-time 30, part-time 34; 43% female; 18% minority; student/faculty ratio 11 to 1.

Degrees conferred: J.D., J.D.-M.B.A., J.D.-M.A.P.A., J.D.-M.A.(Latin American Studies).

RECRUITMENT PRACTICES AND POLICIES. Attends national law school forums. Has on-campus informational sessions. School does have diversity program and actively recruits women/minority applicants.

ADMISSION REQUIREMENTS FOR FIRST-YEAR APPLICANTS. LSDAS law school report, LSAT (not later than December test date, if more than one LSAT, average is used), bachelor's degree from an accredited institution, personal statement, one recommendation, transcripts (must show all schools attended and at least three years of study) required in support of application. Applicants must have received bachelor's degree prior to enrollment. Interview not required; campus visits welcomed. In addition, international applicants whose native language is not English must submit TOEFL (not older than two years). Preference given to state residents. Joint-degree applicants must apply to and be accepted by each school. Apply to Office of Admission after September 30, before February 15. First-year students admitted fall only. Rolling admission process, notification starts in February and is finished by late April. Application fee $40. Phone: (505)277-2146. Fax: (505)277-0068.

ADMISSION REQUIREMENTS FOR TRANSFER APPLICANTS. Accepts transfers from other ABA-accredited schools. Admission limited to space available and state residents. At least one year of enrollment, dean's letter indicating the applicant is in good standing (prefer applicants in the top quarter of first-year class), LSAT, LSDAS, personal statement regarding reason for transfer, current law school transcript including rank in class required in support of application. Apply to Admission Office by June 1. Admission decisions made by late July. Application fee $40. Will consider visiting students.

ADMISSION STANDARDS. Number of full-time applicants 825; number accepted 236; number enrolled 112;

median LSAT 155 (75% of class have a score at or above 150); median GPA 3.24 (A = 4) (75% of class have a GPA at or above 2.91). Attrition rate 2.1%. Gorman rating 2.85; *U.S. News & World Report* ranking is in the second tier of all law schools.

FINANCIAL AID. Scholarships, merit scholarships, minority scholarships, Native American Grants, need-based grants, private and institutional loans; federal loans and Federal WS offered through university's Financial Aid Office. Assistantships may be available for upper divisional joint-degree candidates. For scholarships (selection criteria place heavy reliance on LSAT and undergraduate GPA) apply to Admissions Office after January 1, before March 1. Use school's FA addendum. For all other programs apply to university's Office of Student Financial Aid. Phone: (505)277-2041, 2042. Use FAFSA for all federal programs (Title IV School code #002663). Also submit Financial Aid Transcript, federal income tax forms. Approximately 19% of first-year class received scholarships/grants-in-aid. Approximately 66% of current students receive some form of financial assistance. Average scholarship/grant $3,284.

DEGREE REQUIREMENTS. For J.D.: 86 credits (33 required) with a 2.0 (A = 4) GPA, plus completion of upper divisional writing course; 3-year program. For J.D.-master's: 4-year programs. Law school will accept 6 credits; master's programs will accept 6 credits.

CAREER AND PLACEMENT INFORMATION. About 25–30 employers conducted on-campus interviews. Approximately 84% of graduates are employed in state. More than 69% of graduates are practicing law; 11% are in business; 15% in government; 5% in academia. Approximately 89% of the University of New Mexico's first-time state bar exam takers pass the New Mexico Bar Exam; New Mexico's passage rate for all first-time takers from ABA-approved schools is 92%. Graduates are eligible to take the bar exam in all 50 states.

NEW YORK LAW SCHOOL

57 Worth Street
New York, New York 10013-2960
Phone: (212)431-2100
Internet site: http://www.nyls.edu
E-mail: admissions@nyls.edu

Established 1891. Located in lower Manhattan in TriBeCa (triangle below Canal Street) area. ABA approved since 1954. AALS member. Semester system.

Full-time, part-time study. Law library: 421,500 volumes/microforms; 4,713 current periodicals/subscriptions; 105 computer workstations; has LEXIS, NEXIS, WEST-LAW, LEGALTRAC, OCLC, RLIN. Special facilities: Communications Media Center, Center for New York City Law, Center for International Law. Special programs: Law School exchange with Vermont Law School; externships; judicial internships.

Annual tuition: full-time $21,060, part-time $15,793. No on-campus housing available. Law students live off-campus. Contact New York Law School Housing Office for off-campus information. Phone: (212)431-2166. Off-campus housing and personal expenses: approximately $13,945. Additional costs: books approximately $800.

Enrollment: first-year class 314 full-time, 123 part-time; total full-time 911, part-time 484 (men 57%, women 43%). First-year statistics: 28% out of state, 30 states and foreign countries represented; 43% women; 22% minority; average age 27; 132 undergraduate institutions represented; average first-year section sizes full-time 110 students, part-time 120 students; number of upper division courses offered after first year 82 full-time, 76 part-time.

Faculty: full-time 50, part-time 63; 31% female; 10% minority; student/faculty ratio 23 to 1.

Degrees conferred: B.S.-J.D. (Stevens Institute of Technology) J.D., J.D.-M.B.A. (Baruch College of City University of New York).

RECRUITMENT PRACTICES AND POLICIES. Attends selected national law school forums. Has on-campus informational sessions. School does have diversity program and actively recruits women/minority applicants.

ADMISSION REQUIREMENTS FOR FIRST-YEAR APPLICANTS. LSDAS law school report, LSAT (prefers December test date, if more than one LSAT, average is used), bachelor's degree from an accredited institution, personal statement, two recommendations, transcripts (must show all schools attended and at least three years of study) required in support of application. Applicants must have received bachelor's degree prior to enrollment. In addition, international applicants whose native language is not English must submit TOEFL (not older than two years), certification of degree equivalent to U.S. baccalaureate, certified evaluation of transcript and summation. Joint-degree applicants must apply to and be accepted by both schools. Apply to Office of Admission after September 30, before April 1. First-year students admitted fall only. Rolling admission process. Application

fee $50. Phone: (212)431-2888. E-mail: admissions@nyls.edu.

ADMISSION REQUIREMENTS FOR TRANSFER APPLICANTS. Accepts transfers from other ABA-accredited schools. Admission limited to space available. At least one year of enrollment, dean's letter indicating the applicant is in good standing (prefer applicants in the top quarter of first-year class), LSAT, LSDAS, two recommendations, personal statement regarding reason for transfer, undergraduate transcript, current law school transcript required in support of application. Admits fall, spring, summer. Apply to Admission Office at least two months prior to preferred date of entrance. Admission decision made within one month of receipt of completed application. Application fee $50. Will consider visiting students.

ADMISSION STANDARDS. Number of full-time applicants 3,288, part-time 825; number accepted 1,929 full-time, 356 part-time; number enrolled 314 full–time, 123 part-time; median LSAT 154 (75% of class have a score at or above 151 for both full- and part-time); median GPA 3.01 (A = 4) (75% of class have a GPA at or above 2.80 full-time, 2.78 part-time). Attrition rate 6.3%. Gorman rating 3.36; *U.S. News & World Report* ranking is in the second tier of all law schools.

FINANCIAL AID. Scholarships, merit scholarships, minority scholarships, grants-in-aid, private and institutional loans, federal loans, and Federal WS available. All accepted students are automatically considered for scholarships (selection criteria place heavy reliance on LSAT and undergraduate GPA). Apply to Office of Financial Aid after January 1, before April 15. Phone: (212)431-2828. Use FAFSA for all federal programs (Title IV School code #G02783). Also submit Financial Aid Transcript, federal income tax forms. Approximately 38% (full-time), 19% (part-time) of first-year class received scholarships/grants-in-aid. Approximately 80% of current students receive some form of financial assistance. Average scholarship/grant $7,475 (full-time), $6,770 (part-time). Average debt after graduation $47,000.

DEGREE REQUIREMENTS. For J.D.: 86 credits (38 required) with a 2.0 (A = 4) GPA, plus completion of upper divisional writing course; 3-year full-time program, 4-year part-time program. For J.D.-master's: 4-year program rather than the usual 5-year program needed if both degrees taken separately.

CAREER AND PLACEMENT INFORMATION. About 400–500 employers conducted on-campus interviews.

Approximately 82% of graduates are employed in state. More than 67% of graduates are practicing law; 18% are in business; 14% in government; 1% in academia. Approximately 74% of New York Law School's first-time state bar exam takers pass the New York Bar Exam; New York's passage rate for all first-time takers from ABA-approved schools is 78%. Graduates are eligible to take the bar exam in all 50 states.

NEW YORK UNIVERSITY

New York, New York 10012-1019
Internet site: http://www.nyu.edu

Founded 1831. Located in Greenwich Village at Washington Square. Private control. Semester system. Library: 3,650,000 volumes; 3,240,000 microforms; 28,700 periodicals/subscriptions; 50 computer workstations.

University's other graduate colleges/schools: College of Dentistry, Gallatin School of Individualized Study, Graduate School of Arts and Sciences, Leonard M. Stern School of Business, Robert F. Wagner School of Public Service, School of Continuing Education, School of Education, School of Medicine, Shirley M. Ehrenkranz School of Social Work, Tisch School of the Arts.

Total university enrollment: 33,900.

School of Law
110 West Third Street
New York, New York 10012-1074
Phone: (212)998-6000
Internet site: http://www.nyu.edu/law

Established 1835. Located at the Washington Square campus. ABA approved since 1930. AALS member. Semester system. Full-time, day study only. Law library: 944,500 volumes/microforms; 5,766 current periodicals/subscriptions; 100 computer workstations; has LEXIS, NEXIS, WESTLAW, DIALOG; is a Federal Government Depository. Special facilities and programs: Global Law Program, Center for International Studies, Center for Research in Crime and Justice, Arthur Garfield Hays Civil Liberties Program, Program for Study of Law Philosophy and Social Theory, Program on Philanthropy and the Law, Public Interest Center, Institute for Judicial Administration.

Annual tuition: $25,685. On-campus housing available for both single and married students. Law school has over 400 on-campus accommodations. Annual on-campus housing cost: single students $4,948 (room only), married students $6,500. Contact law school Residence Hall for both on- and off-campus housing information. Many law students live in off-campus housing. Off-campus housing

and personal expenses: approximately $16,225. Additional costs: books approximately $850.

Enrollment: first-year class 420; total full-time 1,342 (men 54%, women 46%); no part-time students. First-year statistics: 70% out of state, 69 states and foreign countries represented; 46% women; 22% minority; average age 25; 226 undergraduate institutions represented; average first-year section size 108 students; number of upper division courses offered after first year 247.

Faculty: full-time 95, part-time 97; 29% female; 8% minority; student/faculty ratio 14 to 1.

Degrees conferred: J.D., J.D.-M.B.A., J.D.-M.P.A. (Princeton University or NYU), J.D.-M.U.P., J.D.-M.S.W., J.D.-LL.M., LL.M.(Corporate Law, International Legal Studies, International Tax Program for Foreign Students, Taxation, Trade Regulations), M.C.J. (only for persons who have completed a basic legal education and received a university degree in law in another country), J.S.D.

RECRUITMENT PRACTICES AND POLICIES. Attends national law school forums. Has on-campus guided tours, self-guided tours of campus available from Admissions Office. School does have diversity program and actively recruits women/minority applicants.

ADMISSION REQUIREMENTS FOR FIRST-YEAR APPLICANTS. LSDAS law school report, LSAT (not later than December test date, if more than one LSAT, average is used), bachelor's degree from an accredited institution, personal statement, one recommendation, transcripts (must show all schools attended and at least three years of study) required in support of application. Applicants must have received bachelor's degree prior to enrollment. In addition, international applicants whose native language is not English must submit TOEFL (not older than two years), certified translation of all foreign transcripts. Apply to Office of Admission after September 1, before February 1. For Early Action apply by October 15, decisions made by December 1. First-year students admitted fall only. Notification starts in mid April. School does maintain a waiting list. Application fee $65. Phone: (212)998-6060. Fax: (212)995-4527.

ADMISSION REQUIREMENTS FOR TRANSFER APPLICANTS. Accepts transfers from other ABA-accredited or AALS-approved schools. Admission limited to space available. At least one year of enrollment, dean's letter indicating that applicant is in good standing and is eligible to return (prefer applicants in the top quarter of first-year class), LSAT, LSDAS, personal statement regarding reason for transfer, current law school transcript including rank in class required in support of application. Admits to fall term only. Apply to Admission Office by July 1. Admission decisions made by early August. Application fee $65. Will consider visiting students.

ADMISSION REQUIREMENTS FOR LL.M., M.C.J. All applicants must hold a first degree in law (J.D. or LL.B) approved by the Section of Legal Education of the ABA. Official transcripts, at least two professional recommendations, résumé or other evidence of significant professional accomplishment, personal statement required in support of graduate application. For international applicants, a bachelor of law degree from a non-U.S. law school approved by an ABA equivalent authority; TOEFL, TWE required for all applicants whose native language is not English. Admits fall only. Apply to Admissions Office by April 1 (full-time domestic), June 1 (part-time domestic), January 1 (international). Application fee $65. Phone: (212)998-6060.

ADMISSION REQUIREMENTS FOR J.S.D. All applicants must apply for, be accepted to, and complete LL.M. program before advancement to candidacy can be considered. See application procedures above.

ADMISSION STANDARDS. Number of full-time applicants 6,525; number accepted 1,480; number enrolled 420; median LSAT 168 (75% of class have a score at or above 165); median GPA 3.67 (A = 4) (75% of class have a GPA at or above 3.53). Attrition rate .6%. Gorman rating 4.76; *U.S. News & World Report* ranking is in the top 6 of all law schools.

FINANCIAL AID. Scholarships, Root-Tilden Snow Scholarships, Sinsheimer Service Scholarships, Public Service Scholarships, Dean's Merit Scholarship, minority scholarships, Soros Criminal Justice Fellowships, need-based grants, private and institutional loans, federal loans, Federal WS available. Assistantships may be available for upper divisional joint-degree candidates. All accepted students are automatically considered for scholarships (selection criteria place heavy reliance on LSAT and undergraduate GPA). Apply to Financial Aid Office after January 1, before February 1. Use FAFSA for all federal programs (Title IV School code #002785). Also submit Financial Aid Transcript, federal income tax forms, Access Disk. Approximately 24% of first-year class received scholarships/grants-in-aid. Approximately 78% of current students receive some form of financial assistance. Average scholarship/grant $12,735. Public service loan repayment program available. Average debt after graduation $51,800.

DEGREE REQUIREMENTS. For J.D.: 82 credits (38 required) with a 2.0 (A = 4) GPA, plus completion of upper divisional writing course; 3-year program. Accelerated J.D. with summer course work. For J.D.-M.B.A., M.U.P., M.P.A., M.S.W.: 4-year programs rather than the usual 5 years needed if both degrees taken separately. For J.D.-M.P.A. (Public Affairs) (Princeton University): 4 years, plus 1 summer rather than 5½ years usually needed if both degrees taken separately. For J.D.-M.A.: 4-year program, less than 4 years if some course work is taken in summer session. For LL.M.(Tax): 24 credits; at least 2 semesters in residence; thesis/nonthesis option. For LL.M. (foreign students), M.C.J. (for lawyers trained in Common Law): 24 credits; at least 2 semesters in full-time residence; Introduction to American Law (generally offered the summer prior to beginning degree program); at least 1 seminar. For J.S.D: an NYU LL.M. required; advancement to candidacy; at least one additional year in residence; thesis proposal; thesis; oral defense.

CAREER AND PLACEMENT INFORMATION. More than 400 employers conducted on-campus interviews. Approximately 75% of graduates are employed in state. More than 93% of graduates are practicing law; 4% are in business; 3% in government. Approximately 94% of New York University's first-time state bar exam takers pass the New York Bar Exam; New York's passage rate for all first-time takers from ABA-approved schools is 78%. Graduates are eligible to take the bar exam in all 50 states.

UNIVERSITY OF NORTH CAROLINA AT CHAPEL HILL
Chapel Hill, North Carolina 27599
Internet site: http://www.unc.edu

Founded 1789. The first state university chartered in the U.S. Public control. Semester system. Library: 3,500,000 volumes; 2,730,000 microforms.

University's other graduate colleges/schools: College of Arts and Sciences, School of Education, School of Information and Library Science, School of Journalism and Mass Communications, School of Nursing, School of Public Health, School of Social Work, Kenan-Flagler Business School, School of Dentistry, School of Medicine, School of Pharmacy.

Total university enrollment: 24,500.

School of Law

Campus Box 3380
101 Van Hecke-Wettach Hall
Chapel Hill, North Carolina 27599-3380
Phone: (919)962-5106
Internet site: http://www.law.unc/edu
E-mail: law_admission@unc.edu

Established 1845. Located on main campus. ABA approved since 1923. AALS member since 1920. Semester system. Full-time, day study only. Law library: 420,000 volumes/microforms; 5,718 current periodicals/subscriptions; 48 computer workstations; has LEXIS, NEXIS, WESTLAW.

Annual tuition: resident $2,881, nonresident $14,743. On-campus housing available for both single and married students. Annual on-campus housing cost: single students $7,340 (room and board), married students $4,560. Contact Director of University Housing for on-campus housing information. Phone: (919)966-5401. Law students tend to live off-campus. Contact Student Family Housing Office for off-campus information. Phone: (919)962-5661. Off-campus housing and personal expenses: approximately $8,950. Additional costs: books approximately $800.

Enrollment: first-year class 240; total full-time 97 (men 54%, women 46%); no part-time students. First-year statistics: 25% out of state, 23 states and 2 foreign countries represented; 46% women; 20% minority; average age 24; 105 undergraduate institutions represented; average first-year section size 80 students; number of upper division courses offered after first year 89.

Faculty: full-time 42, part-time 42; 30% female; 8% minority; student/faculty ratio 18.6 to 1.

Degrees conferred: J.D., J.D.-M.B.A., J.D.-M.P.A., J.D.-M.A.P.P. (Duke University), J.D.-M.P.H., J.D.-M.R.P.

RECRUITMENT PRACTICES AND POLICIES. Attends national law school forums. Has on-campus informational sessions. School does have diversity program and actively recruits women/minority applicants.

ADMISSION REQUIREMENTS FOR FIRST-YEAR APPLICANTS. LSDAS law school report, LSAT (not later than December test date, if more than one LSAT, average is used), bachelor's degree from an accredited institution, personal statement, two recommendations (a third is optional), transcripts (must show all schools attended and at least three years of study) required in support of application. Applicants must have received bachelor's degree prior to enrollment. Interview not required; applicants encouraged to visit law school. In addition, international applicants whose native language is not English must submit TOEFL (not older than two years), transcripts must be translated and verified, evaluated and certified by WES. Joint-degree applicants must apply to and be accepted by both schools. Apply to Office of Admission after September 15, before February 1. First-year students admitted fall only. Rolling admission process, notification starts in late fall and is finished by late April. School does maintain a waiting list. Application fee $60. Phone: (919)962-5109. E-mail: law_admission@unc.edu.

ADMISSION REQUIREMENTS FOR TRANSFER APPLICANTS. Accepts transfers from other ABA-accredited schools. Admission limited to space available. At least one year of enrollment, dean's letter indicating the applicant is in good standing (prefer applicants in the top 10% of first-year class), LSAT, LSDAS, personal statement regarding reason for transfer, two recommendations from current faculty, current law school transcript required in support of application. Apply to Admission Office by April 15. Admission decisions made by mid July. Application fee $60. Will consider visiting students.

ADMISSION STANDARDS. Number of full-time applicants 2,281; number accepted 617; number enrolled 240; median LSAT 162 (75% of class have a score at or above 155); median GPA 3.50 (A = 4) (75% of class have a GPA at or above 3.30). Attrition rate 1.4%. Gorman rating 4.46; *U.S. News & World Report* ranking is in the top 35 of all law schools.

FINANCIAL AID. Chancellor's Scholarships, merit scholarships, minority presence scholarships, grants-in-aid, institutional loans; federal loans and Federal WS offered through university's Financial Aid Office. Assistantships may be available for upper divisional joint-degree candidates. All accepted students are automatically considered for both merit and need-based scholarships (selection criteria place heavy reliance on LSAT and undergraduate GPA). For all other programs apply after January 1, before March 1 to university's Office of Scholarship and Student Aid. Phone: (919)962-8396. Use FAFSA for all federal programs (Title IV School code #002974). Also submit Financial Aid Transcript, federal income tax forms. Approximately 19% of first-year class received scholarships/grants-in-aid. Approximately 50% of current students receive some form of financial assistance. Average scholarship/grant $2,500.

DEGREE REQUIREMENTS. For J.D.: 86 credits (33 required) with a 2.0 (A = 4) GPA, plus completion of 2 upper divisional writing courses; 3-year program. For

J.D.-master's: 4- or 4½-year programs rather than the usual 5- or 5½-year programs needed if both degrees taken separately; an internship may be required by some degree programs.

CAREER AND PLACEMENT INFORMATION. About 240–250 employers conducted on-campus interviews. Approximately 62% of graduates are employed in state. More than 80% of graduates are practicing law; 7% are in business; 12% in government; 1% in academia. Approximately 94% of the University of North Carolina at Chapel Hill's first-time state bar exam takers pass the North Carolina Bar Exam; North Carolina's passage rate for all first-time takers from ABA-approved schools is 85%. Graduates are eligible to take the bar exam in all 50 states.

NORTH CAROLINA CENTRAL UNIVERSITY

Durham, North Carolina 27707-3129
Internet site: http://www.nccu.edu

Founded 1910. Located 20 miles from Raleigh. Public control. Semester system. Library: 624,000 volumes; 536,100 microforms; 4,811 periodicals/subscriptions; 30 computer workstations.

University's Division of Academic Affairs includes: College of Arts and Sciences, School of Business, School of Education, School of Library and Information Sciences.

Total university enrollment: 5,470.

School of Law
1512 South Alston Avenue
Durham, North Carolina 27707
Phone: (919)560-6333
Internet site: http://www.nccu.edu/law

Established 1939. Located on main campus. ABA approved since 1950. AALS member. Semester system. Full-time (day), part-time (evening) study. Law library: 270,250 volumes/microforms; 2,375 current periodicals/subscriptions; 19 computer workstations; has LEXIS, NEXIS, WESTLAW, DIALOG.

Annual tuition: resident $2,070, nonresident $10,939. On-campus housing available for single students only. Annual on-campus housing cost: single students $1,574 (room only), $3,006 (room and board). Housing deadline July 1. Contact Student Housing Office for both on- and off-campus housing information. Phone: (919)560-6517. Law students tend to live off-campus. Off-campus hous-

ing and personal expenses: approximately $7,400. Additional costs: books approximately $700.

Enrollment: first-year class 101 full-time, 32 part-time; total full-time 244, part-time 103 (men 47%,women 53%). First-year statistics: 23% out of state, 53% women; 53% minority; average age 26; range of first-year section sizes 20–55 students; number of upper division courses offered after first year 42 full-time, 13 part-time.

Faculty: full-time 20, part-time 5; 50% female; 45% minority; student/faculty ratio 20 to 1.

Degrees conferred: J.D., J.D.-M.B.A., J.D.-M.L.S.

RECRUITMENT PRACTICES AND POLICIES. Attends selected national law school forums. Has on-campus informational sessions. School does have diversity program and actively recruits women/minority applicants.

ADMISSION REQUIREMENTS FOR FIRST-YEAR APPLICANTS. LSDAS law school report, LSAT (not later than February test date, if more than one LSAT, highest is used), bachelor's degree from an accredited institution, personal statement, two recommendations, transcripts (must show all schools attended and at least three years of study) required in support of application. Applicants must have received bachelor's degree prior to enrollment. Interview not required; campus visits encouraged. In addition, international applicants whose native language is not English must submit TOEFL (not older than two years). Joint-degree applicants must apply to and be accepted by both schools. Apply to Office of Admission after September 30, before April 1. First-year students admitted fall only. Rolling admission process, notification starts in February and is finished by May. Application fee $30. Phone: (919)560-6333.

ADMISSION REQUIREMENTS FOR TRANSFER APPLICANTS. Accepts transfers from other ABA-accredited schools. Admission limited to space available. At least one year of enrollment, dean's letter indicating the applicant is in good standing (prefer applicants in the top half of first-year class), LSAT, LSDAS, personal statement regarding reason for transfer, two recommendations, current law school transcript required in support of application. Apply to Admission Office by July 1. Admission decisions made by mid August. Application fee $30. Will consider visiting students.

ADMISSION STANDARDS. Number of full-time applicants 1,152, part-time 252; number accepted 223 full-time, 49 part-time; number enrolled 101 full-time, 32 part-time; median LSAT 149 (75% of class have a score at or above 146 full-time, 151 part-time); median GPA 3.00 (A = 4) (75% of class have a GPA at or above 2.60 full-time, 2.70 part-time). Attrition rate 3.7%. Gorman rating 2.17; *U.S. News & World Report* ranking is in the fourth tier of all law schools.

FINANCIAL AID. Scholarships, merit scholarships, minority scholarships, private and institutional loans; federal loans and Federal WS offered through university's Financial Aid Office. For scholarships (selection criteria place heavy reliance on LSAT and undergraduate GPA) apply to Admissions Office after January 1, before February 1. Phone: (919)560-6335. Use school's financial assistance application. For all other programs apply to university's Office of Financial Aid. Phone: (919)560-6202. Use FAFSA for all federal programs (Title IV School code #002950). Also submit Financial Aid Transcript, federal income tax forms. Approximately 30% (full-time) of first-year class received scholarships/grants-in-aid. Approximately 68% of current students receive some form of financial assistance. Average scholarship/grant $400. Financial aid available for part-time students.

DEGREE REQUIREMENTS. For J.D.: 88 credits (65 required) with a 2.0 (A = 4) GPA, plus completion of upper divisional writing course; 3-year program, 4-year program (part-time). For J.D.-master's: 4-year program rather than the usual 5-year program needed if both degrees taken separately.

CAREER AND PLACEMENT INFORMATION. About 20–25 employers conducted on-campus interviews. Approximately 90% of graduates are employed in state. More than 77% of graduates are practicing law; 27% are in business; 9% in government; 1% in academia. Approximately 74% of North Carolina Central University's first-time state bar exam takers pass the North Carolina Bar Exam; North Carolina's passage rate for all first-time takers from ABA-approved schools is 85%. Graduates are eligible to take the bar exam in all 50 states.

UNIVERSITY OF NORTH DAKOTA

Grand Forks, North Dakota 58202
Internet site: http://www.und.nodak.edu

Founded 1883. Located in the NE part of the state, 320 miles NW of Minneapolis, 120 miles S of Winnipeg, Manitoba. Public control. Semester system. Library:

2,300,000 volumes; 800,000 microforms; 8,200 periodicals/subscriptions; 150 computer workstations.

University's other graduate colleges/schools: Center for Aerospace, Center for Teaching and Learning, College of Arts and Sciences, College of Business and Public Administration, College of Fine Arts, College of Human Resources, School of Engineering and Mines, School of Nursing, School of Medicine.

Total university enrollment: 11,500.

School of Law

P.O. Box 9003
Centennial Drive
Grand Forks, North Dakota 58202-9003
Phone: (701)777-2104
Internet site: http://www.law.und.nodak.edu

Established 1899. Located on main campus. ABA approved since 1923. AALS member. Semester system. Full-time, day study only. Law library: 230,000 volumes, 60,000 microforms; 2,697 current periodicals/subscriptions; 68 computer workstations; has LEXIS, WESTLAW, ODIN, OCLC; is a Federal Government Depository. Special facilities: Agricultural Law Institute, Center for American Indian Legal Program and Resources. Special programs: summer study abroad at University of Oslo, Norway.

Annual tuition: resident $4,097, Minnesota residents $4,302, residents of contiguous state/provinces $5,213, nonresident $8,533. On-campus housing available for both single and married students. Annual on-campus housing cost: single students $2,750 (room and board), married students $3,300. Contact Residence Hall for on-campus housing information. Phone: (701)777-2104. Law students tend to live off-campus. For apartment information contact Apartment Housing Office. Phone: (701)777-4208. Off-campus housing and personal expenses: approximately $7,300. Additional costs: books approximately $750.

Enrollment: first-year class 68; total full-time 202 (men 49%, women 51%); no part-time students. First-year statistics: 47% out of state, 51% women; 4% minority; average age 26; 85 undergraduate institutions represented; average first-year section size 70 students; number of upper division courses offered after first year 59.

Faculty: full-time 11, part-time 6; 41% female; no minority faculty; student/faculty ratio 15.7 to 1.

Degree conferred: J.D.

RECRUITMENT PRACTICES AND POLICIES. Attends several national law school forums. Has on-campus informational sessions. School does have diversity program and actively recruits women/minority applicants.

ADMISSION REQUIREMENTS FOR FIRST-YEAR APPLICANTS. LSDAS law school report, LSAT (not later than February test date, if more than one LSAT, average is used), bachelor's degree from an accredited institution, personal statement, two recommendations, transcripts (must show all schools attended and at least three years of study) required in support of application. Applicants must have received bachelor's degree prior to enrollment. Reciprocity Participation Agreement required for Minnesota state residents. In addition, international applicants whose native language is not English must submit TOEFL (not older than two years). Apply to Office of Admission after November 1, before April 1. First-year students admitted fall only. Rolling admission process, notification starts in January and is finished by late April. Acceptance of offer and first deposit due date April 1. Application fee $35. Phone: (701)777-2260.

ADMISSION REQUIREMENTS FOR TRANSFER APPLICANTS. Accepts transfers from other ABA-accredited schools. Admission limited to space available. At least one year of enrollment, dean's letter indicating applicant is in good standing (prefer applicants in the top half of first-year class), LSAT, LSDAS, personal statement regarding reason for transfer, undergraduate transcript, current law school transcript required in support of application. Apply to Admission Office by June 1. Admission decisions made by mid July. Application fee $35. Will consider visiting students.

ADMISSION STANDARDS. Number of full-time applicants 315; number accepted 171; number enrolled 68; median LSAT 153 (75% of class have a score at or above 149); median GPA 3.22 (A = 4) (75% of class have a GPA at or above 2.83). Attrition rate 4.2%. Gorman rating 2.35; *U.S. News & World Report* ranking is in the fourth tier of all law schools.

FINANCIAL AID. Scholarships, private and institutional loans; federal loans and Federal WS offered through university's Student Financial Aid Office. For scholarships (selection criteria place heavy reliance on LSAT and undergraduate GPA) use school's special scholarship form. For all other programs apply after January 1, before March 1 to university's Student Financial Aid Office. Phone: (707)777-3121. Use FAFSA for all federal programs (Title IV School code #003005). Also submit Financial Aid Transcript, federal income tax forms. Approximately 20% of first-year class received scholarships/grants-in-aid. Approximately 85% of current students receive some form of financial assistance. Average scholarship/grant $2,530.

DEGREE REQUIREMENTS. For J.D.: 90 credits (33 required) with a 2.0 (A = 4) GPA, plus completion of upper divisional writing course and a professional responsibility course; 3-year program. Accelerated J.D. with summer course work.

CAREER AND PLACEMENT INFORMATION. About 10–15 employers conducted on-campus interviews. Approximately 53% of graduates are employed in state. More than 74% of graduates are practicing law; 15% are in business; 11% in government. Approximately 89% (ND), 85% (MN) of the University of North Dakota's first-time state bar exam takers pass the North Dakota Bar Exam; North Dakota's passage rate for all first time takers from ABA-approved schools is 85% (ND), 91% (MN). Graduates are eligible to take the bar exam in all 50 states.

NORTHEASTERN UNIVERSITY
Boston, Massachusetts 02115-5096
Internet site: http://www.neu.edu

Founded 1898. Public control. Quarter system. Library: 1,810,000 volumes; 1,879,600 microforms; 8,963 periodicals/subscriptions.

University's other graduate colleges/schools: Bouve College of Pharmacy and Health Sciences, College of Computer Science, Graduate School of Arts and Sciences, Graduate School of Business Administration, Graduate School of Professional Accounting, Graduate School of Criminal Justice, Graduate School of Nursing, School of Journalism.

Total university enrollment: 24,600.

School of Law
400 Huntington Avenue
P.O. Box 728
Boston, Massachusetts 02115-0725
Phone: (617)373-5149
Internet site: http://www.slaw.neu/edu
E-mail: admissions@slaw.neu.edu

Established 1898. Located on main campus. ABA approved since 1969. AALS member. Quarter system. Full-time, day study only. Law library: 220,000 volumes/

microforms; 2,509 current periodicals/subscriptions; 89 computer workstations; has LEXIS, NEXIS, WEST-LAW, DIALOG. Special facilities: Urban Law and Public Policy Institute, Center for Artificial Intelligence and Law. Special programs: Cooperative Legal Education Program ("Co-op"), Poverty Law and Practice Program.

Annual tuition: $21,300. On-campus housing available for single students only. Annual on-campus living expenses: $14,900. Contact Housing Office for both on- and off-campus housing information. Phone: (617)373-2814. Law students tend to live off-campus. Off-campus housing and personal expenses: approximately $14,900. Additional costs: books approximately $850.

Enrollment: first-year class 215; total full-time 614 (men 33%,women 67%); no part-time students. First-year statistics: 63% out of state, 40 states and foreign countries represented; 67% women; 26% minority; average age 24; 123 undergraduate institutions represented; average first-year section size 65 students; number of upper division courses offered after first year 75.

Faculty: full-time 31, part-time 32; 43% female; 16% minority; student/faculty ratio 23 to 1.

Degrees conferred: J.D., J.D.-M.B.A., J.D.-M.S. (Accounting).

RECRUITMENT PRACTICES AND POLICIES. Attends national law school forums. Has on-campus informational sessions. School does have diversity program and actively recruits women/minority applicants.

ADMISSION REQUIREMENTS FOR FIRST-YEAR APPLICANTS. LSDAS law school report, LSAT (not later than October [round one], December [round two], February [round three] test date, if more than one LSAT, average is used), bachelor's degree from an accredited institution, personal statement, two recommendations, transcripts (must show all schools attended and at least three years of study) required in support of application. Applicants must have received bachelor's degree prior to enrollment. Interview not required but recommended. Apply to Office of Admission after September 1, before December 1 (round one), January 15 (round two), March 1 (round three). Will accept Law Multi-App in lieu of Northeastern application. Concurrent-degree applicants must apply to and be accepted by both schools. First-year students admitted fall only. Rolling admission process, notification starts in January 15 (round one), March 15 (round two), April 15 (round three). Application fee $55. Phone: (617)373-2395. Fax: (617)373-8865. E-mail: admissions@slaw.neu.edu.

ADMISSION REQUIREMENTS FOR TRANSFER APPLICANTS. Accepts transfers from other ABA-accredited schools. Admission limited to space available. At least one year of enrollment, dean's letter indicating applicant is in good standing (prefer applicants in the top quarter of first-year class), LSAT, LSDAS, personal statement regarding reason for transfer, one recommendation, current law school transcript required in support of application. Apply to Admission Office by June 15. Admission decision made as soon as application is complete. Application fee $55. Will consider visiting students.

ADMISSION STANDARDS. Number of full-time applicants 2,514; number accepted 881; number enrolled 215; median LSAT 157 (75% of class have a score at or above 151); median GPA 3.30 (A = 4) (75% of class have a GPA at or above 3.04). Attrition rate 2.8%. Gorman rating 3.10; *U.S. News & World Report* ranking is in the third tier of all law schools.

FINANCIAL AID. Scholarships, minority scholarships, grants-in-aid, private and institutional loans; federal loans and Federal WS offered through university's Financial Aid Office. Assistantships may be available for upper divisional joint-degree candidates. For scholarships (selection criteria place heavy reliance on LSAT and undergraduate GPA) apply to Graduate/Law Office of Financial Aid after January 1, before April 1. Use university's graduate/law financial aid form. For all loans/WS apply to Office of Financial Aid, Student Loan Department. Phone: (617)373-3386. Use FAFSA for all federal programs (Title IV School code #002199). Also submit Financial Aid Transcript, CSS profile form, federal income tax forms. Approximately 45% of first-year class received scholarships/grants-in-aid. Approximately 71% of current students receive some form of financial assistance. Average scholarship/grant $3,750. Loan deferral and forgiveness program available. Average debt after graduation $56,000.

DEGREE REQUIREMENTS. For J.D.: 99 quarter credits (48 required) with a 2.0 (A = 4) GPA, plus completion of upper divisional writing course; completion of 4 11-week legal "Co-op" internships, 3-year program. For J.D.-M.B.A.: 45-month program rather than the 54 months usually needed if both degrees taken separately. For J.D.-M.S. (Accounting): 42-month program rather than the 48 months usually needed if both degrees taken separately.

CAREER AND PLACEMENT INFORMATION. About 35–40 employers conducted on-campus interviews. Approximately 61% of graduates are employed in state. More than 75% of graduates are practicing law; 16% are in business; 7% in government; 2% in academia. Approximately 85% (MA), 72% (NY) of Northeastern University's first-time state bar exam takers pass the bar exam; the passage rate for all first-time takers from ABA-approved schools is 85% (MA), 78% (NY). Graduates are eligible to take the bar exam in all 50 states.

NORTHERN ILLINOIS UNIVERSITY

Dekalb, Illinois 60115-2854
Internet site: http://www.niu.edu

Founded 1895. Located 65 miles W of Chicago. Public control. Semester system. Library: 1,414,000 volumes; 2,240,000 microforms; 12,700 periodicals/subscriptions.

University's Graduate School includes: College of Business, College of Education, College of Engineering and Engineering Technology, College of Health and Human Sciences, College of Liberal Arts and Sciences, College of Visual and Performing Arts.

Total university enrollment: 22,000.

School of Law
Swen Parson Hall
Dekalb, Illinois 60115
Phone: (815)753-1068
Internet site: http://www.nui.edu/claw/lawhome.html
E-mail: lawadm@niu.edu

Established in 1975 as part of Lewis University, acquired by NIU in 1979. Located on main campus. ABA approved since 1978. AALS member. Semester system. Full-time, day study only. Law library: 195,700 volumes/microforms; 3,100 current periodicals/subscriptions; 25 computer workstations; has LEXIS, NEXIS, WESTLAW, LIS; is a Federal, State, and International Government Depository. Special programs: summer study abroad at University of Bordeaux-Montesquieu, Agen, France; externships.

Annual tuition: resident $5,938, nonresident $10,976. On-campus housing available for both single and married students. Annual on-campus housing cost: single students $4,000 (room and board), married students $2,000. There is a law school floor in housing accommodations. Contact Student Housing Services for both on- and off-campus housing information. Phone: (815)753-1525. Law students can live off-campus. Off-campus housing and personal expenses: approximately $8,462. Additional costs: books approximately $700.

Enrollment: first-year class 104; total full-time 296 (men 58%, women 42%); no part-time students. First-year statistics: 20% out of state, 14 states and foreign countries represented; 42% women; 20% minority; average age 27; 55 undergraduate institutions represented; average first-year section size 50 students; number of upper division courses offered after first year 64.

Faculty: full-time 28, part-time 13; 15% female; 19% minority; student/faculty ratio 14.8 to 1.

Degrees conferred: J.D., J.D.-M.B.A.

RECRUITMENT PRACTICES AND POLICIES. Attends several national law school forums. Has on-campus informational sessions. School does have diversity program and actively recruits women/minority applicants.

ADMISSION REQUIREMENTS FOR FIRST-YEAR APPLICANTS. LSDAS law school report, LSAT (not later than June test date, if more than one LSAT, average is used), bachelor's degree from an accredited institution, personal statement, two recommendations, transcripts (must show all schools attended and at least three years of study) required in support of application. Applicants must have received bachelor's degree prior to enrollment. Interview not required. Campus visits are encouraged. In addition, international applicants whose native language is not English must submit TOEFL (not older than two years). Joint-degree applicants must apply to and be accepted by both schools. Apply to Office of Admission and Financial Aid after September 30, before May 15 (priority deadline). First-year students admitted fall only. Rolling admission process, notification starts in November and is finished by late May. Acceptance of offer and first deposit due April 1. Application fee $35. Phone: (815)753-1420 or (815)753-8595. E-mail: lawadm@niu.edu.

ADMISSION REQUIREMENTS FOR TRANSFER APPLICANTS. Accepts transfers from other ABA-accredited schools. Admission limited to space available. At least one year of enrollment, dean's letter indicating applicant is in good standing (prefer applicants in the top quarter of first-year class), LSAT, LSDAS, personal statement regarding reason for transfer, one letter of recommendation, current law school transcript required in support of application. Apply to Admission and Financial Aid Office by June 30. Admission decisions made by early August. Application fee $35. Will consider visiting students.

ADMISSION STANDARDS. Number of full-time applicants 1,073; number accepted 381; number enrolled

104; median LSAT 156 (75% of class have a score at or above 153); median GPA 3.00 (A = 4) (75% of class have a GPA at or above 2.67). Attrition rate 3.3%. Gorman rating 2.43; *U.S. News & World Report* ranking is in the third tier of all law schools.

FINANCIAL AID. Scholarships, grants-in-aid, private loans, federal loans, Federal WS. Assistantships may be available for upper divisional joint-degree candidates. For scholarships (selection criteria place heavy reliance on LSAT and undergraduate GPA) apply to Admissions and Financial Aid Office after January 1, before March 1. Use NIU's financial aid application. Use FAFSA for all federal programs (Title IV School code #001737). Also submit Financial Aid Transcript, federal income tax forms. Approximately 17% of first-year class received scholarships/grants-in-aid. Approximately 71% of current students receive some form of financial assistance. Average scholarship/grant $2,316. Average debt after graduation $20,000.

DEGREE REQUIREMENTS. For J.D.: 85 credits (33 required) with a 2.0 (A = 4) GPA, plus completion of upper divisional writing course; 3-year program. Accelerated J.D. with summer course work. For J.D.-M.B.A.: 4-year program rather than the usual 5 years needed if both degrees were taken separately.

CAREER AND PLACEMENT INFORMATION. About 10–15 employers conducted on-campus interviews. Approximately 86% of graduates are employed in state. More than 65% of graduates are practicing law; 7% are in business; 28% in government. Approximately 77% of Northern Illinois University's first-time state bar exam takers pass the Illinois Bar Exam; Illinois' passage rate for all first-time takers from ABA-approved schools is 87%. Graduates are eligible to take the bar exam in all 50 states.

NORTHERN KENTUCKY UNIVERSITY
Highland Heights, Kentucky 41099
Internet site: http://www.nku.edu

In 1968 Northern Community College was authorized to operate as a four-year institute, Northern Kentucky State College. Name changed in 1976. Located 7 miles SE of Cincinnati, Ohio. Public control. Semester system. Library: 110,000 volumes; 700,000 microforms; 1,544 periodicals/subscriptions.

University's graduate school is the School of Graduate Programs.

Total university enrollment: 11,637.

Salmon P. Chase
College of Law
Nunn Drive
Highland Heights, Kentucky 41099-6031
Phone: (606)572-5340
Internet site: http://www.nku.edu~chase

Established 1893. Located on main campus. ABA approved since 1954. AALS member. Semester system. Full-time, part-time study. Law library: 241,800 volumes/microforms; 2,328 current periodicals/subscriptions; 26 computer workstations; has LEXIS, NEXIS, WESTLAW, DIALOG. Special facility: Ohio Valley Environmental and Natural Resources Law Institute.

Annual tuition: full-time resident $5,200, nonresident $13,040; part-time resident $4,340, nonresident $10,880. On-campus housing available for single students only. Annual on-campus housing cost: single students $3,608 (room and board). Contact Residential Life Office for both on- and off-campus housing information. Phone (606)572-5676. Law students tend to live off-campus. Off-campus housing and personal expenses: approximately $10,500. Additional costs: books approximately $700.

Enrollment: first-year class 72 full-time, 55 part-time, total full-time 205, part-time 205 (men 62%, and women 38%). First-year statistics: 41% out of state, 14 states and foreign countries represented; 38% women; 9% minority; average age 28; 42 undergraduate institutions represented; range of first-year section sizes 13–77 students; number of upper division courses offered after first year 40 full-time, 72 part-time.

Faculty: full-time 22, part-time 36, 22% female, 2% minority, student/faculty ratio 15.6 to 1.

Degrees conferred: J.D., J.D.-M.B.A.

RECRUITMENT PRACTICES AND POLICIES. Attends national law school forums. Has on-campus open houses. School does have diversity program and actively recruits women/minority applicants.

ADMISSION REQUIREMENTS FOR FIRST-YEAR APPLICANTS: LSDAS law school report, LSAT (not later than February test date, if more than one LSAT, highest is used), bachelor's degree from an accredited institution, personal statement, two recommendations, transcripts (must show all schools attended and at least three years of study) required in support of application. Applicant must have received bachelor's degree prior to enrollment. Interview not required but may be requested during "Open Houses." Apply to Office of Admission after September 30, before May 15 (February 1 priority deadline). First-year students admitted fall only. Rolling admission process, notification starts in February and is finished by late May. Application fee $30. Phone (606)572-6471.

ADMISSION REQUIREMENTS FOR TRANSFER APPLICANTS. Accepts transfers from other ABA-accredited schools. Admission limited to space available. At least one year of enrollment, dean's letter indicating applicant is in good standing, (prefer applicants with a 3.0 [A = 4] average), LSAT, LSDAS, personal statement regarding reason for transfer, two letters of recommendation, current law school transcript required in support of application. Apply to Admission Office by July 1. Admission decisions made by early August. Application fee $30. Will consider visiting students.

ADMISSION STANDARDS. Number of full-time applicants 639, part-time 172; number accepted 248 full-time, 83 part-time; number enrolled 72 full-time, 55 part-time; median LSAT 154 (75% of class have a GPA at or above 2.87 full-time, 2.79 part-time). Attrition rate 3.4%. Gorman rating 2.24; *U.S. News & World Report* ranking is in the fourth tier of all law schools.

FINANCIAL AID. Scholarships, merit scholarships, minority scholarships, tuition reciprocity (four Ohio counties only), grants-in-aid, private and institutional loans; federal loans and Federal WS offered through university's Financial Aid Office. For scholarships (selection criteria place heavy reliance on LSAT and undergraduate GPA) apply to Admissions Office by February 1. Use school's entering student scholarship application. For all other programs apply to university's Financial Aid Office. Use university's financial aid application. Submit FAFSA for all federal programs (Title IV School code #009275. Also submit Financial Aid Transcript, federal income tax forms. Approximately 29% (full-time), 31% (part-time) of first-year class received scholarships/grants-in-aid. Approximately 65% of current students receive some form of financial assistance. Average scholarship/grant $1,500.

DEGREE REQUIREMENTS. For J.D.: 90 credits (41 required) with a 2.0 (A = 4) GPA (2.15 in required and core courses), plus completion of upper divisional writing course; 3-year full-time program, 4-year part-time program. Accelerated J.D. with summer course work. For J.D.-M.B.A.: total 106 credits (J.D. 76 credits, M.B.A. 30 credits).

CAREER AND PLACEMENT INFORMATION. About 15–20 employers conducted on-campus interviews. Approximately 59% of graduates are employed in state. More than 51% of graduates are practicing law; 33% are in business; 16% in government; none in academia. Approximately 83% (KY), 92% (OH) of Northern Kentucky University's first-time state bar exam takers pass the bar exam; the passage rate for all first-time takers from ABA-approved schools is 88% (KY), 90% (OH). Graduates are eligible to take the bar exam in all 50 states.

NORTHWESTERN UNIVERSITY
Evanston, Illinois 60208
Internet site: http://www.nwu.edu

Founded 1851. Located 12 miles N of Chicago. Private control. Semester system. Library: 3,775,500 volumes; 2,887,000 microforms; 38,900 periodicals/subscriptions; 467 computer workstations.

University's other graduate college/schools: College of Arts and Sciences, Division of Interdepartmental Programs, Garret-Evangelical Theological Seminary, Integrated Graduate Programs in the Life Sciences, J. L. Kellogg Graduate School of Management, Robert R. McCormich School of Engineering and Applied Science, School of Education and Social Policy, School of Speech, Dental School, Medical School, Medill School of Journalism, School of Music.

Total university enrollment: 17,900.

School of Law
3357 East Chicago Avenue
P.O. Box 11064
Chicago, Illinois 60611-0064
Phone: (312)503-8462
Internet site: http://www.law1.nwu.edu
E-mail: nulawadm@harold.nwu.edu

Established 1859. Located in downtown Chicago. The national headquarters for ABA and AALS are located in the Northwestern University School of Law complex. ABA approved since 1923. AALS member. Semester system. Full-time, day study only. Law library: 622,000 volumes/microforms; 8,200 current periodicals/subscriptions; 75 computer workstations; has LEXIS, NEXIS, WESTLAW, DIALOG, CCH Access.

Annual tuition: $22,638. On-campus housing available for both single and married students. Annual on-campus living expenses: $13,094. Contact Admission Office for both on- and off- campus housing information. Law students tend to live off-campus. Off-campus housing and personal expenses: approximately $14,808. Additional costs: books approximately $800.

Enrollment: first-year class 204; total full-time 606 (men 55%,women 45%); no part-time students. First-year statistics: 65% out of state, 40 states and 10 foreign countries represented; 45% women; 21% minority; average age 25; 178 undergraduate institutions represented; range of first-year section sizes 50–100 students; number of upper division courses offered after first year 142.

Faculty: full-time 54, part-time 114; 24% female; 4% minority; student/faculty ratio 15.2 to 1.

Degrees conferred: J.D., J.D.-M.M., J.D.-Ph.D. (Anthropology, Economics, History, Political Science, Psychology, Sociology), LL.M. (for persons who have completed a basic legal education and received a university degree in law in another country), S.J.D.

RECRUITMENT PRACTICES AND POLICIES. Attends national law school forums. Has on-campus informational sessions. School does have diversity program and actively recruits women/minority applicants.

ADMISSION REQUIREMENTS FOR FIRST-YEAR APPLICANTS. LSDAS law school report, LSAT (not later than December test date, if more than one LSAT, average is used), bachelor's degree from an accredited institution, personal statement, two recommendations, transcripts (must show all schools attended and at least three years of study) required in support of application. Applicants must have received bachelor's degree prior to enrollment. On-campus interview optional. In addition, international applicants whose native language is not English must submit TOEFL (not older than two years), certified evaluations and translations of all foreign records. Will accept Law Multi-App in lieu of school's application. Joint-degree applicants must apply to and be accepted by both schools. Apply to Office of Admission after September 15, before February 1. First-year students admitted fall only. Rolling admission process. School does maintain a waiting list. Application fee $65, $80 after January 1. Phone: (312)503-8465. E-mail: nulawadm@harold.nwu.edu.

ADMISSION REQUIREMENTS FOR TRANSFER APPLICANTS. Accepts transfers from other ABA-accredited schools. Admission limited to space available. At least one year of enrollment, dean's letter indicating applicant is in good standing (prefer applicants in the top 10% of first-year class), LSAT, LSDAS, personal statement regarding reason for transfer, undergraduate transcript, two letters of recommendation, current law school transcript required in support of application. Apply to Admission Office by May 15. Admission decisions completed by mid July. Application fee $65. Will consider visiting students.

ADMISSION REQUIREMENTS FOR LL.M. Applicants must have a degree in law from a foreign university. Official transcripts with certified translations and evaluations of all foreign credentials, résumé, personal statement, two letters of recommendation; TOEFL, TSE for those who are not native speakers of English required in support of graduate application. Admits fall only. Apply by February 2, January 1 (priority deadline) to Graduate Studies Program. Phone: (312)503-8465. Fax: (312)503-0178. E-mail: nulawadm@harold.law.nwu.edu. Notification of selected candidates by the end of May.

For S.J.D.: in addition to the LL.M. items listed above, copies of two published works (not an undergraduate or master's thesis) written by applicant on legal subject with English translation, a proposed research topic are required. No S.J.D. applicant can be admitted to the law school until at least one faculty member has agreed to supervise the proposed research.

ADMISSION STANDARDS. Number of full-time applicants 4,098; number accepted 842; number enrolled 204; median LSAT 163 (75% of class have a score at or above 159); median GPA 3.49 (A = 4) (75% of class have a GPA at or above 3.26). Attrition rate 1.7%. Gorman rating 4.73; *U.S. News & World Report* ranking is in the top 15 of all law schools.

FINANCIAL AID. All financial aid programs are need based. Scholarships, minority scholarships, grants-in-aid, private and institutional loans, federal loans, Federal WS. Assistantships may be available for upper divisional joint-degree candidates. All accepted students who show need are automatically considered for scholarships (selection criteria place heavy reliance on LSAT and undergraduate GPA); apply by March 15. For all other programs apply to the University's Office of Financial Aid. Phone: (312)503-8722. Use FAFSA for all federal programs (Title IV School code #E000293). Also submit Financial Aid Transcript, federal income tax forms, Access Disk. Approximately 38% of first-year class received scholarships/grants-in-aid. Approximately 70% of current students receive some form of financial assistance. Average scholarship/grant $9,500.

For LL.M.: Fellowships in the form of grants, Graduate-Professional Alternative Loan (GPAL) available. Indicate on admissions application form and complete LL.M. financial aid form. Apply by March 15. If eligible for federal programs, submit FAFSA. No employment opportunities are available.

DEGREE REQUIREMENTS. For J.D.: 86 credits (32 required) with a 2.25 (A = 4) GPA, plus completion of upper divisional writing course; 3-year program. Accelerated J.D. with summer course work. For J.D.-M.M.: a 4-year program with the first year spent in the J. L. Kellogg School of Management. For J.D.-Ph.D.: individualized programs, approximately 6 years for completion of program rather than the 7 to 8 years usually needed if both degrees taken separately. For LL.M.: 20 semester credits; 1 academic year in full-time residence; research project/nonresearch project option (research project must be suitable for publication; a GPA of 2.25 (A = 4) required; all degree requirements must be completed within 2 years. For S.J.D.: At least 1 academic year in residence; thesis; oral defense; all degree requirements must be completed within 5 years.

CAREER AND PLACEMENT INFORMATION. About 250–260 employers conducted on-campus interviews. Approximately 59% of graduates are employed in state. More than 84% of graduates are practicing law; 9% are in business; 6% in government; 1% in academia. Approximately 95% of Northwestern University's first-time state bar exam takers pass the Illinois Bar Exam; Illinois's passage rate for all first-time takers from ABA-approved schools is 87%. Graduates are eligible to take the bar exam in all 50 states.

UNIVERSITY OF NOTRE DAME

Notre Dame, Indiana 46556
Internet site: http://www.nd.edu

Founded 1842. Located 80 miles SE of Chicago, just outside of South Bend. Private control. (Roman Catholic—Congregation of the Holy Cross affiliation.) Semester system. Library: 2,458,000 volumes; 2,661,000 microforms; 23,100 periodicals/subscriptions; 315 computer workstations.

University's other graduate colleges/schools: College of Arts and Letters, College of Engineering, College of Science, School of Architecture, College of Business Administration.

Total university enrollment: 10,300.

School of Law
103 Law Building
Notre Dame, Indiana 46556-0959
Phone: (219)631-6627
Internet site: http://www.nd.ed/~ndlaw
E-mail: law.bulletin.1/nd.edu

Established 1869. Located on main campus. ABA approved since 1925. AALS member. Semester system. Full-time, day study only. Law library: 405,300 volumes/microforms; 5,144 current periodicals/subscriptions; 47 computer workstations; has LEXIS, NEXIS, WESTLAW, DIALOG, VUTEXT. Special facilities: Notre Dame London Law Center, Notre Dame Center for Civil and Human Rights. Special programs: summer study abroad at the London Center; externships.

Annual tuition: $20,427. On-campus housing available for both single and married students. Annual on-campus housing cost: single students $2,050 (room only), married students $3,912. Housing deadline May 1. Contact Housing Office for on-campus housing information. Phone: (219)631-5878. Off-campus housing and personal expenses: approximately $5,150. Additional costs: books approximately $700.

Enrollment: first-year class 172; total full-time 568 (men 63%, women 37%); no part-time students. Statistics: 94% out of state, 37% women; 22% minority; average age 24; 109 undergraduate institutions represented; average first-year section size 90 students; number of upper division courses offered after first year 76.

Faculty: full-time 28, part-time 25; 20% female; 5% minority; student/faculty ratio 15.4 to 1.

Degrees conferred: J.D., J.D.-M.B.A., J.D.-M.S.E. (Engineering and Law), J.D.-M.A. (English and Law, Peace Studies), LL.M. (Comparative and International Law at London Center for both American and non-American students), LL.M. (International Human Rights), J.S.D.

RECRUITMENT PRACTICES AND POLICIES. Attends national law school forums. Has on-campus informational sessions. School does have diversity program and actively recruits women/minority applicants.

ADMISSION REQUIREMENTS FOR FIRST-YEAR APPLICANTS. LSDAS law school report, LSAT (not later than December test date, if more than one LSAT, average is used), bachelor's degree from an accredited institution, résumé, personal statement, two recommendations, transcripts (must show all schools attended and at least three years of study) required in support of application. Applicants must have received bachelor's degree prior to enrollment. In addition, international applicants whose native language is not English must submit TOEFL (not older than two years), certified translation and evaluation of all non-English documents. Joint-degree applicants must apply to and be accepted by both Schools, GMAT/LSAT/GRE required. Apply to Office of Admission after September 30, before March 1. First-year students admitted fall only. Rolling admission process, consideration starts in December and is finished by late April. School does maintain a waiting list. Application fee $50 before February 1, $65 after February 1. Phone: (209)631-6626. Fax: (213)631-6391. E-mail: law.bulletin.1/nd.edu.

ADMISSION REQUIREMENTS FOR TRANSFER APPLICANTS. Accepts transfers from other ABA-accredited schools. Admission limited to space available. At least one year of enrollment, dean's letter indicating applicant is in good standing (prefer applicants in the top quarter of first-year class), LSAT, LSDAS, personal statement regarding reason for transfer, two letters of recommendation, undergraduate transcript, current law school transcript required in support of application. Apply to Admission Office by July 15. Admission decisions made by early August. Application fee $50. Will consider visiting students.

ADMISSION STANDARDS. Number of full-time applicants 2,249; number accepted 591; number enrolled 172; median LSAT 162 (75% of class have a score at or above 160); median GPA 3.40 (A = 4) (75% of class have a GPA at or above 3.09). Attrition rate 1.9%. Gorman rating 4.68; *U.S. News & World Report* ranking is in the top 21 of all law schools.

FINANCIAL AID. Fellowships, scholarships, grants, private and institutional loans; federal loans and Federal WS offered through university's Financial Aid Office. Most financial assistance is need based. Assistantships may be available for upper divisional joint-degree candidates. For fellowships, scholarships, grants (selection criteria place heavy reliance on LSAT and undergraduate GPA) apply to Financial Aid Office at same time as you apply for admission. Use School's FA application. For all other programs apply to Office of Financial Aid. Phone: (213)631-6436. Use FAFSA for all federal programs (Title IV School code #001840). Also submit Financial Aid Transcript, federal income tax forms. Approximately 37% of first-year class received fellowships/grants-in-aid. Approximately 90% of current students receive some form of financial assistance. Average scholarship/grant $4,500. Average debt after graduation $35,000.

DEGREE REQUIREMENTS. For J.D.: 90 credits (63 required) with a 2.0 (A = 4) GPA, plus completion of upper divisional writing course; 3-year program. Accelerated J.D. with summer course work. For J.D.-master's: 4-year programs rather than the usual 5-year programs needed if both degrees taken separately. For LL.M., J.S.D. (International Human Rights): Individualized and interdisciplinary programs combining the resources of the university's Kellogg Institute for International Studies, the Institute for International Peace Studies, and the Department of Government and International Studies; contact the Graduate Office, P.O. Box 0959, Notre Dame, Indiana 46556-0959.

CAREER AND PLACEMENT INFORMATION. About 125–130 employers conducted on-campus interviews. Approximately 10% of graduates are employed in state. More than 83% of graduates are practicing law; 6% are in business; 11% in government. Approximately 97% of the University of Notre Dame's first-time state bar exam takers pass the Indiana Bar Exam; Indiana's passage rate for all first time-takers from ABA-approved schools is 86%. Graduates are eligible to take the bar exam in all 50 states.

NOVA SOUTHEASTERN UNIVERSITY
Fort Lauderdale, Florida 33314-7721
Internet site: http://www.nova.edu

Chartered 1964 as Nova University. Merged with Southeastern University of Health Sciences in 1994. Located 3 miles W of Ft. Lauderdale. Private control. Semester system. Library: 243,300 volumes; 1,050,000 microforms; 7,102 periodicals/subscriptions; 88 computer workstations.

University's other graduate colleges/schools: Abraham S. Fischler Center for the Advancement of Education, Center for Psychological Studies, Oceanography Center, School of Business and Entrepreneurship, School of Computer and Information Sciences, School of Social and Systemic Studies; the Health Professional Division includes the College of Allied Health, College of Optometry, College of Osteopathic Medicine, College of Pharmacy.

Total university enrollment: 15,200.

Shepard Broad Law Center
3305 College Avenue
Fort Lauderdale, Florida 33314-7721
Phone: (954)262-6100

Internet site: http://www.nsulaw.nova.edu
E-mail: admission@law-lib.law.nova.edu

Established 1974. Located on main campus. ABA approved since 1975. AALS member. Semester system. Full-time, part-time study. Law library: 288,700 volumes/microforms; 5,470 current periodicals/subscriptions; 68 computer workstations; has LEXIS, NEXIS, WESTLAW, DIALOG; is a State, Federal, U.N. document Depository. Special programs: Conditional Acceptance (summer session) Program, summer study abroad in Caracas, Venezuela; internships.

Annual tuition: full-time $19,400, part-time $14,550. On-campus housing available for both single and married students. Annual on-campus housing cost: apartment average $4,355 (room only), $6,425 (room and board). Contact Residential Life Office for both on- and off-campus housing information. Phone: (954)475-7052. Law students tend to live off-campus. Off-campus housing and personal expenses: approximately $14,142. Additional costs: books approximately $750.

Enrollment: first-year class 313 full-time, 72 part-time; total full-time 830, part-time 183 (men 62%,women 38%). First-year statistics: 20% out of state, 23 states and foreign countries represented; 38% women; 24% minority; average age 27 full-time, 34 part-time; range of first-year section size 30–60 students; number of upper division courses offered after first year 93.

Faculty: full-time 45, part-time 52; 36% female; 12% minority; student/faculty ratio 20.5 to 1.

Degrees conferred: J.D., J.D.-M.B.A., J.D.-M.S. (Psychology), J.D.-M.U.R.R. (Florida Atlantic University).

RECRUITMENT PRACTICES AND POLICIES. Attends national law school forums. Has on-campus informational sessions and a class visitation program. School does have diversity program and actively recruits women/minority applicants.

ADMISSION REQUIREMENTS FOR FIRST-YEAR APPLICANTS. LSDAS law school report, LSAT and writing sample (not later than February test date, if more than one LSAT, highest is used), bachelor's degree from an accredited institution, résumé, personal statement, two recommendations, transcripts (must show all schools attended and at least three years of study) required in support of application. Applicants must have received bachelor's degree prior to enrollment. In addition, international applicants whose native language is not English must submit TOEFL (not older than two years). Call International Student Advisor for additional information.

Phone: (954)370-5695. Joint-degree applicants must apply to and be accepted by both schools. Apply to Office of Admission after September 30, before March 28 (February 17 priority deadline). First-year students admitted fall only. Rolling admission process, notification starts in March 1 and is finished by late May. Application fee $45. Phone: (954)262-6117. E-mail: admission@law-lib.law.nova.edu.

ADMISSION REQUIREMENTS FOR TRANSFER APPLICANTS. Accepts transfers from other ABA-accredited schools. Admission limited to space available. At least one year of enrollment, dean's letter indicating applicant is in good standing, (prefer applicants with a B or better GPA), LSAT, LSDAS, personal statement regarding reason for transfer, current law school transcript required in support of application. Apply to Admission Office by June 15 (fall), December 1 (spring). Admission decision made within six weeks of receipt of completed application. Application fee $45. Will consider visiting students.

ADMISSION STANDARDS. Number of full-time applicants 1,656, part-time 203; number accepted 926 full-time, 113 part-time; number enrolled 313 full-time, 72 part-time; median LSAT 150 (75% of class have a score at or above 145 full-time, 144 part-time); median GPA 2.93 (A = 4) (75% of class have a GPA at or above 2.67 full-time, 2.55 part-time). Attrition rate 7.5%. Gorman rating 2.55; *U.S. News & World Report* ranking is in the fourth tier of all law schools.

FINANCIAL AID. Merit scholarships, need-based scholarships, minority scholarships, tuition waivers, private and institutional loans; federal loans and Federal WS offered through university's Financial Aid Office. Assistantships may be available for upper divisional joint-degree candidates. For scholarships (selection criteria place heavy reliance on LSAT and undergraduate GPA) apply to Admissions Office after January 1, before April 1 (March 1 priority deadline); use Law Center's financial aid application form. For all other programs apply to university's Office of Financial Aid. Phone: (800)541-6682. Use FAFSA for all federal programs (Title IV School code #001509). Also submit Financial Aid Transcript, federal income tax forms. Approximately 29% (full-time), 6% (part-time) of first-year class received scholarships/grants-in-aid. Approximately 70% of current students receive some form of financial assistance. Average scholarship/grant $6,600 full-time, $3,535 part-time.

DEGREE REQUIREMENTS. For J.D.: 90 credits (34 required) with a 2.0 (A = 4) GPA, plus completion of upper divisional writing course; 3-year full-time program, 4-year part-time program. Accelerated J.D. with 1 summer of course work. For J.D.-master's: a 3½- to 4-year program rather than the usual 5-year program needed if both degrees taken separately.

CAREER AND PLACEMENT INFORMATION. About 18–20 employers conducted on-campus interviews. Approximately 85% of graduates are employed in state. More than 74% of graduates are practicing law; 8% are in business; 16% in government; 2% in academia. Approximately 82% (FL), 77% (NY) of Shepard Broad Law Center's first-time state bar exam takers pass the bar exam; the passage rate for all first time takers from ABA-approved schools is 84% (FL), 78% (NY). Graduates are eligible to take the bar exam in all 50 states.

OHIO NORTHERN UNIVERSITY

Ada, Ohio 45810-1599
Internet site: http://www.onu.edu

Founded 1871. Located 70 miles SE of Toledo. Private control. Semester system. Library: 485,700 volumes; 120,000 microforms; 1,950 periodicals/subscriptions; 63 computer workstations.

Total university enrollment: 2,997.

Claude W. Pettit
College of Law
525 South Main Street
Ada, Ohio 45810
Phone: (419)772-2205
Internet site: http://www.oaw.onu.edu
E-mail: admissions-ug@onu.edu

Established 1885. Located on main campus. ABA approved since 1939. AALS member. Semester system. Full-time, day study only. Law library: 275,300 volumes/microforms; 3,414 current periodicals/subscriptions; 36 computer workstations; has LEXIS, NEXIS, WESTLAW; is a Federal Government Depository. Special program: exchange program with the University of Iceland.

Annual tuition: $20,450. On-campus housing available for single students only. Annual on-campus housing cost: single students $2,440 (room only), $5,020 (room and board). Contact Housing Office for both on- and off-campus housing information. Phone: (419)772-2430. Law students tend to live off-campus. Off-campus housing and personal expenses: approximately $8,700. Additional costs: books approximately $700.

Enrollment: first-year class 125; total full-time 351 (men 65%, women 35%); no part-time students. First-year statistics: 70% out of state, 34 states and foreign countries represented; 35% women; 12% minority; average age 22; 212 undergraduate institutions represented; average first-year section size 41 students; number of upper division courses offered after first year 71.

Faculty: full-time 23, part-time 14, 43% female; 3% minority; student/faculty ratio 15 to 1.

Degrees conferred: B.S.Pharm -J.D., J.D.

RECRUITMENT PRACTICES AND POLICIES. Attends national law school forums. Has on-campus informational sessions. School does have diversity program and actively recruits women/minority applicants.

ADMISSION REQUIREMENTS FOR FIRST-YEAR APPLICANTS. LSDAS law school report, LSAT (not later than December test date, if more than one LSAT, highest is used), bachelor's degree from an accredited institution, personal statement, transcripts (must show all schools attended and at least three years of study) required in support of application. One or two recommendations are optional. Applicants must have received bachelor's degree prior to enrollment. Apply to Office of Admission after September 30, preferably before April 1. First-year students admitted fall only. Rolling admission process, notification starts in December and is finished when class is filled. Acceptance of offer and first deposit due April 1. Application fee $40. Phone: (419)772-2211. Fax: (419)772-1875. E-mail: admissions.ug@onu.edu.

ADMISSION REQUIREMENTS FOR TRANSFER APPLICANTS. Accepts transfers from other ABA-accredited schools. Admission limited to space available. At least one year of enrollment, dean's letter indicating applicant is in good standing (prefer applicants in the top half of first-year class), LSAT, LSDAS, personal statement regarding reason for transfer, current law school transcript including rank in class required in support of application. Admits fall only. Apply to Admission Office by June 15. Admission decision within six weeks of the receipt of completed application. Application fee $40. Will consider visiting students.

ADMISSION STANDARDS. Number of full-time applicants 861; number accepted 549; number enrolled 125; median LSAT 149 (75% of class have a score at or above 144); median GPA 3.06 (A = 4) (75% of class have a GPA at or above 2.64). Attrition rate 7.3%. Gorman rating 2.67; *U.S. News & World Report* ranking is in the fourth tier of all law schools.

FINANCIAL AID. Scholarships, Legal Scholars Program, diversity scholarships, grants-in-aid, private institutional loans; federal loans and Federal WS offered through university's Financial Aid Office. For scholarships (selection criteria place heavy reliance on LSAT and undergraduate GPA) apply after January 1, before March 15 to the Office of Financial Aid. Use university's FA application. For all other programs apply to university's Office of Financial Aid. Phone: (419)882-2272. Use FAFSA for all federal programs (Title IV School code # 003089). Also submit Financial Aid Transcript, federal income tax forms. Approximately 34% of first-year class received scholarships/grants-in-aid. Approximately 82% of current students receive some form of financial assistance. Average scholarship/grant $10,400.

DEGREE REQUIREMENTS. For J.D.: 87 credits (82 required) with a 2.0 (A = 4) GPA, plus completion of upper divisional writing course; 3-year program.

CAREER AND PLACEMENT INFORMATION. About 7–10 employers conducted on-campus interviews. Approximately 35% of graduates are employed in state. More than 72% of graduates are practicing law; 11% are in business; 15% in government; 2% in academia. Approximately 74% (OH), 88% (PA), 73% (NY) of Ohio Northern University's first-time state bar exam takers pass the bar exam; the passage rate for all first-time takers from ABA-approved schools is 90% (OH), 73% (PA), 78% (NY). Graduates are eligible to take the bar exam in all 50 states.

OHIO STATE UNIVERSITY
Columbus, Ohio 43210
Internet site: http://www.ohio-state.edu

Founded 1870. Located 2 miles N of downtown Columbus. Public control. Quarter system. Library: 4,860,000 volumes; 4,005,000 microforms; 33,360 periodicals/subscriptions; 370 computer workstations.

University's other graduate colleges/schools: College of the Arts, College of Biological Sciences, College of Education, College of Engineering, College of Food Agriculture and Environmental Sciences, College of Human Ecology, College of Humanities, College of Mathematical and Physical Sciences, College of Nursing, College of Social and Behavioral Sciences, College of Social Work, Max M. Fisher College of Business, College of Dentistry, College of Medicine, College of Optometry, College of Pharmacy, College of Veterinary Medicine.

Total university enrollment: 54,781.

College of Law
John Deaver Drinko Hall
55 West 12th Avenue
Columbus, Ohio 43210-1391
Phone: (614)292-2631
Internet site: http://www.acs.ohio-state.edu/units/law
E-mail: rsolomon@magnus.acs.ohio-state.edu

Established 1891. Located on main campus. ABA approved since 1923. AALS member. Semester system. Full-time, day study only. Law library: 631,700 volumes/microforms; 7,453 current periodicals/subscriptions; 39 computer workstations; has LEXIS, NEXIS, WESTLAW, DIALOG, OCLC; is a partial Federal Government Depository. Special programs: designated as a Comprehensive Natural Resource Center; a Public Service Fellows Program; summer study abroad at Oxford University, England.

Annual tuition: resident $7,022, nonresident $15,968. On-campus housing available for both single and married students. Annual on-campus housing cost: single students $2,810 (room only), $4,865 (room and board); married students $3,900. Contact Office of Housing Assignments for both on- and off- campus housing information. Phone: (614)292-8266. Law students tend to live off-campus. Off-campus housing and personal expenses: approximately $9,569. Additional costs: books approximately $800.

Enrollment: first-year class 244; total full-time 683 (men 52%, women 48%); no part-time students. First-year statistics: 27% out of state, 33 states and foreign countries represented; 48% women; 17% minority; average age 24; 186 undergraduate institutions represented; range of first-year section sizes 30–80 students; number of upper division courses offered after first year 69.

Faculty: full-time 32, part-time 64; 26% female; 13% minority; student/faculty ratio 17.6 to 1.

Degrees conferred: J.D., J.D.-M.B.A., J.D.-M.H.A., J.D.-M.P.A.

RECRUITMENT PRACTICES AND POLICIES. Attends national law school forums. Has on-campus informational sessions. School does have diversity program and actively recruits women/minority applicants.

ADMISSION REQUIREMENTS FOR FIRST-YEAR APPLICANTS. LSDAS law school report, LSAT (not later than December test date, if more than one LSAT, average is used), bachelor's degree from an accredited institution, personal statement, two recommendations, transcripts (must show all schools attended and at least three years of study) required in support of application. Applicants must have received bachelor's degree prior to enrollment. Interview not required but may be requested by school under unusual circumstances. In addition, international applicants whose native language is not English must submit TOEFL (not older than two years), certified translations and evaluations of all foreign credentials. Joint-degree applicants must apply to and be accepted by both colleges. Apply to university's Office of Admission—Professional Area (Phone: [614]292-3980) after September 15, before March 15, January 31 (deadline for scholarship consideration). First-year students admitted fall only. Rolling admission process, notification starts in late December or early January and is finished by late April. Acceptance of offer and first deposit due April 1. School does maintain a waiting list. Application fee $30. Phone: (614)292-8810 or (614)292-2631. E-mail: rsolomon@magnus.acs.ohio-state.edu.

ADMISSION REQUIREMENTS FOR TRANSFER APPLICANTS. Accepts transfers from other ABA-accredited schools. Admission limited to space available. At least one year of enrollment, dean's letter indicating applicant is in good standing (prefer applicants in the top quarter of first-year class), LSAT, LSDAS, personal statement regarding reason for transfer, current law school transcript required in support of application. Apply to university's Admission Office—Professional Area at least six weeks prior to the beginning of desired semester of enrollment. Admission decision within one month of the receipt of completed application. Application fee $30. Will consider visiting students.

ADMISSION STANDARDS. Number of full-time applicants 1,387; number accepted 582; number enrolled 244; median LSAT 158 (75% of class have a score at or above 155); median GPA 3.48 (A = 4) (75% of class have a GPA at or above 3.16). Attrition rate 3.3%. Gorman rating 4.38; *U.S. News & World Report* ranking is in the top 50 of all law schools.

FINANCIAL AID. Scholarships, merit scholarships, diversity scholarships, grants, private institutional loans; federal loans and Federal WS offered through university's Financial Aid Office. Assistantships may be available for upper divisional joint-degree candidates. All accepted students are automatically considered for scholarships (selection criteria place heavy reliance on LSAT and undergraduate GPA). Apply to university's Admissions Office—Professional Area before January 31. For law school financial aid information call: (614)292-8807. E-mail: iberry@magnus.ohio-state.edu. For all other programs apply before March 15 to university's Financial Aid Office. Phone: (614)282-0300. Use FAFSA for all federal programs (Title IV School code # 003090). Also submit Financial Aid Transcript, federal income tax forms. Approximately 62% of first-year class received scholarships/grants-in-aid. Approximately 70% of current students receive some form of financial assistance. Average scholarship/grant $1,500. Average debt after graduation $30,000.

DEGREE REQUIREMENTS. For J.D.: 91 credits (38 required) with a 2.0 (A = 4) GPA, plus completion of upper divisional writing course; 3-year program. Accelerated J.D. with summer course work. For J.D.-master's: 4-year program (up to 12 semester hours, 18 quarter hours may be accepted toward J.D.) rather than the usual 5-year program needed if degrees taken separately.

CAREER AND PLACEMENT INFORMATION. About 40–50 employers conducted on-campus interviews. Approximately 67% of graduates are employed in state. More than 62% of graduates are practicing law; 16% are in business; 20% in government; 2% in academia. Approximately 93% of Ohio State University's first-time state bar exam takers pass the Ohio Bar Exam; Ohio's passage rate for all first-time takers from ABA-approved schools is 90%. Graduates are eligible to take the bar exam in all 50 states.

OKLAHOMA CITY UNIVERSITY
Oklahoma City, Oklahoma 73106-1402
Internet site: http://www.okcu.edu

Founded 1904. Located about 3 miles from downtown. Private control (Methodist affiliation). Semester system. Library: 274,000 volumes; 577,500 microforms; 4,188 periodicals/subscriptions; 36 computer workstations.

University's other graduate colleges/schools: Petree College of Arts and Sciences, Meinders School of Management and Business Sciences, School of Music and Performing Arts, School of Religion and Church Vocations.

Total university enrollment: 4,660.

School of Law
P.O. Box 61310
Oklahoma City, Oklahoma 73106-1310
Phone: (405)521-5337
Internet site: http://www.okcu.edu/~law/home/htm

Established 1952. Located on main campus. ABA approved since 1969. AALS member. Semester system. Full-time, part-time study. Law library: 242,000 volumes/microforms; 3,768 current periodicals/subscriptions; 20

computer workstations; has LEXIS, NEXIS, WEST-LAW, OCLC, CALI; is a Federal Government Depository. Special facility/programs: Native American Legal Resource Center; internships.

Annual tuition: full-time $13,488, part-time $9,680. On-campus housing available for both single and married students. Annual on-campus housing cost: single students $3,900 (room and board), married students $5,022. Contact Students Personnel Office for on-campus housing information. Phone: (405)521-5377. Law students tend to live off-campus. Contact Cokesbury Court apartments for off-campus information. Phone: (405)524-2600. Off-campus housing and personal expenses: approximately $9,094. Additional costs: books approximately $700.

Enrollment: first-year class 131 full-time, 51 part-time; total full-time 399, part-time 187 (men 63%, women 37%). First-year statistics: 57% out of state, 46 states and foreign countries represented; 37% women; 12% minority; average age 27; 242 undergraduate institutions represented; range of first-year section sizes 20–83 students; number of upper division courses offered after first year 68 full-time, 53 part-time.

Faculty: full-time 32, part-time 33; 25% female; 9% minority; student/faculty ratio 16.7 to 1.

Degrees conferred: J.D., J.D.-M.B.A.

RECRUITMENT PRACTICES AND POLICIES. Attends national law school forums. Has on-campus informational sessions. School does have diversity program and actively recruits women/minority applicants.

ADMISSION REQUIREMENTS FOR FIRST-YEAR APPLICANTS. LSDAS law school report, LSAT (not later than February test date, if more than one LSAT, average is used), bachelor's degree from an accredited institution, two recommendations, transcripts (must show all schools attended and at least three years of study) required in support of application. A two-page personal statement is optional. Applicants must have received bachelor's degree prior to enrollment. In addition, international applicants whose native language is not English must submit TOEFL (minimum 600 score). Apply to Office of Admission after September 1, before August 1 (April 1 guarantees consideration); February 14 for Halton Sumners Scholarship. First-year students admitted fall only. Rolling admission process, notification starts in December and is finished by mid to late June. Application fee $35. Phone: (800)633-7242.

ADMISSION REQUIREMENTS FOR TRANSFER APPLICANTS. Accepts transfers from other ABA-accredited schools. Admission limited to space available.

At least one year of enrollment, dean's letter indicating applicant is in good standing (prefer applicants in the top quarter of first-year class), LSAT, LSDAS, personal statement regarding reason for transfer, two letters of recommendation, current law school transcript required in support of application. Apply to Admission Office at least six weeks in advance of the preferred semester of entrance. Admission decision made within one month after receipt of completed application. Application fee $35. Will consider visiting students.

ADMISSION STANDARDS. Number of full-time applicants 924, part-time 145; number accepted 533 full-time, 111 part-time; number enrolled 131 full-time, 51 part-time; median LSAT 149 (75% of class have a score at or above 144 full-time, 145 part-time); median GPA 2.95 (A = 4) (75% of class have a GPA at or above 2.66 for both full- and part-time). Attrition rate 8.9%. Gorman rating 2.69; *U.S. News & World Report* ranking is in the fourth tier of all law schools.

FINANCIAL AID. Halton W. Sumners Scholarships, merit scholarships, University Scholarships, private and institutional loans; federal loans and Federal WS offered through university's Financial Aid Office. For law school scholarships (selection criteria place heavy reliance on LSAT and undergraduate GPA) apply to Admissions Office after January 1, before February 15. Use school's scholarship application. For all other programs apply to university's Office of Financial Aid. Phone: (800)633-7242, (405)521-5211. Use FAFSA for all federal programs (Title IV School code # 003166). Also submit Financial Aid Transcript, federal income tax forms. Approximately 12% (full-time), 10% (part-time) of first-year class received scholarships. Approximately 89% of current students receive some form of financial assistance. Average scholarship/grant $5,000 (full-time), $3,000 (part-time). Average debt after graduation $42,000.

DEGREE REQUIREMENTS. For J.D.: 90 credits (43 required) with a 4.5 (scale 1–12) GPA, plus completion of upper divisional writing course; 3-year program. For J.D.-M.B.A.: total 114 credits (J.D. 84 credits, M.B.A. 30 credits).

CAREER AND PLACEMENT INFORMATION. About 8–10 employers conducted on-campus interviews. Approximately 54% of graduates are employed in state. More than 71% of graduates are practicing law; 15% are in business; 13% in government; 1% in academia. Approximately 84% (OK), 82% (TX) of Oklahoma City

University's first-time state bar exam takers pass the Oklahoma Bar Exam; Oklahoma's passage rate for all first-time takers from ABA-approved schools is 85% (OK), 82% (TX). Graduates are eligible to take the bar exam in all 50 states.

UNIVERSITY OF OKLAHOMA
Norman, Oklahoma 73019
Internet site: http://www.ou.edu

Founded 1890. Located 18 miles S of Oklahoma. Public control. Semester system. Library: 2,430,000 volumes; 3,394,000 microforms; 17,400 periodicals/subscriptions; 155 computer workstations.

University's other graduate colleges/schools: College of Architecture, College of Arts and Sciences, College of Business Administration, College of Education, College of Engineering, College of Fine Arts, College of Geosciences, College of Liberal Studies. Colleges located in Oklahoma City at Health Sciences Center: College of Allied Health, College of Nursing, College of Public Health, College of Dentistry, College of Medicine, College of Pharmacy.

Total university enrollment: 19,400.

College of Law
300 Timberdell Road
Norman, Oklahoma 73019-5081
Phone: (405)325-4726
Internet site: http://www.law.ou.edu
E-mail: law@hamilton.ou.edu

Established 1911. Law Center formed in 1971. Located on main campus. ABA approved since 1923. AALS member since 1911. Semester system. Full-time, day study only. Law library: 300,800 volumes/microforms; 3,888 current periodicals/subscriptions; 49 computer workstations; has LEXIS, NEXIS, WESTLAW, OCLC. Special facility: American Indian Law and Policy Center. Special programs: summer study abroad Oxford University, England; special summer admissions program.

Annual tuition: resident $4,492, nonresident $13,260. On-campus housing available for both single and married students. Annual on-campus housing cost: single students $3,800 (room and board), married students $3,900. Contact University Housing Office for both on- and off-campus housing information. Phone: (405)325-2511. Law students tend to live off-campus. Off-campus housing and personal expenses: approximately $10,932. Additional costs: books approximately $700.

Enrollment: first-year class 167; total full-time 546 (men 59%, women 41%); no part-time students. First-year statistics: 15% out of state, 27 states and foreign countries represented; 41% women; 14% minority; average age 24; 49 undergraduate institutions represented; range of first-year section size 20–50 students; number of upper division courses offered after first year 155.

Faculty: full-time 37, part-time 14; 26% female; 9% minority; student/faculty ratio 15.2 to 1.

Degrees conferred: J.D., J.D.-M.B.A., J.D.-M.P.H., J.D.-M.S. (Environmental Management, Occupational Health).

RECRUITMENT PRACTICES AND POLICIES. Attends national law school forums. Has on-campus informational sessions. School does have diversity program and actively recruits women/minority applicants.

ADMISSION REQUIREMENTS FOR FIRST-YEAR APPLICANTS. LSDAS law school report, LSAT (not later than February test date, if more than one LSAT, average is used), bachelor's degree from an accredited institution, personal statement, transcripts (must show all schools attended and at least three years of study) required in support of application. Recommendations are welcomed but are optional. Applicants must have received bachelor's degree prior to enrollment. In addition, international applicants whose native language is not English must submit TOEFL (not older than two years), certified translations and evaluations of all foreign transcripts. Apply to Office of Admission after September 30, before April 15. First-year students admitted fall only. Rolling admission process, notification starts in January and is finished by May 1. Application fee $50. Phone: (405)325-4726. E-mail: law@hamilton.ou.edu.

ADMISSION REQUIREMENTS FOR TRANSFER APPLICANTS. Accepts transfers from other ABA-accredited schools. Admission limited to space available. At least one year of enrollment, dean's letter indicating applicant is in good standing (prefer applicant whose academic credentials would have admitted them to OU in their first year), LSAT, LSDAS, personal statement regarding reason for transfer, current law school transcript, supplemental application required in support of application. Apply to Admission Office by June 15. Admission decision made within one month after receipt of completed application. Application fee $50. Will consider visiting students.

ADMISSION STANDARDS. Number of full-time applicants 704; number accepted 291; number enrolled 167; median LSAT 154 (75% of class have a score at or above

150); median GPA 3.30 (A = 4) (75% of class have a GPA at or above 3.05). Attrition rate 1.5%. Gorman rating 3.41; *U.S. News & World Report* ranking is in the third tier of all law schools.

FINANCIAL AID. Scholarships, merit scholarships, diversity scholarships, grants-in-aid, private and institutional loans, state grants; federal loans and Federal WS offered through university's Financial Aid Office. For scholarships (selection criteria place heavy reliance on LSAT and undergraduate GPA) return scholarship questionnaire before March 1. For all other programs apply after January 1, before March 15 to the university's Officer of Financial Aid. Phone: (405)325-4521. Use FAFSA for all federal programs (Title IV School code # 003184). Also submit Financial Aid Transcript, federal income tax forms. Approximately 51% of first-year class received scholarships/grants-in-aid. Approximately 70% of current students receive some form of financial assistance. Average scholarship/grant $1,000.

DEGREE REQUIREMENTS. For J.D.: 90 credits (43 required) with a C average, plus completion of upper divisional writing course; 3-year program. Accelerated J.D. with summer course work. For J.D.-master's: 4-year program rather than the usual 5-year program needed if degrees taken separately.

CAREER AND PLACEMENT INFORMATION. About 30–40 employers conducted on-campus interviews. Approximately 69% of graduates are employed in state. More than 67% of graduates are practicing law; 15% are in business; 17% in government; 1% in academia. Approximately 75% (OK), 75% (TX) of the University of Oklahoma's first-time state bar exam takers pass the bar exam; the passage rate for all first-time takers from ABA-approved schools is 85% (OK), 82% (TX). Graduates are eligible to take the bar exam in all 50 states.

UNIVERSITY OF OREGON
Eugene, Oregon 97403
Internet site: http://www.uoregon.edu

Founded 1871. Located in southern Willamette Valley. Public control. Semester system. Library: 2,082,000 volumes; 1,888,800 microforms; 17,250 periodicals/subscriptions; 200 computer workstations.

University's other graduate colleges/schools: Charles H. Linquist College of Business Administration, College of Arts and Sciences, College of Education, School of Architecture, School of Journalism and Communication, School of Music.

Total university enrollment: 17,100.

School of Law
1221 University of Oregon
Eugene, Oregon 97403-1221
Phone: (514)346-3853
Internet site: http://www.law.uoregon.edu
E-mail: admissions@law.uoregon.edu

Established 1884. Located on main campus. ABA approved since 1923. AALS member. Semester system. Full-time, day study only. Law library: 330,400 volumes/microforms; 3,216 current periodicals/subscriptions; 25 computer workstations; has LEXIS, NEXIS, WEST-LAW; is a Federal Government Depository. Special facility: William K. Knight Law Center will be complete in 1999.

Annual tuition: resident $10,004, nonresident $13,642. On-campus housing available for both single and married students. Annual on-campus housing cost: single students $1,734 (room only), $4,342 (room and board), married students $4,000. Housing deadline February 1. Contact University Housing Office for on-campus housing information. Phone: (541)346-4277. Law students tend to live off-campus. Contact Retail Information Office for off-campus information. Phone: (543)346-3731. Off-campus housing and personal expenses: approximately $7,515. Additional costs: books approximately $700.

Enrollment: first-year class 162; total full-time 499 (men 46%, women 54%); no part-time students. First-year statistics: 47% out of state; 54% women, 16% minority; average age 26; 95 undergraduate institutions represented; average first-year section size 50 students; number of upper division courses offered after first year 85.

Faculty: full-time 31, part-time 19; 28% female; 10% minority; student/faculty ratio 17 to 1.

Degrees conferred: J.D., J.D.-M.B.A., J.D.-M.S. (Environmental Studies Program—Interdisciplinary).

RECRUITMENT PRACTICES AND POLICIES. Attends national law school forums. Has on-campus informational sessions. School does have diversity program and actively recruits women/minority applicants.

ADMISSION REQUIREMENTS FOR FIRST-YEAR APPLICANTS. LSDAS law school report, LSAT (not later than February test date, if more than one LSAT, average is used), bachelor's degree from an accredited institution, résumé, personal statement, two or three recommendations, transcripts (must show all schools attended and at least three years of study) required in support of application. Applicants must have received bachelor's degree prior to enrollment. Interview not required but may be requested by school. In addition, international applicants whose native language is not English must submit TOEFL (not older than two years). Both joint-degree and concurrent-degree applicants must apply to and be accepted by both schools (January 15 deadline for M.S., March 1 deadline for M.B.A.). Apply to Office of Admission after September 30, before April 1. First-year students admitted fall only. Rolling admission process with an early decision process (if application is complete by December 15 admissions decision is sent by January 15), regular notification starts in February and is finished by May. Acceptance of offer and first deposit due April 15. School does maintain a waiting list. Application fee $50. Phone: (541)346-3846. E-mail: admissions@law.uoregon.edu.

ADMISSION REQUIREMENTS FOR TRANSFER APPLICANTS. Accepts transfers from other ABA-accredited schools. Admission limited to space available. At least one year of enrollment, dean's letter indicating applicant is in good standing (prefer applicants in the top quarter of first-year class), LSAT, LSDAS, personal statement regarding reason for transfer, two letters of recommendation, current law school transcript required in support of application. Apply to Admission Office by July 1. Admission decisions made by early August. Application fee $50. Will consider visiting students.

ADMISSION STANDARDS. Number of full-time applicants 1,454; number accepted 550; number enrolled 162; median LSAT 159 (75% of class have a score at or above 155); median GPA 3.40 (A = 4) (75% of class have a GPA at or above 3.13). Attrition rate 2.1%. Gorman rating 3.67; *U.S. News & World Report* ranking is in the second tier of all law schools.

FINANCIAL AID. Scholarships, merit scholarships, minority scholarships, graduate teaching fellowships, grants-in-aid, private institutional loans; federal loans and Federal WS offered through university's Financial Aid Office. Assistantships may be available for upper divisional concurrent- and joint-degree candidates. All accepted students are considered for merit awards and scholarships (selection criteria place heavy reliance on LSAT and undergraduate GPA). Apply to Admissions Office before March 1. For all other programs apply after January 1, before April 1 to university's Office of Financial Aid. Phone: (541)346-3221 or (800)760-6953. Use FAFSA for all federal programs (Title IV School code #003223). Also submit Financial Aid Transcript, federal income tax forms. Approximately 44% of first-year class received scholarships/grants-in-aid. Approximately 80% of current students receive some form of financial assistance. Average scholarship/grant $2,231.

DEGREE REQUIREMENTS. For J.D.: 85 credits (37 required) with a 2.0 (A = 4) GPA, plus completion of upper divisional writing course; 3-year program. For J.D.-M.B.A. (joint degree): a 4-year program rather than the usual 5-year program needed if degrees taken separately. For J.D.-M.S. (concurrent degree): Individualized programs, could take up to 5 years to complete.

CAREER AND PLACEMENT INFORMATION. About 40–50 employers conducted on-campus interviews. Approximately 62% of graduates are employed in state. More than 56% of graduates are practicing law; 14% are in business; 24% in government; 6% in academia. Approximately 77% (OR), 95% (WA) of the University of Oregon's first-time state bar exam takers pass the bar exam; the passage rate for all first-time takers from ABA-approved schools is 85% (OR), 83% (WA). Graduates are eligible to take the bar exam in all 50 states.

PACE UNIVERSITY
New York, New York 10038
Internet site: http://www.pace.edu

Founded 1906. Located in lower Manhattan in the financial district of New York City. Private control. Semester system. Library: 1,000,000 volumes; 655,000 microforms; 2,500 periodicals/subscriptions.

University's other graduate colleges/schools: Dyson College of Arts and Sciences, Lienhard School of Nursing, Lubin School of Business, School of Computer Science and Information Systems, School of Education.

Total university enrollment: 14,100.

School of Law
78 North Broadway
White Plains, New York 10603
Phone: (914)422-4205
Internet site: http://www.law.pace.edu
E-mail: admission@genesis.law.pace.edu

Established 1976. Located in White Plains, Westchester County's seat. ABA approved since 1978. AALS member. Semester system. Full-time, part-time study. Law library: 311,200 volumes/microforms; 3,580 current periodicals/subscriptions; 79 computer workstations; has

LEXIS, NEXIS, WESTLAW, DIALOG, OCLC, VU-TEXT, EPIC, RLIN; is a Federal Government Depository. Special facilities: Social Justice Center, Battered Women's Justice Center, Pace Institute for International Law. Special programs: summer Conditional Admissions Program, study abroad Pace London Program at University of London, England; externships; internships.

Annual tuition: full-time $20,640, part-time $15,490. On-campus housing available for single students. Annual on-campus housing cost: single room $6,360, double room $5,160. Contact law school's residence halls for on-campus housing information. Law students can live off-campus. Contact Admissions Office for off-campus information. Off-campus housing and personal expenses: approximately $13,210. Additional costs: books approximately $800.

Enrollment: first-year class 165 full-time, 81 part-time; total full-time 488, part-time 308 (men 49%, women 51%). First-year statistics: 30% out of state, 51% women; 17% minority; average age 28; 134 undergraduate institutions represented; range of first-year section sizes 20–80 students; number of upper division courses offered after first year 94 full-time, 95 part-time.

Faculty: full-time 51, part-time 40; 37% female; 5% minority; student/faculty ratio 15.6 to 1.

Degrees conferred: J.D., J.D.-M.B.A., J.D.-M.P.A., LL.M. (Environmental Law), S.J.D. (Environmental Law).

RECRUITMENT PRACTICES AND POLICIES. Attends most national law school forums. Has on-campus informational sessions. School does have diversity program and actively recruits women/minority applicants.

ADMISSION REQUIREMENTS FOR FIRST-YEAR APPLICANTS. LSDAS law school report, LSAT (not later than February test date, if more than one LSAT, highest is used), bachelor's degree from an accredited institution, personal statement, two appraisals (recommendations), transcripts (must show all schools attended and at least three years of study) required in support of application. Applicants must have received bachelor's degree prior to enrollment. Interview not required but may be requested by school. In addition, international applicants whose native language is not English must submit TOEFL (600 minimum). Apply to Office of Admission after September 30, before March 15 (February 1 for scholarship consideration). First-year students admitted fall only. Rolling admission process, notification starts in January and is finished by late April. Acceptance of offer and first deposit due April 15. School does maintain a waiting list. Application fee $55. Phone: (914)422-4210. E-mail: admission@genesis.law.pace.edu.

ADMISSION REQUIREMENTS FOR TRANSFER APPLICANTS. Accepts transfers from other ABA-accredited schools. Admission limited to space available. At least one year of enrollment, dean's letter indicating applicant is in good standing (prefer applicants in the top quarter of first-year class), LSAT, LSDAS, personal statement regarding reason for transfer, current law school transcript, copy of school's catalog required in support of application. Apply to Admission Office at least six weeks prior to date of preferred entrance. Admission decision made upon receipt of completed application. Application fee $55. Will consider visiting students.

ADMISSION REQUIREMENTS FOR LL.M., S.J.D. Applicants must hold a final degree in law (J.D., LL.B) approved by the Section of Legal Education of ABA. Submit all official transcripts, at least two professional recommendations, résumé, personal statement to the Admission Office before March 1. Admits to fall only. Application fee $55. S.J.D. applicants must apply to and be accepted for LL.M.; completion of LL.M. program required before advancement to candidacy.

ADMISSION STANDARDS. Number of full-time applicants 1,580 full-time, 427 part-time; number accepted full-time 702, part-time 176; number enrolled full-time 165, part-time 81; median LSAT 155 (75% of class have a score at or above 146 for both full- and part-time); median GPA 3.20 (A = 4) (75% of class have a GPA at or above 3.00 for both full- and part-time). Attrition rate 5.0%. Gorman rating 2.4; *U.S. News & World Report* ranking is in the third tier of all law schools.

FINANCIAL AID. Scholarships, merit scholarships, minority scholarships, grants-in-aid, institutional loans, federal loans, and Federal WS are available. Assistantships may be available for upper divisional joint-degree candidates. For scholarships (selection criteria place heavy reliance on LSAT and undergraduate GPA) apply to Admissions Office by February 1. For all other programs apply to the Financial Aid Office before April 30. Phone: (914)422-4050. Use FAFSA for all federal programs (Title IV School code # 002727). Submit TAP application (New York State residents only). Also submit Financial Aid Transcript, federal income tax forms. Approximately 58% (full-time), 15% (part-time) of first-year class received scholarships/grants-in-aid. Approximately 92% of current students receive some form of financial assistance. Average scholarship/grant $3,000 (full-time), $5,000 (part-time).

DEGREE REQUIREMENTS. For J.D.: 90 credits (40 required) with a 2.0 (A = 4) GPA, plus completion of upper divisional writing course; 3-year full-time program, 4-year part-time program. Accelerated J.D. with summer course work. For J.D.-master's: a 4-year program rather than the usual 5-year program needed if degrees taken separately. For LL.M. (Environmental Law): 24 credits; 1 year full-time, 2 years part-time, major research paper. For S.J.D.: completion of LL.M., advancement to candidacy; 1 year in full-time residence; thesis of publishable quality; oral defense.

CAREER AND PLACEMENT INFORMATION. About 30–40 employers conducted on-campus interviews. Approximately 85% of graduates are employed in state. More than 63% of graduates are practicing law; 30% are in business; 5% in government; 2% in academia. Approximately 80% of Pace University's first-time state bar exam takers pass the New York Bar Exam; New York's passage rate for all first-time takers from ABA-approved schools is 78%. Graduates are eligible to take the bar exam in all 50 states.

UNIVERSITY OF THE PACIFIC

Stockton, California 95211-0197
Internet site: http://www.uop.edu

Founded 1851. Private control. Semester system. Library: 437,000 volumes; 531,000 microforms; 2,652 periodicals/subscriptions; 48 computer workstations.

University's other graduate schools: Conservatory of Music, School of Business and Public Administration, School of Education, School of Dentistry (San Francisco), School of Pharmacy.

Total university enrollment: 5,850.

McGeorge School of Law

5200 Fifth Avenue
Sacramento, California 95817
Phone: (916)739-7169. Fax: (916)739-7111
Internet site: http://www.mcgeorge.edu

Established 1924, amalgamated with the University of the Pacific in 1966. Located in an urban area of the state capital. ABA approved since 1969. AALS member. Semester system. Full-time, part-time study. Law library: 419,300 volumes/microforms; 3,969 current periodicals/subscriptions; 40 computer workstations; has LEXIS, NEXIS, WESTLAW, DIALOG; is a Federal Government Depository. Special facilities: Center for Advanced Study of Law and Policy, Institute for Administrative Justice.

Special programs: study abroad at the University of Salzburg, Austria; externships; internships.

Annual tuition: $18,378, part-time $11,326. On-campus apartments available for both single and married students. Annual on-campus living expenses: $13,300. An early housing application is encouraged. Contact Housing Office for both on- and off-campus housing information. Law students tend to live off-campus. Off-campus housing and personal expenses: approximately $13,910. Additional costs: books approximately $800.

Enrollment: first-year class 312 full-time, 107 part-time; total full-time 855 full-time (men 53%, women 47%). First-year statistics: 25% out of state, 34 states and foreign countries represented; 47% women; 23% minority; average age 24; 215 undergraduate institutions represented; range of first-year section sizes 30–109 students; number of upper division courses offered after first year 81 full-time, 52 part-time.

Faculty: full-time 51, part-time 47; 28% female; 7% minority; student/faculty ratio 23.6 to 1.

Degrees conferred: J.D., J.D.-Accounting, J.D.-M.B.A., J.D.-M.P.P.A., LL.M. (Transnational Business Practice).

RECRUITMENT PRACTICES AND POLICIES. Attends local and national law school forums. Has on-campus informational sessions. School does have diversity program and actively recruits women/minority applicants.

ADMISSION REQUIREMENTS FOR FIRST-YEAR APPLICANTS. LSDAS law school report, LSAT (not later than February test date, if more than one LSAT, average is used), bachelor's degree from an accredited institution, personal statement, transcripts (must show all schools attended and at least three years of study) required in support of application. Letters of recommendation optional. Applicants must have received bachelor's degree prior to enrollment. Interview not required but may be requested by school. In addition, international applicants whose native language is not English must submit TOEFL (not older than two years), transcript evaluation obtained from a credential evaluation agency. Apply to Office of Admission after September 30, before March 15. First-year students admitted fall only. Rolling admission process, notification starts in February and is finished by late early April. Application fee $40. Phone: (916)739-7105.

ADMISSION REQUIREMENTS FOR TRANSFER APPLICANTS. Accepts transfers from other ABA-accredited schools. Admission limited to space available.

At least one year of enrollment, dean's letter indicating applicant is in good standing (prefer applicants in the top quarter of first-year class), LSAT, LSDAS, personal statement regarding reason for transfer, undergraduate transcript, current law school transcript required in support of application. Apply to Admission Office by June 1. Admission decision made by mid July. Application fee $40. Will consider visiting students.

ADMISSION REQUIREMENTS FOR LL.M. Applicants must be graduates of an ABA-approved law school or have gained admission to the bar of a state in the United States, or be a graduate of a faculty of law in a foreign country whose faculty are authorized to issue a degree in law. Official transcripts, two letters of recommendation, curriculum vitae (résumé), statement of purpose, writing sample, four passport photographs required in support of international graduate law application. In addition, TOEFL (550 minimum) required for international applicants whose native language is not English, transcript must have a certified English evaluation and translation. Admits fall and spring. Apply at least two months prior to preferred date of entrance. Application fee $75. Phone: (916)739-7195.

ADMISSION STANDARDS. Number of full- and part-time applicants 2,073; number accepted 1,150 full-time, 149 part-time; number enrolled 310 full-time, 107 part-time; median LSAT 153 (75% of class have a score at or above 150 for both full- and part-time); median GPA 3.01 (A = 4) (75% of class have a GPA at or above 2.75 full-time, 2.70 part-time). Attrition rate 7%. Gorman rating 4.28; *U.S. News & World Report* ranking is in the fourth tier of all law schools.

FINANCIAL AID. Scholarships, merit scholarships, diversity scholarships, grants-in-aid, private and institutional loans, state, federal loans, and Federal WS are offered. Assistantships may be available for upper divisional joint-degree candidates. Financial aid packets are sent to all accepted applicants. File law school's financial aid application as soon as it is received. For scholarships, selection criteria place heavy reliance on LSAT and undergraduate GPA. Submit FAFSA for all federal programs (Title IV School code # G03952). Also submit Financial Aid Transcript, federal income tax forms. Approximately 65% (full-time), 53% (part-time) of first-year class received scholarships/grants-in-aid. Approximately 92% of current students receive some form of financial assistance. Average scholarship/grant $3,351

full-time, $2,257 part-time. Average debt after graduation $64,500.

DEGREE REQUIREMENTS. For J.D.: 88 credits (53 required) with a 2.0 (A = 4) GPA, plus completion of upper divisional writing course; 3-year full-time program, 4-year part-time program. Accelerated J.D. with summer course work. For J.D.-master's: a 4-year program rather than the usual 5-year program needed if degrees taken separately. For LL.M. (Transnational): 24 credits, at least 2 semesters in full-time residence; completion of pre-internships program at University of Salzburg; successful completion of internship; a 2.6 GPA (A = 4) required.

CAREER AND PLACEMENT INFORMATION. About 3–40 employers conducted on-campus interviews. Approximately 78% of graduates are employed in state. More than 67% of graduates are practicing law; 11% are in business; 21% in government; 1% in academia. Approximately 83% of the University of the Pacific's first-time state bar exam takers pass the California Bar Exam; California's passage rate for all first-time takers from ABA-approved schools is 83%. Graduates are eligible to take the bar exam in all 50 states.

THE PENNSYLVANIA STATE UNIVERSITY
University Park, Pennsylvania 16802-1503
Internet site: http://www.pennstate.edu

Founded 1855. Penn State has campuses at Erie, Harrisburg, Hershey, Malvern. Public control. Semester system.

Total university enrollment: 45,000 at all sites.

Dickinson School of Law
of The Pennsylvania State University
150 South College Street
Carlisle, Pennsylvania 17013-2899
Phone: (717)240-5000
Internet site: http://www.dsl.edu
E-mail: dsladmit@psu.edu

Established 1834. Effective July 1, 1997, Dickinson affiliated with Penn State University and is known as Dickinson School of Law of The Pennsylvania State University. ABA approved since 1931. AALS member. Semester system. Full-time, day study only. Law library: 380,000 volumes and equivalent forms; 4,185 current periodicals/subscriptions; 59 computer workstations; has

LEXIS, WESTLAW; is a depository for U.S. government documents. Special facilities: Agricultural Law Research and Education Center. Special programs: ABA-approved summer study abroad at the University of Florence, Italy, and in the cities of Brussels, Strasbourg, and Vienna; externships.

Annual tuition: $14,600. On-campus housing available for single students only. Annual on-campus housing cost: single students $3,000 (room only), $5,680 (room and board). Housing deadline May 15. Law students generally live off-campus. Contact Administrative Services Office forth both on- and off-campus housing information. Phone: (717)240-5000. Off-campus housing and personal expenses: approximately $12,224. Additional costs: books approximately $700.

Enrollment: first-year class 175; total full-time 515 (men 56%, women 44%); no part-time students. First-year statistics: 31% out of state, 34 states and foreign countries represented; 44% women; 9% minority; average age 24; 206 undergraduate institutions represented; range of first-year section sizes 26–60 students; number of upper division courses offered after first year 101.

Faculty: full-time 30, part-time 53; 22% female; 10% minority; student/faculty ratio 23.9 to 1.

Degrees conferred: J.D., J.D.-M.P.A. (Penn State Harrisburg), LL.M (only for persons who have completed a basic legal education and received a university degree in law in another country).

RECRUITMENT PRACTICES AND POLICIES. Attends national law school forums. On-campus informational sessions. School does have diversity program and actively recruits women/minority applicants.

ADMISSION REQUIREMENTS FOR FIRST-YEAR APPLICANTS. LSDAS law school report, LSAT (not later than December test date, if more than one LSAT, average is used), bachelor's degree from an accredited institution, a one-page personal statement, employment record, two recommendations, transcripts (must show all schools attended and at least three years of study) required in support of application. Applicants must have received bachelor's degree prior to enrollment. Interview not required; fall campus visits are strongly encouraged. In addition, international applicants whose native language is not English must submit TOEFL (not older than two years). Apply to Director of Admission after September 30, before March 1. First-year students admitted fall only. Rolling admission process. Acceptance of offer and first deposit due April 15. Application fee $50. Phone: (800)840-1122, (717)240-5207. E-mail: dsladmit@psu.edu.

ADMISSION REQUIREMENTS FOR TRANSFER APPLICANTS. Accepts transfers from other ABA-accredited schools. Admission limited to space available. At least one year of enrollment, dean's letter indicating applicant is in good standing (prefer applicants in the top quarter of first-year class), LSAT, LSDAS, personal statement regarding reason for transfer, one recommendation from a law school professor, current law school transcript, undergraduate transcript required in support of application. Apply to Director of Admission by June 1. Admission decisions made by mid July. Application fee $50. Will consider visiting students.

ADMISSION REQUIREMENTS FOR LL.M. LL.B, J.D. or equivalent from a foreign law school; official transcripts (in English) with certified translation and evaluation; TOEFL (score of 575 minimum required) for applicants whose native language is not English required in support of application. Apply to the Associate Dean at least two months prior to preferred semester of entrance. Application fee $50. E-mail: jqf@psu.edu.

ADMISSION STANDARDS. Number of full-time applicants 1,287; number accepted 663; number enrolled 175; median LSAT 153 (75% of class have a score at or above 148); median GPA 3.4 (A = 4) (75% of class have a GPA at or above 3.07). Attrition rate 3.3%. Gorman rating 3.27; *U.S. News & World Report* ranking is in the third tier of all law schools.

FINANCIAL AID. Scholarships, merit scholarships, diversity achievement awards, grants-in-aid, private loans, federal loans, Federal WS available. For scholarships (selection criteria place heavy reliance on LSAT and undergraduate GPA) apply to Financial Aid Office after January 1, before February 15. Phone: (717)241-3524. Use FAFSA (FAFSA code #G03254). Submit federal income tax form, Financial Aid Transcript, needs Access Disk. Approximately 28% of first-year class received scholarships/grants-in-aid. Approximately 75% of current students receive some form of financial assistance. Average scholarship/grant $4,528. Average debt after graduation $42,000.

DEGREE REQUIREMENTS. For J.D.: 88 credits (41 required) with a 70 (scale 0–100) GPA, plus completion of upper divisional writing course and 1 seminar; 3-year program. Accelerated J.D. with 1 summer of course work. For J.D.-M.P.A.: up to 9 M.P.A. credits may be used for J.D., up to 9 J.D. credits may be used for M.P.A.; must complete first year at Dickinson before beginning M.P.A. program. For LL.M.: 24 credits, at least 2 semesters in residence.

CAREER AND PLACEMENT INFORMATION. About 74 employers conducted on-campus interviews. Approximately 75% of graduates are employed in state. More than 74% of graduates are practicing law; 11% are in business; 14% in government; 1% in academia. Approximately 88% of Dickinson School of Law of the Pennsylvania State University's first-time state bar exam takers pass the Pennsylvania Bar Exam; Pennsylvania's passage rate for all first-time takers from ABA-approved schools is 73%. Graduates are eligible to take the bar exam in all 50 states.

UNIVERSITY OF PENNSYLVANIA

Philadelphia, Pennsylvania 19104
Internet site: http://www.upenn.edu

Founded 1740. Located 2 miles from central Philadelphia. Private control. Semester system. Library: 4,200,000 volumes; 1,500,000 microforms; 33,000 periodicals/subscriptions.

University's other graduate colleges/schools: Annenberg School of Communication, Graduate School of Education, Graduate School of Fine Arts, School of Arts and Sciences, School of Dental Medicine, School of Engineering and Applied Science, School of Medicine, School of Nursing, School of Social Work, School of Veterinary Medicine, Wharton School.

Total university enrollment: 22,100.

Law School

3400 Chestnut Street
Philadelphia, Pennsylvania 19104-6204
Phone: (215)898-7483
Internet site: http://www.law.upenn.edu
E-mail: admissions@oyez.law.upenn.edu

Established 1852. Located on main campus. ABA approved since 1923. AALS member. Semester system. Full-time, day study only. Law library: 611,700 volumes/microforms; 7,100 current periodicals/subscriptions; 96 computer workstations; has LEXIS, NEXIS, WESTLAW, DIALOG, BRS, VUTEXT; is a Federal Government Depository. Special facility: Institute of Law and Economics. Special programs: Public Service Program; externships.

Annual tuition: $24,530. On-campus housing available for both single and married students. Annual on-campus housing cost: single students $7,260 (room only), $10,760 (room and board), married students $10,080. Contact Office of Graduate Housing for both on- and off-campus housing information. Phone: (215)898-8271.

Law students tend to live off-campus. Off-campus housing and personal expenses: approximately $12,000. Additional costs: books approximately $800.

Enrollment: first-year class 280; total full-time 788 (men 59%, women 41%); no part-time students. First-year statistics: 85% out of state, 53 states and foreign countries represented; 41% women; 26% minority; average age 24; 168 undergraduate institutions represented; average first-year section size 80 students; number of upper division courses offered after first year 73.

Faculty: full-time 41, part-time 50; 25% female; 4% minority; student/faculty ratio 18 to 1.

Degrees conferred: J.D., J.D.-M.B.A., J.D.-M.A. (Communication, Economics, History, Islamic Studies, Middle Eastern Studies, Public Policy, Philosophy), J.D.-M.C.P., J.D.-M.S.W., LL.M., S.J.D.

RECRUITMENT PRACTICES AND POLICIES. Attends national law school forums. Has on-campus informational sessions every Monday except in the early fall. School does have diversity program and actively recruits women/minority applicants.

ADMISSION REQUIREMENTS FOR FIRST-YEAR APPLICANTS. LSDAS law school report, LSAT (not later than December test date, if more than one LSAT, average is used), bachelor's degree from an accredited institution, College Certification Form, personal statement, two recommendations, transcripts (must show all schools attended and at least three years of study) required in support of application. Applicants must have received bachelor's degree prior to enrollment. Interview not required, but campus visits are encouraged. In addition, international applicants whose native language is not English must submit TOEFL (not older than two years), certified translation and evaluation of all foreign transcripts. Joint-degree applicants must apply to and be accepted by both schools. Apply to Office of Admission after September 30, before March 1. First-year students admitted fall only. Rolling admission process, notification starts in January and is finished by late April. Acceptance of offer and first deposit due April 1. School does maintain a waiting list. Application fee $65. Phone: (215)898-7400. Fax: (215)573-2025. E-mail: admissions@oyez.law.upenn.edu.

ADMISSION REQUIREMENTS FOR TRANSFER APPLICANTS. Accepts transfers from other ABA-accredited schools. Admission limited to space available. At least one year of enrollment, dean's letter indicating applicant is in good standing (prefer applicants in the top

10% of first-year class), LSAT, LSDAS, personal statement regarding reason for transfer, two letters of recommendation, current law school transcript required in support of application. Apply to Admission Office by July 15. Admission decisions made by late July, early August. Application fee $65. Will consider visiting students.

ADMISSION REQUIREMENTS FOR LL.M., S.J.D. All applicants must have J.D. or LL.B (or the equivalent) from a U.S. ABA/AALS-approved law school. If applicants are from outside the U.S., the law school/faculty must be approved by organization/government agency of comparable standing. Official transcripts, two recommendations, résumé, personal statement, writing sample required in support of graduate application. Admits fall only (new class enrollment is normally between 40 and 50 each fall). Apply by March 1 to Graduate Admissions Office. Application fee $65. Phone: (215)898-9606. For S.J.D.: this degree is normally open only to those candidates who have spent at least one academic year in residence at the law school, have earned a LL.M., and have a fully developed scholarly project before admission. Normally admits between 6 and 7 candidates each year.

ADMISSION STANDARDS. Number of full-time applicants 3,956; number accepted 1,158; number enrolled 280; median LSAT 166 (75% of class have a score at or above 162); median GPA 3.60 (A = 4) (75% of class have a GPA at or above 3.41). Attrition rate 1.8%. Gorman rating 4.83; *U.S. News & World Report* ranking is in the top 11 of all law schools.

FINANCIAL AID. Scholarships, merit scholarships, Public Interest Scholarship Program, minority scholarships, grants-in-aid, private and institutional loans, federal loans, and Federal WS available. Assistantships may be available for upper divisional joint-degree candidates. Submit the university's Financial Aid Form before March 1. The Center for Graduate and Professional Student Finance reviews all applicants requests and supporting documents. After review, the Center forwards the results to the law school for grant and loan consideration. Public Interest Scholar's Program places heavy reliance on LSAT/undergraduate GPA and expressed interest in program. Use FAFSA for all federal programs (Title IV School code # 003378). Also submit Financial Aid Transcript, federal income tax forms. Approximately 31% of first-year class received scholarships/grants-in-aid. Approximately 80% of current students receive some form of financial assistance. Average scholarship/grant $7,850. Public Interest Loan Repayment Assistance program available. Average debt after graduation $54,300.

Financial aid for LL.M. students is extremely limited. Students should be prepared to finance their entire program.

DEGREE REQUIREMENTS. For J.D.: 89 credits (28 required) with a 2.0 (A = 4) GPA, plus completion of upper divisional writing course; 3-year program. Accelerated J.D. with summer course work. For J.D.-master's: most joint-degree programs are 4 years in duration rather than the usual 5 years needed if degree taken separately. LL.M.: 13–20 credits, at least 1 full academic year in residence; thesis/course track. For S.J.D.: at least 1 year in full-time residence after receipt of LL.M.; dissertation of publishable quality; oral defense.

CAREER AND PLACEMENT INFORMATION. About 275 employers conducted on-campus interviews. Approximately 28% of graduates are employed in state. More than 91% of graduates are practicing law; 4% are in business; 4% in government; 1% in academia. Approximately 91% (NY), 84% (PA) of the University of Pennsylvania's first-time state bar exam takers pass the bar exam; the passage rate for all first-time takers from ABA-approved schools is 78% (NY), 73% (PA). Graduates are eligible to take the bar exam in all 50 states.

PEPPERDINE UNIVERSITY
Malibu, California 90263-0001
Internet site: http://www.pepperdine.edu

Founded 1937. Located about 45 minutes from downtown Los Angeles. Private control (Church of Christ affiliation). Trimester system. Library: 377,400 volumes; 229,200 microforms; 4,774 periodicals/subscriptions.

University's other graduate colleges/schools: Graduate School of Education and Psychology, George L. Graziadio School of Business and Management, Seaver College.

Total university enrollment: 7,833.

School of Law
24255 Pacific Coast Highway
Malibu, California 90263
Phone: (310)456-4611
Internet site: http://law-www.pepperdine.edu
E-mail: soladmis@pepperdine.edu

Formerly Orange University College of Law, affiliated with Pepperdine in 1969. Located on main campus. ABA approved since 1972. AALS member. Semester system. Full-time, day study only. Law library: 262,900 volumes/microforms; 3,496 current periodicals/subscriptions; 52 computer workstations; has LEXIS, NEXIS, WEST-

LAW, DIALOG. Special facility: Institute for Dispute Resolution. Special programs: summer study abroad in London, England.

Annual tuition: $21,980. On-campus housing available for single students only. Annual on-campus housing cost: single students $4,030 (room only), $6,860 (room and board). Contact Residential Life Office for both on- and off- campus housing information. Phone: (310)456-4104. Law students tend to live off-campus. Off-campus housing and personal expenses: approximately $15,732. Additional costs: books approximately $800.

Enrollment: first-year class 205; total full-time 680 (men 54%, women 46%); no part-time students. First-year statistics: 26% out of state, 40 states and foreign countries represented; 46% women; 22% minority; average age 27; 215 undergraduate institutions represented; average first-year section size 70 students; number of upper division courses offered after first year 92.

Faculty: full-time 39, part-time 20; 33% female; 11% minority; student/faculty ratio 20 to 1.

Degrees conferred: J.D., J.D.-M.B.A., J.D.-M.D.R., M.D.R.

RECRUITMENT PRACTICES AND POLICIES. Attends national law school forums. Has on-campus informational sessions. School does have diversity program and actively recruits women/minority applicants.

ADMISSION REQUIREMENTS FOR FIRST-YEAR APPLICANTS. LSDAS law school report, LSAT (not later than February test date, if more than one LSAT, highest is used), bachelor's degree from an accredited institution, personal statement, two recommendations, transcripts (must show all schools attended and at least three years of study) required in support of application. Applicants must have received bachelor's degree prior to enrollment. Interview not required; campus visit encouraged. In addition, international applicants whose native language is not English must submit TOEFL (not older than two years). Joint-degree applicants must apply to Office of Admission after September 30, before March 1. First-year students admitted fall only. Rolling admission process, notification starts in February and is finished by late May. Acceptance of offer and first deposit due June 1. School does maintain a waiting list. Application fee $50. Phone: (310)456-4631. E-mail: soladmis@pepperdine.edu.

ADMISSION REQUIREMENTS FOR TRANSFER APPLICANTS. Accepts transfers from other ABA-accredited schools. Admission limited to space available. At least one year of enrollment, dean's letter indicating applicant is in good standing (prefer applicants in the top 15% of first-year class) LSAT, LSDAS, personal statement regarding reason for transfer, current law school transcript required in support of application. Apply to Admission Office by June 1. Admission decisions made by mid July. Application fee $50. Will consider visiting students.

ADMISSIONS REQUIREMENTS FOR M.D.R. Bachelor's degree from an accredited insitution, GRE or LSAT, official transcripts, 3 student evaluations, statement for the study of dispute resolution required in support of application. Apply to the Program Director at least two months prior to preferred entrance date. Admission notification within two weeks of the receipt of completed application. Application fee $50. Phone: (310)456-4655. Fax: (310)456-4437.

ADMISSION STANDARDS. Number of full-time applicants 2,595; number accepted 1,019; number enrolled 205; median LSAT 157 (75% of class have a score at or above 154); median GPA 3.33 (A = 4) (75% of class have a GPA at or above 3.03). Attrition rate 3.1%. Gorman rating 3.68; *U.S. News & World Report* ranking is in the third tier of all law schools.

FINANCIAL AID. Scholarships, Dean's Merit Scholarships, ethnic diversity scholarships, grants-in-aid, institutional and state loans; federal loans and Federal WS offered through university's Financial Aid Office. No formal application required, all accepted students are automatically considered for Dean's Scholarships (selection criteria place heavy reliance on LSAT and undergraduate GPA). For all other programs apply after January 1, before May 13 to university's Financial Aid Office. Phone: (310)456-4633. Submit FAFSA for all federal programs (Title IV School code # 001264). Also submit Financial Aid Transcript, federal income tax forms. Approximately 75% of first-year class received scholarships/grants-in-aid. Approximately 85% of current students receive some form of financial assistance. Average scholarship/grant $8,450. Average debt after graduation $67,000.

DEGREE REQUIREMENTS. For J.D.: 88 credits (57 required) with a 72 (C = 70–73) GPA, plus completion of upper divisional writing course; 3-year program. Accelerated J.D. with 1 summer of course work. For J.D.-M.B.A.: a 4-year program rather than the usual 5-year program needed if degrees taken separately. For J.D.-M.D.R.: 3½- to 4-year program rather than the usual 5-year program needed if degrees taken separately. For M.D.R.: 32 units; thesis/project or externship.

CAREER AND PLACEMENT INFORMATION. About 15–20 employers conducted on-campus interviews. Approximately 81% of graduates are employed in state. More than 74% of graduates are practicing law; 19% are in business; 7% in government. Approximately 86% of Pepperdine University's first-time state bar exam takers pass the California Bar Exam; California's passage rate for all first-time takers from ABA-approved schools is 83%. Graduates are eligible to take the bar exam in all 50 states.

UNIVERSITY OF PITTSBURGH
Pittsburgh, Pennsylvania 15261
Internet site: http://www.pitt.edu

Founded 1787. Located 3 miles from downtown. Public control. Trimester system. Library: 3,296,000 volumes; 3,312,000 microforms; 23,290 periodicals/subscriptions.

University's other graduate colleges/schools: Center for Neuroscience, Faculty of Arts and Sciences, Graduate School of Public and International Affairs, Graduate School of Public Health, Joseph M. Katz Graduate School of Business, School of Dental Medicine, School of Education, School of Engineering, School of Health and Rehabilitation Science, School of Information Sciences, School of Medicine, School of Nursing, School of Pharmacy, School of Social Work.

Total university enrollment: 26,100.

School of Law
202 Law Building
3900 Forbes Avenue
Pittsburgh, Pennsylvania 15260
Phone: (412)648-1400
Internet site: http://www.law.pitt.edu
E-mail: admissions@law.pitt.edu

Established 1895. Located in Oakland area of Pittsburgh. ABA approved since 1923. AALS charter member. Semester system. Full-time, day study only. Law library: 364,400 volumes/microforms; 5,154 current periodicals/subscriptions; 43 computer workstations; has LEXIS, NEXIS, WESTLAW, CALI; is a Federal Government Depository. Special facility: Center for International Legal Education. Special program: externships.

Annual tuition: resident $11,898, nonresident $18,346, LL.M. $16,712. No on-campus housing available in Oakland area. Contact the university's Housing Office for on-campus housing information. Phone: (412)624-4317. Law students live off-campus. Contact Admissions Office for off-campus information. Off-campus housing and

personal expenses: approximately $10,180, the average monthly rent for one bedroom $375, two bedrooms $500. Additional costs: books approximately $750.

Enrollment: first-year class 266; total full-time 722 (men 58%, women 42%); no part-time students. First-year statistics: 39% out of state, 30 states and foreign countries represented; 42% women; 12% minority; average age 24; 136 undergraduate institutions represented; range of first-year section sizes 10–80 students; number of upper division courses offered after first year 122.

Faculty: full-time 45, part-time 39; 36% female; 14% minority; student/faculty ratio 21 to 1.

Degrees conferred: J.D., J.D.-M.A., J.D.-M.B.A., J.D.-M.P.A., J.D.-M.P.I.A., J.D.-M.P.H., J.D.-M.S. (Carnegie Mellon University), J.D.-M.S.I.A. (Carnegie Mellon University), J.D.-M.U.R.P., LL.M. (for persons who have completed a basic legal education and received a university degree in law in another country).

RECRUITMENT PRACTICES AND POLICIES. Attends both local and national law school forums. Has on-campus informational sessions. School does have diversity program and actively recruits women/minority applicants.

ADMISSION REQUIREMENTS FOR FIRST-YEAR APPLICANTS. LSDAS law school report, LSAT (not later than February test date, if more than one LSAT, average is used), bachelor's degree from an accredited institution, personal statement, transcripts (must show all schools attended and at least three years of study) required in support of application. An optional supplementary questionnaire and letters of recommendation may be submitted. Applicants must have received bachelor's degree prior to enrollment. Interview not required. Group interview available and campus visits are encouraged. In addition, international applicants whose native language is not English must submit TOEFL (not older than two years), submit certified translations and evaluations of all foreign credentials. Joint-degree applicants must apply to and be accepted by both schools. The Law Multi-App may be used in lieu of school's application. Apply to Office of Admission after October 1, before March 1. First-year students admitted fall only. Rolling admission process, notification starts in January and is finished by early April. Application fee $40. Phone: (412)648-1412. E-mail: admissions@law.pit.edu.

ADMISSION REQUIREMENTS FOR TRANSFER APPLICANTS. Accepts transfers from other ABA-accredited schools. Admission limited to space available. At least one year of enrollment, dean's letter indicating

applicant is in good standing (prefer applicants in the top quarter of first-year class), LSAT, LSDAS, personal statement regarding reason for transfer, undergraduate transcript, current law school transcript required in support of application. Apply to Admission Office by June 1. Admission decision made by mid July. Application fee $40. Will consider visiting students.

ADMISSION STANDARDS. Number of full-time applicants 1,367; number accepted 861; number enrolled 266; median LSAT 156 (75% of class have a score at or above 152); median GPA 3.24 (A = 4) (75% of class have a GPA at or above 2.89). Attrition rate 6%. Gorman rating 3.75; *U.S. News & World Report* ranking is in the third tier of all law schools.

FINANCIAL AID. Academic scholarships, grants-in-aid, private and institutional loans, PHEAA loans; federal loans and Federal WS offered through university's Financial Aid Office. Assistantships may be available for upper divisional joint-degree candidates. For scholarships (selection criteria place heavy reliance on LSAT and undergraduate GPA) apply to Admissions Office as soon as possible; use school's financial aid application. For all other programs apply by March 1. Phone: (415)648-1415. Submit FAFSA for all federal programs (Title IV School code #008815). Also submit Financial Aid Transcript, federal income tax forms. Approximately 31% of first-year class received scholarships/grants-in-aid. Approximately 95% of current students receive some form of financial assistance. Average scholarship/grant $4,050. Average debt after graduation $45,000.

DEGREE REQUIREMENTS. For J.D.: 88 credits (40 required) with a 2.0 (A = 4) GPA, plus completion of upper divisional writing course; 3-year program. Accelerated J.D. with summer course work. For J.D.-master's: 3½- to 4½-year programs rather than the usual 4 to 5½ years needed if both degrees taken separately. For LL.M. (foreign law graduates): 24 credits, at least 2 semesters in residence; 1 course in legal analysis and writing; writing project; colloquium presentation of research findings.

CAREER AND PLACEMENT INFORMATION. About 50–60 employers conducted on-campus interviews. Approximately 74% of graduates are employed in state. More than 80% of graduates are practicing law; 10% are in business; 10% in government. Approximately 82% of the University of Pittsburgh's first-time state bar exam takers pass the Pennsylvania Bar Exam; Pennsylvania's passage rate for all first-time takers from ABA-approved schools is 73%. Graduates are eligible to take the bar exam in all 50 states.

PONTIFICAL CATHOLIC UNIVERSITY OF PUERTO RICO
Ponce, Puerto Rico 00731-6382

Founded 1948. Located 140 miles S of San Juan. Private control. Semester system. Library: 236,800 volumes; 336,200 microforms; 3,700 periodicals/subscriptions, 8 computer workstations.

University's other graduate colleges/schools: College of Arts and Humanities, College of Business Administration, College of Education, College of Sciences.

Total university enrollment: 11,800.

School of Law
Las Americas Avenue, Ste 543
Ponce, Puerto Rico 00731-6382
Phone: (787)841-2000, Ext. 339, 340.

Established 1961. Located on main campus. ABA approved since 1967. AALS member. Semester system. Full-time, part-time study. Law library:171,800 volumes/microforms; 2,200 current periodicals/subscriptions; 41 computer workstations; has LEXIS, NEXIS, WESTLAW, DIALOG; is a Federal Government and United Nations Depository.

Annual tuition: full-time $8,768, part-time $6,256, per credit $220. On-campus housing available for single students only. Annual on-campus housing cost: single students $1,240 (room only), $3,967 (room and board). Housing deadline July 15. Contact Housing Office for both on- and off-campus housing information. Phone: (787)841-2000, Ext. 232. Law students prefer to live off-campus. Off-campus housing and personal expenses: approximately $8,927. Additional costs: books approximately $700.

Enrollment: first-year class 118 full-time, 52 part-time; total full- and part-time 505 (men 51%, women 49%). First-year statistics: most students are from Puerto Rico, 49% women; 100% minority; average age 24; range of first-year section sizes 20–60 students; number of upper division courses offered after first year 26 full-time, 31 part-time.

Faculty: full-time 17, part-time 14; 28% female;100% minority; student/faculty ratio 21 to 1.

Degrees conferred: J.D., J.D.-M.B.A.

RECRUITMENT PRACTICES AND POLICIES. Has on-campus informational sessions and personal interviews.

ADMISSION REQUIREMENTS FOR FIRST-YEAR APPLICANTS. LSDAS law school report, LSAT (not later than February test date, if more than one LSAT, highest is used), PAEG, bachelor's degree from an accredited institution, personal statement, personal interview, two recommendations, transcripts (must show all schools attended and at least three years of study) required in support of application. Applicants must have received bachelor's degree prior to enrollment. Joint-degree applicants must apply to and be accepted by both schools. Apply to Office of Admission after November 1, before May 15. First-year students admitted fall only. Rolling admission process. Application fee $25. Phone: (787)841-2200, Ext. 339, 340.

ADMISSION REQUIREMENTS FOR TRANSFER APPLICANTS. Accepts transfers from other ABA-accredited schools. Admission limited to space available. At least one year of enrollment, dean's letter indicating applicant is in good standing, LSAT, LSDAS, personal statement regarding reason for transfer, undergraduate transcript, current law school transcript required in support of application. Apply to Admission Officer by June 30. Admission decisions made by early August. Application fee $25. Will consider visiting students.

ADMISSION STANDARDS. Number of full-time applicants 303 full-time, 132 part-time; number accepted 160 full-time, 68 part-time; number enrolled 118 full-time, 52 part-time; median LSAT 133 (75% of class have a score at or above 132 full-time, 131 part-time); median GPA 3.08 (A = 4) (75% of class have a GPA at or above 2.85 full-time, 2.83 part-time). Attrition rate 8.4%. Gorman rating 2.28; *U.S. News & World Report* ranking is in the fourth tier of all law schools.

FINANCIAL AID. Scholarships, merit scholarships, grants-in-aid, private institutional loans; federal loans and Federal WS offered through university's Financial Aid Office. For scholarships apply to Admissions Office after January 1, before April 1. For all other programs apply to university's Office of Financial Aid. Use FAFSA for all federal programs (Title IV School code #003936). Also submit Financial Aid Transcript, federal income tax forms. Approximately 8% (full-time) of first-year class received scholarships/grants-in-aid. Approximately 50% of current students receive some form of financial assistance. Average scholarship/grant $1,520. Financial aid available for part-time students.

DEGREE REQUIREMENTS. For J.D.: 94 credits (82 required) with a 2.0 (A = 4) GPA, plus completion of upper divisional writing course; 3-year full-time program, 4-year part-time program. For J.D.-M.B.A.: a 4-year program rather than the usual 5-year program needed if degrees taken separately.

CAREER AND PLACEMENT INFORMATION. About 10–15 employers conducted on-campus interviews. Approximately 98.6% of graduates are employed in the commonwealth. More than 67% of graduates are practicing law; 11% are in business; 22% in government. Approximately 63% of the Pontifical Catholic University of Puerto Rico's first-time state bar exam takers pass the Puerto Rico Bar Exam; Puerto Rico's passage rate for all first-time takers from ABA-approved schools is 69%. Graduates are eligible to take the bar exam in all 50 states.

UNIVERSITY OF PUERTO RICO, RIO PIEDRAS

Rio Piedras, Puerto Rico 00931

Founded 1903. Located 8 miles S of San Juan. Public control. Semester system. Library: 4,100,000 volumes; 1,637,800 microforms; 4,966 periodicals/subscriptions.

University's other graduate colleges/schools: College of Education, College of Humanities, College of Social Sciences, Faculty of Natural Science, Graduate School of Business Administration, Graduate School of Librarianship, School of Architecture, School of Public Communication.

Total university enrollment: 20,000.

School of Law
P.O. Box 23349
San Juan, Puerto Rico 00931-3349
Phone: (787)764-2680

Established 1913. Located in metropolitan San Juan. ABA approved since 1945. AALS member. Semester system. Full-time, part-time study. Law library: 290,300 volumes/microforms; 4,250 current periodicals/subscriptions; 26 computer workstations; has LEXIS, NEXIS, WESTLAW, DIALOG, COMPUCLERK, CUMPULEY, LEGALTRAC, INFOTRAC; is a selective depository for U.S. Government Documents and European Document Centre. Special programs: exchange program with the University of Arizona and the University of Connecticut, summer study abroad at University of Barcelona; externships.

Annual tuition: full-time $2,450, part-time $1,713. On-campus housing available for single students only. Annual on-campus living expenses: single students $9,975.

Housing deadline June 15. Contact Housing Office for both on- and off-campus housing information. Phone: (787)764-2680, Ext, 5651. Law students tend to live off-campus. Off-campus housing and personal expenses: approximately $8,475. Additional costs: books approximately $700.

Enrollment: first-year class 114 full-time, 46 part-time; total full-time 326, part-time 199 (men 46%, women 54%). First-year statistics: 2% outside of Puerto Rico, 3 states and foreign countries represented; 54% women; 100% minority; average age 24; 20 undergraduate institutions represented; range of first-year section sizes 10–50 students; number of upper division courses offered after first year 60 full-time, 38 part-time.

Faculty: full-time 33, part-time 23; 41% female; 98% minority; student/faculty ratio 24 to 1.

Degrees conferred: J.D., J.D.-M.B.A., J.D.-Lic. en Derecho (University of Barcelona).

RECRUITMENT PRACTICES AND POLICIES. Has on-campus informational sessions.

ADMISSION REQUIREMENTS FOR FIRST-YEAR APPLICANTS. LSDAS law school report, LSAT (not later than February test date, if more than one LSAT, average is used), PAEG, bachelor's degree from an accredited institution, personal statement, two recommendations, transcripts (must show all schools attended and at least three years of study) required in support of application. Applicants must have received bachelor's degree prior to enrollment. Apply to Office of Admission after November 1, before February 17. First-year students admitted fall only. Rolling admission process. Phone: (787)764-1655.

ADMISSION REQUIREMENTS FOR TRANSFER APPLICANTS. Accepts transfers from other ABA-accredited schools. Admission limited to space available. At least one year of enrollment, dean's letter indicating applicant is in good standing (prefer applicants with a 3.3 [A = 4] GPA), LSAT, LSDAS, personal statement regarding reason for transfer, undergraduate transcripts, current law school transcript required in support of application. Apply to Admission Office by July 1. Admission decisions made by early August. Will consider visiting students.

ADMISSION STANDARDS. Number of applicants 449 full-time, 290 part-time; number accepted 136 full-time, 47 part-time; number enrolled 114 full-time, 46 part-time; median LSAT 147 (75% of class have a score at or above 143 full-time, 142 part-time); median GPA 3.46 (A = 4) (75% of class have a GPA at or above 3.26 full-time, 2.95 part-time). Attrition rate 5.9%. Gorman rating 2.32; *U.S. News & World Report* ranking is in the fourth tier of all law schools.

FINANCIAL AID. Scholarships, grants-in-aid, private institutional loans; federal loans and Federal WS administered through university's Office of Financial Aid. For scholarships (selection criteria place heavy reliance on LSAT, PAEG, and undergraduate GPA) and all other programs, apply after January 1, before April 15. Submit FAFSA for all federal programs (Title IV School code #007108). Also submit Financial Aid Transcript, federal income tax forms. Approximately 47% of first-year class received scholarships/grants-in-aid. Approximately 60% of current students receive some form of financial assistance. Average scholarship/grant $1,000.

DEGREE REQUIREMENTS. For J.D.: 92 credits (70 required) with a 2.0 (A = 4) GPA, plus completion of upper divisional writing course; 3-year program. Accelerated J.D. with 1 summer of course work. For J.D.-M.B.A., Lic. en Derecho: 4-year programs rather than the usual 5-year programs needed if degrees taken separately.

CAREER AND PLACEMENT INFORMATION. About 20–25 employers conducted on-campus interviews. Approximately 95% of graduates are employed in Puerto Rico. Approximately 84% of the University of Puerto Rico, Rio Piedras' first-time state bar exam takers pass the Puerto Rico Bar Exam; Puerto Rico's passage rate for all first-time takers from ABA-approved schools is 69%.

CITY UNIVERSITY OF NEW YORK

School of Law at Queens College
58-21 Main Street
Flushing, New York 11367-1358
Phone: (718)575-4200
Internet site: http://www.cuny.edu/colleges/frames/cunylaw/html

Established 1983. Located on the Queens College campus in Flushing. ABA approved since 1885. AALS member. Semester system. Full-time, day study only. Law library: 226,500 volumes/microforms; 2,537 current periodicals/subscriptions; 64 computer workstations; has LEXIS, NEXIS, WESTLAW, DIALOG.

Annual tuition: resident $6,452, nonresident $9,682. No on-campus housing available. Law students live off-campus. Contact Admissions Office for off-campus information. Off-campus housing and personal expenses: approximately $10,351. Additional costs: books approximately $800.

Enrollment: first-year class 162; total full-time 459 (men 40%, women 60%); no part-time students. First-year statistics: 15% out of state, 28 states and foreign countries represented; 60% women; 36% minority; average age 30; 215 undergraduate institutions represented; range of first-year section sizes 20–160 students; number of upper division courses offered after first year 68.

Faculty: full-time 36, part-time 14; 55% female; 34% minority; student/faculty ratio 13.8 to 1.

Degree conferred: J.D.

RECRUITMENT PRACTICES AND POLICIES. Attends selected local law school forums. Has on-campus informational interviews and group sessions. School does have diversity program and actively recruits women/minority applicants.

ADMISSION REQUIREMENTS FOR FIRST-YEAR APPLICANTS. LSDAS law school report, LSAT (not later than February test date, if more than one LSAT, highest is used), bachelor's degree from an accredited institution, personal statement, two recommendations, transcripts (must show all schools attended and at least three years of study) required in support of application. Applicants must have received bachelor's degree prior to enrollment. Interview not required but may be requested by school. In addition, international applicants whose native language is not English must submit TOEFL (not older than two years). Apply to Office of Admission after October 1, before March 14. First-year students admitted fall only. Rolling admission process. Application fee $40. Phone: (718)575-4210.

ADMISSION REQUIREMENTS FOR TRANSFER APPLICANTS. Accepts transfers from other ABA-accredited schools. Admission limited to space available. At least one year of enrollment, dean's letter indicating applicant is in good standing (prefer applicants with a 3.0 [A = 4] GPA), LSAT, LSDAS, personal statement regarding reason for transfer, two recommendations, undergraduate transcripts, current law school transcript required in support of application. Apply to Admission Office by June 1. Admission decisions made by mid July. Application fee $40. Will consider visiting students.

ADMISSION STANDARDS. Number of full-time applicants 1,647; number accepted 521; number enrolled

162; median LSAT 150 (75% of class have a score at or above 142); median GPA 3.00 (A = 4) (75% of class have a GPA at or above 2.76). Attrition rate 2.8%. Gorman rating 2.10; *U.S. News & World Report* ranking is in the fourth tier of all law schools.

FINANCIAL AID. Scholarships, grants-in-aid, private and institutional loans, federal loans, and Federal WS available. For scholarships (selection criteria place heavy reliance on LSAT and undergraduate GPA) apply to Admissions Office after January 1, before March 1. Use CUNY's financial aid form. Also submit Financial Aid Transcript, federal income tax forms. Approximately 51% of first-year class received scholarships/grants-in-aid. Approximately 80% of current students receive some form of financial assistance. Average scholarship/grant $1,575.

DEGREE REQUIREMENTS. For J.D.: 92 credits (70 required) a 2.0 (A = 4) GPA, plus completion of upper divisional writing course; 3-year program.

CAREER AND PLACEMENT INFORMATION. About 8–10 employers conducted on-campus interviews. Approximately 79% of graduates are employed in state. More than 71% of graduates are practicing law; 18% are in business; 9% in government; 2% in academia. Approximately 56% of the City University of New York's first-time state bar exam takers pass the New York Bar Exam; New York's passage rate for all first-time takers from ABA-approved schools is 78%. Graduates are eligible to take the bar exam in all 50 states.

QUINNIPIAC COLLEGE
Hamden, Connecticut 06518-1904
Internet site: http://www.quinnipiac.edu

Founded 1929. Private control. Semester system. Library: 272,800 volumes; 184,400 microforms; 4,586 periodicals/subscriptions; 85 computer workstations.

College's other graduate schools: School of Business, School of Health Sciences, School of Liberal Arts.

Total college enrollment: 5,000.

School of Law
275 Mount Carmel Avenue
Hamden, Connecticut 06518-1948
Phone: (203)287-3200
Internet site: http://www.quinnipiac.edu/law.html
E-mail: cadm@quinnipiac.edu

Founded in 1979 as part of the University of Bridgeport, name changed in 1995 and moved to Hamden. Located on main campus. ABA approved since 1992. AALS member. Semester system. Full-time, part-time study. Law library: 300,500 volumes/microforms; 3,013 current periodicals/subscriptions; 130 computer workstations; has LEXIS, NEXIS, WESTLAW, DIALOG. Special programs: Pre-Admission Summer Program; summer study abroad at Trinity College, University of Dublin, Ireland; externships.

Annual tuition: full-time $19,323, part-time $16,175. No on-campus housing available. Law students live off-campus. Contact Office of Residential Life for off-campus information. Phone: (203)281-8666. Off-campus housing and personal expenses: approximately $13,075. Additional costs: books approximately $750.

Enrollment: first-year class 161 full-time, 74 part-time; total full-time 544, part-time 222 (men 62%, women 38%). First-year statistics: 45% out of state, 31 states and foreign countries represented; 38% women; 12% minority; average age 26; 134 undergraduate institutions represented; range of first-year section sizes 20–80 students; number of upper division courses offered after first year 51 full-time, 47 part-time.

Faculty: full-time 40, part-time 23; 28% female; 8% minority; student/faculty ratio 21 to 1.

Degrees conferred: J.D., J.D.-M.B.A., J.D.-M.H.A.

RECRUITMENT PRACTICES AND POLICIES. Attends all local and selected national law school forums. Has on-campus informational sessions. School does have diversity program and actively recruits women/minority applicants.

ADMISSION REQUIREMENTS FOR FIRST-YEAR APPLICANTS. LSDAS law school report, LSAT (not later than February test date, if more than one LSAT, highest is used), bachelor's degree from an accredited institution, personal statement, transcripts (must show all schools attended and at least three years of study) required in support of application. Two letters of recommendation suggested but not required. Applicants must have received bachelor's degree prior to enrollment. Interview not required but may be requested by school. In addition, international applicants whose native language is not English must submit TOEFL (not older than two years). Joint-degree applicants must apply to and be accepted by both schools. Apply to Office of Admission after September 30, no formal deadlines, early applications encouraged. First-year full-time students admitted fall only, part-time applicants admitted both fall and spring (spring entrance allows students to start and take summer

session to catch up to those admitted in fall). Rolling admission process. Application fee $40. Phone: (203)287-3400. Fax: (203)287-3339. E-mail: cadm@quinnipiac.edu.

ADMISSION REQUIREMENTS FOR TRANSFER APPLICANTS. Accepts transfers from other ABA-accredited schools. Admission limited to space available. At least one year of enrollment, dean's letter indicating applicant is in good standing (prefer applicants in the top half of first-year class), LSAT, LSDAS, personal statement regarding reason for transfer, current law school transcript required in support of application. Apply to Admission Office at least six weeks prior to proposed semester of entrance. Admission decision within one month of the receipt of a completed application. Application fee $50. Will consider visiting students.

ADMISSION STANDARDS. Number of full-time applicants 1,703, part-time 325; number accepted 917 full-time, 145 part-time; number enrolled 161 full-time, 74 part-time; median LSAT 153 (75% of class have a score at or above 147 for both full- and part-time); median GPA 2.85 (A = 4) (75% of class have a GPA at or above 2.5 full-time, 2.6 part-time). Attrition rate 5.9%. Gorman rating 2.22; *U.S. News & World Report* ranking is in the fourth tier of all law schools.

FINANCIAL AID. Scholarships, merit scholarships, diversity scholarships, grants-in-aid, private loans, federal loans, and Federal WS available. Apply to school's Financial Aid Office as soon as possible after January 1. Phone: (203)287-3405. E-mail: lawfinaid@quinnipiac.edu. Use FAFSA for all federal programs (Title IV School code #E00545). Also submit Financial Aid Transcript, federal income tax forms. Financial aid notification date is June 1. Approximately 29% (full-time), 19% (part-time) of first-year class received scholarships/grants-in-aid. Approximately 80% of current students receive some form of financial assistance. Average scholarship/grant $6,050 full-time, $5,000 part-time. Average debt after graduation $67,000.

DEGREE REQUIREMENTS. For J.D.: 86 credits (53 required) with a 2.0 (A = 4) GPA, plus completion of upper divisional writing course; 3-year full-time program, 4-year part-time program. Accelerated J.D. with summer course work. For J.D.-M.B.A.: total 107 credits (J.D. 77 credits, M.B.A. 30). For J.D.-M.H.A.: total 107 credits (J.D. 77 credits, M.H.A. 30 credits).

CAREER AND PLACEMENT INFORMATION. About 20–30 employers conducted on-campus interviews. Approximately 50% of graduates are employed in state. More than 56% of graduates are practicing law; 25% are in business; 19% in government; none in academia. Approximately 76% (CT), 70% (NY) of Quinnipiac College's first-time state bar exam takers pass the bar exam; the passage rate for all first-time takers from ABA-approved schools is 78% (CT),78% (NY). Graduates are eligible to take the bar exam in all 50 states.

REGENT UNIVERSITY
Virginia Beach, Virginia 23464-9800
Internet site: http://www.regent.edu

Founded 1977. Private control (Christian Broadcasting Network affiliation). Semester system. Library: 600,000 volumes; 2,000,000 microforms.

University's other graduate colleges/schools: The Graduate School includes the College of Communication and the Arts, Robertson School of Government, School of Counseling and Human Services, School of Divinity, School of Education.

Total university enrollment: 1,500.

School of Law
1000 Regent University Drive
Virginia Beach, Virginia 23464
Phone: (757)579-4040
Internet site: http://www.regent.edu/acad/schlaw
E-mail: lawschool@regent.edu

Established 1986 as the successor to O. W. Coburn School of Law at Oral Roberts University. Located on main campus. ABA approved since 1989. AALS member. Semester system. Full-time, day study only. Law library: 272,000 volumes/microforms; 4,300 current periodicals/subscriptions; 23 computer workstations; has LEXIS, NEXIS, WESTLAW, DIALOG, INFOTRAC, LEGAL-TRAC.

Annual tuition: $14,198. Law students live off-campus. Contact Admissions Office for off-campus information. Off-campus housing and personal expenses: approximately $10,793. Additional costs: books approximately $550.

Enrollment: first-year class 140; total full-time 364 (men 66%, women 34%); no part-time students. First-year statistics: 50% out of state, 35 states and foreign countries represented; 34% women; 9% minority; average age 26; 118 undergraduate institutions represented; average first-year section size 70 students; number of upper division courses offered after first year 57.

Faculty: full-time 21, part-time 13; 30% female; 9% minority; student/faculty ratio 19 to 1.

Degrees conferred: J.D., J.D.-M.B.A., J.D.-M.A. (Communications, Public Policy).

RECRUITMENT PRACTICES AND POLICIES. Attends several national law school forums. Has on-campus informational sessions. School does have diversity program and actively recruits women/minority applicants.

ADMISSION REQUIREMENTS FOR FIRST-YEAR APPLICANTS. LSDAS law school report, LSAT (not later than February test date, if more than one LSAT, highest is used), bachelor's degree from an accredited institution, personal statement, two recommendations, transcripts (must show all schools attended and at least three years of study) required in support of application. Applicants must have received bachelor's degree prior to enrollment. Interview not required but may be requested by school. In addition, international applicants whose native language is not English must submit TOEFL (not older than two years). Joint-degree applications must apply to and be accepted by both schools. Apply to Office of Admission after September 30, before April 1. First-year students admitted fall only. Rolling admission process, notification starts in January and is finished by late May. Application fee $40. Phone: (757)579-4584. E-mail: lawschool@regent.edu.

ADMISSION REQUIREMENTS FOR TRANSFER APPLICANTS. Accepts transfers from other ABA-accredited schools. Admission limited to space available. At least one year of enrollment, dean's letter indicating applicant is in good standing (prefer applicants in the upper half of first-year class), LSAT, LSDAS, personal statement regarding reason for transfer, current law school transcript required in support of application. Apply to Admission Office by June 15. Admission decisions made by mid July. Application fee $40. Will consider visiting students.

ADMISSION STANDARDS. Number of full-time applicants 426; number accepted 230; number enrolled 140; median LSAT 152 (75% of class have a score at or above 140); median GPA 3.00 (A = 4) (75% of class have a GPA at or above 2.62). Attrition rate 5.5%. Gorman Ranking N/A. *U.S. News & World Report* ranking is in the fourth tier of all law schools.

FINANCIAL AID. Scholarships, merit scholarships, minority scholarships, private institutional loans; federal loans and Federal WS offered through university's Financial Aid Office. For scholarships (selection criteria place heavy reliance on LSAT and undergraduate GPA) and all other programs apply to university's Central Financial Aid Office after January 1, before April 1. Submit FAFSA for all federal programs (Title IV School code #030913). Also submit Financial Aid Transcript, federal income tax forms. Approximately 89% of first-year class received scholarships/grants-in-aid. Approximately 90% of current students receive some form of financial assistance. Average scholarship/grant $2,955.

DEGREE REQUIREMENTS. For J.D.: 90 credits (66 required) with a 2.0 (A = 4) GPA, plus completion of upper divisional writing course; 3-year program. For J.D.-master's: 3½- to 4-year program rather than thc usual 4- to 5-year program needed if degrees taken separately.

CAREER AND PLACEMENT INFORMATION. About 12–15 employers conducted on-campus interviews. Approximately 55% of graduates are employed in state. More than 79% of graduates are practicing law; 9% are in business; 10% in government; 2% in academia. Approximately 69% (VA), 60% (FL), 100% (NC) of Regent University's first-time state bar exam takers pass the bar exam; the passage rate for all first-time takers from ABA-approved schools is 77% (VA), 84% (FL), 85% (NC). Graduates are eligible to take the bar exam in all 50 states.

UNIVERSITY OF RICHMOND
Richmond, Virginia 23173
Internet site: http://www.urich.edu

Founded 1830. Located in a suburban area of Richmond, 6 miles W of downtown. Private control (Baptist affiliation). Semester system. Library: 500,000 volumes; 120,000 microforms; 6,000 periodicals/subscriptions; 100 computer workstations.

University's other graduate schools: the Graduate School, The E. Claiborne Robins School of Business.

Total university enrollment: 4,320.

T.C. Williams
School of Law
Richmond, Virginia 23173
Phone: (804)289-8740
Internet site: http://www.urich.edu/~law
E-mail: admissions@uofrlaw.urich.edu

Established 1870. Located on main campus. ABA approved since 1928. AALS member. Semester system. Full-time, day study only. Law library: 249,200 volumes/

microforms; 4,000 current periodicals/subscriptions; 460 computer workstations; has LEXIS, NEXIS, WESTLAW, DIALOG, VUTEXT. Special programs: summer study abroad at Emmanuel College, Cambridge, England; Caracas, Venezuela; D.C. Summer Environmental Internships program; externships.

Annual tuition: $18,170. No on-campus housing available. Law students live off-campus. Contact Admissions Office for off-campus information. Off-campus housing and personal expenses: approximately $10,000. Additional costs: books approximately $900.

Enrollment: first-year class 152; total full-time 473 (men 54%, women 46%); no part-time students. First-year statistics: 38% out of state, 44 states and foreign countries represented; 46% women; 24% minority; average age 25; 175 undergraduate institutions represented; range of first-year section sizes 75–80 students; number of upper division courses offered after first year 94.

Faculty: full-time 25, part-time 65; 45% female; 11% minority; student/faculty ratio 18 to 1.

Degrees conferred: J.D., J.D.-M.B.A., J.D.-M.H.A. (Virginia Commonwealth University), J.D.-M.S.W. (Virginia Commonwealth University), J.D.-M.U.R.P. (Virginia Commonwealth University).

RECRUITMENT PRACTICES AND POLICIES. Attends national law school forums. Has on-campus admission conferences. School does have diversity program and actively recruits women/minority applicants.

ADMISSION REQUIREMENTS FOR FIRST-YEAR APPLICANTS. LSDAS law school report, LSAT (not later than December test date, October test date for Early Application Opportunity Program, if more than one LSAT, highest is used), bachelor's degree from an accredited institution, narrative statement, transcripts (must show all schools attended and at least three years of study) required in support of application. Letters of recommendation are optional. Applicants must have received bachelor's degree prior to enrollment. Interview not required but a Richmond Applicant Video Essay may be requested by school. In addition, international applicants whose native language is not English must submit TOEFL (not older than two years). Dual-degree applicants must apply to and be accepted by both schools. Apply to Office of Admission after September 30, before February 1; January 1 for Early Application Opportunity Program (applicant starts in summer and can complete degree in 2½ years. First-year students admitted fall only. Rolling admission process, notification starts in January and is finished by mid May. School does maintain a waiting list. Application fee $35. Phone: (804)289-8189. E-mail: admissions@uofrlaw.urich.edu.

ADMISSION REQUIREMENTS FOR TRANSFER APPLICANTS. Accepts transfers from other ABA-accredited schools. Admission limited to space available. At least one year of enrollment, dean's letter indicating applicant is in good standing (prefer applicants in the top quarter of first-year class), LSAT, LSDAS, personal statement regarding reason for transfer, undergraduate transcript, two letters of recommendation from current faculty members, current law school transcript required in support of application. Apply to Admission Office by June 1. Admission decisions made by mid July. Application fee $35. Will consider visiting students.

ADMISSION STANDARDS. Number of full-time applicants 1,296; number accepted 542; number enrolled 152; median LSAT 159 (75% of class have a score at or above 156); median GPA 3.09 (A = 4) (75% of class have a GPA at or above 2.85). Attrition rate 1.7%. Gorman rating 2.64; *U.S. News & World Report* ranking is in the second tier of all law schools.

FINANCIAL AID. Scholarships, merit scholarships, minority scholarships, grants-in-aid, private and institutional loans; federal loans and Federal WS offered through university's Financial Aid Office. Assistantships may be available for upper divisional dual-degree candidates. All accepted students are considered for scholarships (the selection process places heavy reliance on LSAT and undergraduate GPA) and all other programs apply after January 1, before February 15 to the university's Financial Aid Officer. Phone: (804)289-8438. Submit FAFSA prior to February 25 to be considered for all federal programs (Title IV School code #003744). Also submit Financial Aid Transcript, federal income tax forms, and university's Supplementary Financial Aid application. Approximately 75% of first-year class received scholarships/grants-in-aid. Approximately 91% of current students receive some form of financial assistance. Average scholarship/grant $3,200.

DEGREE REQUIREMENTS. For J.D.: 86 credits (38 required) with a 2.0 (A = 4) GPA, plus completion of upper divisional writing course, and a professional responsibility course; 3-year program. Accelerated J.D. with summer course work. For J.D.-master's: 4-year program rather than the usual 5-year program needed if two degrees taken separately.

CAREER AND PLACEMENT INFORMATION. About 45–50 employers conducted on-campus interviews. Approximately 76% of graduates are employed in state. More than 74% of graduates are practicing law; 8% are in business; 16% in government; 2% in academia. Approximately 86% of the University of Richmond's first-time state bar exam takers pass the Virginia Bar Exam; Virginia's passage rate for all first-time takers from ABA-approved schools is 77%. Graduates are eligible to take the bar exam in all 50 states.

ROGER WILLIAMS UNIVERSITY
Bristol, Rhode Island 02809
Internet site: http://www.rwu.edu

Founded 1967. Located on a peninsula in Bristol, 20 miles from Providence. Private control. Semester system. Library: 206,000 volumes; 611,500 microforms; 4,087 periodicals/subscriptions; 90 computer workstations.

University has no other graduate colleges/schools.

Total university enrollment: 1,500.

School of Law
Ten Metacom Avenue
Bristol, Rhode Island 02809
Phone: (800)633-2727, (401)254-4500
Internet site: http://www.rwu.edu/law

Established 1992. Located on main campus. ABA approved since 1995. Semester system. Full-time, part-time study. Law library: 175,400 volumes/microforms; 3,022 current periodicals/subscriptions; 40 computer workstations; has LEXIS, NEXIS, WESTLAW, DIALOG.

Annual tuition: full-time $18,080, part-time $13,873; per credit $567. On-campus housing available for both single and married students. Annual on-campus living expenses: $11,970. Contact the university's Housing Office for both on- and off-campus housing information. Law students tend to live off-campus. Off-campus housing and personal expenses: approximately $13,610. Additional costs: books approximately $750.

Enrollment: first-year class 91 full-time, 81 part-time; total full-time 316, part-time 204 (men 53%, women 47%). First-year statistics: 40% out of state, 17 states and foreign countries represented; 47% women; 10% minority; average age 24 full-time, 31 part-time; 90 undergraduate institutions represented; range of first-year section sizes 20–60 students; number of upper division courses offered after first year 40 full-time, 21 part-time.

Faculty: full-time 26, part-time 24; 33% female; 8% minority; student/faculty ratio 18 to 1.

Degrees conferred: J.D., J.D.-M.C.P.

RECRUITMENT PRACTICES AND POLICIES. Attends local and national law school conferences/forums. Has on-campus informational sessions. School does have diversity program and actively recruits women/minority applicants.

ADMISSION REQUIREMENTS FOR FIRST-YEAR APPLICANTS. LSDAS law school report, LSAT (not later than February test date, if more than one LSAT, highest is used), bachelor's degree from an accredited institution, personal statement, résumé, transcripts (must show all schools attended and at least three years of study) required in support of application. Applicants must have received bachelor's degree prior to enrollment. Interview and recommendations not required. Apply to Office of Admission after September 30, before May 15 (priority deadline). First-year students admitted fall only. Rolling admission process, notification starts in January and is finished when class is filled. Application fee $60. Phone: (800)633-2727, (401)254-4555. Fax: (401)254-4516.

ADMISSION REQUIREMENTS FOR TRANSFER APPLICANTS. Accepts transfers from other ABA-accredited schools. Admission limited to space available. At least one year of enrollment, dean's letter indicating applicant is in good standing (prefer applicants in the upper half of first-year class), LSAT, LSDAS, personal statement regarding reason for transfer, undergraduate transcript, current law school transcript required in support of application. Apply to Admission Office by June 15. Admission decisions made by late July. Application fee $60. Will consider visiting students.

ADMISSION STANDARDS. Number of full-time applicants 468 full-time, 172 part-time; number accepted 285 full-time, 106 part-time; number enrolled 91 full-time, 82 part-time; median LSAT 147 (75% of class have a score at or above 143 full-time, 142 part-time); median GPA 3.08 (A = 4) (75% of class have a GPA at or above 2.75 full-time, 2.70 part-time). Attrition rate 4.6%. Gorman Ranking N/A. *U.S. News & World Report* ranking is in the fourth tier of all law schools.

FINANCIAL AID. Scholarships, merit scholarships, minority scholarships, grants-in-aid, institutional loans, federal loans, and Federal WS offered through university's Financial Aid Office. For scholarships (selection criteria place heavy reliance on LSAT and undergraduate GPA)

apply to Admissions Office after January 1, before April 30. Use school's financial aid form. For all other programs apply to the university's Office of Financial Aid. Phone: (401)254-4656. Submit FAFSA for all federal programs (Title IV School code # 003410). Also submit Financial Aid Transcript, federal income tax forms. Approximately 5% (full-time), 2–6% (part-time) of first-year class received scholarships/grants-in-aid. Approximately 77% of current students receive some form of financial assistance. Average scholarship/grant $3,000 for both full- and part-time.

DEGREE REQUIREMENTS. For J.D.: 90 credits (54 required) with a 2.0 (A = 4) GPA, plus completion of upper divisional writing course; 3-year full-time program, 4-year part-time program. For J.D.-M.C.P.: 4-year program rather than the usual 5-year program needed if degrees taken separately.

CAREER AND PLACEMENT INFORMATION. About 5–8 employers conducted on-campus interviews. Approximately 53% of graduates are employed in state. More than 70% of graduates are practicing law; 23% are in business; 7% in government. Approximately 53% of Roger Williams University's first-time state bar exam takers pass the Rhode Island Bar Exam; Rhode Island's passage rate for all first-time takers from ABA-approved schools is 75%. Graduates are eligible to take the bar exam in all 50 states.

RUTGERS, THE STATE UNIVERSITY OF NEW JERSEY
Camden, New Jersey 08102-1401
Internet site: http://www.cam.rutgers.edu

Founded 1926. Located 2 miles E of Philadelphia. Public control. Semester system. Library: 226,700 volumes; 133,000 microforms.

University's other graduate colleges/schools at Camden: Graduate School, School of Business.

Total university enrollment at Camden campus: 5,000.

School of Law
406 Penn Street
Camden, New Jersey 05102
Phone: (609)225-6191
Internet site: http://www-CamLaw.rutgers.edu
E-mail: dcomuso@crab.rutgers.edu

Established 1926. Located on Camden campus. ABA approved since 1951. AALS member. Semester system.

Full-time, part-time study. Law library: 393,700 volumes/microforms; 3,190 current periodicals/subscriptions; 44 computer workstations; has LEXIS, NEXIS, WESTLAW, RLIN, INNOPAC. Special programs: exchange program with University of Graz, Austria; externships.

Annual tuition: resident $10,062, nonresident $14,288; part-time resident $7,940, nonresident $11,500. On-campus housing available for both single and married students. Annual on-campus housing cost: single students $3,582 (room only), married students $7,440. Contact Housing Division for both on- and off-campus housing information. Phone: (609)225-6471. Law students tend to live off-campus. Off-campus housing and personal expenses: approximately $11,295. Additional costs: books approximately $700.

Enrollment: first-year class 192 full-time, 42 part-time; total full-time 610, part-time 164 (men 56%, women 44%). First-year statistics: 31% out of state, 42 states and foreign countries represented; 44% women; 17% minority; average age 27; 230 undergraduate institutions represented; range of first-year section sizes 40–80 students; number of upper division courses offered after first year 58 full-time, 41 part-time.

Faculty: full-time 39, part-time 56; 27% female; 6% minority; student/faculty ratio 23 to 1.

Degrees conferred: J.D., J.D.-M.B.A., J.D.-M.C.R.P., J.D.-M.P.A., J.D.-M.A. (Political Science).

RECRUITMENT PRACTICES AND POLICIES. Attends selected national law school forums. Has on-campus admissions seminar. Tours and campus visits arranged through Student Bar Association. School does have diversity program and actively recruits women/minority applicants.

ADMISSION REQUIREMENTS FOR FIRST-YEAR APPLICANTS. LSDAS law school report, LSAT (not later than February test date, if more than one LSAT, average is used), bachelor's degree from an accredited institution, personal statement, two recommendations, transcripts (must show all schools attended and at least three years of study) required in support of application. Applicants must have received bachelor's degree prior to enrollment. Interview not required. In addition, international applicants whose native language is not English must submit TOEFL (600 minimum), Rutgers Affidavit of Support Form for International Students. Apply to Office of Admission after September 30, before March 1. First-year students admitted fall only. Rolling admission process. Application fee $40. Phone: (800)466-7561, (609)225-6102. E-mail: dcomuso@crab.rutgers.edu.

ADMISSION REQUIREMENTS FOR TRANSFER APPLICANTS. Accepts transfers from other ABA-accredited schools. Admission limited to space available. At least one year of enrollment, dean's letter indicating applicant is in good standing (prefer applicants in the upper third of first-year class), LSAT, LSDAS, personal statement regarding reason for transfer, current law school transcript including rank in class required in support of application. Apply to Admission Office by July 1 (fall), December 1 (spring). Admission decision made within six weeks of receipt of completed application. Application fee $40. Will consider visiting students.

ADMISSION STANDARDS. Number of full- and part-time applicants 1,656; number accepted 742 full- and part-time; number enrolled 192 full-time, 42 part-time; median LSAT 154 (75% of class have a score at or above 151 for both full- and part-time); median GPA 3.18 (A = 4) (75% of class have a GPA at or above 2.95 full-time, 2.71 part-time). Attrition rate 3.6%. Gorman rating 3.69; *U.S. News & World Report* ranking is in the second tier of all law schools.

FINANCIAL AID. Scholarships, merit scholarships, minority scholarships, grants-in-aid, private institutional loans; federal loans and Federal WS offered through university's Financial Aid Office on Camden Campus. For scholarships (selection criteria place heavy reliance on LSAT and undergraduate GPA) apply on admissions application by checking appropriate box and submit by before March 1. Use university's Institutional Aid Form. For all other programs apply to Office of Financial Aid. Phone: (609)225-6039. Submit FAFSA for all federal programs (Title IV School code #004741). Also submit Financial Aid Transcript, federal income tax forms. Approximately 9% (full-time), 4% (part-time) of first-year class received scholarships/grants-in-aid. Approximately 75% of current students receive some form of financial assistance. Average scholarship/grant $2,250 full-time, $1,500 part-time. Average debt after graduation $45,700.

DEGREE REQUIREMENTS. For J.D.: 84 credits (34 required) with a 2.0 (A = 4) GPA, plus completion of upper divisional writing course and course on professional responsibility; 3-year full-time program, 4-year part-time program. Accelerated J.D. with 1 summer of course work. For J.D.-master's: 4-year program rather than the usual 5-year program needed if degrees taken separately.

CAREER AND PLACEMENT INFORMATION. About 150–155 employers conducted on-campus interviews.

Approximately 60% of graduates are employed in state. More than 72% of graduates are practicing law; 14% are in business; 11% in government; 3% in academia. Approximately 76% (NJ), 68% (PA) of Rutgers' first-time state bar exam takers pass the bar exam; the passage rate for all first-time takers from ABA-approved schools is 78% (NJ), 73% (PA). Graduates are eligible to take the bar exam in all 50 states.

RUTGERS, THE STATE UNIVERSITY OF NEW JERSEY, NEWARK

Newark, New Jersey 07102-3192
Internet site: http://www.rutgers.edu

Founded 1901. Located 8 miles S of New York City. Public control. Semester system. Library: 260,000 volumes/microforms.

University's other graduate colleges/schools at Newark: Graduate School, Graduate School of Management.

Total university enrollment at Newark campus: 4,000.

School of Law

S.I. Newhouse Center for Law and Justice
15 Washington Street
Newark, New Jersey 07102-3192
Phone: (201)648-5561
Internet site: http://www.rutgers.edu/RUSLN
E-mail: geddis@andromeda.rutgers.edu

Established 1908, the oldest law school in New Jersey. Located on Newark campus. ABA approved since 1941. AALS member. Semester system. Full-time, part-time study. Law library: 415,200 volumes/microforms; 3,065 current periodicals/subscriptions; 47 computer workstations; has LEXIS, NEXIS, WESTLAW, CALI, OCLC; is a Federal and New Jersey Government Depository.

Annual tuition: resident $10,037, nonresident $14,263; part-time resident $6,436, nonresident $9,284. On-campus housing available for both single and married students. Annual on-campus living expenses: $9,688. Contact Division of Housing for both on- and off-campus. Phone: (908)935-1002. Law students tend to live off-campus. Off-campus housing and personal expenses: approximately $11,675. Additional costs: books approximately $800.

Enrollment: first-year class 184 full-time, 47 part-time; total full-time 564, part-time 224 (men 56%, women 44%). First-year statistics: 20% out of state, 18 states and foreign countries represented; 44% women; 32% minority; average age 26 full-time, 33 part-time; 128 undergraduate institutions represented; range of first-year section sizes 60–90 students; number of upper division courses offered after first year 78 full-time, 41 part-time.

Faculty: full-time 39, part-time 41; 31% female; 16% minority; student/faculty ratio 19 to 1.

Degrees conferred: J.D., J.D.-M.A. (Criminal Justice, Political Science), J.D.-M.C.R.P.

RECRUITMENT PRACTICES AND POLICIES. Attends selected national law school forums. Has on-campus informational sessions. School does have diversity program and actively recruits women/minority applicants.

ADMISSION REQUIREMENTS FOR FIRST-YEAR APPLICANTS. LSDAS law school report, LSAT (not later than February test date, if more than one LSAT, average is used), bachelor's degree from an accredited institution, personal statement, two recommendations, transcripts (must show all schools attended and at least three years of study) required in support of application. Applicants must have received bachelor's degree prior to enrollment. Interview not required but may be requested by school. In addition, international applicants whose native language is not English must submit TOEFL (not older than two years), Rutgers Affidavit of Support Form for International Students. Apply to Office of Admission after September 30, before March 15. Joint-degree applicants must apply to and be accepted by both schools. First-year students admitted fall only. Rolling admission process. Application fee $40. Phone: (201)648-5557. E-mail: geddis@andromeda.rutgers.edu.

ADMISSION REQUIREMENTS FOR TRANSFER APPLICANTS. Accepts transfers from other ABA-accredited schools. Admission limited to space available. At least one year of enrollment, dean's letter indicating applicant is in good standing (prefer applicants in the upper third of first-year class), LSAT, LSDAS, personal statement regarding reason for transfer, two letters of recommendation, undergraduate transcripts, current law school transcript with rank-in-class required in support of application. Apply to Admission Office by July 1 (fall), December 1 (spring). Admission decision made within six weeks of receipt of completed application. Application fee $40. Will consider visiting students.

ADMISSION STANDARDS. Number of full-time applicants 2,324 full-time, 354 part-time; number accepted 587 full-time, 105 part-time; number enrolled 184 full-time, 47 part-time; median LSAT 157 (75% of class have a score at or above 151 for both full- and part-time); median GPA 3.30 (A = 4) (75% of class have a GPA at or above 3.14 for both full- and part-time). Attrition rate 4%. Gorman rating 3.73; *U.S. News & World Report* ranking is in the second tier of all law schools.

FINANCIAL AID. Scholarships, merit scholarships, minority scholarships, graduate law fellowships, grants-in-aid, institutional loans; federal loans and Federal WS offered through university's Financial Aid Office on the Newark campus. Assistantships may be available for upper divisional joint-degree candidates. For scholarships (selection criteria place heavy reliance on LSAT and undergraduate GPA) apply on admissions application before March 1 by checking the appropriate box. Use Rutgers Institutional Aid Form. For all other programs on Newark campus apply to Office of Financial Aid. Submit FAFSA for all federal programs (Title IV School code #002631). Also submit Financial Aid Transcript, federal income tax forms. Approximately 18% (full-time), 13% (part-time) of first-year class received scholarships/grants-in-aid. Approximately 45% of current students receive some form of financial assistance. Average scholarship/grant $1,500 full-time, $1,500 part-time. Average debt after graduation $49,700.

DEGREE REQUIREMENTS. For J.D.: 84 credits (32 required) with a 2.0 (A = 4) GPA, plus completion of upper divisional writing course and course in professional responsibility; 3-year full-time program, 4-year part-time program. Accelerated J.D. with 1 summer of course work. For J.D.-master's: 4-year program rather than the usual 5-year program needed if degrees taken separately.

CAREER AND PLACEMENT INFORMATION. About 60–70 employers conducted on-campus interviews. Approximately 73% of graduates are employed in state. More than 67% of graduates are practicing law; 27% are in business; 4% in government; 2% in academia. Approximately 75% of Rutgers' first-time state bar exam takers pass the New Jersey Bar Exam; New Jersey's passage rate for all first-time takers from ABA-approved schools is 78%. Graduates are eligible to take the bar exam in all 50 states.

ST. JOHN'S UNIVERSITY
Jamaica, New York 11439
Internet site: http://www.stjohns.edu

Founded 1870. Located in central Queens. Private control (Roman Catholic—St. Augustine affiliation).

Semester system. Library: 1,202,300 volumes; 2,460,600 microforms; 15,171 periodicals/subscriptions; 154 computer workstations.

University's other graduate colleges/schools: College of Business, College of Pharmacy and Allied Health Professions, Graduate School of Arts and sciences, School of Education.

Total university enrollment: 17,400.

School of Law
8000 Utopia Parkway
Jamaica, New York 11439
Phone: (718)990-6600
Internet site: http://www.stjohns.edu/law

Established 1925. Located on Jamaica campus. ABA approved since 1937. AALS member. Semester system. Full-time, part-time study. Law library: 452,100 volumes/microforms; 5,477 current periodicals/subscriptions; 60 computer workstations; has LEXIS, NEXIS, WESTLAW, DIALOG; is a Federal Government Depository.

Annual tuition: full-time $21,000, part-time $15,750. No on-campus housing available. Law students live off-campus. Contact Office of Student Life for off-campus information. Phone: (718)990-6161, Ext. 6573. Off-campus housing and personal expenses: approximately $12,740. Additional costs: books approximately $700.

Enrollment: first-year class 348 full-time, 77 part-time; total full-time 854, part-time 282 (men 63%, women 37%). First-year statistics: 20% out of state, 37% women; 26% minority; average age 26; 118 undergraduate institutions represented; range of first-year section sizes 40–80 students; number of upper division courses offered after first year 73, full-time 48 part-time.

Faculty: full-time 56, part-time 20; 26% female; 19% minority; student/faculty ratio 18 to 1.

Degrees conferred: J.D., J.D.-M.B.A., J.D.-M.A. (Government and Politics).

RECRUITMENT PRACTICES AND POLICIES. Attends selected local and national law school forums. Has on-campus informational sessions. School does have diversity program and actively recruits women/minority applicants.

ADMISSION REQUIREMENTS FOR FIRST-YEAR APPLICANTS. LSDAS law school report, LSAT (not later than December [fall], June [spring] test date, if more than one LSAT, average is used), bachelor's degree from an accredited institution, personal statement, two recommendations, transcripts (must show all schools attended and at least three years of study) required in support of application. Applicants must have received bachelor's degree prior to enrollment. Interview not required but may be requested by school. In addition, international applicants whose native language is not English must submit TOEFL (not older than two years). Apply to Office of Admission after September 30, before March 1 (fall), November 1 (spring). First-year students admitted fall and spring. Rolling admission process. Application fee $50. Phone: (718)990-6611.

ADMISSION REQUIREMENTS FOR TRANSFER APPLICANTS. Accepts transfers from other ABA-accredited schools. Admission limited to space available. At least one year of enrollment, dean's letter indicating applicant is in good standing (prefer applicants in the top quarter of first-year class), LSAT, LSDAS, personal statement regarding reason for transfer, current law school transcript required in support of application. Apply to Admission Office by July 1 (fall), December 1 (spring). Admission decision made within one month from date of the receipt of the completed application. Application fee $50. Will consider visiting students.

ADMISSION STANDARDS. Number of full-time applicants 2,026, part-time 446; number accepted 1,033 full-time, 180 part-time; number enrolled 348 full-time, 77 part-time; median LSAT 155 (75% of class have a score at or above 152 full-time, 151 part-time); median GPA 3.05 (A = 4) (75% of class have a GPA at or above 2.71 full-time, 2.64 part-time). Attrition rate 4.2%. Gorman rating 3.64; *U.S. News & World Report* ranking is in the third tier of all law schools.

FINANCIAL AID. St. Thomas Moore Scholarships, University Scholarship, Law School Scholarships, minority scholarships, private and institutional loans; federal loans and Federal WS offered through university's Financial Aid Office. Assistantships may be available for upper divisional joint-degree candidates. For scholarships (selection criteria place heavy reliance on LSAT and undergraduate GPA) apply to the school's Office of Financial Aid before April 1. For all other programs apply to university's Office of Financial Aid. Phone: (718)990-6403. Submit FAFSA for all federal programs (Title IV School code #002823). Also submit Financial Aid Transcript, federal income tax forms. Approximately 31% (full-time), 24% (part-time) of first-year class received scholarships. Approximately 88% of current students receive some form of financial assistance. Average scholarship/grant $5,000 (full-time), $4,000 (part-time).

DEGREE REQUIREMENTS. For J.D.: 85 credits (61 required) with a 2.0 (A = 4) GPA, plus completion of upper divisional writing course; 3-year full-time program, 4-year part-time program. For J.D.-master's: 3½- or 4-year program rather than the usual 5-year programs needed if degrees taken separately.

CAREER AND PLACEMENT INFORMATION. About 50–60 employers conducted on-campus interviews. Approximately 88% of graduates are employed in state. More than 64% of graduates are practicing law; 14% are in business; 22% in government. Approximately 84% of St. John's University's first-time state bar exam takers pass the New York Bar Exam; New York's passage rate for all first-time takers from ABA-approved schools is 78%. Graduates are eligible to take the bar exam in all 50 states.

ST. LOUIS UNIVERSITY
St. Louis, Missouri 63103-2097
Internet site: http://www.slu.edu

Founded 1818, received charter in 1832, and became first university west of the Mississippi. Located in midtown St. Louis. Private control (Roman Catholic—Jesuit affiliation). Semester system. Library: 1,460,000 volumes; 1,100,000 microforms; 12,800 periodicals/subscriptions.

University's other graduate colleges/schools: College of Arts and Sciences, School of Allied Health Professions, School of Nursing, School of Public Health, School of Social Services, Institute for Leadership and Public Service, School of Business Administration, School of Medicine.

Total university enrollment: 11,200.

School of Law
3700 Lindell Boulevard
St. Louis, Missouri 63108
Phone: (614)977-2766
Internet site: http://www.lawlib.slu.edu/home/htm
E-mail: admissions@lawlib.slu.edu

Established 1842. Located on main campus. ABA approved since 1924. AALS member. Semester system. Full-time, part-time study. Law library: 487,300 volumes/microforms; 6,253 current periodicals/subscriptions; 66 computer workstations; has LEXIS, NEXIS, WESTLAW, DIALOG; is a Federal Government Depository. Special facilities: Center for Health Law Studies, Center for International and Comparative Law, Wefel Center for Employment Law. Special programs: Summer Institute; externships; faculty exchange programs with Sichuan

University in the People's Republic of China, Ruhr University in Bochum, Germany, University of Warsaw, Poland.

Annual tuition: full-time $18,205, part-time $13,580. On-campus housing available for both single and married students. Annual on-campus housing cost: single students $3,030 (room only), $5,790 (room and board), married students $5,000. Housing deadline June 1. Contact Office of Housing for both on- and off-campus housing information. Phone: (314)977-2797. Law students generally live off-campus. Off-campus housing and personal expenses: approximately $9,700. Additional costs: books approximately $700.

Enrollment: first-year class 179 full-time, 77 part-time; total full-time 551, part-time 256 (men 56%, women 44%). First-year statistics: 43% out of state, 43 states and foreign countries represented; 44% women; 18% minority; average age 27; 125 undergraduate institutions represented; range of first-year section sizes 30–90 students; number of upper division courses offered after first year 100 full-time, 28 part-time.

Faculty: full-time 44, part-time 15; 21% female; 4% minority; student/faculty ratio 20 to 1.

Degrees conferred: J.D., J.D.-M.B.A., J.D.-M.H.A., J.D.-M.A. (Public Affairs, Urban Affairs), LL.M. (Health Law, Employment Law), LL.M. (American Law–for foreign lawyers who have completed a basic legal education and received a university degree in law in another country).

RECRUITMENT PRACTICES AND POLICIES. Attends many local and national law school forums. Has on-campus informational sessions. School does have diversity program and actively recruits women/minority applicants.

ADMISSION REQUIREMENTS FOR FIRST-YEAR APPLICANTS. LSDAS law school report, LSAT (not later than December test date, if more than one LSAT, average is used), bachelor's degree from an accredited institution, two recommendations, transcripts (must show all schools attended and at least three years of study) required in support of application. Personal statements optional but strongly recommended. Applicants must have received bachelor's degree prior to enrollment. Interview not required but may be requested by school. In addition, international applicants whose native language is not English must submit TOEFL (not older than two years), certified translation and evaluation of all foreign transcripts. Apply to Office of Admission after September 1, before March 1 (preferential deadline). First-year students

admitted fall only. Rolling admission process, notification starts in January and is finished by June. Acceptance of offer and first deposit due April 15. Application fee $40. Phone: (314)977-2800. E-mail: admissions@lawlib.slu.edu.

ADMISSION REQUIREMENTS FOR TRANSFER APPLICANTS. Accepts transfers from other ABA-accredited schools. Admission limited to space available. At least one year of enrollment, dean's letter indicating applicant is in good standing (prefer applicants in the top quarter of first-year class), LSAT, LSDAS, personal statement regarding reason for transfer, current official law school transcript with rank-in-class included required in support of application. Apply to Admission Office by June 30. Admission decision made within one month from the receipt of a completed application. Application fee $40. Will consider visiting students.

ADMISSION REQUIREMENTS FOR LL.M. (Health, Employment Law). Applicants must have a J.D. from an ABA/AALS accredited/approved law school. Official transcripts from undergraduate, graduate, and law schools, résumé/curriculum vitae, two letters of recommendation, personal statement including interest and career goals required in support of graduate application. Admits fall only. Apply by May 1 to the School of Law—Graduate Programs. Phone: (314)977-3067. Approximately five students accepted each year. Web site: http://www.lawlib.slu.edu.

ADMISSION REQUIREMENTS FOR LL.M. (foreign lawyers). Applicants must have a degree in law from a foreign university. Certified translations and evaluations of all foreign academic credentials, TOEFL (for those whose native language is not English, minimum score required 575), two letters of recommendation, personal statement including interests and career goals, résumé/curriculum vitae required in support of application. Admits fall only. Apply by May 1 to School of Law—Graduate programs. Phone: (314)977-3067.

ADMISSION STANDARDS. Number of full-time applicants 970 full-time, 171 part-time; number accepted 511 full-time, 106 part-time; number enrolled 179 full-time, 77 part-time; median LSAT 155 (75% of class have a score at or above 149 for both full- and part-time); median GPA 3.30 (A = 4) (75% of class have a GPA at or above 3.12 full-time, 2.73 part-time). Attrition rate 2.5%. Gorman rating 3.65; *U.S. News & World Report* ranking is in the second tier of all law schools.

FINANCIAL AID. Academic scholarships, grants-in-aid, private and institutional loans; federal loans and Federal WS offered through university's Financial Aid Office. Assistantships may be available for upper divisional joint-degree candidates. For scholarships (selection criteria place heavy reliance on LSAT and undergraduate GPA) apply to Admissions Office before March 1. For all other programs apply after January 1, before April 1 to the university's Financial Aid Office. Phone: (314)977-2350. Fax: (314)977-3437. Submit FAFSA for all federal programs (Title IV School code #002506). Also submit Financial Aid Transcript, federal income tax forms. Approximately 60% (full-time), 28% (part-time) of first-year class received scholarships/grants-in-aid. Approximately 85% of current students receive some form of financial assistance. Average scholarship/grant $4,000 full-time, $3,000 part-time.

DEGREE REQUIREMENTS. For J.D.: 88 credits (36 required) with a 2.0 (A = 4) GPA, plus completion of upper divisional writing course; 3-year full-time program, 4-year part-time program. Accelerated J.D. with summer course work. For J.D.-master's: 4-year program rather than the usual 5-year program needed if degrees taken separately. For LL.M. (Health Law, Employment Law): 24 credits completed over 2 years, full- and part-time study; thesis of publishable quality; oral defense. For LL.M. (Foreign Lawyers): 24 credits; at least 2 semesters in residence; thesis of publishable quality; oral defense.

CAREER AND PLACEMENT INFORMATION. About 40–50 employers conducted on-campus interviews. Approximately 87% of graduates are employed in state. More than 64% of graduates are practicing law; 21% are in business; 12% in government; 3% in academia. Approximately 88% (MO), 70% (IL) of St. Louis University's first-time state bar exam takers pass the bar exam; the passage rate for all first-time takers from ABA-approved schools is 92% (MO), 87% (IL). Graduates are eligible to take the bar exam in all 50 states.

ST. MARY'S UNIVERSITY OF SAN ANTONIO
San Antonio, Texas 78228-8507
Internet site: http://www.stmarytx.edu

Founded 1852. Private control (Roman Catholic—Society of Mary affiliation). Semester system. Library:

525,000 volumes; 17,000 microforms; 1,400 periodicals/subscriptions; 66 computer workstations.

University's other graduate schools include: the Graduate School, School of Business Administration.

Total university enrollment: 4,000.

School of Law
One Camino Santa Maria
San Antonio, Texas 78228-8602
Phone: (210)436-3424
Internet site: http://www.stmarylaw.edu

Established 1927. Located on main campus. ABA approved since 1948. AALS member. Semester system. Full-time, day study only. Law library: 312,200 volumes/microforms; 3,442 current periodicals/subscriptions; 12 computer workstations; has LEXIS, NEXIS, WESTLAW, DIALOG. Special facilities: Center for Legal and Social Justice, Centre for Conciliation and Arbitration, Center for International Legal Studies, Institute for World Legal Problems in Innsbruch, Austria, Institute for International Human Rights in Guatemala. Special programs: judicial internships.

Annual tuition: J.D. $14,916; LL.M. per credit $523. On-campus housing available for single students only. Annual on-campus housing cost: single students $2,500 (room only), $4,500 (room and board). Contact Housing Office for both on- and off-campus housing information. Phone: (210)436-3534. Law students tend to live off-campus. Off-campus housing and personal expenses: approximately $12,296. Additional costs: books approximately $750.

Enrollment: first-year class 264; total full-time 777 (men 51%, women 49%); no part-time students. First-year statistics: 20% out of state, 38 states and foreign countries represented; 49% women; 36% minority; average age 25; 94 undergraduate institutions represented; average first-year section size 85 students; number of upper division courses offered after first year 159.

Faculty: full-time 34, part-time 26; 30% female; 17% minority; student/faculty ratio 20 to 1.

Degrees conferred: J.D., J.D.-M.B.A., J.D.-M.P.A., J.D.-E.C., J.D.-I.R., J.D.-M.Theo., J.D.-M.C.I.S., LL.M. (International and Comparative Law for U.S. trained attorneys), LL.M. (American Legal Studies—for persons who have completed a basic legal education and received a university degree in law in another country).

RECRUITMENT PRACTICES AND POLICIES. Attends local and national law school forums. Has on-campus informational sessions. School does have

diversity program and actively recruits women/minority applicants.

ADMISSION REQUIREMENTS FOR FIRST-YEAR APPLICANTS. LSDAS law school report, LSAT (not later than February test date, if more than one LSAT, highest is used), bachelor's degree from an accredited institution, personal statement, two recommendations, Application Matching Card (AMC), transcripts (must show all schools attended and at least three years of study) required in support of application. Applicants must have received bachelor's degree prior to enrollment. In addition, international applicants whose native language is not English must submit TOEFL (not older than two years), certified translations and evaluations of all foreign credentials. Apply to Office of Admission after September 30, before March 1. First-year students admitted fall only. Rolling admission process, notification starts in January and is finished by late May. Application fee $45. Phone: (210)436-3523.

ADMISSION REQUIREMENTS FOR TRANSFER APPLICANTS. Accepts transfers from other ABA-accredited schools. Admission limited to space available. At least one year of enrollment, dean's letter indicating applicant is in good standing (prefer applicants in the top half of first-year class), LSAT, LSDAS, personal statement regarding reason for transfer, two letters of recommendation, current law school transcript required in support of application. Apply to Admission Office by June 30. Admission decisions made by early August. Application fee $45. Will consider visiting students.

ADMISSION REQUIREMENTS FOR LL.M. APPLICANTS. All applicants must have earned a law degree from either an ABA-accredited law school or a recognized foreign university. Official transcripts (with certified translations and evaluations along with original credentials), résumé, personal statement, two letters of recommendation required in support of LL.M. application. In addition, applicants for American Legal Studies must submit TOEFL if their native language is not English. Apply by March 31 to Center for International Legal Studies. Phone: (800)468-5529.

ADMISSION STANDARDS. Number of full-time applicants 1,545; number accepted 735; number enrolled 264; median LSAT 153 (75% of class have a score at or above 149); median GPA 2.86 (A = 4) (75% of class have a GPA at or above 2.58). Attrition rate 3.1%. Gorman rating 2.52; *U.S. News & World Report* ranking is in the fourth tier of all law schools.

FINANCIAL AID. Scholarships, minority scholarships, grants-in-aid, private and institutional loans; federal loans and Federal WS offered through university's Financial Aid Office. Assistantships may be available for upper divisional joint-degree candidates. For scholarships (selection criteria place heavy reliance on LSAT and undergraduate GPA) apply to the school's Office of Financial Aid before April 1. For all other programs apply to university's Office of Financial Assistance. Submit FAFSA (not later than February 14) for all federal programs (Title IV School code #003623). Also submit Financial Aid Transcript, federal income tax forms. Approximately 34% of first-year class received scholarships/grants-in-aid. Approximately 80% of current students receive some form of financial assistance. Average scholarship/grant $700. Average debt after graduation $60,000.

DEGREE REQUIREMENTS. For J.D.: 90 credits (46 required) with a a 2.0 (A = 4) GPA, plus completion of upper divisional writing course; 3-year program. Accelerated J.D. with summer course work. For J.D.-masters: 4-year program rather than the usual 5-year program needed if degrees taken separately. For LL.M. (International and Comparative Law): 24 credits, at least 2 semesters in full-time residence; thesis of publishable quality. For LL.M. (American Legal Studies): 24 credits; at least 2 semesters in full-time residence; 3 required courses in U.S. legal system; thesis of publishable quality.

CAREER AND PLACEMENT INFORMATION. About 35–40 employers conducted on-campus interviews. Approximately 87% of graduates are employed in state. More than 78% of graduates are practicing law; 9% are in business; 13% in government. Approximately 80% of St. Mary's University of San Antonio's first-time state bar exam takers pass the Texas Bar Exam; Texas' passage rate for all first-time takers from ABA-approved schools is 82%. Graduates are eligible to take the bar exam in all 50 states.

ST. THOMAS UNIVERSITY
Miami, Florida 33054-6459
Internet site: http://www.stu.edu

Founded 1966. Private control (Roman Catholic affiliation). Semester system. Library: 140,000 volumes; 190,000 microforms; 990 periodicals/subscriptions; 45 computer workstations.

University's School of Graduate Studies includes the Department of Arts and Sciences, Department of Business.

Total university enrollment: 2,500.

School of Law
16400 N.W. 32nd Avenue
Miami, Florida 33504
Phone: (305)623-2320
Internet site: http://www.law.stu.edu

Established 1984. Located on main campus. ABA approved since 1988. AALS member. Semester system. Full-time, day study only. Law library: 247,300 volumes/microforms; 1,725 current periodicals/subscriptions; 63 computer workstations; has LEXIS, NEXIS, WESTLAW, DIALOG.

Annual tuition: $18,985. On-campus housing available for single students only. Annual on-campus housing cost: single students $4,000 (room and board). Housing deadline July 1. Contact university's Housing Office for both on- and off-campus housing information. Phone: (305)628-6692. Law students generally live off-campus. Off-campus housing and personal expenses: approximately $14,120. Additional costs: books approximately $800.

Enrollment: first-year class 217; total full-time 531 (men 63%, women 37%); no part-time students. First-year statistics: 25% out of state, 24 states and foreign countries represented; 37% women; 33% minority; average age 25; 105 undergraduate institutions represented; range of first-year section sizes 30–60 students; number of upper division courses offered after first year 101.

Faculty: full-time 33, part-time 26; 29% female; 16% minority; student/faculty ratio 23 to 1.

Degree conferred: J.D.

RECRUITMENT PRACTICES AND POLICIES. Attends local and selected national law school forums. Has on-campus informational sessions. School does have diversity program and actively recruits women/minority applicants.

ADMISSION REQUIREMENTS FOR FIRST-YEAR APPLICANTS. LSDAS law school report, LSAT (not later than February test date, if more than one LSAT, average is used), bachelor's degree from an accredited institution, personal statement, one recommendation, transcripts (must show all schools attended and at least three years of study) required in support of application. Applicants must have received bachelor's degree prior to enrollment. Interview not required but may be requested by school. Apply to Office of Admission after September 30, before April 30. First-year students admitted fall only. Rolling admission process. Application fee $40. Phone: (305)623-2310.

ADMISSION REQUIREMENTS FOR TRANSFER APPLICANTS. Accepts transfers from other ABA-accredited schools. Admission limited to space available. At least one year of enrollment, dean's letter indicating applicant is in good standing (prefer applicants in the upper half of first-year class), LSAT, LSDAS, personal statement regarding reason for transfer, undergraduate transcript, one letter of recommendation, current law school transcript required in support of application. Apply to Admission Office by June 30. Admission decision made by early August. Application fee $40. Will consider visiting students.

ADMISSION STANDARDS. Number of full-time applicants 1,338; number accepted 782; number enrolled 217; median LSAT 148 (75% of class have a score at or above 145); median GPA 2.70 (A = 4) (75% of class have a GPA at or above 2.37). Attrition rate 10%. Gorman Ranking N/A. *U.S. News & World Report* ranking is in the fourth tier of all law schools.

FINANCIAL AID. Scholarships, minority scholarships, grants-in-aid, private and institutional loans; federal loans and Federal WS offered through university's Financial Aid Office. For scholarships/grants (selection criteria place heavy reliance on LSAT and undergraduate GPA) apply to the Financial Aid Office before March 1 (priority deadline). For all other programs apply to University's Financial Aid Office. Phone: (305)628-6547. Submit FAFSA for all federal programs (Title IV School code # 001468). Also submit Financial Aid Transcript, federal income tax forms. Approximately 25% of first-year class received scholarships/grants-in-aid. Approximately 93% of current students receive some form of financial assistance. Average scholarship/grant $4,500.

DEGREE REQUIREMENTS. For J.D.: 90 credits (49 required) with a a 2.0 (A = 4) GPA, plus completion of upper divisional writing course; 3-year program.

CAREER AND PLACEMENT INFORMATION. About 30–35 employers conducted on-campus interviews. Approximately 80% of graduates are employed in state. More than 77% of graduates are practicing law; 10% are in business; 13% in government. Approximately 79% of St. Thomas University's first-time state bar exam takers pass the Florida Bar Exam; Florida's passage rate for all first-time takers from ABA-approved schools is 84%. Graduates are eligible to take the bar exam in all 50 states.

SAMFORD UNIVERSITY

Birmingham, Alabama 35229-0002
Internet site: http://www.samford.edu

Founded 1941. Private control (Baptist affiliation). Semester system. Library: 523,000 volumes; 308,000 microforms; 5,087 periodicals/subscriptions; 71 computer workstations.

University's other graduate colleges/schools: Beeson School of Divinity, Howard College of Arts and Sciences, Ida V. Moffett School of Nursing, McWorter School of Pharmacy, School of Business, School of Education, School of Music.

Total university enrollment: 4,300.

School of Law

800 Lakeshore Drive
Birmingham, Alabama 35229
Phone: (205)870-2701
Internet site: http://www.samford.edu/schools/law
E-mail: msdavis@samford.edu

Established 1847, acquired by Samford University in 1961. Located on main campus. ABA approved since 1949. AALS member. Semester system. Full-time, day study only. Law library: 232,800 volumes/microforms; 2,300 current periodicals/subscriptions; 28 computer workstations; has LEXIS, NEXIS, WESTLAW, LEGAL-TRAC; is a United Nations Document Depository. Special programs: summer study abroad at University of Durham, England, the University of Victoria, British Columbia; externships.

Annual tuition: $17,700. No on-campus housing available. Law students live off-campus. Contact Office of Residence Life for off-campus housing information. Phone: (205)870-2956. Off-campus housing and personal expenses: approximately $11,089. Additional costs: books approximately $700.

Enrollment: first-year class 214; total full-time 598 (men 65%, women 35%); no part-time students. First-year statistics: 50% out of state, 28 states and foreign countries represented; 35% women; 8% minority; average age 24; 28 undergraduate institutions represented; range of first-year section sizes 5–80 students; number of upper division courses offered after first year 68.

Faculty: full-time 34, part-time 23; 18% female; 14% minority; student/faculty ratio 20 to 1.

Degrees conferred: J.D., J.D.-M.Acc., J.D.-M.A.E. (University of Alabama, Birmingham), J.D.-M.B.A., J.D.-M.P.A., J.D.-M.P.H. (University of Alabama, Birmingham), J.D.-M.S. (Environmental Management), J.D.-M.Div.

RECRUITMENT PRACTICES AND POLICIES. Attends selected local and national law school forums. Has on-campus informational sessions. School does have diversity program and actively recruits women/minority applicants.

ADMISSION REQUIREMENTS FOR FIRST-YEAR APPLICANTS. LSDAS law school report, LSAT (not later than February test date, if more than one LSAT, average is used), bachelor's degree from an accredited institution, personal statement, two recommendations (one from either a clergy or member of community), transcripts (must show all schools attended and at least three years of study) required in support of application. Applicants must have received bachelor's degree prior to enrollment. Interview not required but may be requested by school. Joint-degree applicants must apply to and be accepted by both schools. Apply to Admission Office after October 1, before May 1 (February 28 priority deadline). First-year students admitted fall only. Rolling admission process, notification starts in January and is finished by mid June. Acceptance of offer and first deposit due April 1. Application fee $40. Phone: (800)888-7213. E-mail: msdavis@samford.edu.

ADMISSION REQUIREMENTS FOR TRANSFER APPLICANTS. Accepts transfers from other ABA-accredited schools. Admission limited to space available. At least one year of enrollment, dean's letter indicating applicant is in good standing (prefer applicants in the top half of first-year class), LSAT, LSDAS, personal statement regarding reason for transfer, two recommendations, undergraduate transcript, current law school transcript required in support of application. Apply to Admission Office by July 1. Admission decisions made by early August. Application fee $40. Will consider visiting students.

ADMISSION STANDARDS. Number of full-time applicants 1,030; number accepted 591; number enrolled 214; median LSAT 153 (75% of class have a score at or above 150); median GPA 3.00 (A = 4) (75% of class have a GPA at or above 2.81). Attrition rate 3.8%. Gorman rating 2.70; *U.S. News & World Report* ranking is in the fourth tier of all law schools.

FINANCIAL AID. Scholarships, merit scholarships, grants-in-aid, institutional loans; federal loans and Federal WS offered through university's Financial Aid Office. Assistantships may be available for upper divisional joint-degree candidates. All accepted students are automatically considered for all scholarships (selection criteria place heavy reliance on LSAT and undergraduate GPA). Apply after January 1, before March 1 to the university's Financial Aid Office for all other programs. Submit FAFSA for all federal programs (Title IV School code #001036). Also submit Financial Aid Transcript, federal income tax forms. Approximately 26% of first-year class received scholarships/grants-in-aid. Approximately 85% of current students receive some form of financial assistance. Average scholarship/grant $7,000.

DEGREE REQUIREMENTS. For J.D.: 90 credits (53 required) with a 2.0 (A = 4) GPA, plus completion of upper divisional writing course; 3-year program. Accelerated J.D. with summer course work. For J.D.-master's: 4- or 4½-year program rather than the usual 5- or 5½-year program if degrees taken separately.

CAREER AND PLACEMENT INFORMATION. About 20–25 employers conducted on-campus interviews. Approximately 52% of graduates are employed in state. More than 80% of graduates are practicing law; 5% are in business; 15% in government. Approximately 94% of Samford University's first-time state bar exam takers pass the Alabama Bar Exam; Alabama's passage rate for all first-time takers from ABA-approved schools is 90%. Graduates are eligible to take the bar exam in all 50 states.

UNIVERSITY OF SAN DIEGO
San Diego, California 92110-2492
Internet site: http://www.acusd.edu

Founded 1949. Located approximately 5 miles N of downtown. Private control (Roman Catholic affiliation). Semester system. Library: 828,000 volumes; 1,036,550 microforms; 7,640 periodicals/subscriptions.

University's other schools of graduate colleges/schools: College of Arts and Sciences, Philip Y. Hahn School of Nursing, School of Business Administration, School of Education.

Total university enrollment: 6,400.

School of Law
5998 Alcala Park
San Diego, California 92110-2492
Phone: (619)260-4527
Internet site: http://www.acusd.edu/~usdlaw
E-mail: jdinfo@acusd.edu

Established 1954. Located on main campus. ABA approved since 1961. AALS member. Semester system. Full-time, part-time study. Law library: 394,800 volumes/microforms; 5,182 current periodicals/subscriptions; 28 computer workstations; has LEXIS, NEXIS, WESTLAW, LEGALTRAC, CALI. Special facilities: Institute of International and Comparative Law, Research and Advocacy Institute.

Annual tuition: full-time $19,980, part-time $14,180. On-campus housing available for both single and married students. Annual on-campus apartment cost: $6,880 (room and board). Housing deadline May 1. Contact Resident Life Office for both on- and off-campus housing information. Phone: (619)260-4624. Law students tend to live off-campus. Off-campus housing and personal expenses: approximately $12,538. Additional costs: books approximately $700.

Enrollment: first-year class full-time 225, part-time 85; total full-time 751, part-time 329 (men 60%, women 40%). First-year statistics: 20% out of state, 35 states and 10 foreign countries represented; 40% women; 23% minority; average age 24; 160 undergraduate institutions represented; range of first-year section sizes 20–85 students; number of upper division courses offered after first year 75 full-time, 50 part-time.

Faculty: full-time 60, part-time 40; 34% female; 12% minority; student/faculty ratio 14.5 to 1.

Degrees conferred: J.D., J.D.-M.B.A., J.D.-M.I.B.A., J.D.-M.A. (International Relations), J.D.-LL.M., LL.M. (General, Tax), LL.M. (International Law—for persons who have completed a basic legal education and received a university degree in law in another country).

RECRUITMENT PRACTICES AND POLICIES. Attends local and national law school forums. Has on-campus informational sessions. School does have diversity program and actively recruits women/minority applicants.

ADMISSION REQUIREMENTS FOR FIRST-YEAR APPLICANTS. LSDAS law school report, LSAT (not later than February test date, if more than one LSAT, average is used), bachelor's degree from an accredited institution, personal statement, two recommendations, transcripts (must show all schools attended and at least three years of study) required in support of application. Applicants must have received bachelor's degree prior to enrollment. Interview not required. Campus visits encouraged. In addition, international applicants whose native language is not English must submit TOEFL (not older than two years), certified translations and evaluations of all foreign credentials. Joint-degree applicants must apply to and be accepted by both schools. Apply to Office of Admission after September 30, before February 15. First-year students admitted fall only. Rolling admission process, notification starts in January and is finished by late April. Application fee $40. Phone: (619)260-4528. E-mail: jdinfo@acusd.edu.

ADMISSION REQUIREMENTS FOR TRANSFER APPLICANTS. Accepts transfers from other ABA-accredited schools. Admission limited to space available. At least one year of enrollment, dean's letter indicating applicant is in good standing (prefer applicants in the upper third of first-year class), LSAT, LSDAS, personal statement regarding reason for transfer, two recommendations, undergraduate transcript, current law school transcript required in support of application. Apply to Admissions Office by June 30. Admission decision made within one month of the receipt of a completed application. Application fee $40. Will consider visiting students.

ADMISSIONS REQUIREMENTS FOR LL.M. APPLICANTS. All applicants must possess a J.D. or an equivalent foreign law degree. Official transcripts with rank-in-class, résumé, personal statement with rationale for graduate study required in support of graduate application. In addition, international applicants whose native language is not English must submit TOEFL. Admits fall, spring, summer. Apply by May 1 (fall), November 1 (spring), April 1 (summer) to the Office of Graduate Programs. Application fee $40. Phone: (619)260-4596. Notification of admission decision normally begins within six weeks of receipt of completed application.

ADMISSION STANDARDS. Number of full- and part-time applicants 2,932; number accepted 1,014; number enrolled 225 full-time, 85 part-time; median LSAT 159 (75% of class have a score at or above 157 full-time, 154 part-time); median GPA 3.09 (A = 4) (75% of class have a GPA at or above 2.84 full-time, 2.68 part-time). Attrition rate 2.8%. Gorman rating 3.81; *U.S. News & World Report* ranking is in the second tier of all law schools.

FINANCIAL AID. Scholarships, merit scholarships, diversity scholarships, grants-in-aid, private and institutional loans; federal loans and Federal WS offered through university's Financial Aid Office. Assistantships may be available for upper divisional joint-degree candidates. All accepted students are automatically considered for scholarships (selection criteria place heavy reliance on LSAT and undergraduate GPA). Use School of Law Financial Aid application. For all other programs apply to university Office of Financial Aid after January 1, before March 1. Phone: (619)260-4570. Use university's financial aid application. Submit FAFSA for all federal programs (Title IV School code # G06976). Also submit Financial Aid Transcript, federal income tax forms. Approximately 40% (full-time), 21% (part-time) of first-year class received scholarships/grants-in-aid. Approximately 76% of current students receive some form of financial assistance. Average scholarship/grant full-time $11,497, part-time $6,671. Average debt after graduation $55,000.

DEGREE REQUIREMENTS. For J.D.: 85 credits (48 required) with a a 75 (scale 0–100) GPA, plus completion of upper divisional writing course; 3-year full-time program, 4-year part-time program. Accelerated J.D. with 2 summers of course work. For J.D.-master's: 4- to 4½-year programs rather than the usual 5- to 5½-year programs needed if degrees taken separately. For LL.M.: 24 credits, 2 to 3 semesters in full-time residence; 81 (scale 0–100) or better average required. For J.D.-LL.M.: a 3½-year program rather than the usual 4-year program needed if both degrees taken separately. For LL.M. (International): 24 credits; at least 2 to 3 semesters in residence; 81 (scale 0–100) or better average required.

CAREER AND PLACEMENT INFORMATION. About 40–50 employers conducted on-campus interviews. Approximately 84% of graduates are employed in state. More than 76% of graduates are practicing law; 12% are in business; 11% in government; 1% in academia. Approximately 79% of the University of San Diego's first-time state bar exam takers pass the California Bar Exam; California's passage rate for all first-time takers from ABA-approved schools is 83%. Graduates are eligible to take the bar exam in all 50 states.

UNIVERSITY OF SAN FRANCISCO
San Francisco, California 94117-1080
Internet site: http://www.usfca.edu

Founded 1855. Located adjacent to Golden Gate Park. Private control (Roman Catholic—Jesuit affiliation). Semester system. Library: 747,800 volumes; 775,000 microforms; 2,711 periodicals/subscriptions; 60 computer workstations.

University's other graduate colleges/schools: College of Arts and Sciences, College of Professional Studies, McLaren School of Business, School of Education, School of Nursing.

Total university enrollment: 7,400.

School of Law

2130 Fulton Street
San Francisco, California 94117-1080
Phone: (415)422-6304
Internet site: http://www.usfca.edu

Established 1912. Located on main campus. ABA approved since 1935. AALS member. Semester system. Full-time, part-time study. Law library: 272,250 volumes/microforms; 2,355 current periodicals/subscriptions; 41 computer workstations; has LEXIS, NEXIS, WESTLAW, DIALOG, INNOPAC. Special programs: Asian Pacific Legal Studies Program; summer study abroad at Trinity College, Ireland, Charles University, Czech Republic, Nayana University, Bali; judicial externships.

Annual tuition: full-time $20,000; part-time $14,275. On-campus housing available for single students only. Annual on-campus housing cost: single students $4,154 (room only), $6,554 (room and board). Contact Housing Office for both on- and off-campus housing information. Phone: (415)422-6824. Law students tend to live off-campus. Off-campus housing and personal expenses: approximately $12,850. Additional costs: books approximately $700.

Enrollment: first-year class full-time 181, part-time 53; total full-time 556, part-time 135 (men 47%, women 53%). First-year statistics: 13% out of state, 25 states and foreign countries represented; 53% women; 31% minority; average age 24; 95 undergraduate institutions represented; average first-year section sizes full-time 85 students, part-time 45 students; number of upper division courses offered after first year 57 full-time, 44 part-time.

Faculty: full-time 27, part-time 62; 34% female; 20% minority; student/faculty ratio 21.5 to 1.

Degrees conferred: J.D., J.D.-M.B.A., LL.M. (International Transactions and Comparative Law) (for foreign lawyers who have completed a basic legal education and received a university degree in law in another country); full- and part-time study.

RECRUITMENT PRACTICES AND POLICIES. Attends local and selected national law school forums. Has on-campus informational sessions. School does have diversity program and actively recruits women/minority applicants.

ADMISSION REQUIREMENTS FOR FIRST-YEAR APPLICANTS. LSDAS law school report, LSAT (not later than February test date, if more than one LSAT, average is used), bachelor's degree from an accredited institution, personal statement, two recommendations, transcripts (must show all schools attended and at least three years of study) required in support of application. Applicants must have received bachelor's degree prior to enrollment. Interview not required. Campus visits encouraged. In addition, international applicants whose native language is not English must submit TOEFL (not older than two years, minimum score required 600), certified translations and evaluations of all foreign documents. Joint-degree applicants must apply to and be accepted by each school. Apply to Office of Admission after September 1, before April 1; February 15 is the priority deadline. First-year students admitted fall only. Rolling admission process, notification starts in January and is finished by mid May. Application fee: $40. Phone: (415)422-6586.

ADMISSION REQUIREMENTS FOR TRANSFER APPLICANTS. Accepts transfers from other ABA-accredited schools. Admission limited to space available. At least one year of enrollment, dean's letter indicating applicant is in good standing, LSAT, LSDAS, personal statement regarding reason for transfer, two recommendations, undergraduate transcripts, current law school transcript required in support of application. Apply to Admission Office by July 1. Admission decision made within one month of the receipt of a completed application. Application fee $40. Will consider visiting students.

ADMISSION REQUIREMENTS FOR LL.M. APPLICANTS. All applicants must have a first law degree from a foreign university authorized by the government of the country to confer such a degree and be fluent in English. Official transcripts with certified translations and evaluations, two letters of recommendation (if not in English they should be accompanied by an English translation), personal statement (no more than two double-spaced typewritten pages), résumé, evidence of financial support required in support of LL.M. application. In addition, TOEFL (600 minimum score required) is required for those whose native language is not English. Admits fall only. Apply by June 1. Application fee $60. Phone: (415)422-6946. Fax: (415)422-6433. Attn: LL.M. Director. Web site: www.usfca.edu/law/llm. About 25 students admitted each year.

ADMISSION STANDARDS. Number of full-time applicants 2,661, part-time 235; number accepted 1,053 full-time, 198 part-time; number enrolled 181 full-time, 53 part-time; median LSAT 156 (75% of class have a score at or above 154 full-time, 150 part-time); median GPA 3.08 (A = 4) (75% of class have a GPA at or above 2.90 full-time, 2.80 part-time). Attrition rate 6%. Gorman rating 3.80; *U.S. News & World Report* ranking is in the third tier of all law schools.

FINANCIAL AID. Scholarships, merit scholarships, minority scholarships, grants-in-aid, private and institutional loans, State Graduate Fellowships; federal loans and Federal WS offered through university's Financial Aid Office. Assistantships may be available for upper divisional joint-degree candidates. All accepted students are automatically considered for scholarships (selection criteria place heavy reliance on LSAT and undergraduate GPA). Contact the law school's Financial Aid Office for scholarships information. Phone: (415)422-6210. For all other programs apply as soon as possible after January 1 to the university's Financial Aid Office. Phone: (415)333-6303. Submit FAFSA for all federal programs (Title IV School code # 001325). Also submit Financial Aid Transcript, federal income tax forms. Approximately 70% (full-time), 32% (part-time) of first-year class received scholarships/grants-in-aid. Approximately 85% of current students receive some form of financial assistance. Average scholarship/grant $1,400 full-time, $3,000 part-time. Average debt after graduation $50,000. Loan Repayment Assistance Program for Public Interest Law available.

DEGREE REQUIREMENTS. For J.D.: 86 credits (48 required) with a 2.0 (A = 4) GPA, plus completion of upper divisional writing course; 3-year full-time program, 4-year part-time program. Accelerated J.D. with summer course work. For J.D.-M.B.A.: 4-year program rather than the usual 5-year program needed if degrees taken separately. For LL.M.: 25 course units; at least 2 semesters in full-time residence, 4 semesters in part-time residence.

CAREER AND PLACEMENT INFORMATION. About 50–60 employers conducted on-campus interviews. Approximately 90% of graduates are employed in state. More than 53% of graduates are practicing law; 31% are in business; 14% in government; 2% in academia. Approximately 81% of the University of San Francisco's first-time state bar exam takers pass the California Bar Exam; California's passage rate for all first-time takers from ABA-approved schools is 83%. Graduates are eligible to take the bar exam in all 50 states.

SANTA CLARA UNIVERSITY
Santa Clara, California 95053-0001
Internet site: http://www.scu.edu

Founded 1851. Located 1 mile W of San Jose, 45 miles S of San Francisco. Private control (Roman Catholic affiliation). Semester system. Library: 735,000 volumes; 1,241,000 microforms; 9,529 periodicals/subscriptions; 67 computer workstations.

University's other graduate colleges/schools: College of Arts and Sciences, Division of Counseling Psychology and Education, Leavey School of Business and Administration, School of Engineering.

Total university enrollment: 7,650.

School of Law
500 El Camino Road
Santa Clara, California 95053
Phone: (408)554-4746
Internet site: http://www.scu.edu/law

Established 1912. Located on main campus. ABA approved since 1937. AALS member. Semester system. Full-time, part-time study. Law library: 258,700 volumes/microforms; 3,457 current periodicals/subscriptions; 65 computer workstations; has LEXIS, NEXIS, WESTLAW, OSCAR. Special facilities: Institute of International and Comparative Law, Center for Trial and Appellate Advocacy. Special programs: internships.

Annual tuition: full-time $19,810, part-time $13,800. Limited on-campus housing available. Annual on-campus living expenses: $14,122. Contact Housing Office for both on- and off-campus housing information. Phone: (408)554-4900. Law students tend to live off-campus. Off-campus housing and personal expenses: approximately $15,164. Additional costs: books approximately $800.

Enrollment: first-year class 222 full-time, 68 part-time; total full-time 655, part-time 250 (men 52%, women 48%). First-year statistics: 20% out of state, 27 states and foreign countries represented; 48% women; 37% minority; average age 26 full-time, 38 part-time; 104 undergraduate institutions represented; range of first-year section sizes 60–70 students; number of upper division courses offered after first year 72 full-time, 40 part-time.

Faculty: full-time 33, part-time 47; 44% female; 18% minority; student/faculty ratio 22 to 1.

Degrees conferred: J.D., J.D.-M.B.A.

RECRUITMENT PRACTICES AND POLICIES. Attends local and national law school forums. Has on-campus informational sessions. School does have

diversity program and actively recruits women/minority applicants.

ADMISSION REQUIREMENTS FOR FIRST-YEAR APPLICANTS. LSDAS law school report, LSAT (not later than February test date, if more than one LSAT, highest is used), bachelor's degree from an accredited institution, personal statement, transcripts (must show all schools attended and at least three years of study) required in support of application. Two recommendations optional. Applicants must have received bachelor's degree prior to enrollment. Campus visits encouraged. In addition, international applicants whose native language is not English must submit TOEFL (not older than two years). Joint-degree applicants must apply to and be accepted by both schools, certified translation and evaluation of all foreign documents. Apply to Office of Admission after September 30, before March 1. First-year students admitted fall only. Rolling admission process, notification starts in January and is finished by late April. Application fee $40, $60 international applicants. Phone: (408)554-4800.

ADMISSION REQUIREMENTS FOR TRANSFER APPLICANTS. Accepts transfers from other ABA-accredited schools. Admission limited to space available. At least one year of enrollment, dean's letter indicating applicant is in good standing (prefer applicants in the upper third of first-year class), LSAT, LSDAS, personal statement regarding reason for transfer, current law school transcript required in support of application. Apply to Admission Office at least two months prior to proposed date of matriculation. Admission decision made within one month of the receipt of a completed application. Application fee $40. Will consider visiting students.

ADMISSION STANDARDS. Number of full-time applicants 2,746, part-time 259; number accepted 1,118 full-time, 118 part-time; number enrolled 222 full-time, 68 part-time; median LSAT 156 (75% of class have a score at or above 153 full-time, 152 part-time); median GPA 3.27 (A = 4) (75% of class have a GPA at or above 3.07 full-time, 2.86 part-time). Attrition rate 2.7%. Gorman rating 3.72; *U.S. News & World Report* ranking is in the third tier of all law schools.

FINANCIAL AID. Emery Law Scholarships, merit scholarships, Public Interest Scholarships, diversity scholarships, grants-in-aid, private and institutional loans; federal loans and Federal WS offered through university's Financial Aid Office. Assistantships may be available for upper divisional joint-degree candidates. For scholarships (selection criteria place heavy reliance on LSAT and undergraduate GPA, in some cases an on-campus interview is requested) apply by checking appropriate box on admissions application. For all other programs apply after January 1, before February 18 to university's Office of Financial Aid. Phone: (404)554-4900. Submit FAFSA for all federal programs (Title IV School code # 001326). Also submit Santa Clara University School of Law Aid Form, Financial Aid Transcript, federal income tax forms. Approximately 38% (full-time), 12% (part-time) of first-year class received scholarships/grants-in-aid. Approximately 71% of current students receive some form of financial assistance. Average scholarship/grant $9,000 full-time, $7,000 part-time. Average debt after graduation $61,000.

DEGREE REQUIREMENTS. For J.D.: 86 credits (46 required) with a 2.0 (A = 4) GPA, plus completion of upper divisional writing course; 3-year full-time program, 4-year part-time program. Accelerated J.D. with summer course work. For J.D.-M.B.A.: a 4-year program rather than the usual 5 years needed if degrees taken separately.

CAREER AND PLACEMENT INFORMATION. About 35–40 employers conducted on-campus interviews. Approximately 72% of graduates are employed in state. More than 65% of graduates are practicing law; 25% are in business; 8% in government; 2% in academia. Approximately 82% of Santa Clara University's first-time state bar exam takers pass the California Bar Exam; California's passage rate for all first-time takers from ABA-approved schools is 83%. Graduates are eligible to take the bar exam in all 50 states.

SEATTLE UNIVERSITY
Seattle, Washington 98122
Internet site: http://www.seattleu.edu

Founded 1891. Private control (Roman Catholic—Jesuit affiliation). Semester system. Library: 200,100 volumes; 362,000 microforms; 1,429 periodicals/subscriptions; 26 computer workstations.

University's other graduate colleges/schools: Albers School of Business and Economics, College of Arts and Sciences, College of Nursing, Institute for Theological Studies, Institute for Public Service, School of Science and Engineering.

Total university enrollment: 6,000.

School of Law Norton Clapp Law Center
950 Broadway
Tacoma, Washington 98402-4470
Phone: (206)591-2275
Internet site: http://www.law.seattle.edu
E-mail: lawadmis@seattleu.edu

Established 1972, formerly Puget Sound School of Law. Acquired by Seattle University in 1994. Located on 30 miles S of Seattle, will be moving to Seattle campus in 1999. ABA approved since 1994. AALS member. Semester system. Full-time, part-time study. Law library: 329,400 volumes/microforms; 3,785 current periodicals/subscriptions; 137 computer workstations; has LEXIS, NEXIS, WESTLAW, DIALOG, BRS, VUTEXT, WILSONLINE. Special programs: internships.

Annual tuition: full-time $17,086, part-time $14,232 (all students have option of completing course work in either 9, 12, or 15 months). No on-campus housing available. Law students live off-campus. Contact Admission Office for off-campus information. Off-campus housing and personal expenses: approximately $11,008. Additional costs: books approximately $700.

Enrollment: first-year class 215 full-time, 73 part-time; total full-time 694, part-time 196 (men 51%, women 49%). First-year statistics: 34% out of state, 45 states and foreign countries represented; 49% women; 22% minority; average age 29; 245 undergraduate institutions represented; range of first-year section sizes 60–75 students; number of upper division courses offered after first year 99.

Faculty: full-time 43, part-time 24; 37% female; 12% minority; student/faculty ratio 23 to 1.

Degree conferred: J.D.

RECRUITMENT PRACTICES AND POLICIES. Attends local and selected national law school forums. Has on-campus informational sessions. School does have diversity program and actively recruits women/minority applicants.

ADMISSION REQUIREMENTS FOR FIRST-YEAR APPLICANTS. LSDAS law school report, LSAT (not later than December test date, if more than one LSAT, highest is used), bachelor's degree from an accredited institution, personal statement (no more than three pages), two recommendations, transcripts (must show all schools attended and at least three years of study) required in support of application. Résumés optional but encouraged. Applicants must have received bachelor's degree prior to enrollment. In addition, international applicants whose native language is not English must submit TOEFL (not older than two years), certified translation and evaluation of all foreign documents. Apply to Office of Admission after October 1, before April 1. First-year full-time students admitted summer or fall, Part-time admitted summer only. Rolling admission process, notification starts in mid February and is finished by late May. Application fee $50. Phone: (206)591-2252. Fax: (206)591-6313. E-mail: lawadmis@seattleu.edu.

ADMISSION REQUIREMENTS FOR TRANSFER APPLICANTS. Accepts transfers from other ABA-accredited schools. Admission limited to space available. At least one year of enrollment, dean's letter indicating applicant is in good standing (prefer applicants in the top half of first-year class), LSAT, LSDAS, personal statement regarding reason for transfer, two recommendations, current law school transcript required in support of application. Apply to Admission Office at least six weeks prior to date of proposed of entrance. Admission decision made within one month of the receipt of completed application. Application fee $50. Will consider visiting students.

ADMISSION STANDARDS. Number of full-time applicants 1,223, part-time 145; number accepted 684 full-time, 92 part-time; number enrolled 215 full-time, 73 part-time; median LSAT 156 (75% of class have a score at or above 153 full-time, 150 part-time); median GPA 3.26 (A = 4) (75% of class have a GPA at or above 3.00 full-time, 2.85 part-time). Attrition rate 4.3%. Gorman rating 2.88; *U.S. News & World Report* ranking is in the third tier of all law schools.

FINANCIAL AID. Scholarships, Presidential and Trustee Scholarships, diversity scholarships, grants-in-aid, private and institutional loans; state and federal loans, Federal WS available. All accepted students are automatically considered for all available scholarships (selection criteria place heavy reliance on LSAT and undergraduate GPA). For all other programs apply after January 1, before March 15 to school's Financial Aid Office and complete the Seattle University School of Law Supplemental Information Form. Phone: (206)591-2252. Submit FAFSA for all federal programs (Title IV School code # E00615). Also submit Financial Aid Transcript, federal income tax forms. Approximately 43% (full-time), 24% (part-time) of first-year class received scholarships/grants-in-aid. Approximately 80% of current students receive some form of financial assistance. Average scholarship/grant $4,813 full-time, $3,163 part-time. Average debt after graduation $42,000.

DEGREE REQUIREMENTS. For J.D.: 90 credits (45 required) with a 2.1 (A = 4) GPA, plus completion of upper divisional writing course; 3-year full-time program, 4-year part-time program. Accelerated J.D. with summer course work.

CAREER AND PLACEMENT INFORMATION. About 12–15 employers conducted on-campus interviews. Approximately 89% of graduates are employed in state. More than 59% of graduates are practicing law; 18% are in business; 21% in government; 2% in academia. Approximately 86% of Seattle University's first-time state bar exam takers pass the Washington Bar Exam; Washington's passage rate for all first-time takers from ABA-approved schools is 83%. Graduates are eligible to take the bar exam in all 50 states.

SETON HALL UNIVERSITY
South Orange, New Jersey 07079-2697
Internet site: http://www.shu.edu

Founded 1856. Located 20 miles SW of New York City. Private control (Roman Catholic affiliation). Semester system. Library: 447,000 volumes; 500,000 microforms; 3,200 periodicals/subscriptions; 70 computer workstations.

University's other graduate colleges/schools: College of Arts and Sciences, College of Education and Human Services, College of Nursing, Immaculate Conception Seminary School of Theology, W. Paul Stillman School of Business.

Total university enrollment: 9,600.

School of Law
One Newark Center
Newark, New Jersey 07102-5210
Phone: (201)642-8500
Internet site: http://www.shu.edu/law
E-mail: admitme@lanmail.shu.edu

Established 1951. Located 20 minutes from New York City. ABA approved since 1951. AALS member. Semester system. Full-time, part-time study. Law library: 367,500 volumes/microforms; 5,068 current periodicals/subscriptions; 88 computer workstations; has LEXIS, NEXIS, WESTLAW, DIALOG. Special programs: summer study abroad at University of Parma in Parma, Milan, Florence, Genoa, Italy; internships.

Annual tuition: full-time $18,900, part-time $13,860. No on-campus housing available. Law students live off-campus. Contact Admissions Office for off-campus information. Off-campus housing and personal expenses:

approximately $16,565. Additional costs: books approximately $800.

Enrollment: first-year class 272, part-time 80; total full-time 905, part-time 316 (men 55%, women 45%). First-year statistics: 25% out of state, 25 states and foreign countries represented; 45% women; 17% minority; average age 26; 155 undergraduate institutions represented; average first-year section size 70 students; number of upper division courses offered after first year 100 full-time, 76 part-time.

Faculty: full-time 52, part-time 96; 24% female; 11% minority; student/faculty ratio 24 to 1.

Degrees conferred: J.D., J.D.-M.B.A.

RECRUITMENT PRACTICES AND POLICIES. Attends local and selected national law school forums. Has on-campus informational sessions. School does have diversity program and actively recruits women/minority applicants.

ADMISSION REQUIREMENTS FOR FIRST-YEAR APPLICANTS. LSDAS law school report, LSAT (not later than February test date, if more than one LSAT, average is used), bachelor's degree from an accredited institution, personal statement, two recommendations, transcripts (must show all schools attended and at least three years of study) required in support of application. Applicants must have received bachelor's degree prior to enrollment. Interview not required but may be requested by school. In addition, international applicants whose pre-college language is not in English and with a score of 150 or less on the LSAT must submit TOEFL (not older than two years), certified copies of all transcripts and evaluations of all foreign credentials. Joint-degree applicants must apply to and be accepted by both schools; GMAT for M.B.A. Apply to Office of Admission after September 30, before April 1. First-year students admitted fall only. Rolling admission process, notification starts in January and is finished by early May. Acceptance of offer and first deposit due April 1. Application fee $50. Phone: (201)642-8747. E-mail: admitme@lanmail.shu.edu.

ADMISSION REQUIREMENTS FOR TRANSFER APPLICANTS. Accepts transfers from other ABA-accredited schools. Admission limited to space available. At least one year of enrollment, dean's letter indicating applicant is in good standing (prefer applicants in the top quarter of first-year class), LSAT, LSDAS, personal statement regarding reason for transfer, undergraduate transcript, current law school transcript required in support of application. Apply to Admission Office by July 15. Admission decisions made by mid August. Application fee $50. Will consider visiting students.

ADMISSION STANDARDS. Number of full-time applicants 2,117, part-time 454; number accepted 1,105 full-time, 158 part-time; number enrolled 272 full-time, 80 part-time; median LSAT 154 (75% of class have a score at or above 151 full-time, 152 part-time); median GPA 3.15 (A = 4) (75% of class have a GPA at or above 2.88 full-time, 2.70 part-time). Attrition rate 4%. Gorman rating 3.44; *U.S. News & World Report* ranking is in the second tier of all law schools.

FINANCIAL AID. Centennial Scholarships, need-based merit scholarship, minority scholarships, grants-in-aid, private and institutional loans; federal loans and Federal WS offered through university's Financial Aid Office. Assistantships may be available for upper divisional joint-degree candidates. All accepted students are automatically considered for scholarships (selection criteria place heavy reliance on LSAT and undergraduate GPA). For all other programs apply after January 1, before April 15 to Office of Financial Resource Management. Submit FAFSA for all federal programs (Title IV School code # G09986). Also submit Financial Aid Transcript, federal income tax forms. Approximately 52% (full-time), 75% (part-time) of first-year class received scholarships/ grants-in-aid. Approximately 85% of current students receive some form of financial assistance. Average scholarship/grant $2,260 full-time, $1,850 part-time. Average debt after graduation $51,000.

DEGREE REQUIREMENTS. For J.D.: 85 credits (46 required) with a 2.0 (A = 4) GPA, plus completion of upper divisional writing course; 3-year full-time program, 4-year part-time program. Accelerated J.D. with 1 summer of course work. For J.D.-M.B.A.: total 118 credits (J.D. 73 credits, M.B.A. 45 credits); 4-year full-time program only.

CAREER AND PLACEMENT INFORMATION. About 120–130 employers conducted on-campus interviews. Approximately 74% of graduates are employed in state. More than 76% of graduates are practicing law; 14% are in business; 10% in government. Approximately 78% (NJ), 63% (NY) of Seton Hall University's first-time state bar exam takers pass the bar exam; the passage rate for all first-time takers from ABA-approved schools is 78%(NJ), 78% (NY). Graduates are eligible to take the bar exam in all 50 states.

UNIVERSITY OF SOUTH CAROLINA
Columbia, South Carolina 29208
Internet site: http://www.sc.edu

Founded 1801. Located in downtown Columbia. Public control. Semester system. Library: 2,714,000 volumes; 4,186,700 microforms; 17,940 periodicals/ subscriptions; 289 computer workstations.

University's other graduate colleges/schools: College of Applied Professional Sciences, College of Business Administration, College of Criminal Justice, College of Education, College of Engineering, College of Interdisciplinary Studies, College of Journalism, College of Liberal Arts, College of Library and Information Sciences, College of Nursing, College of Science and Mathematics, College of Social Work, School of Music, School of Public Health, College of Pharmacy, School of Medicine.

Total university enrollment: 26,300.

School of Law
Main and Green Street
Columbia, South Carolina 29208
Phone: (803)777-6857
Internet site: http://www.law.sc.edu
E-mail: usclaw@law.law.sc.edu

Founded 1866. Located on main campus. ABA approved since 1925. AALS member. Semester system. Full-time, day study only. Law library: 383,100 volumes/ microforms; 2,925 current periodicals/subscriptions; 55 computer workstations; has LEXIS, NEXIS, WESTLAW, DIALOG, RLIN, USCAN.

Annual tuition: resident $6,964, nonresident $13,706. On-campus housing available for both single and married students. Annual on-campus housing cost: single students $4,700 (room and board), married students $3,860. Contact University Housing Office for both on- and off-campus housing information. Phone: (803)777-4283. Law students tend to live off-campus. Also contact Office of Student Affairs of the law school for off-campus housing information. Phone: (803)777-8117. Off-campus housing and personal expenses: approximately $11,009. Additional costs: books approximately $700.

Enrollment: first-year class 250; total full-time 750 (men 60%, women 40%); no part-time students. First-year statistics: 15% out of state, 13 states and foreign countries represented; 40% women; 11% minority; average age 26; 81 undergraduate institutions represented; range of first-year section sizes 20–80 students; number of upper division courses offered after first year 108.

Faculty: full-time 44, part-time 25; 10% female; 4% minority; student/faculty ratio 20 to 1.

Degrees conferred: J.D., J.D.-M.Acc., J.D.-M.B.A., J.D.-M.C.P., J.D.-M.P.A., J.D.-M.I.B.S., J.D.-M.A. (Economics), J.D.-M.H.R.

RECRUITMENT PRACTICES AND POLICIES. Attends national law school forums. Has on-campus informational sessions. Phone: (803)777-6605 to schedule visits. School does have diversity program and actively recruits women/minority applicants.

ADMISSION REQUIREMENTS FOR FIRST-YEAR APPLICANTS. LSDAS law school report, LSAT (not later than December test date, if more than one LSAT, average is used), bachelor's degree from an accredited institution, personal statement, two recommendations, transcripts (must show all schools attended and at least three years of study) required in support of application. Applicants must have received bachelor's degree prior to enrollment. In addition, international applicants whose native language is not English must submit TOEFL (not older than two years). Joint-degree applicants must apply to and be accepted by both schools. Apply to Office of Admission after September 30, before February 15 (February 1 for scholarship applicants). First-year students admitted fall only. Rolling admission process, notification starts in January and is finished by late April. Application fee $25 residents, $35 nonresidents. Phone: (803)777-6605. E-mail: usclaw@law.law.sc.edu.

ADMISSION REQUIREMENTS FOR TRANSFER APPLICANTS. Accepts transfers from other ABA-accredited schools. Admission limited to space available. At least one year of enrollment, dean's letter indicating applicant is in good standing (prefer applicants with a 2.8 [A = 4] GPA or better), LSAT, LSDAS, personal statement regarding reason for transfer, two letters of recommendation, undergraduate transcripts, current law school transcript required in support of application. Apply to Admission Office by May 15. Admission decisions made by mid July. Application fee $25 residents, $35 nonresidents. Will consider visiting students.

ADMISSION STANDARDS. Number of full-time applicants 1,294; number accepted 420; number enrolled 250; median LSAT 157 (75% of class have a score at or above 154); median GPA 3.20 (A = 4) (75% of class have a GPA at or above 2.98). Attrition rate 2.2%. Gorman rating 3.44; U.S. News & World Report ranking is in the second tier of all law schools.

FINANCIAL AID. Need-based scholarships, merit scholarship, minority scholarships, grants-in-aid, private and institutional loans; federal loans and Federal WS offered through university's Financial Aid Office. Assistantships may be available for upper divisional joint-degree candidates. For scholarships (selection criteria place heavy reliance on LSAT and undergraduate GPA) apply to Admissions Office after January 1, before April 15 (priority deadline). Use school's scholarship form and university's Institutional Application for Financial Aid. For all other programs apply to the university's Office of Student Financial Aid and Scholarships. Phone: (803)777-8134. E-mail: uscoaid@sc.edu. Submit FAFSA for all federal programs (Title IV School code # 003448). Also submit Financial Aid Transcript, federal income tax forms. Approximately 36% of first-year class received scholarships/grants-in-aid. Approximately 80% of current students receive some form of financial assistance. Average scholarship/grant $1,290. Average debt after graduation $35,000.

DEGREE REQUIREMENTS. For J.D.: 90 credits (46 required) with a 2.0 (A = 4) GPA, plus completion of upper divisional writing course; 3-year program. Accelerated J.D. with 2 summers of course work. For J.D.-master's: 4-year program rather than the usual 5-year program needed if degrees taken separately.

CAREER AND PLACEMENT INFORMATION. About 170–180 employers conducted on-campus interviews. Approximately 91% of graduates are employed in state. More than 83% of graduates are practicing law; 4% are in business; 12% in government; 1% in academia. Approximately 95% of the University of South Carolina's first-time state bar exam takers pass the South Carolina Bar Exam; South Carolina's passage rate for all first-time takers from ABA-approved schools is 81%. Graduates are eligible to take the bar exam in all 50 states.

UNIVERSITY OF SOUTH DAKOTA
Vermillion, South Dakota 57069-2390
Internet site: http://www.usd.edu

Founded 1882. Located 60 miles S of Sioux Falls, South Dakota, 40 miles from Sioux City, Iowa. Public control. Semester system. Library: 667,100 volumes; 645,000 microforms; 8,147 periodicals/subscriptions; 138 computer workstations.

University's other graduate colleges/schools: College of Arts and Sciences, College of Fine Arts, School of Business, School of Education, School of Medicine.

Total university enrollment: 7,750.

School of Law
414 East Clark Street
Vermillion, South Dakota 57069-2390
Phone: (605)377-5443
Internet site: http://www.usd.edu/law
E-mail: request@jurist.law.usd/law

Established 1901. Located on main campus. ABA approved since 1923. AALS member. Semester system. Full-time, day study only. Law library: 176,900 volumes/microforms; 1,282 current periodicals/subscriptions; 24 computer workstations; has LEXIS, NEXIS, WESTLAW, DIALOG, SDLN. Special programs: summer screening program; externships.

Annual tuition: resident $4,715, nonresident $9,979. On-campus housing available for single students in the Graduate and Professional Dormitory and for married students in university-owned apartments. Annual on-campus living expenses: $5,709. Contact Office of Residential Life for both on- and off-campus housing information. Phone: (605)677-5663. Law students tend to live off-campus. Off-campus housing and personal expenses: approximately $8,429. Additional costs: books approximately $700.

Enrollment: first-year class 73; total full-time 213 (men 67%, women 33%); no part-time students. First-year statistics: 35% out of state, 13 states and foreign countries represented; 33% women; 5% minority; average age 27; 29 undergraduate institutions represented; average first-year section size 75 students; number of upper division courses offered after first year 46.

Faculty: full-time 15, part-time 6; 13% female; student/faculty ratio 17.7 to 1.

Degrees conferred: J.D., J.D.-M.Acc., J.D.-M.B.A., J.D.-M.Econ., J.D.-M.P.A., J.D.-M.A. (English, History, Political Science, Psychology).

RECRUITMENT PRACTICES AND POLICIES. Attends local and several national law school forums. Has on-campus informational sessions. School does have diversity program and actively recruits women/minority applicants.

ADMISSION REQUIREMENTS FOR FIRST-YEAR APPLICANTS. LSDAS law school report, LSAT (not later than December test date, if more than one LSAT, average is used), bachelor's degree from an accredited institution, personal statement, two recommendations, transcripts (must show all schools attended and at least three years of study) required in support of application. Applicants must have received bachelor's degree prior to enrollment. In addition, international applicants whose native language is not English must submit TOEFL (not

older than two years). Apply to Office of Admission after September 30, before March 1. First-year students admitted fall only. Rolling admission process, notification starts in January and is finished by late April. Application fee $15. Phone: (605)677-5443. E-mail: request@jurist.law.usd.edu.

ADMISSION REQUIREMENTS FOR TRANSFER APPLICANTS. Accepts transfers from other ABA-accredited schools. Admission limited to space available. At least one year of enrollment, dean's letter indicating applicant is in good standing (prefer applicants in the top quarter of first-year class), LSAT, LSDAS, personal statement regarding reason for transfer, two recommendations, undergraduate transcript, current law school transcript required in support of application. Apply to Admission Office by June 15. Admission decision made within one month of the receipt of a completed application. Application fee $15. Will consider visiting students.

ADMISSION STANDARDS. Number of full-time applicants 351; number accepted 214; number enrolled 73; median LSAT 151 (75% of class have a score at or above 149); median GPA 3.15 (A = 4) (75% of class have a GPA at or above 2.8). Attrition rate 4.9%. Gorman rating 2.48; *U.S. News & World Report* ranking is in the third tier of all law schools.

FINANCIAL AID. Scholarships, merit scholarships, minority scholarships, grants-in-aid, private and institutional loans; federal loans and Federal WS offered through university's Financial Aid Office. Assistantships may be available for second- and third-year joint-degree students. For scholarships (selection criteria place heavy reliance on LSAT and undergraduate GPA) apply to Admissions Office before March 1. For all other programs apply to university's Office of Financial Aid. Phone: (605)677-5446. Submit FAFSA for all federal programs (Title IV School code #003474). Also submit Financial Aid Transcript, federal income tax forms. Approximately 42% of first-year class received scholarships/grants-in-aid. Approximately 75% of current students receive some form of financial assistance. Average scholarship/grant $900.

DEGREE REQUIREMENTS. For J.D.: 90 credits (45 required) with a 70 (scale 0–100) GPA, plus completion of upper divisional writing course; 3-year program. Accelerated J.D. with summer course work. For J.D.-master's: 4-year program (up to 9 credits may be used toward J.D.) rather than the usual 5–6 years needed if degrees taken separately; 75 (scale 0–100) GPA for both degrees.

CAREER AND PLACEMENT INFORMATION. About 10–15 employers conducted on-campus interviews. Approximately 68% of graduates are employed in state. More than 78% of graduates are practicing law; 12% are in business; 10% in government. Approximately 96% of the University of South Dakota's first-time state bar exam takers pass the South Dakota Bar Exam; South Dakota's passage rate for all first-time takers from ABA-approved schools is 91%. Graduates are eligible to take the bar exam in all 50 states.

UNIVERSITY OF SOUTHERN CALIFORNIA
University Park
Los Angeles, California 90089-0913
Internet site: http://www.usc.edu

Founded 1880. Located 3½ miles from downtown Los Angeles. Private control. Semester system. Library: 3,100,000 volumes; 3,900,000 microforms; 38,000 periodicals/subscriptions; 334 computer workstations.

University's other graduate colleges/schools: Annenberg School of Communication, College of Letters, Arts and Sciences, Graduate School of Business Administration, Institute of Safety and Systems Management, Leonard Davis School of Gerontology, School of Architecture, School of Cinema-Television, School of Dentistry, School of Engineering, School of Fine Arts, School of Independent Health Professions, School of Music, School of Pharmacy, School of Public Administration, School of Social Work, School of Theatre, School of Urban and Regional Planning, School of Medicine.

Total university enrollment: 28,000.

Law School
University Park
669 Exposition Boulevard
Los Angeles, California 90089-0071
Phone: (213)740-7331
Internet site: http://www.usc.edu/dept./law-lib
E-mail: admissions@law.usc.edu

Established 1896. Located on main campus in Law Center. ABA approved since 1924. AALS member since 1907. Semester system. Full-time, day study only. Law library: 344,700 volumes/microforms; 4,091 current periodicals/subscriptions; 81 computer workstations; has LEXIS, NEXIS, WESTLAW, DIALOG; is a Federal Government Depository. Special programs: Center for Post-Conviction Justice Project; Faculty exchange programs with Hebrew University, Tel Aviv Universities, Israel, Oxford University, England, China University of

Political Science, People's Republic of China; judicial externships; internships.

Annual tuition: $23,862. On-campus housing available for both single and married students. Annual on-campus living expenses: $11,098. Contact university's Housing Office for both on- and off-campus housing information. Phone: (800)872-4632. Law students tend to live off-campus. Off-campus housing and personal expenses: approximately $12,024. Additional costs: books approximately $800.

Enrollment: first-year class 205; total full-time 610 (men 55%, women 45%); no part-time students. First-year statistics: 38% out of state, 40 states and foreign countries represented; 45% women; 39% minority; average age 24; 125 undergraduate institutions represented; average first-year section size 70 students; number of upper division courses offered after first year 95.

Faculty: full-time 47, part-time 40; 21% female; 7% minority; student/faculty ratio 15 to 1.

Degrees conferred: J.D., J.D.-M.B.A., J.D.-M.B.T., J.D.-M. Phil., J.D.-M.A. (Communications Management, Economics, International Relations, Religion), J.D.-M.R.E.D., J.D.-M.S.W.

RECRUITMENT PRACTICES AND POLICIES. Attends national law school forums. Has on-campus informational sessions. School does have diversity program and actively recruits women/minority applicants.

ADMISSION REQUIREMENTS FOR FIRST-YEAR APPLICANTS. LSDAS law school report, LSAT (not later than December test date, if more than one LSAT, average is used), bachelor's degree from an accredited institution, personal statement, one recommendation (two preferred), transcripts (must show all schools attended and at least three years of study) required in support of application. Applicants must have received bachelor's degree prior to enrollment. In addition, international applicants whose native language is not English must submit TOEFL (not older than two years), certified translations and evaluations of all foreign credentials. Joint-degree applicants must apply to and be accepted by both schools. Apply to Office of Admission after September 30, before February 1. First-year students admitted fall only. Rolling admission process, notification starts in March and is finished by mid May. School does maintain a waiting list. Application fee $60. Phone: (213)740-7331. E-mail: admissions@law.usc.edu.

ADMISSION REQUIREMENTS FOR TRANSFER APPLICANTS. Accepts transfers from other ABA-accredited schools. Admission limited to space available.

At least one year of enrollment, dean's letter indicating applicant is in good standing (prefer applicants in the top 20% of first-year class), LSAT, LSDAS (no photocopies), personal statement regarding reason for transfer, current law school transcript required in support of application. Apply to Admission Office after May 1, before June 15. Admission decision made by late July. Application fee $60. Will consider visiting students.

ADMISSION STANDARDS. Number of full-time applicants 3,674; number accepted 854; number enrolled 205; median LSAT 164 (75% of class have a score at or above 162); median GPA 3.50 (A = 4) (75% of class have a GPA at or above 3.22). Attrition rate 2.4%. Gorman rating 4.44; *U.S. News & World Report* ranking is among the top 15 of all law schools.

FINANCIAL AID. Scholarships, merit scholarships, minority scholarships, grants-in-aid, institutional loans, federal loans, and Federal WS (for second- and third-year students only) available. Assistantships may be available for upper divisional joint-degree candidates. All accepted students are automatically considered for all scholarships (selection criteria place heavy reliance on LSAT and undergraduate GPA). Apply to for all other programs after January 1, before February 15. Phone: (213)740-7331. Use Law School's Financial Aid Form. Use FAFSA for all federal programs and submit to processor by February 15 (Title IV School code #001328). Also submit Financial Aid Transcript, federal income tax forms. Approximately 47% of first-year class received scholarships/ grants-in-aid. Approximately 80% of current students receive some form of financial assistance. USC Loan Repayment Assistance Program for Public Interest Employment available. Average scholarship/grant $10,000. Average debt after graduation $48,000.

DEGREE REQUIREMENTS. For J.D.: 88 credits (33 required) with a 70 (scale 0–100) GPA, plus completion of upper divisional writing course; 3-year program. Accelerated J.D. with summer course work. For J.D.-M.B.A.: 105–121 total credits. For J.D.-M.P.A.: 93 total credits. For J.D.-M.B.T.: 94–110 total credits. For J.D.-M.Phil.: 90 total credits. For J.D.-M.A.: Comunications 88 total credits; Economics 89 total credits; International Relations 94 total credits; Religion 88 total credits. For J.D.-M.R.E.D.: 108 total credits. For J.D.-M.S.W.: 118 total credits.

CAREER AND PLACEMENT INFORMATION. About 175–200 employers conducted on-campus interviews. Approximately 83% of graduates are employed in state.

More than 94% of graduates are practicing law; 1% are in business; 4% in government; 1% in academia. Approximately 84% of the University of Southern California's first-time state bar exam takers pass the California Bar Exam; California's passage rate for all first-time takers from ABA-approved schools is 83%. Graduates are eligible to take the bar exam in all 50 states.

SOUTHERN ILLINOIS UNIVERSITY
Carbondale, Illinois 62901-6806
Internet site: http://www.siu.edu

Founded 1869. Located 100 miles SE of St. Louis, Missouri. Public control. Semester system. Library: 2,000,000 volumes; 2,000,000 microforms; 15,000 periodicals/subscriptions.

University's other graduate colleges/schools: College of Agriculture, College of Business and Administration, College of Education, College of Engineering, College of Liberal Arts, College of Communication and Media Arts, College of Science, School of Social Work, School of Medicine.

Total university enrollment: 11,000.

School of Law
Lesan Law Building
Carbondale, Illinois 62901-6804
Phone: (618)536-7711
Internet site: http://www.siu.edu/~~lawsch/
E-mail: lawadmit@siu.edu

Established 1973. Located on main campus. ABA approved since 1974. AALS member. Semester system. Full-time, day study only. Law library: 328,700 volumes/ microforms; 4,711 current periodicals/subscriptions; 49 computer workstations; has LEXIS, NEXIS, WESTLAW, LEGALTRAC. Special programs: externships.

Annual tuition: resident $5,330, nonresident $13,954. On-campus housing available for both single and married students. Annual on-campus housing cost: single students $3,256 (room and board), married students $3,088. Contact Housing Office for both on- and off-campus housing information. Phone: (618)453-2301. Law students can live off-campus. Off-campus housing and personal expenses: approximately $8,040. Additional costs: books approximately $700.

Enrollment: first-year class 125; total full-time 360 (men 59%, women 41%); no part-time students. First-year statistics: 8% out of state, 23 states and foreign countries represented; 41% women; 21% minority; average age 26; 65 undergraduate institutions represented; range of first-year section sizes 20–65 students; number of upper division courses offered after first year 51.

Faculty: full-time 24, part-time 8; 35% female; 6% minority; student/faculty ratio 13 to 1.

Degrees conferred: J.D., J.D.-M.Acct., J.D.-M.B.A., J.D.-M.P.A., J.D.-M.D.

RECRUITMENT PRACTICES AND POLICIES. Attends selected national law school forums. Has on-campus informational sessions. School does have diversity program and actively recruits women/minority applicants.

ADMISSION REQUIREMENTS FOR FIRST-YEAR APPLICANTS. LSDAS law school report, LSAT (prefers December test date, will accept February; if more than one LSAT, average is used), bachelor's degree from an accredited institution, résumé, personal statement, two recommendations, transcripts (must show all schools attended and at least three years of study) required in support of application. Applicants must have received bachelor's degree prior to enrollment. In addition, international applicants whose native language is not English must submit TOEFL (not older than two years), certified translation and evaluation of all foreign credentials. Joint-degree applicants must apply to and be accepted by both schools. Apply to Office of Admission after September 30, before February 1 (priority deadline). First-year students admitted fall only. Rolling admission process, notification starts in January and is finished by mid May. Application fee $25. Phone: (800)739-9187, (618)453-8767. E-mail: lawadmit@siu.edu.

ADMISSION REQUIREMENTS FOR TRANSFER APPLICANTS. Accepts transfers from other ABA-accredited schools. Admission limited to space available. At least one year of enrollment, dean's letter indicating applicant is in good standing (prefer applicants in the upper half of first-year class), LSAT, LSDAS, personal statement regarding reason for transfer, two letters of recommendation, undergraduate transcripts, current law school transcript required in support of application. Apply to Admission Office by June 15. Admission decision made by mid July. Application fee $25. Will consider visiting students.

ADMISSION STANDARDS. Number of full-time applicants 740; number accepted 365; number enrolled 125; median LSAT 153 (75% of class have a score at or above 147); median GPA 3.08 (A = 4) (75% of class have a GPA at or above 2.63). Attrition rate 4%. Gorman rating 3.16; *U.S. News & World Report* ranking is in the third tier of all law schools.

FINANCIAL AID. Scholarships, tuition waivers, law school employment (available to second- and third-year students), private and institutional loans; federal loans and Federal WS offered through university's Financial Aid Office. Assistantships may be available for upper divisional joint-degree candidates. All accepted students are automatically considered for scholarships (selection criteria place heavy reliance on LSAT and undergraduate GPA). For all other programs apply after January 1, before March 1 to the university's Financial Aid Office. Phone: (618)453-4334. Submit FAFSA for all federal programs (Title IV School code # 001758). Also submit Financial Aid Transcript, federal income tax forms. Approximately 37% of first-year class received scholarships/grants-in-aid. Approximately 90% of current students receive some form of financial assistance. Average scholarship/grant $2,000. Average debt after graduation $35,000.

DEGREE REQUIREMENTS. For J.D.: 90 credits (46 required) with a 2.0 (A = 4) GPA, plus completion of upper divisional writing course; 3-year program. Accelerated J.D. with summer course work. For J.D.-master's: 4-year program rather than the usual 5-year program needed if degrees taken separately. For J.D.-M.D.: a 6-year program rather than the 7-year program needed if both degrees taken separately.

CAREER AND PLACEMENT INFORMATION. About 20–25 employers conducted on-campus interviews. Approximately 74% of graduates are employed in state. More than 72% of graduates are practicing law; 10% are in business; 18% in government; none in academia. Approximately 81% of Southern Illinois University's first-time state bar exam takers pass the Illinois Bar Exam; Illinois' passage rate for all first-time takers from ABA-approved schools is 87%. Graduates are eligible to take the bar exam in all 50 states.

SOUTHERN METHODIST UNIVERSITY
Dallas, Texas 75275
Internet site: http://www.smu.edu

Founded 1911. Located 5 miles N of downtown. Private control (Methodist affiliation). Semester system. Library: 2,950,000 volumes; 704,168 microforms; 6,417 periodicals/subscriptions.

University's other graduate colleges/schools: Dedman College, Edwin L. Cox School of Business, Meadows School of the Arts, Perkins School of Theology.

Total university enrollment: 9,100.

School of Law
P.O. Box 750110
Dallas, Texas 75275-0110
Phone: (214)768-2080
Internet site: http://www.smu.edu/~law
E-mail: lmontes@mail.smu.edu

Established 1925, Graduate program since 1950. Located on main campus. ABA approved since 1927. AALS member. Semester system. Full-time, day study primarily; LL.M. both full- and part-time study. Law library: 478,300 volumes/microforms; 5,052 current periodicals/subscriptions; 89 computer workstations; has LEXIS, WESTLAW; is a Federal Government Depository. Special facilities: Center for Pacific Rim Legal Studies, Center for NAFTA and Latin American Legal Studies. Special programs: summer study abroad at University College, Oxford University, England; externships.

Annual tuition: $19,534. On-campus housing available for both single and married students. Annual on-campus housing cost: single students $3,000 (room only), married students $3,500. Housing deadline May 31. Contact Office of Housing for both on- and off-campus housing information. Phone: (214)768-2407. Law students can live off-campus. Off-campus housing and personal expenses: approximately $9,000. Additional costs: books approximately $930.

Enrollment: first-year class 250; total full-time 762 (men 55%, women 45%); very few part-time students. First-year statistics: 27% out of state, 20 states and foreign countries represented; 45% women; 22% minority; average age 25; 151 undergraduate institutions represented; range of first-year section sizes 75–80 students; number of upper division courses offered after first year 114. LL.M.: full-time 50, part-time 30.

Faculty: full-time 41, part-time 49; 24% female; 9% minority; student/faculty ratio 21 to 1.

Degrees conferred: J.D., J.D.-M.B.A., J.D.-M.A. (Economics), LL.M. (General, Taxation), LL.M. (Comparative and International Law—for persons who have completed a basic legal education and received a university degree in law in another country), S.J.D.

RECRUITMENT PRACTICES AND POLICIES. Attends local and national law school forums. Has on-campus informational sessions. School does have diversity program and actively recruits women/minority applicants.

ADMISSION REQUIREMENTS FOR FIRST-YEAR APPLICANTS. LSDAS law school report, LSAT (not later than December test date, if more than one LSAT, average is used), bachelor's degree from an accredited insti-

tution, personal statement, two recommendations, dean's statement, transcripts (must show all schools attended and at least three years of study) required in support of application. Applicants must have received bachelor's degree prior to enrollment. In addition, international applicants whose native language is not English must submit TOEFL (not older than two years), certified translation and evaluation of foreign credentials. Will accept Law Multi-App in lieu of SMU application. Joint-degree applicants must apply to and be accepted by both schools. Apply to Office of Admission after September 15, before December 15 (Early Decision), February 15 (regular decision), April 1 (late decision). First-year students admitted fall only. Rolling admission process, notification starts in December and is finished by late April. Acceptance of offer and first deposit due April 1. Application fee $50. Phone: (214)768-2550. Fax: (214)768-2549. E-mail: lmontes@mail.smu.edu.

ADMISSION REQUIREMENTS FOR TRANSFER APPLICANTS. Accepts transfers from other ABA-accredited schools. Admission limited to space available. At least one year of enrollment, dean's letter indicating applicant is in good standing (prefer applicants in the top quarter of first-year class), LSAT, LSDAS, personal statement of compelling need regarding reason for transfer, current law school transcript required in support of application. Apply to Admission Office by July 1 (fall), December 1 (spring), May 1 (summer). Admission decision made within one month of the receipt of completed application. Application fee $50. Will consider visiting students.

ADMISSION REQUIREMENTS FOR LL.M. APPLICANTS (General, Taxation). All applicants must have a J.D. from an ABA-accredited law school; must have graduated in the top half of class. Official transcripts including rank-in-class, two letters of recommendation, a statement of interest in graduate study required in support of graduate application. Admits fall and spring, for full- and part-time study. Apply by April 1 (fall), December 1 (spring).

ADMISSION REQUIREMENT FOR LL.M. (Comparative and International Law). Applicants must be graduates of a recognized foreign law school. Official U.S. law school transcripts, or certified translation and evaluation of all foreign credentials; TOEFL for all applicants whose native language is not English, short curriculum vitae, two letters of recommendation, evidence of financial ability to pay degree expenses required in support of graduate application. Admits full-time and fall only.

ADMISSION REQUIREMENTS FOR S.J.D. APPLI-CANTS. Applicants must have an LL.M. degree from any one of the three SMU School of Law graduate programs and already have selected a research project or an appropriate area for advanced study or extended research.

ADMISSION STANDARDS. Number of full-time applicants 1,750; number accepted 720; number enrolled 252; median LSAT 157 (75% of class have a score at or above 154); median GPA 3.16 (A = 4) (75% of class have a GPA at or above 2.85). Gorman rating 4.36; *U.S. News & World Report* ranking is in the second tier of all law schools.

FINANCIAL AID. Scholarships, merit scholarships, minority scholarships, grants-in-aid, private and institutional loans; federal loans and Federal WS offered through university's Financial Aid Office. Assistantships may be available for upper divisional joint-degree candidates. All accepted students are automatically considered for all scholarships/grants (selection criteria place heavy reliance on LSAT and undergraduate GPA) apply to Admissions Office before February 1 for Sumners and Hughes Scholarships. Use school's scholarship application. For all other programs apply after January 1, before March 15 to university's Office of Financial Aid. Phone: (214)768-3417. Fax: (214)768-3878. E-mail: finaid@smu.edu. Submit FAFSA for all federal programs (Title IV School code #003613). Also submit Financial Aid Transcript, federal income tax forms. Approximately 28% of first-year class received scholarships/grants-in-aid. Approximately 45% of current students receive some form of financial assistance. Average scholarship/grant $6,000. Average debt after graduation $60,000. Financial Aid available for part-time students. Limited financial assistance for LL.M. candidate; indicate interest in scholarship assistance on admissions application.

DEGREE REQUIREMENTS. For J.D.: 90 credits (37 required) with a 2.0 (A = 4) GPA, plus completion of upper divisional writing course; 3-year program. Accelerated J.D. with 2 summers of course work. For J.D.-M.B.A.: total 137 credits (J.D. 86 credits, M.B.A. 51 credits). For J.D.-M.A. (Economics): total 111 credits (J.D. 84 credits, M.A. 27 credits). For LL.M. (Taxation): 24 credits, a minimum of 2 semesters in residence; 2.0 (A = 4) GPA required. For LL.M. (General): 24 credits, at least 2 semesters in residence; 2.0 (A = 4) GPA required; completion of degree within 3 years: thesis/nonthesis option. For LL.M. (Comparative and International Law): 24 credits; at least 2 semesters in residence; a GPA of 1.70 (A = 4) required. For S.J.D.: a minimum of 2 years in res-idence; dissertation of publishable quality; oral defense; degree requirement must be completed within 5 years.

CAREER AND PLACEMENT INFORMATION. About 70–75 employers conducted on-campus interviews. Approximately 70% of graduates are employed in state. More than 81% of graduates are practicing law; 16% are in business; 3% in government; none in academia. Approximately 84% of Southern Methodist University's first-time state bar exam takers pass the Texas Bar Exam; Texas' passage rate for all first-time takers from ABA-approved schools is 82%. Graduates are eligible to take the bar exam in all 50 states.

SOUTH TEXAS COLLEGE OF LAW

1303 San Jacinto
Houston, Texas 77002-7000
Phone: (713)659-8040
Internet site: http://www.stcl.edu

Established 1923. ABA approved since 1959. AALS member. Semester system. Full-time, part-time study. Law library: 338,900 volumes/microforms; 4,011 current periodicals/subscriptions; 66 computer workstations; has LEXIS, NEXIS, WESTLAW, DIALOG, Epic. Special facilities: Center for Legal Responsibility. Special program: externships.

Annual tuition: full-time $14,700, part-time $10.000. No on-campus housing available. Law students live off-campus. Contact Admission Office for off-campus information. Off-campus housing and personal expenses: approximately $12,024. Additional costs: books approximately $700.

Enrollment: first-year class 361 full-time, 131 part-time; total full-time 838, part-time 379 (men 59%, women 41%). First-year statistics: 12% out of state, 38 states and foreign countries represented; 41% women; 21% minority; average age 29; 246 undergraduate institutions represented; range of first-year section sizes 20–80 students; number of upper division courses offered after first year 76 full-time, 56 part-time.

Faculty: full-time 58, part-time 36; 20% female; 8% minority; student/faculty ratio 21 to 1.

Degree conferred: J.D.

RECRUITMENT PRACTICES AND POLICIES. Attends local and several national law school forums. Has on-campus informational sessions. School does have diversity program and actively recruits women/minority applicants.

ADMISSION REQUIREMENTS FOR FIRST-YEAR APPLICANTS. LSDAS law school report, LSAT (not later than December test date, if more than one LSAT, highest is used), bachelor's degree from an accredited institution, résumé, personal statement, two recommendations, transcripts (must show all schools attended and at least three years of study) required in support of application. Applicants must have received bachelor's degree prior to enrollment. In addition, international applicants whose native language is not English must submit TOEFL (not older than two years), obtain certified translation and evaluation of foreign credentials. Apply to Office of Admission before March 15 (fall), October 1 (spring). First-year students admitted both fall and spring. Rolling admission process. Acceptance of offer and first deposit due within one month after receipt of acceptance letter. Application fee $40. Phone: (713)646-1810.

ADMISSION REQUIREMENTS FOR TRANSFER APPLICANTS. Accepts transfers from other ABA-accredited schools. Admission limited to space available. At least one year of enrollment, dean's letter indicating applicant is in good standing (prefer applicants in the top half of first-year class), LSAT, LSDAS, personal statement regarding reason for transfer, résumé, two letters of recommendation, current law school transcript required in support of application. Apply to Admission Office by May 15 (fall), October 15 (spring). Admission decision made within one month of the receipt of completed application. Application fee $40. Will consider visiting students.

ADMISSION STANDARDS. Number of full-time applicants 1,429, part-time 613; number accepted 818 full-time, 350 part-time; number enrolled 361 full-time, 131 part-time; median LSAT 153 (75% of class have a score at or above 148 for both full- and part-time); median GPA 2.90 (A = 4) (75% of class have a GPA at or above 2.69 full-time, 2.66 part-time). Attrition rate 6.9%. Gorman rating 2.27; *U.S. News & World Report* ranking is in the fourth tier of all law schools.

FINANCIAL AID. Scholarships, Dean's Merit Scholarship, minority scholarships, grants-in-aid, state grants, private and institutional loans; federal loans and Federal WS available. All accepted students are automatically considered for scholarships (selection criteria place heavy reliance on LSAT and undergraduate GPA). Apply by May 1 (fall), October 1 (spring) to the Office of Scholarship and Financial Aid. Phone: (713)646-1820. Use school's financial aid form. Submit FAFSA for all federal programs (Title IV School code #G04977). Also sub-mit Financial Aid Transcript, federal income tax forms. Approximately 40% (full-time), 30% (part-time) of first-year class received scholarships/grants-in-aid. Approximately 82% of current students receive some form of financial assistance. Average scholarship/grant $1,143 full-time, $1,154 part-time. Average debt after graduation $47,000.

DEGREE REQUIREMENTS. For J.D.: 90 credits (41 required) with a 2.0 (A = 4) GPA, plus completion of upper divisional writing course; 3-year full-time program, 4-year part-time program.

CAREER AND PLACEMENT INFORMATION. About 17–20 employers conducted on-campus interviews. Approximately 94% of graduates are employed in state. More than 67% of graduates are practicing law; 23% are in business; 9% in government; 1% in academia. Approximately 78% of South Texas College of Law's first-time state bar exam takers pass the Texas Bar Exam; Texas' passage rate for all first-time takers from ABA-approved schools is 82%. Graduates are eligible to take the bar exam in all 50 states.

SOUTHERN UNIVERSITY AND AGRICULTURAL AND MECHANICAL COLLEGE

Baton Rouge, Louisiana 70813
Internet site: currently under construction

Founded 1880. Public control. Semester system. Library: 451,700 volumes/microforms.

University's other graduate colleges/schools: College of Arts and Humanities, College of Business, College of Education, College of Sciences, Graduate School, School of Public Policy and Urban Affairs, Special Education Institute, School of Nursing.

Total university enrollment: 9,900.

Law Center
P.O. Box 9294
Baton Rouge, Louisiana 70813
Phone: (504)771-2552, (800)537-1135
Internet site: currently under construction

Established 1947. Located on main campus. ABA approved since 1953. AALS member. Semester system. Full-time, day study only. Law library: 378,900 volumes/microforms; 4,350 current periodicals/subscriptions; 52 computer workstations; has LEXIS, NEXIS, WESTLAW, DIALOG.

Annual tuition: resident $3,128, nonresident $7,728. On-campus housing available for single students only. Annual on-campus housing cost: single students $1,490 (room only), $2,934 (room and board). Housing deadline June 30. Contact Housing Office for both on- and off-campus housing information. Phone: (504)771-3590. Law students tend to live off-campus. Off-campus housing and personal expenses: approximately $9,544. Additional costs: books approximately $700.

Enrollment: first-year class 125; total full-time 335 (men 53%, women 47%); no part-time students. First-year statistics: 15% out of state, 22 states and foreign countries represented; 47% women; 66% minority; average age 27; 59 undergraduate institutions represented; average first-year section size 40 students; number of upper division courses offered after first year 61.

Faculty: full-time 28, part-time 9; 24% female; 70% minority; student/faculty ratio 13 to 1.

Degree conferred: J.D.

RECRUITMENT PRACTICES AND POLICIES. Attends local and several national law school forums. Has on-campus informational sessions. School does have diversity program and actively recruits women applicants.

ADMISSION REQUIREMENTS FOR FIRST-YEAR APPLICANTS. LSDAS law school report, LSAT (not later than February test date, if more than one LSAT, highest is used), bachelor's degree from an accredited institution, personal statement, two recommendations, transcripts (must show all schools attended and at least three years of study) required in support of application. Applicants must have received bachelor's degree prior to enrollment. Apply to Office of Admission after September 30, before March 31. First-year students admitted fall only. Rolling admission process. No application fee. Phone: (504)771-5340, (800)537-1135.

ADMISSION REQUIREMENTS FOR TRANSFER APPLICANTS. Accepts transfers from other ABA-accredited schools. Admission limited to space available. At least one year of enrollment, dean's letter indicating applicant is in good standing (prefer applicants in the top half of first-year class), LSAT, LSDAS, personal statement regarding reason for transfer, two recommendations, current law school transcript required in support of application. Apply to Admission Office by July 1. Admission decisions made by mid August. No application fee. Will consider visiting students.

ADMISSION STANDARDS. Number of full-time applicants 1,122; number accepted 198; number enrolled 125; median LSAT 145 (75% of class have a score at or above 143); median GPA 2.62 (A = 4) (75% of class have a GPA at or above 2.43). Attrition rate 5.2%. Gorman rating 2.08; *U.S. News & World Report* ranking is in the fourth tier of all law schools.

FINANCIAL AID. Scholarship assistance limited, grants-in-aid, private and institutional loans; federal loans and Federal WS offered through university's Financial Aid Office. For scholarships (selection criteria place heavy reliance on LSAT and undergraduate GPA) apply to Scholarship Committee before April 1. For all other programs apply to the University's Office of Financial Aid. Phone: (504)771-2796. Submit FAFSA for all federal programs (Title IV School code #002025). Also submit Financial Aid Transcript, federal income tax forms. Approximately 19% of first-year class received scholarships/grants-in-aid. Approximately 60% of current students receive some form of financial assistance. Average scholarship/grant $4,600.

DEGREE REQUIREMENTS. For J.D.: 96 credits (76 required) with a 2.0 (A = 4) GPA, plus completion of upper divisional writing course; 3-year program.

CAREER AND PLACEMENT INFORMATION. About 40–50 employers conducted on-campus interviews. Approximately 100% of graduates are employed in state. More than 47% of graduates are practicing law; 2% are in business; 24% in government; 18% in academia. Approximately 36% of Southern University Law Center's first-time state bar exam takers pass the Louisiana Bar Exam; Louisiana's passage rate for all first-time takers from ABA-approved schools is 67%. Graduates are eligible to take the bar exam in all 50 states.

SOUTHWESTERN UNIVERSITY SCHOOL OF LAW

675 South Westmoreland Avenue
Los Angeles, California 90005-3992
Phone: (213)738-6717
Internet site: http://www.swlaw.edu
E-mail: admissions@swla.edu

Established 1911. Located in downtown Los Angeles. ABA approved since 1970. AALS member. Semester system. Full-time, part-time study. Law library: 372,900 volumes/microforms; 4,902 current periodicals/subscriptions; 85 computer workstations; has LEXIS, NEXIS, WESTLAW, RLIN, LEGALTRAC, WILSONLINE. Special programs: Southwestern Conceptual Approach to

Legal Education (SCALE, a two-year J.D. program), Part-time Legal Education Alternative at Southwestern (PLEAS, a program designed for students with child-care responsibilities); summer study in Entertainment Law; study abroad in Buenos Aires, Argentina, Vancouver, British Columbia, University of Guanajicato, Mexico; externships.

Annual tuition: full-time $20,050, part-time $12,735. No on-campus housing available. Law students live off-campus. Contact Admissions Office for off-campus housing information. Off-campus housing and personal expenses: approximately $11,430. Additional costs: books approximately $800.

Enrollment: first-year class 296 full-time, 104 part-time; total full-time 806, part-time 354 (men 50%, women 50%). First-year statistics: 15% out of state, 50% women; 33% minority; average age 27; 250 undergraduate institutions represented; range of first-year section sizes 17–95 students; number of upper division courses offered after first year 77 full-time, 56 part-time.

Faculty: full-time 49, part-time 40; 29% female; 20% minority; student/faculty ratio 21.7 to 1.

Degree conferred: J.D.

RECRUITMENT PRACTICES AND POLICIES. Attends local and several national law school forums. Has on-campus informational sessions. School does have diversity program and actively recruits women/minority applicants.

ADMISSION REQUIREMENTS FOR FIRST-YEAR APPLICANTS. LSDAS law school report, LSAT (not later than February test date, if more than one LSAT, highest is used), bachelor's degree from an accredited institution, personal statement, two recommendations, transcripts (must show all schools attended and at least three years of study) required in support of application. Applicants must have received bachelor's degree prior to enrollment. Interview not required except for SCALE applicants. In addition, international applicants whose native language is not English must submit TOEFL (not older than two years), certified translation and evaluation of all foreign credentials. Will accept Law Multi-App in lieu of school's application. Apply to Office of Admission after September 30, before June 30 (May 30 for SCALE applicants). First-year students admitted fall only. Rolling admission process, notification starts in January and is finished by mid July. Application fee $50. Phone: (213)738-6717. E-mail: admissions@swlaw.edu.

ADMISSION REQUIREMENTS FOR TRANSFER APPLICANTS. Accepts transfers from other ABA-accredited schools. Admission limited to space available. At least one year of enrollment, dean's letter indicating applicant is in good standing (prefer applicants in the upper half of first-year class), LSAT, LSDAS, personal statement regarding reason for transfer, undergraduate transcript, current law school transcript required in support of application. Apply to Admission Office at least six weeks prior to proposed semester of entrance. Admission decision made within one month from the receipt of a completed application. Application fee $50. Will consider visiting students.

ADMISSION STANDARDS. Number of full-time applicants 2,252, part-time 436; number accepted 1,200 full-time, 213 part-time; number enrolled 296 full-time, 104 part-time; median LSAT 153 (75% of class have a score at or above 150 for both full- and part-time); median GPA 3.0 (A = 4) (75% of class have a GPA at or above 2.72 full-time, 2.69 part-time). Attrition rate 7.4%. Gorman rating 3.47; *U.S. News & World Report* ranking is in the fourth tier of all law schools.

FINANCIAL AID. Scholarships, minority scholarships, grants, State Graduate Fellowships, private and institutional loans, federal loans and Federal WS available. For scholarships (selection criteria place heavy reliance on LSAT and undergraduate GPA) apply to Financial Aid Office after January 1, before March 1 (priority consideration). Use school's FAF. For all other program considerations apply by April 1. Submit FAFSA by February 1 for all federal programs (Title IV School code #G01295). Also submit Financial Aid Transcript, federal income tax forms. Approximately 9% (full-time), 11% (part-time) of first-year class received scholarships/grants-in-aid. Approximately 85% of current students receive some form of financial assistance. Average scholarship/grant $4,712 full-time, $4,232 part-time. Public Interest Loan Forgiveness Program available.

DEGREE REQUIREMENTS. For J.D.: 87 credits (52 required) with a 2.0 (A = 4) GPA, plus completion of upper divisional writing course; 2-year program (SCALE), 3-year full-time program, 4-year part-time program. Accelerated J.D. with 2 summers of course work.

CAREER AND PLACEMENT INFORMATION. About 30–40 employers conducted on-campus interviews. Approximately 91% of graduates are employed in state. More than 63% of graduates are practicing law; 28% are in business; 8% in government; 1% in academia. Approximately 80% (CA), 88% (NY) of Southwestern University's first-time state bar exam takers pass the bar exam;

the passage rate for all first-time takers from ABA-approved schools is 83% (CA), 78% (NY). Graduates are eligible to take the bar exam in all 50 states.

STANFORD UNIVERSITY

Stanford, California 94305-9991
Internet site: http://www.stanford.edu

Founded 1891. Located near Palo Alto, 30 miles S of San Francisco. Private control. Semester system. Library: 6,500,000 volumes; 4,500,000 microforms; 43,800 periodicals/subscriptions; 600 computer workstations.

The University's other graduate schools: Graduate School of Business, School of Earth Sciences, School of Education, School of Engineering, School of Humanities and Sciences, School of Medicine.

Total university enrollment: 14,000.

Law School

Crown Quadrangle
Stanford, California 94305-8610
Phone: (415)723-2465
Internet site: http://www-leland.stanford.edu/group/law
E-mail: law.admissions@forsythe.stanford.edu

Established 1893. Located on main campus. ABA approved since 1923. AALS member. Semester system. Full-time, day study only. Law library: 447,500 volumes/microforms; 7,030 current periodicals/subscriptions; 50 computer workstations; has LEXIS, NEXIS, WESTLAW; is a Federal Government Depository. Special facilities: Stanford Center in Conflict and Negotiation, Stanford Law and Technology Policy Center. Special program: Stanford Program in International Legal Studies (SPILS).

Annual tuition: $24,276, SPILS $24,276. On-campus housing available for both single and married students. Annual on-campus housing cost: single students $3,822 (room only), $7,396 (room and board), married students $9,070. Housing deadline May 15. Contact Housing Office for both on- and off-campus housing information. Phone: (415)725-2810. Law students tend to live off-campus. Off-campus housing and personal expenses: approximately $15,369. Additional costs: books approximately $1,100. A PC/modem/printer required, approximate cost: $2,500.

Enrollment: first-year class 176; total full-time 550 (men 55%, women 45%); no part-time students. First-year statistics: 50% out of state, 45 states and 6 foreign countries represented; 45% women; 32% minority; average age 24; 152 undergraduate institutions represented; average first-year section size 60 students; number of upper division courses offered after first year 147.

Faculty: permanent 39, visiting 61; 39% female; 15% minority; student/faculty ratio 17 to 1.

Degrees conferred: J.D., J.D.-M.B.A., J.D.-M.I.P.S., J.D.-M.P.A. (Princeton University), J.D.-M.A. (Johns Hopkins University), J.S.M. (only for persons who have received a university degree in law in another country or have an advanced degree in law from outside the U.S. and will be returning overseas upon completion of degree. Emphasis is on international issues), M.L.S. (a nonprofessional degree for those who do not have a law degree but are pursuing a doctoral degree, have earned another advanced degree, or possess exceptional relevant experience), J.S.D.

RECRUITMENT PRACTICES AND POLICIES. Attends local and national law school forums. Has on-campus informational sessions. School does have diversity program and actively recruits women/minority applicants.

ADMISSION REQUIREMENTS FOR FIRST-YEAR APPLICANTS. LSDAS law school report, LSAT (not later than December test date, if more than one LSAT, average is used), bachelor's degree from an accredited institution, dean's statement (Form B), personal statement, two recommendations (Form C), transcripts (must show all schools attended and at least three years of study) required in support of application (Form A). Applicants must have received bachelor's degree prior to enrollment. Interview not required but may be requested by school. In addition, international applicants whose native language is not English must submit TOEFL (not older than two years), certified translations and evaluations of all foreign credentials. Joint/Dual-degree applicants must apply to and be accepted by both schools. Apply to Office of Admission after September 15, before February 1. First-year students admitted fall only. Rolling admission process, consideration starts in January and all first responses will be received by April 30. School does maintain a small waiting list. Application fee $65. Phone: (415)723-4985. E-mail: lawadmissions@forsythe.stanford.edu.

ADMISSION REQUIREMENTS FOR TRANSFER APPLICANTS. Accepts very few transfers and they must be from other ABA-accredited schools. At least one year of enrollment, dean's letter indicating applicant is in good standing (prefer applicants in the top 5% of first-year class), LSAT, LSDAS, personal statement regarding reason for transfer, undergraduate transcript, current law school transcript required in support of application. Apply to Admission Office after May 15, before June 15. Admission decision made by mid July. Application fee $65. Will consider visiting students.

ADMISSION REQUIREMENTS FOR J.S.M., M.L.S. Certified translations and evaluation of all foreign credentials, résumé, personal statement, at least two recommendations, copies of research or published works are required in support of graduate application. Admits to fall only. Apply by April 1 to Stanford Program in International Legal Studies. Phone: (415)723-4985. Fax: (415)725-0253. Selection of SPILS fellows announced by June 1.

ADMISSIONS REQUIREMENTS FOR J.S.D. A J.D. from an approved ABA/AALS law school or equivalent degree required for consideration. Official transcripts, two to three letters of recommendation, résumé or other evidence of significant professional accomplishment, personal statement, proposed dissertation research project required in support of graduate application. Admits fall only. Apply by April 1 to the Office of Graduate Programs. Phone: (415)723-4985.

ADMISSION STANDARDS. Number of full-time applicants 4,034; number accepted 491; number enrolled 176; median LSAT 168 (75% of class have a score at or above 165); median GPA 3.70 (A = 4) (75% of class have a GPA at or above 3.51). Attrition rate .5%. Gorman rating 4.88; U.S. News & World Report ranking is in the top 3 of all law schools.

FINANCIAL AID. All financial aid is need based. There are tuition fellowships, private loans, institutional loans, and federal loans available. Research assistantships and fellowships may be available for upper divisional joint-degree candidates. Apply to Financial Aid Office after January 1, before March 15. Phone: (415)723-9247. For all federal programs submit FAFSA (Title IV School code #E00341). Also submit Financial Aid Transcript, federal income tax forms, and need Access Disk. Approximately 36% of first-year class received scholarships/grants-in-aid. Approximately 75% of current students receive some form of financial assistance. Average tuition fellowship is $9,000. Public Interest Loan Repayment Assistance Program available.

DEGREE REQUIREMENTS. For J.D.: 86 credits (27 required) with a 2.0 (A = 4) GPA, plus completion of upper divisional writing course, 1 course in legal ethics, 1 interdisciplinary course examining the American legal system or examining a foreign or international legal system; 3-year program. Accelerated J.D. with summer course work. For J.D.-M.B.A.: a 4-year program rather than the usual 5-year program needed if degrees taken separately. For J.D.-master's: individually designed programs, normally a 4- to 4½-year program rather than the usual 5- to 5½-year program needed if degrees taken separately. For J.S.M.: 1 core seminar, 3 to 5 advanced courses or seminars, a multidisciplinary research workshop; written research project. For M.L.S.: 30 credits, must be completed within 2 consecutive academic years; 1 writing seminar or directed research project resulting in a written paper. For J.S.D.: at least 1 year in full-time residence; dissertation of publishable quality, oral defense.

CAREER AND PLACEMENT INFORMATION. About 150–175 employers conducted on-campus interviews. Approximately 50% of graduates are employed in state. More than 88% of graduates are practicing law; 6% are in business; 5% in government; 1% in academia. Approximately 91% of Stanford University's first-time state bar exam takers pass the California Bar Exam; California's passage rate for all first-time takers from ABA-approved schools is 83%. Graduates are eligible to take the bar exam in all 50 states.

STETSON UNIVERSITY

Deland, Florida 32720-3781
Internet site: http://www.stetson.edu

Founded 1883. Located 40 miles N of Orlando. Private control. Semester system. Library: 511,400 volumes; 937,500 microforms; 5,949 periodicals/subscriptions.

University's other graduate colleges/schools: College of Arts and Sciences, School of Business.

Total university enrollment: 2,900.

College of Law
1401 61st Street South
St. Petersburg, Florida 33707
Phone: (813)562-7800
Internet site: http://www.law.stetson.edu
E-mail: lawadmit@hermes.law.stetson.edu

Established 1900. Located in South St. Petersburg (Tampa Bay Region). ABA approved since 1930. AALS member. Semester system. Full-time, day study only. Law library: 340,700 volumes/microforms; 4,842 current periodicals/subscriptions; 47 computer workstations; has

LEXIS, NEXIS, WESTLAW, DIALOG. Special programs: Center for Dispute Resolution; internships.

Annual tuition: $19,110. Limited on-campus housing available for single students. Annual on-campus living expenses: $10,270. Housing deadline March 1. Contact Housing Office for both on- and off-campus housing information. Phone: (904)822-7000. Most law students live off-campus. Off-campus housing and personal expenses: approximately $12,470. Additional costs: books approximately $800.

Enrollment: first-year class 220; total full-time 626 (men 49%, women 51%); no part-time students. First-year statistics: 10% out of state, 43 states and foreign countries represented; 51% women; 16% minority; average age 25; 200 undergraduate institutions represented; range of first-year section sizes 30–70 students; number of upper division courses offered after first year 77.

Faculty: full-time 41, part-time 32; 28% female; 5% minority; student/faculty ratio 19 to 1.

Degrees conferred: J.D., J.D.-M.B.A.

RECRUITMENT PRACTICES AND POLICIES. Attends local and selected national law school forums. Has on-campus informational sessions. School does have diversity program and actively recruits women/minority applicants.

ADMISSION REQUIREMENTS FOR FIRST-YEAR APPLICANTS. LSDAS law school report, LSAT (not later than December test date, if more than one LSAT, highest is used), bachelor's degree from an accredited institution, college's questionnaire, personal statement, transcripts (must show all schools attended and at least three years of study) required in support of application. Letters of recommendation not required but are encouraged. Applicants must have received bachelor's degree prior to enrollment. Interview not required. Campus visits encouraged. Joint-degree applicants must apply to and be accepted by both schools, GMAT required. Apply to Office of Admission by March 1 (fall), September 1 (spring), February 1 (summer). First-year students admitted fall, spring, and summer. Rolling admission process. Application fee $45. Phone: (813)562-7802. E-mail: lawadmit@hermes.law.stetson.edu.

ADMISSION REQUIREMENTS FOR TRANSFER APPLICANTS. Accepts transfers from other ABA-accredited schools. Admission limited to space available. At least one year of enrollment, dean's letter indicating applicant is in good standing (prefer applicants in the upper third of first-year class), LSAT, LSDAS, personal statement regarding reason for transfer, current law school transcript including rank-in-class required in support of application. Apply to Admission Office at least six months prior to proposed date of entrance. Admission decision within one month of the receipt of completed application. Application fee $45. Will consider visiting students.

ADMISSION STANDARDS. Number of full-time applicants 1,702; number accepted 726; number enrolled 220; median LSAT 153 (75% of class have a score at or above 149); median GPA 3.20 (A = 4) (75% of class have a GPA at or above 2.95). Attrition rate 5.8%. Gorman rating 2.56; *U.S. News & World Report* ranking is in the third tier of all law schools.

FINANCIAL AID. Stetson Scholarship program, need-based scholarships, state minority scholarships, private and institutional loans; federal loans and Federal WS offered through university's Financial Aid Office. All accepted students are automatically considered for all available scholarships (selection criteria place heavy reliance on LSAT and undergraduate GPA; interviews may be requested). For all other programs, including need-based scholarships, apply to Financial Aid Office after January 1, before March 1 (fall), September 1 (spring), February 1 (summer). Submit FAFSA for all federal programs (Title IV School code # E00342). Also submit Financial Aid Transcript, federal income tax forms. Approximately 45% of first-year class received scholarships. Approximately 90% of current students receive some form of financial assistance. Average scholarship/grant $4,550. Average debt after graduation $62,600.

DEGREE REQUIREMENTS. For J.D.: 88 credits (45 required) with a 2.0 (A = 4) GPA, plus completion of upper divisional writing course; 20 hours of pro bono service required; 3-year program. For J.D.-M.B.A.: a 4-year program rather than the usual 5-year program needed if degrees taken separately.

CAREER AND PLACEMENT INFORMATION. About 15–20 employers conducted on-campus interviews. Approximately 90% of graduates are employed in state. More than 65% of graduates are practicing law; 8% are in business; 27% in government. Approximately 85% of Stetson University's first-time state bar exam takers pass the Florida Bar Exam; Florida's passage rate for all first-time takers from ABA-approved schools is 84%. Graduates are eligible to take the bar exam in all 50 states.

SUFFOLK UNIVERSITY

Boston, Massachusetts 02108-2770
Internet site: http://www.suffolk.edu

Founded 1906. Private control. Semester system. Library: 281,000 volumes; 588,000 microforms; 6,965 periodicals/subscriptions.

University's other graduate colleges/schools: College of Liberal Arts and Sciences, Sawyer School of Management.

Total university enrollment: 6,200.

School of Law

41 Temple Street
Boston, Massachusetts 02114-4280
Phone: (617)573-8155
Internet site: http://www.suffolk.edu/law
E-mail: lawadm@admin.suffolk.edu

Established 1906. Located on Beacon Hill in the heart of historic Boston. ABA approved since 1953. Semester system. Full-time, part-time study. Law library: 300,800 volumes/microforms; 5,830 current periodicals/subscriptions; 45 computer workstations; has LEXIS, NEXIS, WESTLAW, DIALOG; is a Federal Government Depository. Special programs: The Prosecutor Program, Battered Women's Advocacy Program; internships.

Annual tuition: full-time $19,036, part-time $14,278. On-campus housing available for single students only. Annual on-campus housing cost: single students $7,900 (room and board). Contact the Dean of Students Office for both on- and off-campus housing information. Phone: (617)573-8239. Law students tend to live off-campus. Off-campus housing and personal expenses: approximately $14,581. Additional costs: books approximately $800.

Enrollment: first-year class full-time 365, part-time 209; total full-time 1,050, part-time 650 (men 50%, women 50%). First-year statistics: 52% out of state, 50 states and foreign countries represented; 50% women; 11% minority; average age 25; 322 undergraduate institutions represented; average first-year section sizes 100–123 students; number of upper division courses offered after first year 138 full-time, 139 part-time.

Faculty: full-time 60, part-time 95; 30% female; 9% minority; student/faculty ratio 23 to 1.

Degrees conferred: J.D., J.D.-M.B.A., J.D.-M.P.A., J.D.-M.S.F., J.D.-M.S.I.E.

RECRUITMENT PRACTICES AND POLICIES. Attends local and selected national law school forums. Has on-campus informational sessions. School does have diversity program and actively recruits women/minority applicants.

ADMISSION REQUIREMENTS FOR FIRST-YEAR APPLICANTS. LSDAS law school report, LSAT (not later than February test date, if more than one LSAT, highest is used), bachelor's degree from an accredited institution, dean's certification of good standing, personal statement, one recommendation, transcripts (must show all schools attended and at least three years of study) required in support of application. Applicants must have received bachelor's degree prior to enrollment. Interview not required but occasionally may be requested by school. Campus visits are encouraged. In addition, international applicants whose native language is not English must submit TOEFL (not older than two years), certified translations and evaluations of all foreign documents. Joint-degree applicants must apply to and be accepted by both schools. The Law Multi-App may be used in lieu of school's application. Apply to Office of Admission after September 30, before March 3. First-year students admitted fall only. Rolling admission process, notification starts in November and is finished by May. Acceptance of offer and first deposit due April 15. Application fee $50. Phone: (617)573-8144. E-mail: lawadm@admin.suffolk.edu.

ADMISSION REQUIREMENTS FOR TRANSFER APPLICANTS. Accepts transfers from other ABA-accredited schools. Admission limited to space available. At least one year of enrollment, dean's letter indicating applicant is in good standing (prefer applicants in the top half of first-year class), LSAT, LSDAS, personal statement regarding reason for transfer, one letter of recommendation, current law school transcript required in support of application. Apply to Admission Office by June 2. Admission decision made within one month of the receipt of a completed application. Application fee $50. Will consider visiting students.

ADMISSION STANDARDS. Number of full-time applicants 1,533, part-time 464; number accepted 1,096 full-time, 284 part-time; number enrolled 365 full-time, 209 part-time; median LSAT 152 (75% of class have a score at or above 148 full-time, 150 part-time); median GPA 3.15 (A = 4) (75% of class have a GPA at or above 2.91 full-time, 2.82 part-time). Attrition rate 3.3%. Gorman rating 3.12; *U.S. News & World Report* ranking is in the fourth tier of all law schools.

FINANCIAL AID. Merit- and need- based scholarships, fellowships, grants-in-aid, private and institutional loans;

federal loans and Federal WS offered through university's Financial Aid Office. Assistantships may be available for upper divisional joint-degree candidates. For scholarships (selection criteria place heavy reliance on LSAT and undergraduate GPA) apply to law school's Financial Aid Office before March 1. For all other programs apply after January 1, before April 1 to university's Office of Financial Aid. Submit FAFSA for all federal programs prior to March 6 (Title IV School code #E00517). Also submit Financial Aid Transcript, federal income tax forms. Approximately 36% (full-time), 14% (part-time) of first-year class received scholarships/grants-in-aid. Approximately 80% of current students receive some form of financial assistance. Average scholarship/grant $2,500 full-time, $1,500 part-time. Average debt after graduation $60,000.

DEGREE REQUIREMENTS. For J.D.: 84 credits (58 required) with a 2.0 (A = 4) GPA, plus completion of upper divisional writing course; 3-year 6-semester program, 4-year part-time program. Summer course work may be used to reduce the number of credits carried in third year. For J.D.-M.B.A.: total 114 credits (J.D. 72 credits, M.B.A. 42 credits). For J.D.-M.P.A.: total 120 credits (J.D. 80 credits, M.P.A. 40 credits). For J.D.-M.S.F.: total 117 credits (J.D. 78 credits, M.S.F. 39 credits). For J.D.-M.S.I.E.: total 110 credits (J.D. 80 credits, M.S.I.E. 30 credits).

CAREER AND PLACEMENT INFORMATION. About 90–100 employers conducted on-campus interviews. Approximately 78% of graduates are employed in state. More than 51% of graduates are practicing law; 32% are in business; 15% in government; 2% in academia. Approximately 84% of Suffolk University's first-time state bar exam takers pass the Massachusetts Bar Exam; Massachusetts' passage rate for all first-time takers from ABA-approved schools is 85%. Graduates are eligible to take the bar exam in all 50 states.

SYRACUSE UNIVERSITY
Syracuse, New York 13244-0003
Internet site: http://www.syr.edu

Founded 1871. Private control. Semester system. Library: 2,001,000 volumes; 2,069,000 microforms.

University's other graduate colleges/school: College for Human Development, College of Arts and Sciences, College of Nursing, College of Visual and Performing Arts, L.C. Smith College of Engineering and Computer Science, Maxwell School of Citizenship and Public Affairs, S.I. Newhouse School of Public Communication, School of Architecture, School of Education, School of Information Studies, School of Management, School of Social Work.

Total university enrollment: 18,000.

School of Law
Suite 212
Syracuse, New York 13244-1030
Phone: (315)443-1962. Fax: (315)443-9568
Internet site: http://www.law.syr.edu
E-mail: admissions@law.syr.edu

Established 1895. Located on main campus. ABA approved since 1923. AALS charter member. Semester system. Full-time, day study, limited part-time program. Law library: 358,840 volumes/microforms; 5,865 current periodicals/subscriptions; 55 computer workstations; has LEXIS, NEXIS, WESTLAW, DIALOG. Special facilities: Business Law Center, Family Law and Social Policy Center, Center for Global Law and Practice, Center for Law, Technology and Management. Special programs: Law and Economics Program.

Annual tuition: $21,136, part-time $18,249. On-campus housing available for both single and married students. Annual on-campus housing cost: single students $4,680 (room only), $6,591 (room and board), married students $8,544. Housing deadline June 1. Contact Office of South Campus Housing. Phone: (345)443-2567. Off-campus housing and personal expenses: approximately $12,094. Additional costs: books approximately $800.

Enrollment: first-year class 243; total full-time 723, part-time 11 (men 57%, women 43%). First-year statistics: 55% out of state, 40 states and foreign countries represented; 43% women; 24% minority; average age 25; 311 undergraduate institutions represented; average first-year section size 90 students; number of upper division courses offered after first year 127.

Faculty: full-time 40, part-time 34; 30% female; 10% minority; student/faculty ratio 17 to 1.

Degrees conferred: J.D., J.D.-M.B.A., J.D.-M.P.A., J.D.-M.A. (Communications, Economics, History, International Relations, Media), J.D.-M.S. (Accounting, Environmental Science, Engineering, Political Science), J.D.-Ph.D.

RECRUITMENT PRACTICES AND POLICIES. Attends local and national law school forums. Has on-campus informational sessions. School does have

diversity program and actively recruits women/minority applicants.

ADMISSION REQUIREMENTS FOR FIRST-YEAR APPLICANTS. LSDAS law school report, LSAT (not later than February test date, if more than one LSAT, average is used), bachelor's degree from an accredited institution, personal statement, two or three recommendations, transcripts (must show all schools attended and at least three years of study) required in support of application. Applicants must have received bachelor's degree prior to enrollment. Interview not required. In addition, international applicants whose native language is not English must submit TOEFL (not older than two years), certified translation and evaluation of all foreign documents, signed letter of financial support. Joint-degree applicants must apply to and be accepted by both schools. Apply to Office of Admission after September 30, before April 1. First-year students admitted fall only. Rolling admission process, notification starts in December and is finished by early May. School does maintain a waiting list. Application fee $50. Phone: (345)443-1962. E-mail: admissions@ law.syr.edu.

ADMISSION REQUIREMENTS FOR TRANSFER APPLICANTS. Accepts transfers from other ABA-accredited schools. Admission limited to space available. At least one year of enrollment, dean's letter indicating applicant is in good standing (prefer applicants in the top quarter of first-year class), LSAT, LSDAS, personal statement regarding reason for transfer, undergraduate transcript, one letter of recommendation, current law school transcript required in support of application. Apply to Admission Office by June 1. Admission decision made between July 10 and August 10. Application fee $50. Will consider visiting students.

ADMISSION STANDARDS. Number of full-time applicants 1,837, part-time 35; number accepted 1,124 full-time, 15 part-time; number enrolled 234 full-time, 11 part-time; median LSAT 152 (75% of class have a score at or above 147 for both full- and part-time); median GPA 3.25 (A = 4) (75% of class have a GPA at or above 3.00 full-time, 3.03 part-time). Attrition rate 3.9%. Gorman rating 3.82; *U.S. News & World Report* ranking is in the third tier of all law schools.

FINANCIAL AID. Merit scholarships, grants-in-aid, private and institutional loans, state programs, federal loans, and Federal WS available. Assistantships may be available for upper divisional joint-degree candidates. For scholarships (selection criteria place heavy reliance on LSAT and undergraduate GPA) use school's Financial Aid application. For all other programs apply to school's Financial Aid Office after January 1, before March 1. Submit FAFSA (by January 31) for all federal programs (Title IV School code #002882). Also submit Financial Aid Transcript, federal income tax forms. Approximately 57% of first-year class received scholarships/grants-in-aid. Approximately 79% of current students receive some form of financial assistance. Average scholarship/grant $6,300. Average debt after graduation $56,000. Financial aid available for part-time students.

DEGREE REQUIREMENTS. For J.D.: 87 credits (40 required) with a 2.0 (A = 4) GPA, plus completion of upper divisional writing course; 3-year full-time program, 4-year part-time program. Accelerated J.D. with summer course work. For J.D.-M.B.A., M.S. Accounting: a 4-year program rather than the usual 5-year program needed if degrees taken separately. For J.D.-M.P.A.: a 4-year program rather than the usual 5-year program needed if degrees taken separately. For J.D.-M.A.: 3½-year programs rather than the usual 4½-year programs needed if degrees taken separately. For J.D.-M.S.: 3½-year programs rather than the usual 4½-year programs needed if degrees taken separately. J.D.-Ph.D.: a 6-year program rather than the usual 7-year program needed if degrees taken separately.

CAREER AND PLACEMENT INFORMATION. About 40–50 employers conducted on-campus interviews. Approximately 53% of graduates are employed in state. More than 64% of graduates are practicing law; 19% are in business; 16% in government; 1% in academia. Approximately 68% of Syracuse University's first-time state bar exam takers pass the New York Bar Exam; New York's passage rate for all first-time takers from ABA-approved schools is 78%. Graduates are eligible to take the bar exam in all 50 states.

TEMPLE UNIVERSITY
Philadelphia. Pennsylvania 19122
Internet site: http://www.temple.edu

Founded 1894. Located 2 miles N of downtown. State related control. Semester system. Library: 2,265,000 volumes; 2,462,700 microforms; 15,437 periodicals/subscriptions; 400 computer workstations.

University's other graduate colleges/schools: College of Arts and Sciences, College of Education, College of Engineering, College of Health, Physical Education, Recreation and Dance, Ester Boyer College of Music, School of Business and Management, School of Communications and Theater, School of Social Administration, Tyler School of Art. Health Center includes: College of Allied Health Professions, School of Dentistry, School of Medicine, School of Pharmacy.

Total university enrollment: 30,700.

School of Law
1719 North Broad Street
Philadelphia, Pennsylvania 19122
Phone: (800)560-1428
Internet site: http://www.temple.edu/lawschool
E-mail: law@astro.ocis.temple.edu

Established 1895. Located on main campus. ABA approved since 1933. AALS member. Semester system. Full-time, part-time study. Law library: 470,500 volumes/microforms; 2,517 current periodicals/subscriptions; 88 computer workstations; has LEXIS, NEXIS, WESTLAW, DIALOG, RLIN, INNOPAC, CALI; is a Federal Government Depository. Special programs: semester abroad in Tokyo, Japan, summer abroad in Athens, Greece, Rome, Italy, Tel Aviv, Israel; externships.

Annual tuition full-time: resident $8,900, nonresident $15,414; part-time resident $7,182, nonresident $12,392. On-campus housing available for single, married, and LL.M. (about half of entering LL.M. class live on-campus) students. Annual on-campus housing cost: single students $4,344 (room only), married students $6,000. Housing deadline June 1. Contact Office of University Housing for both on- and off-campus housing. Phone: (218)207-7223. J.D. students tend to live off-campus. Off-campus housing and personal expenses: approximately $13,360. Additional costs: books approximately $800.

Enrollment: first-year class full-time 255, part-time 88; total full-time 769, part-time 377 (men 52%, women 48%). First-year statistics: 35% out of state, 63 states and foreign countries represented; 48% women; 26% minority; average age 27; 334 undergraduate institutions represented; range of first-year section sizes 9–87 students; number of upper division courses offered after first year 130 full-time, 57 part-time.

Faculty: 31% female; 12% minority; student/faculty ratio 19.7 to 1.

Degrees conferred: J.D., J.D.-M.B.A., J.D.-LL.M. (Tax, Trial Advocacy), LL.M. (Tax [full- and part-time program]), Trial Advocacy [evening and weekend program], LL.M. (only for international graduates who have completed a basic legal education and received a university degree in law in another country).

RECRUITMENT PRACTICES AND POLICIES. Attends national law school forums. Has on-campus infor-

mational sessions. School does have diversity program and actively recruits women/minority applicants.

ADMISSION REQUIREMENTS FOR FIRST-YEAR APPLICANTS. LSDAS law school report, LSAT (not later than February test date, if more than one LSAT, average is used), bachelor's degree from an accredited institution, personal statement, no more than three recommendations, transcripts (must show all schools attended and at least three years of study) required in support of application. Applicants must have received bachelor's degree prior to enrollment. Interview not required but may be requested by school. In addition, international applicants whose native language is not English must submit TOEFL (not older than two years), certified translations and evaluations of all foreign documents. Dual-degree applicants must apply to and be accepted by both schools. Will accept Law Multi-App in lieu of school's application. Apply to Office of Admission after September 30, before March 1, January 15 for priority consideration. First-year students admitted fall only. Rolling admission process, notification starts in January and is finished by late April. Acceptance of offer and first deposit due April 15. School does maintain a waiting list. Application fee $50. Phone: (800)560-1428. E-mail: law@astro.ocis.temple.edu.

ADMISSION REQUIREMENTS FOR TRANSFER APPLICANTS. Accepts transfers from other ABA-accredited schools. Admission limited to space available. At least one year of enrollment, dean's letter indicating applicant is in good standing (prefer applicants in the top quintile of first-year class), LSAT, LSDAS (certified copies acceptable), personal statement regarding reason for transfer, current law school transcript required in support of application. Apply to Admission Office by June 1. Admission decision made by mid August. Application fee $50. Will consider visiting students.

ADMISSION REQUIREMENTS FOR LL.M. APPLICANTS. For LL.M. (Tax, Trial Advocacy), all applicants must have a J.D. from an ABA-accredited law school. Certified copies of official transcript (for Tax program the transcript must show the successful completion of at least one basic taxation course), résumé, personal statement, two letters of recommendation required in support of LL.M. application. Admits fall and spring. Apply by August 1 (fall), November 30 (spring) to the Office of Graduate Legal Studies. Application fee $25. Phone: (Tax): (215)204-1448. Fax: (215)204-1185. Phone: (Trial Advocacy): (215)204-1231 (Director) or (215)204-5314 (Program Coordinator).

For LL.M. (International Law Graduates), all applicants must have a basic law degree from an approved foreign law school. Official transcripts with certified English translations, personal statement, three letters of recommendation required in support of the LL.M. application. In addition, TOEFL is required for all applicants whose native language is not English. Apply by March 15 to the Office of International Programs. Application fee $25.

ADMISSION STANDARDS. Number of full-time applicants 2,384, part-time 394; number accepted 894 full-time, 143 part-time; number enrolled 255 full-time, 88 part-time; median LSAT 155 (75% of class have a score at or above 149 full-time, 150 part-time); median GPA 3.16 (A = 4) (75% of class have a GPA at or above 2.96 full-time, 2.79 part-time). Attrition rate 2.3%. Gorman rating 3.88; *U.S. News & World Report* ranking is in the second tier of all law schools.

FINANCIAL AID. Need-based partial scholarships, merit scholarships, grants-in-aid, private and institutional loans; federal loans and Federal WS offered through university's Financial Aid Office. Assistantships may be available for upper divisional joint-degree candidates. For need-based, merit scholarships and grants (selection criteria place heavy reliance on LSAT and undergraduate GPA) apply to law school's Financial Aid Office after January 1, before March 1. Use Temple University Financial Aid Institutional Application Form. Phone: (215)204-8943. For all other programs apply to university's Office of Financial Aid. File FAFSA for all federal programs (Title IV School code #E00354). Also submit Financial Aid Transcript, federal income tax forms. Approximately 69% (full-time), 20% (part-time) of first-year class received scholarships/grants-in-aid. Approximately 75% of current students receive some form of financial assistance. Average scholarship/grant $1,957 full-time, $2,318 part-time. There is a Barrack Public Interest Fellowships program for those interested in Public Interest careers.

DEGREE REQUIREMENTS. For J.D.: 83 credits (38 required) with a 2.0 (A = 4) GPA, plus completion of upper divisional writing course; 3-year full-time program, 4-year part-time program. Accelerated J.D. with 1 summer of course work. For J.D.-M.B.A.: 4- to 6-year programs (full- or part-time) rather than the usual 5- to 7-year programs needed if degrees were taken separately. For LL.M. (Tax): 24 credits. For M.C.L. (International): 30 credits; at least 2 semesters in residence; a GPA of 2.5 (A = 4) required.

CAREER AND PLACEMENT INFORMATION. About employers conducted on-campus interviews. Approximately 67% of graduates are employed in state. More than 64% of graduates are practicing law; 22% are in business; 9% in government; 1% in academia. Approximately 72% of Temple University's first-time state bar exam takers pass the Pennsylvania Bar Exam; Pennsylvania's passage rate for all first-time takers from ABA-approved schools is 73%. Graduates are eligible to take the bar exam in all 50 states.

UNIVERSITY OF TENNESSEE
Knoxville, Tennessee 37996
Internet site: http://www.UTK.edu

Founded 1794. Located in the foothills of the Great Smoky Mountains of East Tennessee. Public control. Semester system. Library: 2,000,000 volumes; 2,000,000 microforms; 11,000 periodicals/subscriptions.

University's other graduate colleges/schools: College of Agricultural Sciences and Natural Resources, College of Architecture and Planning, College of Arts and Sciences, College of Business Administration, College of Communications, College of Education, College of Human Ecology, College of Nursing, College of Social Work, College of Veterinary Medicine, School of Biomedical Sciences, School of Information Sciences.

Total university enrollment: 25,700.

College of Law
1505 W. Cumberland Avenue
Knoxville, Tennessee 37996-1810
Phone: (423)974-4241
Internet site: http://www.law.UTK.edu
E-mail: lawadmit@libra.law.utk.edu

Established 1890. Located on main campus. ABA approved since 1925. AALS member. Semester system. Full-time, day study only. Law library: 420,800 volumes/microforms; 5,344 current periodicals/subscriptions; 57 computer workstations; has LEXIS, NEXIS, WESTLAW, INFOTRAC, LegalTrak; is a Federal Government Selective Depository. Special facilities: Center for Entrepreneurial Law, Center for Advocacy and Dispute Resolution.

Annual tuition: resident $4,204, nonresident $10,496. On-campus housing available for both single and married students. Annual on-campus housing cost: single students $2,355 (room only), married students $3,546. Housing deadline February 1. Contact Director of Residence Halls for both on- and off-campus housing information. Phone:

(423)974-3411. Law students tend to live off-campus. Off-campus housing and personal expenses: approximately $10,816. Additional costs: books approximately $700.

Enrollment: first-year class 165; total full-time 468 (men 58%, women 42%); no part-time students. First-year statistics: 20% out of state, 42% women; 12% minority; average age 26; 73 undergraduate institutions represented; average first-year section size 55 students; number of upper division courses offered after first year 75.

Faculty: full-time 31, part-time 22; 27% female; 4% minority; student/faculty ratio 14.5 to 1.

Degrees conferred: J.D., J.D.-M.B.A., J.D.-M.P.A.

RECRUITMENT PRACTICES AND POLICIES. Attends local and selected national law school forums. Has on-campus informational sessions. School does have diversity program and actively recruits women/minority applicants.

ADMISSION REQUIREMENTS FOR FIRST-YEAR APPLICANTS. LSDAS law school report, LSAT (not later than December test date, if more than one LSAT, average is used), bachelor's degree from an accredited institution, résumé, personal statement, two recommendations, transcripts (must show all schools attended and at least three years of study) required in support of application. Applicants must have received bachelor's degree prior to enrollment. Interview not required, but visits to campus are encouraged. In addition, international applicants whose native language is not English must submit TOEFL (not older than two years). Dual-degree applicants must apply to and be accepted by both schools. Apply to Office of Admission after October 1, before February 1. First-year students admitted fall only. Rolling admission process, notification starts in early April and is finished by early May. Acceptance of offer and first deposit due June 1. Application fee $15. Phone: (423)974-4131. Fax: (423)974-1572. E-mail: lawadmit@libra.law.utk.edu.

ADMISSION REQUIREMENTS FOR TRANSFER APPLICANTS. Accepts transfers from other ABA-accredited schools. Admission limited to space available. At least one year of enrollment, dean's letter indicating applicant is in good standing (prefer applicants in the top quarter of first-year class), LSAT, LSDAS, personal statement regarding reason for transfer, two letters of recommendation, undergraduate transcripts, current law school transcript required in support of application. In addition,

a catalog from a current law school must be sent to Admission Office. Apply to Admission Office by June 15 (fall), September 15 (spring), April 15 (summer). Admission decision made within one month of the receipt of a completed application. Application fee $15. Will consider visiting students.

ADMISSION STANDARDS. Number of full-time applicants 1,062; number accepted 384; number enrolled 165; median LSAT 156 (75% of class have a score at or above 153); median GPA 3.43 (A = 4) (75% of class have a GPA at or above 3.14). Attrition rate 2.7%. Gorman rating 2.95; *U.S. News & World Report* ranking is in the top 45 of all law schools.

FINANCIAL AID. Need-based scholarships, merit scholarships, minority scholarships, research assistantships/fellowships, private and institutional loans; federal loans and Federal WS offered through university's Financial Aid Office. Assistantships may be available for upper divisional joint-degree candidates. All accepted students are automatically considered for scholarships (selection criteria place heavy reliance on LSAT and undergraduate GPA). For all other programs apply after January 1, before February 15 to the university's Office of Financial Assistance. Use the university's Financial Aid Application and submit FAFSA for all federal programs (Title IV School code #006725). Also submit Financial Aid Transcript, federal income tax forms. Approximately 22% of first-year class received scholarships/grants-in-aid. Approximately 70% of current students receive some form of financial assistance. Average scholarship/grant $4,200.

DEGREE REQUIREMENTS. For J.D.: 89 credits (41 required) with a 2.0 (A = 4) GPA, plus completion of upper divisional writing course; 3-year program. Accelerated J.D. with summer course work. For J.D.-master's: 4-year programs rather than the usual 5-year programs needed if degrees taken separately.

CAREER AND PLACEMENT INFORMATION. About 20–30 employers conducted on-campus interviews. Approximately 76% of graduates are employed in state. More than 76% of graduates are practicing law; 15% are in business; 8% in government; 1% in academia. Approximately 85% of the University of Tennessee's first-time state bar exam takers pass the Tennessee Bar Exam; Tennessee's passage rate for all first-time takers from ABA-approved schools is 81%. Graduates are eligible to take the bar exam in all 50 states.

TEXAS SOUTHERN UNIVERSITY

Houston, Texas 77004-4584

Internet site: http://www.tsu.edu

Founded 1947. Located 7 miles S of downtown Houston. Public control. Semester system. Library: 465,200 volumes; 363,500 microforms; 1,950 periodicals/subscriptions; 60 computer workstations.

University's other graduate colleges/schools: College of Arts and sciencess, College of Education, School of Business, School of Technology, College of Pharmacy and Health Sciences.

Total university enrollment: 9,500.

Thurgood Marshall
School of Law

3100 Cleburne Avenue

Houston, Texas 77004-3216

Phone: (713)313-1075

Internet site: http://www.tsulaw.edu

E-mail: cgardner@tsulaw.edu

Established 1947. Located on main campus. ABA approved since 1949. AALS member. Semester system. Full-time, day study only. Law library: 371,100 volumes/microforms; 2,448 current periodicals/subscriptions; 30 computer workstations; has LEXIS, NEXIS, WESTLAW, DIALOG. Special programs: externships; internships.

Annual tuition: resident $4,367, nonresident $8,007. On-campus housing available for both single and married students. Annual on-campus housing cost: single students $3,360 (room only), married students $4,000. Housing deadline July 15. Contact Director of Housing for both on- and off-campus housing information. Phone: (713)527-7205. Law students tend to live off-campus. Off-campus housing and personal expenses: approximately $9,872. Additional costs: books approximately $800.

Enrollment: first-year class 300; total full-time 600 (men 55%, women 45%); no part-time students. First-year statistics: 10% out of state, 34 states and foreign countries represented; 45% women; 85% minority; average age 29; 139 undergraduate institutions represented; average first-year section size 65 students; number of upper division courses offered after first year 68.

Faculty: full-time 37, part-time 20; 32% female; 71% minority; student/faculty ratio 22.8 to 1.

Degree conferred: J.D.

RECRUITMENT PRACTICES AND POLICIES. Attends local and selected national law school forums. Has on-campus informational sessions. School does have diversity program and actively recruits women applicants.

ADMISSION REQUIREMENTS FOR FIRST-YEAR APPLICANTS. LSDAS law school report, LSAT (not later than February test date, if more than one LSAT, highest is used), bachelor's degree from an accredited institution, personal statement, two letters of evaluation, transcripts (must show all schools attended and at least three years of study) required in support of application. Applicants must have received bachelor's degree prior to enrollment. Interview not required but in rare cases may be requested by school. In addition, international applicants whose native language is not English must submit TOEFL (not older than two years), certified translations and evaluations of all foreign credentials. Apply to Office of Admission after September 30, before April 1. First-year students admitted fall only. Rolling admission process, notification starts in January and is finished by May. Acceptance of offer and first deposit due upon receipt of letter of acceptance. Application fee $40. Phone: (713)313-7114. E-mail: cgardner@tsulaw.edu.

ADMISSION REQUIREMENTS FOR TRANSFER APPLICANTS. Accepts transfers from other ABA-accredited schools. Admission limited to space available. At least one year of enrollment, dean's letter indicating applicant is in good standing, LSAT, LSDAS, personal statement regarding reason for transfer, two letters of evaluation, undergraduate transcript, current law school transcript required in support of application. Apply to Admission Office at least one semester prior to date of anticipated transfer. Admission decision made within six weeks of receipt of completed application. Application fee $40. Will consider visiting students.

ADMISSION STANDARDS. Number of full-time applicants 1,378; number accepted 571; number enrolled 300; median LSAT 143 (75% of class have a score at or above 140); median GPA 2.74 (A = 4) (75% of class have a GPA at or above 2.41). Attrition rate 19%. Gorman rating 2.33; *U.S. News & World Report* ranking is in the fourth tier of all law schools.

FINANCIAL AID. Scholarships, assistantships, grants-in-aid, private and institutional loans, federal loans, and Federal WS available. For scholarships (selection criteria place heavy reliance on LSAT and undergraduate GPA) apply to Office of Financial Aid after January 1, before May 1. Use TSU's General Financial Aid Application. For all other programs submit FAFSA (Title IV School code #003642). Also submit Financial Aid Transcript, federal income tax forms, Institutional Verification Form. Approximately 41% of first-year class received scholarships/grants-in-aid. Approximately 90% of current students receive some form of financial assistance. Average scholarship/grant $1,800.

DEGREE REQUIREMENTS. For J.D.: 90 credits (70 required) with a 2.0 (A = 4) GPA, plus completion of upper divisional writing course; 3-year program.

CAREER AND PLACEMENT INFORMATION. About 30–40 employers conducted on-campus interviews. Approximately 92% of graduates are employed in state. More than 98% of graduates are practicing law; 2% in government. Approximately 75% of Texas Southern University's first-time state bar exam takers pass the Texas Bar Exam; Texas' passage rate for all first-time takers from ABA-approved schools is 82%. Graduates are eligible to take the bar exam in all 50 states.

TEXAS TECH UNIVERSITY
Lubbock, Texas 79409
Internet site: http://www.ttu.edu

Founded 1923. Public control. Semester system. Library: 507,000 volumes; 287,000 microforms; 17,556 periodicals/subscriptions; 170 computer workstations.

University's other graduate colleges/schools: College of Agricultural Sciences and Natural Resources, College of Architecture, College of Arts and Sciences, College of Business Administration, College of Education, College of Engineering, College of Human Sciences.

Total university enrollment: 24,200.

School of Law
P.O. Box 40004
Lubbock, Texas 79409-0004
Phone: (806)742-3793
Internet site: http://www.law.ttu.edu
E-mail: xylaw@ttacs.ttu.edu

Established 1967. Located on main campus. ABA approved since 1969. AALS member since 1969. Semester system. Full-time, day study only. Law library: 251,200 volumes/microforms; 2,136 current periodicals/subscriptions; 232 computer workstations; has LEXIS, NEXIS, WESTLAW, CALI. Special programs: Summer Entrance Program; internships.

Annual tuition: resident $6,195, nonresident $10,335. On-campus housing available for single students only. Annual on-campus housing cost: single students $3,963 (room and board). Housing deadline June 1. Contact Housing Office for on-campus housing information. Phone: (806)742-2661. Law students tend to live off-campus. Contact Student Association for off-campus information. Phone: (806)742-3631. Off-campus housing and personal expenses: approximately $9,190. Additional costs: books approximately $700.

Enrollment: first-year class 227; total full-time 642 (men 63%, women 37%); no part-time students. First-year statistics: 5% out of state, 37% women; 15% minority; average age 25; 136 undergraduate institutions represented; range of first-year section sizes 60–70 students; number of upper division courses offered after first year 83.

Faculty: full-time 22, part-time 12; 19% female; 10% minority; student/faculty ratio 27.5 to 1.

Degrees conferred: J.D., J.D.-M.B.A., J.D.-M.P.A., J.D.-M.S. (Accounting, Agricultural Economics), J.D.-M.Tax.

RECRUITMENT PRACTICES AND POLICIES. Attends local and selected national law school forums. Has on-campus informational sessions. School does have diversity program and actively recruits women/minority applicants.

ADMISSION REQUIREMENTS FOR FIRST-YEAR APPLICANTS. LSDAS law school report, LSAT (prefers December, will accept February test, if more than one LSAT, average is used), bachelor's degree from an accredited institution, résumé, personal statement, Residency Oath, transcripts (must show all schools attended and at least three years of study) required in support of application. Applicants must have received bachelor's degree prior to enrollment. Joint-degree applicants must apply to and be accepted by both schools. An Early Action Program is available. Apply to Office of Admission Office after September 1, before February 1. First-year students admitted fall only. Rolling admission process. School does maintain a waiting list. Application fee $50. Phone: (806)742-3985. E-mail: xylaw@ttacs.ttu.edu.

ADMISSION REQUIREMENTS FOR TRANSFER APPLICANTS. Accepts transfers from other ABA-accredited schools. Admission limited to space available. At least one year of enrollment, dean's letter indicating applicant is in good standing (prefer applicants in the top quarter of first-year class), LSAT, LSDAS, personal statement regarding reason for transfer, undergraduate transcript, current law school transcript required in support of application. Apply to Admission Office by June 1. Admission decisions made by mid-summer. Application fee $50. Will consider visiting students.

ADMISSION STANDARDS. Number of full-time applicants 1,376; number accepted 578; number enrolled 227; median LSAT 154 (75% of class have a score at or above 151); median GPA 3.41 (A = 4) (75% of class have a GPA at or above 3.18). Attrition rate 4.5%. Gorman rating 3.18; *U.S. News & World Report* ranking is in the third tier of all law schools.

FINANCIAL AID. Scholarships, merit scholarships, minority scholarships, grants-in-aid, institutional loans, federal loans, and Federal WS offered through university's Financial Aid Office. Assistantships may be available for upper divisional joint-degree candidates. For scholarships (selection criteria place heavy reliance on LSAT and undergraduate GPA) apply to Admissions Office before February. Use scholarship application in admissions materials. For all other programs apply as soon as possible after January 1 to university's Office of Student Financial Aid. Phone: (806)742-3681. Submit FAFSA for all federal programs (Title IV School code #003644). Also submit Financial Aid Transcript, federal income tax forms. Approximately 47% of first-year class received scholarships/grants-in-aid. Approximately 60% of current students receive some form of financial assistance. Average scholarship/grant $3,000.

DEGREE REQUIREMENTS. For J.D.: 90 credits (55 required) with a 2.0 (A = 4) GPA, plus completion of upper divisional writing course; 3-year program. Accelerated J.D. with summer course work. For J.D.-master's: 4-year programs rather than the usual 5-year programs needed if degrees taken separately.

CAREER AND PLACEMENT INFORMATION. About 30–40 employers conducted on-campus interviews. Approximately 97% of graduates are employed in state. More than 94% of graduates are practicing law; 1% are in business; 4% in government; 1% in academia. Approximately 92% of Texas Tech University's first-time state bar exam takers pass the Texas Bar Exam; Texas' passage rate for all first-time takers from ABA-approved schools is 82%. Graduates are eligible to take the bar exam in all 50 states.

UNIVERSITY OF TEXAS AT AUSTIN
Austin, Texas 78712-7666
Internet site: http://www.utexas.ed

Founded 1883. Austin is state capital. Public control. Semester system. Library: 7,016,500 volumes; 4,220,800 microforms; 78,446 periodicals/subscriptions.

University's other graduate colleges/schools: College of Business, College of Communication, College of Education, College of Engineering, College of Fine Arts, College of Liberal Arts, College of Natural Sciences, College of Pharmacy, Graduate School of Library and Information Science, Lyndon B. Johnson School of Public Affairs, School of Architecture, School of Nursing, School of Social Work.

Total university enrollment: 47,900.

School of Law
P.O. Box 149105
Austin, Texas 78714-9105
Phone: (512)471-4800
Internet site: http://www.utexas.edu/law
E-mail: admissions@mail.law.utexas.edu

Established 1883. Located on main campus. ABA approved since 1923. AALS member since 1907. Semester system. Full-time, day study only. Law library: 907,400 volumes/microforms; 9,515 current periodicals/subscriptions; 126 computer workstations; has LEXIS, NEXIS, WESTLAW, DIALOG, CALI; is a State and Federal Document Depository. Special facilities: Center for Public Policy Dispute Resolution, Public Interest Law Center. Special programs: summer study abroad at the University of London, England, University of São Paulo, Brazil, University of Tokyo, Japan; internships.

Annual tuition: resident $6,300, nonresident $13,300, LL.M. $12,000. Limited on-campus housing available. Law students generally prefer to live off-campus. Contact University of Texas Housing Division for off-campus information. Phone: (512)471-3136. Off-campus housing and personal expenses: approximately $10,444. Additional costs: books approximately $800.

Enrollment: first-year class 488; total full-time 1,471 (men 58%, women 42%); no part-time students. First-year statistics: 20% out of state; 42% women; 25% minority; average age 25; 250 undergraduate institutions represented; average first-year section size 100 students; number of upper division courses offered after first year 141.

Faculty: full-time 67, part-time 47; 27% female; 9% minority; student/faculty ratio 18.7 to 1.

Degrees conferred: J.D., J.D.-M.B.A., J.D.-M.P.A., J.D.-M.A. (Latin American Studies, Post Soviet and

East European Studies, Middle Eastern Studies), J.D.-M.S.C.R.P., LL.M. (for foreign law school graduates who have completed a basic legal education and received a university degree in law in another country).

RECRUITMENT PRACTICES AND POLICIES. Attends local and national law school forums. Has on-campus informational sessions. School does have diversity program and actively recruits women/minority applicants.

ADMISSION REQUIREMENTS FOR FIRST-YEAR APPLICANTS. LSDAS law school report, LSAT (not later than October test for Early Decision Program, December test date for regular admission program, if more than one LSAT, average is used), bachelor's degree from an accredited institution, résumé (not to exceed three pages), personal statement (limited to two double-spaced pages), transcripts (must show all schools attended and at least three years of study) required in support of application. Three letters of recommendation from employer or faculty encouraged. Applicants must have received bachelor's degree prior to enrollment. Interview not required but may be requested by school. In addition, international applicants whose native language is not English must submit TOEFL (500 minimum score), certified translation and a course-by-course evaluation. Joint-degree candidates must apply to and be accepted by both schools. Apply to Office of Admission after September 30, before November 1 (Early Decision), February 1 regular decision deadline. First-year students admitted fall only. Rolling admission process, notification starts by January 15 (Early Decision), regular notification will be finished by May 15. Acceptance of offer and first deposit due April 15. School does maintain a waiting list. Application fee $65. Phone: (512)471-8268. E-mail: admissions@mail.law.utexas.edu.

ADMISSION REQUIREMENTS FOR TRANSFER APPLICANTS. Accepts transfers from other ABA-accredited schools. Admission limited to space available. At least one year of enrollment, dean's letter indicating applicant is in good standing (prefer applicants in the top 10% of first-year class), LSAT, LSDAS, résumé. personal statement regarding reason for transfer, undergraduate transcripts, current law school transcript required in support of application. Apply to Admission Office by June 1. Admission decision made by mid July. Application fee $65. Will consider visiting students.

ADMISSION REQUIREMENTS FOR LL.M. (Foreign Law Graduates). All applicants must have the foreign equivalent of an American J.D. with distinction. Official transcripts with certified translations and evaluation, three letters of recommendation, personal statement including the purpose for graduate study required in support of graduate application. TOEFL is required for all applicants whose law degrees were earned where English was not the principal language of instruction. Admits fall only. Apply by March 1 to Graduate Admissions Coordinator at the School of Law. Application fee $75. Approximately 10–12 candidates are accepted each year.

ADMISSION STANDARDS. Number of full-time applicants 3,910; number accepted 1,105; number enrolled 488; median LSAT 162 (75% of class have a score at or above 159); median GPA 3.59 (A = 4) (75% of class have a GPA at or above 3.40). Attrition rate 1.6%. Gorman rating 4.76; *U.S. News & World Report* ranking is in the top 20 of all law schools.

FINANCIAL AID. Law school scholarships, Townes-Rice Scholarship, minority scholarships, Texas Grants, law school and private loans, federal loans, and Federal WS offered through university's Financial Aid Office. Assistantships may be available for upper divisional joint-degree candidates and second- and third-year law students. For scholarships (selection criteria place heavy reliance on LSAT and undergraduate GPA) apply to Loans and Scholarships Office after January 1, before March 31. For all other programs apply to university's Office of Student Financial Services, Wooldridge Hall, 600 W 24th Street, 78714. Phone: (512)475-6282. Submit FAFSA for all federal programs (Title IV School code #003658). Also submit Financial Aid Transcript, federal income tax forms. Approximately 76% of first-year class received scholarships/grants-in-aid. Approximately 80% of current students receive some form of financial assistance. Average scholarship/grant $1,650. Average debt after graduation $30,532. No financial aid available for LL.M. students.

DEGREE REQUIREMENTS. For J.D.: 86 credits (39 required) with a 2.0 (A = 4) GPA, plus completion of upper divisional writing seminar, 1 course in professional responsibility; (28 Month Early Entrance Program), 3-year program. Accelerated J.D. with 2 summers of course work. For J.D.-master's: 4-year programs rather than the usual 5-year programs needed if degrees taken separately. For LL.M. (foreign law graduates): 24 credits; at least 2 semesters in residence; satisfactory completion of "Introduction to U.S. Law and Legal Research"; completion of a substantial paper.

CAREER AND PLACEMENT INFORMATION. About 500 employers conducted on-campus interviews. Approximately 80% of graduates are employed in state. More than 84% of graduates are practicing law; 5% are in business; 10% in government; 1% in academia. Approximately 92% (TX), 100% (CA), 100% (NY) of the University of Texas at Austin's first-time state bar exam takers pass the bar exam; the passage rate for all first-time takers from ABA-approved schools is 82% (TX), 83% (CA), 78% (NY). Graduates are eligible to take the bar exam in all 50 states.

TEXAS WESLEYAN UNIVERSITY
Fort Worth, Texas 76105-1536
Internet site: http://www.txwesleyan.edu

Founded 1890. Private control (Methodist affiliation). Semester system. Library: 239,000 volumes; 51,000 microforms; 1,511 periodicals/subscriptions; 25 computer workstations.

University's other graduate programs: Business Administration, Education, and Health Sciences.

Total university enrollment: 2,800.

School of Law
1515 Commerce Street
Fort Worth, Texas 76102
Phone: (817)212-4100
Internet site: http://www.txwesleyan.edu

Established 1989, became part of Texas Wesleyan University in 1992. School of Law moved to its current site in 1997. ABA approved since 1994 (provisional). AALS member. Semester system. Full-time, part-time study. Law library: 142,000 volumes/microforms; 2,517 current periodicals/subscriptions; 20 computer workstations; has LEXIS, NEXIS, WESTLAW. Special programs: externships.

Annual tuition: full-time $12,074, part-time $8,674. University housing available for both single and married students. Annual on-campus housing cost: single students $3,454 (room only), married students $3,600. Contact Director of Housing for university-owned housing. Phone: (817)531-4432. Law students generally live off-campus. Contact Admissions Office for off-campus information. Off-campus housing and personal expenses: approximately $8,506. Additional costs: books approximately $1,000.

Enrollment: first-year class full-time 144, part-time 105; total full-time 376, part-time 323 (men 58%, women 42%). First-year statistics: 5% out of state; 42% women; 19% minority; average age 30; 86 undergraduate institutions represented; average first-year section sizes full-time students 77, part-time students 110; number of upper division courses offered after first year 46 full-time, 37 part-time.

Faculty: full-time 25, part-time 21; 35% female; 6% minority; student/faculty ratio 23 to 1.

Degree conferred: J.D.

RECRUITMENT PRACTICES AND POLICIES. Attends local and selected national law school forums. Has on-campus informational sessions. School does have diversity program and actively recruits women/minority applicants.

ADMISSION REQUIREMENTS FOR FIRST-YEAR APPLICANTS. LSDAS law school report, LSAT (June test acceptable, if more than one LSAT, highest is used), bachelor's degree from an accredited institution, résumé, personal statement, two recommendations, transcripts (must show all schools attended and at least three years of study) required in support of application. Applicants must have received bachelor's degree prior to enrollment. Apply to Office of Admission after September 30, preference given to those who apply by February 15, later application may be considered. First-year students admitted fall only. Rolling admission process; notification generally completed May 15. Application fee $50. Phone: (800)733-9529, (972)579-5751. Fax: (972)579-5929.

ADMISSION REQUIREMENTS FOR TRANSFER APPLICANTS. Accepts transfers from other ABA-accredited schools. Admission limited to space available. At least one year of enrollment, dean's letter indicating applicant is in good standing (prefer applicants in the top half of first-year class), LSAT, LSDAS, personal statement regarding reason for transfer, two letters of recommendation, undergraduate transcript, current law school transcript required in support of application. Apply to Admission Office at least two months prior to preferred date of entrance. Admission decision made within one month of the receipt of completed application. Application fee $50. Will consider visiting students.

ADMISSION STANDARDS. Number of full-time applicants 783, part-time 226; number accepted 418 full-time, 141 part-time; number enrolled 144 full-time, 105 part-time; median LSAT 144 (75% of class have a score at or above 143 full-time, 144 part-time); median GPA 2.91 (A = 4) (75% of class have a GPA at or above 2.59 full-time, 2.69 part-time). Attrition rate 12%. No Gorman rating or *U.S. News & World Report* ranking.

FINANCIAL AID. Scholarships, grants-in-aid, private and institutional loans, federal loans, and Federal WS may be offered through university's Financial Aid Office. For scholarships (selection criteria place heavy reliance on LSAT and undergraduate GPA) apply to Admissions Office as soon as possible after January 1. Use School's FAF. Submit FAFSA for all federal programs (Title IV School code # 003645). Also submit Financial Aid Transcript, federal income tax forms. Approximately 45% (full-time), 44% (part-time) of first-year class received scholarships/grants-in-aid. Approximately 75% of current students receive some form of financial assistance. Average scholarship/grant $2,200 (full-time), $1,600 (part-time).

DEGREE REQUIREMENTS. For J.D.: 88 credits (33 required) with a 70 (scale 0–100) GPA, plus completion of upper divisional writing course; 3-year full-time program, 4-year part-time program. Accelerated J.D. with summer course work.

CAREER AND PLACEMENT INFORMATION. About 5–10 employers conducted on-campus interviews. Approximately 100% of graduates are employed in state. More than 56% of graduates are practicing law; 39% are in business; 5% in government. Approximately 48% of Texas Wesleyan University's first-time state bar exam takers pass the Texas Bar Exam; Texas' passage rate for all first-time takers from ABA-approved schools is 82%. Graduates are eligible to take the bar exam in all 50 states.

THOMAS M. COOLEY LAW SCHOOL

217 S Capital Avenue
P.O. Box 13038
Lansing, Michigan 48901-3038
Phone: (517)371-5140
Internet site: http://www.cooley.edu
E-mail: cooleyadm@aol.com

Established 1972. Located in downtown Lansing ½ block from state capital. Private control. ABA approved since 1978. AALS member. Trimester system, a year-round educational program. Full-time, part-time study. Law library: 350,000 volumes/microforms; 5,509 current periodicals/subscriptions; 58 computer workstations; has LEXIS, NEXIS, WESTLAW, CALI. Special facility: 60 Plus Law Center, Michigan Indian Law Center.

Annual tuition: full-time $14,110, part-time $10,090. No on-campus housing available. Law students live off-campus. Contact Admission Office for off-campus information. Off-campus housing and personal expenses: approximately $15,571. Additional costs: books approximately $800.

Enrollment: first-year class full-time 106, part-time 982; total full-time 152, 1,671 part-time students (men 65%, women 35%). First-year statistics: 72% out of state; 35% women; 15% minority; average age 26; average first-year section size 80 students; number of upper division courses offered after first year 94.

Faculty: full-time 65, part-time 100; 30% female; 5% minority; student/faculty ratio 24 to 1.

Degree conferred: J.D.

RECRUITMENT PRACTICES AND POLICIES. Attends local and selected national law school forums. Has on-campus informational sessions. School does have diversity program and actively recruits women/minority applicants.

ADMISSION REQUIREMENTS FOR FIRST-YEAR APPLICANTS. LSDAS law school report, LSAT (not later than February test date, if more than one LSAT, highest is used), bachelor's degree from an accredited institution, transcripts (must show all schools attended and at least three years of study) required in support of application. Applicants must have received bachelor's degree prior to enrollment. In addition, international applicants whose native language is not English must submit TOEFL (not older than two years). Apply for admission only if applicant meets the 180 Index Requirement. The Admissions Index is arrived at by multiplying fifteen times UGPA (A = 4) and adding LSAT score. If qualified, submit application at least two months prior to proposed term of entrance. First-year students admitted September morning session (Michaelmas Term), January afternoon session (Hilary Term), May evening session (Trinity Term). Rolling admission process. Application fee $50. Phone: (517)371-5140. Fax: (517)334-5718. E-mail: cooleyadm@aol.com.

ADMISSION REQUIREMENTS FOR TRANSFER APPLICANTS. Accepts transfers from other ABA-accredited schools. Admission limited to space available. At least one year of enrollment, dean's letter indicating applicant is in good standing, LSAT, LSDAS, personal statement regarding reason for transfer, undergraduate transcript, current law school transcript required in support of application. Apply to Admission Office at least two months prior to the beginning of the preferred term; September—morning session, January—afternoon session, May—evening session. Admission decision made within one month of the receipt of completed application. Application fee $50. Will consider visiting students.

ADMISSION STANDARDS. Number of full-time applicants 727; number accepted 547; number enrolled 209; part-time applicants 1,391; number accepted 1,063; number enrolled 550; median LSAT 145 full-time, 144 part-time (75% of class have a score at or above 143 full-time, 142 part-time); median GPA 2.82 full-time, 2.78 part-time (A = 4) (75% of class have a GPA at or above 2.56 full-time, 2.54 part-time). Attrition rate 32%. Gorman rating 2.90; *U.S. News & World Report* ranking is in the fourth tier of all law schools.

FINANCIAL AID. Scholarships, merit scholarships, Martin Luther King, Jr. Scholarships, Rosa Parks Minority Scholarship, grants-in-aid, private and institutional loans, federal loans, and Federal WS available. All accepted students are automatically considered for scholarships (selection based on Admission Index, i.e., 219 or above 100% scholarship, 218 equals 90% scholarship). For all other programs apply at least three months prior to beginning of preferred term. Phone: (517)371-5140. Fax: (517)371-5716. Submit FAFSA for all federal programs (Title IV School code #G12627). Also submit Financial Aid Transcript, federal income tax forms. Approximately 3% of first-year class received scholarships/grants-in-aid. Approximately 85% of current students receive some form of financial assistance. Average scholarship/grant full-time $2,205, part-time $1,078.

DEGREE REQUIREMENTS. For J.D.: 90 credits (74 required) with a 2.0 (A = 4) GPA, plus completion of upper divisional writing course; 24-month full-time program, 32-month full-time program, 36-month part-time program, 48-month part-time program.

CAREER AND PLACEMENT INFORMATION. About 20–30 employers conducted on-campus interviews. Approximately 56% of graduates are employed in state. More than 66% of graduates are practicing law; 16% are in business; 17% in government; 1% in academia. Approximately 61% (MI), 63% (NY) of Thomas M. Cooley Law School's first-time state bar exam takers pass the bar exam; the passage rate for all first-time takers from ABA-approved schools is 85% (MI), 78% (NY). Graduates are eligible to take the bar exam in all 50 states.

THOMAS JEFFERSON SCHOOL OF LAW

2121 San Diego Avenue
San Diego, California 92110
Phone: (619)297-9700
Internet site: http://www.jeffersonlaw.edu
E-mail: info@tjsl.edu

Established 1969. Located in historic Old Town section of San Diego. ABA approved since 1996 (provisional). AALS member. Semester system. Full-time (day), part-time (day or evening) study. Law library: 107,900 volumes/microforms; 2,413 current periodicals/subscriptions; 33 computer workstations; has LEXIS, NEXIS, WESTLAW. Special programs: externships.

Annual tuition: full-time $19,920, part-time $13,500. No on-campus housing available. Law students live off-campus. Contact the Admissions Office for off-campus information. Off-campus housing and personal expenses: approximately $13,973. Additional costs: books approximately $700.

Enrollment: first-year class 70 full-time, 61 part-time; total full- and part-time 564 (men 60%, women 40%). First-year statistics: 15% out of state, 24 states and foreign countries represented; 40% women; 24% minority; average age 26; 115 undergraduate institutions represented; range of first-year section sizes 20–80 students; number of upper division courses offered after first year 47.

Faculty: full-time 22, part-time 40; 37% female; 2% minority; student/faculty ratio 20 to 1.

Degree conferred: J.D.

RECRUITMENT PRACTICES AND POLICIES. Attends local and selected national law school forums. Has on-campus informational sessions. School does have diversity program and actively recruits women/minority applicants.

ADMISSION REQUIREMENTS FOR FIRST-YEAR APPLICANTS. LSDAS law school report, LSAT (not later than June [fall], December [spring] test date), if more than one LSAT, highest is used), bachelor's degree from an accredited institution, résumé, personal statement, two recommendations, transcripts (must show all schools attended and at least three years of study) required in support of application. Applicants must have received bachelor's degree prior to enrollment. Interview not required but both phone and personal interviews are available. In addition, international applicants whose native language is not English must submit TOEFL (not older than two years). The Admissions Committee admits continuously, therefore there are no application deadlines. First-year students admitted fall, spring. Rolling admission process. Application fee $35. Phone: (800)936-7529, (619)297-9700 Ext. 1600. E-mail: info@ tjsl.edu.

ADMISSION REQUIREMENTS FOR TRANSFER APPLICANTS. Accepts transfers from other ABA-accredited schools. Admission limited to space available. At least one year of enrollment, dean's letter indicating applicant is in good standing, LSAT, LSDAS, personal statement regarding reason for transfer, undergraduate transcript, current law school transcript required in support of application. The Admission Committee meets continuously year round, therefore, there are no admission deadlines. Application fee $35. Will consider visiting students.

ADMISSION STANDARDS. Number of full-time applicants 208; number accepted 139 full-time, 89 part-time; number enrolled 70 full-time, 61 part-time; median LSAT 148 (75% of class have a score at or above 145 for both full- and part-time); median GPA 2.73 (A = 4) (75% of class have a GPA at or above 2.48 for both full- and part-time). Attrition rate 15%. No Gorman rating or *U.S. News & World Report* ranking available.

FINANCIAL AID. Scholarships, merit scholarships, minority scholarships, private loans, state grants, federal loans, and Federal WS available. All accepted students are considered for scholarships (selection criteria place heavy reliance on LSAT, a student with a score of 150 of higher automatically receives either a partial or full scholarship). Apply as soon as possible after January 1. Phone: (619)279-9700, Ext. 1350. For all federal programs submit FAFSA (Title IV School code #013780). Also submit Financial Aid Transcript, federal income tax forms. Approximately 42% (full-time), 32% (part-time) of first-year class received scholarships/grants-in-aid. Approximately 70% of current students receive some form of financial assistance. Average scholarship/grant $3,702 full-time, $2,530 part-time.

DEGREE REQUIREMENTS. For J.D.: 88 credits (33 required) with a 2.0 (A = 4) GPA, plus completion of upper divisional writing course; 3-year full-time program, 4-year part-time program. Accelerated J.D. with summer course work.

CAREER AND PLACEMENT INFORMATION. About 10–15 employers conducted on-campus interviews. Most graduates are employed in state. More than 74% of graduates are practicing law; 15% are in business; 10% in government; 1% in academia. Approximately 48% of Thomas Jefferson School of Law's first-time state bar exam takers pass the California Bar Exam; California's passage rate for all first-time takers from ABA-approved schools is 83%. Graduates are eligible to take the bar exam in all 50 states.

UNIVERSITY OF TOLEDO
Toledo, Ohio 43606-3398
Internet site: http://www.utoledo.edu

Founded 1872. Located western edge of Toledo. Public control, became a state university in 1967. Quarter system. Library: 1,600,000 volumes; 1,487,000 microforms; 6,650 periodicals/subscriptions; 32 computer workstations.

University's other graduate colleges/schools: College of Arts and Sciences, College of Education and Allied Professions, College of Engineering, College of Pharmacy, Graduate School of Business.

Total university enrollment: 22,000.

College of Law
2801 West Bancroft
Toledo, Ohio 43606-3390
Phone: (419)530-2882
Internet site: http://www.utoledo.edu/law
E-mail: law0046/uoft01.utoledo.edu

Established 1906. Located on main campus. ABA approved since 1939. AALS member. Semester system. Full-time, part-time study. Law library: 301,000 volumes/ microforms; 3,374 current periodicals/subscriptions; 63 computer workstations; has LEXIS, NEXIS, WESTLAW. Special programs: Legal Institute of the Great Lakes, judicial clerkships.

Annual tuition: full-time resident $6,970, nonresident $13,406, part-time resident $5,808, nonresident $11,172. No on-campus housing available. Law students live off-campus. Contact university's Office of Off-Campus Living for information. Phone: (419)537-8521. Off-Campus housing and personal expenses: approximately $9,639. Additional costs: books approximately $800.

Enrollment: first-year class full-time 154, part-time 46; total full-time 436, part-time 198 (men 56%, women 44%). First-year statistics: 35% out of state, 25 states and foreign countries represented; 44% women; 10% minority; average age 26; 200 undergraduate institutions represented; range of first-year section sizes 20–50 students; number of upper division courses offered after first year 46 full-time, 36 part-time.

Faculty: full-time 36, part-time 25; 24% female; 2% minority; student/faculty ratio 18.8 to 1.

Degrees conferred: J.D., J.D.-M.B.A.

RECRUITMENT PRACTICES AND POLICIES. Attends local and selected national law school forums. Has on-campus informational sessions. School does have diversity program and actively recruits women/minority applicants.

ADMISSION REQUIREMENTS FOR FIRST-YEAR APPLICANTS. LSDAS law school report, LSAT (not later than December test date, if more than one LSAT, highest is used), bachelor's degree from an accredited institution, résumé, two recommendations, transcripts (must show all schools attended and at least three years of study) required in support of application. A personal statement is optional. Applicants must have received bachelor's degree prior to enrollment. Interview not required. Campus visits are encouraged. In addition, international applicants whose native language is not English must submit TOEFL (not older than two years). Joint-degree applicants must apply to and be accepted by both schools. Apply to Office of Admission after September 30, before March 15 (full-time), May 15 (part-time). First-year students admitted fall only. Rolling admission process. Application fee $30. Phone: (419)530-4131. E-mail: law0046@uoft01.utoledo.edu.

ADMISSION REQUIREMENTS FOR TRANSFER APPLICANTS. Accepts transfers from other ABA-accredited schools. Admission limited to space available. At least one year of enrollment, dean's letter indicating applicant is in good standing (prefer applicants in the upper half of first-year class), LSAT, LSDAS, personal statement regarding reason for transfer, undergraduate transcript, current law school transcript required in support of application. Apply to Admission Office at least three months prior to the beginning of the semester. Admission decision made within six week of the receipt of the completed application. Application fee $30. Will consider visiting students.

ADMISSION STANDARDS. Number of full-time applicants 765, part-time 163; number accepted 488 full-time, 93 part-time; number enrolled 154 full-time, 46 part-time; median LSAT 153 full-time, 150 part-time (75% of class have a score at or above 150 full-time, 148 part-time); median GPA 3.05 full-time, 3.03 part-time (A = 4) (75% of class have a GPA at or above 2.67 full-time, 2.69 part-time). Attrition rate 5.4%. Gorman rating 2.49; *U.S. News & World Report* ranking is in the fourth tier of all law schools.

FINANCIAL AID. Scholarships, merit scholarships, minority scholarships, grants-in-aid, private and institutional loans; federal loans and Federal WS offered through university's Financial Aid Office. For scholarships (selection criteria place heavy reliance on LSAT and undergraduate GPA) apply as soon as possible after January1. For all other programs apply by April 1 to university's Office of Financial Aid. Phone: (419)537-2056. Submit FAFSA for all federal programs (Title IV School code #003131). Also submit Financial Aid Transcript, federal income tax forms. Approximately 25% (full-time) 8% (part-time) of first-year class received scholarships/grants-in-aid. Approximately 88% of current students receive some form of financial assistance. Average scholarship/grant $3,206 full-time, $1,000 part-time.

DEGREE REQUIREMENTS. For J.D.: 87 credits (42 required) with a 2.0 (A = 4) GPA, plus completion of upper divisional writing course; 3-year full-time program, 4-year part-time program. Accelerated J.D. with summer course work. For J.D.-M.B.A.: a 4-year program rather than the usual 5-year program needed if degrees taken separately.

CAREER AND PLACEMENT INFORMATION. About 10–15 employers conducted on-campus interviews. Approximately 66% of graduates are employed in state. More than 65% of graduates are practicing law; 17% are in business; 14% in government; 3% in academia. Approximately 92% (OH), 80% (MI) of the University of Toledo's first-time state bar exam takers pass the Ohio Bar Exam; Ohio's passage rate for all first-time takers from ABA-approved schools is 90% (OH), 85% (MI). Graduates are eligible to take the bar exam in all 50 states.

TOURO COLLEGE
JACOB D. FUCHSBERG LAW CENTER

300 Nassau Road
Huntington, New York 11743
Phone: (516)421-2244
Internet site: http://www.tourolaw.edu
E-mail: admissions@tourolaw.edu

Established 1976. Located on Long Island's north shore approximately 30 miles E of New York City. Private control. Semester system. ABA approved since 1983. AALS member. Semester system. Full-time, part-time study. Law library: 336,600 volumes/microforms; 3,408 current periodicals/subscriptions; 50 computer workstations; has LEXIS, NEXIS, WESTLAW, DIALOG, OCLC, DOWJONES, AUTO-CITE. Special facilities: Institute of Local and Suburban Law, Institute of Jewish Law. Special programs: summer study abroad at Moscow State University, Soviet Union, Shimla, India; international internships.

Annual tuition: full-time $19,600, part-time $15,300. On-campus apartments available for both single and married students. Annual on-campus living expenses: $15,089. Law students tend to live off-campus. Contact Admissions Office for both on- and off-campus information. Off-campus housing and personal expenses: approximately $15,545. Additional costs: books approximately $700.

Enrollment: first-year class full-time 113, part-time 107; total full-time 448, part-time 331 (men 60%, women 40%). First-year statistics: 10% out of state, 15 states and 4 foreign countries represented; 40% women; 25% minority; average age 30; 109 undergraduate institutions represented; range of first-year section sizes 15–78 students; number of upper division courses offered after first year 47 full-time, 35 part-time.

Faculty: full-time 40, part-time 24; 31% female; 8% minority; student/faculty ratio 16.5 to 1.

Degrees conferred: J.D., J.D.-M.B.A. (with Dowling College), J.D.-M.P.A. (Long Island University, C.W. Post College), J.D.-M.S. (Tax), LL.M. (full- or part-time for foreign lawyers who have completed a basic legal education and received a university degree in law in another country).

RECRUITMENT PRACTICES AND POLICIES. Attends local and selected national law school forums. Has on-campus informational sessions. School does have diversity program and actively recruits women/minority applicants.

ADMISSION REQUIREMENTS FOR FIRST-YEAR APPLICANTS. LSDAS law school report, LSAT (not later than December test date, if more than one LSAT, highest is used), bachelor's degree from an accredited institution, personal statement, transcripts (must show all schools attended and at least three years of study) required in support of application. Recommendations are optional. Applicants must have received bachelor's degree prior to enrollment. Campus visits are encouraged. In addition, international applicants whose native language is not English must submit TOEFL (not older than

five years), certified translations and evaluations of all foreign credentials. Joint-degree applicants must apply to and be accepted by both colleges/university. Apply to Office of Admission after September 30, before May 1 (priority deadline). First-year students admitted fall only. Rolling admission process, notification starts within four to six weeks from the time application is complete and continues until class is filled. Application fee $50. Phone: (516)421-2244, Ext. 312. Fax: (516)421-2675. E-mail: admissions@tourolaw.edu.

ADMISSION REQUIREMENTS FOR TRANSFER APPLICANTS. Accepts transfers from other ABA-accredited schools. Admission limited to space available. At least one year of enrollment, dean's letter indicating applicant is in good standing (prefer applicants in the top half of first-year class), LSAT, LSDAS, personal statement regarding reason for transfer, undergraduate transcript, current law school transcript required in support of application. Admits to fall, spring. Apply to Admissions Office at least six weeks prior to preferred semester of entrance. Admission decision made within one month of the receipt of the completed application. Application fee $50. Will consider visiting students.

ADMISSION REQUIREMENTS FOR LL.M. (Foreign Lawyers). All applicants must have the foreign equivalent of an American J.D. Official transcript with certified translation and evaluations, two letters of recommendation, personal statement required in support of LL.M. application. TOEFL required for those applicants whose native language is not English. Admits fall only. Full-time day, part-time day, part-time evening study available. Apply to Admissions Office at least three months prior to preferred date of entrance. Application fee $50.

ADMISSION STANDARDS. Number of full-time applicants 1,232, part-time 443; number accepted 418 full-time, 218 part-time; number enrolled 113 full-time, 107 part-time; median LSAT 148 (75% of class have a score at or above 144 full-time, 147 part-time); median GPA 3.0 (A = 4) (75% of class have a GPA at or above 2.69 full-time, 2.55 part-time). Attrition rate 5.3%. Gorman rating 2.13; *U.S. News & World Report* ranking is in the fourth tier of all law schools.

FINANCIAL AID. Scholarships, Dean's Fellowships, merit scholarships and Incentive Awards, private and institutional loans, summer Public Interest Fellowships, state grants (TAP), federal loans, and Federal WS available. All accepted students are automatically considered for scholarships (selection criteria place heavy reliance on LSAT and undergraduate GPA). Apply to Admissions

Office as soon as possible after January 1. Phone: (516)421-2244, Ext. 322. For all federal programs submit FAFSA by May 1. Also submit Financial Aid Transcript, federal income tax forms. Approximately 42% (full-time), 26% (part-time) of first-year class received scholarships/grants-in-aid. Approximately 85% of current students receive some form of financial assistance. Average scholarship/grant $4,000 full-time, $2,500 part-time. Public Interest Loan Repayment Program available.

DEGREE REQUIREMENTS. For J.D.: 87 credits (44–46 required) with a 2.0 (A = 4) GPA, plus completion of upper divisional writing course; 3-year full-time program, 4-year part-time program. Accelerated J.D. with 2 summers of course work. For J.D.-master's: 4-year program rather than the usual 5-year program needed if degrees taken separately. For LL.M. (Foreign Lawyers): 27 credits, at least 2 semesters in residence; successful completion of "Introduction to the U.S. Legal System."

CAREER AND PLACEMENT INFORMATION. About 15–20 employers conducted on-campus interviews. Approximately 91% of graduates are employed in state. More than 67% of graduates are practicing law; 24% are in business; 9% in government. Approximately 65% of Touro College's first-time state bar exam takers pass the New York Bar Exam; New York's passage rate for all first-time takers from ABA-approved schools is 78%. Graduates are eligible to take the bar exam in all 50 states.

TULANE UNIVERSITY
New Orleans, Louisiana 70118-5669
Internet site: http://www.tulane.edu

Founded 1834. Private control. Semester system. Library: 2,200,000 volumes; 2,405,300 microforms; 14,846 periodicals/subscriptions.

University's other graduate colleges/schools: Graduate School, A.B. Freeman Business School, School of Architecture, School of Engineering, School of Medicine, School of Public Health and Tropical Medicine, School of Social Work.

Total university enrollment: 11,100.

Law School
John Giffen Weinmann Hall
6329 Freret Street
New Orleans, Louisiana 70118-5670
Phone: (504)865-5939
Internet site: http://www.law.tulane.edu
E-mail: admissions@law.tulane.edu

Established 1847. Located on main campus. ABA approved since 1925. AALS member. Semester system. Full-time, day study only. Law library: 484,400 volumes/microforms; 5,584 current periodicals/subscriptions; 140 computer workstations; has LEXIS, NEXIS, WESTLAW, DIALOG, EELS, ORBIT, QUICKLAW, VU-TEXT; is a Federal Government Depository. Special facilities: Maritime Law Center, Eason Weinmann Center for Comparative Law, Institute for Environmental Law. Special programs: summer study abroad at McGill University, Canada, Trinity College Cambridge, England, Tulane Institute of European Legal Studies, Paris, France, Hebrew University, Israel, University of Siena, Italy, Tulane Center for European Union Law, Amsterdam, the Netherlands; externships.

Annual tuition: $22,940, LL.M. $22,940. On-campus housing available for both single and married students. Annual on-campus housing cost: single students $4,420 (room only), $7,273 (room and board), married students $4,680. Housing deadline March 24. Contact Director of Housing for both on- and off- campus housing information. Phone: (504)865-5724. Law students tend to live off-campus. Off-campus housing and personal expenses: approximately $11,200. Additional costs: books approximately $800.

Enrollment: first-year class 327; total full-time 994 (men 53%, women 47%); no part-time students. First-year statistics: 84% out of state, 54 states and foreign countries represented; 47% women; 24% minority; average age 24; 300 undergraduate institutions represented; range of first-year section sizes 40–100 students; number of upper division courses offered after first year 162.

Faculty: full-time 58, part-time 58; 27% female; 9% minority; student/faculty ratio 17.6 to 1.

Degrees conferred: J.D., J.D.-M.B.A., J.D.-M.H.A., J.D.-M.P.H., J.D.-M.S.P.H., LL.M. (General, Admiralty, Energy and Environmental Law), LL.M.-M.S.P.H., M.C.L. (International and Comparative Law—for persons who have completed a basic legal education and received a university degree in law in another country.) LL.M.-M.A. (Latin American Studies), S.J.D.

RECRUITMENT PRACTICES AND POLICIES. Attends local and national law school forums. Has on-campus informational sessions. School does have diversity program and actively recruits women/minority applicants.

ADMISSION REQUIREMENTS FOR FIRST-YEAR APPLICANTS. LSDAS law school report, LSAT (not later than December test date, if more than one LSAT, average is used), bachelor's degree from an accredited institution, résumé, personal statement, two recommendations, transcripts (must show all schools attended and at least three years of study) required in support of application. Applicants must have received bachelor's degree prior to enrollment. Interview not required but may be arranged with law school personnel. In addition, international applicants whose native language is not English must submit TOEFL (not older than two years), certified translations and evaluations of all foreign credentials. Joint-degree applicants must apply to and be accepted by both schools. Apply to Office of Admission after October 1, before March 1. First-year students admitted fall only. Rolling admission process, notification starts in December and is finished by May. School does maintain a waiting list. Application fee $45. Phone: (504)865-5930. Fax: (504)865-6710. E-mail: admissions@law.tulane.edu.

ADMISSION REQUIREMENTS FOR TRANSFER APPLICANTS. Accepts transfers from other ABA-accredited schools. Admission limited to space available. At least one year of enrollment, dean's letter indicating applicant is in good standing (prefer applicants in the top quarter of first-year class), LSAT, LSDAS, personal statement regarding reason for transfer, two letters of recommendation from current faculty members, undergraduate transcripts, current law school transcript required in support of application. Apply to Admission Office by June 1. Admission decisions made by mid July. Application fee $45. Will consider visiting students.

ADMISSION REQUIREMENTS FOR LL.M. APPLICANTS. All applicants must have obtained a J.D. (equivalent) from a U.S. law school or the first (basic) law degree from a foreign law school approved by Tulane's Committee on Graduate Admission. Official transcripts (a certified translation and evaluation in addition to original international credentials for international applicants), two letters of recommendation, personal statement required in support of Graduate Programs in Law application. In addition, international candidates whose native language is not English and have attended a law school in a non-English speaking countries must submit TOEFL. The TSE is strongly encouraged although not required. Admits fall only. Apply after September 1, before May 1 (preferred deadline March 31, especially for international candidates). Application fee $50. Phone: (504)865-5930.

ADMISSION REQUIREMENTS FOR S.J.D. APPLICANTS. All applicants should have an LL.M. earned within the past five years. Official transcripts, two letters of recommendation, detailed proposal for research to be undertaken, as well as any work already written or pub-lished required in support of S.J.D. application. TOEFL required for all applicants whose native language is other than English. In addition, each candidate should have contacted a Tulane Law School faculty member to be a sponsor for research project. Admits fall only. Apply to Office of Graduate Programs in Law. Application fee $75. Phone: (504)865-5930.

ADMISSION STANDARDS. Number of full-time applicants 2,945; number accepted 1,492; number enrolled 327; median LSAT 158 (75% of class have a score at or above 156); median GPA 3.28 (A = 4) (75% of class have a GPA at or above 3.03). Attrition rate 4.1%. Gorman rating 4.42; *U.S. News & World Report* ranking is in the top 50 of all law schools.

FINANCIAL AID. Scholarships, merit scholarships, minority scholarships, tuition waivers, private and institutional loans, federal loans, and Federal WS offered through university's Financial Aid Office. Assistantships may be available for upper divisional joint-degree candidates. All accepted students who submit school's financial aid application are automatically considered for scholarships (selection criteria place heavy reliance on LSAT and undergraduate GPA). Submit the Financial Aid Information Request Form at the same time as admissions application but before February 15. All financial aid offers must be confirmed by the university's Director of Financial Aid. Submit FAFSA to processor not later than February 15 (Title IV School code #002029). Also submit Financial Aid Transcript, federal income tax forms. Approximately 40% of first-year class received scholarships/grants-in-aid. Approximately 70% of current students receive some form of financial assistance. Average scholarship/grant $5,000. Summer public interest jobs available. Average debt after graduation $60,000. Loan Repayment Assistance Program available (LRAPS).

Financial aid for LL.M. students. Scholarships, partial tuition waivers, Graduate Fellowships, private loans, federal loans (for eligible candidates submit FAFSA) available. Submit the Financial Data and Scholarships Form to school's Financial Aid Office. Contact school's Financial Aid Office for more specific information and deadlines. Phone: (504)865-5931. E-mail: sjohnson@law.tulane.edu.

DEGREE REQUIREMENTS. For J.D.: 88 credits (31 required) with a 2.0 (A = 4) GPA, plus completion of upper divisional writing course; 20 hours of pro bono work required; 3-year program. Accelerated J.D. with summer course work. For J.D.-master's: 4-year program rather than the usual 5-year program needed if degrees taken separately. Law school accepts up to 9 credits toward degree, the other programs will accept between 12–15 credits. For LL.M.: 24 credits up to 1 year of full-time study. For M.C.L. (International and Comparative Law): 30 credits, at least 2 semesters in residence; successful completion of 1 3-week "Introduction to American Law" course. LL.M.-M.S.P.H.: 52 credits, 2-year program (LL.M. 24 credits, M.S.P.H. 28 credits), M.C.L.-M.A.: 30 credits; 1½-year program (M.C.L. 15 credits, M.A. 15 credits). For S.J.D.: complete all requirements for LL.M.; at least 1 semester in full-time residence; dissertation; oral defense.

CAREER AND PLACEMENT INFORMATION. About 150–160 employers conducted on-campus interviews. Approximately 31% of graduates are employed in state. More than 73% of graduates are practicing law; 12% are in business; 15% in government. Approximately 53% (LA), 55% (CA), 64% (MD), 85% (NY), 84% (PA) of Tulane University's first-time state bar exam takers pass the bar exam; the passage rate for all first-time takers from ABA-approved schools is 67% (LA), 83% (CA), 75% (MD), 78% (NY), 73% (PA). Graduates are eligible to take the bar exam in all 50 states.

UNIVERSITY OF TULSA

Tulsa, Oklahoma 74104-3189
Internet site: http://www.utulsa.edu

Founded 1894. Private control. Semester system. Library: 790,000 volumes; 2,414,300 microforms; 7,424 periodicals/subscriptions; 87 computer workstations.

University's other graduate colleges/schools: College of Arts and Sciences, College of Business Administration, College of Engineering and Applied Sciences.

Total university enrollment: 4,400.

College of Law
3120 East Fourth Place
Tulsa, Oklahoma 74104-2499
Phone: (918)631-2401
Internet site: http://www.utulsa.edu/AcademicColleges/
   Collegeoflaw.html
E-mail: law_vls@centum.utulsa.edu

Established 1923. Located on main campus. ABA approved since 1950. AALS member. Semester system. Full-time, part-time study. Law library: 263,700 volumes/microforms; 3,869 current periodicals/subscriptions; 56 computer workstations; has LEXIS, NEXIS, WEST-LAW, DIALOG, LegalTrack. Special programs: legal and judicial internships.

Annual tuition: full-time $15,314 (31 credits), part-time $10,264 (21 credits). On-campus housing available for both single and married students. Annual on-campus housing cost: single students $3,500 (room only), $5,500 (room and board); married students $4,500, $6,500 (room and board). Contact Director of Housing for both on- and off-campus housing information. Phone: (918)631-2378. Law students tend to live off-campus. Off-campus housing and personal expenses: approximately $7,050. Additional costs: books approximately $700.

Enrollment: first-year class full-time 154, part-time 58; total full-time 480, part-time 128 (men 61%, women 39%). First-year statistics: 56% out of state, 45 states and foreign countries represented; 39% women; 15% minority; average age 24; 175 undergraduate institutions represented; average first-year section size 76 students; number of upper division courses offered after first year 89 full-time, 30 part-time.

Faculty: full-time 38, part-time 30; 28% female; 10% minority; student/faculty ratio 16.8 to 1.

Degrees conferred: J.D., J.D.-M.Acc., J.D.-M.B.A., J.D.-M.Tax., J.D.-M.A. (Anthropology, History, Industrial and Organizational Psychology, Clinical Psychology), J.D.-M.S. (Biological Sciences, Geosciences).

RECRUITMENT PRACTICES AND POLICIES. Attends local and selected national law school forums. Has on-campus informational sessions. School does have diversity program and actively recruits women/minority applicants.

ADMISSION REQUIREMENTS FOR FIRST-YEAR APPLICANTS. LSDAS law school report, LSAT (not later than December test date, if more than one LSAT, highest is used), bachelor's degree from an accredited institution, résumé, personal statement, two recommendations, transcripts (must show all schools attended and at least three years of study) required in support of application. Applicants must have received bachelor's degree prior to enrollment. Interview not required, campus visits encouraged. In addition, international applicants whose native language is not English must submit TOEFL (not older than two years), certified translations and evaluations of all foreign credentials by Educational Credential Evaluator, Milwaukee, Wisconsin, 53211. Phone: (414)289-3400. Joint-degree applicants must apply to and be accepted by both schools. Apply to Office of Admission after September 30, before January 15 (for full scholarship consideration; no official deadline). First-year students admitted fall only. Rolling admission process, all complete applications received by February 1 will be notified by March 31. Acceptance of offer and first deposit due April 1. Application fee $30. Phone: (918)631-2709. Fax: (918)631-2406. E-mail: law_vls@centum.utulsa.edu.

ADMISSION REQUIREMENTS FOR TRANSFER APPLICANTS. Accepts transfers from other ABA-accredited schools. Admission limited to space available. At least one year of enrollment, dean's letter indicating applicant is in good standing (prefer applicants in the top half of first-year class), LSAT, LSDAS, personal statement regarding reason for transfer, two letters of recommendation, undergraduate transcript, current law school transcript required in support of application. Apply to Admission Office at least six weeks prior to beginning of the semester. Admission decision made within one month of the receipt of a complete application. Application fee $30. Will consider visiting students.

ADMISSION STANDARDS. Number of full-time applicants 793, part-time 110; number accepted 516 full-time, 84 part-time; number enrolled 154 full-time, 58 part-time; median LSAT 152 (75% of class have a score at or above 148 full-time, 145 part-time); median GPA 3.03 (A = 4) (75% of class have a GPA at or above 2.75 for both full- and part-time). Attrition rate 4.2%. Gorman rating 3.21; *U.S. News & World Report* ranking is in the fourth tier of all law schools.

FINANCIAL AID. Need-based scholarships, merit scholarships, minority scholarships, state-funded grants, private and institutional loans; federal loans and Federal WS offered through university's Financial Aid Office. Assistantships may be available for upper divisional joint-degree candidates. Complete College of Law Need Application Form for scholarships (selection criteria place heavy reliance on LSAT and undergraduate GPA) by January 15 for full consideration. For all other programs complete university's Financial Aid Application and send to the university's Student Financial Services Office. Phone: (918)631-2526. Use FAFSA for all federal programs (Title IV School code #003185). Also submit Financial Aid Transcript, federal income tax forms. Approximately 34% (full-time), 28% (part-time) of first-year class received scholarships/grants-in-aid. Approximately 75% of current students receive some form of financial assistance. Average scholarship/grant $3,875 full-time, $2,800 part-time. Average debt after graduation $52,600.

DEGREE REQUIREMENTS. For J.D.: 88 credits (42 required) with a 2.0 (A = 4) GPA, plus completion of upper divisional writing course; 3-year full-time program, 4-year part-time program. Accelerated J.D. with summer course work. For J.D.-M.B.A., M.Acc., M.S.Tax.: 102 total credits (J.D. 78 credits, other degrees 24 credits). For J.D.-M.A., M.S.: 102–105 total credits (J.D. 78 credits, other degrees 24–27 credits). For J.D.-M.A. (Clinical Psychology): 114 total credits (J.D. 78 credits, M.A. 36 credits).

CAREER AND PLACEMENT INFORMATION. About 35–40 employers conducted on-campus interviews. Approximately 64% of graduates are employed in state. More than 65% of graduates are practicing law; 24% are in business; 11% in government. Approximately 78% (OK), 82% (TX), 100% (MO) of the University of Tulsa's first-time state bar exam takers pass the bar exam; the passage rate for all first-time takers from ABA-approved schools is 75% (OK), 82% (TX), 92% (MO). Graduates are eligible to take the bar exam in all 50 states.

UNION UNIVERSITY
Schenectady, New York 12308-2311
Internet site: http://www.union/edu

Founded 1795. Located across the Hudson River from Albany. Private control. Semester system. Library: 500,000 volumes; 618,600 microforms; 1,970 periodicals/subscriptions.

University's other graduate colleges/schools: Union College, Albany Medical School, Albany College of Pharmacy.

Total university enrollment: 2,300.

Albany Law School
80 New Scotland Avenue
Albany, New York 12208
Phone: (518)445-2311
Internet site: http://www.als.edu
E-mail: admissions@mail.als.edu

Established 1851. Located in the state capital of New York. ABA approved since 1930. AALS member. Semester system. Full-time, day study, very limited part-time study. Law library: 489,300 volumes/microforms; 3,819 current periodicals/subscriptions; 86 computer workstations; has LEXIS, NEXIS, WESTLAW, DIALOG. Special facility: Government Law Center. Special program: externships.

Annual tuition: full-time $18,905, part-time $14,206. Limited on-campus housing available for single students only. Annual on-campus housing cost: single students $5,800 (room and board). Law students tend to live off-campus. Contact Admissions Office for both on- and off-campus information. Off-campus housing and personal expenses: approximately $10,070. Additional costs: books approximately $700.

Enrollment: first-year class 247; total full-time 727, part-time 36 (men 49%, women 51%). First-year statistics: 15% out of state, 28 states and foreign countries represented; 51% women; 18% minority; average age 26; 28 undergraduate institutions represented; range of first-year section size 25–92 students; number of upper division courses offered after first year 99.

Faculty: full-time 40, part-time 37; 39% female; 11% minority; student/faculty ratio 24 to 1.

Degrees conferred: J.D., J.D.-M.B.A. (with the College of St. Rose, Union College, Rensselaer Polytechnic University, the Sages Colleges), J.D.-M.P.A. (with the University at Albany, SUNY).

RECRUITMENT PRACTICES AND POLICIES. Attends local and selected national law school forums. Has on-campus informational sessions. School does have diversity program and actively recruits women/minority applicants.

ADMISSION REQUIREMENTS FOR FIRST-YEAR APPLICANTS. LSDAS law school report, LSAT (not later than December test date, if more than one LSAT, average is used), bachelor's degree from an accredited institution, résumé, personal statement, two recommendations, transcripts (must show all schools attended and at least three years of study) required in support of application. Applicants must have received bachelor's degree prior to enrollment. Campus visits encouraged. In addition, international applicants whose native language is not English must submit TOEFL (not older than two years). Joint-degree applicants must apply to and be accepted by both colleges/university. Apply to Office of Admission after September 30, before March 15. First-year students admitted fall only. Rolling admission process. Application fee $50. Phone: (518)445-2326. E-mail: admissions@mail.als.edu.

ADMISSION REQUIREMENTS FOR TRANSFER APPLICANTS. Accepts transfers from other ABA-accredited schools. Admission limited to space available. At least one year of enrollment, dean's letter indicating applicant is in good standing (prefer applicants in the top half of first-year class), LSAT, LSDAS, personal statement regarding reason for transfer, two letters of recommendation from current faculty members, undergraduate transcripts, current law school transcript required in support of application. Apply to Admission Office by June 1. Admission decisions made by mid July. Application fee $50. Will consider visiting students.

ADMISSION STANDARDS. Number of full-time applicants 1,297; number accepted 875; number enrolled 247; median LSAT 151 (75% of class have a score at or above 147); median GPA 3.08 (A = 4) (75% of class have a GPA at or above 2.78). Attrition rate 3.7%. Gorman rating 4.35; *U.S. News & World Report* ranking is in the third tier of all law schools.

FINANCIAL AID. Scholarships, merit scholarships, minority scholarships, state grants, private and institutional loans, federal loans, and Federal WS available. For scholarships (selection criteria place heavy reliance on LSAT and undergraduate GPA) apply as soon as possible after January 1; use Albany Law School Request for Financial Assistance. For other programs submit FAFSA (Title IV School code # G02886). Also submit Financial Aid Transcript, federal income tax forms. Approximately 48% of first-year class received scholarships/grants-in-aid. Approximately 85% of current students receive some form of financial assistance. Average scholarship/grant $4,000. Average debt after graduation $60,000.

DEGREE REQUIREMENTS. For J.D.: 87 credits (30 required) with a 2.0 (A = 4) GPA, plus completion of upper divisional writing course; 3-year full-time program, 4-year part-time program. Accelerated J.D. with 2 summers of course work. For J.D.-master's: 4-year program rather than the usual 5-year program needed if degrees taken separately.

CAREER AND PLACEMENT INFORMATION. About 50–60 employers conducted on-campus interviews. Approximately 78% of graduates are employed in state. More than 57% of graduates are practicing law; 20% are in business; 17% in government; 1% in academia. Approximately 93% of Union University's first-time state bar exam takers pass the New York Bar Exam; New York's passage rate for all first-time takers from ABA-approved schools is 78%. Graduates are eligible to take the bar exam in all 50 states.

UNIVERSITY OF UTAH

Salt Lake City, Utah 84112-9401
Internet site: http://www.utah.edu

Founded 1850. Public control. Semester system. Library: 3,089,400 volumes; 3,126,000 microforms; 21,807 periodicals/subscriptions; 186 computer workstations.

University's other graduate colleges/schools: College of Engineering, College of Fine Arts, College of Health, College of Humanities, College of Mines and Earth Sciences, College of Nursing, College of Science, College of Social and Behavioral Science, Graduate School of Architecture, Graduate School of Business, Graduate School of Education, Graduate School of Social Work, College of Pharmacy, School of Medicine.

Total university enrollment: 27,100.

College of Law

Admissions Office
Salt Lake City, Utah 84112
Phone: (801)571-6833
Internet site: http://www.law.utah.edu
E-mail: admissions@law.utah.edu

Established 1914. Located on main campus. ABA approved since 1927. AALS member. Semester system. Full-time, day study only. Law library: 286,300 volumes/microforms; 4,395 current periodicals/subscriptions; 62 computer workstations; has LEXIS, NEXIS, WESTLAW, VUTEXT; is a State Government Depository. Special facility: Wallace Stegner Center for Land, Resources and the Environment. Special programs: externships.

Annual tuition: resident $4,524, nonresident $10,122. On-campus housing available for both single and married students. Annual on-campus housing cost: single students $1,800 (room only), married students $5,241. Contact Office of Residential Living for both on- and off-campus housing information. Phone: (801)581-6611. Law students tend to live off-campus. Off-campus housing and personal expenses: approximately $12,246. Additional costs: books approximately $700.

Enrollment: first-year class 101; total full-time 366 (men 62%, women 38%); no part-time students. First-year statistics: 32% out of state, 43 states and 11 foreign countries represented; 38% women; 14% minority; average age 28; 138 undergraduate institutions represented; range of first-year section sizes 10–50 students; number of upper division courses offered after first year 81.

Faculty: full-time 29, part-time 36; 29% female; 12% minority; student/faculty ratio 14.8 to 1.

Degrees conferred: J.D., J.D.-M.B.A., J.D.-M.P.A., LL.M. (Environmental and Natural Resource Law).

RECRUITMENT PRACTICES AND POLICIES. Attends local and selected national law school forums. Has on-campus informational sessions. School does have diversity program and actively recruits women/minority applicants.

ADMISSION REQUIREMENTS FOR FIRST-YEAR APPLICANTS. LSDAS law school report, LSAT (not later than December test date, if more than one LSAT, average is used), bachelor's degree from an accredited institution, personal statement, one Letter of Evaluation Form (no more than three), transcripts (must show all schools attended and at least three years of study) required in support of application. Applicants must have received bachelor's degree prior to enrollment. Interview not required. In addition, international applicants whose native language is not English must submit TOEFL (not older than two years), certified translations and evaluations of all foreign credentials. Joint-degree applicants must apply to and be accepted by both schools. Apply to Office of Admission after November 1, before March 1, preference given to applications received by January 15. First-year students admitted fall only. Rolling admission process, notification starts in February and is finished by late April. School does maintain a waiting list. Application fee $40. Phone: (800)444-8638, (801)581-7479. E-mail: admissions@law.utah.edu.

ADMISSION REQUIREMENTS FOR TRANSFER APPLICANTS. Accepts transfers from other ABA-accredited schools. Admission limited to space available. At least one year of enrollment, dean's letter indicating applicant is in good standing (prefer applicants in the top third of first-year class), LSAT, LSDAS, personal statement regarding reason for transfer, one letter of evaluation, undergraduate transcript, current law school transcript required in support of application. Admits fall only. Apply to Admission Office by July 15. Admission decisions made by early August. Application fee $40. Will consider visiting students.

ADMISSION REQUIREMENTS FOR LL.M. APPLICANTS. All applicants must possess a J.D. or equivalent degree from an ABA-approved American law school or from an approved foreign law school. Official transcripts with rank-in-class, résumé, personal statement with rationale for graduate study required in support of graduate application. In addition, international applicants whose native language is other than English must submit TOEFL and certified translations and evaluations of foreign credentials. Admits fall only. Apply by May 1 to the

Office of Admissions. Application fee $40. Phone: (801)581-7479.

ADMISSION STANDARDS. Number of full-time applicants 810; number accepted 300; number enrolled 101; median LSAT 159 (75% of class have a score at or above 154); median GPA 3.38 (A = 4) (75% of class have a GPA at or above 3.11). Attrition rate 2.5%. Gorman rating 4.40; *U.S. News & World Report* ranking is in the top 40 of all law schools.

FINANCIAL AID. Scholarships, merit scholarships, minority scholarships, diversity intern stipends, grants-in-aid, private and institutional loans; federal loans and Federal WS offered through university's Financial Aid Office. Assistantships may be available for upper divisional joint-degree candidates. For scholarships (selection criteria place heavy reliance on LSAT and undergraduate GPA) apply to the Office of Financial Aid after January1, before February 15; submit the Supplemental Financial Aid Application (UU98). For all other programs apply to university's Financial Aid Office. Phone: (801)585-5828. Use FAFSA for all federal programs and mail to federal Student Aid programs, Iowa City (Title IV School code #003675). Also submit Financial Aid Transcript, federal income tax forms. Approximately 41% of first-year class received scholarships/grants-in-aid. Approximately 75% of current students receive some form of financial assistance. Average scholarship/grant $3,266. Loan forgiveness program for graduates who work in the public sector. Average debt after graduation $30,000.

DEGREE REQUIREMENTS. For J.D.: 88 credits (40 required) with a 2.0 (A = 4) GPA, plus completion of upper divisional writing course; 3-year program. Accelerated J.D. with summer course work. For J.D.-master's: 4-year programs rather than the usual 5-year programs needed if degrees taken separately. For LL.M. (with American J.D.): 24 credits, 17 credits in required courses; at least 2 semesters in full-time residence; 1 seminar requiring major research and writing project; LL.M. seminar. For LL.M. (with foreign law degree): 24 credits; at least 2 semesters in full-time residence; 2 courses in U.S. Law; 15–17 credits in approved courses; thesis; LL.M. seminar; a GPA of 2.75 (A = 4) required.

CAREER AND PLACEMENT INFORMATION. About 30–40 employers conducted on-campus interviews. Approximately 77% of graduates are employed in state. More than 75% of graduates are practicing law; 18% are in business; 12% in government. Approximately 93% of the University of Utah's first-time state bar exam takers pass the Utah Bar Exam; Utah's passage rate for all first-time takers from ABA-approved schools is 93%. Graduates are eligible to take the bar exam in all 50 states.

VALPARAISO UNIVERSITY
Valparaiso, Indiana 46383-6493
Internet site: http://www.valpo.edu

Founded 1859. Located 55 miles SE of Chicago. Private control (Lutheran affiliation). Semester system. Library: 531,000 volumes; 333,100 microforms; 3,753 periodicals/subscriptions; 106 computer workstations.

University's graduate division: College of Nursing, programs in Education, Liberal Studies, Music, Psychology, Sociology.

Total university enrollment: 3,500.

School of Law
Wesemann Hall
Valparaiso, Indiana 46383
Phone: (219)465-7829
Internet site: http://www.valpo.edu/law
E-mail: valpolaw@wesemann.law.valpl.edu

Established 1879. Located on main campus. ABA approved since 1929. AALS member. Semester system. Full-time, part-time study. Law library: 255,800 volumes/microforms; 3,223 current periodicals/subscriptions; 41 computer workstations; has LEXIS, NEXIS, WESTLAW, DIALOG. Special programs: summer study abroad at Valparaiso University's Cambridge Centre, England; summer Academic Support Program; externships; internships.

Annual tuition: full-time $16,920; part-time $12,940. No on-campus housing available. Law students live off-campus. Contact Admissions Office for off-campus information. Off-campus housing and personal expenses: approximately $10,370. Additional costs: books approximately $700.

Enrollment: first-year class full-time 141, part-time 17; total full-time 398, part-time 57 (men 55%, women 45%). First-year statistics: 46% out of state, 32 states and foreign countries represented; 45% women; 19% minority; average age 25; 161 undergraduate institutions represented; range of first-year section sizes 45–70 students; number of upper division courses offered after first year 67.

Faculty: full-time 16, part-time 16; 39% female; 6% minority; student/faculty ratio 22.7 to 1.

Degree conferred: J.D.

RECRUITMENT PRACTICES AND POLICIES. Attends local and selected national law school forums. Has on-campus informational sessions. School does have diversity program and actively recruits women/minority applicants.

ADMISSION REQUIREMENTS FOR FIRST-YEAR APPLICANTS. LSDAS law school report, LSAT (not later than February test date, if more than one LSAT, highest is used), bachelor's degree from an accredited institution, personal statement, transcripts (must show all schools attended and at least three years of study) required in support of application. Two recommendations (no more than three) optional but encouraged. Applicants must have received bachelor's degree prior to enrollment. Interview not required. In addition, international applicants whose native language is not English must submit TOEFL (not older than two years). Apply to Office of Admission after September 30, before April 15. First-year students admitted fall only. Rolling admission process, first review begins in January, second review starts in late spring and is finished by summer. Acceptance of offer and first deposit due April 15. Application fee $30. Phone: (800)262-0656, (219)465-7829. E-mail: valpolaw@wsmann.law.valpo.edu.

ADMISSION REQUIREMENTS FOR TRANSFER APPLICANTS. Accepts transfers from other ABA-accredited schools. Admission limited to space available. At least one year of enrollment, dean's letter indicating applicant is in good standing, LSAT, LSDAS, personal statement regarding reason for transfer, undergraduate transcript, current law school transcript required in support of application. Apply to Admission Office by July 15. Admission decision made within one month of receipt of completed application. Application fee $30. Will consider visiting students.

ADMISSION STANDARDS. Number of full-time applicants 736, part-time 47; number accepted 514 full-time, 30 part-time; number enrolled 141 full-time, 17 part-time; median LSAT 152 (75% of class have a score at or above 147 full-time, 146 part-time); median GPA 3.25 (A = 4) (75% of class have a GPA at or above 2.85 full-time, 2.70 part-time). Attrition rate 5.4%. Gorman rating 3.60; *U.S. News & World Report* ranking is in the fourth tier of all law schools.

FINANCIAL AID. Scholarships, merit scholarships, diversity scholarships, Public Service Grants, private and institutional loans; federal loans and Federal WS offered through university's Financial Aid Office. For scholarships (selection criteria place heavy reliance on LSAT and undergraduate GPA) apply before March 1. For all other programs apply to university's Office of Financial Aid. Phone: (800)348-2611. Submit FAFSA for all federal programs (Title IV School code #001842). Also submit Financial Aid Transcript, federal income tax forms. Approximately 65% (full-time), 30% (part-time) of first-year class received scholarships/grants-in-aid. Approximately 90% of current students receive some form of financial assistance. Average scholarship/grant $3,000 full-time, $2,000 part-time.

DEGREE REQUIREMENTS. For J.D.: 90 credits (49 required) with a 2.0 (A = 4) GPA, plus completion of upper divisional writing course; 20 hours of pro bono work; 3-year full-time program, 4-year part-time program. Accelerated J.D. with summer course work.

CAREER AND PLACEMENT INFORMATION. About 40–50 employers conducted on-campus interviews. Approximately 42% of graduates are employed in state. More than 71% of graduates are practicing law; 11% are in business; 16% in government; 2% in academia. Approximately 82% (IN), 77% (IL) of Valparaiso University's first-time state bar exam takers pass the bar exam; the passage rate for all first-time takers from ABA-approved schools is 86% (IN), 87% (IL). Graduates are eligible to take the bar exam in all 50 states.

VANDERBILT UNIVERSITY
Nashville, Tennessee 37240-1001
Internet site: http://www.vanderbilt.edu

Founded 1873. Located 1½ miles W of downtown Nashville, the state capital. Private control. Semester system. Library: 2,000,000 volumes; 1,800,000 microforms; 16,000 periodicals/subscriptions.

University's other graduate colleges/schools: Divinity School, Graduate School, Owen Graduate School of Management, Peabody College, School of Engineering, School of Medicine, School of Nursing.

Total university enrollment: 10,000.

School of Law
21st Avenue South
Nashville, Tennessee 37240
Phone: (615)322-2615
Internet site: http://www.vanderbilt.edu/Law
E-mail: admissions@law.vanderbilt.edu

Established 1873. Located on main campus. ABA approved since 1925. AALS member. Semester system.

Full-time, day study only. Law library: 499,800 volumes/ microforms; 6,065 current periodicals/subscriptions; 40 computer workstations; has LEXIS, NEXIS, WEST-LAW, INFOTRAC; is a Federal Government Depository. Special facilities: Vanderbilt Institute for Public Policy Studies, Freedom Forum First Amendment Center. Special programs: Transnational Legal Studies Program; clerkships; internships.

Annual tuition: $21,971. On-campus housing available for both single and married students. Annual on-campus housing cost: single students $4,260 (room only), married students $5,022. Housing deadline May 1. Contact Office of Residential and Judicial Affairs for both on- and off-campus housing. Law students tend to live off-campus. Off-campus housing and personal expenses: approximately $13,500. Additional costs: books approximately $800.

Enrollment: first-year class 184; total full-time 550 (men 62%, women 38%); no part-time students. First-year statistics: 85% out of state, 48 states and foreign countries represented; 38% women; 21% minority; average age 25; 203 undergraduate institutions represented; range of first-year section sizes 30–90 students; number of upper division courses offered after first year 77.

Faculty: full-time 34, part-time 33; 24% female; 4% minority; student/faculty ratio 20 to 1.

Degrees conferred: J.D., J.D.-M.B.A., J.D.-M.T.S., J.D.-M.Div., Concurrent M.A., Ph.D. available through the Graduate School.

RECRUITMENT PRACTICES AND POLICIES. Attends local and national law school forums. Has on-campus informational sessions. School does have diversity program and actively recruits women/minority applicants.

ADMISSION REQUIREMENTS FOR FIRST-YEAR APPLICANTS. LSDAS law school report, LSAT (not later than December test date, if more than one LSAT, average is used), bachelor's degree from an accredited institution, personal statement, two recommendations, transcripts (must show all schools attended and at least three years of study) required in support of application. Applicants must have received bachelor's degree prior to enrollment. Interview not required. In addition, international applicants whose native language is not English must submit TOEFL (not older than two years), certified translations and evaluations of all foreign credentials. Joint-degree applicants must apply to and be accepted by both schools. Accepts Law Multi-App in lieu of institution's application. Apply to Office of Admission after October 1, before February 1. First-year students admitted

fall only. Rolling admission process, notification starts in November and is finished by April 1. Acceptance of offer and first deposit due April 15. School does maintain a waiting list. Application fee $50. Phone: (615)322-6452. E-mail: admissions@law.vanderbilt.edu.

ADMISSION REQUIREMENTS FOR TRANSFER APPLICANTS. Accepts transfers from other ABA-accredited schools. Admission limited to space available. At least one year of enrollment, dean's letter indicating applicant is in good standing (prefer applicants in the top quintile of first-year class), LSAT, LSDAS, personal statement regarding reason for transfer, two letters of recommendation, undergraduate transcript, current law school transcript required in support of application. Apply to Admissions Office by June 1. Admission decision made within one month of the receipt of complete application. Application fee $50. Will consider visiting students.

ADMISSION STANDARDS. Number of full-time applicants 2,452; number accepted 736; number enrolled 184; median LSAT 162 (75% of class have a score at or above 159); median GPA 3.56 (A = 4) (75% of class have a GPA at or above 3.36). Attrition rate .9%. Gorman rating 4.71; *U.S. News & World Report* ranking is in the top 20 of all law schools.

FINANCIAL AID. Need-based scholarships, merit scholarships, minority scholarships, grants-in-aid, private and institutional loans, federal loans, and Federal WS available. Assistantships may be available for upper divisional joint-degree candidates. For scholarships in general all accepted students are automatically considered (selection criteria place heavy reliance on LSAT and undergraduate GPA); however for the John W. Wade, Philip G. Davidson III, and Elliot Cheatham Scholarships use special financial aid form supplied with admissions application. For all other programs apply after January 1, before March 1. Submit FAFSA for all federal programs (Title IV School code #E00529). Also submit Financial Aid Transcript, federal income tax forms. Approximately 51% of first-year class received scholarships/grants-in-aid. Approximately 85% of current students receive some form of financial assistance. Average scholarship/grant $8,493. Loan Repayment Assistance Program available.

DEGREE REQUIREMENTS. For J.D.: 88 credits (34 required) with a 2.0 (A = 4) GPA, plus completion of upper divisional writing course; 3-year program. Accelerated J.D. with summer course work. For J.D.-M.B.A., M.T.S.: 4-year program rather than the usual 5-year program needed if degrees taken separately. For J.D.-M.Div.: a 5-year program rather than the usual 6-year program needed if degrees taken separately.

CAREER AND PLACEMENT INFORMATION. About 340–350 employers conducted on-campus interviews. Approximately 27% of graduates are employed in state. More than 85% of graduates are practicing law; 10% are in business; 5% in government. Approximately 90% (TN), 91% (NY) of Vanderbilt University's first-time state bar exam takers pass the Tennessee Bar Exam; Tennessee's passage rate for all first-time takers from ABA-approved schools is 79% (TN), 78% (NY). Graduates are eligible to take the bar exam in all 50 states.

VERMONT LAW SCHOOL

P.O. Box 96
Chelsea Street
South Royalton, Vermont 05506-0096
Phone: (802)763-8303
Internet site: http://www.vermontlaw.edu
E-mail: admiss@vermontlaw.edu

Established 1972. Located in a national historic district along the White River. ABA approved since 1975. AALS member. Private control. Semester system. Full-time, day study only. Law library: 206,900 volumes/microforms; 2,710 current periodicals/subscriptions; 20 computer workstations; has LEXIS, NEXIS, WESTLAW, DIALOG; is a U.S. Government Selective Depository. Special facility: Environmental Law Center. Special programs: Law School Exchange Program; internships.

Annual tuition: $18,565. On-campus housing available for single students only. Annual on-campus housing cost: single students $2,025 (room only). Contact Business Office for both on- and off-campus housing information. Phone: (802)763-8303. Law students tend to live off-campus. Off-campus housing and personal expenses: approximately $13,375. Additional costs: books approximately $800.

Enrollment: first-year class 176; total full-time 505 (men 55%, women 45%); no part-time students; new M.S.E.L. students 26. First-year statistics: 90% out of state, 46 states and foreign countries represented; 44% women; 6% minority; average age 27; 298 undergraduate institutions represented; average first-year section size 80 students; number of upper division courses offered after first year 92.

Faculty: full-time 32, part-time 27; 22% female; 3% minority; student/faculty ratio 21 to 1.

Degrees conferred: J.D., J.D.-M.E.S.L., M.E.S.L.

RECRUITMENT PRACTICES AND POLICIES. Attends local and selected national law school forums. Has on-campus informational sessions. School does have diversity program and actively recruits women/minority applicants.

ADMISSION REQUIREMENTS FOR FIRST-YEAR APPLICANTS. LSDAS law school report, LSAT (not later than February test date, if more than one LSAT, average is used), bachelor's degree from an accredited institution, résumé, essay/personal statement, two recommendations, transcripts (must show all schools attended and at least three years of study) required in support of application. Applicants must have received bachelor's degree prior to enrollment. Campus visits encouraged. In addition, international applicants whose native language is not English must submit TOEFL (not older than two years), certified translations, and evaluations of all foreign credentials. Apply to Office of Admission after September 30, before February 1. First-year students admitted fall only. Rolling admission process, notification starts in November and is finished by early May. School does maintain a waiting list. Application fee $50. Phone: (800)227-1395. E-mail: admiss@vermontlaw.edu.

ADMISSION REQUIREMENTS FOR TRANSFER APPLICANTS. Accepts transfers from other ABA-accredited schools. Admission limited to space available. At least one year of enrollment, dean's letter indicating applicant is in good standing (prefer applicants in the top half of first-year class), LSAT, LSDAS, statement of objectives and goals including the reason for transfer, two recommendations, current law school transcript required in support of application. Admits fall, spring. Apply to Admission Office at least six weeks prior to semester of entrance. Admission decision made within one month of receipt of completed application. Application fee $50. Will consider visiting students.

ADMISSION REQUIREMENT FOR M.E.S.L. All applicants must have a bachelor's degree from an accredited institution. Official transcripts, personal statement, two letters of recommendation, LSAT or GRE required in support of M.E.S.L. application. In addition, TOEFL required for all international applicants whose native language is not English. Admits fall only. Apply by February 15 to Environmental Law Center's Admissions Office. Application fee $50. Phone: (800)227-1395, (802)763-8303. E-mail: elcinfo@vermontlaw.edu.

ADMISSION STANDARDS. Number of full-time applicants 992; number accepted 773; number enrolled 176;

median LSAT 155 (75% of class have a score at or above 152); median GPA 3.13 (A = 4) (75% of class have a GPA at or above 2.83). Attrition rate 3.7%. Gorman rating 2.51; *U.S. News & World Report* ranking is in the third tier of all law schools.

FINANCIAL AID. Scholarships, tuition grants, private and institutional loans, federal loans, and Federal WS available. For scholarships (selection criteria place heavy reliance on LSAT and undergraduate GPA) apply before February 1 (recommended deadline; use the Application for Student Financial Aid). For all other programs submit FAFSA. Also submit Financial Aid Transcript, federal income tax forms. Approximately 39% of first-year class received scholarship/grants-in-aid. Approximately 85% of current students receive some form of financial assistance. Average scholarship/grant $5,650. Average debt after graduation $66,000. Loan Repayment Assistance Program available.

DEGREE REQUIREMENTS. For J.D.: 84 credits (44 required) with a 2.0 (A = 4) GPA, plus completion of upper divisional writing course; 3-year program. Accelerated J.D. with summer course work. For J.D.-M.E.S.L.: 105 total credits; at least 8 semesters in full-time residence; a GPA of 2.0 (A = 4) required. For M.E.S.L.: 30 credits, at least 3 semesters in full-time residence; a GPA of 2.0 (A = 4) required.

CAREER AND PLACEMENT INFORMATION. About 20–25 employers conducted on-campus interviews. Approximately 26% of graduates are employed in state. More than 68% of graduates are practicing law; 20% are in business; 11% in government; 1% in academia. Approximately 81% (VT), 94% (NY) of the Vermont School of Law's first-time state bar exam takers pass the bar exam; the passage rate for all first-time takers from ABA-approved schools is 78% (VT), 78% (NY). Graduates are eligible to take the bar exam in all 50 states.

VILLANOVA UNIVERSITY

Villanova, Pennsylvania 19085-1699
Internet site: http://www.vill.edu

Founded 1843. Located 10 miles W of Philadelphia. Private control (Roman Catholic—Order of St. Augustine affiliation). Semester system. Library: 900,000 volumes; 1,694,000 microforms; 4,000 periodicals/subscriptions; 122 computer workstations.

University's other graduate colleges/schools: College of Commerce and Finance, College of Engineering, College of Nursing, Graduate School of Liberal Arts and Sciences.

Total university enrollment: 10,525.

School of Law
299 North spring Mill Road
Villanova, Pennsylvania 19085
Phone: (610)519-7000
Internet site: http://www.law.vill.edu/vls

Established 1953. Located on main campus. ABA approved since 1954. AALS member. Semester system. Full-time, day study only. Law library: 421,500 volumes/microforms; 3,915 current periodicals/subscriptions; 198 computer workstations; has LEXIS, NEXIS, WESTLAW, DIALOG, CALI; is a Federal Government Depository. Special facility: Center for Information Law and Policy.

Annual tuition: $18,780. No on-campus housing available. Law students live off-campus. Contact Admission Office for off-campus information. Off-campus housing and personal expenses: approximately $13,440. Additional costs: books approximately $800.

Enrollment: first-year class 236; total full-time 712 (men 60%, women 40%); no part-time students. First-year statistics: 50% out of state, 27 states and foreign countries represented; 40% women; 22% minority; average age 24; 116 undergraduate institutions represented; average first-year section size 100 students; number of upper division courses offered after first year 97.

Faculty: full-time 41, part-time 34; 24% female; 6% minority; student/faculty ratio 21 to 1.

Degrees conferred: J.D., J.D.-M.B.A., J.D.-Ph.D. (Psychology with Allegheny University), LL.M. (Tax).

RECRUITMENT PRACTICES AND POLICIES. Attends local and selected national law school forums. Has on-campus informational sessions. School does have diversity program and actively recruits women/minority applicants.

ADMISSION REQUIREMENTS FOR FIRST-YEAR APPLICANTS. LSDAS law school report, LSAT (not later than December test date, scores older than three years not considered, if more than one LSAT, average is used), bachelor's degree from an accredited institution, personal statement, transcripts (must show all schools attended and at least three years of study) required in support of application. Applicants must have received bachelor's degree prior to enrollment. Recommendations optional. Interview not required. Campus visits encouraged. In addition, international applicants whose native language is not English must submit TOEFL (not older than two years). Joint-degree applicants must apply to and be accepted by both schools; GRE/GMAT required. Apply to Office of Admission after September 1, before January 31. First-year students admitted fall only. Rolling admission process. School does maintain a waiting list. Application fee $75. Phone: (610)519-7010.

ADMISSION REQUIREMENTS FOR TRANSFER APPLICANTS. Accepts transfers from other ABA-accredited schools. Admission limited to space available. At least one year of enrollment, dean's letter indicating applicant is in good standing (prefer applicants in the top third of first-year class), LSAT, LSDAS, personal statement regarding reason for transfer, undergraduate transcript, current law school transcript required in support of application. Apply to Admission Office by June 1. Admission decisions made by mid July. Application fee $75. Will consider visiting students.

ADMISSION REQUIREMENTS FOR LL.M. Applicants must have earned an acceptable GPA and have a J.D. or its equivalent from an ABA-approved law school. Applicants who did not attend law school in the U.S. must demonstrate that they have completed all of the educational requirements and other prerequisites for the practice of law in a foreign country. Official transcripts required in support of graduate application. Admits fall, spring, summer. Apply to Graduate Tax Program at least two months prior to term of expected entrance. Application fee $25. Phone: (610)519-4533.

ADMISSION STANDARDS. Number of full-time applicants 1,270; number accepted 693; number enrolled 236; median LSAT 158 (75% of class have a score at or above 150); median GPA 3.40 (A = 4) (75% of class have a GPA at or above 3.16). Attrition rate 2.9%. Gorman rating 3.7; *U.S. News & World Report* ranking is in the third tier of all law schools.

FINANCIAL AID. Need-based scholarships, merit scholarships, Disadvantaged Students Scholarships, fellowships, private and institutional loans, federal loans, and Federal WS available. Assistantships may be available for upper divisional joint-degree candidates. All accepted students are automatically considered for scholarships (selection criteria place heavy reliance on LSAT and undergraduate GPA), apply to the Office of Financial Aid before March 1 (priority deadline). Phone: (610)519-7015. For all other programs submit FAFSA (Title IV School code #E00428). Also submit Financial Aid Transcript, federal income tax forms. Approximately 8% of first-year class received scholarships/grants-in-aid. Approximately 78% of current students receive some form of financial assistance. Average scholarship/grant $8,875. Financial aid available for LL.M. students. Contact law school's Financial Aid Office. Phone: (610)519-7015.

DEGREE REQUIREMENTS. For J.D.: 87 credits (53 required) with a 2.0 (A = 4) GPA, plus completion of upper divisional writing course; 3-year program. Accelerated J.D. with summer course work. For J.D.-M.B.A.: a 4-year program rather than the usual 5-year program needed if degrees taken separately. Each school will accept up to 12 credits. For J.D.-Ph.D.: a 6-year program rather than the usual 7-year program needed if degrees taken separately. For LL.M. (Tax): 24 credits (14 required); successful completion of Professional Responsibility Symposium; a GPA of 2.5 (A = 4) required.

CAREER AND PLACEMENT INFORMATION. About 90–100 employers conducted on-campus interviews. Approximately 80% of graduates are employed in state. More than 82% of graduates are practicing law; 12% are in business; 6% in government. Approximately 75% of Villanova University's first-time state bar exam takers pass the Pennsylvania Bar Exam; Pennsylvania passage rate for all first-time takers from ABA-approved schools is 73%. Graduates are eligible to take the bar exam in all 50 states.

UNIVERSITY OF VIRGINIA
Charlottesville, Virginia 22903-3196
Internet site: http://www.virginia.edu

Founded 1819. Located 66 miles W of Richmond, 120 miles SW of Washington, D.C. Public control. Semester system. Library: 4,165,800 volumes; 4,386,000 microforms; 39,084 periodicals/subscriptions; 325 computer workstations.

University's other graduate colleges/schools: Colgate Darden Graduate School of Business Administration, Curry School of Education, Graduate School of Arts and Sciences (includes McIntire School of Commerce), School of Architecture, School of Engineering and Applied Science, School of Medicine, School of Nursing.

Total university enrollment: 17,700.

School of Law
580 Massie Road
Charlottesville, Virginia 22903-1789
Phone: (804)924-7354
Internet site: http://www.law.virginia.edu/index.htm

Established 1825. Located on main campus. ABA approved since 1923. AALS member. Semester system. Full-time, day study only. Law library: 753,500 volumes/microforms; 10,588 current periodicals/subscriptions; 112 computer workstations; has LEXIS, NEXIS, WESTLAW; is a Federal Government Depository. Special programs: clerkships.

Annual tuition: resident $13,954, nonresident $19,870; LL.M. $19,870. On-campus housing available for single students only. Annual on-campus housing cost: single students $3,374 (room only), $5,484 (room and board). Housing deadline February 20. Contact Housing Office for both on- and off-campus housing information. Phone: (804)924-6873. Law students tend to live off-campus. Off-campus housing and personal expenses: approximately $10,760. Additional costs: books approximately $800.

Enrollment: first-year class 361; total full-time 1,148 (men 63%, women 37%); no part-time students. First-year statistics: 44% out of state, 45 states and foreign countries represented; 37% women; 14% minority; average age 25; 251 undergraduate institutions represented; range of first-year section sizes 32–128 students; number of upper division courses offered after first year 148.

Faculty: full-time 62, part-time 64; 20% female; 6% minority; student/faculty ratio 17.4 to 1.

Degrees conferred: J.D., J.D.-M.S. (Accounting at the Graduate School of Arts and Sciences), J.D.-M.P.A. (Public Affairs in the Woodrow Wilson School of Public and International Affairs at Princeton University), J.D.-M.A. (International Relations and International Economics at Johns Hopkins University School of Advanced International Studies), J.D.-M.A.L.D. (Law and Diplomacy in the Fletcher School of Law and Diplomacy at Tufts University), LL.M. (three quarters of accepted students are foreign lawyers), S.J.D.

RECRUITMENT PRACTICES AND POLICIES. Attends local and national law school forums. Has on-campus informational sessions. School does have diversity program and actively recruits women/minority applicants.

ADMISSION REQUIREMENTS FOR FIRST-YEAR APPLICANTS. LSDAS law school report, LSAT (not later than December test date, if more than one LSAT, average is used), bachelor's degree from an accredited institution, personal statement, Dean's Certification Form, two letters of reference, transcripts (must show all schools attended and at least three years of study) required in support of application. Résumé optional. Applicants must have received bachelor's degree prior to enrollment. Interview not required, but personal interviews are accommodated between October 1 and January 31. In addition, international applicants whose native language is not English must submit TOEFL (not older than two years), certified translations and evaluations of all foreign credentials. Joint-degree applicants must apply to and be accepted by both colleges/universities. Apply to Office of Admission after September 30, before January 15. First-year students admitted fall only. Rolling admission process, Admissions Office will attempt to notify all "timely" applicants by April 15. School does maintain a waiting list. Application fee $40. Phone: (804)924-7351.

ADMISSION REQUIREMENTS FOR TRANSFER APPLICANTS. Accepts transfers from other ABA-accredited schools. Admission limited to space available. At least one year of enrollment, dean's letter indicating applicant is in good standing (prefer applicants in the top 5% of first-year class), LSAT, LSDAS, personal statement regarding reason for transfer, two letters of reference, undergraduate transcripts, current law school transcript required in support of application. Apply to Admission Office by June 1. Admission decisions made by mid July. Application fee $40. Will consider visiting students.

ADMISSION REQUIREMENTS FOR LL.M. All applicants must have received J.D. or equivalent first professional degree in law from an accredited U.S. law school or comparable foreign law school. Official transcripts with rank in class, two letters of recommendation required in support of LL.M. application. In addition, international applicants whose native language is not English must submit TOEFL and certified translations and evaluations of all foreign credentials. Personal interviews may be arranged with the Director of LL.M. Program. Admits fall only. Apply by April 1 to Graduate Studies Office. Application fee $40. Phone: (804)924-3154. E-mail: gradadmit@law. virginia.edu.

ADMISSION REQUIREMENTS FOR S.J.D. Applicants must submit all materials required for LL.M. In addition, a personal statement expressing the rationale for pursuing the S.J.D. and its relevance to the applicant's planned career; submit dissertation proposal and candidate research plan with an endorsement of the proposal by a resident faculty member who has agreed to supervise the research and writing of dissertation; most candidates have completed the School of Law's LL.M.

ADMISSION STANDARDS. Number of full-time applicants 3,782; number accepted 980; number enrolled 361; median LSAT 165 (75% of class have a score at or above 162); median GPA 3.64 (A = 4) (75% of class have a GPA at or above 3.49). Attrition rate 1.3%. Gorman rating 4.72; *U.S. News & World Report* ranking is in the top 10 of all law schools.

FINANCIAL AID. Need-based scholarships, merit scholarships, minority scholarships, grants, private and institutional loans, federal loans, and Federal WS available. Assistantships may be available for upper divisional joint-degree candidates. All accepted students are considered for all available aid (selection criteria place heavy reliance on LSAT and undergraduate GPA). Submit the school's Financial Aid Form before February 1. Phone: (804)924-7805. For all federal programs submit FAFSA by early February (Title IV School code #003745). Also submit Financial Aid Transcript, federal income tax forms. Approximately 30% of first-year class received scholarships/grants-in-aid. Approximately 67% of current students receive some form of financial assistance. Average scholarship/grant $6,500. Limited aid for LL.M. applicants. Contact Director of Graduate Studies for information and consideration.

DEGREE REQUIREMENTS. For J.D.: 86 credits (27 required) with a 2.0 (A = 4) GPA, plus completion of upper divisional writing course; 6 semesters in residence program. For J.D.-M.S. (Accounting): 98 total credits (J.D. up to 12 credits, M.S. up to 6 credits). For J.D.-M.A.L.D., M.A., M.P.A.: individualized programs at each university; up to 14 credits may be applied to the J.D. and 1 semester of residence. For LL.M.: 24 credits, at least 2 semesters in full-time residence; substantial written work either within a seminar or as supervised research; specialization in Oceans Law and Policy requires 30 credits. For S.J.D.: completion of an LL.M.; at least 1 year in full-time study; dissertation must make an original contribution to legal literature and be of publishable quality; oral defense.

CAREER AND PLACEMENT INFORMATION. About 500–600 employers conducted on-campus interviews. Approximately 20% of graduates are employed in state. More than 93% of graduates are practicing law; 3% are in business; 3% in government; 1% in academia. Approximately 88% (VA), 93% (NY) of the University of Virginia's first-time state bar exam takers pass the Virginia Bar Exam; Virginia's passage rate for all first-time takers

from ABA-approved schools is 77% (VA), 78% (NY). Graduates are eligible to take the bar exam in all 50 states.

WAKE FOREST UNIVERSITY
Winston-Salem, North Carolina 27109
Internet site: http://www.wfu.edu

Founded 1834. Located 3 miles N of Winston-Salem. Private control (Baptist affiliation). Semester system. Library: 1,299,800 volumes; 1,602,300 microforms; 17,585 periodicals/subscription; 100 computer workstations.

University's other graduate colleges/schools: Graduate School, Babcock Graduate School of Management, Bowman Gray School of Medicine.

Total university enrollment: 5,750.

School of Law
P.O. Box 7206
Winston-Salem, North Carolina 27109
Phone: (910)759-5435
Internet site: http://www.law.wfu.edu
E-mail: admissions@law.wfu.edu

Established 1984. Located on main campus. ABA approved since 1935. AALS member. Semester system. Full-time, day study only. Law library: 308,100 volumes/microforms; 5,140 current periodicals/subscriptions; 99 computer workstations; has LEXIS, NEXIS, WESTLAW, DIALOG, EPIC, ACES. Special programs: Sister School program in Pecs, Hungary; summer study abroad in London, England, Venice, Italy.

Annual tuition: $19,500; LL.M. $19,750. No on-campus housing available. Law students live off-campus. Contact the Admissions Office for off-campus housing information. Off-campus housing and personal expenses: approximately $11,700. Additional costs: books approximately $800.

Enrollment: first-year class 160; total full-time 460 (men 60%, women 40%); no part-time students. First-year statistics: 69% out of state, 39 states and foreign countries represented; 40% women; 10% minority; average age 25; 177 undergraduate institutions represented; average first-year section size 40 students; number of upper division courses offered after first year 72.

Faculty: full-time 34, part-time 36; 26% female; 6% minority; student/faculty ratio 15.3 to 1.

Degrees conferred: J.D., J.D.-M.B.A., LL.M. (American Law—for foreign lawyers who have completed a basic legal education and received a university degree in law in another country).

RECRUITMENT PRACTICES AND POLICIES. Attends local and selected national law school forums. Has on-campus informational sessions. School does have diversity program and actively recruits women/minority applicants.

ADMISSION REQUIREMENTS FOR FIRST-YEAR APPLICANTS. LSDAS law school report, LSAT (not later than December test date, if more than one LSAT, average is used), bachelor's degree from an accredited institution, personal statement, one academic recommendation, Dean's Certification, transcripts (must show all schools attended and at least three years of study) required in support of application. Applicants must have received bachelor's degree prior to enrollment. Personal interview not required but may be arranged with School of Law personnel. Campus visits encouraged. In addition, international applicants whose native language is not English must submit TOEFL (not older than two years), certified translations and evaluations of all foreign credentials. Apply to Office of Admission and Financial Aid after September 30, before March 15 (application deadline) April 15 (deadline for receipt of completed files). First-year students admitted fall only. Rolling admission process, notification starts in November and is finished by May 1. Acceptance of offer and first-deposit due April 17. School does maintain a waiting list. Application fee $60. Phone: (910)759-5437. E-mail: admissions@law.wfu.edu.

ADMISSION REQUIREMENTS FOR TRANSFER APPLICANTS. Accepts transfers from other ABA-accredited schools. Admission limited to space available. At least one year of enrollment, dean's letter indicating applicant is in good standing (prefer applicants in the top 10% of first-year class), LSAT, LSDAS, personal statement regarding reason for transfer, one letter of recommendation, undergraduate transcript, current law school transcript required in support of application. Apply to Admission Office by June 1. Admission decision made by mid July. Application fee $60. Will consider visiting students.

ADMISSION REQUIREMENTS FOR LL.M. APPLICANTS. All applicants must have a law degree from an approved degree-granting institution in the applicant's home country. Official transcripts (in the language of the institution and certified English translation), two recommendations (one from a current or former faculty member), documentation of financial resources from bank or sponsor required in support of LL.M. application. In addition, TOEFL is required for those whose native language is not English (minimum score 550). Admits fall only. Apply by March 15 to Director LL.M. Program. Phone: (910)758-6116. E-mail: llm-admission@law.wfu.edu.

ADMISSION STANDARDS. Number of full-time applicants 1,492; number accepted 599; number enrolled 158; median LSAT 161 (75% of class have a score at or above 158); median GPA 3.29 (A = 4) (75% of class have a GPA at or above 3.04). Attrition rate 4.4%. Gorman rating 3.14; *U.S. News & World Report* ranking is in the top 30 of all law schools.

FINANCIAL AID. Need-based scholarships, merit scholarships, minority scholarships, assistantships, private and institutional loans, federal loans, Federal WS available for second- and third-year students only. Assistantships may be available for upper divisional joint-degree candidates. All accepted students are automatically considered for scholarships (selection criteria place heavy reliance on LSAT and undergraduate GPA). For all other programs apply to Admissions and Financial Aid Office after January 1, before May 1. Submit FAFSA for all federal programs (Title IV School code #E00514). Also submit Financial Aid Transcript, federal income tax forms. Approximately 25% of first-year class received scholarships/grants-in-aid. Approximately 78% of current students receive some form of financial assistance. Average scholarship/grant $9,562. Average debt after graduation $43,000.

DEGREE REQUIREMENTS. For J.D.: 89 credits with a GPA of at least a 73 (scale 0–100), plus completion of upper divisional writing course; 3-year program, 4-year program (part-time). Accelerated J.D. with summer course work. For J.D.-M.B.A.: a 4-year program rather than the usual 5-year program needed if degrees taken separately. For LL.M. (foreign lawyers): 24 credits, at least 2 semesters in residence; "Introduction to American Law" course; thesis/seminar paper; a GPA of 73 (scale 0–100) required.

CAREER AND PLACEMENT INFORMATION. About 90–100 employers conducted on-campus interviews. Approximately 58% of graduates are employed in state. More than 75% of graduates are practicing law; 15% are in business; 9% in government; 1% in academia. Approximately 90% of Wake Forest University's first-time state bar exam takers pass the North Carolina Bar Exam; North Carolina's passage rate for all first-time takers from ABA-approved schools is 85%. Graduates are eligible to take the bar exam in all 50 states.

WASHBURN UNIVERSITY

Topeka, Kansas 66621
Internet site: http://www.washburn.edu

Began as Lincoln College in 1865, changed name to Washburn in 1868. Located 60 miles W of Kansas City. Public control. Semester system. Library: 900,000 volumes; 2,000,000 microforms; 5,400 periodicals/subscriptions; 100 computer workstations.

University's other graduate colleges/schools: College of Arts and Sciences, School of Business.

Total university enrollment: 6,400.

School of Law

1700 College Ave.
Topeka, Kansas 66621
Phone: (913)231-1010
Internet site: http://www.washburnlaw.wuacc.edu
E-mail: washburn.admissions@law.wuacc.edu

Established 1903. Located on main campus. Topeka is the state capital. ABA approved since 1923. AALS member since 1905. Semester system. Full-time, day study only. Law library: 289,800 volumes/microforms; 3,666 current periodicals/subscriptions; 63 computer workstations; has LEXIS, WESTLAW; is a Kansas and Federal Government Depository. Special facility: Rural Law Center.

Annual tuition: resident $6,396, nonresident $9,476. On-campus housing available for both single and married students. Annual on-campus housing cost: single students $3,410 (room and board), married students $2,160. Contact Housing Office for both on- and off-campus housing information. Phone: (913)231-1065. Most law students live off-campus. Off-campus housing and personal expenses: approximately $10,918. Additional costs: books approximately $700.

Enrollment: first-year class 182; total full-time 442 (men 57%, women 43%); no part-time students. First-year statistics: 40% out of state, 39 states and foreign countries represented; 43% women; 13% minority; average age 26; 159 undergraduate institutions represented; range of first-year section sizes 30–90 students; number of upper division courses offered after first year 79.

Faculty: full-time 27, part-time 9; 32% female; 16% minority; student/faculty ratio 16.8 to 1.

Degree conferred: J.D.

RECRUITMENT PRACTICES AND POLICIES. Attends local and selected national law school forums. Has on-campus informational sessions. School does have diversity program and actively recruits women/minority applicants.

ADMISSION REQUIREMENTS FOR FIRST-YEAR APPLICANTS. LSDAS law school report, LSAT (LSAT must have been taken within the last five years, if more than one LSAT, highest is used), bachelor's degree from an accredited institution, personal statement, two recommendations, transcripts (must show all schools attended and at least three years of study) required in support of application. Applicants must have received bachelor's degree prior to enrollment. Interview not required, but campus and law class visitations are encouraged. Admits fall, spring. Apply to Office of Admission before March 1 (fall), September 15 (spring). First-year students admitted fall only. Rolling admission process. Fall notification starts in January and is finished by late May. Spring notification starts in August and is finished by late November. School does maintain a waiting list. Application fee $30. Phone: (888)WASHBURN. E-mail: washburn.admissions@law.wuacc.edu.

ADMISSION REQUIREMENTS FOR TRANSFER APPLICANTS. Accepts transfers from other ABA-accredited schools. Admission limited to space available. At least one year of enrollment, dean's letter indicating applicant is in good standing (prefer applicants in the top half of first-year class), LSAT, LSDAS, personal statement regarding reason for transfer, two letters of recommendation, current law school transcript required in support of application. Apply to Admission Office by June 30 (fall), December 1 (spring). Admission decision made within one month of the receipt of completed application. Application fee $30. Will consider visiting students.

ADMISSION STANDARDS. Number of full-time applicants 719; number accepted 432; number enrolled 182; median LSAT 153 (75% of class have a score at or above 149); median GPA 3.34 (A = 4) (75% of class have a GPA at or above 2.91). Attrition rate 4.1%. Gorman rating 3.20; *U.S. News & World Report* ranking is in the third tier of all law schools.

FINANCIAL AID. Scholarships, merit scholarships, minority scholarships, research assistant position (second- and third-year students only), private and institutional loans; federal loans and Federal WS offered through university's Financial Aid Office. All accepted students are considered for scholarships (selection criteria place heavy reliance on LSAT and undergraduate GPA). Use school's Financial Aid Form and submit with admission application. For all other programs submit FAFSA (Title IV School code #001949). Also submit Financial Aid

Profile Service, Financial Aid Transcript, federal income tax forms. Approximately 36% of first-year class received scholarships/grants-in-aid. Approximately 88% of current students receive some form of financial assistance. Average scholarship/grant $2,000. Average debt after graduation $30,000.

DEGREE REQUIREMENTS. For J.D.: 90 credits (34 required) with a 2.0 (A = 4) GPA, plus completion of upper divisional writing course; 3-year program. A 2½- or 3-year program available for spring semester entrants.

CAREER AND PLACEMENT INFORMATION. About 20–30 employers conducted on-campus interviews. Approximately 62% of graduates are employed in state. More than 62% of graduates are practicing law; 15% are in business; 23% in government. Approximately 71% of Washburn University's first-time state bar exam takers pass the Kansas Bar Exam; Kansas' passage rate for all first-time takers from ABA-approved schools is 82%. Graduates are eligible to take the bar exam in all 50 states.

WASHINGTON AND LEE UNIVERSITY
Lexington, Virginia 24450
Internet site: http://www.wlu.edu

Founded 1749 as Liberty Hall, named changed in 1865 to Washington and Lee. Located 50 miles NE of Roanoke in the Blue Ridge Mountains of Virginia. Private control. Semester system. Library: 651,700 volumes; 825,600 microforms; 6,769 periodicals/subscriptions; 109 computer workstations.

Total university enrollment: 2,000.

School of Law
Lewis Hall
Lexington, Virginia 24450-0303
Phone: (540)463-8400
Internet site: http://www.wlu.edu
E-mail: lawadm@wlu.edu

Established 1849. Located on main campus. ABA approved since 1923. AALS member. Semester system. Full-time, day study only. Law library: 339,700 volumes/microforms; 4,374 current periodicals/subscriptions; 73 computer workstations; has LEXIS, NEXIS, WEST-LAW. Special programs: summer internships; judicial clerkships; International Environmental Law Program.

Annual tuition: $17,211. On-campus housing available for single students only. Annual on-campus housing cost: single students $2,660 (room only) $4,545 (room and board). Housing deadline April 15. Contact Housing Office for both on- and off-campus housing information. Phone: (540)463-8405. Law students tend to live off-campus. Off-campus housing and personal expenses: approximately $10,085. Additional costs: books approximately $700.

Enrollment: first-year class 120; total full-time 360 (men 60%, women 40%); no part-time students. First-year statistics: 78% out of state, 46 states and foreign countries represented; 40% women; 13% minority; average age 25; 179 undergraduate institutions represented; range of first-year section sizes 20–60 students; number of upper division courses offered after first year 68.

Faculty: full-time 34, part-time 7; 20% female; 7% minority; student/faculty ratio 9.8 to 1.

Degree conferred: J.D.

RECRUITMENT PRACTICES AND POLICIES. Attends local and selected national law school forums. Has on-campus informational sessions. School does have diversity program and actively recruits women/minority applicants.

ADMISSION REQUIREMENTS FOR FIRST-YEAR APPLICANTS. LSDAS law school report, LSAT (not later than December test date, if more than one LSAT, average is used), bachelor's degree from an accredited institution, personal statement, two recommendations, transcripts (must show all schools attended and at least three years of study) required in support of application. Applicants must have received bachelor's degree prior to enrollment. Interview not required but campus visits encouraged. Apply to Admission Office after September 30, before February 1. First-year students admitted fall only. Rolling admission process, notification starts in December and is finished by mid March. School does maintain a waiting list. Application fee $40. Phone: (540)463-8504. E-mail: lawadm@wlu.edu.

ADMISSION REQUIREMENTS FOR TRANSFER APPLICANTS. Accepts transfers from other ABA-accredited schools. Admission limited to space available. At least one year of enrollment, dean's letter indicating applicant is in good standing (prefer applicants in the top quarter of first-year class), LSAT, LSDAS, personal statement regarding reason for transfer, two letters of recommendation, undergraduate transcripts, current law school transcript required in support of application. Apply to Admission Office by May 1. Admission decision made within one month of the receipt of a completed application. Application fee $40. Will consider visiting students.

ADMISSION STANDARDS. Number of full-time applicants 1,844; number accepted 513; number enrolled 120; median LSAT 165 (75% of class have a score at or above 161); median GPA 3.51 (A = 4) (75% of class have a GPA at or above 3.11). Attrition rate 3.5%. Gorman rating 2.93; *U.S. News & World Report* ranking is in the top 25 of all law schools.

FINANCIAL AID. Need-based scholarships, merit scholarships, Virginia Tuition Assistance Grants, private and institutional loans; federal loans and Federal WS offered through university's Financial Aid Office. All accepted students are automatically considered for scholarships (selection criteria place heavy reliance on LSAT and undergraduate GPA). For all other programs apply after January 1, before February 15 to University's Office of Financial Aid. Phone: (540)463-8729. Submit FAFSA for all federal programs (Title IV School code #003768). Also submit Financial Aid Transcript, federal income tax forms. Approximately 66% of first-year class received scholarships/ grants-in-aid. Approximately 87% of current students receive some form of financial assistance. Average scholarship/grant $7,000. Average debt after graduation $48,000.

DEGREE REQUIREMENTS. For J.D.: 85 credits (37 required) with a 2.0 (A = 4) GPA, plus completion of upper divisional writing course; 3-year program.

CAREER AND PLACEMENT INFORMATION. About 30–40 employers conducted on-campus interviews. Approximately 32% of graduates are employed in state. More than 90% of graduates are practicing law; 5% are in business; 5% in government. Approximately 81% of Washington and Lee University's first-time state bar exam takers pass the Virginia Bar Exam; Virginia's passage rate for all first-time takers from ABA-approved schools is 76%. Graduates are eligible to take the bar exam in all 50 states.

WASHINGTON UNIVERSITY

St. Louis, Missouri 63130-4899
Internet site: http://www.wustl.edu

Founded 1853. Private control. Semester system. Library: 3,000,000 volumes; 2,700,000 microforms; 19,000 periodicals/subscriptions.

University's other graduate colleges/schools: Graduate School of Arts and Sciences, George Warren Brown School of School Work, School of Architecture, School of Art, School of Engineering and Applied Science, School of Medicine.

Total university enrollment: 11,600.

School of Law
Campus Box 1120
One Brookings Drive
St. Louis, Missouri 63130-4899
Phone: (314)935-6400
Internet site: http://www.ls.wustl.edu
E-mail: admiss@wulaw.wustl.edu

Established 1867. Oldest private law school west of the Mississippi, moved to new facilities in 1997. Located on main campus. ABA approved since 1923. AALS member. Semester system. Full-time, day study only. Law library: 546,400 volumes/microforms; 6,312 current periodicals/ subscriptions; 56 computer workstations; has LEXIS, NEXIS, WESTLAW, LEGISLATE, Congressional Information Systems.

Annual tuition: $21,715, LL.M. $21,715. No on-campus housing available. Law students live off-campus. Contact University Housing Office for off-campus information. Phone: (314)935-5050, or University Apartment Referral Service. Phone: (314)935-5092. Off-campus housing and personal expenses: approximately $10,490. Additional costs: books approximately $800.

Enrollment: first-year class 212; total full-time 647 (men 53%, women 47%); no part-time students. First-year statistics: 60% out of state, 36 states and foreign countries represented; 47% women; 23% minority; average age 24; 110 undergraduate institutions represented; average first-year section size 35 students; number of upper division courses offered after first year 99.

Faculty: full-time 44, part-time 38; 32% female; 10% minority; student/faculty ratio 18.6 to 1.

Degrees conferred: J.D., J.D.-M.B.A., J.D.-M.H.A., J.D.-M.A. (Asian Studies, European Studies, Environmental Policy, Political Science), J.D.-M.S. (Engineering and Policy), J.D.-M.S.W., M.J.S. (limited to 5 students per year), LL.M. (Tax), LL.M. (for international students who have completed a basic legal education and received a university degree in law in another country), LL.M.-J.S.D.

RECRUITMENT PRACTICES AND POLICIES. Attends local and national law school forums. Has on-campus informational sessions. School does have diversity program and actively recruits women/minority applicants.

ADMISSION REQUIREMENTS FOR FIRST-YEAR AND M.J.S. APPLICANTS. LSDAS law school report, LSAT (not later than December test date, if more than one LSAT, highest is used), bachelor's degree from an accredited institution, personal statement, transcripts (must show all schools attended and at least three years of study) required in support of application. Recommendations are optional. Applicants must have received bachelor's degree prior to enrollment. Interviews are not granted or required, but campus visits are encouraged. In addition, international applicants whose native language is not English must submit TOEFL (not older than two years). Joint-degree applicants must apply to and be accepted by both schools; GRE/GMAT may be required for specific programs. Apply to Office of Admission after September 15, before March 1. First-year students admitted fall only. Rolling admission process, notification starts in November and is finished by late April. Acceptance of offer and first-deposit due April 15. Application fee $50. Phone: (314)935-4525. Fax: (314)935-6959. E-mail: admiss@wulaw.wustl.edu.

ADMISSION REQUIREMENTS FOR TRANSFER APPLICANTS. Accepts transfers from other ABA-accredited schools. Admission limited to space available. At least one year of enrollment, dean's letter indicating applicant is in good standing (prefer applicants in the top 10% of first-year class), LSAT, LSDAS, personal statement regarding reason for transfer, undergraduate transcripts, current law school transcript required in support of application. Apply to Admission Office by June 1. Admission decision made by mid summer. Application fee $50. Will consider visiting students.

ADMISSION REQUIREMENTS FOR LL.M. APPLICANTS. For LL.M. (Tax): all applicants must have received the LL.B. or J.D. from a law school approved by AALS. Official undergraduate transcripts, official law school transcripts with rank-in-class, verification of LSAT, personal statement, résumé required in support of graduate application. Apply to LL.M. Tax Program. Application fee $50. Phone: (314)935-4525. For LL.M. (international applicants): all applicants must have the basic law degree recognized in their own country. Official transcripts with certified translations and evaluations, TOEFL (minimum score required 600) for those whose native language is not English, letter of credit indicating sufficient financial support required in support of graduate application. Personal interviews may be requested. Admits fall only. Apply to LL.M. Program for International Students. Application fee $50. Phone: (314)935-6404.

ADMISSION REQUIREMENTS FOR LL.M.-J.S.D. APPLICANTS (Research Degree). All applicants must have received LL.B. or J.D. from a law school approved by AALS. Official undergraduate transcripts, official law school transcripts with rank-in-class, verification of LSAT, personal statement, résumé required in support of

graduate application. Admits fall only. Apply to graduate program by March 15. Application fee $50. Phone: (314)935-4525.

ADMISSION STANDARDS. Number of full-time applicants 1,665; number accepted 949; number enrolled 212; median LSAT 160 (75% of class have a score at or above 156); median GPA 3.26 (A = 4) (75% of class have a GPA at or above 2.95). Attrition rate 2.7%. Gorman rating 4.30; *U.S. News & World Report* ranking is in the top 25 of all law schools.

FINANCIAL AID. Scholars-in-Law, fellowships, merit scholarships, diversity scholarships (Farmer Scholarships, Buder Scholarships, Olin Scholarships, American Indian Fellowships), grants-in-aid, institutional and private loans, federal loans, and Federal WS available. Assistantships may be available for upper divisional joint-degree candidates. For scholarships/fellowships (selection criteria place heavy reliance on LSAT and undergraduate GPA), applications for special scholarships/fellowships are due before February 1. For all other programs apply as soon as possible after January 1. Use university's Financial Aid Application Form. Submit FAFSA for all federal programs (Title IV School code #002520). Also submit Financial Aid Transcript, federal income tax forms. Approximately 60% of first-year class received scholarships/grants-in-aid. Approximately 75% of current students receive some form of financial assistance. Average scholarship/grant $6,500. Average debt after graduation $50,000. Scholarships, need-based and credit-based loans available for LL.M. (Tax) accepted students.

DEGREE REQUIREMENTS. For J.D.: 85 credits (36 required) with a 75 (scale 0–100) GPA, plus completion of upper divisional writing course; 3-year program. Accelerated J.D. with summer course work. For J.D.-master's: 3½- to 4-year programs rather than the usual 4- to 5-year programs needed if degrees taken separately. For M.J.S.: 30 credits; all credits in residence; thesis of publishable quality; all course work completed in 4 years; thesis must be completed within 1 year of the completion of course work. For LL.M. (Tax): 24 credits, at least 2 semesters in full-time residence, 4 semesters in residence for part-time (evening and weekends); research paper; GPA of 75 (scale 0–100) or better required. For LL.M. (international students): 24 credits; at least 2 semesters in residence; 1 seminar; passing grades in all courses. For LL.M.-J.S.D.: Individually designed degree programs; must have completed all requirements for LL.M.; at least 1 year in full-time residence beyond LL.M.; thesis of publishable quality; oral defense.

CAREER AND PLACEMENT INFORMATION. About 115–120 employers conducted on-campus interviews. Approximately 41% of graduates are employed in state. More than 69% of graduates are practicing law; 16% are in business; 14% in government; 1% in academia. Approximately 94% (MO), 89% (IL) of Washington University's first-time state bar exam takers pass the bar exam; the passage rate for all first-time takers from ABA-approved schools is 92% (MO), 87% (IL). Graduates are eligible to take the bar exam in all 50 states.

UNIVERSITY OF WASHINGTON

Seattle, Washington 98195
Internet site: http://www.washington.edu

Founded 1861. Located 3 miles from downtown Seattle. Public control. Quarter system. Library: 5,400,700 volumes; 6,255,700 microforms; 56,700 periodicals/subscriptions; 531 computer workstations.

University's other graduate colleges/schools: College of Architecture and Urban Planning, College of Arts and Sciences, College of Education, College of Engineering, College of Forest Resources, College of Ocean and Fishery Sciences, Graduate School of Library and Information Sciences, Graduate School of Public Affairs, School of Business Administration, School of Nursing, School of Public Health and Community Medicine, School of Social Work, School of Dentistry, School of Medicine.

Total university enrollment: 35,600.

School of Law

316 Condon Hall
Seattle, Washington 98105-6617
Phone: (206)543-4551
Internet site: http://www.law.washington.edu
E-mail: admit@law.washington.edu

Established 1899. Located on main campus. ABA approved since 1924. AALS member. Quarter system. Full-time, day study only. Law library: 462,000 volumes/microforms; 7,686 current periodicals/subscriptions; 61 computer workstations; has LEXIS, NEXIS, WESTLAW, DIALOG. Special facility: Center for Advanced Study and Research on Intellectual Property.

Annual tuition: resident $5,388, nonresident $13,293. On-campus housing available for both single and married students. Annual on-campus housing cost: single students $3,279 (room only), $4,455 (room and board); married students $4,392. Housing deadline May 1. Contact Housing Services Office for both on- and off-campus housing information. Phone: (206)543-4059. Law students tend to live off-campus. Off-campus housing and personal expenses: approximately $11,271. Additional costs: books approximately $880.

Enrollment: first-year class 172; total full-time 530 (men 51%, women 49%); no part-time students. First-year statistics: 30% out of state, 20 states and foreign countries represented; 49% women; 34% minority; average age 24; 90 undergraduate institutions represented; range of first-year section sizes 30–120 students; number of upper division courses offered after first year 152.

Faculty: full-time 44, part-time 26; 41% female; 13% minority; student/faculty ratio 14 to 1.

Degrees conferred: J.D., J.D.-M.B.A., J.D.-M.A. (International Studies), LL.M. (Asian Law, Law and Marine Affairs, International Environmental Law, Law of Sustainable International Development, Taxation).

RECRUITMENT PRACTICES AND POLICIES. Attends local and selected national law school forums. Has on-campus informational sessions. School does have diversity program and actively recruits women/minority applicants.

ADMISSION REQUIREMENTS FOR FIRST-YEAR APPLICANTS. LSDAS law school report, LSAT (not later than December test date, if more than one LSAT, average is used), bachelor's degree from an accredited institution, personal statement, Dean's Certification (Form B) transcripts (must show all schools attended and at least three years of study) required in support of application (Form A). Two recommendations optional, use Form C. Applicants must have received bachelor's degree prior to enrollment. Interview not required, visits and meetings with Admissions Staff encouraged. In addition, international applicants whose native language is not English must submit TOEFL (not older than two years), certified translations and evaluation of foreign credentials; all recommendations must be in English. Concurrent-degree applicants must apply to and be accepted by both schools. Apply to Office of Admission after October 1, before January 15. First-year students admitted fall only (October quarter). Rolling admission process, notification starts in January 15 and is finished by April 1. Acceptance of offer and first-deposit due June 1. Application fee $50. Phone: (206)543-4972. E-mail: admit@law.washington.edu.

ADMISSION REQUIREMENTS FOR TRANSFER APPLICANTS. Accepts transfers from other AALS approved schools. Admission limited to space available. At least one year of enrollment, dean's letter indicating applicant is in good standing (prefer applicants in the top

10% of first-year class), LSAT, LSDAS, personal statement regarding reason for transfer, undergraduate transcript, current law school transcript required in support of application. Apply to Admission Office by July 15. Admission decisions made by mid August. Application fee $50. Will consider visiting students.

ADMISSION REQUIREMENT FOR LL.M. APPLICANTS. All applicants must hold a J.D. or equivalent degree from a law school that is a member of AALS and is approved by ABA. International applicant must have a first law degree or equivalent and must receive permission from Director of Graduate Admission. Original Application, one official transcript and application fee of $45 should be sent to the Office of Graduate Admission, Box 351280. A second official transcript including rank-in-class, one or two letters of recommendation, a statement of purpose, a current résumé and the goldenrod copy of the application should be sent to the Law School Graduate Admission Office. Admits to all quarters. Deadlines—fall quarter, July 1 (full- and part-time), winter quarter, November 1 (part-time only), spring quarter, February 1 (part-time only), summer quarter, May 15 (part-time only). Phone: (206)616-5964. Fax: (206)685-4469.

ADMISSION STANDARDS. Number of full-time applicants 1,960; number accepted 498; number enrolled 172; median LSAT 163 (75% of class have a score at or above 157); median GPA 3.58 (A = 4) (75% of class have a GPA at or above 3.38). Attrition rate 0.0%. Gorman rating 4.45; *U.S. News & World Report* ranking is in the top 30 of all law schools.

FINANCIAL AID. Need-based scholarships, private and institutional loans; federal loans and Federal WS offered through university's Office of Student Financial Aid. All accepted students are automatically considered for scholarships (selection criteria place heavy reliance on LSAT and undergraduate GPA). For information on School of Law Scholarships contact Financial Aid Coordinator. Phone: (206)543-4552. For all other programs apply before February 28 to Office of Student Financial Aid. Phone: (206)543-6101. Submit FAFSA for all federal programs (Title IV School code #003798). Also submit Financial Aid Transcript, federal income tax forms. Approximately 51% of first-year class received scholarships/grants-in-aid. Approximately 70% of current students receive some form of financial assistance. Average scholarship/grant $1,300.

DEGREE REQUIREMENTS. For J.D.: 135 quarter credits with a 2.0 (A = 4) GPA, plus completion of upper divisional writing course; 60 hours of public service; 3-year program. Accelerated J.D. with summer course work. For LL.M. (Asian and Comparative Law): 36 quarter credits; 1 Comparative Law seminar; 1 graduate research course; research project. For LL.M. (International Environmental Law): 40 quarter credits, at least 15 credits earned in law school; seminar on problems in international environmental law; research paper. For LL.M. (Sustainable International Development): 40 quarter credits, at least 15 credits earned in law school; seminar in legal problems of economic development; research paper. For LL.M. (Law and Marine Affairs): 40 quarter credits, at least 15 credits earned in law school; 1 course in marine affairs (courses must be at the 500 level); Ocean Policy and Resource Seminar. For LL.M. (Tax): 36 quarter credits.

CAREER AND PLACEMENT INFORMATION. About 30–40 employers conducted on-campus interviews. Approximately 74% of graduates are employed in state. More than 67% of graduates are practicing law; 16% are in business; 15% in government; 2% in academia. Approximately 86% of the University of Washington's first-time state bar exam takers pass the Washington Bar Exam; Washington's passage rate for all first-time takers from ABA-approved schools is 83%. Graduates are eligible to take the bar exam in all 50 states.

WAYNE STATE UNIVERSITY
Detroit, Michigan 48202
Internet site: http://www.wayne.edu

Founded 1868. Located about 4 miles from downtown. Public control. Semester system. Library: 2,904,600 volumes; 3,374,100 microforms; 24,785 periodicals/subscriptions.

University's other graduate colleges/schools: College of Education, College of Engineering, College of Fine, Performing and Communication Arts, College of Liberal Arts, College of Nursing, College of Science, College of Urban, Labor and Metropolitan Affairs, School of Business Administration, School of Social Work, College of Pharmacy, School of Medicine.

Total university enrollment: 32,100.

Law School
468 W. Ferry Mall
Detroit, Michigan 48202
Phone: (313)577-3937
Internet site: http://www.wayne.edu/~law
E-mail: inquire@novell.law.wayne.edu

Established 1927. Located on main campus. ABA approved since 1927. AALS member. Semester system. Full-time (day), part-time (day or evening) study. Law library: 541,100 volumes/microforms; 4,631 current periodicals/subscriptions; 52 computer workstations; has LEXIS, NEXIS, WESTLAW, CALI. Special facilities: Intellectual Property Law Institute, Center for Legal Studies. Special programs: summer study abroad at the Academy of International Law the Hague, the Netherlands; the London Law Programme; exchange program with the School of Law, University of Warwick, England; Summer Institute Program; internships.

Annual tuition: full-time resident $6,578, nonresident $13,802; part-time resident $4,738, nonresident $9,898. University-owned apartments available for both single and married students. Annual living expenses: $10,000. Contact university's Housing Office for both on- and off-housing information. Law students tend to live off-campus. Off-campus housing and personal expenses: approximately $10,000. Additional costs: books approximately $800.

Enrollment: first-year class full-time 150, part-time 77; total full-time 522, part-time 215 (men 52%, women 48%). First-year statistics: 5% out of state, 13 states and foreign countries represented; 48% women; 16% minority; average age 25; 99 undergraduate institutions represented; range of first-year section sizes 25–80 students; number of upper division courses offered after first year 49 full-time, 27 part-time.

Faculty: full-time 33, part-time 34; 28% female; 6% minority; student/faculty ratio 26 to 1.

Degrees conferred: J.D., J.D.-M.B.A., J.D.-M.A. (History, Public Policy), J.D.-M.A.D.R. (Dispute Resolution), LL.M. (Corporate and Finance Law, Labor Law).

RECRUITMENT PRACTICES AND POLICIES. Attends local and selected national law school forums. Has on-campus informational sessions. School does have diversity program and actively recruits women/minority applicants.

ADMISSION REQUIREMENTS FOR FIRST-YEAR APPLICANTS. LSDAS law school report, LSAT (not later than February test date, if more than one LSAT, average is used), bachelor's degree from an accredited institution, personal statement, one recommendation, transcripts (must show all schools attended and at least three years of study) required in support of application. Applicants must have received bachelor's degree prior to enrollment. Interview not required. In addition, international applicants whose native language is not English must submit TOEFL (not older than two years), certified

translations and evaluations of all foreign documents. Apply to Office of Admission after October 1, before March 15. First-year students admitted fall only. Rolling admission process. Application fee $20, noncitizen $30. Phone: (313)577-3937. E-mail: inquire@novell.law.wayne.edu.

ADMISSION REQUIREMENTS FOR TRANSFER APPLICANTS. Accepts transfers from other ABA-accredited schools. Admission limited to space available. At least one year of enrollment, dean's letter indicating applicant is in good standing (prefer applicants in the top quarter of first-year class), LSAT, LSDAS, personal statement regarding reason for transfer, undergraduate transcript, current law school transcript required in support of application. Apply to Admission Office by July 1. Admission decision made within one month of the receipt of a completed application. Application fee $20. Will consider visiting students.

ADMISSION REQUIREMENTS FOR LL.M. APPLICANTS. All applicants must have a equivalent J.D. (LL.B.) degree from a common law–based country or have completed a distinguished academic record in legal studies from a non–common law country approved by the Director of Graduate Studies. Official transcripts, a personal statement, résumé, recommendations (optional) required in support of the graduate application. In addition, international students must submit TOEFL, if English is not their native language; submit a special Graduate International Application, and a statement of financial support. Admits fall, winter, spring/summer. Apply by July 1 (fall), November 1 (winter), March 15 (spring/summer) to the Office of University Admissions. Contact the Director of Graduate Studies, Law Program for information. Phone: (313)577-3947. Fax: (313)577-1060. E-mail: jfriedl@novell.law.wayne.edu. International applicants should contact the Office of University Admissions for specific admissions information. Phone: (313)577-3577.

ADMISSION STANDARDS. Number of full-time applicants 735, part-time 314; number accepted 382 full-time, 108 part-time; number enrolled 150 full-time, 77 part-time; median LSAT 155 (75% of class have a score at or above 152 full-time, 151 part-time); median GPA 3.28 (A = 4) (75% of class have a GPA at or above 3.07 full-time, 2.94 part-time). Attrition rate 5.2%. Gorman rating 3.66; *U.S. News & World Report* ranking is in the second tier of all law schools.

FINANCIAL AID. Need-based scholarships, minority (Kenneth Cockrel, Wade McCree) scholarships, law alumni fellowships, Board of Governor's Grants, private and institutional loans; federal loans and Federal WS offered through university's Financial Aid Office. Assistantships may be available for upper divisional joint-degree candidates. All accepted students are automatically considered for scholarships (selection criteria place heavy reliance on LSAT and undergraduate GPA), for scholarship information contact the law school. Phone: (313)577-5142. For all other programs apply to university's Office of Financial Aid after January 1, before April 23. Phone: (313)577-2172. Submit FAFSA for all federal programs (Title IV School code #E00435). Also submit Financial Aid Transcript, federal income tax forms. Approximately 70% of first-year class received scholarships/grants-in-aid. Approximately 85% of current students receive some form of financial assistance. Average scholarship/grant $1,500. Limited financial assistance for part-time students. Average debt after graduation $24,100.

DEGREE REQUIREMENTS. For J.D.: 86 credits (36 required) with a 2.0 (A = 4) GPA, plus completion of upper divisional writing course; 3-year full-time program, 4–6 year part-time program. Accelerated J.D. with summer course work. For J.D.-master's: 3½- to 4-year programs rather than the usual 4- to 5-year programs needed if degrees taken separately. For LL.M. (Tax): primarily a part-time evening program; 26 credits, at least 16 credits taken in the law school; 3.0 (A = 4) GPA required; master's essay.

CAREER AND PLACEMENT INFORMATION. About 40–50 employers conducted on-campus interviews. Approximately 93% of graduates are employed in state. More than 65% of graduates are practicing law; 18% are in business; 14% in government; 3% in academia. Approximately 96% of Wayne State University's first-time state bar exam takers pass the Michigan Bar Exam; Michigan's passage rate for all first-time takers from ABA-approved schools is 85%. Graduates are eligible to take the bar exam in all 50 states.

WESTERN NEW ENGLAND COLLEGE
Springfield, Massachusetts 01119-2654
Internet site: http://www.wnec.edu

Founded 1919 as the Springfield Division of Northeastern University. Chartered as Western New England College in 1951. Located 25 miles N of Hartford, 90 miles W of Boston. Private control. Semester system. Library: 277,600 volumes; 1,081,600 microforms; 4,275 periodicals/subscriptions; 94 computer workstations.

College's other graduate schools: School of Business, School of Engineering.

Total college enrollment: 4,250.

School of Law
1215 Wilbraham Road
Springfield, Massachusetts 01119-2689
Phone: (413)782-1412
Internet site: http://www.law.wnec.edu
E-mail: lawadmis@wnec.edu

Established 1919. Located on main campus. ABA approved since 1974. AALS member. Semester system. Full-time, part-time study. Law library: 325,200 volumes/microforms; 4,328 current periodicals/subscriptions; 48 computer workstations; has LEXIS, NEXIS, WESTLAW, DIALOG, OCLC. Special programs: judicial clerkships; internships.

Annual tuition: full-time $17,366, part-time $12,820. No on-campus housing available. Law students live off-campus. Contact Admissions Office Housing Coordinator for off-campus information. Off-campus housing and personal expenses: approximately $8,750. Additional costs: books approximately $700.

Enrollment: first-year class full-time 137, part-time 74; total full-time 422, part-time 267 (men 51%, women 49%). First-year statistics: 54% out of state, 27 states and foreign countries represented; 49% women; 10% minority; average age 26; 200 undergraduate institutions represented; average first-year section size 80 students; number of upper division courses offered after first year 53.

Faculty: full-time 26, part-time 29; 28% female; 5% minority; student/faculty ratio 20 to 1.

Degrees conferred: J.D., J.D.-M.R.P. (University of Massachusetts at Amherst).

RECRUITMENT PRACTICES AND POLICIES. Attends local and selected national law school forums. Has on-campus informational sessions. School does have diversity program and actively recruits women/minority applicants.

ADMISSION REQUIREMENTS FOR FIRST-YEAR APPLICANTS. LSDAS law school report, LSAT (not later than February test date, if more than one LSAT, highest is used), bachelor's degree from an accredited institution, personal statement, two recommendations, transcripts (must show all schools attended and at least three years of study) required in support of application. Applicants must have received bachelor's degree prior to enrollment. Interview not required but may be requested by school. Joint-degree applicants must apply to and be accepted by both college/university. Apply to the Director of Admission after September 30, before March 1 (preferred deadline). First-year students admitted fall only. Rolling admission process, notification starts in January and is finished by May. Application fee $35. Phone: (800)782-6665, (413)752-1406. E-mail: lawadmis@wnec.edu.

ADMISSION REQUIREMENTS FOR TRANSFER APPLICANTS. Accepts transfers from other ABA-accredited schools. Admission limited to space available. At least one year of enrollment, dean's letter indicating applicant is in good standing, LSAT, LSDAS, personal statement regarding reason for transfer, two letters of recommendation, undergraduate transcript, current law school transcript required in support of application. Apply to the Director of Admission by July 1. Admission decision made within one month of the receipt of a completed application. Application fee $35. Will consider visiting students.

ADMISSION STANDARDS. Number of full-time applicants 1,181, part-time 225; number accepted 725 full-time, 155 part-time; number enrolled 134 full-time, 74 part-time; median LSAT 151 (75% of class have a score at or above 147 full-time, 146 part-time); median GPA 2.98 (A = 4) (75% of class have a GPA at or above 2.71 full-time, 2.69 part-time). Attrition rate 6%. Gorman rating 2.68; *U.S. News & World Report* ranking is in the fourth tier of all law schools.

FINANCIAL AID. Limited full and partial scholarships, grants-in-aid, private and institutional loans, federal loans, and Federal WS available. All accepted applicants are automatically considered for scholarships (selection criteria place heavy reliance on LSAT and undergraduate GPA). Apply to college's Student Administrative Services Office as soon as possible after January 1. Phone: (413)796-2080; use college's Financial Aid Form. For most other programs submit FAFSA (Title IV School code #002226). Also submit Financial Aid Transcript, federal income tax forms. Approximately 10% (full-time), 6% (part-time) of first-year class received scholarships/grants-in-aid. Approximately 80% of current students receive some form of financial assistance. Average scholarship/grant $2,291 full-time, $1,803 part-time. Average debt after graduation $42,000.

DEGREE REQUIREMENTS. For J.D.: 88 credits (45 required) with a 2.0 (A = 4) GPA, plus completion of upper divisional writing course; 3-year full-time program, 4- or 4½-year program (part-time). Accelerated J.D. with summer course work. For J.D.-M.R.P.: a 4-year program rather than the usual 5-year program needed if degrees taken separately.

CAREER AND PLACEMENT INFORMATION. About 20–25 employers conducted on-campus interviews. Approximately 32% of graduates are employed in state. More than 53% of graduates are practicing law; 23% are in business; 22% in government; 2% in academia. Approximately 85% of Western New England College's first-time state bar exam takers pass the Massachusetts Bar Exam; Massachusetts' passage rate for all first-time takers from ABA-approved schools is 78%. Graduates are eligible to take the bar exam in all 50 states.

WEST VIRGINIA UNIVERSITY
Morgantown, West Virginia 26506-6009
Internet site: http://www.wvu.edu

Founded 1867. Located 70 miles S of Pittsburgh. Public control. Semester system. Library: 1,344,200 volumes; 2,512,100 microforms; 10,800 periodicals/subscriptions; 120 computer workstations.

University's other graduate colleges/schools: College of Agriculture and Forestry, College of Business and Economics, College of Creative Arts, College of Engineering and Mineral Resources, College of Human Resources and Education, Eberly College of Arts and Sciences, Perley Isaac Reed School of Journalism, School of Dentistry, School of Medicine, School of Nursing, School of Pharmacy, School of Physical Education, School of Social Work.

Total university enrollment: 21,500.

College of Law
P.O. Box 6130
Morgantown, West Virginia 26506-6130
Phone: (304)293-3199
Internet site: http://www.wvu.edu/~law
E-mail: devince@wvnvm.wvnet.edu

Established 1878. Located on main campus. ABA approved since 1923. AALS member since 1914. Semester system. Full-time day and limited part-time study. Law library: 233,300 volumes/microforms; 2,925 current periodicals/subscriptions; 53 computer workstations; has LEXIS, WESTLAW, CALI; is a Federal Government Depository. Special facility: Appalachian Center for Law and Public Service.

Annual tuition: resident $5,062, nonresident $12,104. On-campus housing available for both single and married students. Annual on-campus housing cost: single students $4,300 (room only), married students $4,800. Contact university's On-campus Housing Office for information. Phone: (304)293-3621. Law students tend to live off-campus. Contact university's Off-campus Housing Office for off-campus information. Phone: (304)293-5613. Off-campus housing and personal expenses: approximately $10,212. Additional costs: books approximately $800.

Enrollment: first-year class 148; total full-time 419 (men 51%, women 49%); limited part-time study. First-year statistics: 13% out of state; 49% women; 5% minority; average age 26; average first-year section size 72 students; number of upper division courses offered after first year 59.

Faculty: full-time 29, part-time 17; 31% female; 5% minority; student/faculty ratio 14.3 to 1.

Degrees conferred: J.D., J.D.-M.B.A., J.D.-M.P.A.

RECRUITMENT PRACTICES AND POLICIES. Attends local and selected national law school forums. Has on-campus informational sessions. School does have diversity program and actively recruits women/minority applicants.

ADMISSION REQUIREMENTS FOR FIRST-YEAR APPLICANTS. LSDAS law school report, LSAT (not later than February test date, if more than one LSAT, average is used), bachelor's degree from an accredited institution, personal statement, three recommendations, transcripts (must show all schools attended and at least three years of study) required in support of application. Applicants must have received bachelor's degree prior to enrollment. Interview not required. Joint-degree applicants must apply to and be accepted by both schools. Apply to Admission Office after September 30, before March 1. First-year students admitted fall only. Rolling admission process, notification starts in January and is finished by late April. Acceptance of offer and first deposit due April 1. School does maintain a waiting list. Application fee $45. Phone: (304)293-5304. E-mail: devince@wvnvm.wvnet.edu.

ADMISSION REQUIREMENTS FOR TRANSFER APPLICANTS. Accepts transfers from other ABA-accredited schools. Admission limited to space available. At least one year of enrollment, dean's letter indicating applicant is in good standing (prefer applicants in the top half of first-year class), LSAT, LSDAS, personal statement regarding reason for transfer, three recommendations, undergraduate transcript, current law school transcript required in support of application. Apply to Admission Office by July 1. Admission decision made within one month of the receipt of a completed application. Application fee $45. Will consider visiting students.

ADMISSION STANDARDS. Number of full-time applicants 539; number accepted 296; number enrolled 148; median LSAT 153 (75% of class have a score at or above 149); median GPA 3.36 (A = 4) (75% of class have a GPA at or above 3.09). Attrition rate 2.1%. Gorman rating 3.19; *U.S. News & World Report* ranking is in the third tier of all law schools.

FINANCIAL AID. Scholarships, tuition waivers, W.E.B. DuBois Fellowships, private and institutional loans; federal loans and Federal WS offered through university's Financial Aid Office. Assistantships may be available for upper divisional joint-degree candidates. All accepted students are considered for scholarships/fellowships, tuition waivers (selection criteria place heavy reliance on LSAT and undergraduate GPA). For additional financial aid information contact College of Law. Phone: (304)293-5302. For all other programs apply to university's Financial Aid Office before March 1. Phone: (304)293-5242. Submit FAFSA for all federal programs (Title IV School code #003827). Also submit Financial Aid Transcript, federal income tax forms. Approximately 24% of first-year class received scholarships/fellowships/tuition waivers. Approximately 80% of current students receive some form of financial assistance. Average scholarship/grant $3,140. Average debt after graduation $24,000. Financial aid available for part-time students.

DEGREE REQUIREMENTS. For J.D.: 93 credits (52 required) with a 2.0 (A = 4) GPA, plus completion of upper divisional writing course; 3-year full-time program, 4-year part-time program. For J.D.-master's: 4-year program rather than the usual 5-year program needed if degrees taken separately.

CAREER AND PLACEMENT INFORMATION. About 25–30 employers conducted on-campus interviews. Approximately 79% of graduates are employed in state. More than 72% of graduates are practicing law; 9% are in business; 15% in government; 4% in academia. Approximately 78% of West Virginia University's first-time state bar exam takers pass the West Virginia Bar Exam; West Virginia's passage rate for all first-time takers from ABA-approved schools is 79%. Graduates are eligible to take the bar exam in all 50 states.

WHITTIER COLLEGE
Whittier, California 90608-0634
Internet site: http://www.whittier.edu

Chartered 1887. Located adjacent to Los Angeles. Private control (Quaker affiliation). Semester system. Library: 200,000 volumes; 300,000 microforms; 1,000 periodicals/subscriptions.

College has other graduate programs in education.

Total college enrollment: 2,000.

School of Law

3333 Harbor Blvd.

Costa Mesa, California 92626

Phone: (213)938-3621

Internet site: http://www.law.whittier.edu

E-mail: info@law.whittier.edu

Founded in 1966 as Beverly Law School, merged with Whittier College in 1975. Now located in Costa Mesa, Orange County, two blocks N of the San Diego Freeway. ABA approved since 1978. AALS member since 1987. Semester system. Full-time, part-time study. Law library: 283,000 volumes/microforms; 4,915 current periodicals/subscriptions; 68 computer workstations; has LEXIS, NEXIS, WESTLAW, DIALOG. Special facility: Center for Children's Rights. Special programs: Summer Performance Program.

Annual tuition: full-time $20,014, part-time $12,022. No on-campus housing available. Law students live off-campus. Contact Office of the Assistant Dean for off-campus information. Off-campus housing and personal expenses: approximately $14,958. Additional costs: books approximately $800.

Enrollment: first-year class full-time 186, part-time 70; total full-time 406, part-time 229 (men 50%, women 50%). First-year statistics: 40% out of state, 42 states and 3 foreign countries represented; 50% women; 35% minority; average age 25; 107 undergraduate institutions represented; range of first-year section sizes 70–90 students; number of upper division courses offered after first year 41 full-time, 35 part-time.

Faculty: full-time 30, part-time 23; 33% female; 10% minority; student/faculty ratio 21 to 1.

Degree conferred: J.D.

RECRUITMENT PRACTICES AND POLICIES. Attends local and selected national law school forums. Has on-campus informational sessions. School does have diversity program and actively recruits women/minority applicants.

ADMISSION REQUIREMENTS FOR FIRST-YEAR APPLICANTS. LSDAS law school report, LSAT (not later than February (fall), June (spring) test date, if more than one LSAT, highest is used), bachelor's degree from an accredited institution, personal statement (not to exceed three pages), two recommendations, transcripts (must show all schools attended and at least three years of

study) required in support of application. Applicants must have received bachelor's degree prior to enrollment. Interview not part of admissions process. Visits and tours of campus are encouraged. In addition, international applicants whose native language is not English must submit TOEFL (not older than two years), certified translations and evaluations of all foreign credentials. Use the Credential Evaluation Service, 5353 West Third Street, Los Angeles, California 90020. Phone: (310)390-6276. Apply to Office of Admission by March 15 (fall), November 1 (spring). First-year students admitted fall and spring. Rolling admission process, notification starts in February (fall), September (spring). Acceptance of offer and first deposit due April 1 (fall). Application fee $50. Phone: (800)808-8188, (213)938-3621, Ext.123. E-mail: info@law.whittier.edu.

ADMISSION REQUIREMENTS FOR TRANSFER APPLICANTS. Accepts transfers from other ABA-accredited schools. Admission limited to space available. At least one year of enrollment, dean's letter indicating applicant is in good standing, LSAT, LSDAS, personal statement regarding reason for transfer, two letters of recommendation, undergraduate transcript, current law school transcript required in support of application. Apply to Admission Office by June 1. Admission decisions made by late July. Application fee $50. Will consider visiting students.

ADMISSION STANDARDS. Number of full-time applicants 2,140, part-time 381; number accepted 1,045 full-time, 183 part-time; number enrolled 186 full-time, 70 part-time; median LSAT 150 (75% of class have a score at or above 147 full-time, 148 part-time); median GPA 2.90 (A = 4) (75% of class have a GPA at or above 2.65 for both full- and part-time). Attrition rate 12%. Gorman rating 2.53; *U.S. News & World Report* ranking is in the fourth tier of all law schools.

FINANCIAL AID. Need-based scholarships, merit scholarships, diversity scholarships, private and institutional loans, state grants, federal loans, and Federal WS available. All accepted students who have signed and returned the preliminary financial aid applications with the admissions application are automatically considered for scholarships (selection criteria place heavy reliance on LSAT and undergraduate GPA). For all other programs apply by June 1 (Fall), November 1 (spring). Phone: (213)938-3621, Ext. 114. Submit FAFSA for all federal programs (Title IV School code #E00480). Also submit Financial Aid Transcript, federal income tax forms. Approximately 26% (full-time), 26% (part-time) of first-year class received scholarships/grants-in-aid. Approximately 78% of current students receive some form of financial assistance. Average scholarship/grant $5,000 full-time, $3,000 part-time. Average debt after graduation $65,000.

DEGREE REQUIREMENTS. For J.D.: 87 credits (40 required) with a 77 or higher (C = 77–84) GPA, plus completion of upper divisional writing course; 3-year full-time program, 4-year plus 2 summer sessions part-time program. Accelerated J.D. with summer course work.

CAREER AND PLACEMENT INFORMATION. About 15–20 employers conducted on-campus interviews. Approximately 89% of graduates are employed in state. More than 62% of graduates are practicing law; 28% are in business; 8% in government; 2% in academia. Approximately 72% of Whittier College's first-time state bar exam takers pass the California Bar Exam; California's passage rate for all first-time takers from ABA-approved schools is 83%. Graduates are eligible to take the bar exam in all 50 states.

WIDENER UNIVERSITY
Chester, Pennsylvania 19013-5792
Internet site: http://www.widener.edu

Founded 1921. Widener University has two separate law schools, one located in Wilmington, Delaware, the other located outside of Harrisburg, Pennsylvania. Widener University is located 15 miles S of Philadelphia. Private control. Semester system. Library: 728,600 volumes/microforms.

University's other graduate colleges/schools: College of Arts and Sciences, School of Engineering, School of Human Service Professions, School of Management, School of Nursing.

Total university enrollment at main campus: 8,500.

School of Law
4601 Concord Pike
P.O. Box 7474
Wilmington, Delaware 19803-0474
Phone: (302)477-2100
Internet site: http://www.widener.edu/law/law.html
E-mail: law.admissions@law.widener.edu

Founded 1971, affiliated with Widener University in 1975. ABA approved since 1975. AALS member. Semester system. Full-time, part-time day study. Law library: 385,000 volumes/microforms; 5,634 current periodicals/

subscriptions; 100 computer workstations; has LEXIS, NEXIS, WESTLAW, DIALOG, LEGALTRAC, INFO-TRAC. Special facilities: Health Law Institute, Trial Advocacy Institute. Special programs: summer study abroad at the International Law Institute, University of Geneva, Switzerland, the International Law Institute, University of Nairobi (Kenya), the International Law Institute, Macquarie University (Sydney, Australia); prosecutors extern program; judicial externships.

Annual tuition: full-time $17,820, part-time $13,380. On-campus housing available. Annual on-campus living expenses $11,170. Law students tend to live off-campus. Contact Admissions Office for both on- and off-campus information. Off-campus housing and personal expenses: approximately $11,620. Additional costs: books approximately $800.

Enrollment: first-year class full-time 285, part-time 155; total full-time 818, part-time 454 (men 57%, women 43%). First-year statistics: 80% out of state, 33 states and foreign countries represented; 43% women; 6% minority; average age 27; 364 undergraduate institutions represented; range of first-year section sizes 25–110 students; number of upper division courses offered after first year 85.

Faculty: full-time 39, part-time 35; 38% female; 9% minority; student/faculty ratio 23.9 to 1.

Degrees conferred: J.D., J.D.-M.B.A., J.D.-Psy.D., LL.M. (Corporate Law and Finance, Health Law).

RECRUITMENT PRACTICES AND POLICIES. Attends local and selected national law school forums. Has on-campus informational sessions. School does have diversity program and actively recruits women/minority applicants.

ADMISSION REQUIREMENTS FOR FIRST-YEAR APPLICANTS. LSDAS law school report, LSAT (not later than February test date, if more than one LSAT, highest is used), bachelor's degree from an accredited institution, personal statement, two recommendations, transcripts (must show all schools attended and at least three years of study) required in support of application. Applicants must have received bachelor's degree prior to enrollment. Interview not required. Campus visits encouraged. In addition, international applicants whose native language is not English must submit TOEFL (not older than two years). Apply to Office of Admission after September 30, before May 15. First-year students admitted fall only. Rolling admission process, notification starts in January and is finished by late April. Application fee $60. Phone: (302)477-2162.

ADMISSION REQUIREMENTS FOR TRANSFER APPLICANTS. Accepts transfers from other ABA-accredited schools. Admission limited to space available. At least one year of enrollment, dean's letter indicating applicant is in good standing, LSAT, LSDAS, personal statement regarding reason for transfer, undergraduate transcript, personal interview, current law school transcript required in support of application. Apply to Admission Office by July 1. Admission decision made within one month of the receipt of a completed application. Application fee $60. Will consider visiting students.

ADMISSION REQUIREMENTS FOR LL.M. APPLICANTS. All applicants must have a J.D. or equivalent from an ABA-accredited law school. Official transcript, two letters of recommendation, personal statement, résumé required in support of Graduate Legal Studies Application. Apply by May 15 to the Director of Graduate Legal Studies. Application fee $60.

ADMISSION STANDARDS. Number of full-time applicants 1,221, part-time 330; number accepted 813 full-time, 211 part-time; number enrolled 285 full-time, 155 part-time; median LSAT 149 (75% of class have a score at or above 147 for both full- and part-time); median GPA 2.99 (A = 4) (75% of class have a GPA at or above 2.75 full-time, 2.62 part-time). Attrition rate 7.8%. Gorman rating 2.07; *U.S. News & World Report* ranking is in the fourth tier of all law schools.

FINANCIAL AID. Full and half scholarships, state scholarships, grants-in-aid, private and institutional loans, federal loans, and Federal WS available. Assistantships may be available for upper divisional joint-degree candidates. All accepted students are automatically considered for all scholarships (selection criteria place heavy reliance on LSAT and undergraduate GPA); use school's Institutional Data Form. For all other programs apply as soon as possible after January 1. Submit FAFSA for all federal programs (Title IV School code #003313). Also submit Financial Aid Transcript, federal income tax forms. Approximately 8% (both full- and part-time) of first-year class received scholarships/grants-in-aid. Approximately 80% of current students receive some form of financial assistance. Average scholarship/grant $8,425 full-time, $6,320 part-time. Average debt after graduation $48,000. Loan Repayment Assistance Program available.

DEGREE REQUIREMENTS. For J.D.: 87 credits (44 required) with a 2.3 (A = 4) GPA, plus completion of upper divisional writing course; 3-year full-time program, 4-year part-time program. Accelerated J.D. with summer course work. For J.D.-M.B.A.: total 102 credits (J.D. 78 credits, M.B.A. 24 credits). For J.D.-Psy.D.: total 172 credits (J.D. 78 credits, Psy.D. 97 credits). For LL.M. (Corporate Law and Finance, Health Law): 24 credits, at least 2 semesters in residence full-time; at least 4 semesters part-time.

CAREER AND PLACEMENT INFORMATION. About 20–25 employers conducted on-campus interviews. Approximately 20% of graduates are employed in Delaware. More than 64% of graduates are practicing law; 26% are in business; 9% in government; 1% in academia. Approximately 65% (PA) of Widener University's first-time state bar exam takers pass the Bar Exam; the passage rate for all first-time takers from ABA-approved schools is 73% (PA). Graduates are eligible to take the bar exam in all 50 states.

School of Law

3800 Vartan Way
P.O. Box 69381
Harrisburg, Pennsylvania 17106-9381
Phone: (717)541-3900
Internet site: http://www.widener.edu/law/law.html

Established 1989. Located 7 miles from Pennsylvania's state capital. Semester system. Full-time, part-time study. Law library: 188,600 volumes/microforms; 4,207 current periodicals/subscriptions; 52 computer workstations; has LEXIS, NEXIS, WESTLAW, DIALOG, LEGALTRAC, INFOTRAC. Special programs: students have same access to facilities and programs as those students at Wilmington campus.

Annual tuition: full-time $17,820, part-time $13,380. No on-campus housing available. Law students live off-campus. Contact Admissions Office for off-campus information. Off-campus housing and personal expenses: approximately $11,700. Additional costs: books approximately $800.

Enrollment: first-year class full-time 107, part-time 48; total full-time 389, part-time 149 (men 61%, women 39%). First-year statistics: 10% out of state, 39% women; 4% minority; average age 27; range of first-year section sizes 50–140 students; number of upper division courses offered after first year 41 full-time, 43 part-time.

Faculty: full-time 22, part-time 13; 38% female; 3% minority; student/faculty ratio 18.5 to 1.

Degrees conferred: J.D., LL.M. (Corporate Law and Finance, Health Law).

RECRUITMENT PRACTICES AND POLICIES. Attends some local law school forums. Has on-campus informational sessions. School does have diversity program and actively recruits women/minority applicants.

ADMISSION REQUIREMENTS FOR FIRST-YEAR APPLICANTS. LSDAS law school report, LSAT (not later than February test date, if more than one LSAT, highest is used), bachelor's degree from an accredited institution, personal statement, two recommendations, transcripts (must show all schools attended and at least three years of study) required in support of application. Applicants must have received bachelor's degree prior to enrollment. Interview not required. Campus visits encouraged. Apply to Office of Admission after September 30, before May 15 (March 31 is preferred date). First-year students admitted fall only. Rolling admission process, notification starts in January and is finished by late April. Application fee $60. Phone: (717)541-3903.

ADMISSION REQUIREMENTS FOR TRANSFER APPLICANTS. Accepts transfers from other ABA-accredited schools. Admission limited to space available. At least one year of enrollment, dean's letter indicating applicant is in good standing, LSAT, LSDAS, personal statement regarding reason for transfer, personal interview, current law school transcript required in support of application. Apply to Admission Office by July 1. Admission decision made within one month of the receipt of completed application. Application fee $60. Will consider visiting students.

ADMISSION REQUIREMENT FOR LL.M. APPLICANTS. All applicants must have a J.D. or equivalent from an ABA-accredited law school. Official transcripts, two letters of recommendation, personal statement, résumé required in support of Graduate Legal Studies Application. Apply May 15 to the Director of Graduate Legal Studies. Application fee $60.

ADMISSION STANDARDS. Number of full-time applicants 346, part-time 103; number accepted 243 full-time, 67 part-time; number enrolled 107 full-time, 48 part-time; median LSAT 148 (75% of class have a score at or above 145 full-time, 149 part-time); median GPA 2.95 (A = 4) (75% of class have a GPA at or above 2.64 full-time, 2.68 part-time). Attrition rate 7.2%. Gorman rating 2.07; *U.S. News & World Report* ranking is in the fourth tier of all law schools.

FINANCIAL AID. Full and half scholarships, state scholarships, grants-in-aid, private and institutional loans, federal loans, and Federal WS available. All accepted students are automatically considered for scholarships (selection criteria place heavy reliance on LSAT and undergraduate GPA); use school's Institutional Data Form. For all other programs apply as soon as possible after January 1. Submit FAFSA for all federal programs (Title IV School code #E00651). Also submit Financial Aid Transcript, federal income tax forms. Approximately 8% (full-time), 11% (part-time) of first-year class received scholarships/grants-in-aid. Approximately 80% of current students receive some form of financial assistance. Average scholarship/grant $11,620 full-time, $8,020 part-time. Average debt after graduation $48,000. Loan Repayment Assistance Program available.

DEGREE REQUIREMENTS. For J.D.: 87 credits (44 required) with a 2.3 (A = 4) GPA, plus completion of upper divisional writing course; 3-year full-time program, 4-year part-time program. Accelerated J.D. with summer course work. For LL.M. (Corporate Law and Finance, Health Law): 24 credits, at least 2 semesters in residence full-time, at least 4 semesters part-time.

CAREER AND PLACEMENT INFORMATION. About 20–25 employers conducted on-campus interviews. Approximately 72% of graduates are employed in state. More than 55% of graduates are practicing law; 17% are in business; 25% in government; 3% in academia. Approximately 65% of Widener University's first-time state bar exam takers pass the Pennsylvania Bar Exam; Pennsylvania's passage rate for all first-time takers from ABA-approved schools is 73%. Graduates are eligible to take the bar exam in all 50 states.

WILLAMETTE UNIVERSITY

Salem, Oregon 97301-3931
Internet site: http://www.willamette.edu

Founded 1842. Located 42 miles S of Portland. Private control. Semester system. Library: 374,300 volumes; 142,300 microforms; 3,231 periodicals/subscriptions; 50 computer workstations.

University's other graduate schools/programs: George H. Atkinson School of Management, Graduate Teaching Program.

Total university enrollment: 2,525.

College of Law
245 Winter Street, SE
Salem, Oregon 97301-3922
Phone: (503)370-6402
Internet site: http://www.willamette.edu/wucl
E-mail: law-admission@willamette.edu

Established 1883. Located on main campus. ABA approved since 1938. AALS member. Semester system. Full-time, day study only. Law library: 266,700 volumes/microforms; 4,264 current periodicals/subscriptions; 44 computer workstations; has LEXIS, NEXIS, WESTLAW, DIALOG, CALI. Special facility: Center for Dispute Resolution. Special programs: summer study abroad in the People's Republic of China; Ecuador.

Annual tuition: $17,100. On-campus housing available for single students only. Annual on-campus housing cost: single students $2,600 (room only), $5,200 (room and board). Housing deadline June 1. Contact Office of Residential Life for both on- and off-campus housing information. Phone: (503)370-6212. Law students tend to live off-campus. Off-campus housing and personal expenses: approximately $10,820. Additional costs: books approximately $1,000.

Enrollment: first-year class 140; total full-time 438 (men 55%, women 45%); no part-time students. First-year statistics: 57% out of state; 45% women; 12% minority; average age 26; range of first-year section sizes 30–120 students; number of upper division courses offered after first year 77.

Faculty: full-time 31, part-time 16; 28% female; 3% minority; student/faculty ratio 19 to 1.

Degrees conferred: J.D., J.D.-M.Mt.

RECRUITMENT PRACTICES AND POLICIES. Attends local and selected national law school forums. Has on-campus informational interviews and tours. School does have diversity program and actively recruits women/minority applicants.

ADMISSION REQUIREMENTS FOR FIRST-YEAR APPLICANTS. LSDAS law school report, LSAT (not later than February test date, if more than one LSAT, average is used), bachelor's degree from an accredited institution, résumé, personal statement, two recommendations, transcripts (must show all schools attended and at least three years of study) required in support of application. Applicants must have received bachelor's degree prior to enrollment. Interview not required but may be requested by school. In addition, international applicants whose native language is not English must submit TOEFL (not older than two years, minimum score 575), certified translation and evaluation of all foreign documents, documentation of financial support. Joint-degree applicants must apply to and be accepted by both schools. Apply to Office of Admission after September 30, before March 15. First-year students admitted fall only. Rolling admission process, notification starts in mid March and is finished by June 1. Acceptance of offer and first deposit

due June 15. Application fee $50. Phone: (503)370-6287. E-mail: law-admission@willamette.edu.

ADMISSION REQUIREMENTS FOR TRANSFER APPLICANTS. Accepts transfers from other ABA-accredited schools. Admission limited to space available. At least one year of enrollment, dean's letter indicating applicant is in good standing (prefer applicants in the top half of first-year class), LSAT, LSDAS, résumé, personal statement regarding reason for transfer, two letters of recommendation, undergraduate transcripts, current law school transcript required in support of application. Apply to Admission Office by July 1. Admission decisions made by early August. Application fee $50. Will consider visiting students.

ADMISSION STANDARDS. Number of full-time applicants 1,037; number accepted 554; number enrolled 136; median LSAT 156 (75% of class have a score at or above 152); median GPA 3.21 (A = 4) (75% of class have a GPA at or above 2.84). Attrition rate 5%. Gorman rating 3.61; *U.S. News & World Report* ranking is in the third tier of all law schools.

FINANCIAL AID. Scholarships, Trustee Scholarships, grants-in-aid, private and institutional loans; federal loans and Federal WS offered through university's Financial Aid Office. Assistantships may be available for upper divisional joint-degree candidates. All accepted students are automatically considered for scholarships (selection criteria place heavy reliance on LSAT and undergraduate GPA); apply to Admissions Office after January 1, no later than January 31. For all other programs apply to the university's Office of Financial Aid. Phone: (503)370-6273. Submit FAFSA for all federal programs (Title IV School code #003227). Also submit Financial Aid Transcript, federal income tax forms. Approximately 24% of first-year class received scholarships/grants-in-aid. Approximately 85% of current students receive some form of financial assistance. Average scholarship/grant $7,000.

DEGREE REQUIREMENTS. For J.D.: 88 credits (37 required) with a 2.0 (A = 4) GPA, plus completion of upper divisional writing course; 3-year program. Accelerated J.D. with summer course work. For J.D.-M.Mt.: a 4-year program rather than the usual 5-year program needed if both degrees taken separately.

CAREER AND PLACEMENT INFORMATION. About 40–50 employers conducted on-campus interviews. Approximately 66% of graduates are employed in state. More than 70% of graduates are practicing law; 16% are in business; 13% in government; 1% in academia. Approximately 74% of Williamette University's first-time state bar exam takers pass the Oregon Bar Exam; Oregon's passage rate for all first-time takers from ABA-approved schools is 77%. Graduates are eligible to take the bar exam in all 50 states.

THE COLLEGE OF WILLIAM AND MARY

Williamsburg, Virginia 23187-8795
Internet site: http://www.wm.edu

Founded 1693. Located 50 miles SE of Richmond in historic Williamsburg. Public control. Semester system. Library: 1,127,400 volumes; 1,880,800 microforms; 10,272 periodicals/subscriptions; 50 computer workstations.

College's other graduate schools: Faculty of Arts and Sciences, School of Business, School of Education, School of Marine Science/Virginia Institute of Marine Science.

Total college enrollment: 7,700.

Marshall-Wythe

School of Law

P.O. Box 8795
Williamsburg, Virginia 23187-8795
Phone: (757)221-3800
Internet site: http://www.wm.edu/law
E-mail: lawadm@facstaff.wm.edu

Established 1779. Located on main campus. ABA approved since 1932. AALS member. Semester system. Full-time, day study only. Law library: 331,340 volumes/microforms; 5,146 current periodicals/subscriptions; 62 computer workstations; has LEXIS, NEXIS, WESTLAW, DIALOG; is a Federal Government Depository. Special facility: Institute of Bill of Rights Law. Special programs: summer study abroad at University of Exeter, Devonshire, England, University of Madrid, Spain, University of Adelaide, Australia; externships.

Annual tuition: resident $7,758, nonresident $17,574. On-campus housing available for both single and married students. Annual on-campus housing cost: single students $2,860 (room only), $4,860 (room and board), married students $5,460. Contact Resident Life Office for both on- and off-campus housing information. Phone: (757)221-4314. Law students tend to live off-campus. Off-campus housing and personal expenses: approxi-

mately $12,830. Additional costs: books approximately $900.

Enrollment: first-year class 200; total full-time 532 (men 54%, women 46%); no part-time students. First-year statistics: 35% out of state, 37 states and foreign countries represented; 46% women; 21% minority; average age 25; 204 undergraduate institutions represented; average first-year section size 70 students; number of upper division courses offered after first year 97.

Faculty: full-time 30, part-time 38; 30% female; 14% minority; student/faculty ratio 18.5 to 1.

Degrees conferred: J.D., J.D.-M.B.A., J.D.-M.P.P., J.D.-M.A. (American Studies), LL.M. (American Legal System—for foreign attorneys who have completed a basic legal education and received a university degree in law in another country).

RECRUITMENT PRACTICES AND POLICIES. Attends national law school forums. Has on-campus group informational sessions. School does have diversity program and actively recruits women/minority applicants.

ADMISSION REQUIREMENTS FOR FIRST-YEAR APPLICANTS. LSDAS law school report, LSAT (not later than February test date, if more than one LSAT, average is used), bachelor's degree from an accredited institution, personal statement, two recommendations, transcripts (must show all schools attended and at least three years of study) required in support of application. Applicants must have received bachelor's degree prior to enrollment. Interview not required but will be granted upon request. In addition, international applicants whose native language is not English must submit TOEFL (not older than two years), certified translations and evaluations of all foreign credentials. Joint-degree applicants must apply to and be accepted by both schools. Apply to Office of Admission after September 1, before March 1. First-year students admitted fall only. Rolling admission process. Application fee $40. Phone: (757)221-3785. Fax: (757)221-3261. E-mail: lawadm@facstaff.wm.edu.

ADMISSION REQUIREMENTS FOR TRANSFER APPLICANTS. Accepts transfers from other ABA-accredited schools. Admission limited to space available. At least one year of enrollment, dean's letter indicating applicant is in good standing (prefer applicants in the top 10% of first-year class), LSAT, LSDAS, personal statement regarding reason for transfer, two letters of recommendation, current law school transcript with rank in class required in support of application. Apply to Admission Office by July 1. Admission decisions made by early

August. Application fee $40. Will consider visiting students.

ADMISSION REQUIREMENTS FOR LL.M. APPLICANTS. All applicants must have a basic law degree from a country other than the U.S.; the institution must be fully accredited and recognized by the relevant educational authority of that country. Applicant must not be a permanent resident or U.S. citizen. Original or certified copies of all official transcripts/academic records, certified English translations of all non-English credentials, two letters of recommendation, personal statement required in support of LL.M. application. Admits fall only. Apply by February 1 to the School of Law's Admissions Office. Application fee $40.

ADMISSION STANDARDS. Number of full-time applicants 2,681; number accepted 776; number enrolled 200; median LSAT 163 (75% of class have a score at or above 160); median GPA 3.28 (A = 4) (75% of class have a GPA at or above 3.02). Attrition rate 3.1%. Gorman rating 3.45; U.S. News & World Report ranking is in the top 35 of all law schools.

FINANCIAL AID. Need-based scholarships, merit scholarships, grants-in-aid, private and institutional loans, federal loans, and Federal WS offered through college's Financial Aid Office. Assistantships may be available for upper divisional joint-degree candidates. All accepted students are automatically considered for scholarships (selection criteria place heavy reliance on LSAT and undergraduate GPA). For all other programs apply to the college's Financial Aid Office after January 1, before February 15. Phone: (575)224-2420. Use the Institutional Financial Aid Application. Submit FAFSA for all federal programs (Title IV School code #003705). Also submit Financial Aid Transcript, federal income tax forms. Approximately 42% of first-year class received scholarships/grants-in-aid. Approximately 88% of current students receive some form of financial assistance. Average scholarship/grant $2,000. Several funding/forgiveness programs available for students who accept public service positions.

DEGREE REQUIREMENTS. For J.D.: 90 credits (36 required) with a GPA of at least a 2.0 (A = 4) GPA, plus completion of upper divisional writing course; 3-year program. Accelerated J.D. with summer course work. For J.D.-M.B.A., -M.P.P.: 4-year programs rather than the usual 5-year program needed if degrees taken separately. For J.D.-M.A. (American Studies): a 3½-year program rather than the usual 4-year program needed if both degrees taken separately. For LL.M. (Foreign Attorneys): 24 credits, at least 2 semesters in residence; major research paper; a GPA of 2.5 (A = 4) required.

CAREER AND PLACEMENT INFORMATION. About 60–70 employers conducted on-campus interviews. Approximately 54% of graduates are employed in state. More than 85% of graduates are practicing law; 8% are in business; 7% in government. Approximately 92% of The College of William and Mary's first-time state bar exam takers pass the Virginia Bar Exam; Virginia's passage rate for all first-time takers from ABA-approved schools is 77%. Graduates are eligible to take the bar exam in all 50 states.

WILLIAM MITCHELL COLLEGE OF LAW

875 Summit Avenue
St. Paul, Minnesota 55105-3076
Phone: (612)227-9171
Internet site: http://www.wmitchell.edu
E-mail: admissions@wmitchell.edu

Established 1900. Located in downtown St. Paul. Private control. Semester system. ABA approved since 1938. AALS member. Semester system. Full-time, part-time study. Law library: 267,600 volumes/microforms; 4,565 current periodicals/subscriptions; 74 computer workstations; has LEXIS, WESTLAW.

Annual tuition: full-time (3-year program) $16,280, part-time (4-year program) $11,830. No on-campus housing available. Law students live off-campus. Contact Student Services Office for off-campus information. Off-campus housing and personal expenses: approximately $11,060. Additional costs: books approximately $500.

Enrollment: first-year class full-time 168, part-time 126; total full-time 353, part-time 531 (men 55%, women 45%). First-year statistics: 12% out of state, 45% women; 9% minority; average age 27; average first-year section size 79 students; number of upper division courses offered after first year 43 full-time, 76 part-time.

Faculty: full-time 31, part-time 24; 36% female; 6% minority; student/faculty ratio 23 to 1.

Degrees conferred: J.D., LL.M. (Tax; this degree program will be ended effective the fall of 1999).

RECRUITMENT PRACTICES AND POLICIES. Attends local and selected national law school forums. Has on-campus informational sessions. School does have diversity program and actively recruits women/minority applicants.

ADMISSION REQUIREMENTS FOR FIRST-YEAR APPLICANTS. LSDAS law school report, LSAT (not later than February test date, if more than one LSAT, highest is used), bachelor's degree from an accredited institution, résumé, personal statement, two recommendations, transcripts (must show all schools attended and at least three years of study) required in support of application. Applicants must have received bachelor's degree prior to enrollment. Interview is optional, campus tours are encouraged. Apply to Office of Admission after September 30, before July 1, April 1 (preferred deadline). First-year students admitted fall only. Rolling admission process, notification is generally within 4–6 weeks of the receipt of a completed application. Application fee $45. Phone: (612)290-3429. E-mail: admissions@wmitchell. edu.

ADMISSION REQUIREMENTS FOR TRANSFER APPLICANTS. Accepts transfers from other ABA-accredited schools. Admission limited to space available. At least one year of enrollment, dean's letter indicating applicant is in good standing, LSAT, LSDAS, personal statement regarding reason for transfer, two letters of recommendation, undergraduate transcript, current law school transcript required in support of application. Apply to Admission Office by July 1. Admission decision made within one month of the receipt of a completed application. Application fee $45. Will consider visiting students.

ADMISSION STANDARDS. Number of full- and part-time applicants 1,200; number accepted 799; number enrolled full-time 168, part-time 126; median LSAT 154 (75% of class have a score at or above 150 full-time, 148 part-time); median GPA 3.13 (A = 4) (75% of class have a GPA at or above 2.90 full-time, 2.82 part-time). Attrition rate 4.7%. Gorman rating 2.91; *U.S. News & World Report* ranking is in the third tier of all law schools.

FINANCIAL AID. Need-based scholarships, merit scholarships, minority scholarships, grants-in-aid, private loans, federal loans, and Federal WS available. All accepted students are automatically considered for scholarships (selection criteria place heavy reliance on LSAT and undergraduate GPA). For all other programs apply as soon as possible after January 1. Phone: (612)290-6403. Submit FAFSA for all federal programs (Title IV School code #G02391). Also submit Financial Aid Transcript, federal income tax forms. Approximately 35% (full-time), 23% (part-time) of first-year class received scholarships/grants-in-aid. Approximately 90% of current students receive some form of financial assistance. Average scholarship/ grant $5,340 full-time, $4,170 part-time. Average debt after graduation $44,000.

DEGREE REQUIREMENTS. For J.D.: 86 credits (45 required) with a 2.0 (A = 4) GPA, plus completion of upper divisional writing course; 3-year full-time program, and 4-year part-time program. Accelerated J.D. with summer course work. For LL.M. (Tax): 24 credits.

CAREER AND PLACEMENT INFORMATION. About 20–30 employers conducted on-campus interviews. Approximately 91% of graduates are employed in state. More than 56% of graduates are practicing law; 25% are in business; 13% in government; 6% in academia. Approximately 85% of William Mitchell College of Law's first-time state bar exam takers pass the Minnesota Bar Exam; Minnesota's passage rate for all first-time takers from ABA-approved schools is 90%. Graduates are eligible to take the bar exam in all 50 states.

UNIVERSITY OF WISCONSIN

Madison, Wisconsin 53706-1380
Internet site: http://www.wisc.edu

Founded 1848. Located 120 miles N of Chicago. Public control. Semester system. Library: 5,530,000 volumes; 4,100,000 microforms; 46,100 periodicals/ subscriptions.

University's other graduate colleges/school: College of Agriculture and Life Sciences, College of Engineering, College of Letters and Science, Institute for Environmental Studies, Institute for Molecular Biology, School of Business, School of Education, School of Family Resources and Consumer Sciences, School of Pharmacy, Medical School, School of Nursing, School of Veterinary Medicine.

Total university enrollment: 40,300.

Law School

975 Bascom Mall
Madison, Wisconsin 53706
Phone: (608)262-2240
Internet site: http://www.law.wisc.edu
E-mail: thomas@law.wisc.edu

Established 1868. Located on main campus. ABA approved since 1923. AALS charter member. Semester system. Full-time, day study, limited part-time study. Law library: 454,650 volumes/microforms; 4,961 current periodicals/subscriptions; 60 computer workstations; has LEXIS, NEXIS, WESTLAW, DIALOG. Special facility:

Center for Public Representation. Special programs: Criminal Justice Administration Program; The Legal Assistance to Institutionalized Persons Program (LAIP); Public Intervenor's Program; internships.

Annual tuition: resident $5,910, nonresident $15,442. On-campus housing available for both single and married students. Annual on-campus living expenses: $9,100. Contact Officer of University Housing for on-campus housing information. Phone: (608)252-2522. Law students tend to live off-campus. Contact Campus Assistance Center for off-campus information. Phone: (608)262-2400. Contact the Family Housing Office for off-campus married housing information. Phone: (608)262-2789. Off-campus housing and personal expenses: approximately $9,725. Additional costs: books approximately $700.

Enrollment: first-year class 250; total full-time 785 (men 53%, women 47%); limited part-time study. First-year statistics: 20% out of state, 28 states and foreign countries represented; 47% women; 24% minority; average age 25; 89 undergraduate institutions represented; range of first-year section sizes 20–90 students; number of upper division courses offered after first year 202.

Faculty: full-time 52, part-time 11; 33% female; 7% minority; student/faculty ratio 20 to 1.

Degrees conferred: J.D., J.D.-M.B.A., J.D.-M.P.A., J.D.-M.A. (Ibero-American Studies), J.D.-M.S. (Environmental Studies), J.D.-M.L.I., J.D.-M.L.S., LL.M., M.L.I. (for foreign law graduates only), S.J.D.

RECRUITMENT PRACTICES AND POLICIES. Attends local and national law school forums. Has on-campus informational sessions. School does have diversity program and actively recruits women/minority applicants.

ADMISSION REQUIREMENTS FOR FIRST-YEAR APPLICANTS. LSDAS law school report, LSAT (not later than February test date, if more than one LSAT, average is used), bachelor's degree from an accredited institution, personal statement, "Record of Residence" form, Financial Aid Request Form (if requesting financial aid), transcripts (must show all schools attended and at least three years of study) required in support of application. Letters of recommendation are optional. Applicants must have received bachelor's degree prior to enrollment. Interview not required but may be requested by school. In addition, international applicants whose native language is not English must submit TOEFL (not older than two years), certified translations and evaluations of all foreign credentials. Apply to Office of Admission after September 15, before February 1 (strictly enforced). First-year students admitted fall only. Rolling admission process, notification starts in November and is finished by late April. Acceptance of offer and first deposit due April 1. School does maintain a waiting list. Application fee $45. Phone: (608)262-5914. Fax: (608)262-5485. E-mail: thomas@law.wisc.edu.

ADMISSION REQUIREMENTS FOR TRANSFER APPLICANTS. Accepts transfers from other ABA-accredited schools. Admission limited to space available. At least one year of enrollment, dean's letter indicating applicant is in good standing (prefer applicants in the top 15% of first-year class), LSAT, LSDAS, personal statement regarding reason for transfer, undergraduate transcript, current law school transcript required in support of application. Apply to Admission Office by June 1 (fall), December 1 (spring). Preference given to Wisconsin residents. Admission decision made within one month of the receipt of a completed application. Application fee $45. Will consider visiting students.

ADMISSION REQUIREMENTS FOR LL.M., S.J.D. APPLICANTS. For LL.M.: all applicants must hold a J.D. or equivalent law degree. Official transcripts, three letters of recommendation, a plan of work (at least four double-spaced typed pages, including a statement of objective, outline of proposed research and explanation of courses/seminar needs), consent of a faculty member of the law school to act as the principal academic advisor required in support of LL.M. application. In addition, holders of law degrees from foreign countries must submit proof of completion of all academic work necessary for entering a law profession in the applicant's home country; TOEFL (minimum score 625) required for all international applicants whose native language is other than English. Apply by March 15 (fall), November 15 (spring) to Committee on Academic Programs. Application fee $45. Phone: (608)262-9120.

For S.J.D.: all applicants must hold a J.D. or an equivalent law degree and usually an LL.M. from the University of Wisconsin. Official transcript, three letters of recommendation, LL.M. thesis or equivalent project, at least six double-spaced typed pages outlining objective, methodology, required materials and timetable, consent of a faculty member of the law school faculty to act as the principal academic advisor required in support of S.J.D. application. In addition, holders of law degrees from foreign countries must submit proof of completion of all academic work necessary for entering a law profession in the applicant's home country; TOEFL (minimum score

625) required for all international applicants whose native language is other than English. Apply by March 15 (fall), November 15 (spring) to Committee on Graduate Programs. Application fee $45. Phone: (608)262-9120.

ADMISSION STANDARDS. Number of full-time applicants 1,947; number accepted 754; number enrolled 282; median LSAT 158 (75% of class have a score at or above 153); median GPA 3.52 (A = 4) (75% of class have a GPA at or above 3.13). Attrition rate 3.2%. Gorman rating 4.49; *U.S. News & World Report* ranking is in the top 40 of all law schools.

FINANCIAL AID. Need-based scholarships, grants-in-aid, private loans, federal loans, and Federal WS offered through university's Financial Aid Office. Assistantships may be available for upper divisional joint-degree candidates. Apply to the Law School Financial Aid Office for all scholarships (selection criteria place heavy reliance on LSAT and undergraduate GPA), after January 1 before March 1. Phone: (608)262-1815. For all other programs apply to university's Office of Student Financial Services. Phone: (608)262-3060. Submit FAFSA for all federal programs (Title IV School code #003895). Also submit Financial Aid Transcript, federal income tax forms. Approximately 12% of first-year class received scholarships/grants-in-aid. Approximately 65% of current students receive some form of financial assistance. Average scholarship/grant $9,000. Average debt after graduation $31,700. Financial aid available for part-time students.

DEGREE REQUIREMENTS. For J.D.: 90 credits (30–31 required) with a 77 (scale 0–100) GPA, plus completion of upper divisional writing course; 2½–3 year program. Accelerated J.D. with summer course work. For J.D.-master's: 3½- to 4-year programs rather than the usual 4- to 5-year programs needed if both degrees taken separately. For LL.M.: 24–30 credits, at least 2 semesters in full-time residence; thesis (equivalent in quality and substance to a substantial law review article); program must be completed no later than 1 calendar year after the residence period. For S.J.D.: a minimum of 24 credits beyond the LL.M., at least 2 semesters in full-time residence; dissertation; degree must be completed no later than 3 calendar years after the residence period.

CAREER AND PLACEMENT INFORMATION. About 90–100 employers conducted on-campus interviews. Approximately 65% of graduates are employed in state. More than 77% of graduates are practicing law; 10% are in business; 12% in government; 1% in academia. Ad-

mission to the Wisconsin State Bar is automatic if one has a J.D. from a Wisconsin law school and the required upper divisional courses are successfully completed, Graduates are eligible to take the bar exam in all 50 states.

UNIVERSITY OF WYOMING
Laramie, Wyoming 82071
Internet site: http://www.uwyo.edu

Founded 1886. Located in southeastern Wyoming. Public control. Semester system. Library: 1,134,000 volumes; 2,270,700 microforms; 12,150 periodicals/subscriptions; 75 computer workstations.

University's other graduate colleges/schools: College of Agriculture, College of Arts and Sciences, College of Business, College of Education, College of Engineering, College of Health Sciences.

Total university enrollment: 11,300.

College of Law
P.O. Box 3035
Laramie, Wyoming 82071-3035
Phone: (307)766-6416
Internet site: http://www.uwyo.edu/law/law.htm
E-mail: candid@uwyo.edu

Established 1920. Located on main campus. ABA approved since 1923. AALS member. Semester system. Full-time, day study only. Law library: 198,150 volumes/microforms; 2,504 current periodicals/subscriptions; 26 computer workstations; has LEXIS, NEXIS, WESTLAW, INFOTRAC; is a Federal Government Depository. Special programs: Wyoming Defender Aid Program, Legal Services Program, Wyoming Prosecution Assistance Program.

Annual tuition: resident $4,234, nonresident $9,322. On-campus housing available for single students only. Annual on-campus housing cost: single students $1,512 (room only), $3,530 (room and board). Housing deadline May 30. Contact Director of Housing for both on- and off-campus housing information. Phone: (800)228-7232 (in Wyoming), (800)423-5809 (outside Wyoming). Law students tend to live off-campus. Off-campus housing and personal expenses: approximately $8,500. Additional costs: books approximately $700.

Enrollment: first-year class 79; total full-time 212 (men 57%, women 43%); no part-time students. First-year statistics: 30% out of state, 29 states and foreign countries represented; 43% women; 6% minority; average age 24; 70 undergraduate institutions represented; range of first-year section sizes 20–80 students; number of upper division courses offered after first year 53.

Faculty: full-time 12, part-time 17; 30% female; student/faculty ratio 14.7 to 1.

Degrees conferred: J.D., J.D.-M.B.A., J.D.-M.P.A.

RECRUITMENT PRACTICES AND POLICIES. Attends local and selected national law school forums. Has on-campus informational sessions. School does have diversity program and actively recruits women/minority applicants.

ADMISSION REQUIREMENTS FOR FIRST-YEAR APPLICANTS. LSDAS law school report, LSAT (not later than February test date, if more than one LSAT, average is used), bachelor's degree from an accredited institution, personal statement, transcripts (must show all schools attended and at least three years of study) required in support of application. Letters of recommendation optional. Applicants must have received bachelor's degree prior to enrollment. Interview not required. Joint-degree applicants must apply to and be accepted by both schools. Apply to Office of Admission Office after October 1, before April 1. First-year students admitted fall only. Rolling admission process, notification starts in February and is finished by early May. Application fee $35. Phone: (307)766-6416. E-mail: candid@uwyo.edu.

ADMISSION REQUIREMENTS FOR TRANSFER APPLICANTS. Accepts transfers from other ABA-accredited schools. Admission limited to space available. At least one year of enrollment, dean's letter indicating applicant is in good standing (prefer applicants in the upper quarter of first-year class), LSAT, LSDAS, personal statement regarding reason for transfer, undergraduate transcripts, current law school transcript required in support of application. Apply to Admissions Office by July 1 (fall), December 1 (spring). Admission decision made by within six weeks of the receipt of the completed application and all supporting documentation. Application fee $35. Will consider visiting students.

ADMISSION STANDARDS. Number of full-time applicants 548; number accepted 257; number enrolled 78; median LSAT 154 (75% of class have a score at or above 150); median GPA 3.33 (A = 4) (75% of class have a GPA at or above 3.06). Attrition rate 8.4%. Gorman rating 2.59; *U.S. News & World Report* ranking is in the third tier of all law schools.

FINANCIAL AID. Scholarships, merit scholarships, minority scholarships, grants-in-aid, institutional loans; federal loans and Federal WS offered through university's Financial Aid Office. Assistantships may be available for upper divisional joint-degree candidates. Apply to the Admissions Office after January 1, before June 1 for scholarships (selection criteria place heavy reliance on LSAT and undergraduate GPA). Use college's scholarship application. For all other programs apply to Office of Student Financial Aid by May 1. Submit FAFSA for all federal programs (Title IV School code #003932). Also submit Financial Aid Transcript, federal income tax forms. Approximately 26% of first-year class received scholarships/grants-in-aid. Approximately 80% of current students receive some form of financial assistance. Average scholarship/grant $1,668. Average debt after graduation $30,000.

DEGREE REQUIREMENTS. For J.D.: 88 credits (52 required) with a 2.0 (A = 4) GPA, plus completion of upper divisional writing course; 3-year program. Accelerated J.D. with summer course work. For J.D.-M.B.A.: Law School will accept up to 6 credits, M.B.A. will accept up to 9 credits; a 4½-year program rather than the usual 5-year program needed if degrees taken separately. For J.D.-M.P.A.: Law School will accept up to 6 credits, M.P.A. will accept up to 6 credits; a 4½-year program rather than the usual 5-year program needed if degrees taken separately.

CAREER AND PLACEMENT INFORMATION. About 15–20 employers conducted on-campus interviews. Approximately 61% of graduates are employed in state. More than 80% of graduates are practicing law; 9% are in business; 11% in government. Approximately 81% of the University of Wyoming's first-time state bar exam takers pass the Wyoming Bar Exam; Wyoming's passage rate for all first-time takers from ABA-approved schools is 76%. Graduates are eligible to take the bar exam in all 50 states.

YALE UNIVERSITY
New Haven, Connecticut 06520
Internet site: http://www.yale.edu

Founded 1701. Located 80 miles NE of New York City. Private control. Semester system. Library: 10,600,000 volumes; 5,000,000 microforms; 55,000 periodicals/subscriptions.

University's other graduate colleges/schools: Divinity School, Graduate School of Arts and Sciences, School of Architecture, School of Art, School of Drama, School of Forestry and Environmental Studies, School of Management, School of Medicine, School of Music, School of Nursing.

Total university enrollment: 11,000.

Law School

P.O. Box 208329
New Haven, Connecticut 06520-8329
Phone: (203)432-1660
Internet site: http://www.law.yale.edu
E-mail: admissions@mail.law.yale.edu

Established 1801. Located on main campus. ABA approved since 1923. AALS member. Semester system. Full-time, day study only. Law library: 941,200 volumes/microforms; 9,147 current periodicals/subscriptions; 73 computer workstations; has LEXIS, NEXIS, WESTLAW, DIALOG, OCLC; is a Federal Government Depository. Special facilities: Center for Law Economics and Public Policy, Orville H. Schnell, Jr. Center for International Human Rights.

Annual tuition: for J.D., LL.M., M.S.L. $23,940; J.S.D. $3,812 per term. On-campus housing available for both single and married students. Annual on-campus living expenses: $10,816. Housing deadline June 1. Contact Housing Department for both on- and off-campus housing information. Phone: (203)432-9756. Law students tend to live off-campus. Off-campus housing and personal expenses: approximately $11,556. Additional costs: books approximately $800.

Enrollment: first-year class 198; total full-time 582 (men 57%, women 43%); no part-time students. First-year statistics: 90% out of state, 68 states and foreign countries represented; 43% women; 28% minority; average age 24; 174 undergraduate institutions represented; range of first-year section sizes 15–90 students; number of upper division courses offered after first year 112.

Faculty: full-time 48, part-time 54; 23% female; 11% minority; student/faculty ratio 10.9 to 1.

Degrees conferred: J.D., J.D.-M.P.A., J.D.-M.A., J.D.-M.P.P.M., J.D.-M.E.S., J.D.-M.F.S., J.D.-M.Div., J.D.M.D., J.D.-Ph.D., LL.M. (generally open for those committed to law teaching as a career), LL.M. (for persons who have completed a basic legal education and received a university degree in law in another country), M.S.L. (Masters of Studies in Law, for nonlawyers), J.S.D. (open to LL.M. graduates from Yale only).

RECRUITMENT PRACTICES AND POLICIES. Attends local and national law school forums. Has on-campus tours and class visitations encouraged. School does have diversity program and actively recruits women/minority applicants.

ADMISSION REQUIREMENTS FOR FIRST-YEAR APPLICANTS. LSDAS law school report, LSAT (not later than December test date, if more than one LSAT, average is used), bachelor's degree from an accredited institution, short essay, personal statement, two recommendations, transcripts (must show all schools attended and at least three years of study) required in support of application. Applicants must have received bachelor's degree prior to enrollment. Interviews are not part of the admissions process but a personal appointment may be requested by applicant. In addition, international applicants whose native language is not English must submit TOEFL (not older than two years). Joint-degree applicants must apply to and be accepted by both schools. Apply to Director of Admission as soon as possible after October 1. First-year students admitted fall only. Rolling admission process. School does maintain a waiting list. Application fee $65. Phone: (203)432-4995. E-mail: admissions@mail.law.yale.edu.

ADMISSION REQUIREMENTS FOR TRANSFER APPLICANTS. Accepts about 10–12 transfers each year from other ABA-accredited schools. At least one year of enrollment, dean's letter indicating applicant is in good standing (applicants must have maintained a weighted B average), LSAT, LSDAS, personal statement regarding reason for transfer, two letters of recommendation, undergraduate transcripts, current law school transcript required in support of application. Apply to Director of Admission after May 1, before July 20. Admission decisions made by the first week of August. Application fee $65. Will consider visiting students.

ADMISSION REQUIREMENTS FOR LL.M. APPLICANTS. All applicants must have graduated from either an AALS member law school or an ABA-accredited law school with a high rank-in-class. If from another country, the applicant must have graduated with high rank from a law school or law faculty with standards substantially equivalent to those of U.S. applicants. Official undergraduate college/university transcripts, official law school transcript, résumé, proposed study plan, personal statement, two letters of recommendation required in support of graduate application. In addition, TOEFL for those whose native language is not English; all transcripts and recommendations must be in English or accompanied by an English translation. Admits fall only. Apply by December 15 to Graduate Programs Office. Application $60. Phone: (203)432-1693. E-mail: couture@mail.law.yale.edu.

ADMISSION STANDARDS. Number of full-time applicants 3,811; number accepted 253; number enrolled 198; median LSAT 172 (75% of class have a score at or above 168); median GPA 3.84 (A = 4) (75% of class have a GPA at or above 3.73). Attrition rate .3%. Gorman rating 4.91; *U.S. News & World Report* ranking is the number 1 law school in U.S.

FINANCIAL AID. Need-based scholarships, merit scholarships, minority scholarships, grants-in-aid, private institutional loans, summer Public Interest Funding, federal loans, and Federal WS available. Assistantships may be available for upper divisional joint-degree candidates. For all financial aid, complete the need Access Disk (must arrive at Yale no later than April 15) and submit FAFSA (Title IV School code #E00444) as soon as possible after January 1, but no later than March 15. In addition, also submit Financial Aid Transcript, federal income tax forms. Approximately 42% of first-year class received scholarships/grants-in-aid. Approximately 74% of current students receive some form of financial assistance. Average scholarship/grant $9,300. Average debt after graduation $45,000. Loan Forgiveness Program and Career Options Assistance Program (COAP) available.

DEGREE REQUIREMENTS. For J.D.: 82 units (19 required) with a 2.0 (A = 4) GPA, plus completion of 2 upper divisional writing courses and lectures on professional responsibility; 3-year program. Accelerated J.D. with summer course work. For J.D.-master's: most joint-degree programs reduce the time needed to complete both degrees by up to 1 year. For LL.M.: 18 units plus 6 units of independent research and writing. For M.S.L.: 27 units; at least 2 semesters; 1 year terminal degree. For J.S.D.: at least 1 additional year in full-time study beyond the LL.M.; thesis that makes a substantial contribution to legal scholarship.

CAREER AND PLACEMENT INFORMATION. About 400–500 employers conducted on-campus interviews. Approximately 4% of graduates are employed in state. More than 90% of graduates are practicing law; 5% are in business; 4% in government; 1% in academia. Approximately 97% of Yale University's first-time state bar exam takers pass the New York Bar Exam; New York's passage rate for all first-time takers from ABA-approved schools is 78%. Graduates are eligible to take the bar exam in all 50 states.

YESHIVA UNIVERSITY
New York, New York 10033-3201
Internet site: http://www.yu.edu

Founded 1886. Private control. Semester system. Library: 1,013,700 volumes; 1,120,000 microforms; 10,100 periodicals/subscriptions; 200 computer workstations.

University's other graduate colleges/schools: Albert Einstein College of Medicine, Azrieli Graduate School of Jewish Education and Administration, Bernard Revel Graduate School, Ferkauf Graduate School of Psychology, Wurzweiler School of Social Work.

Total university enrollment: 5,400.

Benjamin N. Cardozo
School of Law
55 Fifth Avenue
New York, New York 10003-4391
Phone: (212)790-0200
Internet site: http://www.yu.edu/csl/law
E-mail: lawinfo@yul.yu.edu

Established 1976. Located at the foot of Fifth Avenue in historic Greenwich Village. ABA approved since 1978. AALS member. Semester system. Full-time, day study only. Law library: 400,500 volumes/microforms: 5,786 current periodicals/subscriptions: 87 computer workstations; has LEXIS, NEXIS, WESTLAW, OCLC. Special programs: clerkships; externships; internships.

Annual tuition: $20,000. No on-campus housing available. Law students live off-campus. Contact Admissions Office for off-campus information. Off-campus housing and personal expenses: approximately $18,038. Additional costs: books approximately $800.

Enrollment: first-year class in September 250, in January 40, in May 40; total full-time 975 (men 53%, women 47%); no part-time students. First-year statistics: 40% out of state, 26 states and 12 foreign countries represented; 46% women; 16% minority; average age 23; 177 undergraduate institutions represented; range of first-year section sizes 12–105 students; number of upper division courses offered after first year 134.

Faculty: full-time 45, part-time 87%, 31% female; 3% minority; student/faculty ratio 21 to 1.

Degree conferred: J.D.

RECRUITMENT PRACTICES AND POLICIES. Attends local and selected national law school forums. Has on-campus informational sessions. School does have diversity program and actively recruits women/minority applicants.

ADMISSION REQUIREMENTS FOR FIRST-YEAR APPLICANTS. LSDAS law school report, LSAT (not later than February [for May and September admission], October [for January admission] test date, if more than one LSAT, average is used), bachelor's degree from an accredited institution, personal statement, Dean's Certification Form, two recommendations, transcripts (must show all schools attended and at least three years of study) required in support of application. Applicants must have received bachelor's degree prior to enrollment. Interview not required but may be requested by school. In addition, international applicants whose native language is not English must submit TOEFL (not older than two years), Foreign Student Questionnaire, financial support documentation, all transcripts must have certified translations and evaluations. Apply to Office of Admission Office after September 1, before December 1 (January), April 1 (May and September). First-year students admitted January (Accelerated Entry Program), May (Accelerated Entry Plan) and September. Rolling admission process. Application fee $60. Phone: (212)790-0274. E-mail: lawinfo@yul.yu.edu.

ADMISSION REQUIREMENTS FOR TRANSFER APPLICANTS. Accepts transfers from other ABA-accredited schools. Admission limited to space available. At least one year of enrollment, dean's letter indicating applicant is in good standing, LSAT, LSDAS, personal statement regarding reason for transfer, two letters of recommendation, undergraduate transcript, current law school transcript required in support of application. Apply to Admission Office by August 10 (fall term), January 1 (spring term), April 15 (May term). Admission decision made within two weeks of the receipt of a completed application. Application fee $60. Will consider visiting students.

ADMISSION STANDARDS. Number of full-time applicants 2,205; number accepted 1,062; number enrolled 332; median LSAT 156 (75% of class have a score at or above 152); median GPA 3.21 (A = 4) (75% of class have a GPA at or above 2.94). Attrition rate 1.3%. Gorman rating 3.76; *U.S. News & World Report* ranking is in the second tier of all law schools.

FINANCIAL AID. Need-based scholarships, partial merit scholarships, grants-in-aid, private and institutional loans, state TAP grants; federal loans and Federal WS offered through university's Office of Financial Assistance. All accepted students are automatically considered for scholarships (selection criteria place heavy reliance on LSAT and undergraduate GPA). Apply as soon as possible after January 1. Phone: (212)790-0392. Use university's Application for Financial Assistance. For all other programs apply to the Office of Student Financial Assistance. Submit FAFSA for all federal programs (Title IV School code #002903). Also submit Financial Aid Transcript, federal income tax forms. Approximately 53% of first-year class received scholarships/grants-in-aid. Approximately 80% of current students receive some form of financial assistance. Average scholarship/grant $4,000. Average debt after graduation $67,900.

DEGREE REQUIREMENTS. For J.D.: 84 credits (33 required) with a 2.0 (A = 4) GPA, plus completion of upper divisional writing course; 2½-year program (Accelerated Entry Program, entrance in January and May), 3-year program. Accelerated J.D. with summer course work.

CAREER AND PLACEMENT INFORMATION. About 40–50 employers conducted on-campus interviews. Approximately 81% of graduates are employed in state. More than 69% of graduates are practicing law; 16% are in business; 11% in government; 4% in academia. Approximately 76% of Yeshiva University's first-time state bar exam takers pass the New York Bar Exam; New York's passage rate for all first-time takers from ABA-approved schools is 78%. Graduates are eligible to take the bar exam in all 50 states.

Alphabetical Listing of All Law Schools

A

University of Akron, School of Law
The University of Alabama, School of Law
Albany Law School. *See* Union University
American University, Washington College of Law
Arizona State University, College of Law
University of Arizona, College of Law
University of Arkansas, Fayetteville, School of Law
University of Arkansas at Little Rock, School of Law

B

University of Baltimore, School of Law
Baylor University, School of Law
Benjamin N. Cardozo School of Law. *See* Yeshiva University
Boalt Hall. *See* University of California, Berkeley
Boston College, Law School
Boston University, School of Law
Brigham Young University, J. Reuben Clark Law School
Brooklyn Law School
University at Buffalo, State University of New York School of Law

C

University of California at Berkeley School of Law (Boalt Hall)
University of California, Davis, School of Law
University of California, Hastings College of the Law
University of California Los Angeles, School of Law
California Western School of Law
Campbell University, Norman Adrian Wiggins School of Law
Capital University, Law School
Case Western Reserve University, School of Law
The Catholic University of America, Columbus School of Law
Chicago-Kent College of Law. *See* Illinois Institute of Technology
University of Chicago, Law School
University of Cincinnati, College of Law
Cleveland State University, Cleveland–Marshall College of Law
University of Colorado, School of Law

Columbia University, School of Law
University of Connecticut, School of Law
Cooley Law School. *See* Thomas M. Cooley Law School
Cornell University, Law School
Creighton University, School of Law
Cumberland School of Law. *See* Samford University

D

University of Dayton, School of Law
University of Denver, College of Law
DePaul University, College of Law
Detroit College of Law at Michigan State University
University of Detroit Mercy, School of Law
Dickinson School of Law. *See* The Pennsylvania State University
University of the District of Columbia, School of Law
Drake University, Law School
Duke University, School of Law
Duquesne University, School of Law

E

Emory University, School of Law

F

The Florida State University, College of Law
University of Florida, College of Law
Fordham University, School of Law
Franklin Pierce Law Center

G

George Mason University, School of Law
George Washington University, Law School
Georgetown University, Law Center
Georgia State University, College of Law
University of Georgia, School of Law
Golden Gate University, School of Law
Gonzaga University, School of Law

S

St. John's University, School of Law
St. Louis University, School of Law
St. Mary's University, School of Law
St. Thomas University, School of Law
Salmon P. Chase College of Law. *See* Northern Kentucky
   University
Samford University, Cumberland School of Law
University of San Diego, School of Law
University of San Francisco, School of Law
Santa Clara University, School of Law
Seattle University, School of Law
Seton Hall University, School of Law
Shepard Broad Law Center. *See* Nova Southeastern
   University
University of South Carolina, School of Law
University of South Dakota, School of Law
South Texas College of Law
University of Southern California, Law School
Southern Illinois University, Carbondale, School of Law
Southern Methodist University, School of Law
Southern University, Law Center
Southwestern University, School of Law
Stanford University, Law School
Stetson University, College of Law
Suffolk University, Law School
Syracuse University, College of Law

T

Temple University, School of Law
University of Tennessee, College of Law
University of Texas, Austin, School of Law
Texas Southern University, Thurgood Marshall School of
   Law
Texas Tech University, School of Law
Texas Wesleyan University, School of Law
Thomas Jefferson School of Law
Thomas M. Cooley Law School
University of Toledo College of Law
Touro College–Jacob D. Fuchsberg Law Center

Tulane University Law School
University of Tulsa, College of Law

U

Union University, Albany Law School
University of Utah, College of Law

V

Valparaiso University, School of Law
Vanderbilt University, School of Law
Vermont Law School
Villanova University, School of Law
University of Virginia, School of Law

W

Wake Forest University, School of Law
Washburn University, School of Law
Washington and Lee University, School of Law
Washington College of Law. *See* American University
Washington University, School of Law
University of Washington, School of Law
Wayne State University, Law School
West Virginia University, College of Law
Western New England College, School of Law
Whittier College, Law School
Widener University, Harrisburg, School of Law
Widener University, Wilmington, School of Law
Willamette University, College of Law
College of William and Mary, School of Law
William Mitchell College of Law
University of Wisconsin, Law School
University of Wyoming, College of Law

Y

Yale University, Law School
Yeshiva University, Benjamin N. Cardozo School of Law

Law Schools by Region and Geographic Location

PACIFIC NORTHWEST

Washington

Seattle—Population: 516,250
University of Washington

Spokane—Population: 177,200
Gonzaga University

Tacoma—Population: 176,600
Seattle University

Oregon

Eugene—Population: 112,700
University of Oregon

Portland—Population: 437,300
Lewis & Clark College

Salem—Population: 107,800
Willamette University

WEST COAST AND HAWAII

California

Los Angeles—Population: 3,485,400
University of California, Los Angeles
Loyola University, Los Angeles
Pepperdine University
University of Southern California
Southwestern University
Whittier College

Sacramento—Population: 369,300
University of California, Davis
McGeorge School of Law, University of
    the Pacific

San Diego—Population: 1,110,500
California Western School of Law
University of San Diego
Thomas Jefferson School of Law

San Francisco—Population: 723,950
University of California, Berkeley
University of California, Hastings School
    of Law
Golden Gate University
University of San Francisco
Stanford University

Santa Clara—Population: 93,600
Santa Clara University

Hawaii

Honolulu—Population: 365,200
University of Hawaii

ROCKY MOUNTAINS

Idaho

Moscow—Population: 18,519
University of Idaho

Utah

Provo—Population: 86,800
Brigham Young University

Salt Lake City—Population: 159,900
University of Utah

Arizona

Tempe—Population: 141,800
Arizona State University

Tucson—Population: 405,400
University of Arizona

Montana

Missoula—Population: 42,900
University of Montana

Wyoming

Laramie—Population: 26,700
University of Wyoming

Colorado

Boulder—Population: 83,300
University of Colorado

Denver—Population: 467,600
University of Denver

New Mexico

Albuquerque—Population: 384,700
University of New Mexico

WEST NORTH CENTRAL

North Dakota

Grand Forks—Population: 49,500
University of North Dakota

South Dakota

Vermillion—Population: 10,000
University of South Dakota

Nebraska

Lincoln—Population: 192,000
University of Nebraska

Omaha—Population: 335,800
Creighton University

Kansas

Lawrence—Population: 65,900
University of Kansas

Topeka—Population: 120,000
Washburn University

Iowa

Des Moines—Population: 193,200
Drake University

Iowa City—Population: 59,800
University of Iowa

Missouri

Columbia—Population: 69,100
University of Missouri, Columbia

Kansas City—Population: 435,100
University of Missouri, Kansas City

St. Louis—Population: 396,700
St. Louis University
Washington University

WEST SOUTH CENTRAL

Oklahoma

Norman—Population: 80,171
University of Oklahoma

Oklahoma City—Population: 444,800
Oklahoma City University

Tulsa—Population: 367,300
University of Tulsa

Texas

Austin—Population: 465,600
University of Texas, Austin

Dallas—Population: 1,006,800
Southern Methodist University

Houston—Population: 1,630,500
University of Houston
South Texas College of Law
Texas Southern University

Irving—Population: 155,000
Texas Wesleyan University

Lubbock—Population: 186,200
Texas Tech University

San Antonio—Population: 936,000
St. Mary's University

Waco—Population: 103,600
Baylor University

Arkansas

Fayetteville—Population: 42,100
University of Arkansas, Fayetteville

Little Rock—Population: 175,800
University of Arkansas, Little Rock

Louisiana

Baton Rouge—Population: 219,500
Louisiana State University

New Orleans—Population: 497,000
Loyola University, New Orleans
Tulane University

EAST NORTH CENTRAL

Minnesota

Minneapolis/St. Paul—Population: 368,400
Hamline University
University of Minnesota
William Mitchell College of Law

Wisconsin

Madison—Population: 191,250
University of Wisconsin

Milwaukee—Population: 628,100
Marquette University

Illinois

Carbondale—Population: 27,000
Southern Illinois University

Champaign—Population: 63,500
University of Illinois

Chicago—Population: 2,783,700
University of Chicago
DePaul University
Illinois Institute of Technology, Chicago-Kent
John Marshall Law School
Loyola University, Chicago
Northwestern University

Dekalb—Population: 34,900
Northern Illinois University

Michigan

Ann Arbor—Population: 109,500
University of Michigan

Detroit—Population: 1,028,000
University of Detroit Mercy
Wayne State University

Lansing—Population: 127,300
Detroit College of Law
Thomas M. Cooley Law School

Indiana

Bloomington—Population: 60,600
Indiana University, Bloomington

Indianapolis—Population: 731,300
Indiana University, Indianapolis

South Bend—Population: 105,500
University of Notre Dame

Valparaiso—Population: 24,400
Valparaiso University

EAST SOUTH CENTRAL

Kentucky

Highland Heights—Population: 4,223
Northern Kentucky University

Lexington—Population: 225,400
University of Kentucky

Louisville—Population: 269,100
University of Louisville

Tennessee

Knoxville—Population: 165,100
University of Tennessee

Memphis—Population: 610,300
University of Memphis

Nashville—Population: 488,400
Vanderbilt University

West Virginia

Morgantown—Population: 25,900
West Virginia University

Virginia

Arlington—Population: 171,000
George Mason University

Charlottesville—Population: 40,300
University of Virginia

Lexington—Population: 7,000
Washington and Lee University

Richmond—Population: 203,100
University of Richmond

Virginia Beach—Population: 393,100
Regent University

Williamsburg—Population: 11,500
College of William & Mary

SOUTHEAST AND PUERTO RICO

Mississippi

Jackson—Population: 196,700
Mississippi College

Oxford—Population: 10,000
University of Mississippi

Alabama

Birmingham—Population: 266,000
Samford University

Tuscaloosa—Population: 77,800
University of Alabama

North Carolina

Buies Creek—Population: 2,000
Campbell University

Chapel Hill—Population: 38,700
University of North Carolina

Durham—Population: 136,600
Duke University
North Carolina Central University

Winston-Salem—Population: 143,500
Wake Forest University

South Carolina

Columbia—Population: 98,000
University of South Carolina

Georgia

Athens—Population: 45,700
University of Georgia

Atlanta—Population: 394,000
Emory University
Georgia State University

Macon—Population: 106,600
Mercer University

Florida

Coral Gables—Population: 40,100
University of Miami

Ft. Lauderdale—Population: 149,400
Nova Southeastern University

Gainesville—Population: 84,800
University of Florida

Miami—Population: 358,600
St. Thomas University

St. Petersburg—Population: 238,600
Stetson University

Tallahassee—Population: 124,800
Florida State University

Puerto Rico

Ponce—Population: 187,800
Pontifical Catholic University

San Juan—Population: 437,800
Inter American University
University of Puerto Rico

MID ATLANTIC AND NEW YORK

New York

Albany—Population: 101,100
Union University

Buffalo—Population: 328,100
University at Buffalo, SUNY

Hempstead—Population: 725,600
Hofstra University

Huntington—Population: 18,200
Touro College

Ithaca—Population: 29,500
Cornell University

New York City—Population: 7,322,500
Brooklyn Law School

City University of New York, Queens
  College
Columbia University
Fordham University
New York Law School
New York University
St. John's University
Yeshiva University

Syracuse—Population: 163,700
Syracuse University

White Plains—Population: 48,700
Pace University, School of Law

Pennsylvania

Carlisle—Population: 18,400
Pennsylvania State University, Dickinson
  School of Law

Harrisburg—Population: 52,400
Widener University

Philadelphia—Population: 1,585,600
University of Pennsylvania
Temple University

Pittsburgh—Population: 370,000
Duquesne University
University of Pittsburgh

New Jersey

Camden—Population: 87,492
Rutgers University, Camden

Newark—Population: 275,200
Rutgers University, Newark
Seton Hall University

Maryland

Baltimore—Population: 736,000
University of Maryland

Delaware

Wilmington—Population: 71,500
Widener University

District of Columbia

Washington—Population: 606,900
American University
Catholic University of America
District of Columbia University
Georgetown University
George Washington University
Howard University

NEW ENGLAND

Vermont

South Royalton—Population: 2,500
Vermont Law School

Massachusetts

Boston—Population: 574,300
Boston College
Boston University
Harvard University
New England School of Law

Northeastern University
Suffolk University

Springfield—Population: 157,000
Western New England College

Connecticut

Bridgeport—Population: 141,700
Quinnipiac College

Hartford—Population: 140,000
University of Connecticut

New Haven—Population: 130,500
Yale University

Rhode Island

Bristol—Population: 21,600
Roger Williams University

New Hampshire

Concord—Population: 36,000
Franklin Pierce Law Center

Maine

Portland—Population: 64,400
University of Maine

Law Schools by State

ALABAMA

University of Alabama
Samford University

ARIZONA

Arizona State University
University of Arizona

ARKANSAS

University of Arkansas, Fayetteville
University of Arkansas, Little Rock

CALIFORNIA

University of California, Berkeley
University of California, Davis
University of California, Los Angeles
University of California, Hastings College of Law
California Western School of Law
Golden Gate University
Loyola Marymount University
University of the Pacific, McGeorge School of Law
Pepperdine University
University of San Diego
University of San Francisco
Santa Clara University
University of Southern California
Southwestern University
Stanford University
Whittier College

COLORADO

University of Colorado
University of Denver

CONNECTICUT

University of Connecticut
Quinnipiac College
Yale University

DELAWARE

Widener University

DISTRICT OF COLUMBIA

American University
Catholic University of America
George Washington University
Georgetown University
Howard University

FLORIDA

Florida State University
University of Florida
University of Miami
Nova Southeastern University
Stetson University

GEORGIA

Emory University
Georgia State University
University of Georgia
Mercer University

HAWAII

University of Hawaii, Manoa

IDAHO

University of Idaho

ILLINOIS

University of Chicago
DePaul University
Illinois Institute of Technology
University of Illinois
John Marshall Law School
Loyola University, Chicago
Northern Illinois University
Northwestern University
Southern Illinois University

INDIANA

Indiana University, Bloomington
Indiana University, Indianapolis
University of Notre Dame
Valparaiso University

IOWA

Drake University
University of Iowa

KANSAS

University of Kansas
Washburn University

KENTUCKY

University of Kentucky
University of Louisville
Northern Kentucky University

LOUISIANA

Louisiana State University
Loyola University, New Orleans
Southern University
Tulane University

MAINE

University of Maine

MARYLAND

University of Baltimore
University of Maryland

MASSACHUSETTS

Boston College
Boston University
Harvard University
New England School of Law
Northeastern University
Suffolk University
Western New England College

MICHIGAN

Detroit College of Law at Michigan State
   University
University of Detroit
University of Michigan
Thomas M. Cooley Law School
Wayne State University

MINNESOTA

Hamline University
University of Minnesota
William Mitchell College of Law

MISSISSIPPI

Mississippi College
University of Mississippi

MISSOURI

University of Missouri, Columbia
University of Missouri, Kansas City
St. Louis University
Washington University

MONTANA

University of Montana

NEBRASKA

Creighton University
University of Nebraska

NEW HAMPSHIRE

Franklin Pierce Law Center

NEW JERSEY

Rutgers University, Camden
Rutgers University, Newark
Seton Hall University

NEW MEXICO

University of New Mexico

NEW YORK

Brooklyn Law School
University at Buffalo, State University of
   New York
City University of New York at Queens
   College
Columbia University
Cornell University
Fordham University
Hofstra University
New York Law School
New York University
Pace University
St. John's University
Syracuse University
Touro College
Union University, Albany Law School
Yeshiva University

NORTH CAROLINA

Campbell University
Duke University
North Carolina Central University
University of North Carolina
Wake Forest University

NORTH DAKOTA

University of North Dakota

OHIO

University of Akron
Capital University
Case Western Reserve University
University of Cincinnati
Cleveland State University
University of Dayton
Ohio Northern University
Ohio State University
University of Toledo

OKLAHOMA

Oklahoma City University
University of Oklahoma
University of Tulsa

OREGON

Lewis and Clark College
University of Oregon
Willamette University

PENNSYLVANIA

Duquesne University
Pennsylvania State University, Dickinson
   School of Law
University of Pennsylvania
University of Pittsburgh
Temple University
Villanova University

SOUTH CAROLINA

University of South Carolina

SOUTH DAKOTA

University of South Dakota

TENNESSEE

University of Memphis
University of Tennessee
Vanderbilt University

TEXAS

Baylor University
University of Houston
South Texas College of Law
Southern Methodist University
St. Mary's University

Texas Southern University
Texas Tech University
University of Texas

UTAH

Brigham Young University
University of Utah

VERMONT

Vermont Law School

VIRGINIA

George Mason University
University of Richmond
University of Virginia
Washington and Lee University
College of William and Mary

WASHINGTON

Gonzaga University
Seattle University
University of Washington

WEST VIRGINIA

West Virginia University

WISCONSIN

Marquette University
University of Wisconsin

WYOMING

University of Wyoming

Law Schools by Type
(Public or Private)

These are the ABA-approved law schools as of October 1, 1997. The first list contains all of the public ABA-approved law schools. The second list contains all of the private ABA-approved law schools.

PUBLIC

Akron, University of
Alabama, University of
Arizona State University
Arizona, University of
Arkansas-Fayetteville, University of
Arkansas-Little Rock, University of
Baltimore, University of
Buffalo, University at, State University of
   New York
California-Berkeley, University of
California-Davis, University of
California-Hastings, University of
California-Los Angeles, University of
Cincinnati, University of
City University of New York-Queens
   College
Cleveland State University
Colorado, University of
Connecticut, University of
District of Columbia School of Law
Florida State University
Florida, University of
George Mason University
Georgia State University
Georgia, University of
Hawaii, University of
Houston, University of
Idaho, University of
Illinois, University of
Indiana University-Bloomington
Indiana University-Indianapolis
Iowa, University of
Kansas, University of
Kentucky, University of
Louisiana State University

Louisville, University of
Maine, University of
Maryland, University of
Memphis State University
Michigan, University of
Minnesota, University of
Mississippi, University of
Missouri-Columbia, University of
Missouri-Kansas City, University of
Montana, University of
Nebraska, University of
New Mexico, University of
North Carolina Central University
North Carolina, University of
North Dakota, University of
Northern Illinois University
Northern Kentucky University
Ohio State University
Oklahoma, University of
Oregon, University of
Pennsylvania State University, Dickinson
   School of Law
Pittsburgh, University of
Puerto Rico, University of
Rutgers University-Camden
Rutgers University-Newark
South Carolina, University of
South Dakota, University of
Southern Illinois University
Southern University
Temple University
Tennessee, University of
Texas Southern University
Texas Tech University
Texas, University of
Toledo, University of
Utah, University of
Virginia, University of
Washburn University
Washington, University of
Wayne State University
West Virginia University
William and Mary, College of
Wisconsin, University of
Wyoming, University of

PRIVATE

American University
Baylor University
Boston College
Boston University
Brigham Young University
Brooklyn Law School
California Western School of law
Campbell University
Capital University
Case Western University
Catholic University of America
Chicago, University of
Columbia University
Cornell University
Creighton University
Dayton, University of
Denver, University of
DePaul University
Detroit College of Law at Michigan State
   University
Detroit Mercy, University of
Drake University
Duke University
Duquesne University
Emory University
Fordham University
Franklin Pierce Law Center
George Washington University
Georgetown University
Golden Gate University
Gonzaga University
Hamline University
Harvard University
Hofstra University
Howard University
Illinois Institute of Technology, Chicago-
   Kent
Inter-American University of Puerto Rico
John Marshall Law School
Lewis and Clark College
Loyola University-Chicago
Loyola University-Los Angeles
Loyola University-New Orleans

Marquette University
Mercer University
Miami, University of
Mississippi College
New England School of Law
New York Law School
New York University
Northeastern University
Northwestern University
Notre Dame, University of
Nova Southeastern University
Ohio Northern University
Oklahoma City University
Pace University
Pacific, University of the, McGeorge
   School of Law
Pennsylvania, University of
Pepperdine University
Pontifical Catholic University of Puerto
   Rico
Quinnipiac College School of Law
Regent University

Richmond, University of
Roger Williams University
Samford University
San Diego, University of
San Francisco, University of
Santa Clara University
Seattle University (formerly Puget Sound
   School of Law)
Seton Hall University
South Texas College of Law
Southern California, University of
Southern Methodist University
Southwestern University
St. John's University
St. Louis University
St. Mary's University
St. Thomas University
Stanford University
Stetson University
Suffolk University
Syracuse University
Texas Wesleyan University

Thomas Jefferson School of Law
Thomas M. Cooley Law School
Touro College
Tulane University
Tulsa, University of
Union University, Albany Law School
Valparaiso University
Vanderbilt University
Vermont Law School
Villanova University
Wake Forest University
Washington and Lee University
Washington University, St. Louis
Western New England College
Whittier College
Widener University (Wilmington)
Widener University (Harrisburg)
Willamette University
William Mitchell College of Law
Yale University
Yeshiva University

Law Schools Participating in Law Multi-App

American University
Boston College
Boston University
California-Berkeley, University of
California-Davis, University of
California-Hastings, University of
California-Los Angeles, University of
California Western School of law
Catholic University
Chicago, University of
Columbia University
Cornell University
Duke University
Emory University
Fordham University
George Washington University
Georgetown University
Golden Gate University
Harvard University
Hofstra University

Howard University
Illinois, University of
Iowa, University of
Loyola University, Los Angeles
Michigan, University of
Minnesota, University of
New York Law School
New York University
North Carolina, University of
Northeastern University
Northwestern University
Pace University
University of the Pacific, McGeorge
    School of Law
Pennsylvania, University of
Pepperdine University
Pittsburgh, University of
Rutgers University-Camden
Rutgers University-Newark
St. John's University

San Diego, University of
San Francisco, University of
Santa Clara University
Seton Hall University
Southern California, University of
Southern Methodist University
Southwestern University
Stanford University
Temple University
Texas, University of
Touro College
Tulane University
Vanderbilt University
Virginia, University of
Washington and Lee University
Washington, University of
Whittier College
Widener University
William and Mary, College of
Yale University

Joint-Degree Programs in American Law Schools

J.D. -A.M. (HISTORY, PUBLIC POLICY)

University of Chicago

J.D. -D.V.M.

University of Illinois

J.D. -MAÎTRISE EN DROIT

Cornell University

J.D. -M.A.

John Marshall Law School
University of Maine

J.D. -M.A. (AGRICULTURAL ECONOMICS)

Drake University
Texas Tech University

J.D. -M.A. (AMERICAN INDIAN STUDIES)

University of Arizona

J.D. -M.A. (AMERICAN STUDIES)

College of William and Mary

J.D. -M.A. (ANTHROPOLOGY)

Columbia University
Duke University
University of Tulsa

J.D. -M.A. (ASIAN STUDIES)

Washington University

J.D. -M.A. (CLINICAL PSYCHOLOGY)

University of Tulsa

J.D. -M.A. (COMMUNICATION/JOURNALISM/MEDIA)

Boston University
University of California, Berkeley
Columbia University
Drake University
Loyola University, New Orleans
University of Pennsylvania
Regent University
University of Southern California
Syracuse University

J.D. -M.A. (CRIMINAL JUSTICE)

University of Maryland
Rutgers University, Newark
University of South Carolina

J.D. -M.A. (ECONOMICS)

University of California, Berkeley
Catholic University
University of Chicago (A.M.)
Columbia University
University of Denver
Duke University
Florida State University
University of Kansas
University of Michigan
University of Nebraska, Lincoln
University of Pennsylvania
University of South Carolina
University of South Dakota
Southern Methodist University
Syracuse University
University of Washington
Yale University

J.D. -M.A. (ENGLISH)

Duke University
University of South Dakota

J.D. -M.A. (EUROPEAN STUDIES)

Washington University

J.D. -M.A. (GOVERNMENT AND POLITICS)

St. John's University

J.D. -M.A. (HISTORY)

Case Western Reserve University
Catholic University
University of Chicago (A.M.)

Columbia University
Duke University
University of Houston
University of Iowa
University of Pennsylvania
University of South Dakota
Syracuse University
University of Tulsa
Wayne State University

J.D. -M.A. (IBERO-AMERICAN STUDIES)

University of Wisconsin

J.D. -M.A. (INDUSTRIAL AND ORGANIZATIONAL PSYCHOLOGY)

University of Tulsa

J.D. -M.A. (INDUSTRIAL RELATIONS)

Loyola University, Chicago

J.D. -M.A. (INTERNATIONAL AFFAIRS/RELATIONS)

American University
Boston University
University of California, Berkeley
University of California, Los Angeles
Columbia University
Cornell University
Florida State University
George Washington University
Marquette University
University of San Diego
University of Southern California
Syracuse University
University of Virginia
University of Washington

J.D. -M.A. (ISLAMIC STUDIES)

University of Pennsylvania

J.D. -M.A. (LATIN AMERICAN STUDIES)

University of New Mexico
University of Texas
Tulane University

J.D. -M.A. (MIDDLE EASTERN STUDIES)

University of Pennsylvania

J.D. -M.A. (MODERN MIDDLE EASTERN AND NORTH AFRICAN STUDIES)

University of Michigan

J.D. -M.A. (PEACE STUDIES)

University of Notre Dame

J.D. -M.A. (PHILOSOPHY)

Catholic University
Columbia University
Duke University
University of Iowa
University of Kansas
University of Pennsylvania
University of Southern California
(M. Phil.)
University of Washington

J.D. -M.A. (POLITICAL SCIENCE)

Brooklyn Law School
Catholic University
Columbia University
Drake University
Duke University
Loyola University, Chicago
Marquette University
University of Maryland
University of Nebraska
Rutgers University, Camden
Rutgers University, Newark
University of South Dakota
Washington University
Wayne State University

J.D. -M.A. (PUBLIC AFFAIRS)

St. Louis University

J.D. -M.A. (PSYCHOLOGY/SOCIOLOGY)

Columbia University
Duke University
University of Iowa
University of South Dakota

J.D. -M.A. (RELIGIOUS STUDIES)

Loyola University, New Orleans

J.D. -M.A. (URBAN AFFAIRS)

St. Louis University

J.D. -M.A. (URBAN PLANNING)

Loyola University, New Orleans

J.D. -M.A. (WOMEN'S STUDIES)

University of Cincinnati

J.D. -M.ACC.

Brigham Young University
Gonzaga University
University of Iowa
Northeastern University
University of the Pacific
Samford University
University of South Carolina
University of South Dakota
Southern Illinois University, Carbondale

J.D. -M.A.E. (ENGINEERING)

Samford University

J.D. -M.A.L.I.R (LABOR AND INTERNATIONAL RELATIONS)

University of Illinois

J.D. -M.A.L.D. (LAW AND DIPLOMACY)

University of Virginia

J.D. -M.B.A.

University of Akron
University of Alabama
American University
Arizona State University
University of Arizona
University of Arkansas, Little Rock
University of Baltimore
Baylor University
Boston College
Boston University
Brigham Young University
Brooklyn Law School
University at Buffalo, State University of New York
University of California, Berkeley
University of California, Davis
University of California, Hastings
University of California, Los Angeles
Campbell University
Capital University
Case Western Reserve University
University of Chicago
University of Cincinnati
Cleveland State University
University of Colorado
Columbia University
University of Connecticut
Cornell University
Creighton University
University of Dayton
University of Denver
DePaul University
Detroit College of Law
University of Detroit Mercy
Drake University
Duke University
Duquesne University
Emory University
Florida State University
Fordham University
George Washington University
Georgia State University
University of Georgia
Golden Gate University
Gonzaga University
Hamline University
Harvard University
University of Hawaii
University of Houston
Hofstra University
Howard University
Illinois Institute of Technology
University of Illinois
Indiana University, Bloomington

Indiana University, Indianapolis
University of Iowa
John Marshall School of Law
University of Kansas
University of Kentucky
University of Louisville
Loyola Marymount University
Loyola University, Chicago
Loyola University, New Orleans
Marquette University
University of Memphis
Mercer University
University of Miami
University of Michigan
University of Minnesota
University of Mississippi
University of Missouri, Columbia
University of Missouri, Kansas City
University of Nebraska
University of New Mexico
New York Law School
New York University
North Carolina Central University
University of North Carolina
Northeastern University
Northern Illinois University
Northern Kentucky University
University of Notre Dame
Nova Southeastern University
Ohio State University
Oklahoma City University
University of Oregon
Pace University
University of the Pacific
University of Pennsylvania
Pepperdine University
University of Pittsburgh
Pontifical Catholic University of Puerto Rico
University of Puerto Rico
Quinnipiac College
Regent University
University of Richmond
Rutgers University, Camden
Rutgers University, Newark
Samford University
University of San Diego
University of San Francisco
Santa Clara University
Seton Hall University
Southern Illinois University
Southern Methodist University
St. John's University
St. Louis University
St. Mary's University
University of South Carolina
University of South Dakota
University of Southern California
Stanford University
Stetson University
Suffolk University
Syracuse University

Temple University
University of Tennessee
Texas Tech University
University of Texas
University of Toledo
Touro College
Tulane University
University of Tulsa
Union University
University of Utah
Vanderbilt University
Villanova University
Wake Forest University
Washington University
University of Washington
Wayne State University
West Virginia University
Widener University, Wilmington
College of William and Mary
University of Wisconsin
University of Wyoming

J.D. -M.B.T. (BUSINESS TAXATION)

University of Southern California

J.D. -M.C.P. (CITY PLANNING)

University of Cincinnati
University of Pennsylvania
Rogers Williams University

J.D. -M.C.R.P.

Rutgers University, Camden
Rutgers University, Newark

J.D. -M.D.

Duke University
Duquesne University
University of Illinois
Southern Illinois University, Carbondale
Yale University

J.D. -M.DIV.

Emory University
Harvard University
University of Louisville
Oklahoma City University
Samford University
Vanderbilt University
Yale University

J.D. -M.D.R. (DISPUTE RESOLUTION)

Pepperdine University

J.D. -M.ED.

Boston College
Brigham Young University
University of California, Hastings
Harvard University
University of Illinois

J.D. -M.E.M. (ENVIRONMENTAL MANAGEMENT)

Duke University

J.D. -M.F. (FORESTRY)

Duke University

J.D. -M.F.A.

Columbia University

J.D. -M.F.S. (FORESTRY SCIENCE)

Yale University

J.D. -M.H.A.

Indiana University, Indianapolis
University of Iowa
Ohio State University
Quinnipiac College
University of Richmond
St. Louis University
Tulane University
Washington University

J.D. -M.H.P. (HISTORIC PRESERVATION)

University of Georgia

J.D. -M.H.S.A. (HEALTH SERVICES ADMINISTRATION)

Arizona State University
George Washington University

University of Kansas
University of Michigan

J.D. -M.I.A. (INTERNATIONAL AFFAIRS)

Columbia University

J.D. -M.I.B.A. (INTERNATIONAL BUSINESS ADMINISTRATION)

University of San Diego

J.D. -M.I.B.S. (INTERNATIONAL BUSINESS STUDIES)

University of South Carolina

J.D. -M.I.M. (INTERNATIONAL MANAGEMENT)

University of Denver

J.D. -M.I.P. (INTELLECTUAL PROPERTY)

Franklin Pierce Law Center

J.D. -M.L.S. (LIBRARY/INFORMATION SCIENCE)

Brooklyn Law School
Catholic University of America
University of Connecticut
Indiana University, Indianapolis
University of Iowa
North Carolina Central University
University of Wisconsin

J.D. -M.M.

Northwestern University
Willamette University

J.D. -M.N.O. (NONPROFIT ORGANIZATIONS)

Case Western Reserve University

J.D. -M.O.B. (ORGANIZATIONAL BEHAVIOR)

Brigham Young University

J.D. -PHARM.D.

Drake University
Ohio Northern University

J.D. -M.P.A.

University of Akron
University of Arizona
University of Baltimore
Brigham Young University
Brooklyn Law School
Cleveland State University
University of Colorado
Columbia University
University of Connecticut
University of Dayton
Drake University
Emory University
Florida State University
Georgia State University
Golden Gate University
Harvard University
Indiana University, Bloomington
Indiana University, Indianapolis
John Marshall School of Law
University of Kansas
University of Kentucky
Louisiana State University
Loyola University, New Orleans
University of Minnesota
University of Montana
University of Nebraska
New York University
University of North Carolina
Ohio State University
Pace University
Pennsylvania State University
University of Pittsburgh
Rutgers University, Camden
St. Louis University
St. Mary's University
Samford University
University of South Carolina
University of South Dakota
Southern Illinois University
Suffolk University
Syracuse University
University of Tennessee
Texas Tech University
University of Texas
Union University
University of Utah
University of Virginia

West Virginia University
University of Wisconsin
University of Wyoming
Yale University

J.D. -M.P.H.

Boston University
Columbia University
University of Connecticut
George Washington University
University of Houston
University of North Carolina
University of Oklahoma
University of Pittsburgh
Samford University
Tulane University

J.D. -M.P.P.

University of California, Berkeley
University of Chicago
Duke University
Harvard University
University of Michigan
University of Minnesota
University of North Carolina
Vanderbilt University
College of William and Mary

J.D. -M.P.P.A.

Baylor University
The University of the Pacific

J.D. -M.P.P.M.

University of California, Hastings
Yale University

J.D. -M.R.E.D. (REAL ESTATE DEVELOPMENT)

University of Southern California

J.D. -M.S. (ACCOUNTING)

University of Florida
Syracuse University
University of Tulsa
University of Virginia

J.D. -M.S. (ENGINEERING)

Syracuse University

J.D.-M.S. (ENVIRONMENTAL MANAGEMENT/STUDIES/ SCIENCES)

Duke University
Duquesne University
University of Hawaii
Illinois Institute of Technology
Indiana University, Bloomington
University of Maryland
University of Montana
University of Oklahoma
University of Oregon
Pace University
Samford University
Vermont Law School
Washington University
University of Wisconsin
Yale University

J.D. -M.S. (FINANCE)

Suffolk University

J.D. -M.S. (GEOSCIENCES)

University of Tulsa

J.D. -M.S. (NATURAL RESOURCES)

University of Michigan

J.D. -M.S. (OCCUPATIONAL HEALTH)

University of Oklahoma

J.D. -M.S. (POLITICAL SCIENCE)

University of Florida

J.D. -M.S. (SOCIOLOGY)

University of Florida

J.D. -M.S., -M.R.P, -M.U.R.P.

Brooklyn Law School
University of California, Berkeley
University of California, Los Angeles
Columbia University
Cornell University
University of Florida

University of Illinois
University of Iowa
University of Kansas
New York University
North Carolina University
Nova Southeastern University
University of Pittsburgh
University of Richmond
Rutgers University, Camden
Rutgers University, Newark
Syracuse University

J.D. -M.S. (PSYCHOLOGY)

Nova Southeastern University

J.D. -M.S. (TAX)

Texas Tech University
Touro College

J.D. -M.S.A. (SPORTS ADMINISTRATION)

Capital University

J.D. -M.S.E. (ENGINEERING)

University of Notre Dame

J.D. -M.S.E.L. (ENVIRONMENTAL LAW)

Vermont School of Law

J.D. -M.S.I.E. (INDUSTRIAL ENGINEERING)

Suffolk University

J.D. -M.S.P.H. (PUBLIC HEALTH)

Tulane University

J.D. -M.S.S.A. (SOCIAL ADMINISTRATION)

Case Western Reserve University

J.D. -M.S.W.

New York University
University of North Carolina
University of Pennsylvania
Washington University

J.D. -M.TAX.

University of Akron
Baylor University
University of Tulsa

J.D. -M.THEO.

St. Mary's University

J.D. -M.T.S. (THEOLOGICAL STUDIES)

Emory University
Vanderbilt University

Graduate Programs in American Law Schools

J.D. -LL.M.

Cornell University
Duke University
Illinois Institute of Technology (Financial
  Services, Taxation)

J.S.D.

University of California, Berkeley
University of Chicago
Cornell University
University of Illinois
New York University
Northwestern University
Notre Dame University (International
  Human Rights)
Stanford University
Washington University
Yale University

J.S.M. (FOREIGN LAWYERS)

Stanford University

LL.M. (ADMIRALTY LAW)

Tulane University

LL.M. (AGRICULTURAL LAW)

University of Arkansas

LL.M. (AMERICAN COMMON LAW LEGAL SYSTEM)

Temple University

LL.M. (AMERICAN LAW, FOREIGN LAWYERS)

St. Louis University
Wake Forest University

LL.M. (AMERICAN LEGAL STUDIES/SYSTEMS)

St. Mary's University
Touro College
College of William and Mary

LL.M. (ASIAN AND COMPARATIVE LAW)

University of Washington

LL.M. (BANKING, CORPORATE AND FINANCE LAW)

Boston University
Fordham University

LL.M. (CHILD LAW)

Loyola University, Chicago

LL.M. (COMMON LAW, FOREIGN ATTORNEYS)

Georgetown University

LL.M. (COMPARATIVE LAW, FOREIGN LAWYERS)

Boston University
Brigham Young University
University of California, Los Angeles
University of Connecticut
Pennsylvania State University, Dickinson
  School of Law
University of Florida
University of Miami
University of San Diego
Temple University

LL.M. (COMPARATIVE AND INTERNATIONAL LAW)

Southern Methodist University

LL.M. (COMPARATIVE LEGAL STUDIES)

John Marshall Law School

LL.M. (CORPORATE LAW)

New York University
Wayne State University
Widener University, Wilmington
Widener University, Harrisburg

LL.M. (ENERGY AND ENVIRONMENTAL LAW)

Tulane University

LL.M. (ENERGY, ENVIRONMENT AND NATURAL RESOURCES LAW)

University of Houston

LL.M. (ENVIRONMENTAL LAW)

George Washington University
Pace University

LL.M. (ENVIRONMENTAL AND NATURAL RESOURCES LAW)

Lewis and Clark College

LL.M. (ENVIRONMENTAL AND RESOURCE LAW)

University of Utah

LL.M. (ESTATE PLANNING)

University of Miami

LL.M. (FINANCIAL SERVICES LAW)

Illinois Institute of Technology

LL.M. (FOREIGN LAWYERS PROGRAM)

University of Houston
University of Minnesota
Northwestern University
University of Pittsburgh
University of Texas
University of Virginia
Washington University
Yale University

LL.M. (GENERAL)

University of California, Berkeley
University of California, Hastings

University of Chicago
Cleveland State University
Cornell University
Emory University
George Washington University
Georgetown University
University of Georgia
Harvard University
University of Illinois
Indiana University, Bloomington
Louisiana State University
University of Michigan
University of Missouri, Kansas City
New York University
University of Pennsylvania
University of South Dakota
Southern Methodist University
Temple University
Tulane University
Wayne State University
University of Wisconsin
Yale University

LL.M. (GOVERNMENT PROCUREMENT LAW)

George Washington University

LL.M. (HEALTH LAW)

DePaul University
University of Houston
Loyola University, Chicago
St. Louis University
Widener University, Wilmington
Widener University, Harrisburg

LL.M. (INTELLECTUAL PROPERTY LAW)

Franklin Pierce Law Center
George Washington University
University of Houston
John Marshall Law School

LL.M. (INTER-AMERICAN LAW)

University of Miami

LL.M. (INTERNATIONAL BUSINESS AND TRADE LAW)

Fordham University

LL.M. (INTERNATIONAL AND COMPARATIVE LAW)

Duke University
George Washington University
Georgetown University
Illinois Institute of Technology
University of Iowa
University of Miami
University of Pittsburgh
University of South Dakota
St. Mary's University

LL.M. (INTERNATIONAL ECONOMIC LAW)

University of Houston

LL.M. (INTERNATIONAL ENVIRONMENTAL LAW)

University of Washington

LL.M. (INTERNATIONAL HUMAN RIGHTS LAW)

University of Notre Dame

LL.M. (INTERNATIONAL LEGAL STUDIES)

New York University

LL.M. (LABOR AND EMPLOYMENT LAW)

Georgetown University

LL.M. (LABOR LAW)

Wayne State University

LL.M. (LAW AND MARINE AFFAIRS)

University of Washington

LL.M. (OCEAN AND COASTAL LAW)

University of Miami

LL.M. (REAL PROPERTY, LAND DEVELOPMENT AND FINANCE LAW)

University of Miami

LL.M. (REAL ESTATE LAW)

John Marshall Law School

LL.M. (SECURITIES AND FINANCIAL REGULATIONS LAW)

Georgetown University

LL.M. (SUSTAINABLE INTERNATIONAL DEVELOPMENT LAW)

University of Washington

LL.M. (TAXATION)

University of Alabama
Boston University
Capital University
Case Western Reserve University
University of Denver
DePaul University
University of Florida
Georgetown University
Golden State University
University of Houston
Illinois Institute of Technology
John Marshall Law School
University of Miami
University of Missouri, Kansas City
New York University
University of South Dakota
Southern Methodist University
Temple University
Villanova University
Washington University
University of Washington
Wayne State University
William Mitchell College of Law

LL.M. (TRIAL ADVOCACY)

Temple University

LL.M. (U.S. LEGAL STUDIES)

Case Western Reserve University

LL.M. (U.S. LAW FOR INTERNATIONAL STUDENTS)

Duke University

LL.M. (URBAN STUDIES)

Washington University

LL.M. -M.P.H.

George Washington University

LL.M. -S.J.D.

University of Michigan

M.C.J. (COMPARATIVE JURISPRUDENCE, FOREIGN LAWYERS)

New York University

M.C.L. (COMPARATIVE LAW, FOREIGN LAWYERS)

University of Alabama
Indiana University, Bloomington
Louisiana State University
University of Michigan

Samford University
Tulane University

M.COMP./ D.COMP.

University of Chicago

M.J. (CHILD LAW)

Loyola University, Chicago

M.J. (HEALTH LAW)

Loyola University, Chicago

M.L.S. (LEGAL STUDIES FOR STUDENTS WITHOUT A J.D.)

University of Nebraska, Lincoln
Stanford University

M.S.L. (STUDIES IN LAW FOR STUDENTS WITHOUT A J.D.)

Yale University

S.J.D.

Duke University
George Washington University
Georgetown University
Harvard University
University of Illinois
Indiana University, Bloomington
Loyola University, Chicago (Health Law)
University of Michigan
Pace University (Environmental Law)
University of Pennsylvania
Southern Methodist University
Tulane University
University of Virginia
University of Wisconsin

Law Schools with Largest Graduate Enrollments

Below is 1996 data from the ABA indicating the top twenty law schools according to the size of their graduate law programs. It is obvious this information is somewhat dated. However, it is hoped the reader will be able to use it to make a very preliminary judgment concerning the receptivity of certain graduate law programs.

School/College	Private/Public Control	Enrollment
New York University	Private	726
Georgetown University	Private	549
George Washington University	Private	251
Harvard University	Private	196
Villanova University	Private	195
Boston University	Private	188
American University	Private	171
John Marshall Law School	Private	171
Golden State University	Private	160
Wayne State University	Public	146
Columbia University	Private	137
University of Miami	Private	128
Temple University	Public	128
University of Houston	Public	122
University of Washington	Public	115
University of San Diego	Private	98
Judge Advocate General's School	Public	81
University of Florida	Public	79
University of Pennsylvania	Private	79
Tulane University	Private	76

Directory of State
Bar Admissions Offices

Includes passage rates for each state for first-time bar exam takers from all law schools.

ALABAMA

Board of Bar Examiners
Alabama State Bar
P.O. Box 671
Montgomery, AL 36101
Phone: (205)269-1515
Passage Rate: 83%

ALASKA

Committee of Law Examiners
Alaska Bar Association
P.O. Box 100279
Anchorage, AK 99510
Phone: (902)272-7469
Passage Rate: N/A

ARIZONA

Committee on Examinations
   and Character and Fitness
111 W. Monroe
Phoenix, AZ 85003-1742
Phone: (602)340-7295
Passage Rate: 84%

ARKANSAS

State Board of Law Examiners
2400 Justice Building
625 Marshall
Little Rock, AR 72201
Phone: (501)374-1855
Passage Rate: 84%

CALIFORNIA

The State Bar of California
Office of Admissions
555 Franklin Street
San Francisco, CA 94102
Phone: (415)561-8303
Passage Rate: 73%

COLORADO

Supreme Court
Board of Law Examiners
600 17th St., Ste. 520-S
Denver, CO 80202
Phone: (303)893-8096
Passage Rate: 87%

CONNECTICUT

Connecticut Bar Examining Committee
287 Main Street
East Hartford, CT 06118-1885
Phone: (203)568-3450
Passage Rate: 83%

DELAWARE

Board of Bar Examiners for the State of
   Delaware
200 W. Ninth St., Ste. 300-B
Wilmington, DE 19801
Phone: (302)658-7309
Passage Rate: N/A

DISTRICT OF COLUMBIA

Director of Admissions
D. C. Court of Appeals
Room 4200

500 Indiana Avenue, N.W.
Washington, D.C. 20001
Phone: (202)879-2710
Passage Rate: 75%

FLORIDA

Florida Board of Bar Examiners
1891 Elder Court
Tallahassee, FL 32399-1750
Phone: (904)487-1292
Passage Rate: 84%

GEORGIA

Supreme Court of Georgia
Office of Bar Admissions
P.O. Box 38466
Atlanta, GA 30334-0466
Phone: (404)656-3490
Passage Rate: 81%

HAWAII

Bar Admission Attorney
Supreme Court of Hawai'i
Ali'i lani Hale
417 South King Street
Honolulu, HI 96813-2912
Phone: (808)539-4977
Passage Rate: 70%

IDAHO

Admissions Administrator
Idaho State Bar
P.O. Box 895
525 West Jefferson
Boise, ID 83701
Phone: (208)334-4500
Passage Rate: 75%

ILLINOIS

Illinois Board of Admissions to the Bar
430 First of America Center
Springfield, IL 62701
Phone: (217)522-5917
Passage Rate: 87%

INDIANA

Indiana State Board of Law Examiners
South Tower, Suite 1070
115 W. Washington St., #1070
Indianapolis, IN 46204-3417
Phone: (317)232-2552
Passage Rate: 86%

IOWA

Clerk
Supreme Court of Iowa
State Capitol Building
Des Moines, 1A 50319
Phone: (515)281-5911
Passage Rate: 87%

KANSAS

Kansas Board of Law Examiners
Kansas Judicial Center
301 S. West 10th Ave., Rm. 374
Topeka, KS 66612
Phone: (913)296-8410
Passage Rate: 82%

KENTUCKY

Kentucky Board of Bar Examiners
1510 Newtown Pike, Suite X
Lexington, KY 40511
Phone: (606)246-2381
Passage Rate: 82%

LOUISIANA

Louisiana Committee on Bar Admissions
601 St. Charles Avenue
New Orleans, LA 70130
Phone: (504)566-1600
Passage Rate: 55%

MAINE

Maine Board of Bar Examiners
P.O. Box 30
Augusta, ME 04332-0030

Phone: (207)623-2464
Passage Rate: 82%

MARYLAND

State Board of Law Examiners People's
 Resource Center
100 Community Pl., Rm. 1210
Crownsville, MD 21032-2026
Phone: (410)514-7044
Passage Rate: 75%

MASSACHUSETTS

Massachusetts Board of Bar Examiners
77 Franklin Street
Boston, MA 02110-1593
Phone: (617)482-4466, 4467
Passage Rate: 83%

MICHIGAN

Michigan Board of Law Examiners
200 Washington Square North
P.O. Box 30104
Lansing, MI 48909
Phone: (517)334-6992
Passage Rate: 79%

MINNESOTA

Minnesota State Board of Law
 Examiners
Minnesota Judicial Center
25 Constitution Avenue, Suite 110
St. Paul, MN 55155
Phone: (612)297-1800
Passage Rate: 90%

MISSISSIPPI

Mississippi Board of Bar Admissions
P.O. Box 1449
Jackson, MS 39215-1449
Phone: (601)354-6055
Passage Rate: 87%

MISSOURI

Missouri State Board of Law Examiners
P.O. Box 150
Jefferson City, MO 65102
Phone: (573)751-4144
Passage Rate: 92%

MONTANA

Board of Bar Examiners
Room 315, Justice Building
215 North Sanders
Helena, MT 59620
Phone: (406)444-2621
Passage Rate: 90%

NEBRASKA

Nebraska State Bar Commission
635 South 14th Street
P.O. Box 81809
Lincoln, NE 68501
Phone: (402)475-7091
Passage Rate: 94%

NEVADA

State Bar of Nevada
201 Las Vegas Blvd. South
Suite 200
Las Vegas, NV 89101
Phone: (702)382-2200
Passage Rate: N/A

NEW HAMPSHIRE

Clerk of the Supreme Court
Supreme Court Building
Noble Drive
Concord, NH 03301
Phone: (603)271-2646
Passage Rate: 79%

NEW JERSEY

New Jersey Board of Bar Examiners,
 CN 973
Trenton, NJ 08625
Phone: (609)984-7785
Passage Rate: 78%

NEW MEXICO

New Mexico State Board of Bar
 Examiners
9420 Indian School Rd. NE
Albuquerque, NM 87112
Phone: (505)271-9706
Passage Rate: 92%

NEW YORK

New York State Board of Law Examiners
7 Executive Centre Drive

Albany, NY 12203
Phone: (518)452-8700
Passage Rate: 78%

NORTH CAROLINA

Board of Bar Examiners
P.O. Box 2946
208 Fayetteville Street
Raleigh, NC 27602
Phone: (919)828-4886
Passage Rate: 85%

NORTH DAKOTA

State Bar Board
1st Floor, Judicial Wing
600 East Boulevard Avenue
Bismarck, ND 58505-0530
Phone: (701)328-4201
Passage Rate: 85%

OHIO

Ohio Board of Bar Examiners
Rhodes State Office Tower
30 East Broad Street, 2nd Floor
Columbus, OH 43215-3414
Phone: (614)466-1541
Passage Rate: 93%

OKLAHOMA

Oklahoma Board of Bar Examiners
P.O. Box 53036
Oklahoma City, OK 73152
Phone: (405)524-2365
Passage Rate: 75%

OREGON

5200 SW Meadows Road
P.O. Box 1689
Lake Oswego, OR 97035-0889
Phone: (503)620-0222, Ext. 410
Passage Rate: 85%

PENNSYLVANIA

Pennsylvania Board of
Law Examiners
5035 Ritter Road
Mechanicsburg, PA 17055
Phone: (717)795-7270
Passage Rate: 78%

PUERTO RICO

Commonwealth of Puerto Rico
Supreme Court
P.O. Box 2392
San Juan, PR 00902-2392
Phone: (809)725-5030
Passage Rate: 68%

RHODE ISLAND

Chief Deputy Clerk/Bar
Providence County Court House
250 Benefit Street
Providence, RI 02903
Phone: (401)277-3272
Passage Rate: 71%

SOUTH CAROLINA

South Carolina State Board of Law
   Examiners
P.O. Box 11330
Columbia, SC 29211
Phone: (803)734-1080
Passage Rate: 92%

SOUTH DAKOTA

South Dakota Board of Bar Examiners
500 East Capitol
Pierre, SD 57501
Phone: (605)773-4898
Passage Rate: 91%

TENNESSEE

Nashville City Center
511 Union Street, Suite 1420
Nashville, TN 37243-0740
Phone: (615)741-3234
Passage Rate: 79%

TEXAS

Texas Board of Law Examiners
P.O. Box 13486
Austin, TX 78711-3486
Phone: (512)463-1621
Passage Rate: 82%

UTAH

Utah State Bar
645 South 200 East
Salt Lake City, UT 84111-3834

Phone: (801)531-9077
Passage Rate: 92%

VERMONT

Board of Bar Examiners
109 State Street
Montpelier, VT 05609-0702
Phone: (802)828-3281
Passage Rate: 79%

VIRGINIA

Virginia Board of Bar Examiners
Shockoe Center, Suite 225
11 South 12th Street
Richmond, VA 23219
Phone: (804)786-7490
Passage Rate: 76%

WASHINGTON

Washington Board of Bar Examiners
500 Westin Building
2001 Sixth Avenue
Seattle, WA 98121-2599
Phone: (206)727-8209
Passage Rate: 83%

WEST VIRGINIA

West Virginia Board of Law Examiners
Building 1, E-400
1900 Kanawha Blvd., E.
Charleston, WV 25305-0837
Phone: (304)558-7815
Passage Rate: 89%

WISCONSIN

Board of Bar Examiners
119 Martin Luther King, Jr. Boulevard,
   Room 405
Madison, WI 53703-3355
Phone: (608)266-9760
Passage Rate: N/A

WYOMING

State Board of Law Examiners of
   Wyoming
P.O. Box 109
Cheyenne, WY 82003-0109
Phone: (307)632-9061
Passage Rate: 59%

FOR THE BEST IN PAPERBACKS, LOOK FOR THE

In every corner of the world, on every subject under the sun, Penguin represents quality and variety—the very best in publishing today.

For complete information about books available from Penguin—including Puffins, Penguin Classics, and Arkana—and how to order them, write to us at the appropriate address below. Please note that for copyright reasons the selection of books varies from country to country.

In the United Kingdom: Please write to *Dept. EP, Penguin Books Ltd, Bath Road, Harmondsworth, West Drayton, Middlesex UB7 0DA.*

In the United States: Please write to *Penguin Putnam Inc., P.O. Box 12289 Dept. B, Newark, New Jersey 07101-5289* or call 1-800-788-6262.

In Canada: Please write to *Penguin Books Canada Ltd, 10 Alcorn Avenue, Suite 300, Toronto, Ontario M4V 3B2.*

In Australia: Please write to *Penguin Books Australia Ltd, P.O. Box 257, Ringwood, Victoria 3134.*

In New Zealand: Please write to *Penguin Books (NZ) Ltd, Private Bag 102902, North Shore Mail Centre, Auckland 10.*

In India: Please write to *Penguin Books India Pvt Ltd, 11 Panchsheel Shopping Centre, Panchsheel Park, New Delhi 110 017.*

In the Netherlands: Please write to *Penguin Books Netherlands bv, Postbus 3507, NL-1001 AH Amsterdam.*

In Germany: Please write to *Penguin Books Deutschland GmbH, Metzlerstrasse 26, 60594 Frankfurt am Main.*

In Spain: Please write to *Penguin Books S. A., Bravo Murillo 19, 1° B, 28015 Madrid.*

In Italy: Please write to *Penguin Italia s.r.l., Via Benedetto Croce 2, 20094 Corsico, Milano.*

In France: Please write to *Penguin France, Le Carré Wilson, 62 rue Benjamin Baillaud, 31500 Toulouse.*

In Japan: Please write to *Penguin Books Japan Ltd, Kaneko Building, 2-3-25 Koraku, Bunkyo-Ku, Tokyo 112.*

In South Africa: Please write to *Penguin Books South Africa (Pty) Ltd, Private Bag X14, Parkview, 2122 Johannesburg.*